WE SHALL
BE ALL

Arise, ye prisoners of starvation!
Arise, ye wretched of the earth!
For Justice thunders condemnation.
A better world's in birth.

No more tradition's chains shall bind us;
Arise, ye slaves! No more in thrall!
The earth shall stand on new foundations;
We have been *naught*—We shall be *All!*

WE SHALL
BE ALL

A HISTORY OF THE

Industrial Workers of the World

BY

MELVYN DUBOFSKY

SECOND EDITION

UNIVERSITY OF ILLINOIS PRESS

Urbana and Chicago

For David and Lisa

© 1969, 1988 by Melvyn Dubofsky
Manufactured in the United States of America
C 5 4 3 2 1

This book is printed on acid-free paper.

Library of Congress Cataloging-in-Publication Data

Dubofsky, Melvyn, 1934–
    We shall be all: a history of the Industrial Workers of the World
/ Melvyn Dubofsky.—2nd ed.
        p.   cm.
    Bibliography: p.
    Includes index.
    ISBN 0-252-01408-1 (alk. paper)
    1. Industrial Workers of the World—History.   I. Title.
HD8055.I5D8   1988
331.88′6′0973—dc 19   87-16725
                            CIP

(Paperback edition published in 1973 by Quadrangle/
The New York Times Book Co., ISBN 0-8129-6234-6)

PREFACE TO THE
1973 PAPERBACK EDITION

Authors do not usually have the opportunity to revise ideas or interpretations once committed to print. Fortunately the paperback edition of *We Shall Be All* affords me a chance to clarify several aspects of the original book that have troubled critics, friends, and also me.

Soon after completing the book, one of the main organizing themes I used—Oscar Lewis's concept of the "culture of poverty"—began to vex me for several reasons. First, the United States from 1890 to 1920 could scarcely be considered equivalent to the societies that Lewis examined in India, Mexico, Cuba, and Puerto Rico and from which he derived cultural categories and typologies. The world's leading industrial capitalist economy, which the United States was by the end of the 1890s, cannot be equated with underdeveloped or developing societies. Second, as much recent criticism of Lewis has suggested, his subjects suffered from social and economic, not cultural, deprivation. The conditions that Lewis defined as the "culture of poverty" might, in other words, better be described as the "economics and politics of poverty," a problem more suited to investigations in political economy than cultural anthropology.

If Lewis was mistaken in his description of the "culture of poverty" and I erred in applying the concept to aspects of IWW history, does that mean that both Lewis and I have led our readers down an intellectual dead end? I think not. Let me explain why. However different the mature United States industrial society was from India, Mexico, or Cuba, the privileged classes in all cases tended to perceive the poor as "culturally deprived"—as the cause of their own personal failure, not as victims of social and economic exploitation. The dominant ideology used to rationalize poverty in Lewis's more backward societies also justified it in the United States. The problem which Lewis addressed and which the IWW struggled to solve was how to break the vicious circle in which the results of social and economic oppression are interpreted as the causes. It is clear that the men and women the IWW tried to organize, like Lewis's Cubans, Mexicans, and Puerto Ricans, lacked social, economic, and political power. Moreover, the Wobblies, rather than being "culturally deprived," maintained values in conflict with the individualistic, money-oriented culture of the dominant classes in the United States. Because of their lack of effective power, however, many potential IWW recruits had formed negative self-images, which rendered them unable to conceive of themselves as the potential builders of a more humane, egalitarian social order.

Lewis, who sympathized with the oppressed in backward societies, concluded that the poor would liberate themselves only after they began to conceive of themselves as important and powerful—that is, after they had formed positive self-images. This, too, was precisely what the IWW understood. Wobblies insisted that the poor must first organize themselves, then use organization to build effective economic power, and finally through power, which alone would transform the exploited from failures into victors, alter their self-images and lay the foundation for a culture of equality, not poverty. In sum, Lewis and the Wobblies realized that organization by the oppressed and the power that flows from it are the only means to end social and economic deprivation.

Those who read this book for the first time should also bear in mind a point not emphasized sufficiently in the original edition. The IWW was a movement in the American mainstream, never an alien aberration. In their most systematic form, syndicalist ideas may have been European in origin, but the IWW had its roots firmly planted in the United States and its ideas and values corresponded to the realities of American working-class life. That millions of American workers shared the concerns of the IWW, if not common membership in a radical organization, was indicated by the history of direct labor union action between 1909 and 1922. As the IWW asserted, American workers cared more about daily life on the shop floor than stuffing pieces of paper into ballot boxes once a year. The mass strikes and violent labor conflicts, which punctuated American history so frequently between 1909 and 1922, showed that the Wobblies comprehended the psychology of the American worker, be he a militant IWW, a moderate AFL craft unionist, or a nonunion laborer. Direct action, not parliamentary politics, symbolized the spirit of American labor.

Two further points need to be made. First, however much the Wobblies swam in the American mainstream, they were not, as another recent historian of the organization, Joseph R. Conlin, asserts in *Bread and Roses Too* (1969), mere reformers, non-revolutionaries who would have become good CIO men had they been born three decades later. True, they fought long and hard for reforms in working conditions, sometimes suffering and even dying to achieve them, but reform and revolution need not be mutually exclusive. At any given historical moment, to be sure, tangible reforms may vitiate the spirit of revolution among masses of workers. But that in no way lessened the dedication of the typical IWW leader to ultimate revolutionary goals. Struggling for improvements in laboring conditions so that workers could live better today, Wobblies always sought tomorrow's utopia.

Finally, though I observed in the original epilogue that internal factors were as responsible as external repression for the failure of the IWW, I must again caution readers that there is no way of knowing what would have happened to the Wobblies in the absence of official and unofficial, legal and illegal suppression. Events in the years since I completed the book serve to remind us how persistently society's dominant classes and government use repression as an effective instrument to control social crises and stifle radicalism. Wobblies would well understand and sympathize with the plight of the New Left and student radicals in the late 1960s and early 1970s. The history of the IWW, then, is part of the continuing struggle in the United States between radicals who challenge the existing distribution of wealth and power in society and privileged groups who combat threats to their political, economic, and social hegemony. The history of the Wobblies is also part of the never-ending struggle to humanize conditions in the workplace by creating a social system in which workers, through their own democratic institutions, determine the nature and goals of work. Many decades ago Wobblies sensed that growth was not necessarily good, more was not better, and the quality of a society rested on its moral imperative as much as its productive capacities.

PREFACE
TO THE FIRST EDITION

On September 5, 1917, in a series of nationwide raids, agents from the Department of Justice ransacked the halls and headquarters of the Industrial Workers of the World. They seized correspondence, journals, pamphlets, and office furnishings; everything from desks and typewriters to paper clips. Shortly thereafter, federal, local, and state authorities herded hundreds of men into the jails of Chicago, Wichita, Omaha, Tulsa, Spokane, Seattle, and many other American cities. A year later many of those arrested took up more permanent residence in the federal penitentiary at Leavenworth, Kansas.

Well before and for some time after the 1917 IWW raids and arrests, leading American businessmen, the President of the United States, his Secretaries of War, Labor, and Justice, the United States Army and Navy, state governors, and local district attorneys pondered the "Wobbly" menace.[1] In some fevered minds, IWW "subversion" ranked with German imperialism and Russian bolshevism as an immediate danger to national security. Indeed, so feared were the Wobblies that probably no group of labor agitators before or since has as suddenly or as disastrously experienced the full wrath of state and national authorities.

But neither has any labor group ever caught the American imagination in quite the same way. Beginning in 1912, when immigrant textile workers left the Lawrence, Massachusetts, mills, fighting their employers and taking to the streets under IWW leadership, American newspaper and magazine readers were treated to an unending stream of literature about "the Wobbly menace." Scholarly journals published learned treatises; less serious publications delighted, and sometimes frightened, their audiences with more popularized versions of the IWW story. Although more "respectable" labor organizations may have had larger membership lists and more flourishing treasuries, none enjoyed the national publicity—perhaps "notoriety" would be more accurate—accorded the IWW.

But almost as meteorically as the menacing IWW had risen in the official and unofficial public mind, it faded from view. The organization continued to exist after its repression in 1917–1918, as indeed it still does today, but only on the fringes of American society. Many of its leaders had been lynched or imprisoned; others died or deserted to more promising causes; and the remnants of the organization gradually vanished into what one writer has called the "haunted halls" of American labor history. Meanwhile, in the 1920's Americans became preoccupied with the "Great Bull Market," in the 1930's with depression and the New Deal, in the 1940's with world war, and in the 1950's with the threat, internal and external, of communism. Little time remained to consider an organization that for all intents and purposes was defunct. Why worry about old and tired Wobblies when younger and more dangerous radicals were on the scene? J. Edgar Hoover, who had risen in the Justice Department hierarchy by diligently harassing Wobblies, learned in the 1930's and after that greater political mileage was to be had in apprehending Dillingers and prosecuting communists.

Yet even as public officials and private citizens forgot about the radical labor crusaders of an earlier era, the IWW's intrinsic romantic qualities were seized upon by novelists and its songs by folklorists. One of the first to rediscover and romanticize the Wobbly past was John Dos Passos, whose prototypical Wobbly hero, Mac, in *The 42nd Parallel,* deserts the girl he loves and makes pregnant to join the class war at Goldfield, Nevada (1906–1908), one of the earliest IWW battles. There Mac edits the *Nevada Workman* (an actual IWW paper) and listens to "Big Bill" Haywood speak to a crowd in which "a cheering and stocky Bohemian miner that smelt so bad next them was clapping and the oneeyed Pole on the other side was clapping and the bunch of Wops were clapping and the little . . . Jap was clapping and the sixfoot ranchman who'd come in hopes of seeing fight was clapping. 'Ain't the sonofabitch some orator,' he was saying again and again." Or, as an old-timer tells a younger army recruit in James Jones's *From Here to Eternity:* "*You* don't remember the Wobblies. You were too young. Or else not even born yet. There has never been anything like them before or since. They called themselves materialist-economists but what they really were was a religion. They were work-stiffs and bindlebums like you and me, but they were welded together by a vision we don't possess." And that unique Wobbly vision gave the theme for Wallace Stegner's novel *The Preacher and the Slave,* and Barrie Stavis' play *The Man Who Would Not Die,* both based upon the life of Joe Hill, the Swedish-born

IWW organizer, bard, and martyr who, as he faced a Utah firing squad, melodramatically declaimed: "Don't mourn for me. Organize!" [2]

Wobblies were also, as one writer has phrased it, "Troubadors of Discontent." [3] They sang as they organized; their bards composed lyrics on picket lines and in prison cells. These songs were collected in the famous *Little Red Song Book*, where they were rediscovered by a new generation of rebellious folk singers who put Wobbly lyrics to a different use.[4] Instead of fanning the flames of discontent among oppressed workers, by the late 1950's IWW songs were stirring protesting civil rights marchers. But there was no real incongruity here, for the Wobblies' ultimate cause was the same as the civil rights crusaders': freedom and dignity for man. The "Wobs" had their dream a half-century before Martin Luther King.

They also had a certain sardonic streak reminiscent of contemporary "black humor." Wobblies referred to their enemy simply and symbolically as "The Iron Heel." Only a Wobbly organizing Arizona copper miners during the First World War could close a letter with this salutation: "Here's to mud on the stick of the boss."

But the IWW is too important to be left solely to the novelists and folk singers. Its history reveals much about American society before the bloody baptism of the First World War, still more about the strengths and weaknesses of native radicalism. Nor is the Wobbly experience without many lessons for today.

Unfortunately, for almost fifty years professional scholars neglected the IWW. The standard studies of the organization were written just before and immediately after the First World War. John Graham Brooks's *American Syndicalism: The IWW* (1913) was an immediate response to the Lawrence strike and the public's avid desire for more knowledge of the labor uprising's full implications. Paul F. Brissenden's *The IWW: A Study of American Syndicalism* (1919), a reaction to wartime persecution of Wobblies, defended the organization against charges of subversion and treason. Although these books were written by astute scholars who witnessed firsthand the IWW's emergence and growth and who knew many of the IWW leaders personally, both lack the historical perspective that only time makes available.

Not until 1932 would another major work on the IWW appear: John S. Gambs's *The Decline of the IWW.* This volume, however, represented little more than the autopsy of a corpse, for Gambs begins his survey with the year 1919, after the disastrous federal raids.

Brissenden's version of IWW history went virtually unchallenged for four decades. Recently, however, scholars have taken a fresh look at the IWW. Perhaps reflecting a contemporary sense of disenchantment with the drift of American society, perhaps responding to an increasing demand by the young for new culture heroes cast in an anti-bourgeois, anti-authoritarian mold, scholars and journalists have revived academic and popular interest in the Wobblies. In 1965 Philip Foner published the fourth volume of his history of the American labor movement—a book devoted entirely to the history of the IWW from 1905 to 1917. Two years later Patrick Renshaw, a young English journalist, brought out *The Wobblies,* a briefer but chronologically fuller treatment of the organization. Meanwhile, articles and essays about the Wobblies appeared in *American Heritage,* daily newspapers, and scholarly journals. And 1967 witnessed the publication of yet another book-length study: Robert F. Tyler's *Rebels of the Woods,* an analysis of the Wobblies' stormy history in the Pacific Northwest.

These recent studies all reveal that although IWW theory added little or nothing to Marxism and continental syndicalism, and while the organization admittedly failed to show much for its efforts in terms of membership rolls and abundant treasuries, it did have a dream of a better America where poverty—material and spiritual—would be erased and where all men, regardless of nationality or color, would walk free and equal. More than a half-century ago the Wobblies tried in their own ways to grapple with issues that still plague the nation in a more sophisticated, knowledgeable, and prosperous era.

Sixty years before Lyndon B. Johnson, the IWW offered its own version of the Great (New) Society to be built within the shell of the old. At a time when the Negro in America was being lynched wholesale and submerged socially, the IWW promised him hope through organization. At a time when civil liberties had only a precarious hold on the national conscience, the IWW challenged local authorities through campaigns of civil disobedience, time and again extending the realm of free speech and free assembly. At a time when non-white Americans and "new" immigrants formed an oppressed and submerged proletariat within an increasingly prosperous America, the

IWW attempted to stir them from lethargy and lift them from the mudsill of society. The IWW taught society's orphans and outcasts that power—society's motive force—comes through organization, and hence that the poor must organize to help themselves. Thus, to all who desire social change in America, the history of the IWW is fraught with lessons and warnings.

More than half a century ago, when the Wobblies still posed a threat to the existing order, Paul F. Brissenden, in a report prepared for the United States Commission on Industrial Relations, wondered whether the IWW's challenge to the wage system, capitalism, or, indeed, to the whole twentieth century was valid. "It might conceivably be true," he wrote, "that the I.W.W. is dangerous only to systems socially antiquated. The question has not really been decided." [5]

Given the rebirth of interest in the IWW reflected and stimulated by recent publications, and the organization's contemporary relevance, a detailed, documented, and objective history of the IWW is much in order. I hope the following account of the Wobblies' place in the American past meets those specifications. It seeks to analyze and answer on their merits some of the questions first posed by Brissenden. I must admit that some aspects of the IWW interest me far more than others—among them, the organization's revolutionary commitment, its struggles on street corners and picket lines for free speech and better working conditions, and its courageous activities and the ensuing repression by government during the First World War. The book naturally reflects such personal preferences. Despite this admitted (and I trust reasonable) selectivity, I hope the reader will find the book marked not merely by detachment and objectivity, but also by sympathy and compassion for an old cause that still exists.

ACKNOWLEDGMENTS

As with most products of scholarship, this one could not have been completed without the assistance of many institutions and individuals. The American Council of Learned Societies, the American Philosophical Society, and the Dean's Fund of Northern Illinois University provided, through grants-in-aid, funds which made possible research trips to various parts of the country.

Many libraries and historical societies helped me at every stage of the work. I owe particular debts of gratitude to Merle Wells of the Idaho State Historical Society; Richard Berner, Archivist at the University of Washington Library (Seattle); and Joseph Howerton of the Social and Economic Division, National Archives. The staffs at the Montana State Historical Society, Helena; the Bancroft Library, University of California at Berkeley; the Colorado State Archives, Denver; the State Historical Society of Wisconsin, Madison; AFL-CIO Headquarters, Washington, D.C.; the Manuscript Division of the New York Public Library; the Tamiment Institute Library, New York City; and the Legal, Diplomatic, and Financial Branch, National Archives, all offered me unstinting service.

Graduate students in my seminars at Northern Illinois University shared with me their discoveries about the history of the Wobblies and radical labor in America, especially my good friends among them: Michael L. Johnson, Clyde Tyson, and Warren Van Tine, without whose critical observations my own work would have been all the poorer. To Fred Thompson, Carl Keller, Walter Westman, and Richard Brazier I cannot offer sufficient thanks for sharing with me their own personal experiences as members of the IWW, and for always tolerating my own less romantic and more critical estimate of the Wobblies. Philip Mason and Stanley Solvick of the Wayne State University Labor Archives continually brought to my attention fresh items concerning the IWW, and Dr. Mason generously provided many of the illustrations for this book.

The editors of *Labor History* permitted me to draw upon my article "The Origins of Western Working Class Radicalism, 1890–1905"

(Spring 1966) for some of the material that appears in Chapters Two through Four of the book. Northern Illinois University Press and Alfred Young, editor of *Dissent: Explorations in the History of American Radicalism*, graciously allowed me to use my essay "The Radicalism of the Dispossessed: William D. Haywood and the IWW," parts of which appear in Chapters Seven and Ten.

My friend Paul Boyer, who patiently read the entire manuscript with a critical eye for style and substance, provided a boost in spirit that only a tired author can appreciate. Mrs. Joyce Emerle and Mrs. Andrea Bassignani rendered typing assistance when it was most needed. My editor, Ivan Dee, patiently and carefully nurtured and transformed a rough manuscript into a printed book. No words can adequately compensate my wife, Joan, who worked with me at every stage of the project, from musty archives to editing and proofreading the final copy.

CONTENTS

WE SHALL
BE ALL

Introduction

CHAPTER

I

A Setting for Radicalism,
1877–1917

THE history of the Industrial Workers of the World can be understood only in relation to the economic and social changes which between 1877 and 1917 transformed the United States into the world's leading industrial nation. IWW members, whether American-born or foreign-born, were first-generation immigrants to that industrial society. Hence they mirrored the perplexities and confusions, the strivings and ambitions of a generation compelled to contend with a world it had never made, a world it sometimes barely understood.

The social and economic changes which transformed America in the late nineteenth century left nothing untouched: the state, the churches, the family—all were altered because the bases of existence itself were being changed.[1]

Nothing altered the circumstances of life more than the building of cities and the growth of industries. Americans' original dream of creating an agrarian Arcadia, happily free from Europe's urban sores, had died early. Throughout the first half of the nineteenth century, in what remained ostensibly an agrarian society, Americans slowly urbanized and industrialized. Well before the Civil War and Radical Reconstruction completed the victory of industrial capitalism, citizens had laid the foundation for a modern industrial society.

With the end of the Civil War, Americans shifted their energies from waging battles to building steel mills, digging coal, packing

5

meat, and constructing cities. In the process of accomplishing all this, they created a new urban nation. In 1870 only about one of every four Americans lived in what the Census Bureau defined as an urban area; by 1900 the proportion had increased to more than two of every five; and by 1920 more than half the population resided in urban areas.[2]

Americans also built immense industrial combinations. Between 1897 and 1904 the so-called first American trust movement spawned its corporate colossi. Wall Street analyst John Moody in 1904 reported the existence of 318 important and active industrial trusts with a capital of over $7 billion, representing the consolidation of over 5,300 distinctive plants in every line of production. The acme of industrial combination came in 1901 when J. P. Morgan purchased Andrew Carnegie's iron and steel holdings, merging them with his own Federal Steel Company to form United States Steel, the first billion-dollar corporation in American history. What Carnegie and Morgan did for steel, Rockefeller did for oil, Gustavus Swift for meat packing, James Duke for tobacco, Henry Clay Frick for coal mining, James Pillsbury for grain processing, and Messrs. Ward and Roebuck for merchandising.[3]

These corporate concentrations cut across industrial lines. Carnegie's original empire of steel included not only coal and iron mines but blast furnaces and finishing mills, railroads and oreships. Rockefeller's even larger domain encompassed oil fields and refineries, the mining and smelting of copper, a Western steel complex in Pueblo, Colorado, transcontinental railroads, local utilities, and New York investment banks. Morgan, the era's Prince of Finance, as the price of providing funds for needy industrialists, placed his own lieutenants on the boards of directors of the nation's leading corporations. By the turn of the century, then, not only was America the wealthiest of industrial nations, but the agencies of that wealth—the investment banks and insurance companies, the railroads and other public utilities, the basic production and distribution industries—were dominated by a small coterie of powerful men.

Free competition in the marketplace between small producers and small buyers, none of whom could control the price level—the classical economists' laissez-faire ideal—had given way to imperfect competition between corporate giants, each of whom influenced the level of supply and demand. Oligopoly became the economic order of the day.

6

While America's total wealth increased enormously, its distribution remained uneven. The more wealth Henry George discovered, the more dismal poverty he perceived, leading him to conclude that progress and poverty went hand in glove. Jacob Riis also found no signs of affluence among his "Other Half" in New York's slums. Nor did Jane Addams at Hull House; nor Lillian Wald at her settlement house on Henry Street. The nation's great wealth, so impressive in the aggregate, was being distributed very unevenly among the various groups making up American society.

Although the standard of living improved for most American workers between 1877 and 1917, poverty remained a fact of life for most working-class families and a condition of existence for many, if not for most. Robert Hunter, in his classic study *Poverty*, published in 1904, reported that not less than 14 per cent of the people in prosperous times, and not less than 20 per cent in bad times, suffered from dire poverty, with unemployment causing the bulk of the distress. Hunter agreed with the British economist John Hobson, whom he quoted, that: "Modern life has no more tragical figure than the gaunt, hungry laborer wandering about the crowded centres of industry and wealth, begging in vain for permission to share in that industry, and to contribute to that wealth; asking in return, not the comfort and luxuries of civilized life, but the rough food and shelter for himself and his family, which would be practically secured to him in the rudest form of savage society.". [4]

Other observers of working-class life in early twentieth-century America found conditions reminiscent of the worst features of nineteenth-century industrial England. At a twine factory in New York City, a social worker watched the women file out at day's end: "Pale, narrow-chested, from hand to foot . . . covered with fibrous dust. . . . They were the types of factory workers—pale, haggard feeders of machines—like those described in the days of a century past in England." [5]

Not all workers labored for a pittance. For the skilled, who were always in scarce supply, a seller's market guaranteed high wages. And the influx into industry of millions of non-English-speaking immigrants from peasant cultures created numerous well-paid supervisory plant positions for those who could read and write English. Native Americans and acculturated immigrants could move from the blast furnace or the work bench to the foreman's post. And their children could wear a white collar in place of the blue one. Their skills and their relative scarcity also enabled these workers to establish potent trade unions.

And what of the workers who did not qualify for membership in labor's aristocracy? Occupying a position somewhere between the elite and the *lumpenproletariat,* these workers probably received just enough from the system in good times to keep them contented. So, as long as the promise of improvement beckoned and opportunity for it existed, the great mass of American workers had no irreconcilable quarrel with capitalism.

But if most workers benefited to a greater or lesser degree from American capitalism, a significant minority appeared to be bypassed altogether by industrial progress. Of these, none had a stronger grievance against the system than the American Negro. Freed at last from the bondage of chattel slavery, he found new forms of economic subservience waiting for him. At a time when industry cried for manpower, the Negro saw himself in desperate, unsuccessful competition for factory employment with the immigrant millions arriving in America from Eastern and Southern Europe. The black man thus typically remained in the Southland of his birth, there to work a white man's land with a white man's plow, a white man's mule, and a white man's money.[6] When industrial America finally did call him, it was too often to serve as a strikebreaker.

The new immigrants fared better than the Negro, but they too were "second-class citizens" in relation to native whites. Every survey of immigrant earnings shows that the latest arrivals ranked at the bottom of the economic ladder, the less industrialized their country of origin the lower their earnings in America. Only the Negro's presence kept the Italian, the Pole, and the Slav above society's mudsill.

Although most recent immigrants found life in the New World sweeter than what they had known in the Old, sometimes they concluded, as did a Rumanian immigrant: "This was the boasted American freedom and opportunity—the freedom for respectable citizens to sell cabbages from hideous carts, the opportunity to live in those monstrous dirty caves [tenements] that shut out the sunshine." [7]

One native American group with higher status than Negroes or immigrants also fared ill in the land that bred it. If the first half of the nineteenth century had been the golden age of the farmer in America, then the second half was his time of testing. The farms of New England, New York, and Pennsylvania now had to compete with the vast, fertile prairies of the West. And in the West, whether in Illinois, Iowa, or Kansas, economic adversity separated the superior farmer from his less efficient competitor. For those who had the competence but not the capital, the costs of farm-making were prohibitive. An older son might inherit the established family farm—but what of his younger brothers? From the noncompetitive farms of the Northeast, the foreclosed farms of the South and West, and from some successful farms everywhere thousands of young men were pushed off the land to search for other means of sustenance. Eventually many of them drifted into the growing ranks of migratory workers: the men who followed the wheat harvest north from Texas to Canada; picked the fruits, vegetables, and hops of the West Coast; labored in the mines, construction camps, and lumber camps of the West; always ready to move on with the job to a new region, a new camp, a new life. But the region, the camp, and the life too often turned out to be the same as the old: primitive, brutal, lonely, drudging, and poorly paid.[8]

From such as these—oppressed American Negroes, immigrants disillusioned with America's promise, native Americans forced off the land—the Industrial Workers of the World attempted to forge a movement to revolutionize American society. Negroes, immigrants, and migratories always served as the major objects of the IWW's efforts and (such as they were) the sources of its strength. Of the three groups, the migratories were to prove the most militant, revolutionary, and loyal.

If American capitalism in the best of times provided just adequately for most citizens and hardly that well for millions more, in the worst of times it failed to provide even the fortunate with jobs, income, and security. Industrial depressions and recessions occurred like clockwork in the half-century following Appomattox: first from 1873 to 1878, then again in 1883–1885, 1893–1897, 1907–1909, and 1913–

1915. Always the story was the same: Poverty in the midst of plenty. Idle men and idle capital. Sullen discontent and sporadic protest by the workers; gnawing fear by the middle and upper classes; harsh repression by the authorities.

Many Americans, especially workers, thus began to question the humanity and the social efficiency of the new industrial order. One letter writer in 1877 undoubtedly voiced the doubts of many others unable to articulate them: "Haven't these men [the strikers of 1877] a right to demand bread and warmth for their wives and little ones, while many of their fellow citizens revel in luxury and have more of the good things of this life than they can possibly make use of?" he asked. "If not, what is the definition of humanity? One fact is apparent. . . . In a land where there is more than enough for all, all should have at least enough." [9]

Desiring a measure of security in a time of economic fluctuation, workers sought to organize. The founders of the modern American labor movement learned the cardinal lesson of industrial society: the imperviousness of its basic problems to individual solution. For workers, this knowledge dictated the pooling of strength in trade unions and the creation of a national labor movement.

The wonder of labor history in the late nineteenth century is not that unions emerged but rather that they were so weak and that so few workers joined them. But a little reflection shows why. Although American society was hardly classless, it lacked the traditional bonds which tied European workers together into a class characterized by common patterns of thought and behavior. Indeed, America's working class was most notable for its religious and ethnic heterogeneity. Native American workers had nothing but contempt for Irish Catholic immigrants; and Irish workers in turn looked down upon the late-coming Poles, Slavs, and Italians. Whites feared Negroes; Jews suspected Gentiles. Employers easily played off one group against another and shrewdly mixed their labor forces to weaken group solidarity.

What judicious mixing could not accomplish, economic conditions and the law did. Too many workers had only their brawn to sell, and in a labor market periodically flooded by immigrants, brawn commanded a low premium. Better to win approval of one's boss by avoiding labor agitators and their unions than to lose one's job to a greenhorn or a scab! Those with skills to sell faced other barriers to union organization. American law sanctioned employers' anti-union

1 0

devices but outlawed basic trade-union tactics. The American judiciary, it has been said, tied one hand (and sometimes both) behind the worker's back before sending him into the Darwinian ring to fight a more powerful adversary.[10]

The whole American environment seemed to conspire against the labor movement. From 1877 to 1893 social mobility was writ large. Everywhere one looked, evidence emerged of poor boys who had "made good." Perhaps they were the exception, but men live by fantasies as much as by reality, and if the reality of great wealth eluded a worker, he could still dream about it for his son.

So when times were good and opportunities abounded, the ambitious worker showed slight interest in trade unions or in any institution which threatened to alter America's social structure. With depression, however, opportunities shriveled and dreams faded, driving the worker into the embrace of the union organizer; but unions, barely able to survive in prosperity, often collapsed at the first hint of depression. Union builders found themselves caught in an unenviable dilemma: the smallest possible following when times were most propitious for the labor movement; a much larger following when unions had least to offer.

The first important national labor organization to appear in industrial America was the Knights of Labor. Organized initially as a local secret society in 1869, made public and national in 1878, it invited all producers to join. Only capitalists, lawyers, gamblers, and drunkards were excluded from membership. Proclaiming universality of membership as its guiding principle, and solidarity—"An injury to one is the concern of all"—as its motto, the Knights functioned as a conventional labor organization. Most members were wage workers who joined to fight for higher wages and better working conditions.

As the only prominent, national labor organization in existence, the Knights grew rapidly during the prosperous years from 1879 to 1886. By 1886 membership approached one million, and some middle-class Americans came to fear the organization's Grand Master Workman, Terence Powderly—a mild-mannered, narcissistic, administratively incompetent, constitutionally ineffective, teetotaling bumbler— much as later Americans feared the post–New Deal generation of powerful labor leaders.

But the Knights lacked real substance and power. Its membership diminished after 1886 as rapidly as it had previously increased. By 1888 the organization, if not dead, was certainly dying. The age demanded planning, executive ability, and a rational grasp of the issues. The Knights lacked all three.

Some elements in the labor movement did dwell on efficiency and results, notably the national trade unions which in 1886 reorganized themselves as the American Federation of Labor. A rival national labor center competing with the Knights for members and for survival, the AFL lived and eventually thrived while the Knights declined and died.

What happened was that the trade unions recognized and acted upon what *was;* the Knights proposed what *could be.* The Knights, one historian has written, "tried to teach the American wage-earner that he was a wage-earner first and a bricklayer, carpenter, miner, shoemaker after; that he was a wage-earner first and a Catholic, Protestant, Jew, white, black, Democrat, Republican after. This meant that the Order was teaching something that was not so in the hope that sometime it would be." [11] But the AFL affiliates organized carpenters as carpenters, bricklayers as bricklayers, and so forth, teaching them all to place their own craft interests before those of other workers. While the Knights practiced solidarity as well as preaching it, the trade unions preached it and practiced *sauve qui peut.* Deciding that the wage system was here to stay, the craft unions assembled a working-class elite, retreated to a safe position, and weathered the storm.[12]

More and more after 1900, as the AFL under Samuel Gompers' leadership grew and prospered, it sought to sell itself to employers and to government officials as *the* conservative alternative to working-class radicalism. It could do so because its members were by and large those organized workers most satisfied with the status quo, those least alienated. In return for the good treatment accorded to the skilled elite dominant in the AFL, the Federation became in time one of the strongest defenders of the American system. So long as wages rose, and they did, hours fell, and they did, security increased, and it appeared to, the AFL could grow fat while neglecting millions of laborers doomed to lives of misery and want. As trustee of labor's aristocracy, the AFL achieved a ringing success by making certain that its reach never exceeded its grasp.

Here the IWW entered the picture, for it offered to do that which the AFL declined to attempt: organize the Negroes, the new immigrants, and the workers in mass-production industries where craft lines dissolved under the pressures of technology. The IWW, like the

Knights before it, told men and women that they were workers first and Jews, Catholics, whites or blacks, skilled or unskilled second. And the IWW would also try to teach "something that was not so, in the hope that sometime it would be."

Workers, however, were not the only Americans dissatisfied with the prevailing industrial order. This was also the era of Populism, Progressivism, and the rise of American socialism: The Age of Reform. While it lasted, all manner of things seemed possible in America. A myriad of reformers hoped to transform America into a just and good, if not "Great," society.

Arising out of the agrarian depression of the 1880's and 1890's, Populism presented the first effective challenge to thirty years of political complacency and drift. Discontent united the Populists. They agreed that production for profit, not for use, made the few rich at the expense of the many. They sensed that to compel men to obey "natural" laws of supply and demand turned them into just another commodity, like lumps of coal or sacks of flour. Populists saw no sense in an economic order which forced farmers off the land because they produced a surplus, yet could not feed hungry millions; they saw less sense in a system which laid off millions of workers because they could not consume what they had produced; and they found no sense at all in a political order which repressed the discontents of the masses but did little to curb the excesses, follies, and even tyrannies of great wealth. Populists instead proposed to keep the farmer on the land, the worker at his bench, and to return government to the service of the many, not the few. They proposed that man, meaning the masses, control the system for the benefit of society.[13]

But whereas discontent united the Populists, remedies for it divided them. One Populist's gain was another's loss. To the farmer, Populism promised inflation and higher farm prices—which to the worker meant higher prices and reduced real wages. To the worker, Populism included protection for unions and higher wages—which to a farmer implied costlier manufactured goods for himself and his family. While agrarians and workers might preach sympathy for each other's plight, their particular objectives proved mutually exclusive. Even before Populism merged with William Jennings Bryan's version of Democracy in 1896, left-wing socialist Daniel DeLeon correctly perceived its limitations. "Populist farmers are to get free silver at sixteen to one, so that they may pay their debts with depreciated money and thus become capitalists," he wrote. "The Populist politicians will get the spoils of office, while the Populist wage earners will mop their foreheads and rub their empty stomachs with a glittering generality." [14]

Although Populism died after the Democratic defeat in 1896 and the return of prosperity, reform survived. Progressivism followed. More urban, much more successful economically and socially, and much less alienated, Progressives nonetheless were well aware of the inadequacies and injustices rooted in American society. Through reform of the prevailing order, which they considered by and large to be satisfactory, Progressives sought to eliminate the occasion for future working-class uprisings or Populist revolts.[15]

Progressive era reforms included a little something for everyone: stricter anti-trust laws and business regulation for the small manufacturer, merchant, and farmer; lower tariffs for the agrarians of the South and West, and also for consumers; rural free delivery, postal savings banks, federal farm land banks, and other measures for the nation's farmers. Nor were workers and immigrants excluded from the bounty of Progressive reform. For them, Progressives provided factory and social welfare legislation. Child labor was restricted; women workers gained new legal protection; factories were made safer and cleaner; workers gained compensation and liability laws; some states moved in the direction of minimum-wage legislation; and many cities began to tidy up their noisome slums.

Taken together, these reforms appear conservative. Viewing them from the perspective of the present, one historian has concluded that "conservative solutions to the emerging problems of an industrial society were almost uniformly applied. The result was a conservative triumph in the sense that there was an effort to preserve the basic social and economic relations essential to a capitalistic society . . ." [16] Such a judgment, however, misreads the essence of the Progressive era. Progressivism did of course terminate in a conservative *cul de sac*. But that was not the intention of most reformers. The capitalism they sanctioned was clearly not that of J. P. Morgan, Henry Frick, or George F. Baer; they favored a vague, undefined democratic version. Perhaps capitalism was not compatible with the Progressive reformers' notions of a democratic and just society, but they could not know that

14

until the nation had tried their reforms. Many reformers in fact for a time had more in common with socialists than with the businessmen and major party politicians of the period. One prominent Progressive wrote to Morris Hillquit, Socialist theoretician, politician, and party boss: "What I feel about Socialism is that it is a very important element in the whole Progressive movement." [17]

Indeed, during the Progressive years socialism enjoyed its only period of sustained nationwide political success. Socialists benefited from the nation's awakened social conscience. To citizens alarmed about unrestrained and unregulated industrial capitalism, only the Socialist party offered a complete blueprint for a fundamentally different and, it believed, better America.

Socialism in this period also became Americanized. Previously thought of as the importation of European intellectuals and workers, the Socialist party's complexion appeared to change after 1900. Eugene Debs, its outstanding leader, though the child of immigrant parents, was himself American to the core, born and bred in the Midwest. Countless other prominent native Americans followed Debs into the party: the muckraking journalist Charles Edward Russell, Walter Lippmann, Florence Kelley, Frances Perkins, Upton Sinclair, John and Anna Sloan, Theodore Dreiser, and Max Eastman were only a few of the many Americans who found in socialism an antidote to their alienation from American society.[18]

Americanization brought votes. Debs's presidential campaigns of 1904, 1908, and 1912 spread socialism's message broadcast. Locally, where the possibilities of electoral victory were greater than at the national level, Socialists did exceedingly well. By 1911, as they captured the cities of Berkeley, Scranton, Bridgeport, Butte, and Schenectady, among others, articles were appearing in popular magazines as well as in academic journals voicing alarm at the "rising tide of socialism." [19] Socialists picked up votes in the most unlikely places: rural Kansas and Oklahoma, the piney woods of Louisiana and Texas, the mining cities of the Mountain West, as well as the immigrant-saturated industrial communities of the Northeast. After 1913 the Socialist tide began to recede, but in the areas of largest voter concentration the party continued to gain votes and win office.[20]

Political success, however, only obscured basic weaknesses. Within the Socialist party, factionalism and personality clashes ran riot. Although factions and individuals usually united or divided on specific issues without much attention to ideological consistency, a right (reformist) and a left (revolutionary) wing struggled for party ascendancy. More important than factionalism was the party's inability to widen its ethnic appeal beyond a limited number of new immigrants —Jews, most notably—and its consequent abysmal failure to win mass support from Catholic workmen. American socialism never captured the primary bastion of the labor movement, the AFL, as most European socialists had done in their native lands.[21]

While the age of reform lasted, millions of Americans challenged the old capitalist order. The system as described fifty years earlier by Marx and Engels was dying throughout the industrial world, the United States included, and various social groups were struggling to shape the economic order to come. None was absolutely certain of what the future would hold, but all wanted it to accord with their conceptions of a just and good society. In America, many options then *appeared* to exist, for in the 1890's and early 1900's the triumph of the modern corporation and the corporate state did not seem final, or inevitable. Among those Americans who opted for an alternative to the capitalist system were the many Western workers who became the backbone of the Industrial Workers of the World.

PART ONE

Origins,
1890–1905

CHAPTER

2

The Urban-Industrial Frontier, 1890–1905

NOWHERE in the late nineteenth century were the economic and social changes which produced American reform and radicalism so rapid and so unsettling as in the mining West. There, in a relatively short time, industrial cities replaced frontier boom camps and heavily capitalized corporations displaced grubstaking prospectors. The profitable mining of refractory ores (gold and silver) and base metals (lead, zinc, copper) required railroads, advanced technology, large milling and smelting facilities, and intensive capitalization. "The result," in the words of Rodman Paul, "was that [by 1880] many mining settlements were carried well beyond any stage that could reasonably be called the frontier. They became, instead, industrial islands in the midst of forest, desert, or mountain . . ."[1] During the 1890's and early 1900's, continued economic growth carried Western mining communities still further beyond the frontier stage.

Elsewhere in America it took as long as two centuries for the transformation from handicraft economy to machine production, from individual proprietor to impersonal corporation, from village to city. Even with this slow pace of development in older communities, the shock of change had proved unsettling to millions. In the West, where

1 9

communities grew from villages to industrial cities, mining enterprises evolved from primitive techniques to modern technology, from the small business to the giant corporation, if not overnight, at least within a generation; and this transformation proved even more disruptive of old habits and traditional attitudes.

As early as 1876 Colorado, though sparsely settled and far distant from the nation's primary industrial centers, had been colonized by corporations and company towns. Leadville, for example, stood as a monument to the urban frontier in America. Eighty air miles southwest of Denver, nearly two miles above sea level, surrounded by towering mountain peaks and shrouded in low-lying clouds (from which it derived its other name, "Cloud City"), it was by 1880 the metropolis of a Lake County mining community with 35,000 people. Leadville had had a varied history. Gold, discovered in 1858, had first attracted to the mountain settlement called Oro City all the odds and ends of society commonly found in rowdy mining camps. Oro City was at first no more urban or industrial than the California mining camps immortalized in the stories of Bret Harte and Mark Twain. As had happened in many of California's boom camps, dreams of fortune founded upon gold soon dissolved. In Oro City this occurred in 1876, the year Colorado was admitted to the Union. In 1878, however, newly unearthed rich sources of another mineral caused Oro City to be renamed Leadville. Within three years, the population soared from 200 to 14,280.[2]

Now publicized as the "greatest silver camp in the world," Leadville became by 1880 a leading producer of lead-silver ores, products requiring large-scale processing, intensive capitalization, and skilled labor. Such wide-ranging capitalists as Chicago's Marshall Field and Philadelphia's Meyer Guggenheim added their investments to those of local entrepreneurs James J. Brown (immortalized as the husband of "unsinkable Molly Brown") and H. A. W. Tabor (Baby Doe's spouse). The booming economy attracted skilled miners and smelter workers. Tradesmen came to serve the growing population, attorneys arrived to expound the subtleties of the law, medical men to succor the ill, and newspapers to inform the citizens of local and national happenings. Tabor built an opera house for his Baby Doe and for other members of Leadville's growing middle and upper classes; smaller businessmen operated bars and other less cultural resorts for the community's hard-working and hard-drinking laborers. Within a few years Leadville had developed into a middle-sized urban settlement with a heterogeneous population, a varied social structure, a thriving economy, and ample educational and cultural institutions.[3]

Cripple Creek, a once isolated region hidden by Pike's Peak, grew more rapidly than Leadville. In 1891 Bob Womack, the legendary Western cowpuncher and prospector, discovered gold in Poverty Gulch, though he himself died poor. That same year W. S. Stratton, a local building contractor, struck the Independence vein on the site of what later became Victor, Colorado; unlike the cowboy Womack, Stratton the entrepreneur died rich, leaving a fortune of $20 million. By 1893 Cripple Creek was known far and wide as the "greatest gold camp in America." Its gold output, valued at $1,903 in 1891, increased to more than $2 million by 1893, and rose each year thereafter until it peaked at $18,199,736 in 1900. By then Cripple Creek proudly was advertising its ten thousand inhabitants, three railroads, trolleys, electric lights, hospitals, and schools.[4]

Montana repeated the Colorado pattern. Its production of ores, valued at $41 million in 1889, made it the nation's leading mining state, while Butte, "the richest hill in the world," had become America's copper capital.[5] Idaho, on a lesser scale, recapitulated the developmental pattern of Montana and Colorado. And Arizona, in the 1890's and early 1900's still a territory (it did not become a state until 1912), proved remarkably similar in social evolution to its northern neighbors. At Bisbee, near the Mexican border and hard by Tombstone, where the Earps shot it out with the Clantons at the O.K. Corral, Phelps Dodge Corporation built an industrial city. Like company towns everywhere, it had its corporation-owned church, hospital, store, recreation center, and homes.[6]

The industrial cities of the mining West represented in microcosm the emerging conditions of life in urbanized, industrial America rather than the simpler social arrangements of the passing frontier. These mill and smelter towns, with their shoddy company houses and stores, their saloons, and their working-class populations, bore a distinct resemblance to their Eastern industrial counterparts. With this additional difference—that in the West the very rapidity of economic growth brought greater unrest, conflict, violence, and radicalism.

Together with men in search of adventure and fortune, large corporate enterprises took Horace Greeley's advice and went West. Domestic and foreign capital rushed to exploit Western opportunities. In Colorado, for example, between 1893 and 1897, 3,057 new mining corporations were organized, each capitalized at over $1 million. By 1895 all of Colorado's larger cities boasted mining exchanges, and in 1899 the Colorado Springs Mining Exchange alone handled over 230 million mining shares valued at over $34 million. New Yorkers and Chicagoans, Englishmen and Scotsmen poured their funds into the American West. W. S. Stratton sold his fabulous Independence Mine to British investors in 1899, and at about the same time Phelps Dodge, an established Eastern firm, seized control of Arizona copper mining, just as the Rockefeller interests were doing in Montana.[7]

The high costs associated with discovering, extracting, processing, and transporting metal ores led inevitably to large-scale business operation. Corporate concentration offered both economic efficiencies and important noneconomic advantages. The large corporation could more easily finance its own geological surveys and then exploit its findings more fully and cheaply. As prices declined and the cost of extracting ores from deeper beneath the earth's surface rose, only operations able to spread fixed capital costs over increased productivity could survive. Large corporations were also in a better position than their smaller competitors to exact favorable rates from railroads, smelters, and refineries.[8] So, in the West as in the East, large corporations devoured smaller, less efficient, or less capitalized firms.

In constructing its mining empire in the Arizona territory, Phelps Dodge colonized a region known more for its badmen and buttes, its Apaches and U.S. Cavalry, than for its mineral riches. But Phelps Dodge had the capital and the business skills requisite to turn a barren frontier into an industrial citadel. Unlike small local enterprises that could work only rich surface ores and that faced insuperable refining and transportation barriers, Phelps Dodge worked the deeper refractory ores and erected its own refining and transportation facilities. The company literally built the cities of Bisbee and Warren, while the neighboring community of Douglas, a refining center, bore the company president's name. Between 1885 and 1908 Phelps Dodge extracted over 730 million pounds of copper from its famous Copper Queen mine at Bisbee, reaping dividends of over $30 million.[9]

Not satisfied with economic hegemony in the Warren district, Phelps Dodge gained control of copper production further north at Morenci. There it established an even larger, more efficient smelting operation. Large-scale investment raised Morenci's production from about seven million pounds in 1897 to over eighteen million in 1902, and twenty-four million by 1908. By 1910 the Arizona territory was a world leader in copper production; only seven years later, on the eve of the First World War, a handful of companies, led by Phelps Dodge, controlled the new state's mining economy.[10]

Corporate concentration had far-reaching implications for Western workers. As national corporations replaced local enterprises, Western workers and labor leaders suddenly began fondly to recall how easy it had once been to see the head of a local concern and work out amicable arrangements to settle most disputes. Giant corporations, by contrast, did not allow local managers to make ultimate labor policy, while workers and union spokesmen could rarely interview the general officers, who were usually situated in distant cities. Local managers would refuse to settle disputes, claiming they could not go beyond their instructions from the home office. The home office in turn would pass the buck back to its local agents. Workers and union negotiators were caught uncomfortably in the middle. This divorce between ownership and local management, this geographical gulf between the worker and his ultimate employer, led to violent industrial conflict; conflict made even more bitter by the nature of the Western worker.

The workers who filled the industrial cities of the West shared a common language, a certain degree of ethnic similarity, and a tradition of union organization. Unions organized by miners in the 1860's on the Comstock Lode in Nevada had grown and prospered, defending existing wages in bad times and obtaining increases in good times. From there the union idea had spread to other mining districts. ". . . The Virginia City Miners' union became the training center of hard rock miners unionism," wrote Vernon Jensen. "Miners learned the new techniques in mining developed at this place and carried them throughout the West. They also carried the idea of unionism wherever they went." [11]

Ethnic ties increased union solidarity. Census statistics disclose that, unlike other American industrial centers of that era, all the major mining districts in Colorado, Idaho, and Montana were dominated by native-born majorities. Moreover, the foreign-born came largely from the British Isles (including Ireland) and Scandinavia, and were hardly representative of the more recent waves of immigration. An unusually large number of foreign-born workers in the West also became naturalized citizens. Of 528 miners imprisoned in Idaho's Coeur d'Alenes during the labor dispute of 1899, 132 were American-born and 208 naturalized citizens. As late as 1903–1904 Emma F. Langdon, a union sympathizer and participant in that year's Cripple Creek labor war, considered the local miners mostly American-born, with a smattering of German, Irish, and Swedish immigrants. A look at the names published in the Western Federation of Miners (WFM) directory of officers printed regularly by the *Miners' Magazine* demonstrates the overwhelmingly Anglo-Saxon origins of the organization's local and national leadership.[12]

The miners, foreign-born and American, were also skilled workers. Cornishmen who had mined lead in their home country were brought to America for their known skills. Irishmen, too, were recruited primarily as skilled miners. And many a native American had long since forsaken prospecting and the hope of "striking it rich" for the steadier returns of skilled wage labor. There is every reason to believe that as mining became more complex and costly, mine and smelter operators preferred skilled, regular workmen to "pioneers" or "frontiersmen," and that wage differentials attracted European and Eastern miners to the American West.[13] John Calderwood, the first union leader at Cripple Creek, entered the coal mines at the age of nine and thereafter devoted his life to mining, including brief attendance at mining school. Ed Boyce, the first successful president of the WFM (1896–1903) and an Irish immigrant, worked as a miner from 1884 until his election to the union presidency; his successor, Charles Moyer, had been a skilled worker in the Lead, South Dakota, smelter complex. And the most famous of all Mountain West labor leaders, William D. "Big Bill" Haywood, entered the mines as a teen-ager and worked in them until his election as secretary-treasurer of the WFM in 1901.[14]

Although the workers of the Mountain West were not wild and woolly frontiersmen, they did differ in important respects from their counterparts in the East and in Europe. Fred Thompson, former editor of the IWW's *Industrial Worker,* has expressed these differences as he remembers them from his own experiences as a "working stiff":

Their [Western workers'] speech was different—much more seasoned, and even their cussing was original and avoided stereotype. I think they shunned stereotype in all things. Their frontier was a psychological fact—a rather deliberate avoidance of certain conventions, a break with the bondage to the past. Yet there was far more "etiquette" on the job than I had observed back east. . . . In the bunkhouse or jungle or job there was this considerateness that was rare back east. Individuality and solidarity or sense of community flourished here together, and with a radical social philosophy . . . [they] demanded more respect for themselves and accorded more respect to each other than I found back east.

Thompson ascribes Western working-class uniqueness to the inherent character or personality of the worker. He believes the Western working force was made up of men who had consciously chosen to cut loose from unprofitable farms, strikebound Eastern factories, or the security of immigrant enclaves. Then a further winnowing—essentially a process of environmental adaptation—occurred as the worker made his own way west: drifting, working, striking, and moving on. Thompson states his rude social Darwinism in these words: "I believe there was a process of selection whereby those who least tolerated the ways of the east, went west. There most of them did not become settled or tied in a specific location—there weren't enough females to tie them. They were footloose." [15]

Although Thompson apparently perceives a direct relationship between the extent of footlooseness and the growth of radicalism, other factors are more important in accounting for Western differences. First, labor was scarcer in the West, and this scarcity encouraged footlooseness (not vice versa); workers moved where wages were highest and conditions best. In other words, Western workers were no more instinctively mobile than those in the East; they simply had greater opportunities and incentive to move on. Second, ethnic divisions were not as sharp in the West. Though employers attempted to recruit heterogeneous work forces to reduce labor solidarity, they did not succeed as completely as they did in the East. When Eastern and Southern Europeans were introduced into the Western work force, they never dominated a community quite as they had in the coal-mining and steel-making communities of Pennsylvania; instead, they were quickly either socially ostracized or integrated into the Western community of English-speaking workers. (Ethnic conflict was not altogether absent among Western workers; no two nationalities disliked each other more intensely than Cornishmen and Irishmen.) [16] Third, social institutions were not as firmly established in the West. Just as the original colonial settlements were at least to some degree liberated from the European past, so Western settlements were to some degree unencumbered by the Eastern past. Western workers shared that freedom with all the region's inhabitants. Finally, most Western workers lived in mining communities, where men derived their sustenance by daily risking their lives in the bowels of the earth. Western mining centers shared with mining communities the world over the group solidarity and radicalism derived from relative physical isolation and dangerous, underground work.

Owing largely to the ethnic composition and solidarity of Western mining communities and to the reliance of local merchants and professionals upon miners' patronage, workers and local businessmen were not at first split into hostile factions. Local businessmen and farmers often supported the miners in their struggle for union recognition and higher wages. In Idaho's mineral-rich Coeur d'Alenes the local residents—farmer and merchant, journalist and physician, public official and skilled worker—sympathized with striking miners. A leading Idaho attorney and Democratic politician, Boise's James H. Hawley, defended indicted strikers from 1892 to 1894, referring to them as friends and allies and even importuning President Grover Cleveland to provide several with patronage appointments.[17] East of the Continental Divide, in Montana, the copper kings, battling among themselves, wooed their workers with promises of union recognition, higher wages, the eight-hour day, and improved working conditions.[18] Even Bill Haywood admitted that in Colorado's Cripple Creek district before the 1903–1904 conflict, miners and businessmen associated with each other, belonged to the same fraternal societies, and were united by ethnic ties. Mediation hearings held by Colorado Governor James Peabody in 1903 clearly demonstrated the friendlier attitude toward labor held by local employers as compared to national corporations.[19]

But mining communities had no fences to sit on during industrial disputes. With few exceptions, local residents depended upon either workers or employers for subsistence. Consequently, when conflict came, sides had to be chosen.

Into these mining communities the modern corporation intruded to disrupt the local peace and to drive a wedge between workers and their non-working-class allies. The 1890's was an uneasy decade for American business, and for none more so than mining, milling, and smelting. The falling price of silver, the Depression of 1893, the repeal of the Sherman Silver Purchase Act, and the inherent instability of extractive industries made mine owners and smelter operators eager to reduce production costs and consequently less tolerant of labor's demands. Mining corporations formed associations to pressure railroads by threatening to close down mining properties and cease shipments unless shipping rates declined. But capitalists found it easier to make savings by substituting capital for labor.

Technological innovations increased productivity but in so doing diluted the importance of traditional skills and disrupted established patterns of work. Although technological change did not usually decrease total earnings, it tended to lower piece rates and to reduce some formerly skilled workers to unskilled positions with lower earning potential. Since the mining enterprise competed in a common product and labor market, all Western mining communities experienced similar pressures on piece rates, job categories, and established skills. In Bill Haywood's hyperbolic language: "There was no means of escaping from the gigantic force that was relentlessly crushing all of them beneath its cruel heel. The people of these dreadful mining camps were in a fever of revolt. There was no method of appeal; strike was their only weapon." [20]

Haywood exaggerated only slightly. The modernization and corporatization of the mining industry indeed aggravated the miners' traditional job grievances. If technological innovation did not irritate miners, company-owned stores, saloons, and boarding houses charging noncompetitive prices did. If miners accepted changing job classifications and skill dilutions, they refused to tolerate false economies achieved by providing insufficient mine ventilation and timbering, and by cutting down on other safety measures.

Whatever their grievances, Western miners discovered that only through organization could they obtain redress. Employers, however, failed to appreciate the benefits of union organization. Hence for a decade and a half, miners and mine owners struggled for economic power and security.

Modern miners' unions first emerged in Butte in 1878, when on June 13 local workers organized the Butte Miners' Union (later to become Local 1 in the WFM, its largest and richest affiliate) to defend workers against proposed wage reductions and to maintain the $3.50 daily minimum for underground workers. The union grew rapidly, succeeded in its defense of prevailing wage rates, and accumulated a full treasury. Labor leaders trained in Butte and money accumulated there were later to play a prominent role in union organization elsewhere.[21]

Not for another decade, however, did an association of miners' unions develop. Then, in 1888 or 1889, Idaho miners in the Coeur d'Alene camps of Burke, Gem, Mullan, and Wardner formed the Coeur d'Alene Executive Miners' Union.[22] Here violent labor conflict was to occur; and here labor organization began to cross state lines as Butte miners provided legal counsel and strike funds for their Idaho comrades.

Before the 1880's the immensely rich Coeur d'Alene district was hidden in a northern Idaho mountain wilderness. The whole area, consisting of a narrow east-west belt thirty miles long and ten miles wide, was surrounded on all sides by the peaks of the Coeur d'Alene Mountains. The main canyon was barely wide enough to contain a railroad, and subsidiary canyons leading to the main mine sites were even narrower. Such mining towns as Gem and Mullan consisted of a single street, with homes and saloons backed up against mountain walls.[23]

In 1887, a narrow-gauge railroad finally made its way into the main canyon, inaugurating the growth of large-scale mining. Three years later the Northern Pacific and the Union Pacific reached the district, making operations even more profitable. With the railroads came new investors. The most productive local mine, the Bunker Hill and Sullivan, was purchased in 1887 by the Portland, Oregon, capitalist Simeon G. Reed. Not long thereafter, Reed sold out to a San Francisco–New York capitalist combine organized by John Hays Hammond, a world-famous mining engineer. These outside investors transformed the Coeur d'Alenes by 1890 into a productive and profitable mining area.[24]

But large-scale investment also brought to the region new mine managers eager to discipline local labor. Almost as soon as Simeon Reed had assumed ownership of the Bunker Hill, his resident manager advised: ". . . There is a general feeling in the community to rob us whenever and wherever they can and they are like a swarm of hungry coyotes . . . this I propose to stop and they shant rob us out of a dollar —this can only be brought about by a systematic manner in conducting the affairs of the Co. . . . I want the privilege to employ one confidential man, who quietly and unostentatiously reports to me all about our employees . . . his salary would be a trifle compared with the services he might render us." [25] And so labor spies came to the district. Two years later, Reed's next manager, Victor Clement, reported that local mine owners had formed an association for mutual benefit and protection, particularly in dealing with railroads and smelters. But Clement added: "Will also endeavor to regulate many abuses in the labor question . . ." [26]

The labor "abuses" referred to were caused by the policies of the Coeur d'Alene Executive Miners' Union. This local labor organization, generally moderate in its attitudes and policies, sought to maintain the union shop, minimum wages for underground workers regardless of skill, and its own union-financed and -controlled hospitals and medical services.

Mine managers, faced with competition from other nonunion lead-silver districts as well as with railroad and smelter rates they considered too high, decided to crack down on labor. In order to reduce labor costs through increased productivity, they had introduced air drills, an innovation which forced many miners to accept less skilled jobs.* But the unions had insisted upon and won a $3.50 daily mini-

---

* A single miner with an air drill could produce considerably more per unit of time, thus increasing the demand for less skilled workers (muckers) to shovel the ore more rapidly—a prime reason the unions made two men to a drill a major bargaining demand.

mum for all underground workers. Obviously the mine owners could not reduce costs sufficiently while local unions remained so powerful. Employers again looked to private detectives to assist them in breaking labor's hold on the district; in this endeavor they turned to Charlie Siringo, the self-proclaimed "Cowboy Detective." Given employment at the Gem Mine under the assumed name of Allison, Siringo joined the local union. Ingratiating himself with union men by his generosity, Allison-Siringo won election as recording secretary of the Gem local of the Coeur d'Alene Executive Miners' Union. With full access to union records, he transmitted to the mine owners detailed reports of union tactics and policies.[27]

Knowing in advance what to expect from the unions, the mine owners promptly cracked down on their workers. On New Year's Day, 1892, district mines announced an impending shutdown to remain in effect until local railroads reduced their shipping charges. Within two weeks of the announcement every district mine had closed, leaving unemployed workers to contend with a sub-zero northern Idaho winter. Although managers hoped their action would lead to fairer rates from the railroads, they were equally certain that a winter of discontent would weaken the local unions and make a wage reduction easier to effect. On March 19, 1892, having achieved their first objective of reduced shipping charges, mine owners agreed to reopen their properties on or before April 1. But simultaneously they alleged that depressed market conditions required a reduced wage scale. So on March 27 employers reduced the minimum wage for underground work from $3.50 to $3 a day.

Winter unemployment, however, had failed to weaken the union's will or its power. Miners still demanded the "traditional" $3.50, no less! Informed by Siringo that the unions would not compromise, the owners withdrew their wage offer of March 27, and rather than work their mines at what they deemed too high a cost (especially given the depressed market for lead-zinc ores), they decided to keep them closed until June 1.[28]

At this point, April–May 1892, the miners and their unions remained in control of the primary sources of local power. Few, if any, local men would scab. The major district newspapers, the county government whose sheriff and deputy were union men elected by union votes, and the local justices of the peace, who also were either union men or sympathizers, supported the miners' unions. Similar support came from many area merchants, doctors, lawyers, and even farmers. Moreover, the Butte Miners' Union had amassed a $5,000 cash loan for the Coeur d'Alene miners, and it had also assessed its own members $5 monthly for a strike fund.[29]

Employers, of course, were aware of their workers' strength. If the district mines were to be reopened at the reduced wage scale, outside labor would have to be imported. This is just what John Hays Hammond did, transporting California miners to northern Idaho, arming them, and barricading them in his Bunker Hill mine. But the mass importation of strikebreakers proved impossible. The district's limited points of entry and the narrowness of its canyons made it easy for union men to patrol all access routes. Local law officers (some of them union members), joined by deputized union men, worked together to root out strikebreakers who slipped by the union patrols. In addition, Idaho law forbade the importation of armed forces, an expedient for a time considered by mine owners besides Hammond.[30]

Yet the employers possessed two important and, in the last analysis, determining weapons: money and influence. Unable to control the local law or to sway the district's non-working-class population, they approached federal judges and the governor of the state for assistance. From one such judge, James H. Beatty, mine owners in May 1892 obtained an injunction which forbade union members to trespass upon company property, interfere in any way with mining operations, or intimidate company employees. In effect, this and subsequent injunctions restricted picketing and all union efforts to induce strikebreakers to leave the mines.[31] But court decrees could not provide labor to work the mines. For this employers looked to the Governor, from whom they hoped to obtain federal troops to protect unarmed workers imported to Idaho on a mass scale. Governor Norman H. Willey responded to the mine owners' requests. Only President Benjamin Harrison's refusal to send federal troops to an area where there had been no violence that could not be controlled by the state (there had in fact been no violence at all) and no violations of federal laws stood between the mine owners and their plans to smash the unions.[32]

At this point the labor conflict took a strange and violent turn. From March through early July the unemployed miners had maintained a united but peaceful front. Knowing their employers were unable to secure an adequate supply of strikebreakers, the union men quietly waited for their bosses to surrender. But on July 11 the strike-lockout stalemate was unexpectedly altered. *What* happened on that

3 1

day is clear; *why* it happened is not. Union members, who had been peaceful and law-abiding for three months, suddenly armed themselves, formed into an attacking force, and seized two mines. During the attack two men were killed, six injured, and company property destroyed. The circumstances of the July 11 incident are suspicious, to say the least. Only a few days before, employers had learned from Governor Willey that President Harrison had turned down their request for troops because the Coeur D'Alene district was peaceful. Allegedly, the mine owners had been taken by surprise, enabling the miners to capture the two mines so easily. Yet Siringo was at the time a trusted union member, who would certainly have had knowledge of a premeditated union attack, and he would just as certainly have passed such knowledge on to his employers well before July 11. His role as a company spy was not in fact discovered until that very day (July 11), when he made a hasty and ignominious escape from union headquarters and fled the district. Yet Siringo, who had been reporting to the employers regularly on union tactics, forwarded no advance notice of the most important single step allegedly planned by the miners.

Whatever the circumstances, the events of July 11 decisively altered the local balance of power, turning it away from the unions and toward the mine owners. If the employers neither planned nor provoked the violent attack, they were nevertheless its only beneficiaries. Immediately after the July 11 union attack, mine owners demanded aid from Willey and from Idaho's congressional delegation. With each passing hour the employers appeared to become more frantic, as did Willey's own attorney general, who telegrammed Idaho's U.S. senators: "The mob must be crushed by overwhelming force. We can't retreat now." Still more panicky a little later, he added: ". . . Gatling guns and small howitzers . . . should be sent. The woods may have to be shelled. Nothing but overwhelming force will . . . prevent serious fight." [33] Under these circumstances—an outburst of violence by long-suffering workers (or perhaps instigated by their employers) and a great deal of rhetorical blood and thunder drummed up by employers and state officials—Willey and the mine owners obtained from the White House the federal troops they desired.

Within three days of the initial union "outbreak" (which passed as suddenly as it had come), federal troops had the situation well in hand. At Governor Willey's suggestion, the military authorities acted decisively, arresting over 600 men, 350 of whom were held in custody between July 16–20. The arrestees included top union officials; Justices of the Peace George Pettibone and William Frazier; and Peter Breen, the liaison between the Butte Miners' Union and the Coeur d'Alene unions, who had been extradited from Montana. Where once employers had complained to the Governor about a union-created "reign of terror," miners now railed against the "terror" inflicted on them by a powerful government-business alliance.[34]

There was some justice in the miners' complaints, for the federal troops on duty in the Coeur d'Alenes clearly made themselves a union-busting tool for employers. State and federal officials offered the imimprisoned union men their freedom—but only on condition they implicate their organization in the July 11 violence and renounce future union activity. To a man, the prisoners refused the offer, insisting instead that they had broken no law and would not sign an anti-union declaration even if it meant an additional ten years in prison.[35]

Federal and state authorities meanwhile prosecuted a select group of prisoners. In two separate federal trials, Judge Beatty found seventeen union men guilty of violating his injunctions; thirteen of them he declared guilty of contempt of court, a civil offense, and sentenced to short terms in the Ada County Jail; but he found the other four guilty of criminal conspiracy, sentencing them to two years' imprisonment at the Detroit House of Correction. Almost simultaneously the state brought murder charges against forty-two strikers. But here the prosecution had to depend upon a jury verdict (Beatty had handed down his decisions from the bench), and it lacked the evidence to convict. Losing the first in a planned series of murder trials, the state never tried another defendant.[36] Even Beatty's verdicts did not go unchallenged. James H. Hawley, attorney for the miners' unions, appealed Beatty's criminal convictions to the United States Supreme Court, which in March 1893 overturned them. The Supreme Court majority declared that Beatty had abused his authority by using federal power to punish men for violation of what could only be considered a state law.[37]

The mine owners lost more than the legal cases arising out of the Coeur d'Alene conflict. Despite their use of strikebreakers, injunctions, and troops, they also failed to break the local unions. By 1894, in fact, miners' unions had re-established themselves more strongly than ever in all but one (Bunker Hill) of the district mines. Most important, the owners' aggressive anti-union tactics served to bring into the open conditions that would plague Western labor relations for the next decade. The first war of the Coeur d'Alenes demonstrated the degree to which miners' unions dominated the local community, its news sources, its law agencies, its sympathies. Employers as a result resorted to strikebreakers. But imported workers only increased community hostility toward employers and led to yet sharper conflict. The ensuing violence, in turn, permitted employers to request and usually to obtain state and federal assistance. Troops, martial law, and trials followed inevitably, and whatever the immediate result, a heritage of hatred and class resentment was left behind.

Labor disputes, often initially erupting over minor economic grievances, would shortly reach basic issues of economic power: not how much would be paid, but who would decide the rate; not how many hours would be worked, but who would determine the day's length. Minor grievances could be compromised; given the customary beliefs of most American businessmen, power could not. Employers in their search for security turned to the state and its coercive power; workers resorted to union organization. The more successful the capitalists were in using the power of the state, the less interested labor was in politics, and the more it determined to depend upon its own internal resources.

The Coeur d'Alene labor leaders, imprisoned in Ada County Jail, had ample time to consider mine labor's plight. They perceived, with the advice of their lawyer, Hawley, that the dominance of the mining industry by national corporations had drastically altered the miner's existence, and they soon agreed among themselves that only a national organization of hard-rock miners could defend labor's rights against powerful interstate corporations.[38] Hence agitation for a new labor organization began in earnest in March 1893. Soon thereafter, the Butte Miners' Union issued a call to Western hard-rock miners to convene in Butte on May 15. On that day, delegates from Idaho, Nevada, Utah, Colorado, Montana, and South Dakota arrived in Butte. Within five days they adopted a constitution, elected permanent officers, and created the Western Federation of Miners.[39]

The infant WFM, in the spirit of other labor organizations of the era, grandiloquently proclaimed as its purpose: "to unite the various miners' unions of the west into one central body; to practice those virtues that adorn society and remind man of his duty to his fellow men; the elevation of the position and the maintenance of the rights

34

of the miner." [40] Selig Perlman and Philip Taft have aptly described the miners' baby at birth:

Like the typical American union of the period, it was job conscious and, instead of dreaming of either self-employment through co-operation, the dream of the Knights of Labor, or of socialism, it announced to the world that it sought to maintain friendly relations with the employer, preferring voluntary arbitration and conciliation to strikes. This union thus began as a purely job protective organization.[41]

Reading such modest goals in 1893, no one could have foreseen that four years later a WFM president would call for union rifle clubs and for the establishment of a dual Western labor organization; nor that seven years later the WFM would endorse socialism; nor that in 1905 it would father the Industrial Workers of the World. Indeed, the WFM almost died in infancy. When its second convention met in 1894, the organization was barely viable; 1895 proved no better: that year two presidents of the WFM failed to complete their terms in office. (In August 1895, for the second time in less than a year, the WFM lacked a leader.) The prospect for 1896 looked equally bleak. But the 1896 convention elected Ed Boyce as president, and his firm leadership, combined with the return of prosperity, restored life to the organization. By 1899 the WFM had entered a period of brief but impressive growth.[42]

But as it grew, the WFM more often came into conflict with its business opponents and their allies in the courthouses and statehouses, and even in the White House. For a full decade, 1894–1904, violent labor conflict shattered the peace of the Mountain States. From the fires of these struggles emerged the radicals who ultimately founded the IWW.

CHAPTER
3

The Class War on the Industrial Frontier, 1894–1905

Born in the aftermath of a violent labor conflict in which the combined power of private business, state authorities, and federal troops had subdued rebellious miners, the Western Federation of Miners matured during a series of even more explosive industrial wars. Scarcely a year passed from 1894 to 1904 without WFM affiliates becoming involved in disputes with employers—disputes which often resulted in violence, loss of property and life, and military intervention.

These industrial conflicts molded Western labor's attitudes toward employers, society, and the state. From these battles the WFM members drew lessons about class realities in a capitalist society which they could never have derived from Marxist treatises or even from revolutionary tracts. Scarred and embittered by a decade of industrial warfare, many Western workers turned violently against the existing social order, found both an explanation and a remedy for their predicament in Marxian theory, and became in time the most radical and militant sector of the American labor movement.

During the ten years from 1894 to 1904, Western miners literally waged armed war with their capitalist adversaries. Miners' unions sometimes purchased and stocked rifles and ammunition, drilled in military fashion and prepared if all else failed to achieve their objectives with rifle, torch, and dynamite stick. This resort to violence did not lack substantial reason, for mine operators proved equally martial, and usually less compromising, than their labor-union foes. Businessmen also stored arms and ammunition; they, too, on occasion resorted to dynamite, hired Pinkerton men and utilized *agents provocateurs,* and paid private armies to defend their properties when public authorities refused to provide such protection. Given the preparations and precautions undertaken by business and labor combatants, it is no wonder that contending armies clashed on the industrial battlefield at Cripple Creek in 1894; that mines were put to the torch at Leadville in 1896; or that armed miners seized a train and destroyed an ore concentrator in the Coeur d'Alenes in 1899.[1]

These Western labor conflicts seemed to epitomize the Marxian class war—no holds barred, no quarter given. But initially it was a most peculiar variety of class war, for in most mining communities local farmers, businessmen, and professionals allied with labor unionists; and public officials, including judges, elected by union votes, often supported labor's goals. Instead of class being pitted against class, local communities united in coalitions cutting across class lines to combat "foreign" capitalists.[2]

Businessmen, however, as we have seen in one Idaho case, soon learned to counterattack with state and federal power. After watching helplessly as Governor Davis "Bloody Bridles" Waite used militia to disarm their private army at Cripple Creek in 1894, mine owners vowed that never again would the power of the state be placed at labor's disposal. And two years later at Leadville, businessmen used Colorado's state government to break a miners' strike. Then, in 1899, state and federal power combined to crush unionism in the Coeur d'Alenes.

But crushing strikes was not enough. Businessmen also sought to isolate labor from its non-working-class local allies. Their success is

clearly demonstrated in the case of James H. Hawley, the Idaho
lawyer-politician who had defended the Coeur d'Alene miners' unions
from 1892 to 1894. At that time Hawley had viewed Idaho's miners
not only as oppressed workers and political allies in the Democratic
party, but also as personal friends. He had even advised the leaders
among them to establish the WFM. Yet by 1899 he was prosecuting
his former friends and allies, now labeling them either criminals or
"un-American" radicals. Hawley's transformation—from friend of
labor to advocate of the turn-of-the-century business version of "law
and order"—was repeated by hundreds of other men in the mining
West as corporate capitalism extended its grip and widened its influence over the region.[3]

When the mine owners had solidified their power locally as well
as nationally, the workers' only alternative to submission became real
class warfare. As the WFM waged one battle after another, it learned
that the state was allied to capital, that Democrats were no better
than Republicans, and that old friends could not be trusted. Only
through internal organization and class solidarity could labor hope to
find immediate security and ultimate salvation.

For a time, despite or possibly even because of the opposition's
strength, the WFM thrived. The years between the unsuccessful 1899
struggle in the Coeur d'Alenes and the resumption of labor warfare
in Colorado in 1903 were the union's golden age. In November 1901
the *Miners' Magazine* reported that the preceding six months had been
the most prosperous in the union's life, with almost all of its affiliates
increasing their membership and twenty new locals added. The WFM
chartered another twenty locals the following year, and even considered the possibility of extending the organization across the border
to Mexico. Early in 1903, on the eve of a brutal and decisive conflict
in Colorado, the executive board reported that membership had increased by another one-third. It also placed high on its agenda future
organizing efforts in Missouri, Arkansas, Minnesota, Michigan, and
Wisconsin, in order to reduce the importation of strikebreakers into
the West. At the same session the board recommended that the
union's ritual and constitution be translated into Italian, Slavic, and

Finnish to encourage solidarity among nationalities which had become increasingly important in the industry.[4]

In the spring of 1903, then, the WFM's future seemed bright. Yet a year later the organization lay in a shambles. What happened in so short a time to turn success into failure, a glowing future into a despairing present?

The answer is not hard to find. As the WFM increased in strength and enjoyed continued success, Western employers became more anxious and hostile. Large nationwide corporations with Western interests particularly desired to weaken the miners' union before it became strong enough to demand a share of economic power in the industry. Consequently, business interests in Colorado decided to force the issue with the unions.

WFM leaders saw what was happening. They knew that in 1902 Colorado's mine owners had formed a statewide association to combat the miners' unions with money, propaganda, and Pinkertons. They also knew that larger corporate interests, through a combination of economic pressure and appeals to class loyalty, were enlisting local businessmen and professionals, previously allied to the miners, in a growing anti-union coalition. So it was hardly surprising when in February 1903 Charles Moyer, Boyce's successor as WFM president, complained: "We are being attacked on all sides by the Mill Trust and Mine Owners' Association."[5]

Yet union officials reacted cautiously. Moyer emphasized that the WFM's purpose was to build, not to destroy: to avoid by all honorable means a war between employer and employee. At the same time, Haywood probably described the union's position more accurately when he stated: "We are not opposed to employers, and it is our purpose and aim to work harmoniously and jointly with employers as best we can under this system, and we intend to change the system if we get sufficiently organized and well enough educated to do so."[6]

WFM leaders clearly distinguished their long-term from their immediate goals. Whatever their ultimate objectives—and by 1902 they included a socialist society—their immediate demands hardly differed from those commonly sought by AFL affiliates.

But corporate interests in Colorado, like those elsewhere in America, disliked the short-term AFL goals as much as they detested the WFM's ultimate objectives. Corporations would not compromise with labor, in the short or the long run. Company attorneys routinely referred to labor as simply another commodity to be bought and sold in the open marketplace; and Western company managers denied to the state and to the public, as well as to unions, any right to intervene in internal company affairs, including the formulation of corporate labor-relations policies.[7] Thus, between management's deepest commitments and even the minimal objectives of the WFM, compromise was impossible. Consequently, the delicately balanced *modus vivendi* between capital and labor collapsed in Colorado's mining districts and a miniature civil war erupted. It is well to examine why.

Secure in their control of most of Colorado's mining regions, in 1902–1903 WFM leaders tried to carry organization a stage further by increasing union membership among the men who toiled in the state's mills and smelters. Compared to miners, millmen and smelter-men were poorly paid and overworked. By 1903 Colorado miners had had an eight-hour day for almost a decade; mill and smelter workers still labored up to ten and twelve hours daily. Miners maintained a $3.50 daily minimum wage; refinery workers' wages began at $1.80. Underground miners were well organized, mill workers barely organized. Among miners, solidarity prevailed over craft and ethnic divisions; among the more heterogeneous mill hands, differences of skill and nationality were pronounced.[8] Mine owners, moreover, had learned at least a minimal tolerance of trade unions; refining and reduction companies still refused to deal with organized labor.

The WFM chose as its new organizing target the reduction plants at Colorado City, where they chartered a smeltermen's local in August 1902. Colorado City was chosen because three major companies—Portland, Telluride, and Standard (the latter a subsidiary of United States Reduction and Refining)—refined ores shipped there from the Cripple Creek district. More important, as a working-class suburb of Colorado Springs it had a local power structure sympathetic to unionism.[9]

As soon as the local union had been organized, however, the refining companies, led by the Standard, counterattacked. Standard's general superintendent, J. D. Hawkins, immediately hired a Pinkerton agent who infiltrated the new local, reporting its activities and the names of its members to the company. As Hawkins learned the names of the employees who had joined the union, they were promptly fired.[10]

It was to combat this anti-union tactic that William D. Haywood himself came to Colorado City in October 1902 to *demand* Hawkins' permission to organize the mills. Haywood minced no words in expounding his union's position. He bluntly accused the superintendent of discharging workers solely on the basis of their union membership. Hawkins just as bluntly conceded the truth of Haywood's charges, emphasizing that the company would use its full powers to prevent union organization. Hawkins explained that, while he did not oppose unions in principle, he disliked having unionists among his employees, "talking to the men and bringing them to an opinion that they were unfairly treated by the Company as to wages or any other form of treatment." Haywood responded sharply yet moderately, castigating the company's inhumane policies but conceding that under existing conditions the union had to bargain harmoniously with employers, whom it did not intend to antagonize.[11]

Unfortunately for the prospects of compromise, Hawkins and Haywood spoke different languages. The plant superintendent, who claimed to sanction unions in principle, still insisted upon the immediate discharge of any worker carrying a WFM card. To which Haywood threatened: "Whether you like it or not, Mr. Hawkins, these mills are going to be organized." Unmoved, Hawkins retorted: "Well, it is up to you. Go ahead." [12]

The WFM did go ahead, and so did management. As rapidly as the union organized men, the company discharged them. Finally, in February 1903, matters came to a head. The Standard, which until then had been firing union men one at a time, now removed twenty-three at once. The local union reacted immediately, on February 14 declaring a strike against all three Colorado City mills. The next day the smeltermen's local presented its demands to General Manager Charles M. McNeill of Standard, allowing him ten days to reply. In retrospect, the union's manifesto seems exceedingly moderate: "We . . . desire the prosperity of the company and so far as our skill and labor go will do all we can to promote its interests. We cannot understand how any fair and reasonable company should discriminate against union labor . . ." [13]

But McNeill answered the union's moderation with recalcitrance and bitter hostility, and industrial conflict came to Colorado City. This minor skirmish on the frontier of capitalism was not only to undermine the WFM but also to result in the birth of the Industrial Workers of the World. Thus it is essential that we understand clearly why conflict erupted in Colorado City, then spread to Cripple Creek, and finally infected almost all of Colorado's mining districts.

With one notable exception, most accounts of the Colorado labor
conflict of 1903–1905 seriously misjudge its cause. They mistakenly
trace the roots of working-class unrest to organized labor's unsuccessful effort to obtain statewide eight-hour legislation. True, for many
years before 1903 Colorado's labor movement had vainly sought to
win an eight-hour law from the state legislature. Labor had achieved
success in 1899, only to have the state supreme court declare the
statute unconstitutional. Now seeking a constitutional amendment,
trade unionists, with the support of the state's two major parties,
placed on the 1902 ballot an amendment granting the legislature
power to establish an eight-hour day. An overwhelming majority
voted in favor of the amendment, but again the reformers were
frustrated. In 1902 and 1903 corporate influence in the legislature
subverted all attempts to pass an eight-hour law. It is not surprising,
then, that the traditional accounts should picture organized labor,
unable to obtain its objectives through political action and the ballot
box, turning to direct action and the picket line.[14]

But the traditional explanations are in error. The conflict in
Colorado City, as we have seen, began well before the November
1902 election: it started when management first began to fire union
members and grew more intense with the October interview between Hawkins and Haywood. Moreover, the Colorado City strike
began on February 14, 1903, when the legislature was still in session
and the prospects for passage of an eight-hour bill seemed excellent.
Defeat of the eight-hour movement can hardly be blamed for that
conflict.

The relationship of the eight-hour movement to class conflict in
Colorado's mining districts is even more tenuous. Most miners had
already had the eight-hour day for ten years. Of all the workers in
Colorado, they were the least hurt by defeat of an eight-hour bill,
yet they, too, struck while chances for passage of just such a bill
remained bright.

The real nature of the conflict at Colorado City and elsewhere in
the state was the same as it had been earlier in the Coeur d'Alenes,
Leadville, and Cripple Creek: a raw struggle between employers and

42

employees for economic power. Bosses, on the one hand, wanted the undiluted freedom to hire and fire men and to set wages and working conditions as dictated by the demands of the market rather than human needs. Workers, on the other hand, wanted the right to organize unions of their own choosing which would interpose labor's power between employers and the demands of the marketplace. In Colorado City, as elsewhere, employers refused to concede to labor the right to organize freely; and even where businessmen did, in theory, concede the right to unionize, they refused, in practice, to negotiate with unions. Moyer tersely and accurately stated the cause of the Colorado City strike. The Standard mill, he said, discriminated against and discharged men for no other reason than their union membership. "I would say that so far as I am informed, that was the cause leading up to the strike." [15]

Adamant employers, then, forced upon the WFM a struggle it did not seek. Testifying afterward before a gubernatorial advisory commission, Haywood grimly emphasized that the workers in Colorado City had not been sufficiently organized to strike, and that the WFM had accordingly used every means available to avoid a conflict. He suggested, however, that someone other than union officials had been interested in fomenting a strike—perhaps the company, which could then use the strike to break a weak union.[16] But whoever instigated the struggle for economic power, whether aggressive company officials or militant union members, both sides ultimately committed their total resources to the conflict.

The Colorado City strike followed the pattern already well established in Western labor conflicts. When the workers walked out on February 14 they effectively closed down refining operations. Supported by the local community and its public officials, union pickets and deputy sheriffs patrolled the town and stopped strikebreakers from entering the area. But employers, also following the traditional script, outflanked labor, appealing for assistance to Republican Governor James H. Peabody, from whom, on March 3, they obtained state troops. Three days after dispatching the militia for strike duty,

Peabody explained to a mill official his unique brand of impartiality. "The placing of the troops at Colorado City," the Governor wrote, "was as much for the protection of workmen as the operators." Yet Peabody had ordered his militia officers to protect only the workers still in the mills, not those on strike; in fact, he had ordered the troops to curb most picketing.[17] What the Governor defined as impartiality, the union rightly took as anti-labor policy. Moreover, the actions taken by militia commanders stationed at Colorado City made even Peabody look good to the WFM.

Consequently, union leaders anxiously sought to settle the strike they had never wanted, asking only that the mills not discriminate against union men and that those workers already discharged for union membership be reinstated without prejudice. Even Governor Peabody agreed that these were reasonable demands, and he urged McNeill to accept the WFM's revised terms.[18]

The Governor eventually succeeded in arranging a conference between labor and management which might have been productive had it not been for McNeill of Standard. After an all-day and all-evening session with Peabody on March 14, WFM officials and representatives of the Portland and Telluride mills agreed to settle the dispute on the basis of union proposals. More important, both companies consented to bargain with a union committee—in itself a major triumph for the principle of union recognition.[19] But McNeill remained obdurate. As Haywood remembered the event, McNeill "had the air of having been dragged in by the hair of the head to a meeting to which he was opposed before it started." According to Big Bill, "this one wretched little autocrat was able to strangle our efforts." Still insistent upon dictating to the union on a take-it-or-leave-it basis, McNeill absolutely refused to recognize any union committee.[20]

In bringing the Portland and Telluride mills to terms with the union, Peabody had been labor's friend. He seemed more so on March 19 when he withdrew the militia from Colorado City. But on that same day the Governor described to a wealthy New York banker how he actually felt: "I feel sure that my action in enforcing law and order in Colorado, and notifying the lawless and law-violating element [i.e., WFM members] that they must obey the mandates of legal authority, has received the approval of the investing class of people, not only in Colorado, but throughout the country, and I can assure you . . . there will be no destruction to life and property if I can prevent it." [21]

Moyer and Haywood, both well aware of the Governor's basic anti-labor attitude, realized they could not trust Peabody to bring McNeill closer to the WFM's bargaining position. So they warned the Governor that unless McNeill negotiated with the union, Cripple Creek's miners might strike in sympathy with the millmen. Publicly, Moyer and Haywood declared:

The Governor is now intimating that we promised there would be no strike in the Cripple Creek district. . . . We gave the Governor to understand that we would fight McNeill to the finish, and under no circumstances could he construe our meaning that a strike would not be declared upon the mines that would ship ore to unfair mills. We have been willing and are now willing to arbitrate with Manager McNeill. He has refused to arbitrate with us as an organization and he alone is responsible for the situation that confronts the people of the Cripple Creek district.[22]

Cripple Creek's unions indeed had already threatened to strike mines which shipped ore to any of the Standard's mills. But first they allowed district businessmen an opportunity to persuade McNeill to accept the WFM's terms. When he still refused to budge, Cripple Creek's mine owners were left with an unpalatable alternative: either stop shipping ore to the Standard mill or be shut down by a sympathetic strike.

District businessmen who had lived peacefully with the miners' union for a decade saw no reason why McNeill could not do the same. They saw even less reason why an unnecessary labor conflict arising from the Standard manager's intransigence should cause mine owners to suffer hardship. Failing to persuade McNeill to negotiate with the union, Cripple Creek's businessmen next promised employment to any union member discharged by the Standard. Meanwhile, they pleaded with Peabody to bring the Colorado City disputants together again for another attempt to settle the strike.[23]

The Governor decided upon one last effort to end the dispute. On March 19 he invited union leaders and company officials to appear before an advisory commission established to investigate the entire dispute. Both the union and the company, though less than enthusiastic about the idea, consented to appear before the Governor's commission.[24]

While powerless to enforce their findings, Peabody's commissioners hoped that open hearings might result in a mutually satisfactory understanding between the company and the WFM. But this could not be. The commissioners, in fact, soon found themselves investigating a labor dispute whose very existence was denied by the attorney for the United States Reduction Company. Claiming that the Standard "mill is full of men contented and anxious to remain in the employ of the company," the attorney denied that there were any issues about which to bargain.[25] Moyer, however, continued to represent men who were discontented, who had been discharged for union membership, and who had struck but had never been reinstated. He again insisted that the company recognize the rights of the aggrieved workers and bargain with the union.[26]

Unable to resolve these basic differences through public sessions, the advisory commission met privately on March 28–29 in Colorado Springs with union and company officials. At these closed sessions a settlement was finally hammered out which concentrated on two points: reinstatement of union members and strikers, and union recognition. McNeill finally consented to treat with Moyer and any union members in his employ, provided there was no reference to their union affiliation. In short, McNeill would meet with union officials but he would not negotiate with a trade union. Moyer, desperately eager to avert the full-scale labor war impending in the Cripple Creek district, accepted this compromise formula, which promised ultimate re-employment for union members and indirect union recognition.[27]

Moyer's acceptance, however, was conditional. First, he questioned McNeill's willingness to deal justly with organized labor, suggesting that McNeill's propositions had been drafted "to furnish loopholes through which he might escape, if emergencies arose." Second, Moyer stated that although his union scarcely approved the settlement terms as it interpreted them, it would accept them reluctantly to demonstrate its "feeling of appreciation for the public, the business interests of Colorado, and the members of the Advisory Board." Third, Moyer warned that his union would hold the board as well as the Governor responsible for McNeill's carrying out the spirit as well as the letter of the settlement. "The Western Federation of Miners . . . are willing that you place . . . McNeill on probation and give him until the 18th day of May 1903 to carry out the beliefs and impression of the Advisory Board," declared the union president, adding: "You may give him a fair trial and an opportunity to reinstate the men involved and thereby prove his sincerity as to his conduct toward organized labor in the future." [28]

But after agreeing to reinstate discharged union men and to employ union members without discrimination, McNeill procrastinated. When Moyer and the WFM repeatedly protested delays in rehiring union men, McNeill insisted that productivity was too low to increase employment, and that the company could not remove loyal nonunion workers to make work for union members. It seems clear that the Standard official remained committed to his original intention of smashing the union.[29]

Unable to weaken McNeill's resistance, WFM leaders now decided to throw their entire union's resources into the struggle for the right to organize and the principle of union recognition. This meant using union strength in Colorado's mining districts—most notably Cripple Creek.

The WFM mistakenly believed that in Cripple Creek it dealt from a strong hand, even a stacked deck. With some few exceptions, most notably the mayor of the town of Victor (himself a mine owner), the union controlled district public officials. Most local merchants, moreover, did a rousing business with the well-paid and free-spending miners. The local unions owned substantial buildings, had ample treasuries, and members who (as Haywood later remembered them) were "widely read men, and as of high a standard of intelligence, as could be found among workingmen anywhere." [30]

But the employers now dealt from an even more carefully stacked deck. Through the spring of 1903 they had diligently been organizing a common businessmen's front to combat unionism and to win the assistance of the state government. In this they had been encouraged immeasurably by McNeill's successful resistance to the Western Federation. As their counterpart to the WFM, Colorado businessmen had on April 9, 1903, inaugurated the "Citizens' Alliance" movement. Soon nearly every mining community in the state had its Alliance; by October 25, 1903, when a statewide organization was born, the Alliance movement boasted a membership of over thirty thousand. In theory, the Alliances supported legitimate labor and harmonious employer-employee relations; in practice, the Alliances intended to destroy the WFM and other labor organizations. To members of these new businessmen's organizations, the "open shop" meant a company closed to union members, "proper" bargaining implied no negotiations with unions, and opposition to "class legislation" was applied to laws benefiting labor, never to measures favoring capital.[31]

In whatever they did or proposed, the Alliances had the active encouragement of Colorado's governor. James H. Peabody possessed all the traits and ideas anti-labor employers could possibly desire in the occupant of a statehouse. No governor in the United States more conscientiously fought labor. To Peabody, no welfare legislation ever seemed justified, no merely halfway restrictions upon trade unions satisfactory. He had worked himself up from shopkeeper to shop owner to bank president to governor; why could not Colorado's workers do the same for themselves without the aid of labor unions? [32]

Here was a governor who opposed what the voters of Colorado had so obviously mandated: the eight-hour law. Here was a governor who, while opposing eight-hour legislation, asked the legislature to pass a bill outlawing strikes, boycotts, and almost all trade-union economic activities.[33] Peabody's attitude toward labor is worth noting with some care. In a letter to another "friend" of labor, Harrison Gray Otis, the anti-union publisher of the *Los Angeles Times*, the Governor wrote:

I cannot convince myself to believe in the idea that a laboring man who has several little bodies to clothe and hungry mouths to feed, may be compelled to labor no more than eight hours if he be perfectly willing to labor ten or twelve hours for the maintenance of his family. I disclaim the right of any individual or organization to compel him to cease when the clock strikes the eighth hour, and I will not permit it *if it requires the entire power of the state and the Nation to prevent it* [italics added].[34]

To a United Mine Workers' organizer, Peabody stated his attitude more boldly:

[My] advice to you and your union, your federation [he did not distinguish the UMW from the WFM] and your associates, is to become once and for all law abiding, peaceable citizens, controlling your own personal interests and ambitions, and permitting all others to do likewise.

If you wish to idle, that is your right, but you should not compel some other person who desires to labor, to remain idle with you. You are looking at the labor question from an entirely erroneous point of view, and so long as you maintain your present feelings of belligerency and of opposition to law and order, you will find life an unpleasant one to live, and your associations with mankind will be mixed with malice, revenge and unpleasantness and will cause you worry and annoyance.[35]

The Governor personally meant to give organized labor in Colorado all the unpleasantness, worry, and annoyance it could take—and then some.

Publicly pledged to battle for his principles, Peabody cooperated with the Citizens' Alliance movement and even helped to organize an Alliance in his home town of Canyon City. In Colorado it became hard to determine whether the Republican Party was a branch of the Alliance or *vice versa*. In the Governor's mind there was no doubt: the two were identical! He advised Colorado Republicans to take as their slogan "the maintenance of law and order within our boundaries."[36] His firm stance elicited admiring letters from all over the nation. "All the conservative interests in the country are deeply interested in your fight,"[37] one admirer assured him.

That Peabody meant precisely what he said soon became evident to WFM leaders. The Governor had sent the militia when Colorado City mill managers had complained about largely nonexistent labor violence, but some months later, when WFM members were forcibly and brutally deported from Idaho Springs by the local mine owners' association, Peabody found the state's power unequal to the occasion. Apparently, Colorado could protect scabs' right to employment but not union members' right to dwell peaceably in their own community.[38]

Under attack all over Colorado by a business-government alliance, the WFM decided to put its power to the test. On August 8, 1903, WFM members in the Cripple Creek district struck mines which had continued to ship ore to nonunion mills. That decision, not taken without grave misgivings, unleashed one of the most brutal class conflicts in American history, one about which an early historian wrote with grim vindictiveness: "The strike may be summarized thus: The unions sowed class consciousness, and it sprang up and destroyed them."[39] But the facts in the matter were otherwise. Governor Peabody, the Citizens' Alliances, and the Mine Owners' Association had sown class consciousness fully as much as the union, and they had proved even more aggressive. The WFM had responded to challenges from the other side, particularly as reflected in McNeill's anti-union crusade. Moyer's explanation of why his union chose to fight at Cripple Creek was a simple one: "The miners who compose the Western Federation . . . have taken an obligation and pledged themselves to support their fellow workmen in any part of this jurisdiction, whether they be men who are producing ore or whether they be the men who are reducing the ore." [40]

The Cripple Creek strike at first appeared in no way out of the ordinary. Throughout August, although the mines remained shut and both sides held fast to their pre-conflict positions, peace prevailed. Strikers, supported by the sheriff, patrolled roads and depots, successfully keeping strikebreakers out of the district.

But Peabody and his conservative "law and order" backers could not allow labor to triumph. On September 2 Cripple Creek businessmen petitioned the Governor for troops, and the following day Peabody dispatched an investigating committee to the district. Interviewing mine owners, businessmen, and the few anti-union politicians available (while studiously avoiding union members and their sympathizers), Peabody's investigators on September 4 recommended that the Governor send troops to Cripple Creek. That same day, despite the opposition of union officials, Teller County's commissioners, the county sheriff, and the Victor city council, all of whom denied any collapse in local law and order, Peabody dispatched the militia.

The officer in charge was General Sherman Bell, who promptly won a notorious place in American labor history.[41] Bell's command preserved neither law nor order; nor did it apprehend criminals. Instead, when it served their purposes the troops violated the law, including the state and federal constitutions. Bell regularly appealed to "military necessity which recognizes no laws, either civil or social." Major McClelland, his junior officer, remarked: "To hell with the constitution, we aren't going by the constitution." Bell stated the purpose of his mission with terse brutality: "I came to do up this damned anarchistic federation." [42]

And why shouldn't he "do it up"? Peabody had arranged with the Mine Owners' Association to pay the cost of placing the militia in the field. Colorado's troops clearly served private capital more than the public interest. To the Governor, of course, the state and capitalism were synonymous. So intensely anti-labor was the motivation underlying the use of the militia in Colorado that even a military journal was led to comment: "It was a rank perversion of the whole theory and purpose of the National Guard, and far more likely to incite disorder than to prevent it." [43]

Peabody's critics could not have been more correct. No significant violence had occurred before the militia's arrival, and union members proved just as peaceable after its coming. The troops nevertheless arrested men without warrant, willfully disregarded duly elected local officials, and even flaunted judicial decisions with impunity. When cases did come to court, armed troops brought the accused before the bar while General Bell surrounded the courthouse with Gatling guns. To a Wall Street correspondent, Peabody defended even this approach, arguing, "I . . . hope that public sentiment will grasp the idea that it is better to suppress wrong-doing, without loss of life and destruction of property, than to wait until damage is accomplished and then attempt to punish the offenders." [44]

Yet despite military repression, employers could not break the strike. Union benefits kept the miners contented while union cooperatives kept them fed and clothed. Some miners left the district and found union work elsewhere; and five hundred returned to work under a union contract at the Portland mine operated by James Burns, a local employer who retained his former sympathies. Only a few drifted back to work on a nonunion basis.

Meanwhile, halfway across the state in the isolated mountain mining region of Telluride, another conflict between the WFM and the Citizens' Alliance was getting under way. Here, where no sympathetic strike was involved, the union struggled to maintain the eight-hour day and the traditional minimum wage. Here capital was again the aggressor, as mine owners and local bankers, encouraged by Peabody, prepared to make war upon the WFM. Again the Governor, who sympathized openly with Telluride's businessmen, intervened in a labor dispute, preparing to open a second front in his preventive class war. [45]

Peabody conceived his own scheme for strikebreaking in Telluride. Advising his militia commanders to arrest all unemployed men (i.e., strikers) on vagrancy charges, the Governor offered WFM members a simple choice: return to work on the owners' terms, be punished for vagrancy, or leave the county. In addition, Peabody informed Major Zeph Hill that if the courts interfered with the new anti-union tactics the Governor would declare the county under martial law, thus doing away with the right of *habeas corpus*. [46]

5 1

Martial law and suspension of *habeas corpus* were also just what Peabody had been intending for Cripple Creek. Since the Colorado labor conflict had widened at Cripple Creek in August 1903, and even after its spread to Telluride, no appreciable violence had occurred in any strike area. Union members had been arrested on numerous charges, but none had been found guilty in court. This tranquillity could not be expected to last, particularly if the Governor planned to declare martial law.

Prophetically, the *Miners' Magazine* reported on November 12:

It is very probable that the Mine Owners' Association at their next meeting will make arrangements to employ a few corporation dynamiters who will startle the different mining camps in the district by nocturnal explosions. . . . Such actions would be in accordance with other acts of vandalism that points its finger of suspicion in the direction of the mine operators.[47]

Two days later, someone tried to wreck a train carrying nonunion miners home from work. A week after that, on November 21, an explosion at the Vindicator Mine killed two men. The Mine Owners' Association then promptly issued a circular charging the WFM's "inner circle" with the two crimes and offering a $5,000 reward for apprehension of the criminals. The union, however, was probably correct about the Vindicator incident, remarking in effect that if there had been no strike it would have been dismissed as a routine mine disaster. Colorado's Commissioner of Mines verified the union's belief. The attempted train wreck, for which union members were later indicted, tried, and acquitted, turned out on the basis of evidence presented during the trial to have been an attempt by company detectives, acting as *agents provocateurs*, to implicate the union in violence, setting the stage for its final repression.[48]

Nevertheless, these incidents supplied Peabody with a pretext for declaring martial law. On December 4, 1903, acting on a strained interpretation of the 1899 Coeur d'Alene precedent, he declared Teller County "in a state of insurrection and rebellion." Military rule thereupon supplanted civil authority, *habeas corpus* was suspended, and a general vagrancy order, similar to the one in effect at Telluride, was issued.[49]

By December, then, Peabody was firmer than ever in his determination to crush the Western Federation of Miners. Nothing and no one would stand in his way. Of the Portland mine owner who continued to employ union men, the Governor remarked: "I anticipate Mr. Burns will be permanently deposed, and I hope obliterated from that vicinity." [50] In Peabody's world, what was good for capital was good for the worker. Throughout the protracted struggle the Governor saw no difference between public power and private power, between the state of Colorado and corporate capitalism. Preparing to use Pinkertons for espionage purposes at Telluride, Peabody informed Major Hill that the state had had similar assistance in Cripple Creek. But the Governor also suggested to the Major that the Pinkertons, though employed by the state, should be paid and supervised by the Mine Owners' Association (as had been done at Cripple Creek), because mine owners were better able to cope with a strike situation. [51]

The Western Federation seemed doomed. From January through March 1904 affairs went from bad to worse for the union. More and more union men left the Cripple Creek district or returned to work there without their union cards as the mines resumed operations under military protection. Finally, on March 29, Cripple Creek employers announced the introduction of a permit system of employment intended to deny work to union members. At Telluride, meanwhile, union men continued to be "vagged" (arrested on charges of vagrancy) or deported. By March 10 that region was so placid that Peabody lifted martial law. Yet the Governor simultaneously discarded all pretense that the militia was serving the community by appointing Bulkeley Wells, manager of Telluride's largest mine, as commander of a local militia unit composed entirely of area businessmen. Two weeks later Sherman Bell placed Telluride back under martial law, allowing Wells the opportunity to doff his mine manager's hat for a militia commander's cap. A few days later Bell and Wells arrested union president Moyer on a trumped-up charge of desecrating the American flag. In addition to being separated from their former local business and professional allies and denied due process of law, Colorado's striking miners had now been isolated from their union president, who was kept in prison despite union efforts to secure his release through writs of *habeas corpus*. All this caused a Telluride merchant who was deported by the military because of his socialist and pro-union sympathies to write:

> Colorado, it is of thee,
> Dark land of tyranny,
>   Of thee I sing;
> Land wherein labor's bled
> Land from which law has fled
> Bow down thy mournful head,
>   Capital is king. [52]

With Moyer in prison, the union and its sympathetic strike both nearly crushed, and the 1904 WFM convention approaching, the union's executive board on May 20 resolved: "If the life of Charles H. Moyer be sacrificed to appease the wrath of corporate and commercial hate, then there will be forced upon the peaceful, law-abiding, and liberty-loving membership of our organization, the ancient words in the old, Mosaic law: 'An eye for an eye, and a tooth for a tooth . . .'" [53] This somber rhetoric foreshadowed the worst incident of the entire Colorado conflict.

Early on the morning of June 6, as WFM delegates caroused in Denver's saloons and Governor Peabody rested quietly in a St. Louis hotel room (he was attending the World's Fair), a railroad train slowly moved into the Independence depot at Cripple Creek, where a large number of nonunion miners were waiting to board it. As the train approached the platform, a powerful bomb exploded. Arms, legs, and torsos scattered about the depot like windblown leaves; piercing cries shot from all directions through the still night air. Union men, local officials, militiamen, indeed, almost everyone in town rushed to the station to see what had happened. They were revolted by what they saw, including General Bell, who promptly wired Peabody: "14 men now dead, many more dying, and others wounded and mangled!" [54]

As the Governor mulled over the latest Colorado tragedy, his secretary informed him that the state supreme court had just sanctioned his earlier use of martial law as a preventive legal instrument, ruling, according to the Governor's secretary, that "courts should not interfere with you [sic] that you have power to kill and imprison . . ." [55] From Peabody's point of view, the court could not have chosen a more opportune moment to define his authority.

Even before the damage at the Independence depot could be assessed, state officials and Citizens' Alliance members declared the WFM guilty. That same morning, local mine owners, assisted by the militia, took the law into their own hands. Because the county sheriff declined to arrest union men without evidence, employers organized a vigilante group which deposed the sheriff and then, joined by the troops, marched upon the union's headquarters in Victor. Armed union members briefly fought back, but, surrounded and outnumbered, they soon dropped their arms and surrendered to the businessmen's law.

Just after midnight, local justice was put into effect. Special kangaroo courts established for the occasion by the Citizens' Alliance deported union members, and the militia escorted them from the district. Only later was martial law reinstituted to give a thin legal veneer to obviously illegal actions in Cripple Creek.[56]

The WFM had been soundly whipped in Colorado. On June 10 Bell issued a general deportation order, under which seventy-nine men were shipped to Kansas and others banished to desert regions in New Mexico and elsewhere. Stranded without funds or food, the deportees were warned never to return to Cripple Creek, even those who had wives and children there. Simultaneously, mobs ransacked the WFM's cooperative stores, the troops placed union sympathizers under tight surveillance, and the authorities hampered all efforts to aid the deportees. When national newspapers, which had treated the deportation story as front-page news, either criticized Peabody or demanded an explanation for the state's actions, the Governor replied cavalierly that military necessity sometimes superseded legal right.[57]

The WFM had nowhere to turn. The courts would not protect it against Peabody when the Governor refused to execute legal decisions favorable to the union. President Roosevelt, having sent investigators to the scene, refused Moyer's demand that he intervene on the union's behalf. Without officially ending its strikes in Cripple Creek and Telluride, the WFM watched impotently as its local unions were destroyed.

Governor Peabody, meanwhile, glowed in the approval showered upon him by the Colorado and Eastern businessmen whom he had served so well. Later, after rethinking the whole tragic management-labor conflict, the Governor concluded: ". . . They [the unions] learned once for all that I would not recede from the stand I had taken by reason of righteousness being behind me, and that Socialism, Anarchy, and its attending evils would not be tolerated in Colorado." [58]

From the ruins of Colorado's miners' unions, however, would arise an even more radical challenge to American capitalism and society: the Industrial Workers of the World. As John Graham Brooks, one of Roosevelt's investigators of the Colorado struggle, wrote in his 1913 study of American syndicalism: "The I.W.W. was hammered out in the fires of that conflict." [59] But it must not be forgotten that the Coeur d'Alene, Leadville, and other earlier Western conflicts also provided crucibles in which the later ideology of the IWW was forged. What Selig Perlman and Philip Taft in 1936 interpreted as a "class war without a class ideology" [60] may have existed in 1892 or 1894, but well before the last blow in the Western labor war had been struck, class conflict had produced class consciousness and a class ideology. Even in its beginnings, Western class conflict was not (as Perlman and Taft supposed) the response of pioneer individualists to frontier conditions. The WFM, as we have seen, never consisted primarily of erstwhile prospectors or frontiersmen. It was not "permeated with the independent and often lawless spirit of the frontier," nor did its radicalism spring from "a lack of respect for the social distinctions of a civilized life." [61] Quite the contrary! What the miners struggled to obtain was precisely those civilized amenities they felt were being denied them. The violent Western conflicts occurred not on an undeveloped frontier but in a citadel of American industrialism and capitalism.

Western working-class history, then, is not the story of the breakdown of social polarization, but of its creation. In the mining communities of the early West, labor and business had initially united to combat "alien" capital and "foreign" business. Local merchants who sold to mine and mill workers; doctors, lawyers, and dentists who treated and served them; politicians who owed office to union votes; and farmers who fed them at first helped labor in its struggle against corporations. The key development in Western labor history was the success of big businessmen in separating labor from its quondam allies and in the process polarizing society and politics to the disadvantage of the Western worker. The class war in the West ultimately created a class ideology. It became a Marxist ideology for the simple reason that the Mountain West from 1890 to 1905 seemed to follow the classic Marxian pattern of monopoly capitalist development.

It was the actions of their employers which convinced Western workers that labor and capital could never coexist peacefully. The betrayal of labor's cause by local businessmen and once friendly politicians reinforced the miners' conviction that workers must trust to themselves and to their own power. The hostility of the state to labor and the disregard of popular mandates by Peabody and other officeholders convinced many workers that the ballot box was a fraud, and, indeed, that the only hope for improvement lay in economic organization and direct industrial action. In short, a decade of class war taught lessons not easily forgotten to many Western workers, among them men who founded, joined, and long remained loyal to the IWW. Ten years of industrial violence led such men to move from "pure and simple" unionism to industrial unionism to socialism and finally to syndicalism.

5 6

CHAPTER

4

From "Pure and Simple Unionism" to Revolutionary Radicalism

O F all the strains which went into the making of the Industrial Workers of the World, none was more important than that represented by Western workers. Initially the Western miners gave the IWW the bulk of its membership and its finances. Later they contributed the IWW's two most famous leaders: Vincent St. John and William D. Haywood. Most important of all, the IWW's ideology and tactics owed more to the Western miners and their experiences in the Mountain States than to any other source.

At first glance the Western Federation of Miners appeared much like any other American trade union. Its original constitution, its by-laws, its objectives, its rhetoric were all quite ordinary. It waged strikes to protect wages, reduce hours, or gain union recognition— not, certainly, to make a revolution. Although the WFM originated as an industrial union, opening membership to all men who worked in and around the mines, it did not differ in any basic respect from the United Mine Workers of America, which organized all those laboring in and around the coal mines. Even so famous an American radical as Big Bill Haywood, during his early years as an official of the Silver City, Idaho, local of the WFM (1896–1900), concerned himself with

5 7

enrolling all working miners in the union and not with revolution.[1]
Yet before it was five years old the WFM had easily become the
nation's most militant labor organization, and before its tenth birthday
it had become the most radical.

The Westerners' radicalism derived directly from their economic
and social environment. With other individuals and groups pushed
by corporate capitalism to the bottom of the ladder, Western miners
asserted their claim to more decent treatment and a better place in
the American system. To gain control over their situation Western
workers joined the Knights of Labor, crusaded with Populists, and
eventually united with Eastern socialists. Nurtured on the utopianism
of the Knights, their hopes stoked by the promise of Populism, and
victimized by the corporations, they refused to accept the labor program expounded by Samuel Gompers, who drifted from militant,
class-conscious unionism in the 1890's to "pure and simple unionism"
in the 1900's.

By the mid-1890's Western workers, then, had absorbed the spirit
of solidarity and the anti-capitalist ethic of the Knights of Labor,
the industrial unionism of the WFM, and the politics of Populism.
Though most miners probably joined the Knights simply to gain
better conditions or job security, many just as likely became imbued
with that organization's spirit of solidarity. Certainly, the WFM continued the Knights' belief in the unity of all workers, regardless of
skill; or as Haywood put it: "All for One, One for All." These same
union members learned their political lessons in Populist schools, for
Populism in the Mountain West was a working-class movement.
Labor organizations there courted farmers. In Montana, for example,
the major Populist newspapers were labor journals, and state labor
conferences and Populist conventions generally met simultaneously in
the same city and were attended by the same delegates. The Silver
Bow (Butte) Trades and Labor Assembly called upon the farmers to
"join hands with the wage earners. . . . The People's party," it said,
"is organized by those from the humble walks of life to destroy
monopoly and give equal and exact justice to all." The Montana
Populist State Committee chairman was an official of the American

Railway Union, and party candidates in Silver Bow County were mostly union members. And in Idaho's Coeur d'Alenes, local labor groups were indistinguishable from the Populists: Ed Boyce was a power in both the union and People's party, serving as a Populist representative in the state assembly. At its 1895 convention, during the depths of depression, the WFM not unexpectedly endorsed "the party [Populist] advocating the principles contained in the Omaha platform." [2]

Western miners, like farmers elsewhere, learned that politics paid. Across the Mountain West, mining districts elected candidates to local office on labor or, more usually, Populist tickets. Silver Bow County in Montana, Lake and Teller Counties in Colorado, and the major cities in each of these counties were dominated politically by the People's party. On occasion working-class Populists even held the balance of power in statewide elections.[3]

Western workers created a radical Populism which was the industrial counterpart of the rural agrarian type. Mountain States Populists endorsed all the usual party planks, including free silver and nationalization of telephones, telegraphs, railroads, and mines. But they also emphasized specific labor reforms. They demanded legislative enactment of the eight-hour day; sanitary inspection of workshops, mills, and homes; employers' liability laws; abolition of the contract system of public works; and abolition of the sweating system. Western workers wanted no part of an ideology which allowed the marketplace and the so-called law of supply and demand to determine the conditions of their existence. Instead they proposed to guarantee that supply and demand, instead of bringing unemployment and misery to the many, brought a decent standard of living to all, not just the fortunate few.[4]

No wonder, then, that after the Populist party coalesced with the Silver Democrats in 1896, and William Jennings Bryan lost that year's presidential election, WFM President Ed Boyce, speaking at his union's 1897 convention, denounced the free-silver fraud and Populism in words recalling those uttered by socialist revolutionary Daniel DeLeon. Capitalism, Boyce had discovered, was indivisible; if Wall Street was the enemy, so was the Colorado Springs Mining Exchange; if John D. Rockefeller was to be fought, so was John Hays Hammond, the Western mining enterpreneur. Boyce demanded from his union followers more intelligent and effective political action, a request which could lead in only one direction—toward socialism.[5]

So, at the end of the nineteenth century, just as the AFL turned

59

away from socialism and independent political action to follow the narrower path of "pure and simple" trade unionism, the Western Federation moved toward socialism, political action, and the broader road of radical unionism.

Having begun as an open, inclusive union, the Western Federation became even more so. This highly democratic labor organization devoted itself to the open-union concept and the universal union card, accepting any member of a bona fide union without initiation fee upon presentation of his union card. The WFM never demanded a closed shop or an exclusive employment contract. It supported no apprenticeship rules, having no intention of restricting union membership. It wanted jobs for all, not merely for the organized few. As Boyce said in 1897: "Open our portals to every workingman, whether engineer, blacksmith, smelterman, or millman. . . . The mantle of fraternity is sufficient for all." Three years later he expanded his concept of fraternity: "We will at all times and under all conditions espouse the cause of the producing masses, regardless of religion, nationality or race . . ." Boyce's successor, Charles Moyer, urging better-paid and more skilled miners to support smelter and mill hands, warned that labor is only as strong as its weakest link. "The unskilled now constitute [the] weakest link in the chain of the labor movement. It is our duty and interest to strengthen it." He also put his argument in moral terms, strange perhaps to an AFL member, but not to a former Knight or to a follower of Eugene Debs. Moyer insisted that the true trade unionist was his brother's keeper and that it was the *obligation* of the highly skilled to use their power to aid the less skilled.[6]

The WFM's belief in solidarity and fraternity went deeper than platform oratory. The organization practiced it: recall the Colorado labor war of 1903–1904 and its origin in the WFM's decision to call out skilled miners in order to protect the mill hands' right to organize trade unions and bargain collectively. This commitment to industrial unionism and solidarity led the Western organization into conflict with the American Federation of Labor. In 1896 the WFM had affiliated with the AFL; a year later it let its affiliation lapse. In the interval, during the unsuccessful WFM struggle at Leadville, Boyce had pleaded in vain with Gompers and the AFL for financial assistance. In company with another executive board member, Boyce even attended the 1896 AFL convention to carry the WFM's appeal for aid directly to the American Federation's membership. But the convention proved a grave disappointment to the WFM delegates, who subsequently lost what little interest they had in the AFL.[7]

By 1896–1897, though Gompers and the AFL had won their battle against the Knights of Labor, they were not without labor critics outside the confines of Western labor. Foremost among the opponents of the AFL within the labor movement was Eugene Victor Debs, the martyr of the 1894 Pullman strike, whose name was soon to become synonymous with American socialism. In 1896 Debs allied with Ed Boyce, and the two men worked closely during the final stages of the Leadville strike. Sometimes with Boyce, and sometimes on his own, Debs moved toward dual unionism, socialism, and finally to the creation of the Industrial Workers of the World.

The son of Alsatian immigrant parents, Eugene Debs was born in 1855 and grew up in Terre Haute, Indiana, in respectable, if not affluent, circumstances. His should have been a typically nineteenth-century bourgeois life. Debs hardly seemed cut out for the career, or more properly crusade, he chose to lead, which would eventually find him five times Socialist party candidate for President and twice imprisoned for challenging the authority of the federal government.[8]

Young Debs at first accomplished much within the American tradition of success. Although he left school at fourteen to work as a railroader, he rose rapidly in the esteem of fellow workers and his native townsmen. In 1875 Debs founded the first local lodge of the Brotherhood of Locomotive Firemen, but later, despite his activities as a "labor agitator," he was elected city clerk and then to the state legislature. Unsatisfied by his activities as a grocery clerk, city official, and Democratic legislator, Debs returned to the labor movement, becoming in 1880 grand secretary and treasurer of the Brotherhood of Locomotive Firemen as well as editor and manager of the *Firemen's Magazine* (both at a substantial salary). As secretary-treasurer of a successful national trade union he could lead the life his wife so much desired. They built a lavish home in a fine Terre Haute neighborhood and stuffed it with expensive Victorian bric-a-brac.

Behind Debs's respectable American Victorian façade, a radical conscience rested uneasily. No man could serve the American labor movement in the 1870's and 1880's without a nagging concern over its future. Beginning in 1877 as a defender of the existing order and foe of that year's railroad strikers and rioters, over the succeeding fifteen years Debs became an opponent of unjust laws and the enemy of an iniquitous social order. Between 1877 and 1894 he discovered that the labor movement served only some workers, not all. He had witnessed members of the Railway Engineers break a strike waged by Firemen; and then he had seen the Firemen do the same, helping the Burlington Railroad break the 1888 Engineers' strike. Deciding that divided unions could not combat united employers, Debs tried to unite the separate railroad brotherhoods. When the unions rejected solidarity, he resorted to a different course of action. In 1893 he resigned his positions with the Locomotive Firemen, sacrificed his $4,000 annual salary, and went where his conscience directed. He determined to establish a new labor organization that would open its doors to all railroad workers—operating and nonoperating, skilled and unskilled. Thus was born the American Railway Union (ARU), an industrial organization for all railway workers. Thus Eugene Debs took his first giant step on the road to radicalism.

Not only unskilled railroad workers flocked to the new union, but also many of the skilled, seeing in solidarity their best hope for betterment. In its first strike the ARU challenged and defeated James J. Hill's Great Northern Railway by compelling that corporation to rescind a recent wage cut. Success brought in more members from all over the nation, including the South.

But Debs had still to learn the lesson that Boyce and the Western miners were discovering: unions fought not only employers but also the state. In the summer of 1894 the ARU found itself in a battle it had not sought: the Pullman strike. Debs knew his infant union should not strike in sympathy with Pullman employees who had recently affiliated with the ARU, and he advised against it. But Debs and fellow delegates at the ARU's 1894 Chicago convention could not close their hearts to the sufferings recounted by George M. Pullman's workers. So Debs and the ARU committed their total resources to the ensuing labor struggle. But Pullman had more resources to commit, including the support of the united Midwestern railroads and the power of the federal government. When President Grover Cleveland intervened on behalf of the boycotted railroads, the end of the Pullman strike was no longer in doubt. The ARU was destroyed, and Debs spent six months in a Woodstock, Illinois, prison.

It has been said that "Debs entered Woodstock Jail a labor union-ist, and . . . came out a Socialist . . ." [9] Debs himself maintained that it was in prison he first read Laurence Gronlund, Edward Bellamy, and especially Karl Kautsky, whose writings converted him to social-ism. But it must have been a strange conversion, for in 1896 he cam-paigned for William Jennings Bryan, and a few years later, after publicly declaring for socialism, he beseeched "Christian Gentleman" John D. Rockefeller for a contribution to aid in establishing the Co-operative Commonwealth. Rockefeller naturally refused.

Debs's own Social Democratic party, established in the summer of 1897, was anything but Marxist. Far from seeking to revolutionize American society, the Social Democrats proposed to go off into the wilderness (preferably to some unsettled Western territory) and es-tablish the perfect society, thereby setting an example others would irresistibly follow. Still espousing the "utopian socialism" that Marx fifty years earlier had so savagely ridiculed, as a socialist Debs still had much to learn.

But by 1897 he had come a long way as a radical, and was pre-pared to go much further. Debs had already moved from craft unionism to militant industrial unionism; now he was ready to move from utopian to Marxian socialism—which he did in 1901 when his Social Democrats united with Morris Hillquit's and Job Harriman's Socialist Labor party insurgents to form the Socialist Party of Amer-ica. (These insurgents were Socialists dissatisfied with Daniel DeLeon's dogmatic control of the Socialist Labor party, and his war with Gompers and the trade unions.) Five times the new party would nominate Debs for President, including 1920 when he was once again in prison, this time for opposing America's involvement in the First World War.

For a quarter of a century Debs personified American socialism and radicalism. Not because he was socialism's best theorist or most creative organizer; quite the contrary. Although a great orator and a stirring personality, Debs had a shallow intellect and proved a poor party organizer. Too often at Socialist party conventions, or when sectarianism threatened to split the party, Debs was at home, sick or drunk. But he had unusual credentials for an American socialist. In a party dominated by German immigrants and Jewish lawyers and den-tists, Debs was American born and, though a professed nonbeliever, a Christian almost by instinct. Debs Americanized and Christianized the socialist movement. By doing so he made it acceptable, respectable, almost popular. For many followers who still retained traditional religious beliefs, Debs personified the essence of the Christ figure: the simple, humble carpenter who sacrifices himself to redeem a corrupt society. Standing on the speaker's platform, tall, gaunt, balding, slightly stooped, his eyes expressing years of suffering, his haunting voice piercing his audience's emotions, Debs played this role to the hilt. He once expressed this role in these words:

. . . I did not believe that Christ was meek and lowly, but a real living, vital agitator who went into the Temple with a lash and a knout and whipped the oppressors of the poor, routed them out of doors and spilled their blood-got silver on the floor. He told the robbed and misruled and exploited and driven people to disobey their plunderers! He denounced the profiteers, and it was for this that they nailed his quivering body to the cross and spiked it to the gates of Jerusalem, not because he told men to love one another. . . . I did the same thing in a different way . . . but I fared better than Christ. They nailed him to the cross and they threw me in here [Atlanta Penitentiary].[10]

Among those with whom Debs agitated for a better society were Ed Boyce and his associates in the WFM. Both Debs and Boyce had discarded the limitations of craft unionism for what they saw as the greater possibilities of industrial unionism; both also came to see that industrial unionism alone was not enough to bring a new society into existence. Sharing the experience of unhappy relations with Gompers and the AFL, Debs and Boyce decided to create a new federated labor organization.

Immediately after his disillusioning experience at the 1896 AFL convention, Boyce visited Debs in Terre Haute. Early the following January, Debs arrived in Leadville, and for the next three months he and Boyce spent a considerable amount of time together. Although no records or papers describing these meetings exist, it seems reasonable to assume that they discussed the state of labor, its apparent weakness in the face of corporate capital, and the utter inability of the AFL to comprehend the evolving American social and economic order. From their discussions both labor leaders probably came away convinced that a new national labor organization was needed to accomplish what the AFL could not or would not do, and that this new labor organization must pledge itself to the destruction of American capitalism.

At the same time, Boyce was engaged in bitter correspondence with Samuel Gompers, who feared the threatened emergence of a rival national labor organization. On March 16, 1897, Boyce wrote to a worried Gompers to deny that the WFM intended to leave the AFL. But the tone of Boyce's letter could hardly have allayed Gompers' anxieties, for Boyce criticized the AFL for talking about conservative action while four million idle men and women tramped the highways. These unemployed, said Boyce, were victims of a vicious system of government which would continue to repress them "unless they have the *manhood to get out and fight with the sword* or use the ballot with intelligence." Still more threateningly, Boyce declared: "You know that *I am not a trade unionist;* I am fully convinced that their day of usefulness is past." Gompers pleaded with Boyce to remember the importance of labor unity and to keep the WFM within the fold. He further reminded Boyce that the American labor movement rejected force and revolution as the means to achieve a better life, and angrily advised him to become a loyal trade unionist or leave the movement. Boyce took Gompers' advice. Reaffirming that he was not a trade unionist by Gompers' definition, Boyce assured him that Western miners would not take hasty action calculated to injure the labor movement, but coldly concluded: ". . . Now, as .ever, I am strongly in favor of a Western organization." [11]

Boyce went to his own union's 1897 convention eager to put his increasing militancy into effect. First, he advised delegates that the WFM should purchase and operate its own mines because only then would miners achieve equality and freedom. Second, Boyce warned that if employers and the state continued to use military force to subjugate strikers, miners should assert their constitutional right to keep and bear arms. "I entreat you," he proclaimed, "to take action . . . so that in two years we can hear the inspiring music of the martial tread of twenty-five thousand armed men in the ranks of labor." Significantly, Boyce asserted that American workingmen would never regain their full rights through "trades unionism." "With this knowledge and the bitter experience of the past [Leadville, for example]," he concluded, "surely it is time for workingmen to see that trades unionism is a failure." [12] The WFM delegates took their president's advice. Voting to stop per capita payments to the AFL, they laid preliminary plans for the creation of a Western labor organization.

By 1897, as we have seen, Western labor interests had merged with those of other radical reformers and labor leaders. Debs, for example, convened a national labor conference in Chicago in September 1897, whose participants included, along with Boyce, J. A. Ferguson, president of the Montana State Federation of Labor, and Daniel MacDonald, representing the Silver Bow Trades and Labor Assembly. The next month the Montana State Trades and Labor Council acted to bring Western trade unionists into a new coalition. And in December 1897 the WFM's executive board invited all Western unions to attend a meeting in Salt Lake City to found a new organization.[13]

On May 10, 1898, Boyce watched labor union delegates from Montana, Idaho, and Colorado meet in Salt Lake City. The next day they voted to organize the Western Labor Union, and on May 12 they elected Dan MacDonald president of the new organization. A loyal AFL man in attendance described the new Western federation to Gompers as "only the Western Federation of Miners under another name. . . . Boyce dominated everything. . . . Boyce's influence with the miners is unquestionably strong. The majority believe him sincerely, and all of them fear to oppose him." [14]

What manner of man was this Ed Boyce whom Western workers both respected and feared? As with so many other labor leaders, little beyond the barest facts are known about Boyce's life—and of these only a few details can be known with any certainty. He was born in Ireland in 1862, the youngest of four children whose father died at an early age. Educated in Ireland, Boyce arrived in Boston, the Irish immigrants' "Promised City," in 1882, but Boston attracted him only briefly. Less than a year later he went west, first to Wisconsin, and then to Colorado, where in 1883 he went to work for the Denver and Rio Grande Western Railroad. The railroad job brought him to Leadville, where he worked in the mines and first made contact with the labor movement; in 1884, he joined the local miners' union, then a Knights of Labor affiliate.

Like so many other Western workers, Boyce continued to drift from place to place and from job to job, seeking better conditions and greater opportunities, until in June 1887 he settled in the recently opened Coeur d'Alene mining district. There he became a local union leader and a key participant in the 1892 strike—a role which led to his arrest, imprisonment, and blacklisting. Released from prison early in 1893, Boyce attended the WFM's founding convention. By 1894

66

he was back at work in the Coeur d'Alenes, where he was the leading official of the Coeur d'Alene Executive Miners' Union as well as an influential figure in statewide Populist politics. Only two years later, still working in a local mine, Boyce was elected WFM president, an office he held until his voluntary retirement in 1902.[15]

Boyce, in short, grew up with the Western mining industry and its labor movement. Like most miners he had even prospected on his own. Unlike most miners, however, he succeeded grandly in whatever he chose to do; he even struck it rich while prospecting! But even after he acquired wealth and retired, Boyce never rejected the labor movement that had nurtured him, the union men who had befriended him, or the socialist movement that had promised him a better world.

Haywood remembers Boyce in 1897 as tall and slender, with a fine head of thin hair, good features, and prominent buck teeth, caused, according to Big Bill, by years of handling quicksilver in Idaho's quartz mines. Others remember him as energetic and fearless, intelligent but never above conversing in the lingo of the miners, a man who wrote more fluently than he spoke, and a natural leader who was undaunted by the powerful mine owners with whom he negotiated.[16]

Under Boyce's aggressive leadership, the differences between Western labor and the AFL intensified. The Western Labor Union became more, not less, radical. Even those Western workers who retained sympathy for the AFL's position did so as missionaries for the Western point of view, not as true believers in Gompers' version of the labor movement. Although some Westerners realized that labor should unite in the face of united capital, they insisted that "we must try to teach our benighted brothers in the 'jungles of New York' and the East what we have learned here in the progressive, enterprising West." [17] Underneath the whimsy lay a perfectly serious conviction.

Western workers were careful to spell out their points of difference with Gompers. Where the AFL emphasized skills and crafts, the Westerners demanded a policy "broad enough in principle and sufficiently humane in character to embrace every class of toil . . . in one great brotherhood." Where the AFL stressed the national craft union and complete union autonomy, the Westerners favored the industrial union, free transfer from union to union, and labor solidarity. Where the AFL sought to close America's gates to immigrants, the Westerners welcomed most newcomers, except Asians. Where the AFL preferred to seek betterment through the use of strikes, boycotts, and collective bargaining, the Westerners initially claimed that industrial technology and corporate concentration had made those tactics obsolete, leaving the working class but one recourse: ". . . the free and intelligent use of the ballot." [18]

Boyce's rhetoric, which his followers relished, neatly incorporated their view of American society. "There can be no harmony between organized capitalists and organized labor. . . . There can be no harmony between employer and employee; the former wants long hours and low wages; the latter wants short hours and high wages . . ." Boyce told Butte's miners, whom he also reminded: "Our present wage system is slavery in its worst form. The corporations and trusts have monopolized the necessities of society and the means of life, that the laborer can have access to them only on the terms offered by the trust." He ended by proclaiming, "Let the rallying cry be: 'Labor, the producer of all wealth, is entitled to all he creates, the overthrow of the whole profit-making system, the extinction of monopolies, equality for all and the land for the people.'" [19]

A great many Western workers echoed Boyce's indictment of the American system. Testifying before a congressional committee investigating industrial conditions in 1900, one worker asserted: ". . . Our present social system is based upon a fundamental injustice, namely, private ownership of land . . ." Another said: "The great principle of [labor] organization is to remove the wage-earners from competition with each other, substitute the cooperative system for the competitive system, and remove the wage-earners from the competitive state to the cooperative state." Yet another ordinary miner testified simply that the answer to America's ills was unlimited government ownership of the means of production.[20]

To achieve their better society, Western workers at first preferred political to economic action, the ballot and the statute to the strike and the boycott. As a Gibbsonsville, Idaho, miner wrote to the *Miners' Magazine:* ". . . The majority of our members are beginning to realize . . . that strikes and lockouts are ineffectual weapons to use against capital. They are firm believers in political action. . . . Let labor break loose from the old parties and make itself a party of pure social democracy. Let its principles and purposes be, the earth for the people; to every man according to his needs and for every man the product of his own labor; products for all, but profits for none." A Declaration of Principles adopted at the WFM convention in 1900 proposed, among other items, public ownership of the means of production and distribution, abolition of the wage system, and the study of socialist political economy by union members. Agreeing with these principles, a union member in Granite, Montana, commented: "In government ownership we have a remedy for the trust which will minimize its evils and maximize its benefits; a remedy which will make the largest projects in the industrial world the most beneficial and will cause the inventive genius of the centuries to be applied for the benefit of all instead of for the benefit of the few." [21]

The 1900 presidential election saw the *Miners' Magazine* endorse the Socialist party unity candidates, Debs and Harriman, who, as Boyce noted, "come nearer representing the views of the Western Federation of Miners as expressed in its set of principles" than any other candidates. Only a year later, the WFM's adopted child, the Western Labor Union, publicly denounced the American government, "the very foundation of which is crumbling to decay, through the corruption and infamy of the self-constituted governing class . . ." In addition, the Western organization professed its readiness to spill every drop of its members' blood at bayonet point before submitting to further capitalist aggressions. Revolutionary pronunciamentos increasingly filled Boyce's speeches and the columns of the *Miners' Magazine*, culminating in a demand by delegates at the 1901 WFM convention for "a complete revolution of present social and economic conditions . . ." [22]

Boyce's 1902 farewell address to the WFM convention summarized what by then had become the Western organization's guiding philosophy. Conceding that the major purpose of the union, like that of all labor organizations, was to raise wages and lower hours, Boyce nevertheless cautioned that permanent improvements would not come until miners recognized that pure and simple trade unionism would inevitably fail. The only answer to labor's predicament, he stressed, was "to abolish the wage system which is more destructive of human rights and liberty than any other slave system devised." [23]

In keeping with Boyce's advice, the convention delegates voted to unite their organization with the Socialist Party of America. Early the following year the union's executive board under its new president, Charles Moyer, reaffirmed the WFM's radicalism by promising to make the union "an organization of class-conscious political workers that constitute the vanguard of the army that is destined to accomplish the economic freedom of the producers of all wealth." [24]

The growing radicalism of Western labor overjoyed some American radicals. "I have always felt that your organization is the most radical and progressive national body in the country," Debs wrote Boyce in January 1902, "and . . . in my mind . . . it is to take a commanding part, if it does not lead, in the social revolution that will insure final emancipation to the struggling masses." [25]

The conflict between Western workers and the AFL was not primarily because of the Westerners' radicalism or socialism. Gompers and the AFL would have tolerated socialism in the West if it had been divorced from the labor movement, or if it had found a home within the AFL. What irked Gompers was the WFM's decision not only to go it alone but to establish a rival labor center in the West. At the WLU's birth in 1898 the AFL was still a fragile institution just over ten years old, a mere infant which Gompers desperately wanted to survive beyond childhood. If the WFM managed to live and thrive outside the AFL, other large national labor organizations, such as the United Mine Workers, might also choose to leave. It was to combat what he conceived to be dual unionism, not to destroy radicalism, that Gompers fought Western labor's radicals.

After 1900, AFL organizers suddenly appeared in the previously neglected Mountain States to compete with their WLU-WFM counterparts. Gompers' agents in the West attempted to convince workers that the future of the American labor movement was with the AFL, not the WLU. When AFL men failed thus to win over Western Labor Union locals, they tried to wreck them by organizing dual unions of their own, even offering employers inducements to deal with the AFL rather than the WLU.[26]

The Westerners, by contrast, maintained that they had no quarrel with the AFL. Their fight was with employers, not with other workers. Emphasizing its attempts to organize the unorganized within its territory, the WLU's executive board informed the AFL that Western labor was too occupied battling corporations to seek a fight with another labor organization.[27]

But AFL officials were firmly convinced that the American nation was unable to support two labor movements, however noncompetitive. Hence the AFL demanded that the WFM (which it held responsible for all Western separatism) disband all "dual unions" in Denver, abolish the WLU, and reaffiliate with the AFL. To accomplish those ends, Gompers sent two representatives to the WFM convention in 1902. But, far from submitting to what amounted to an AFL ultimatum, Western workers only became more aggressive. Cataloguing the indignities which the WFM had borne with patience, they warned: ". . . There comes a time in the history of all such imposition when patience ceases to be a virtue, and this juncture for the Western Federation of Miners has now arrived." The *Miners' Magazine* informed Gompers' two emissaries: "The Western Federation . . . and the Western Labor Union are ready to join forces with any labor organization that offers a remedy, but they don't propose to be led like sheep into a slaughter pen to await the butcher's knife without a struggle." [28]

Instead of dissolving the WLU and returning to Gompers' waiting arms, the WFM transformed the Western Labor Union into the American Labor Union and embraced socialism more firmly than before. In part, this action was a tacit recognition that the WLU had never amounted to much, that, apart from locals among a handful of restaurant workers and other minor city trades, the organization had almost nothing to show for five years' effort. Conceding the failure of the WLU as a regional labor organization and letting it die an unmourned death, Western workers now decided to carry their challenge directly to the AFL by forming a national labor body—the American Labor Union—which would compete with the AFL for members on a nation-wide basis.

The ALU began where the Western Labor Union left off—but with one important difference. The ALU sent organizers east into traditional AFL territory and invited AFL affiliates; especially the Brewery Workers, to join the new national labor center. Although ALU leaders proclaimed their desire to live in peace with the AFL, they had every intention of weakening, if not destroying, the older national labor organization.[29]

What did the American Labor Union offer workers that could not be obtained through AFL membership? First, the ALU offered its members unswerving loyalty to socialist principles and to the Socialist party. Second, it offered members a constitutional structure more democratic than that of the AFL, one under which basic principles and policies would be established by membership referendum rather than by "irresponsible" officers. Third, it promised Western workers the assistance the AFL so often in the past had denied them.[30] Most important, however, the American Labor Union opened its membership to those neglected by the AFL: the semi-skilled and the unskilled in America's basic industries, women, and immigrants ignored by the established labor unions.

Dan MacDonald, the ALU's president, argued the case for the unorganized, whose "position . . . is more exposed to the influence of unjust conditions and subject to greater impositions and greater burdens than the organized." D. C. Coates, labor leader, former lieutenant governor of Colorado, and later an IWW founder, put the ALU's case for the unorganized more directly and precisely:

We find there is no need of aristocratic unions standing aloof from the common laborer as the craftsman is fast passing away . . . our aim is not so much to help the fellow on the inside, but to help every wage worker. . . . Our plan is progressive, it will help every child and woman worker; in fact, it will solve the labor problem by capturing the government for the workers.[31]

Haywood summarized the ALU's advocacy of industrial unionism and its critique of the American Federation of Labor. He emphasized that the AFL was merely a council of loosely affiliated trade unions representing a small minority of workers who, inculcated with the spirit of craft selfishness, continually engaged in jurisdictional warfare to monopolize union benefits for the favored few. In times of crisis, he said, the AFL had always proved impotent to aid its affiliates, usually sacrificing them on the "sacred altar of contract." To Gompers' impassioned defense of craft unionism, trade autonomy, and exclusive jurisdiction, Haywood retorted:

The diversity of labor is incapable of craft distinction; thus pure and simple trade unions become obsolete. The machine is the apprentice of yesterday, the journeyman of today. But [the] industrial union is the evolution of the labor movement, confronting and competing with the strides of the machine in industrial progress . . . it is also the open door of organized labor. . . . With twenty millions of unorganized wage earners the material presents itself for a progressive, compact, militant organization, the local unions of which will be lyceums for the discussion of political economy, teaching the working class to understand their position in life.[32]

In keeping with its emphasis on industrial unionism, the ALU, though employing the rhetoric of political socialism, stressed the primacy of economic action—which the IWW would later label direct action. The ALU, for example, never required political conformity on the part of its members; in fact, it allowed each man to ride his favorite political hobby horse to exhaustion. Moreover, the organization's constitution barred any member from holding union office if he also held political office, regardless of party affiliation. ". . . The A.L.U. is not a political organization. . . . With regard to its political character, it amounts to this: it simply recommends to the worker what to do and how to do it," claimed ALU officials, seeking to distinguish their organization from Daniel DeLeon's dual union, the Socialist Trades and Labor Alliance, which made membership in the Socialist Labor party a requisite for membership. The ALU, its spokesmen maintained, would concentrate on the industrial field, leaving politics to other organizations.[33]

From the first, the ALU cherished the two tenets most characteristic of the post-1908 IWW: the primacy of economic over political action and a belief in the syndicalist organization of the new society. As the ALU *Journal* expressed the organization's philosophy:

The economic organization of the proletariat is the heart and soul of the Socialist movement. . . . The purpose of industrial unionism is to organize the working class in approximately the same departments of production and distribution as those which will obtain in the co-operative commonwealth, so that if the workers should lose their franchise, they would still retain an economic organization intelligently trained to take over and collectively administer the tools of industry and the sources of wealth for themselves.[34]

Western workers adopted still another principle later characteristic of the IWW: opposition to time contracts. Moyer, for example, informed WFM convention delegates in 1903: ". . . It behooves us at all times to be free to take advantage of any opportunity to better our condition. Nothing affords the majority of corporations more satisfaction than to realize that they have placed you in a position where you are powerless to act for a period of years." [35] The WFM and the ALU by 1903–1904, like the IWW thereafter, believed that no agreement with employers was legally or morally binding, and that workers could achieve their objectives only by remaining free to strike at will.

Clearly, then, what later would become the distinguishing traits of the IWW had been formed in the American West by 1903. The combination of industrial unionism, labor solidarity, political nonpartisanship, direct economic action, and syndicalism, so characteristic of the IWW, had already been subscribed to by the WFM and its offspring, the American Labor Union. Contrary to what some historians have asserted, neither a Daniel DeLeon, nor an Algie Simons,* nor a William Trautmann, nor European labor radicals provided the ideological framework for the IWW. True, European radicals in France and Italy—and to a lesser extent in England and Germany—were moving at the same time toward syndicalist principles; granted that DeLeon, Simons, and Trautmann were familiar with continental developments and European radical ideology, and propagandized about them in America; nevertheless, it was primarily the experiences Western workers had lived through in America—the failure of Populism, bloody industrial warfare, capital's use of the state to repress labor—that created among the more radical their belief in industrial unionism, solidarity, and syndicalism.

For all its radical rhetoric and militant principles, however, the ALU lacked substance. Like its predecessor, the Western Labor Union, its strength, funds, and membership came mainly from the WFM. In addition, its leading officials, Daniel MacDonald and Clarence Smith, were simply inherited from the Western Labor Union. Only in its grander ambitions and its more radical tone did the ALU differ.

Insubstantial as the ALU in fact was, both the Socialist party and the AFL feared and even fought it. Although the ALU enlisted fervently, if not uncritically, in the socialist crusade, Socialist party members did not always respond in kind. After all, as we have already seen, in its publications and propaganda the ALU emphasized that union interests would always take precedence over party considerations, victory in the shop precedence over victory at the ballot box. To some American Socialists—among them, such Socialist party leaders as Victor Berger, Morris Hillquit, and Max Hayes—the ALU seemed uncomfortably radical and revolutionary. These Socialists naturally welcomed the ALU's endorsement of their party, but they deprecated Western labor's war with the AFL, compared the ALU to DeLeon's infamous Socialist Trades and Labor Alliance, and refused to sanction the ALU's existence as a national organization.[36]

Socialist party leaders were in fact gambling their party's future upon an alliance with the AFL, the trade unions, and the skilled workers. The party's dominant faction believed that its best hope lay in capturing the AFL and its affiliates from within; thus anything

---

* Simons was one of the outstanding intellects in the Socialist party, founder and editor of the *International Socialist Review*, and a leader of the party's alleged left wing.

which weakened that strategy by vitiating Socialist strength inside the AFL had perforce to be condemned. In terms of party strategy, they believed, Socialists best served the cause by staying in Gompers' organization, not by deserting it to join the ALU. So many American Socialists, following Gompers' lead, fought the American Labor Union. This Socialist strategy proved wrong; the AFL was beyond capture, but American Socialists could not foresee in 1904 what today seems to have been so inevitable.

Whether a Socialist party alliance with the ALU and its successor, the IWW, would, as some Socialists believed, have altered the future course of American socialism remains debatable. But Eugene Debs and others in the party's "left wing" were willing to wager their future on the radical horse. Criticizing the ALU's Socialist adversaries, Debs wrote: "The class-conscious movement of the West is historic in origin and development and every Socialist should recognize its mission and encourage its growth. It is here that the tide of social revolution will reach its flood and thence roll into other sections, giving impetus where needed and hastening the glorious day of triumph." [37] But most Socialists still preferred to work within the AFL.

Despite opposition, the Western Federation tried to build a substantial, independent radical labor organization devoted to industrial unionism. Recognizing the failure of the WLU and regional radicalism, the WFM had created the American Labor Union. But only a year after the ALU's birth—perhaps stillbirth would be a more accurate description—the Western Federation had to concede another failure. For just when the WFM became involved in the most serious crisis of its existence—the 1903–1904 Colorado labor war described earlier— the ALU proved incapable of saving the Western Federation from utter defeat. The defeat in Colorado convinced WFM leaders of their absolute need for a radical new national labor organization, one which could truly revolutionize American society. Guy E. Miller, a union leader during the Colorado struggle, drew the following conclusions from his experiences:

The man who is a slave in the industrial economy of society can not . . . be other than a slave in its political life. . . . The lives of workers are consumed, eaten up in the creation of dividends. Modern industry is veneered cannibalism. That is the tragedy of the workers locked in the torture halls of the damned so long as the wage system endures. . . . Always and everywhere the few have used some combination of force and fraud to keep the many in subjection. . . . We have seen the private ownership of the revenues of society corrupt the state and reduce it to a vassal in the service of corporate wealth.[38]

To alter life as Miller had experienced it, the WFM in 1904 initiated conferences that led the following year to the founding of the Industrial Workers of the World.

The WFM's twelfth annual convention, meeting in Denver in June 1904 as the Colorado labor conflict moved toward its violent climax, instructed its executive board to plan "for the amalgamation of the entire working class into one general organization." Soon thereafter Haywood and Moyer met informally with Dan MacDonald of the ALU and George Estes of the United Railway Workers, which represented the scattered remnants of Debs's American Railway Union. That November six men conferred secretly in Chicago—since June 1904 the ALU's headquarters—to discuss a general reformation of the American labor movement. The six included Clarence Smith, secretary of the ALU; Thomas Hagerty, editor of *The Voice of Labor*, then the ALU's official journal; George Estes and W. L. Hall, representing the United Railway Workers; Isaac Cowen of the Amalgamated Society of Engineers;° and William E. Trautmann, recently deposed editor of the *Bräuer Zeitung*, official organ of the Brewery Workers. Invited but unable to attend were Eugene Debs and Charles O. Sherman.[39]

The six conferees immediately agreed, as Clarence Smith later remembered it, that America must have "a labor organization that would correspond to modern industrial conditions." On November 29, 1904, they addressed a letter to some thirty individuals known to favor industrial unionism, socialism, and a reformation of the labor movement. The addressees included members of the Socialist party and the Socialist Labor party, industrial unionists and craft unionists, non-AFL members and AFL members, as well as men who can only be labeled fellow travelers in the cause of radicalism and unionism. Although no professed anarchists or known syndicalists received the letter, it contained the kernel of what later became the IWW's syndi-

---

° An American branch of the English organization of the same name, then engaged in a jurisdictional dispute with the American International Association of Machinists, as well as with Gompers and the AFL.

calist ideology. Opening with the predictable blast at the AFL, the letter went on:

Believing that working class political expression, through the Socialist ballot, in order to be sound, must have *its economic counterpart in a labor organization builded as the structure of Socialist society, embracing within itself the working class in approximately the same groups and departments and industries that workers would assume in the working class administration of the Co-operative Commonwealth* [italics added] . . .

It concluded by inviting the addressees "to meet with us in Chicago, Monday, January 2, 1905, in secret conference to discuss ways and means of uniting the working people of America on correct revolutionary principles . . . as will insure its [labor's] integrity as a real protector of the interests of the workers." [40]

Most of those invited—twenty-two, to be exact—did attend the January conference. Twelve others who endorsed the conference's purposes begged off for various reasons. Among the latter were Debs, who pleaded poor health, D. C. Coates, and Ed Boyce. As for Debs, Hagerty and Trautmann reported that they had met privately with him in Terre Haute, and that he enthusiastically supported the conference's purpose. Daniel DeLeon, soon to become the most contentious personality in the early IWW, was not even invited to the January session. [41]

Two men refused to attend, and their refusal carried great significance. They were Victor Berger and Max Hayes, both influential in the Socialist party. Berger did not even reply, while Hayes's response reflected prevailing Socialist party attitudes. Most Socialists, it was obvious, still pinned their hopes on winning over the AFL and its skilled working-class membership. Hayes, himself a craft unionist and also an AFL member, proved no exception. "If I am correct," he wrote to W. L. Hall concerning the proposed labor conference, ". . . it means another running fight between Socialists . . . and all other partisans. Let me say frankly that under no circumstances will I permit myself to be dragged into any more secession movements or fratricidal war between factions of workers. . . . If there is any fighting to be done, I intend to use my energies and whatever ability I may possess to bombard the common enemy—capitalism." Taking an optimistic view of the AFL's future, Hayes preferred for strategic reasons to "be inside the fort and take chances to secure the adoption of my plans than be outside and be regarded as an enemy." [42] His position, which

Berger shared, portended an equivocal and unsatisfactory future relationship between the Socialist party and the IWW.

Without Berger, Hayes, or the blessings of the Socialist party, twenty-one men and one woman—the famous Mother Jones*—met secretly at 122 Lake Street, Chicago, on January 2, 1905. The only significant union group present came from the American West: the WFM sent Haywood, Moyer, and John O'Neill, while MacDonald, Smith, and Hagerty represented the ALU (which was in fact only a WFM subsidiary). The others in attendance spoke only for themselves or for fractional, insignificant labor groups. Trautmann, one of the most influential men at the meeting, had just been deposed as editor of the *Bräuer Zeitung* because of his acidulous anti-AFL, anti–craft-union editorials. Like most of the conferees, he was more a propagandist than a labor leader or union organizer.[43]

For three days this motley assortment of radicals thrashed out their differences, at last agreeing upon eleven principles for reforming the labor movement. Of these the following were the most significant: (1) creation of a general industrial union embracing all industries; (2) the new organization to be founded on recognition of the class struggle and administered on the basis of an irrepressible conflict between capital and labor; (3) all power to reside in the collective membership; (4) universal free transfer of union cards; and (5) a call for a general convention to form a national labor organization in accordance with the conference's basic principles.[44]

Considerable confusion remained hidden within the eleven principles. The proposed organization ostensibly devoted to industrial unionism, for example, was also dedicated in advance to: "craft autonomy locally; industrial autonomy internationally; working class unity, generally." Just how the conferees expected to retain craft autonomy and industrial unionism, industrial autonomy and working-class solidarity, went unexplained. Apparently, some strange labor metaphysics made some working-class concerns peculiar to certain industries, crafts, or localities, in which case autonomy would prevail. Nor did the conferees reach a consensus about the proper political role for their proposed organization. Socialists saw it essentially as a branch of the party (the SLP, if they were DeLeonites); yet the Westerners, while claiming to be socialists, remained suspicious of politics,

---

* Mother Jones had won her fame in the labor movement as the grandmotherly organizer of coal miners and flaming advocate of their rights during tempestuous UMW strikes in which she had taken a leading role.

politicians, and the state. Representing the Western influence predominant at the January sessions, Hagerty pushed through the following resolution: "That this Union be established as the economic organization of the working class without affiliation with any political party." [45] Hardly a position to excite Socialist party politicians!

But uncertainties and conflicts dissolved in the euphoric atmosphere of the Chicago conference, which, at its end, adopted the famous and widely quoted Industrial Union Manifesto. This manifesto reflected a Marxist view of the evolution of society, a view which Trautmann, Algie Simons, and Hagerty had derived from books, and which Western workers had derived from experience. It also distilled into a few terse paragraphs the signatories' scorn for AFL-type craft unionism. The manifesto, which might be considered the IWW's Old Testament, merits extended quotation.

The worker wholly separated from the land and the tools with his skill or craftsmanship rendered useless is sunk in the uniform mass of wage slaves. He sees his power of resistance broken by craft divisions, perpetuated from outgrown industrial stages. His wages constantly grow less as his hours grow longer and monopolized prices go higher. Shifted hither and thither by the demands of the profit takers, the laborer's home no longer exists. In his helpless condition, he is forced to accept whatever humiliating conditions his master may impose. . . . Laborers are no longer classified by differences in trade skill, but the employer assorts them according to the machines to which they are attached. These divisions, far from representing differences in skill, or interests among laborers, are imposed by the employers that workers may be pitted against one another . . . and that all resistance to capitalist tyranny may be weakened by artificial, fratricidal distinctions.

. . . [Craft unionism] offers only a perpetual struggle for slight relief within wage slavery. It is blind to the possibility of establishing an industrial democracy wherein there shall be no wage slavery, but where the workers will own the tools which they operate and the products of which they alone will enjoy.[46]

To change this obnoxious craft-union system, the manifesto asked all true believers in industrial unionism to meet in Chicago on June 27, 1905, to establish a new national labor organization based upon the Marxist concept of the class struggle and committed to the construction of the cooperative commonwealth. This invitation was sent to American radicals and trade unionists, and to European labor organizations, among whom it engendered especially acute interest and heated debate. Max Hayes continued to criticize these proposals and to deny that Socialists had formulated them. (On the last point he was more than half right.) Even Samuel Gompers joined the debate, devoting three issues of the *American Federationist* to an attack upon the so-called industrial unionists, whom he labeled "union smashers." [47] Algie Simons and Frank Bohn, both participants in the January conference, debated the significance of the manifesto in the *International Socialist Review*. Conceding the importance of the approaching industrial union convention, as well as the failure of the AFL to adjust to contemporary economic life, Simons yet wondered: ". . . Is the present the proper time for such a change to come? If it is not, then this organization will be a thing born out of due time, a cause of disorder, confusion, and injury." For a time, Simons surmounted his doubts and favored the new challenge to the AFL. His reservations nevertheless illustrate just how tenuous indeed was the connection between the Socialist party's anti-AFL faction and the birth of the IWW; only two years after the IWW's birth, Simons' skepticism regarding the new industrial union movement, combined with his reluctance to fight the established unions, led him to desert the Wobblies. Frank Bohn, then a Socialist Labor party member, answered Simons' questions, and in so doing demonstrated why his party, rather than the Socialist party, linked itself tightly to the IWW. Denying the possibility of capturing the old unions by boring from within, Bohn considered the occasion ripe for industrial unionism. Hence he called upon his friends within the SLP and also within the craft unions to enter the proposed new labor organization, scuttle trade unionism, and adopt class-conscious industrial unionism. [48]

Western labor leaders, like Bohn, never hesitated in their choice. John O'Neill wrote innumerable *Miners' Magazine* editorials endorsing the January manifesto and the proposed industrial union convention. Moyer and Haywood advised their followers to study the manifesto so that the 1905 WFM convention could ratify it. Local unions added their endorsements to those of their officials. Not surprisingly, the 1905 WFM convention voted overwhelmingly in favor of participating in the proposed Chicago convention, and elected Moyer and Haywood their delegates. [49] Debs, too, added his powerful voice to the chorus of industrial union advocates, proclaiming that the new labor organization would not seek to rival the AFL but rather that its sole aim would be "to advance the material interests of the working class and ultimately to emancipate that class from wage slavery." [50]

On the hot early-summer day of June 27, 1905, in a stuffy, over-crowded, smoke-filled, boisterous auditorium in Brand's Hall on Chicago's near north side, Bill Haywood called to order "the Continental Congress of the Working Class." As the 203 delegates listened intently, Haywood proclaimed:

We are here to confederate the workers of this country into a working class movement that shall have for its purpose the emancipation of the working class from the slave bondage of capitalism. . . . The aims and objects of this organization should be to put the working class in possession of the economic power, the means of life, in control of the machinery of production and distribution, without regard to capitalist masters. The American Federation of Labor, which presumes to be the labor movement of this country, is not a working class movement. It does not represent the working class . . . this organization will be formed, based and founded on the class struggle, having in view no compromise and no surrender, and but one object and one purpose and that is to bring the workers of this country into the possession of the full value of the product of their toil.[51]

The delegates delighted in Haywood's every phrase, for who could better voice their common detestation of the AFL and their ultimate desire for a better world? But on few other matters were they agreed. What else could be expected? Sixty-one delegates represented nobody but themselves. Seventy-two belonged to labor unions with a collective membership of more than ninety thousand—but they did not represent those trade unions, and in effect also spoke only for themselves. Seventy delegates represented slightly over fifty thousand union members, but of these seventy, only Moyer and Haywood, representing the forty thousand members of the WFM and the ALU, spoke for any significant number of union members. The two Westerners outvoted all other convention delegates by ten to one. (The ALU claimed 16,750 members, but many of these were fictional, or only Western Federation members counted twice.) Only five tiny AFL locals came to Chicago prepared to affiliate with the new organization; indeed, most AFL men at the convention represented themselves, not their unions.[52] Under these circumstances, headstrong or exceptional men such as Debs, Haywood, Hagerty, Trautmann, and even Daniel DeLeon (though his role has been repeatedly exaggerated) exerted a disproportionate influence.

Most students of the IWW's history have on one occasion or another tried their hands at distinguishing the various factions and ideologies represented at the founding convention, usually emphasizing the alleged role of a so-called syndicalist component. Probably the most accurate analysis of the factions, however, is that produced by a nonacademic analyst, Ben H. Williams, editor of *Solidarity* from 1909 to 1916, who was also perhaps the most astute IWW theoretician. In his memoirs Williams distinguishes three groups present at the founding convention. First, the WFM and other union veterans. This group was earnest in its desire to create an industrial union initially unattached to any political party but which could in due time develop its own "political reflex." (This faction in time became the syndicalist component, but it had not yet reached that ideological point.) Second, the DeLeonites, who aimed to place the new organization under the tutelage of the SLP. Third, the Socialist party politicians prepared to bypass the new organization if it failed to follow their vote-getting program. Williams also describes a fourth faction: the "also-rans," comprised of would-be craft-union leaders ambitious to get back in the labor game for possible personal gain. Unfortunately, it was from this last faction that the IWW selected its first and only president: Charles O. Sherman.[53]

It is noteworthy that Williams' spectrum of factions includes neither anarchists (though Lucy Parsons, wife of Haymarket martyr Albert Parsons, was an honored guest) nor syndicalists. Almost all the delegates, as Williams himself knew from firsthand experience, were in 1905 committed to some form of socialist politics. The seeds of syndicalism, as we have already seen, were sown well before 1905, but they did not flower until several years after.

On the surface, despite the presence of so many factions known for their disputatious character, unity seemed to prevail at the convention. At first, SLP members, Socialist party members, and trade unionists buried their differences in fevered anti-AFL, anti–Sam Gompers oratory. Trautmann began this type of speechmaking by indicting the AFL for its class collaboration and its leaders (the "labor lieutenants of capitalism") for joining with the captains of industry to exploit the unskilled—be they women, children, or immigrants. Debs, DeLeon, and Hagerty followed Trautmann to the rostrum, each adding his own scathing comments about the AFL's "labor fakirs." Debs and DeLeon, sectarian enemies of long and bitter standing, even complimented each other's sudden conversion to good sense. Debs offered "to take by the hand every man, every woman who comes here, totally regardless of past affiliation," while DeLeon sententiously announced that he and Debs "had shaken hands over the bloody chasm of the past." All of which led an obscure but happy delegate to chime in: "Where I see such intellectual giants from the East as DeLeon, from the West as Haywood, Moyer, and O'Neill . . . and from the Central West [as] Debs [and] Simons . . . the results of this convention must have a gratifying and inspiring effect upon the workers of the world." [54]

This kind of harmony, certainly abundant during the convention's first five days, fled the hall on the sixth. As the temperature rose and tempers flared, delegates began to discuss just what their new organization was to do, and how it would do it.

Two questions—decisive ones having to do with the new organization's politics and structure—particularly divided the convention as it went about the business of drawing up a constitution. Some Socialists had assumed, naturally though unwisely, that the delegates would endorse the Socialist party. Had they paid closer attention to the preconvention debates, these Socialists might have remembered the following warning printed in the *Miners' Magazine:* "Experience has taught us that the economic organization and the political organization must be distinct and apart from each other. . . . To our mind it becomes necessary to unite the workers upon the industrial domain, before it is possible to unite them in the political arena." To which the ALU's journal had added: ". . . It would seem that the industrial labor organization must come first, for here we can have a force with which to defend the rights of the workers at the shop, mine, and factory, every working day of the year . . ." [55] The Westerners, who were dominant at the convention, agreed with this preconvention advice, and also with Hagerty's comment during convention debate: "The ballot box is simply a capitalist concession. Dropping pieces of paper into a hole in a box never did achieve emancipation for the working class, and to my mind never will achieve it." Union delegates from the West, given their immense voting power, could easily have eliminated all reference to politics from the new organization's constitution. Instead, as a concession to Socialists from both parties whom they desired to keep in the fold, the Westerners approved the second, or political, paragraph of the IWW constitution preamble, which

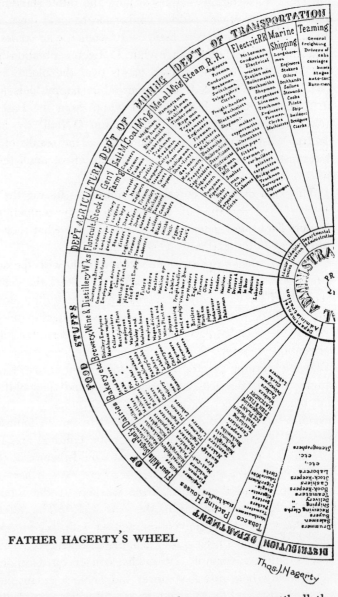

FATHER HAGERTY'S WHEEL

Thos. J. Hagerty

read: "Between these two classes a struggle must go on until all the toilers come together on the political, as well as the industrial field, and take hold of that which they produce by their labor through an economic organization of the working class, without affiliation with any political party." [56] One convention delegate found this clause beyond comprehension. Totally confused, he remarked: ". . . I cannot

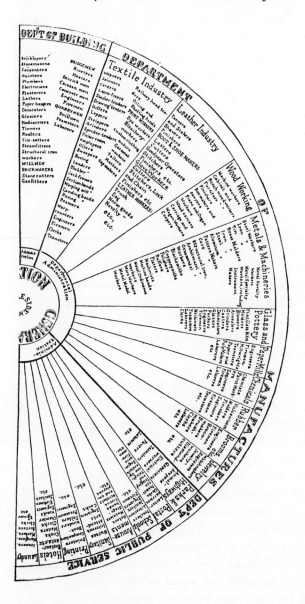

afford to have Brother DeLeon [the convention's leading ideologue] along with me every time I meet a man to explain what this paragraph means." [57] Obscurity was, of course, the precise purpose of the political clause, so as to make it acceptable simultaneously to incipient syndicalists, Socialist party advocates, and SLP members.

Equally controversial was Hagerty's plan for the structure of the organization, the so-called "Wheel of Fortune" involving a "general administration" at the hub, five departments at the circumference, and thirteen industrial divisions in between. None of the delegates really knew what the Wheel meant or how Hagerty proposed to effect it. Haywood openly opposed its elaborately arranged categories and sub-categories; he proposed instead a simple plan of industrial unionism in which workers would be grouped by the industries in which they worked, not by the tools they used. Haywood even went as far as to demand complete autonomy for the various individual industrial unions he envisioned as the IWW's essence.[58] Shades of Sam Gompers!

Debate waxed hot and heavy on Hagerty's proposal. Although many delegates felt that adoption of the Wheel would result in the kind of organizational chaos that had destroyed the Knights of Labor, the convention finally endorsed Hagerty's organizational scheme. Why delegates voted as they did is not clear; perhaps they did so partly because the Wheel, like the political clause, could be interpreted differently to every individual's own satisfaction; perhaps because they perceived that it would always remain only a confusing diagram, never a fact of organization life.

Considerably less trouble and debate went into selecting the new organization's name and its general officers. Without dissent, delegates agreed to call their creation the Industrial Workers of the World. Then, possibly to deflate the overwhelming numerical preponderance of Western workers, but more likely because Moyer and Haywood felt unable to serve two organizations simultaneously and chose to remain in executive office with the WFM, the delegates chose two Easterners, Charles O. Sherman and William Trautmann, as president and secretary-treasurer respectively. (The IWW's first executive board more accurately reflected Western influence and power.)[59]

The convention had sought to achieve what Haywood had defined as its primary objective: "We are here for the purpose of organizing a *Labor Organization,* an organization broad enough to take in all the working class. What I want to see from this organization is an uplifting of the fellow that is down in the gutter . . . *realizing that society can be no better than its most miserable*" (italics added).[60] In order to carry out Haywood's recommendation, the IWW's constitution opened membership to all workers, skilled and unskilled, native and immigrant, child and adult, male and female, black, white, and even yellow. It provided for low, uniform initiation fees, still lower dues, and free universal transfer of union cards. Although it vested in the executive board sole authority to declare strikes, the constitution, by making convention decisions subject to open membership referenda, placed ultimate power in the general membership.

Having adopted a name, endorsed an organizational Wheel, and written a constitution, on the afternoon of July 8 the convention adjourned *sine die*. Algie Simons, writing soon afterward, claimed that the sessions had marked "a decisive turning point in American working class history." Samuel Gompers' hired informant, Luke Grant, although less laudatory, reported to his employer: "The convention did better than I expected, for I hardly believed it possible that the delegates would agree among themselves long enough to adopt a constitution or a name for the thing and they did both." [61]

The birth of the IWW confirmed, or so its founding fathers hoped, a prophecy made by Friedrich Engels in 1893. "In America, at least," Engels had written, "I am strongly inclined to believe that the fatal hour of capitalism will have struck as soon as a native American working class will have replaced a working class composed in its majority by foreign immigrants." [62] The men who created the IWW were by and large native Americans, or the most Americanized of immigrants, committed to interring capitalism in America. Unaware that Engels' prediction and their desires could not have been more ephemeral, the IWW's founders looked forward in 1905 to indefinitely spinning out their radical dreams on Hagerty's "Wheel of Fortune." They looked forward to liberating men from the bondage of wage slavery, abolishing the capitalist system in which man exploited man, and creating the new society in which man would truly be his brother's keeper. These were the yearnings that, in good times and in bad, sustained the men and women who led the IWW through great triumphs and tragic defeats.

PART TWO

Formative Years,
1905–1908

CHAPTER

5

The IWW Under Attack,
1905–1907

I NITIALLY it appeared that the history of the IWW would be synonymous with the life of Father Thomas J. Hagerty, one of the most unusual and colorful figures behind its creation. Hagerty had been the principal author of the January 1905 manifesto, the preamble to the IWW constitution, and the creator of the "Wheel of Fortune." After 1905 he vanished from the radical scene.

Hagerty's connection with the IWW seems at first glance inexplicable.[1] Only three years before the IWW's founding convention, Thomas J. Hagerty quietly pursued his vocation as a Roman Catholic priest (assistant to the rector of Our Lady of Sorrows Catholic Church in Las Vegas, New Mexico), saying Mass, hearing confessions, and baptizing infants. Having finished seminary training in 1895, he had served briefly at a Chicago parish, and at two other parishes in Texas, before moving to Las Vegas.

That Hagerty was an unusual priest soon became clear. At one Texas parish he championed exploited Mexican railroad workers. When railroad managers complained of his agitation, Hagerty is said to have replied: "Tell the people who sent you here that I have a brace of Colts and can hit a dime at twenty paces." Shortly after this incident Hagerty was transferred to the Archdiocese of Santa Fe, where his activities became even more peculiar. After only a few months at his new assignment, Hagerty attended the 1902 joint convention of the Western Federation of Miners and the Western Labor Union, urging delegates to endorse the Socialist party. Then, instead of returning to his parish duties, he toured Colorado's mining camps to propagandize for the American Labor Union and socialism, pausing at Telluride to advise his audience: "That railroad is yours; those large business blocks and office buildings downtown that bring in big rent are yours; if you want them, go and take them." Singular advice from a man of God!

While absent from New Mexico, Hagerty had been suspended from his priestly duties, for when word of his stand reached Church superiors, the Archbishop disowned his radical priest. Hagerty, insisting that Marxism and Catholicism were compatible, settled in Van Buren, Arkansas, still claiming to be a priest in good standing. As he put it to an Indiana audience: "I am a Catholic priest, as much a Catholic as the Pope himself."

The Socialist party naturally expected to make use of this rare priest who found Marxian tenets compatible with Church dogma. Winning Catholic workmen to the cause was an obstacle American Socialists had never surmounted; perhaps Father Hagerty could aid them. A striking figure on the rostrum, well over six feet tall, ruggedly handsome, with a booming and compelling voice, he proved to be one of the party's most popular orators. In a 1903 national lecture tour he attracted record crowds wherever he spoke, whether in New York, Milwaukee, or Butte. Hagerty's triumphant lecture tour led Debs to comment: "Tall, massive, erect, he would command attention anywhere. . . . He has ready language, logic, wit, sarcasm, and at times they roll like a torrent and thrill the multitude like a bugle call to charge." Coming from the master himself, this was no mean praise.

But the Socialist party soon became too tame for Hagerty. Impatient with parliamentary-reform socialists, whom he labeled "slowcialists," Hagerty began to advise lecture audiences: "We must have revolution, peaceable if possible, but, to tell the truth, we care not how we get it." These more radical views brought Hagerty the editorship of the American Labor Union's monthly, *The Voice of Labor*. At the first IWW convention, Hagerty joined the more radical delegates who belittled political action and ballot-box reform; with them he fought for action at the point of production initiated by the industrial unions, which would, in time, become the foundation blocks for erecting a new society within the shell of the old.

After his triumph at the June 1905 convention, Hagerty disappeared from sight. In August he failed to appear for IWW meetings in New York and Newark. Never again would he write for the radical press or take to the lecture platform to preach revolution. Just as he had never explained how a Catholic priest had become a Marxist convert, Hagerty never accounted for his separation from American radicalism; indeed, never again did he speak or write publicly. None of his old radical acquaintances even saw him until 1917, when Ralph Chaplin, editor of *Solidarity*, found a man resembling Hagerty living in Chicago under the name Ricardo Moreno, eking out a bare existence by teaching Spanish. By 1920 Moreno, *né* Hagerty, had joined the multitude of derelicts filling Chicago's skid row on West Madison Street, outcasts whom even the IWW ignored. Here, not far from IWW headquarters, the ex-priest and radical survived on the benevolence of the Salvation Army, private charities, individual handouts, barber colleges, and mission societies. The man who had sought to revolutionize the society which produced outcasts himself became just such an outcast.

What happened to Father Hagerty after 1905 was a portent for the organization he helped found. The ex-priest's radicalism failed to survive the June convention. The product of that convention, the IWW, beset by enemies without and within, scarcely survived its first two years.

The IWW expected opposition from the AFL and Gompers, and received it. Gompers first reacted to the new labor organization with somewhat uneasy ridicule. He had employed a special agent to attend the June 1905 convention and to keep him informed of developments in Chicago. Afterward, Gompers' informant remained in contact with the IWW leaders and reported regularly to his employer. Hence the AFL president could write to another labor leader curious about the new movement: "Yes, I have been kept fairly well informed as to the action of the Industrial Workers of the World and am reminded very much of the three tailors of Tooley Street, London, who issued the famous proclamation in the name of, 'We, the people of England.' They [the IWW founders] showed completely their inability to be of a constructive capacity. It is not even a house of cards, they have not even made the cards stand. The whole scheme is fanciful and chimerical and absolutely impossible . . ." But, Gompers added, "although there is not anything to fear from that source yet the greatest interest for the trade unions must be exercised, for rest assured they will concentrate their efforts in the trade unions, either to capture it or dominate it." [2]

Luke Grant, Gompers' agent, meanwhile sent further reports detailing the chaotic state of the IWW. Its very chaos, he claimed, largely accounted for his delays in providing the information Gompers desired. Apparently on the best of terms with president-elect Sherman and secretary-treasurer-elect Trautmann, who provided him with essential IWW data, Grant did his best to reassure an obviously troubled Gompers that the IWW was not a threat to the AFL. No one in Chicago, he reported, neither trade unionists nor socialists, endorsed the industrial union scheme, which seemed destined for an early demise. Grant also informed Gompers of divisions in the new organization between Socialist party and SLP men and between American Labor Union members and followers of DeLeon's Socialist Trades and Labor Alliance. [3]

But these reports did not put Gompers' mind to rest. He still feared an effort to crush the AFL. Gompers thus wrote to an English correspondent puzzled by the AFL leader's almost instinctive fear of socialists and radicals: "Just think of it, of DeLeon, the representative of the socialist labor party, and Debs the Presidential candidate of the socialist party in two campaigns joining hands, declaring themselves fast friends, and concentrating their efforts to disrupt the trade union movement . . . The history of the socialistic attitude toward the trade unions of the United States is a record of industrial crime, against which the trade unions of America will contend to the end." [4] To Gompers, in other words, the IWW was nothing less than a creation of American socialists intended to replace the AFL.

Consequently, Gompers and his executive council warned all AFL affiliates to guard against IWW infiltration and to refuse to cooperate with members of the new organization. AFL members were told not to support IWW strikes; they were also absolved from the sin of crossing IWW picket lines. In Montana the State Federation of Labor and the Silver Bow Trades and Labor Council purged WFM locals because of their affiliation with the IWW. [5] Gompers personally delivered a blistering attack upon the WFM at the AFL convention in 1905, accusing WFM leaders, especially Haywood, whom he subjected to exceptionally bitter invective, of transferring to the IWW funds the AFL had donated for the defense of WFM members persecuted in Colorado. With scarcely a murmur of dissent, the AFL convention voted to discontinue all defense aid to the WFM.[6]

While most AFL affiliates cooperated in the war against the IWW, a few refused. Two, the Cloth Hat and Cap Makers' Union and the International Ladies' Garment Workers' Union, found themselves engaged in bitter battles with insurgent members who led pro-IWW secessionist movements.[7] Although Algie Simons later claimed that the essential idea of the January 1905 conference "was to form a new central body, into which existing unions and unions to be formed could be admitted, but not to form rival unions," the IWW initially did seek to organize men already in AFL affiliates, concentrating particularly on establishing dual organizations of coal miners and brewery workers. Thus, while Gompers assured AFL members that the industrial-union convention had "labored and brought forth a mouse, and a very silly little mouse at that," he nevertheless urged his followers to remain constantly on the alert against their IWW enemies.[8]

Less expected by the IWW's founders was opposition from the Socialist party. After all, the leading Socialist personality, Eugene Debs, and a prominent party theoretician, Algie Simons, had attended the 1905 convention. Moreover, the IWW had succeeded by the Debs-DeLeon axis in uniting the divided American socialist movement and promised to add new strength to the radical cause.

But most Socialists suspected the new labor organization on two grounds. First, they could not quiet their suspicions of DeLeon and his motives. They were convinced that DeLeon would once again split the socialist movement, as he had done in 1897. Second, most Socialists still dreamed of capturing the AFL from within, and viewed those comrades who deserted to the IWW as weakening left-wing strength within the Federation. Socialists could not bed down with enemies of the AFL and expect Federation members to endorse socialism! As a result, the Socialist party and press, dominated by among others Victor Berger, Max Hayes, and Morris Hillquit, fought to avoid any connection between the Socialist party and the IWW. Gompers' informant found a special pleasure in the Socialist attitude, which he deemed as anti-IWW as that of Gompers himself.[9]

Left-wing Socialists like Simons and Debs tried to defend the IWW. Simons claimed that the IWW had no wish to involve the party in internecine labor strife, though every IWW official was a Socialist party member. If trouble should come, he warned, "it will be because of those who are so anxious to gain the favor of the A.F. of L. officials that they must heap their abuse on every one who does not kow-tow to their pure and simple god." To Simons, Socialist chances of capturing the AFL then seemed slim; Gompers' machine of 1905–1906 was simply too well entrenched to be overthrown. Debs agreed. He could not understand how Socialists could remain in the pro-capitalist AFL. "The choice," Debs wrote, "is between the A.F. of L. and capitalism on one side and the Industrial Workers and Socialism on the other. How can a Socialist hesitate in his choice for an instant? The way to serve the working class through the A. F. of L. is to get out of it and leave the capitalist class and their henchmen in undisputed control." [10]

Despite the arguments of Debs and Simons, most Socialists preferred to remain within and support the AFL. Soon Simons himself would leave the IWW, and a short time later Debs would follow suit. Both learned in somewhat rude fashion that while the IWW's leaders endorsed socialism, they were unwilling to subject the new labor organization to Socialist party discipline or to accept unquestioningly Socialist programs and ideology. Thus the IWW and the Socialist party maintained an uneasy, tenuous relationship—sometimes fighting, sometimes cooperating, but seldom understanding each other.

Under attack by trade unionists and by many Socialists, the IWW suddenly confronted hostile government authorities and public opinion. Events in Idaho, which in fact had little to do with the IWW, nevertheless deeply affected the Wobblies and their cause.

Ice covered the streets of Caldwell, Idaho, the hometown of former Governor Frank Steunenberg, on the afternoon of Saturday, December 30, 1905. Before strolling his daily mile from Caldwell's business district to his home, Steunenberg paused as always in the lobby of the Saratoga Hotel, rocking for a while in his favorite chair, reading the newspapers, and talking to admiring friends. Financially secure thanks to business contacts he had made during his term as governor (1897–1901), Steunenberg was Caldwell's leading citizen. President of the local bank, speculator in sheep and timber, he led a comfortable but inconsequential life. No longer was he the stern governor who had fought the WFM in the Coeur d'Alenes, driven its members out of the mines, and sent one of its officers to prison. Almost everyone had forgotten his role as strikebreaker in 1899; those in Caldwell who did remember applauded his decision at the time to repress "lawless, unAmerican" labor. But on that cold December day the Coeur d'Alenes became more than a distant memory. As Steunenberg read and rocked, a furtive stranger watched intently. Unbeknowst to all, that stranger, a drifter known as Harry Orchard, had for several weeks been observing the movements and habits of the ex-Governor. Twice during that period he had tried to shoot Steunenberg. Failing in those attempts, Orchard decided upon a change in tactics. When Steunenberg entered the hotel lobby on December 30, Orchard hastened to the ex-Governor's home, where he planted a bomb rigged to explode upon the opening of the front gate. Even before the stranger had returned to his room in the Saratoga, Steunenberg had opened his front gate, triggering an explosion which echoed throughout Caldwell. A few moments later, he died without regaining consciousness.

The assassination stunned Caldwell. Immediately public officials acted. Municipal authorities forbade anyone to leave town, while Governor Frank Gooding and other state officials rushed to Caldwell. By then the sheriff had arrested some of the more promising local suspects, among them Harry Orchard.

Orchard had courted arrest. He had lived at the Saratoga for several months without visible means of support. Supposedly a sheep buyer, he bought no sheep. After the murder he made no attempt to escape. Indeed, he made himself more conspicuous. When local police arrested him on January 1, 1906, they easily discovered in his room the ingredients used in the lethal bomb.[11]

Such behavior was puzzling, if not inexplicable. Orchard was either incredibly stupid, or eager to be arrested and punished for his deed. The former explanation scarcely fits the man who could plan so ingenious an assassination (and who later claimed to have murdered more than a score of other men). The latter possibility seems just as unlikely in the case of a professional criminal who later confessed to having been a hired assassin, a cold-blooded amoral killer. Perhaps a psychotic personality disorder led Orchard into a life of violence, perhaps that same disorder eventually caused him to seek penance for his (mis)deeds. His actual motive for Steunenberg's assassination is probably as much within the province of psychopathologists as of historians and amateur detectives.

Idaho officials professed little difficulty in discovering the alleged assassin's motives. Ever since the 1899 Coeur d'Alene conflict they had been convinced that an "inner circle" controlled the WFM, and that this "inner circle" plotted the destruction of property as well as the assassination of capitalists and public officials opposed to the union. Had not Frank Steunenberg been just such an opponent? So reasoned Idaho's officials. The state's problem, then, was not to find a motive for Orchard's deed; rather it was to connect the "hired" assassin to his employers, the "inner circle" of the WFM.[12] To this problem Governor Gooding turned his attention.

Precedent guided Gooding. Thirty years earlier, Pennsylvania had destroyed a similar "inner circle," that of the notorious Molly Maguires. The man responsible for the apprehension and execution of nineteen Mollies, James McParland, was near at hand in 1906. McParland's success in Pennsylvania had transformed the Pinkerton National Detective Agency, for which he worked, into the principal institution to which private employers and public officials turned for discreet and effective anti-labor espionage.[13] McParland, in fact, now managed Pinkerton's Denver office, which Governor Gooding contacted on January 8, asking McParland to direct Idaho's investigation with the purpose of linking Orchard to the WFM's "inner circle." [14] Almost simultaneously, Gooding also appointed James H. Hawley and William Borah—the men who had prosecuted the WFM in 1899—to prosecute the union once again. Thus, even before Orchard confessed, state officials knew whom they were after: Charles Moyer and William D. Haywood.

Once on the job, McParland ingratiated himself with Orchard. The Pinkerton agent had the prisoner moved from the small Caldwell jail to the larger Ada County prison in Boise for softening up.[15] Here for ten days the authorities kept Orchard in solitary confinement, offering him little to eat and drink, all the while plying him with dire threats. Half starved and apparently deeply frightened, Orchard was finally introduced to McParland, who, during an exquisitely prepared luncheon followed by fine cigars, told him the story of "Kelly the Bum." According to McParland, Kelly was a confessed murderer whom the prosecution in Pennsylvania had paid to leave the country after he delivered testimony fatal to the Mollies. The seed planted,

McParland left Orchard alone to smoke fine Havanas and to mull over the fate of "Kelly the Bum." [16] During a second private interview, McParland introduced the prisoner to the subtleties of morality and God. Upon obtaining from Orchard an admission of belief in God and an afterlife, McParland reminded him that King David had been an adulterer and a murderer, and St. Paul an executioner. The Pinkerton official intimated that even a multiple murderer like Orchard could receive both the grace of God and the clemency of the state. Later that afternoon, as McParland relates in his official report, Orchard simultaneously found God, truth, and a reprieve from the gallows. In other words, the prisoner agreed to save himself by implicating the WFM in Steunenberg's assassination. Advised by McParland that if he cooperated with the authorities "the sentiment that now existed would be reversed, that instead of looking upon him as a notorious murderer they [the public] would look upon him as a saver, not only of the State of Idaho, but of all States where the blight of the Inner Circle of the Western Federation of Miners had struck," the frightened Orchard agreed to make a full confession in the hope of escaping the gallows.[17]

Idaho promptly showed appreciation for its "savior." Orchard was moved from his prison cell into a little bungalow where he dined on superior food and received new clothing, spending money, and an ample supply of his favorite cigars. To encourage his newfound piety, the state even provided religious and philosophical works. Governor Gooding personally visited Orchard, called him Harry, and shook his hand.

Day and night for the next month, McParland and Orchard labored over the details of the confession. Together they made certain that almost every unsolved crime associated with labor conflict in the Mountain West was laid at the door of the WFM. As sleuth and slayer constructed this curious "confession" (in which fact and fiction were strangely bound), the states of Colorado and Idaho plotted still more unorthodox actions.

None of the WFM's so-called "inner circle"—neither Moyer, Haywood, George A. Pettibone (a former union member, now a small Denver retailer and good friend of union officials), nor L. J. Simpkins (a member of the WFM general executive board representing Idaho miners)—had been in Idaho at the time of Steunenberg's murder. This was known to Idaho officials, who also knew that under the laws of Colorado and the United States, though not those of Idaho, Moyer,

9 9

Haywood, and Pettibone could not be extradited. The law notwithstanding, Idaho and Colorado officials hatched a scheme to extradite the three suspects (all then Denver residents) by abduction. Working together under McParland's guidance, the governors of Idaho and Colorado executed their scheme.[18] On February 15 Colorado Governor MacDonald honored extradition papers, authorizing the union leaders' immediate arrest. In order to prevent the accused from instituting *habeas corpus* proceedings, authorities delayed until Saturday evening, February 17, before making arrests. That night Moyer was seized at a Denver railroad station and Pettibone at home, Haywood, in a bizarre twist, was apprehended in a brothel. (McParland, indeed, seemed more shocked by Big Bill's marital infidelities than by his alleged part in mass violence and murder.) At dawn the next day, Denver police brought the three manacled prisoners unobtrusively to the railroad depot, where they were placed on a specially made-up train which sped them to the Boise prison and a date with the hangman. After their dubious extradition and forcible abduction they had not been allowed to communicate with friends, families, or attorneys.

Union attorneys finally learned of their clients' abduction on February 22. They filed for *habeas corpus* writs in state and federal courts. But all courts, including the United States Supreme Court, refused relief. The various appeals courts ruled that Idaho's loosely drawn extradition statutes provided a legal basis for the abductions of Haywood, Moyer, and Pettibone. The Supreme Court majority argued, moreover, that the method of extradition, even if illegal, was immaterial to the issue at hand: the presence within Idaho's jurisdiction of three defendants properly indicted on charges of conspiracy to commit murder. Only one Supreme Court dissenting justice, Joseph McKenna, condemned the extradition methods.[19] Despite protests from organized labor, respected liberals, notable radicals, and most socialists (Debs even threatened armed revolution if Haywood were convicted), the prisoners were indicted for Steunenberg's murder on March 6, and remanded to jail to await their fate.

For the next year they languished in prison while McParland desperately sought evidence and witnesses to corroborate Orchard's confession. Under Idaho law, without corroboration, Orchard's testimony would by itself be insufficient to prove conspiracy. McParland proceeded in two ways. First, he tried the tactics which had already drawn a confession from Orchard. When a purported accomplice in the Steunenberg assassination, one Steve Adams, was arrested on

February 20, 1906, McParland threatened him with execution unless he corroborated Orchard's confession. Like Orchard, the new prisoner confessed and received the benevolence of the state, including a private bungalow and friendly visits from Gooding, Hawley, and Borah. McParland, still uncertain of his case, next decided that the best policy would be to obtain a confession from a member of the "inner circle" itself. He looked to Charles Moyer as his man. McParland had heard rumors about a rift between Moyer and Haywood, and even gossip of an unsuccessful plot by Haywood and Pettibone to assassinate the "dangerously garrulous" WFM president.[20] But much as he worked on Moyer, McParland failed to win a third convert.

Meanwhile, much to McParland's chagrin, Steve Adams retracted his corroborating confession. Soon after Adams' arrest, Clarence Darrow, the famed Chicago lawyer, had been appointed chief defense attorney. Knowing how McParland had inveigled Adams' confession, Darrow assured the prisoner that if he retracted, Idaho would be unable to convict him of murder. Won over by Darrow's impressive arguments, Adams repudiated his confession. He was then rearrested for the murder of two missing claim-jumpers, and his trial was set for February 1907 in Wallace, Idaho—in the Coeur d'Alenes, where the whole bloody business had begun fifteen years earlier.

The first Adams trial previewed the subsequent Haywood case. James H. Hawley prosecuted and Darrow and Edmund Richardson, the WFM's Denver attorney, defended: the identical legal lineup which would meet again during the Haywood trial. When the defense's case unfolded, McParland perceived immediately what was happening. "You can see from the whole course of Richardson's and Darrow's arguments that they are simply trying the Moyer, Haywood, and Pettibone cases," he reported, "and all they fear is that Adams will be convicted, taken down to the penitentiary, where no doubt . . . he would return to his original statements." [21] The defense won a technical victory in Wallace, the jury dividing evenly. But even with its corroborating witness now lost, Idaho decided to prosecute Haywood and the others.

During the year and a half that the three prisoners had remained in the Ada County Jail, their friends and critics outside had made vociferous protest. While Debs threatened revolution, even Samuel Gompers, certainly neither a radical nor any very great friend of the WFM-IWW alliance, denounced the mine owners' conspiracy in the *American Federationist* as well as from the floor of the 1906 AFL convention. Colorado Socialists demonstrated their belief in Haywood's innocence by nominating him for governor of the state. Labor unions and radical groups across the nation offered unsolicited donations for the defense.[22] The defenders of the status quo, of course, did not remain silent. Newspapers daily tried and convicted the three accused men through a process of guilt by association: the WFM was equated with socialism, socialism with anarchism, anarchism with assassination. President Theodore Roosevelt enlisted in the "law-and-order" crusade, publicly branding the accused "undesirable citizens." [23]

America impatiently awaited the trial, which was finally scheduled to open in Boise on May 9, 1907. Correspondents and free-lancers jammed the courtroom to hear the confession of Harry Orchard, converted by the grace of God and the wit of McParland, and to observe the response of William D. Haywood. Haywood was chosen by the state to be prosecuted first because he seemed more irascible and more fearsome than the other two defendants, and thus less likely to elicit sympathy from a jury. The journalists also came to observe one of the most impressive arrays of legal talent ever assembled in a Western courtroom: Hawley, the dean of Idaho lawyers, and Borah, a rising young star in the Republican party, for the prosecution; Richardson, perhaps Denver's outstanding attorney, and Darrow, just then approaching the acme of his career, for the defense.

Even before the trial opened, both defense and prosecution perceived conspiracies everywhere. While attorneys examined prospective jurors in court, Pinkerton men and agents for the defense investigated them outside. Both sides skirted the edges of legality in approaching and examining veniremen. But defense and prosecution finally overcame their suspicions sufficiently to settle on a jury of twelve elderly men—all farmers over fifty, none of whom had ever been a WFM member or worked in a mine.[24] Meanwhile, the prosecution uncovered further "conspiracies"; nothing, it seemed, was beyond the WFM's power. Borah had just been indicted on a federal land-fraud charge, leading Hawley to conclude that the United States Justice Department had acted in collusion with Haywood's friends! [25]

While the prosecution fantasized nonexistent WFM conspiracies, it continued to hatch quite genuine plots of its own. Still hopeful that he could break Moyer, McParland indirectly approached the union president. He sent Moyer fine cigars, together with daily newspaper reports of Orchard's unshakable testimony. A prison guard suggested to the WFM president: "I know . . . you love your wife, and you are still a comparatively young man and if I were in your place I would make at least an effort to save myself not caring what the world might say. . . . I know at least one person who is friendly to you and thinks you were more sinned against than sinning. . . . If you wanted to see McParland . . . I could make arrangements . . ." McParland believed he could convert Moyer partly because of Orchard's claim that Moyer opposed Haywood, partly because the union president's wife hated Big Bill, and partly because he suspected that Moyer harbored ambitions to become a conservative and "respected" labor leader, much on the order of John Mitchell of the United Mine Workers.[26] But Moyer refused to talk. He would not see McParland, and his estrangement from Haywood, which was later to have major repercussions, for the moment remained private and muted.

Thus the prosecution based its entire case on Orchard's testimony, which, in the event, proved too good by half. The eager Orchard confessed to crimes the defense easily established he could never have committed. Described by a sympathetic journalist as like nothing so much as the neighborhood milkman—"round-headed, ruddy-faced, sandy-mustached . . . good natured"—the defendant was in fact revealed during Defense Attorney Richardson's brilliant cross-examination to be not only a thief and a murderer but also a perjurer, a bigamist, and an *agent provocateur*. During the Cripple Creek conflict of 1903–1904 he had, for a time, been in the employ of the Pinkerton Agency. How such a man had unexpectedly come to Christ, the truth, and salvation, Richardson and Darrow let the jury of twelve farmers decide.[27]

On July 27, after more than two months of testimony and cross-examination, the jury finally retired to consider a verdict. The prosecution appeared optimistic, the defense pessimistic. Shortly before the trial ended, Hawley wrote to a friend: "I think by the time we are through with this all good citizens will be satisfied that the prosecution is right. . . . I am absolutely convinced of the guilt of these men, and even favorable action by the jury in their behalf would not alter my convictions." Ten days later he added· "We have our case well in hand and think we are going to secure a conviction. . . . All our people are feeling good over the chances." [28] But when the jury returned its verdict in the early morning of July 28, Hawley's optimism vanished. Haywood was found not guilty! A shaken Hawley could only comment: "I have just come from the Court House where . . . we received a verdict of acquittal in the Haywood case. It was very unexpected both by the prosecution and defense . . ." In fact, as a juror later remarked to a reporter, most of the jury considered Haywood innocent throughout the trial, feeling "that there was nothing against the accused but inference and suspicion." [29]

But Hawley, McParland, and the state remained convinced of the WFM's guilt. Rather than dismiss the charges still pending against Moyer and Pettibone, they decided to try Pettibone next, after again inveigling corroborating evidence from a muddled Steve Adams. But once again Adams repudiated a confession and eluded the toils of "justice," beating old murder charges in Idaho as well as new ones in Colorado.[30] Without Adams' testimony Idaho failed to convict Pettibone, whom a jury acquitted in January 1908.

The two jury verdicts failed to establish definitely the veracity, or the falsity, of Orchard's confession, which had remained basically unshaken, even under cruel cross-examination. Many of Orchard's contemporaries, aside from Pinkertons and prosecutors, were impressed by the man's manner on the witness stand and the impressive detail of his sworn testimony. George Kibbe Turner, reporting the trial for *McClure's,* noted that Orchard "impressed me, as he has practically everyone who has observed him, with three things—his absolute and level sanity, his extraordinary and detailed candor, and his utter vacancy of fear." Several historians have also found Orchard's confession largely credible, if not entirely accurate. During the trials it was clearly established that the defendant had been associated on at least several occasions with Haywood and Pettibone (less so in Moyer's case). Moreover, all of the crimes to which Orchard confessed, apart from the assassination of Steunenberg, had been directly or indirectly connected with explosive labor conflicts involving the WFM. Despite Orchard's admission under questioning that he had once served as an *agent provocateur* for private detective agencies, a highly suspicious, if not incriminating, chain of circumstantial evidence linked his criminal deeds to the executive officers of the WFM. Hence Orchard's prosecutors (and admirers) remained convinced that his confession had proved their worst suspicions to be true: that the WFM leadership had indeed hatched a vile criminal conspiracy.

Instead of suggesting to Hawley the weaknesses of the state's case, the acquittals merely confirmed in his mind the true extent of the WFM "conspiracy." The Western Federation of Miners, according to the Idaho prosecutor, not only assassinated its enemies, it also corrupted and terrorized juries. Losing all faith in the perspicacity of twelve honest men, Hawley now claimed that Idaho juries consisted of socialists, "people who are afraid, those who are bought up, and the criminal element." [31] This being the case, the prosecution reluctantly decided to drop its charges against Moyer, thus terminating the great Idaho labor conspiracy trials.

Haywood, Moyer, and Pettibone had been exonerated, and the $140,000 raised for their defense was well spent. Although failing to achieve its immediate objectives, the prosecution effort was not without effect. The months of newspaper publicity, the testimony of Orchard, and the knowledge that labor violence and murders had occurred regularly during Western industrial disputes fixed in the public mind an image of the WFM and the IWW as violent, antisocial organizations synonymous with anarchism and bloody revolution. The trials also transformed small fissures within the WFM and the IWW into gaping holes. The incarceration of Moyer and Haywood removed just when they were most needed the IWW's most experienced, capable, and popular leaders. Their long imprisonment also deeply affected the two men, though in quite different ways. It impelled Haywood further in the direction of radicalism, while it led Moyer toward a more conservative position. This was the change McParland had perceived and tried to exploit. With Haywood in jail, the more conservative influences within the WFM, those to whom Moyer was being drawn and who wanted to make both the Western Federation and the IWW more "respectable" and less revolutionary, gained control. The eventual result of the conservatives' rise to power was civil war within the WFM and its departure from the IWW.

At the birth of the IWW in June 1905, the organization appeared to be relatively powerful, including three major departments—Mining, Metals and Machinery, and Transportation; numerous scattered locals and industrial councils; recruiting unions attached directly to general headquarters; and the remnants of the American Labor Union. As to membership, General President Sherman and Secretary-Treasurer Trautmann agreed that in June 1906, despite some setbacks, it stood at sixty thousand, counting all departments and directly affiliated locals.[32] Beneath this impressive façade, however, glaring weaknesses would soon be revealed.

In fact, the IWW was so poor at birth that it operated initially with books, furniture, and office methods inherited from the defunct ALU. Of the three departments ostensibly a part of the organization, two scarcely existed. The Transportation Department never had the three thousand paid-up members required for departmental status (let alone one thousand actual members); and the 1906 convention would refuse to recognize that department's existence. The Metal and Machinery Department began life with somewhat brighter promise. Almost immediately, however, one of its major components seceded; Isaac Cowen, leader and founder of the American branch of the Amalgamated Society of Engineers, having led his men into the IWW, soon led them back out again. With Cowen's secession, the Metals and Machinery Department lacked sufficient numbers for legal existence as a department, and it, too, was denied departmental status by the 1906 convention. Only the WFM, with 27,000 paid-up members, constituted a valid department (Mining), and after the 1906 convention it also would secede, leaving the IWW, only a year after its creation, close to death. Vincent St. John's 1911 estimate of the IWW's paid-up membership in 1905–1906 as 14,000 (including the WFM) was probably not far off.[33]

Weak though the IWW was, it did not shrink, as we have already seen, from combatting either the AFL or the Socialist party. It engaged in countless unnecessary strikes, as Trautmann led the IWW in repeated attempts to capture AFL affiliates, particularly among coal miners and brewery workers. By January 1906 the IWW had become so aggressive in its incursions upon AFL affiliates that Max Hayes feared the imminent outbreak of civil war within the labor movement.[34]

War with the AFL was hardly the proper strategy for a weak new labor organization. Neither was recurrent industrial conflict. But just such activities caused Trautmann to report at the 1906 convention that the IWW had lost almost every strike it had waged, partly because of improper preparation and partly because of strained finances.[35] Much, if not all, of the IWW's impotence and failure, however, resulted from incompetent leadership. Neither Sherman nor Trautmann was qualified to administer a large labor organization.

Little is known about the life or career of Charles O. Sherman. What is known reflects slight credit on the man. According to Samuel

Gompers, Sherman had been a blacklist victim of the 1894 Pullman strike, and Gompers, feeling sympathy for a victimized trade unionist and upon the recommendation of friends, had commissioned Sherman as an AFL organizer in 1902 or 1903. Sherman promptly created a paper union—the United Metal Workers International Union—which, upon receiving an AFL charter, turned upon its benefactor, declaring jurisdictional war on other AFL international unions. Sherman and his paper organization refused to abide by AFL executive council decisions, Sherman claiming that through oversight he had failed to inform Gompers that the United Metal Workers had withdrawn from the AFL.[36]

But Sherman was hardly neglectful or forgetful. Duplicity seems a better word to describe what he had been up to. From November 1904 he participated in the conferences which led to the formation of the IWW, yet on December 27, 1904, he informed Gompers that the United Metal Workers was still a legal AFL affiliate.[37] A week later, he signed the Industrial Union Manifesto. Unable to build his union empire within the AFL, Sherman entered the IWW to become that organization's first and only president. His record as IWW president was in keeping with his efforts as an AFL organizer. Once again he used a union position to increase his personal power and line his own pockets. He personally selected all IWW organizers, most of whom proved more notable for the expenses they accumulated than for the number of their recruits. He also contracted with a firm in which he had a direct financial interest for union labels and other IWW insignia. Even Sherman's allies within the IWW made no effort to deny his extravagance, high-handedness, or corruption.[38]

Charles Sherman, in brief, represented that faction at the first IWW convention described by Ben Williams as "also-ran, would be craft union leaders, who were ambitious to get back in the game, for possible personal gain or emolument." In philosophy and approach, Sherman barely differed from Gompers and other AFL chieftains. Like them, he insisted that revolution and the cooperative commonwealth were for the future, if at all; that today the majority of workers wanted to hear only of bread and butter, ". . . and that is what I emphasize."[39] In his diagnosis of what most American workers wanted, Sherman was undoubtedly right. But in stressing bread-and-butter unionism and the irrelevance of revolution, he was telling a substantial number of Wobblies what they refused to hear or believe. To accept what Sherman said would have meant for the IWW to disclaim its *raison d'être*. This its members would not do. Instead they would resort to a little revolution of their own and purge Sherman from the IWW's presidency.

More revolutionary, perhaps more principled than Sherman, Trautmann was hardly a more capable administrator. He may have been an effective editor, essayist, and polemicist, but he was no executive. Born of German-American parents in New Zealand in 1869 (the same year as Haywood), he participated in the labor and socialist movements of Russia and Germany (from which he was expelled under Bismarck's anti-socialist laws) before coming to the United States. Here he organized for the Brewery Workers' Union in Massachusetts, edited the *Bräuer Zeitung*, translated Marx into English, wrote industrial-union propaganda tracts, and participated in the founding of the IWW. As secretary-treasurer of the IWW, Trautmann failed to maintain accurate membership records of either individuals or local unions, and his financial accounts were in even worse shape. At the 1906 convention he could not even produce a financial report.[40] A year later, as the IWW's first general organizer, he organized no one. By 1913, having already figured in two IWW purges, Trautmann himself left the IWW to become a full-time propagandist for Daniel DeLeon's schismatic, paper IWW.

Under such leadership it is small wonder that the IWW made no progress its first year and began its second year with its only significant affiliate, the WFM, alienated. Even capable leaders would have had difficulty holding together an infant organization under attack by the AFL, the bulk of the Socialist party, and the state of Idaho. Even Gompers would have had trouble trying to organize workers while simultaneously expending organization resources to free imprisoned leaders. Anyone would have met almost insuperable obstacles in attempting to weld together an organization composed of Socialist party members, Socialist Labor party followers, pure industrial unionists, and incipient anarcho-syndicalists. Sherman and Trautmann were certainly not the men to do it.

As early as January 1906, Max Hayes reported than an internal battle loomed within the IWW—with industrialists and Socialists on one side and DeLeonists and anarchists on the other. Rumors abounded that Sherman and the WFM had soured on DeLeon, Trautmann, and their adherents. Hayes quoted an IWW member as saying: "If a convention were held next month . . . I predict the academic vagaries forced upon us by the DeLeon-Anarchist combine will be dropped for a plain fighting program that everybody can understand and conjure with." [41] Part of Hayes's report represented the wishful thinking of an anti-DeLeon, anti-IWW Socialist, but a substantial portion reflected reality.

Indeed, by midsummer 1906 the predicted conflict had erupted. In July an IWW member suggested in the *Industrial Worker* that the organization had no need of a president, nor even of department heads. About the same time a Chicago-based group spearheaded an effort to revise drastically the IWW's constitution and structure. On August 14, sixteen locals, representing the Metal and Machinery Department, the Transportation Department, bookbinders, printers, and cigarmakers, met in Chicago and resolved unanimously to seek to abolish the office of president. [42]

Simultaneously, other divisive issues emerged. Debs and DeLeon may have shaken hands across the bloody chasm of the past, but their respective followers clearly had not. Within the IWW, SLP members and SP members began to fight with sectarian virulence. The *Miners' Magazine*, despite the complaints of SLP members, endorsed Socialist party candidates. In retaliation for SLP opposition, John O'Neill, editor of the *Miners' Magazine*, warned his critics:

It is now apparent to us that S.L.P.'ism has hooked itself to the Industrial Workers of the World, in order that it might gather sustenance to prolong the life of an invalid that is almost a corpse. *The convention at Chicago must either get rid of the fanatics and disrupters or the I.W.W. is slated for destruction* [italics added]. [43]

Thus, as the IWW prepared for its second convention, one faction linked to the WFM and the Socialist party rallied around President Sherman in opposition to DeLeon's influence and the demands of the so-called "revolutionaries." A second faction, tied to the SLP and including prominent WFM members, schemed to remove Sherman, abolish his office, and purge the IWW of all "anti-revolutionary" sentiments—whatever precisely was meant by that. The convention would determine which faction was to predominate. Would the IWW remain united, or was it indeed, as later described by Ben Williams, a house built with unsuitable materials "and without first excavating and laying the foundation"? [44]

On Monday morning, September 17, President Charles O. Sherman called to order in Chicago the second annual convention of the Industrial Workers of the World. The four-man WFM delegation again controlled the largest number of convention votes (436); Daniel De-Leon once more led the ideologues who were in attendance. Notably absent were Moyer, Haywood, Father Hagerty, Eugene Debs, and Algie Simons. Not a single delegate among the thirty-two purported Socialist party members ranked high in the party hierarchy. But the thirty delegates who belonged to the Socialist Labor party included the party tyrant, DeLeon, and many of his lieutenants. Whereas a spirit of unity had marked the founding convention, the second session was rent by dissension.

Even before the proceedings officially began, delegates clashed with President Sherman over two major issues. First, claiming that Sherman and his "reactionary" clique had intentionally chosen a small hall for the meeting in order to keep their opponents out, delegates voted overwhelmingly (55 to 3) to move the convention to the more spacious Brand's Hall. Second, delegates refused to allow a Sherman-appointed credentials committee to seat disputed delegates. On a motion by DeLeon, the convention voted 315 to 118 to meet as a committee of the whole in order to weigh the cases of disputed delegates.[45]

For the next five days pro- and anti-Sherman factions waged war. Led by DeLeon, who served as their parliamentary tactician, the insurgents succeeded in denying convention seats to disputed pro-Sherman delegates representing the Metal-Machinery and the Transportation departments. Instead the insurgents awarded seats to delegates representing locals in those two departments hostile to Sherman. This, in effect, gave the insurgents a solid convention majority.[46]

Unexpectedly triumphant, many so-called revolutionary delegates now found themselves the victims of economic retribution. Representing only themselves or weak unions, they were given, at best, a meager mileage allowance; at worst, no allowance at all. The pro-

Sherman delegates, by contrast, received a generous expense allowance, much of it drawn from the organization's treasury. The Shermanites now struggled to delay convention proceedings in order to weaken their opponents, many of whom might soon be forced by lack of funds to leave Chicago for home. To avert just such a contingency, one of the "revolutionary" delegates proposed that he and his needy brethren receive $1.50 a day from the IWW's treasury.[47]

As this proposal approached a vote, the IWW's chief executives, Sherman and Trautmann, joined the verbal war. The president took the floor to appeal for moderation and reason, while the secretary-treasurer sounded the tocsin for revolution. Trautmann demanded that the convention purge forthwith the "conservative" Sherman and his "reactionary" followers in order to transform the IWW into a pristine revolutionary organization. Responding to Trautmann's call, the convention majority rammed through the proposal to pay a *per diem* to needy (read: anti-Sherman) delegates. In the face of powerful opposition from more conservative, anti-Socialist WFM delegates led by Butte's John McMullen, DeLeon rallied the "revolutionary" forces behind his leadership to vote for a suspension of the IWW constitution.[48]

This vote made the convention schism irrevocable. Charles Mahoney, acting president of the WFM and also acting convention chairman, after being regularly thwarted in rulings by what he thought to be deluded and dangerous DeLeonites, confided to John O'Neill, editor of the *Miners' Magazine,* that the convention majority's arrogance would result either in the immediate withdrawal of the WFM from the IWW or in the disruption of the entire organization. As WFM delegates Vincent St. John and Al Ryan continued to vote with DeLeon, Mahoney's despondency deepened. "From what I can learn," he informed O'Neill, "there is no question in my mind but that a plan is being laid to tear down the Western Federation of Miners." [49]

Mahoney's critics thought they detected a far different conspiracy: a scheme by WFM conservatives to tear down the IWW. To avoid that possibility the "revolutionaries" abolished the office of IWW president, echoing the words of a DeLeonite delegate: ". . . If we have not got the funds to support a king we might as well use the funds to support ourselves." [50] When Mahoney, asserting his authority as convention chairman, declared the vote to abolish Sherman's office out of order, an SLP member retorted: "It is a revolution." To which John

McMullen angrily remarked: "All right, if you want a revolution have it." And a revolution the delegates had, overruling Mahoney by a vote of 342 to 276.[51]

So ended the façade of IWW unity. McMullen, speaking for the "conservative" WFM faction, criticized the proceedings as unconstitutional. He insisted that he and his supporters could not and would not remain any longer in Chicago. Fred Heslewood, a WFM alternate delegate, rose to answer McMullen: "If he means the reactionists are going to leave this convention I hope to God they do, and I wish they had never come." At this juncture Sherman spoke a bitter farewell to the organization he had led for only a year. Denouncing the "conspiracy" which had surrendered the IWW to DeLeon, the deposed president pronounced burial rites, declaiming, as much in sadness as in anger, that the IWW is "today a corpse . . . as an organization it is now ready for the funeral." [52]

The final crisis came on the morning of October 2, when the convention majority declared all constitutional amendments in force and proceeded to elect new officials. Overruled once again, Mahoney bolted the convention and took several WFM men out with him. Unable to win their battle within the convention, these men carried their fight to the WFM, where their chances for victory were distinctly better. For the next year and a half, the struggle which had raged on the floor of Brand's Hall would be repeated within the ranks of the Western Federation.[53]

With Sherman deposed and his office now abolished, Trautmann became the official leader of the IWW with the title of general organizer. DeLeon, who had dominated the convention debates, retired to the background, assuming no official position in the organization, though several of his followers were elected to the new executive board, along with Heslewood and St. John of the WFM. In a closing address, DeLeon put his stamp of approval upon the convention, proclaiming: "The danger was great. The conspiracy was deep laid. . . . It was a conspiracy to squelch the revolution in this convention and to start over again an A. F. of L." [54]

Was DeLeon correct in his estimate of what had happened? What, indeed, caused the IWW to rupture at the 1906 convention? Despite all the talk of conspiracies, revolutionaries, and reactionaries, such terms in fact shed little light on the convention. Clearly, there were no conspiracies, as delegates moved freely back and forth in their voting patterns, "revolutionaries" and "reactionaries" drawing together and breaking apart in odd coalitions. Ideological disputation was largely absent from convention debates, which focused more on personality and rhetoric than on issues and programs. The convention "reactionaries" scarcely fit the ordinary meaning of that term, for all of them professed belief in industrial unionism, a radical notion at the time, and save a few avid supporters of McMullen, many of them remained socialists. The "revolutionaries" apparently were distinguished more by their rhetoric, replete with sinister similes and menacing metaphors, than their policies, which also stressed industrial unionism and socialism. No one denied that Sherman had been derelict in his presidential duties, yet the anti-revolutionaries found themselves defending this disreputable union careerist and self-seeker. This was partly because their opponents had arrogantly breached convention rules as well as the IWW's constitution, and partly because they frowned upon violent, revolutionary oratory—oratory which just then might prejudice the approaching trials of Haywood and Moyer. Several delegates perhaps also shared McMullen's essential conservatism, with its antipathy to socialism, fear of violent revolution, and eagerness to effect a rapprochement with the AFL. These were doubtless only too happy to see the IWW split.

The victory of the "revolutionaries" at first seemed Pyrrhic, for not only did it splinter the IWW's largest affiliate, with the bulk of the organization's paid-up membership, but the Sherman faction simply refused to accept defeat. Indeed, for a time the deposed Sherman operated his own IWW! Backed by Mahoney and the WFM executive board, Sherman called his preconvention executive board into session, expelled Trautmann from office, ruled the 1906 convention's action null and void, declared the unamended 1905 constitution still in force, and asked that all per capita payments be sent to his "legal" IWW. Sherman and his cohorts also seized physical control of IWW headquarters and books, while awaiting the funds which would enable them to fight their opponents in court.[55]

When St. John, Heslewood, and W. I. Fisher, representing the executive board elected at the 1906 convention, went to IWW headquarters at 148 West Madison Street on the morning of October 4, they found a strange sight. Inside the offices were their organizational enemies, claiming to be in legal possession of IWW properties; outside were private detectives entrusted with protecting the office from the anti-Sherman faction. St. John described what followed. "When Brothers Heslewood, Fisher, and myself ascended to the fifth floor of the hall that morning we did not meet anybody belonging to the organization that had a card in the Industrial Workers of the World." Demanding to know by what right or authority the guards refused IWW officers admission to their own headquarters, St. John received his answer from a slingshot loaded with lead. "At that juncture," St. John later recalled, "I realized this much, that there was a frame-up that was deeper than appeared on the surface . . . and I concluded that the wisest course to pursue . . . would not be to force the issue on the staircase . . ." Not long after St. John and his associates fled, the Chicago police, answering a call from Sherman, arrived on the scene.[56]

The next step in the factional feud involved an unusual bit of historical irony. The contending IWW factions, both purportedly hating capitalism, resorted to capitalist courts to press their respective legal claims. Sherman's group, represented by Seymour Stedman, a Socialist party lawyer, asked the judiciary to validate its possession of IWW properties, including furnishings, books, ledgers, membership lists, and the official journal. Trautmann's faction, finding itself without so much as a postage stamp, asked the courts to declare the 1906 convention decisions binding and to order Sherman to turn all IWW properties over to the officers elected and installed at the second convention. The courts eventually ruled in Trautmann's favor—capitalist justice thus giving "revolutionary wage slaves" at least one victory.

No supporter of radical working-class politics, or even of industrial unionism, could take much pleasure in the 1906 IWW convention split and its bizarre aftermath. Gompers and the AFL, of course, could and did. More unionists probably shared the mixed feelings of Max Hayes, who commented: "If there are any working people who looked with hope to the Industrial Workers of the World to escape from the reactionary and conservative tactics that are enervating the American Federation of Labor they were surely doomed to disappointment. After an experiment of a little over a year the I.W.W. appears to have gone the same route as the late lamented S. T. and L. A. . . . That the I.W.W. received its death blow at Chicago and will gradually disintegrate no careful observer of labor affairs will attempt to dispute." [57]

The Trautmann and Sherman factions, however, continued to struggle for control of the corpse. Forced by the courts to relinquish his claims to the presidency and to the physical assets of the organization, Sherman took his case to the WFM, hoping it would endorse a re-established IWW. To present his claims fully, for a time Sherman published the *Industrial Worker* at Joliet, Illinois, carrying on the sheet's masthead the magic names of Eugene Debs, Algie Simons, John O'Neill, Jack London, and William D. Haywood, among others. In retaliation, Trautmann issued a series of special IWW bulletins. The rivals also carried on their quarrel in the columns of the *Miners' Magazine,* striving desperately to elicit endorsement from the imprisoned Moyer and Haywood, as well as from 27,000 loyal WFM members.[58]

Just after the 1906 convention adjourned, the Trautmann faction plainly asked WFM members: "Which do you want? Pure and simple unionism, more corrupt and rotten than in the American Federation of Labor, or straight revolutionary workingclass solidarity as proclaimed in the Manifesto and Preamble of the I.W.W.?"[59] Most WFM members were probably uncertain what they wanted. A minority, led by McMullen, undoubtedly desired pure-and-simple industrial unionism; pork chops, in other words, without revolution. Another minority group, this one led by St. John, Heslewood, and Al Ryan, unabashedly chose revolution.

From October 1906 to May 1907 these factions fought a war of words in the *Miners' Magazine.* The anti-Trautmann group, favored by editor O'Neill, received most of the space in the union journal. Rather than directing its critique against Trautmann, or at St. John and Heslewood (both popular with the WFM rank and file), McMullen's faction aimed at DeLeon, a more vulnerable target. "Daniel DeLeon will never preach any funeral orations over this organization if it is possible for me to prevent it," vowed Charles Mahoney. O'Neill reserved his choice editorial epithets for DeLeon, sometimes stooping to the vilest anti-Semitic canards, as he had done earlier when the WFM was fighting Gompers. In O'Neill's hyperbole, Sherman was deposed because he refused to accept "the 'hot-air' peddled by a bunch of tramps, that became infuriated at every laboring man that did not

recognize DeLeon as the triple-crowned pope of the labor movement . . ." O'Neill warned WFM members not to follow the encyclicals
emanating from the New York Vatican of "Foxy Grandpa" (DeLeon),
who edited the "Mud-Hole Gazette" (*Daily People*).[60] To such emo-
tionalism, St. John could only reply that DeLeon had not controlled
the 1906 convention, pointing out that he and Al Ryan, neither by any
means a DeLeon puppet, had cast 109 convention votes each, and
that thirty-two Socialist party delegates (as compared with thirty from
the SLP) had attended the convention.

St. John was correct in his assertion that DeLeon never controlled
a voting majority, but he did provide the parliamentary tactics the
majority needed. DeLeon used the majority's votes for his own purposes, as it employed his knowledge for its own ends. It was much
easier, however, for critics of the 1906 IWW session to ignore the
complexities involved at the convention and center their criticism on
DeLeon, long a controversial personality in the ranks of American
radicalism.[61]

The rift in the IWW and WFM also caused dissension behind
prison walls. In the Ada County Jail, Moyer and Haywood reacted
quite differently to the events of September–October 1906. As we
have already seen, an estrangement had developed between the two
WFM officials. On October 2, the day Mahoney and McMullen
walked out of the IWW convention, Moyer wrote WFM Acting Secretary James Kirwan: "I want to serve notice on those calling themselves revolutionists that their program will never receive my
endorsement, nor that of the Western Federation of Miners, if in my
power to prevent it. By the gods, I have suffered too much, worked
too hard to ever tamely submit to the Western Federation of Miners
being turned over to Mr. Daniel DeLeon . . ." Hence Moyer castigated
the Trautmann faction, intimated endorsement of Sherman's position,
and demanded a membership referendum on the IWW convention's
actions.[62]

Although Haywood also condemned DeLeonism and the convention majority's failure to put its constitutional changes to a membership referendum, he minimized DeLeon's influence in the proceedings.
Writing to Kirwan, Haywood noted: "He [DeLeon] is getting a lot of
cheap advertising when you take into consideration at the present
time that it is difficult for the Socialist Labor Party to muster one
thousand . . . Those who made up the majority were not S.L.P.'s; to
my way of thinking, it demonstrates a decided fallacy to halloo

DeLeon! DeLeon! when he and his followers were an insignificant minority." Haywood, unlike Moyer, preferred to withhold final judgment about the IWW controversy until he had more substantial information, though he did advise the WFM to remain within the IWW. Before long he made his opinion in the controversy known, condemning the Sherman faction without condoning the 1906 IWW majority, which, in his words, was "entirely too harsh . . . the Gordian, presidential and other knots that you cut with a broad axe, were only slipknots that could have been easily untied . . ." [63] Above all, Haywood wanted to avoid personalities and to make sacrifices for labor unity. Believing that Trautmann and St. John were in the right, he nevertheless implied that the insurgents could have accomplished their objectives without dividing both the IWW and the WFM. Yet Haywood had to confess that "I have been unable to devise any means of effecting a reconciliation." [64]

Those who suggest that a free Moyer and Haywood might have been able to repair the breach are far from the mark. Quite the reverse would have been more likely. Moyer and Haywood had drifted toward irreconcilable ideological and organizational positions —the former toward an accommodation with the established American order and more businesslike union methods; the latter toward more militant radicalism and revolutionary union tactics. Had they been liberated from prison, they probably would have carried their differences to the WFM's membership and intensified rather than relieved the bitter factionalism in the union's ranks. With Haywood commanding the St. John-Heslewood-Ryan troika, it would have been a more effective force and a greater threat to the WFM establishment. The Western Federation would then probably have split into two groups—one led by Moyer, divorced from the IWW, and on the road to a reconciliation with the AFL; the other led by Haywood, tied to the Trautmann IWW, and a virulent foe of the AFL.

But with Moyer and Haywood in prison, the anti-IWW faction dominated the WFM. Mahoney and Kirwan notified all union locals in November 1906 not to participate in a referendum on the 1906 convention being conducted by Trautmann. The following month the WFM executive board declined to pay per capita dues to *either* IWW faction and announced that a membership referendum had overwhelmingly declared the acts of the 1906 IWW convention invalid.[65]

In response, the Trautmann IWW on January 15, 1907, suspended the Mining Department (WFM), at the same time announcing the results of its *own* referendum vote, which overwhelmingly (3,812 to 154) endorsed the 1906 convention and the new IWW officials. Trautmann demonstrated, moreover, that when the votes in the IWW referendum were combined with those in the WFM election, a majority of the total endorsed the 1906 convention (5,712 in favor, 2,912 opposed).[66]

Meanwhile, an increasingly moderate WFM leadership had to contend with its critics. Before the 1907 national convention of the union, rumors of compromise spread. In March, Haywood wrote to St. John: "I fear more than anything else a repetition of the useless and meaningless wrangle at the coming convention. . . . It must be prevented. It is just to demand the retirement of the officers of both factions of the Industrial Workers of the World, if by so doing, an amalgamation of the rank and file ·can be brought around." [67] But Trautmann's supporters would not compromise, and they brought their case before the 1907 WFM convention, the longest and bitterest in the organization's history.

For almost a month delegates debated the IWW question. St. John, Heslewood, Ryan, Percy Rawlings, and Frank Little (who would later figure prominently in IWW history) led the convention radicals; Mahoney, O'Neill, Kirwan, and McMullen guided the moderates. When Acting President Mahoney and a majority of the resolutions committee opposed affiliation with either IWW faction, the radicals vowed to continue their struggle within the WFM until they prevailed. The solid moderate majority constantly raised the spectre of DeLeon. Robert Randall of Goldfield, Nevada, warned, for example: "I hope you will do nothing to place the Western Federation of Miners where Daniel DeLeon can get his hands on it. For God's sake, don't, or we may go the same road as the Socialist Labor Party and the Socialist Trades and Labor Alliance." [68]

The moderates won by an overwhelming majority—more than two to one on important issues (239½ to 114). Magnanimous in triumph, the majority voted to ask both IWW factions, the United Brewery Workers, and all other unions ready to accept the principles of the January 1905 manifesto to meet with the WFM in Chicago on October 1, 1907, to re-establish and strengthen the IWW. The WFM's radicals, however, refused to sanction the peace conference. St. John and Rawlings declined nomination as conference delegates, with the former denouncing the proposal as "an infamous effort to misdirect the efforts of the working class to emancipate themselves . . ." [69]

The WFM compromise proposal was indeed chimerical. By July 1907 the Sherman IWW no longer existed. The Brewery Workers had no intention of joining any IWW, re-established or not. The McMullen faction within the WFM also had no intention of recreating a radical, revolutionary labor organization. Most important, the Trautmann IWW, which was functioning and claimed several thousand members, insisted that it had nothing to compromise, and would "continue to oppose the insidious, ignorant misleaders and fakirs in the labor movement." [70]

The October peace conference did not convene as scheduled. Mahoney postponed it until the first week in January 1908, but again nothing happened. Once more it was rescheduled, this time for April 6. But as the IWW's official sheet later put it, April 6 came and went, but no industrial conference met. So ended, with a whimper, the WFM's flirtation with revolutionary unionism.

The IWW now appeared doomed. With its largest affiliate gone and no replacement in sight, what remained? Even Haywood announced publicly: "As to the reconstruction of the I.W.W. nothing will be done until the time is ripe for it, and that will not be until organized labor in general offers less opposition to the movement . . ." O'Neill, always less reserved, proclaimed: "The I.W.W. is but a reminiscence. It is dead, and the sooner we forget the stench the better." [71]

But Trautmann and his supporters vowed to demonstrate that the Industrial Workers of the World was a very lively corpse, willing and able to resist those who wished to bury it. Whether Trautmann or O'Neill was the better prophet, only the subsequent history of the IWW would determine.

CHAPTER
6

The IWW in Action, 1906–1908

FROM 1906 to 1908 the IWW, though often interred by its enemies, never took to the grave. Despite manifold weaknesses, it waged industrial conflicts in cities as far removed as Skowhegan, Maine, and Portland, Oregon; Bridgeport, Connecticut, and Goldfield, Nevada. It organized workers in textiles, lumber, mining, and other trades. It survived lost strikes, withstood the economic panic and ensuing recession of 1907–1908, and endured a second internal split. By the end of 1908 the IWW had assumed what thereafter remained its basic characteristics and purposes.

During these formative years the IWW also created enduring myths about itself and committed mistakes which it never overcame. The organization, like a failed psychoanalytic patient, never liberated itself totally from the traumatic experiences of infancy.

One of the most enduring IWW myths is of an alleged "Golden Age," associated with organizational success in the isolated Nevada mining camp of Goldfield, where, within four years of its founding in 1902, the IWW had organized all the workers in the community except for a handful of AFL building tradesmen. Newsboys, waiters, bartenders, cooks, clerks, maids, hard-rock miners, reporters—John Dos Passos' Mac in *The 42nd Parallel* first gives his loyalty to the IWW in Goldfield—all carried the red IWW card. No more complete amalgamation of workers had ever existed in the American labor movement;

never before was an injury to one so obviously the concern of all. In the IWW's first official history, Vincent St. John writes of Goldfield:

The highest point of efficiency for any labor organization was reached by the I.W.W. and the W.F. of M. in Goldfield, Nevada. No committees were ever sent to any employers. The union adopted wage scales and regulated hours. The secretary posted the same on a bulletin board outside of the union hall, and it was the LAW. The employers were forced to come and see the union committees.[1]

Goldfield could better be called the IWW's "Gilded Age." Never achieving anything approaching complete success, the IWW left Goldfield in total defeat.

With only minor variations, the Goldfield story repeated the theme of class warfare earlier played out in similar Idaho and Colorado mining towns. Miners early joined the WFM, which quickly established the upper hand in employer-employee relationships. For a time, unionism flourished as workers maintained an unusual degree of economic and job security.

After the founding of the IWW in 1905 and the affiliation of the WFM as its Mining Department, the Wobblies invaded the camp. Goldfield's WFM Local 220 already included some of that union's most radical members, many of them refugees from the bitter 1903–1904 Cripple Creek and Telluride conflicts. The creation of the IWW enabled these "radicals" to extend their organizational hold over the community. The IWW captured a local town workers' federal union formerly affiliated with the AFL. Renamed Local 77, IWW, it claimed to represent all Goldfield's town workers, and also those in the neighboring mining community of Tonopah. It was in those two towns that IWW Local 77 won from employers the union-enforced "LAW" about which St. John later boasted.[2]

Events in Goldfield stimulated local Wobblies to further successes. On September 10, 1906, at a time when the national leaderships of the IWW and the WFM were drawing apart, both organizations' Goldfield affiliates amalgamated—the town workers and the miners merging into an enlarged WFM-IWW Local 220. Even after the WFM seceded from the IWW in January 1907, Goldfield's workers remained united in a Wobbly-dominated coalition. The allies functioned aggressively. On December 20, 1906, they struck local mines to obtain higher wages and shorter hours, and within three weeks the miners gained their major objectives as well as added fringe benefits.

By March 1907 the amalgamated union claimed three thousand dues-paying members, and it felt secure enough to order all local businesses to go on the eight-hour day—a request promptly accepted. Not satisfied with domination of the mines and local businesses, Local 220 waged war with an AFL carpenters' local, demanding that all carpenters take out red cards or be denied employment in and around the mines. This attack against the AFL carpenters marked the farthest penetration of the IWW-WFM coalition in Goldfield.[3]

Shortly thereafter, a unique concatenation of circumstances drove a wedge between the town workers and the miners, thereby destroying unionism in Goldfield. In the spring of 1907, with Haywood coming to trial, Goldfield opponents of the WFM and IWW asserted that they now had evidence to prove that they were combating not a labor union but a criminal conspiracy. Simultaneously, internecine conflict immobilized the WFM as a result of its secession from the IWW. The battle between Western miners and Wobblies exacerbated an already wretched union situation in Nevada. Moreover, the AFL chose this moment to attack the WFM-IWW axis in Goldfield, and Gompers dispatched a special organizer to the area to join with mine owners and conservative WFM members in fighting the IWW and reasserting AFL hegemony. Soon economic panic and recession would make this bad union scene even worse.[4]

The counterattack by mine owners and local businessmen, well aware that Local 220's conservatives and radicals were bitterly fighting among themselves, came in March 1907. Forming a Businessmen's and Mine Owners' Association, they refused to employ IWW members. On March 15, supported by the AFL, they closed all local places of business, then reopened them three days later without IWW employees. Throughout March and most of April, local mines remained closed as owners and WFM moderates sought to purge Wobblies from the miners' union.[5]

At this stage Goldfield's class lines had become hopelessly confused. Only one thing was certain: Goldfield was no longer an IWW utopia. On one side, local businessmen and mine owners stood with AFL members and conservative miners; on the other, radical town workers and miners sympathetic to the IWW held fast to their position. Both sides went armed, and a precarious peace prevailed as local officials, immobilized by their own divided loyalties, kept hands off.

A majority of the miners and employers, rather than risk open warfare in such a confused situation, came to terms on April 22, 1907. The miners' union protected its prevailing rate of wages and won jurisdiction over all employees working in and around the mines. Employers in return gained a promise that town labor disputes would not be allowed to interfere with mine operations. The agreement, intended to last for two years, brought labor peace through the summer and early fall of 1907.[6]

With the IWW apparently beaten, the mine owners became more aggressive. Goldfield businessmen professed to have fought the Industrial Workers of the World partly because Wobblies were "subversive radicals" and partly because they were alleged criminal conspirators. There seemed, in fact, some basis for such fears. Federal investigators, while criticizing the actions of the mine owners and also the governor of Nevada, reported to the President that "by permitting their organization [Local 220] to be managed and controlled by men of violent tendencies, the union as a body has . . . laid itself open to the reproach of being a vicious organization, and has furnished a foundation for the fear existing in Goldfield . . ."[7] But in fact it was organized labor *per se,* not criminal conspirators, the employers were seeking to combat. They cooperated with the AFL only because that group had never organized local miners or town workers, and therefore posed no threat to employers' economic power. The IWW, by organizing workers successfully, had effectively restricted management's prerogatives. Hence mine owners attacked the IWW and the WFM to reduce labor's economic power, not solely to curb murderers and criminals. In short, employers opposed the IWW in Goldfield in 1907 (as they would in many other cities at other times) not only because it was radical, or violent, or un-American, but because it organized workers, levied economic demands upon employers, and successfully curtailed management's power.

Goldfield's mine owners publicly revealed their anti-union attitude in November 1907, when they broke their April agreement with the miners' union. Using the panic of that year and the subsequent monetary stringency as a pretext, the owners announced they would stop cash payments to their workers. Rejecting union compromise offers, they declared total war against organized labor.

At this juncture, Nevada's public authorities were in no position to aid Goldfield's employers: the state lacked either militia or police for the job. Goldfield's businessmen also realized that town and county officials could not be relied upon to combat labor. Thus, employers devised a scheme with Governor John Sparks to bring in federal troops.[8] In a secret meeting on December 2, 1907, the mine owners and the Governor agreed that Sparks, upon receipt of a coded wire, would request federal troops. No Goldfield town or county officials were informed of these ` arrangements. Immediately upon their return to Goldfield, mine owners dispatched the prearranged code message to Sparks, who on December 3 asked President Roosevelt for troops. After a brief legal contretemps between the Governor and the President, Roosevelt ordered the soldiers to Goldfield two days later.[9] On December 6 federal troops arrived in what to all appearances was an orderly, peaceful community. Only two weeks later, on December 20, agents sent by Roosevelt to investigate the situation wired the President: "Our investigation so far completely has failed to sustain the general and sweeping allegations by the governor in calling for troops. . . . We do find no evidence that any condition then existed not easily controlled by the local authorities." Goldfield, the agents went on, "had been for at least six months previously as free from disturbances as any mining town of similar situation and conditions. There had been no organized opposition to law." [10] But the federal agents soon discovered why mine owners and the Governor wanted federal troops. The mine owners, they learned, had determined to reduce wages and also to refuse to employ WFM members—steps they feared to take without military protection. The federal troops, Roosevelt's investigators concluded, "were part of a general plan of the mine owners to establish their independence of the union . . ." [11]

Aware of all this, Roosevelt nevertheless maintained the federal presence in Goldfield. The troops had been dispatched when there was no need for them, but the mine owners soon created that need, for the President's investigators went on to report that a wage reduction and new "yellow-dog" contracts, posted December 12, would cause the miners' union to resort to violence if the troops were withdrawn. Roosevelt, convinced that Haywood and the WFM "Inner Circle" were murderers, thought the worst of Goldfield's miners. Federal troops thus remained on duty to preserve Goldfield's peace until March 1908, when state police, recently provided for by a special session of the Nevada legislature, replaced them.[12]

The miners' union was by now a shambles. On April 3, when it finally voted to end its strike, only 115 men cast ballots, the remainder having left the union or the area. What had befallen the WFM and the IWW in Goldfield was summed up in 1911 by one of the mine owners who had helped destroy the union in 1907–1908. "The Western Federation of Miners and the I.W.W. are now eliminated from the camp of Goldfield," he wrote, "and always will be as long as I am identified with it." [13]

So ended the IWW's "Golden Age"—and with it the dreams of quick and easy organization of American workers into One Big Union powerful enough to dictate to employers. The Wobblies now knew what to expect in the future. Both the AFL and the WFM would fight them, and its members would scab on them; employers would take advantage of labor's internal divisions; and public authorities would be hostile and repressive. Most important, it became obvious that the more successful the IWW was in achieving its economic goals, the more it would meet employer and public opposition. Radicalism and revolutionary rhetoric were tolerable as long as they were not translated into actual economic power.

The defeat in Nevada notwithstanding, Wobblies liked to look back upon the Goldfield experience as a time when they had demonstrated, temporarily at least, that the One Big Union idea really worked, that laborers from many different occupations *could* be united into one organization, that an injury to one *could* be made the concern of all. A romanticized version of Goldfield became the ideal to be realized. This ideal kept the IWW alive from 1906 to 1908, as it tried to organize workers hitherto thought unorganizable.

The Goldfield debacle convinced some Wobblies that the organization should concentrate upon recruiting members in the urban-industrial East. Ben H. Williams, a member of the general executive board, maintained that Eastern workers, though less imbued than their Western brothers with the spirit of revolutionary industrial unionism, were also less mobile and hence superior material for stable organization.[14]

Williams' observation did not pass unheeded. In 1907–1908, articles in the *Industrial Union Bulletin* described IWW-led industrial conflicts in Bridgeport, Connecticut, in Skowhegan, Maine, and in Schenectady, New York. The Bridgeport and Schenectady strikes are particularly important for what they reveal about IWW methods and principles. In Bridgeport the Wobblies welded together unskilled Hungarian immigrants and skilled native Americans in a united front which in August 1907 won several important concessions from the American Tube and Stamping Company. Even the AFL organizer sent to Bridgeport to keep the International Association of Machinists from supporting the dual union's strike was impressed by the IWW's hold on the Hungarians. ". . . The devotion of these Hunks to the dual union is pathetic," he informed Gompers. "They sit at strike meetings listening to speakers whose speeches they cannot understand and join in the applause at the end louder than any of the others." [15] At the General Electric works in Schenectady, the IWW demonstrated what it meant by direct industrial action. On December 10, 1906, when the company refused to reinstate three discharged Wobblies, three thousand union members sat down inside the plant. As a local paper reported: "They did not walk out but remained at their places, simply stopping production." [16] Wobblies thus initiated the first recorded sitdown strike in American history.

These two conflicts foreshadowed the IWW's future course. They demonstrated that the primary aim of industrial action was immediate improvements in wages and working conditions and the redress of specific grievances. For most Wobblies the revolution was in the future—the empty belly was today's concern. Bridgeport and Schenectady also revealed the IWW's ability to do the unexpected and dramatic, as well as to attract previously neglected, unskilled immigrants into the same organization with skilled native Americans.

The IWW made its deepest Eastern inroads among textile workers. In Paterson, New Jersey, by March 1907 the Silk Workers' Industrial Union No. 152 had over one thousand members whose job classifications cut across craft lines. At the year's end, General Organizer Trautmann informed an executive board session that the IWW had organized about five thousand textile workers: thirty-five hundred in Paterson, seven hundred in New Bedford, fifty in Lawrence, and the remainder scattered among Providence, Woonsocket, Fall River, Hoboken, and Lancaster. Acting upon Trautmann's suggestion, the general executive board issued a call (published in English, French, German, and Italian) for a convention to be held on May Day 1908 in Paterson's IWW Hall to establish a National Industrial Union of Textile Workers.[17]

Twenty-two delegates, representing textile workers from Paterson, Providence, Woonsocket, New Bedford, Lawrence, and Lowell, attended this convention. Three days of discussion and debate produced the National Industrial Union of Textile Workers, the first such national industrial organization established within the IWW structure. Although the NIUTW opened membership to wage workers in every branch of textile production, its constitution allowed for union sub-divisions based upon either language or production unit (somewhat like the arrangements existing in the semi-industrial International Ladies' Garment Workers' Union, in which members belonged to locals based upon craft distinction, production unit, or the English, Yiddish, and Italian languages). The constitution also recognized the Textile Union's subordination to the IWW's general executive board on all vital issues.[18] In later years, this organization would wage several of the IWW's most notable struggles.

Concentration upon Eastern workers did not cause the IWW to neglect the Westerners responsible for the organization's birth. Quite the contrary. Appeals and demands for the organization of migratory farm workers filled the IWW press. Correspondents also urged the IWW to recruit among West Coast Asian workers. Unlike the AFL (or for that matter all other American labor organizations), which refused to organize Asians and sought through legislation to exclude them from the country, the IWW opposed exclusion laws and actively sought Asian recruits. J. H. Walsh, a West Coast organizer, reported that the Japanese-American newspaper *The Revolution* had opened its columns to the IWW, and that he, Walsh, was hot on the trail of two Chinese socialists. Meanwhile, the Wobblies' journal, *IUB*, editorially welcomed Japanese laborers to America, commenting: ". . . Japanese workmen already hold cards in the I.W.W. and more are coming. They are welcome." Early in 1908 the IWW ran a full-page article by organizer Walsh entitled "Japanese and Chinese Exclusion or Industrial Organization, Which?" Walsh's answer, of course, was industrial organization, for "They [the Chinese] can be organized as rapidly, if not more so, than any other nationality on earth." [19]

The Western work first brought to notice Elizabeth Gurley Flynn, destined as "the rebel girl" to become the most publicized of all IWW personalities. In 1907, though still only a teen-ager, Miss Flynn carried the industrial union message west to Duluth and up and down the Mesabi Iron Range. A Duluth paper described her platform manner as follows: "Socialistic fervor seems to emanate from her expressive eyes, and even from her red dress. She is a girl with a 'mission.'" Encountering timidity and fear on the part of the miners, she promised to make a second speaking tour in order to keep alive the interest in the IWW aroused by her messianic speeches.[20]

But in these early years, as also in its later life, the IWW proved most successful in reaching the lumber workers of the Far West. These loggers, commonly referred to as "timber beasts" in the IWW press, worked in an anarchic industry. West Coast lumbermen were as competitive and as ruthless in their business practices as the New York City garment manufacturers who had spawned the nation's worst sweatshops. In lumber as in the garment industry, labor was the chief cost of production; thus intense business competition brought downward pressure on wages and working conditions—at times reducing wages to the barest sustenance level. The inescapable physical hardships and deprivations associated with the lumber industry— particularly the isolation deep within the rain forests, miles from cities and the amenities of civilized life—made working conditions an even more miserable burden than low wages.[21]

James P. Thompson, an IWW lumber industry organizer, explained to a federal commission why the man who worked in the woods was called a "timber beast":

Now, the logger, he walks out in the woods and he looks around at a wilderness of trees. He works hard in there. And what does he get? He gets wages that are below the dead line, I say dead line in wages means below the line necessary to keep him alive. . . . They are being murdered on the installment plan . . . they breathe bad air in the camps. That ruins their lungs. They eat bad food. That ruins their stomachs. The foul conditions shorten their lives and make their short lives miserable.

. . . It rains a great deal and they work in the rain. . . . When they come in from the camps, they are wet. . . . They go into a dark barn, not as good as where the horses are, and the only place to dry their clothes is around the hot stove. . . . Those in the top bunk suffer from heat; those far away, from the cold. . . . business is business. And so the logger, he finds that he is nothing but a living machine. . . .[22]

This the IWW sought to alter by transforming the "timber beast" into a man.

But the lumber industry proved tough to organize. Employer attitudes toward labor were as primitive as the working conditions and as aggressive as the competition between companies. Shortsightedness proved the rule. When profits were good and labor scarce, employers "pampered" the loggers. But as an owner of the Puget Mill Company put it: "Later on when we are in a position to command, we can settle old scores." Puget Mill, like other companies in the industry, refused to countenance labor organizations or strikes. "Such practices are, in my opinion," wrote the Puget Mill's manager, "not fit subjects for arbitration." No labor union could be permitted to stand between an employer and his "right to employ whoever he sees fit, and to discharge an employee who is not in his opinion doing his duty . . ." [23] Such employers exerted their full power to keep labor organizers, especially from the IWW, away from their men.

Yet loggers were perfect IWW recruits. Mostly native Americans or northern Europeans, they spoke English, lived together, drank together, slept together, whored together, and fought together. Isolated in the woods or in primitive mill towns, they were bound by ties much stronger than their separate skill or job classifications. Whether skilled or unskilled, they wanted room to dry their clothes, clean bunks, decent bedding, and good food. They were tired of carrying bindles* on their backs as they moved from job to job and camp to camp. The IWW promised loggers bindle-burning parties and decent working conditions to be won through industrial solidarity. Within a year of its founding, the IWW local in Seattle had over eight hundred members, and by March 1907 had established new locals in the mill and lumber-port towns of Portland, Tacoma, Aberdeen, Hoquiam, Ballard, North Bend, Astoria, and Vancouver. The union idea was becoming contagious. "Unions seem to be the order of the day," one company official reported to his home office in August 1906.[24]

Employers, of course, were aware of the IWW's penetration into the lumber industry, but the public was not; not, that is, until March 1, 1907, when the IWW took command of a spontaneous walkout by Portland's mill workers. The IWW appeared on the Portland scene after a few mill hands had walked out following an unanswered call for higher wages and shorter hours. Fred Heslewood and Joseph Ettor soon went to work. Within a week they closed almost every mill in town and had over two thousand men out on strike. Claiming over eighteen hundred members, the IWW's Portland local (No. 319) formulated demands for a nine-hour day and a $2.50 minimum daily wage.

Like all the early IWW strikes, this one had immediate objectives. Ettor and Heslewood educated the strikers to the realities of the class

* The bindle consisted of the bedding the logger was required to provide wherever he worked, giving rise to the nickname "bindlestiff."

struggle but persistently urged their followers to be orderly and re-strained. The two agitators mentioned revolution only as a future possibility, never as an imminent prospect.[25]

Yet even the struggle over present realities intensely disturbed employers. Again, what vexed them more than questions of wages and working conditions was the issue of power. A Portland mill owner informed a Washington State friend of his fears that socialists and labor leaders would spread labor troubles throughout the Northwest if successful in Portland. "I have never seen such a feeling," he wrote. "It is not alone a question of wages . . . but it is a question of union-izing the mills and ultimately causing no end of trouble. . . . We pro-pose to fight the thing out . . ."[26] Washington's employers fervently hoped that the IWW offensive could be confined to the Portland area, but whatever happened, West Coast lumbermen intended to present a united front against the IWW. One company official, castigating the IWW as an organization which had "been started by a lot of socialists and anarchists . . . with the lowest class of laborers," asserted that all the lumbermen should stand together and refuse to operate with IWW workers. "It looks to me," he noted, "as though the Columbia River people ought to make the fight and that all the other mill companies in the North ought to stand by them in case the movement goes to their mills."[27]

The cards in this instance were stacked in favor of manage-ment. The Portland mills maintained their unity and, with support from lumber firms to the north, held fast against the strikers. Local AFL affiliates refused to cooperate with the strikers; indeed, the AFL Central Labor Council and the Portland building trades unions co-operated with employers to fight the IWW. "Federated Trades have taken a very decided stand against the Industrial Workers, and undoubtedly they have greatly hurt the cause of the strikers," com-mented the Puget Mill's manager. In fact, the Portland mills, with local AFL approval, successfully recruited nonunion workers, and by March 18 one employer concluded: ". . . The strike forces have dis-integrated . . ."[28] The next day Portland's mills reopened, and ten days later the strike had been completely crushed.

IWW organizers attempted to minimize their defeat. Heslewood claimed the conflict had resulted in improved working conditions for the strikers as well as having given IWW agitators forty days in which to educate workers to the necessity of revolutionary industrial unionism.[29] He had a point. The IWW may have lost the immediate conflict, but the strikers and most other workers in the lumber industry did benefit from the Portland struggle. Shock waves were felt throughout the trade from the California redwood forests to the Washington State Douglas fir camps. In the aftermath of the Portland strike the Puget Mill Company decided that it would "be well for the company to do everything in its power to have things pleasant for the men. . . . The days of the cabins and the man with the blankets is over, and I [Will Ames] presume that we have got to furnish better accommodations for our employees than in past times." [30] In the future, Western loggers would remember that it was the IWW, not the AFL, which had improved the conditions of their work and life.

Despite its coast-to-coast industrial activities, the IWW had painfully little in the way of organizational results to show for its efforts of 1907 and 1908. At the uneventful 1907 convention, Trautmann reported that the organization had 31,000 members. But of that number, at most only 10,000 paid monthly dues, and half the membership regularly moved in and out of the organization, leading to considerable double counting. A year later, Trautmann reported that the IWW, despite its well-conducted strikes at Bridgeport and Skowhegan, had not only lost all its members in those cities but also its prestige as an organization. Vincent St. John offered the 1908 convention equally disquieting news, for he estimated that since the 1907 convention the IWW had organized seventy-six locals and three district councils, but over the same period sixty-three locals had disbanded.[31]

The IWW's failure to progress was scarcely alleviated by the 1907 panic. Economic decline aggravated an already grievous organizational collapse. In December 1907, Trautmann reported that organization revenues had fallen by half. Appeal after appeal to delinquent locals and members to pay indebtedness brought no answer. The general executive board levied a special assessment but could not collect it. Printing and office bills grew, receipts dropped—still no relief was forthcoming. The general executive board finally curtailed all administrative expenses, including organizing activity, in order to preserve publication of the *Industrial Union Bulletin,* which, the board told itself, could spread the gospel of industrial unionism better than organizers. Even so, financial stringency compelled the board to reduce the publication of its journal from a weekly to a biweekly.[32]

Economic conditions certainly did not help matters any, but a large share of the IWW's failure must be laid directly at the organization's doorstep. Even before the economic downturn of 1907–1908, the IWW had proved unwilling to correct internal deficiences. The minutes of a September 1907 executive board meeting revealed that the IWW could not, or at any rate would not, finance its organizers. Organizers were expected to support themselves through commissions earned on the sale of IWW literature. As the year ended the board decided against employing additional organizers. Only those who could sustain themselves were allowed to remain in the field; that left five men —Walsh, Ettor, Williams, Heslewood, and Thompson—to organize workers from Maine to California.[33] Furthermore, IWW locals and members refused to pay their dues to general headquarters. ". . . When the industrial panic struck," Trautmann complained, ". . . it was found that those who were hollering loudest for 'voluntary' support of the organization, not based on the system of regular dues paid by members, were the foremost in blocking the efforts of the general secretaries to collect moneys for the sustenance of the organization." [34]

Organizational chaos worsened the financial problems. At a general executive board meeting in December 1907, James Thompson, then organizing in New England, explained the difficulties he faced because the IWW constitution lacked provision for national industrial unions. Then and there, without recorded discussion or debate, the general executive board resolved that three thousand members engaged in the same industry but organized in not less than seven different localities constituted a national industrial union. But most IWW members, unaffected by such grandiose paper schemes, remained in mixed locals which disbanded regularly because of barren treasuries, incompetent leaders, or both. Other aspects of the IWW's internal organization were open to criticism. Ettor, for example, found Wobblies prone to ridicule all union officials as tin gods, and he witnessed IWW locals practicing unrestrained rotation in office: each weekly meeting would elect a new set of officials. Untempered democracy, Ettor concluded, resulted in poorly administered locals, impulsive and ill-planned strikes, and the consequent disillusionment of the workers whom the IWW wished to reach.[35]

St. John was convinced that the IWW could produce no results until it obtained the funds necessary to saturate an industry with organizers as well as the power to protect IWW members against hostile employers. He confessed his own inability to break the vicious circle plaguing the IWW: no funds meant no organizers meant no members—no members meant no funds meant no organizers. St. John readily conceded: "Popularity is today a question of power. If the adherents of Industrial Unionism are going to wait until it has the power to make itself popular, before granting to it their allegiance, there is little hope for any movement that aims at the overthrow of the present system." [36] How to gain popularity, members, and money without effective power was a problem the IWW never resolved.

Although leaders like St. John, Trautmann, and Williams perceived their organization's basic weaknesses, they could not quite bring themselves to admit that these weaknesses were the result of chronic internal ailments; instead, they sought scapegoats. While not actually subscribing to what has been called the devil or conspiratorial theory of history, they nevertheless needed devils, in the form of sinister men, to blame for the organization's failures and thereby assuage their own wounded egos. They found their devil in Daniel DeLeon; indeed, if he had not existed, they would have had to invent him.

DeLeon was never an easy man to get along with. Desiring to be an American Lenin, he compelled uniformity among his disciples. He shared Lenin's iron will as well as his intense desire to command men and to make history. But DeLeon sought to make his revolution in a distinctly nonrevolutionary society.

Claiming to have been born in Curaçao in December 1852, the son of a Dutch Jewish colonial family, DeLeon was apparently American born.[37] So fully and relentlessly did he distort the circumstances of his birth and early life that little that is historically sound is known about DeLeon's youth. What passes for biography is largely a composite of his own peculiar fictions, the product of what one scholar has characterized as the mind of a pathological liar. DeLeon apparently obtained a law degree from Columbia University in 1878, lectured there in Latin American history in 1883, participated in reformer Henry George's 1886 New York City mayoralty campaign, and then flirted with the Knights of Labor and Edward Bellamy's Nationalist movement. This checkered course ultimately brought him to the Socialist Labor party, whose high priest he became in 1892 as editor of *The People,* the party's journal. As Marxian socialism's principal advocate in America, DeLeon would make more heretics than converts.

Once in firm control of the SLP, DeLeon sought to capture the remnants of the dying Knights of Labor. Failing in this, he modestly decided to seize the AFL. Again he was repelled, this time more swiftly. He never took defeat lightly. Unable to control the AFL, he determined to destroy it. In order to do so, DeLeon established the Socialist Trades and Labor Alliance in 1895.

At this stage in his life, DeLeon maintained that his revolution must come through political action, that the economic organization (that is, the trade union) must be subordinate to the political party.[38] When members of the SLP disagreed with DeLeon's dogmatism on the trade-union issue and still tried to bore within the AFL, they were promptly expelled. Tolerating no dissent, DeLeon was beset by enemies on all sides. Gompers was a bitter, vindictive critic; Debs, Berger, and most Midwestern socialists wanted no part of New York's "Red Pope of Revolution"; and even the majority of New York socialists finally realized that they could no longer remain in the same party with DeLeon. By 1900 he was left with a declining SLP and a moribund Trades and Labor Alliance.

Despite adversity, DeLeon refused to change his ideology or his tactics—that is, until the founding of the IWW in 1905 offered him a new opportunity. Here was his chance to win new allies, including Debs and the radical Western workers. DeLeon now suddenly discovered that economic action was more important than political action, and that the industrial union, not the political party, was the instrument of revolution. With his SLP-STLA followers, he joined the IWW.

DeLeon went only where he could lead; he wanted disciples not allies, sycophants not comrades. Hence, DeLeon and his lieutenants at once set about to transform the IWW into an adjunct of the Socialist Labor party. SLP men promoted the propaganda of politics at the expense of industrial unionism; they recruited for the party, not for the union; and wherever DeLeonites were active, factionalism and political argumentation weakened IWW locals. IWW leaders who had joined the SLP, as did Ben Williams in 1906, rapidly learned why a long-time DeLeon associate, after being expelled from the SLP's inner sanctum, described his one-time leader DeLeon as "like a legendary

South American who started a 'revolution' with twenty men, cut off the heads of nineteen and continued the revolution all by himself." [39]

Most Wobblies, indeed, had little in common with DeLeon or his party. Western workers, still a major influence in the organization, had shed none of their deeply ingrained suspicions about the efficacy of political action. From their own experiences, they were convinced that the state was usually their enemy and that politics more often than not had brought them no relief. "If you ignore the ballot box and put your efforts into the building up of the Industrial Workers of the World," an Arizona miner informed the 1907 WFM convention, "you can get all the good things of life. . . . When you meet in a political session what you achieve will be a reflex of what you have previously done on the economic field." Frank Little added: ". . . I do not believe that you can get the ends we are fighting for through a pure and simple political ballot party. . . . We can never do it as long as we depend upon going out and sticking a piece of white paper into a capitalist ballot box." [40]

But DeLeon and his SLP disciples gave only lip service to industrial unionism. When they spoke at IWW meetings or circulated literature during strikes, they concentrated upon criticizing the Socialist party. Not unexpectedly, the IWW general executive board warned all IWW representatives in June 1907 against introducing political fights into union affairs. Directing its message specifically toward SLP members, the general executive board warned: "No organizer or representative of the I.W.W. can . . . use his position . . . for any act of hostility . . . against such other organizations, even though individual members of the latter may be opposed to the I.W.W." The *IUB* made this warning even clearer: "In the very nature of the problem, political parties are subordinate to the economic organism of the class whose freedom is sought." [41]

The fight with DeLeon finally erupted openly in December 1907. James Connolly, later to become a martyr in the 1916 Dublin Easter Rising, was an IWW organizer in New York City in 1907, when he asked for an emergency general executive board meeting to discuss the possibility of recruiting large numbers of New York workers. But before the session could be held, DeLeon demanded a secret conference on "a matter of importance." His "important matter" turned out to be a warning that Connolly was an unreliable maverick hostile to the SLP. At the special secret meeting, DeLeon delivered an invective-filled tirade, which became so bitter that Ben Williams, chairing the session, declared DeLeon out of order. At that point, Williams later recalled, "the secret session adjourned with the chairman meeting a baleful eye from his majesty of the SLP." [42]

The internal struggle was now in earnest. Speaking before a New York SLP audience in March 1908, Williams angrily declared that experience had taught him that the IWW received a hearing and a response from workers only in proportion to its ability to avoid political entanglements and hairsplitting. Insisting that the political party was but a reflex of the industrial union, Williams concluded: ". . . We say to those who cannot adjust themselves to the I.W.W. position, 'Hands Off!' whether such individuals belong to one or the other of the two Socialist Parties." [43] Adding fuel to the ideological fire, Justus Ebert, a former SLP theorist, announced in a letter of resignation from the party in April: "The I.W.W., hampered in its growth by the illogical posture of the S.L.P., is compelled to serve notice in big, black type that it has no political affiliations of any sort." That same month James Connolly emphasized: ". . . The conquest of political power by the working class waits upon the conquest of economic power . . ." Williams terminated the anti-DeLeon, anti-SLP struggle in a letter to the editor of the *IUB*, which declared: "The I.W.W. is a way out of which everything else will develop. Let us 'make straight the *way*.'" [44]

How rank-and-file nonintellectuals reacted to the debate raging between DeLeon and his critics was best expressed in a letter from Heslewood to Trautmann. ". . . Any more of this damn dope about DeLeon or S.L.P. will be very obnoxious to me and to hundreds of others that are the life of the I.W.W. We want something to read in the Bulletin that is instructive. . . . I . . . say it costs money to be harping on . . . such trash, as there is more important work to be done." [45] Heslewood and his Western supporters came to the fourth IWW convention determined to clean DeLeon and his SLP supporters out of the organization. On this issue, they were supported by such IWW intellectuals as Trautmann, Ebert, and Williams.

As the 1908 convention approached, the DeLeonites made one last effort to dominate the IWW. Paying up their back dues by the hundreds, they packed the IWW mixed local in New York and selected

DeLeon and his adherents as the city's convention delegation. But the DeLeonites failed to take into account rank-and-file hostility to them and their plans.

Two thousand miles from the convention city of Chicago, in Portland, Oregon, IWW organizer John H. Walsh started a movement which ensured DeLeon's defeat. Walsh described his tactics in dispatches to the *IUB*. On September 1, 1908, nineteen men gathered in the Portland railroad yards, he wrote, "all dressed in black overalls and jumpers, black shirts and red ties, with an I.W.W. book in his [sic] pocket and an I.W.W. button on his [sic] coat." Seizing a cattle car, they started on their side-door coach journey east to Chicago. Northward went the "Overalls Brigade" as their "Red Special" took them first to Centralia, Washington, and then to an unexpected overnight stay in Seattle's jail. Undeterred by imprisonment, they hopped a second freight which carried them through Spokane; Sand Point, Idaho; Missoula, Montana, and points east. All along the route Walsh held propaganda meetings and sold literature to keep his brigade fed. After two weeks on the road his army suffered a net loss of only one man, and it expected to arrive in Chicago in time for the convention, then only three weeks off.

These Westerners sang their way across Montana, eating in the "jungles," preaching revolution in the prairie towns they besieged, and singing constantly. Walsh conceded that the Industrial Union Singing Club's lyrics "may not be as scientifically revolutionary as some would like, but it certainly has its psychological effect upon the poor wage slave that . . . has starvation army dope poured into his ears about five times a week." In five weeks of riding the rods the "Overalls Brigade" and its singing platoon traveled over 2,500 miles, held thirty-one meetings, and sold more than $175 worth of literature and about $200 in song sheets (the parent of the now famous *Little Red Song Book*).[46]

Other anti-DeLeonites converged upon Chicago from the east. Ben Williams arrived in town to find Vincent St. John fearful of bringing the DeLeon-SLP issue before the convention. Williams argued that confining the issue to New York, as St. John hoped to do, was impossible, for the future of the entire IWW hinged upon the relationship between the concept of industrial unionism, the ideology of the SLP, and the role of politics in bringing about the revolution. Hence he demanded that the entire New York controversy be laid before the convention. After much hesitation, St. John finally agreed.[47]

The stage was now set for the great struggle over DeLeon's role in the IWW. Williams and the Eastern intellectuals would provide anti-DeLeon ideological ammunition; Walsh's Western Brigade would provide votes and militancy.

The fourth IWW convention differed considerably from its three predecessors. For the first time since the organization's founding, the West Coast was well represented, having sent delegates from Seattle, Portland, and Los Angeles. Notable by their absence were Socialist party members and intellectual fellow travelers. The *IUB* afterward proudly commented: ". . . the fourth annual convention was probably the first revolutionary convention ever held in Chicago that was composed purely of wage workers." [48] Entirely true or not, it was hardly a hospitable environment for DeLeonism!

The convention opened on September 21, with chairman St. John calling upon Walsh's "Overalls Brigade" to sing "The Marseillaise." The martial spirit aroused, the delegates heard Trautmann ask them to march to war against DeLeon and the SLP, as he defined the central issue confronting the convention: Would the IWW become a tail to a political kite, or would it be left free to organize workers into industrial unions? [49]

Not until its fourth day did the convention come to grips with this central issue. On that day, September 24, the Credentials Committee recommended by a vote of three to one that DeLeon not be seated because he belonged to the wrong local. DeLeon had claimed that union membership should be based on the tool used, not the industry involved; in other words, he spoke for the craft autonomy practiced by the AFL, while the Credentials Committee insisted upon the industrial unionism preached by the IWW. DeLeon was given an opportunity to argue his case before the delegates. The *IUB* later published excerpts from his defense and St. John's rebuttal, respectively (and interestingly) titled: "The Intellectual Against the Worker," and "The Worker Against the Intellectual." Resorting to personal invective as usual, DeLeon claimed that his enemies were the men who had retarded the industrial-union movement, and that the convention, instead of "sticking the knife into me . . . should stick it into Trautmann and Williams." But the delegates proceeded to stab DeLeon, voting 40 to 21 to adopt the Credentials Committee recommendation.[50]

With DeLeon ousted, the delegates quarreled cantankerously over their organization's political role. Ideological lines became more confused than ever. A clear majority had removed DeLeon because of his ideological stress on political action, yet the Constitution Committee voted to recommend that the IWW preamble be left untouched, overruling a minority which had insisted that it be amended to remove all reference to political action. Fred Heslewood, who earlier had led the Western attack against DeLeonism and politics in unions, now moved that the majority report be adopted. Throughout the day Heslewood and his adversaries debated the political issue: the critics insisting that political action was a dead end for workers, Heslewood rejoining that elimination of the political clause would leave the IWW open to criticism as an anarchist organization composed in the main of dynamiters. The final vote on the question was as close and as confused as the heated debate preceding it. At least twelve delegates who had voted against DeLeon balloted in favor of retaining the IWW preamble as it stood. A bare three-vote majority (35 to 32) deleted political action from the preamble. Stranger yet, only three days later, both the advocates and the critics of the amended preamble joined in a resolution which rejected all direct or indirect alliances with political parties or with *anti-political sects*.[51] Again, as in 1905, it would have taken an expert on medieval theology to define the IWW's position on political action.

The convention's decision to drop all reference to politics from the preamble did, as Heslewood had predicted, open the IWW to the criticism that it was simply an anarchist organization composed of dynamiters. DeLeon was among the first to attack the "new" IWW on just those grounds, calling Wobblies "bums, anarchists, and physical force destroyers." He even formed his own IWW,* ostentatiously dedicated to orderly, peaceful action through political and parliamentary tactics. DeLeon's unrestrained war of words against the IWW later provided the IWW's enemies with ample justification for their fears of the terrible Wobblies.

But DeLeon and others who accepted his critique of the post-1908

---

* The so-called Detroit IWW, in contradistinction to the Chicago organization, which published its own journal, led a couple of strikes, and, aside from its links to the SLP, existed largely on paper.

IWW misunderstood what the convention had done. The delegates had simply put the IWW where the AFL had been since 1895. Both labor organizations now refused direct endorsement of, or alliance with, any political party; both also declined to join anti-political crusades. Moreover, the IWW, like the AFL, did not and could not determine rank-and-file attitudes or actions on political issues. Delegates to the 1908 convention recognized, as Gompers had over a decade earlier, that political debates between socialist factions wrecked union locals and undermined labor's morale. Hence, the Wobblies decided to keep political debate within the party, where it belonged, and to promote industrial action within the IWW whereby workers could improve their lives. Ben Williams answered DeLeon's charges for the IWW in February 1909. Neither directly nor inferentially, Williams remarked, did the amended preamble compel Wobblies to avoid the ballot box. That remained an individual decision, best kept out of internal union affairs for tactical reasons. Only the misguided, he wrote, could refer to the IWW as "a purely physical force organization" committed to advocacy of "dynamite." [52]

Other equally erroneous misconceptions about the IWW arose as a result of the 1908 convention. Critics of the IWW, especially DeLeon, emphasized the role of the "Overalls Brigade," or "Proletarian Rabble and Bummers." Consequently they overlooked the vital influence exerted by Williams, Trautmann, Ebert, and St. John. Charging that the "slum proletariat" and the "bum brigade" had taken over the organization, DeLeon asserted that because of this the IWW would never achieve stability, since "hoboes" would neither pay adequate dues nor tolerate competent officials. IWW rhetoric, particularly as printed in the *IUB*, appeared to substantiate DeLeon's charges. Again and again editorials referred to the hobo worker as the backbone of the IWW, the only true revolutionary in America, made so as a result of his ability to leave a job whenever conditions did not suit him. As the *IUB* stated its case: "He is the leaven of the revolutionary industrial union movement in the West, and his absence . . . from the East, accounts in large measure for the slowness of the Eastern workers to awaken from their lethargy." [53] Yet the "hobo" delegates at the 1908 convention, quite unlike those imagined by DeLeon, opposed dues reduction and urged instead that they be raised. Walsh reported that the Western rank and file considered dues reduction a cheap proposition and wondered how an organization could exist without adequate funds. Other Western delegates agreed with their leader's comment.[54] Although IWW propagandists may have romanticized the character of the migratory worker and naively transformed the hobo into the revolutionary hero incarnate, Western Wobblies themselves never doubted that an organization needed funds and effective leaders to survive and grow.

Unfortunately, neither Westerners nor Easterners, neither rank and file nor leaders, could do anything about industrial depression, unemployment, and delinquent dues payment. The 1908 convention thus sanctioned the established practice of using only those organizers who sustained themselves through the sale of literature and buttons. Indeed, only a week after the convention adjourned, the new general executive board pleaded for funds to carry on organization activities and to print the *Industrial Union Bulletin.* Pleas accomplished little. In November 1908 the executive board suspended publication of the *IUB*, partly because of a lack of money and partly because of a fight with the Socialist Labor party, which sought to have the IWW journal denied second-class mail privileges on the basis of the *IUB's* alleged espousal of anarchist principles.[55]

The reconstituted IWW thus began its life inauspiciously. When St. John assumed office as general organizer (Trautmann was demoted to secretary-treasurer), he found the IWW practically without income and deeply in debt. The membership consisted of a few mixed foreign-language locals in the East and a few hundred seasonal workers in the West. The WFM, the AFL, and both Socialist parties assailed the IWW as an aggregation of "anarchists and bums." Eugene Debs quietly allowed his IWW membership to lapse. When St. John suspended publication of the *IUB* in March 1909, he could not even hint at a possible date for resumption of publication. Even limited organizing activity ground to a complete halt.[56]

Yet it was this post-1908 organization which was able to contribute "something new to the labor movement." It was in the period after 1908 that the IWW, according to James P. Cannon, played its "best revolutionary part." "That is the enduring story," he notes, "the rest is anti-climax." [57]

During most of those years the IWW's fortunes were guided by

Vincent St. John as general organizer (1908–1915), and its philosophy and approach were expounded by Ben Williams, editor of *Solidarity,* the official IWW journal, from 1909 until his retirement in March 1917. To these two men, about whom Americans know so little, the IWW owed much of its successes and influence in the years before World War I.

Vincent St. John, better known to his friends and associates as "the Saint," commanded the total respect and allegiance of the young rebels who flocked to the IWW. Elizabeth Gurley Flynn later wrote of him: "I never met a man I admired more." James Cannon, a rebellious youth just then beginning a radical journey which was to take him from the IWW to the Communist party and thence to the Trotskyite Socialist Workers party, remembered how all his young friends trusted and swore by "the Saint," always certain of a square deal (or more) from St. John. "Like attracted like," Cannon wrote of St. John, "and he created an organization in his own image. . . . The Saint lived his ideas and methods. He radiated sincerity and integrity, and unselfishness free from taint of ostentation. The air was clean in his presence." [58]

Born in Newport, Kentucky, on July 16, 1876, of Irish-Dutch ancestry, St. John had an unsettled home life. Between 1880 and 1895 he moved with his family to New Jersey, Colorado, Washington State, and California. At nineteen Vincent returned alone to Colorado to begin a tempestuous life as a miner, prospector, and union organizer. As president of the Telluride Miners' Union, he managed the successful 1901 strike; shortly after this, he became a local hero by risking his life in a mining disaster to save others. But he was no hero to local mine managers, who accused him of assassinating the manager of the Smuggler Union mine. For two years (1902–1903) local and state authorities hounded St. John. Lacking evidence, public officials could not prosecute him, but private employers could and did blacklist him throughout Colorado.[59] As a WFM hero and also a close associate of the union's national officers, he was implicated in the Steunenberg case; McParland included St. John among the members of the "Inner Circle" and even provided Colorado authorities with loose circumstantial evidence sufficient to bring St. John to trial for murder. He moved from one scrape with the law to another. A leader in the anti-Sherman IWW factional fight of 1906, he battled with private detectives and city police. A strong advocate of the IWW, unlike some other WFM leaders, St. John went to Goldfield in 1906 to lead the

IWW town workers and their WFM allies, only to be shot in the right hand, which as a result became permanently crippled. Finally, in 1917, though no longer associated with the IWW in any official capacity, St. John, with other IWW officials, was arrested, indicted, tried, and convicted by federal authorities.

Vincent St. John's bitter experiences as a worker and as a union official, and not books or theories, shaped his thoughts and actions. As Cannon put it: ". . . His school was his own experience and observation, and his creed was action." St. John shared with fellow Westerners the feeling that "a man was what he did." Blessed with an unusual ability to act immediately and effectively without undue philosophizing or procrastinating, he obtained the best from his subordinates, in whom he instilled his own ability to act under fire. Decisiveness suited St. John. Under his direction the IWW became noted for its tactics of direct action and its avoidance of political action, though St. John had once been a Socialist party member and even a party candidate for public office. Experience, not European syndicalist ideas, convinced him that political activities disrupted union organization, and that labor's betterment lay in militant industrial unionism. Hence, he struggled to save the IWW from Daniel DeLeon on the one hand and from the "anarchist freaks" on the other.[60]

When after eight years' effort as general organizer St. John saw the IWW no closer to the promised land of industrial unionism than when he assumed that office in 1908, he yielded to the lure of prospecting and decided to return to the West. Resigning from office in 1915 and finding a financial backer in Frank Walsh (the prominent reform Democrat, attorney for radical causes, and chairman of Woodrow Wilson's Commission on Industrial Relations, whom St. John impressed as a witness in 1914), he went off to Jicarilla, New Mexico, in a vain search for gold. Prospecting failed to diminish his enthusiasm for the IWW. Short of money, he headed north to Colorado in search of work and wages. Forced to take an assumed name as a result of the 1901 blacklist there, St. John commented: "The mine owners have forgotten my looks in the past 15 years but the name would no doubt be remembered so to play safe took a new one for the occasion. Great Country!"[61] When federal authorities arrested him in October 1917, he was back prospecting around Jicarilla.

St. John's physique and manner scarcely accorded with the life of the man of action he was. Short and slight, he moved quickly and gracefully. Always in conflict with union opponents, employers, and the law, he was nevertheless quiet, self-contained, and modest. Life finally took its toll upon him. Crippled in one hand, afflicted with chronic bronchitis from years of labor beneath the earth's surface, worn out from eluding the law and serving time in prison, St. John died unnoticed and unmourned in 1929.

Ben H. Williams, the second influential figure during the IWW's early years, led a similarly nomadic life. Williams, like St. John, traveled extensively and had a firsthand experience of a broad spectrum of American life. But while St. John derived his ideas largely from personal experience, Williams' ideas originated as much in reading and reasoning. While "the Saint's" life always tended toward action, Williams more and more turned to a life of thought and theory. While St. John administered general headquarters, Williams edited the official journal, providing the IWW with whatever formal ideological structure it had.

Like St. John, Williams was American to the core. Born in the slate-quarry town of Monson, Maine, in 1877, he was named Benjamin Hayes in honor of the recently elected Republican President. When his father deserted the family in 1888, young Williams moved with his mother to Bertrand, Nebraska, where a half-brother ran a small print shop. Here his kinsman introduced him to the realities of exploitation, driving the young apprentice printer to exhaustion. Here Williams introduced himself to radicalism, later recalling about those Nebraska days: "The Western farmers' revolt was in full swing with the Farmers' Alliance. My brother supported the movement in his paper, and as a result, got all kinds of radical publications on exchange. Before my twelfth year, I was introduced to all the social philosophies—anarchism, socialism, communism, direct legislation, and Alliance programs—absorbing the ideas of a New America and a better world." [62] From this Williams moved on to a closer reading of Bellamy, Marx, and Thomas Henry Huxley, linking together in his own mind Bellamy's utopianism, Marx's materialistic revolutionary credo, and Huxley's evolutionary schema. Williams even managed to squeeze in a formal education at Tabor College in Iowa in the late 1890's.[63]

Learning led Williams to seek action in the world. In 1898 he interested himself in DeLeon's SLP and its effort to organize workers through the Socialist Trades and Labor Alliance. A little later he met Frank Bohn and Father Hagerty, who further influenced him to devote his life to working-class organization. By 1904 he was lecturing

144

and organizing for the SLP, and he naturally followed his party into the IWW in 1905. As a Wobbly, Williams organized unions in the redwood forests around Eureka, California, all the time growing increasingly disillusioned with the SLP's emphasis on political action and its neglect of union organization. As the months passed, he became more active in organizing for the IWW and less active in propagandizing for the SLP. Elected to the general executive board at the 1907 convention, he became its unofficial chairman. As an opponent of DeLeon he led the 1908 struggle which culminated in DeLeon's ouster. When his term on the board ended in 1909, Williams hoboed to New Castle, Pennsylvania, where he became editor of *Solidarity,* the job he held until he left the IWW in 1917.[64]

Williams arrived in New Castle looking every bit the radical intellectual. Short and slight, he had narrow sloping shoulders and a sensitive face more suited for life in the study than in the mine pit or on the picket line. With clear, piercing eyes, topped by thin eyebrows, a fine straight nose, well-formed thin lips, a clear complexion, and a well-trimmed Van Dyke complemented by sideburns and a narrow mustache, he looked like a soft-grained American version of Lenin and other Bolshevik revolutionaries.

Although he would later become disillusioned with the direction the IWW took under Haywood and his successors, Williams never lost his firm belief in the need for revolutionary social change. In the 1920's, reverting to his earlier Bellamyite enthusiasm, Williams found his utopia in the Technocracy movement, becoming its leader in the Cleveland area. Shortly before his death in 1965, at the age of eighty-eight, he still seemed optimistic about the prospects for revolution: "The conditions for the advance toward a New World of General Welfare are ripening toward speedy conclusion," he wrote. "We are convinced beyond a doubt that the One Big Union is about to come to fulfillment and to make certain humanity's permanent freedom from the 'curse of Adam': 'In the sweat of thy face' (and under the goad of the slave master's whip) 'shalt thou eat bread.'" [65]

CHAPTER

7

Ideology and Utopia:
The Syndicalism of the IWW

ROM 1909 to 1919 a legend enveloped the IWW. Many Americans, especially during World War I and the postwar Red Scare, became convinced that the Wobblies were "cut-throat, pro-German, or . . . bolshevik, desperadoes who burn harvest-fields, drive iron spikes into fine timber and ruin saw-mills, devise bomb plots, who obstruct the war and sabotage the manufacture of munitions—veritable supermen, with a superhuman power for evil, omnipresent and almost omnipotent."[1] The hobo Wobbly had replaced the bearded, bomb-carrying anarchist as a bogeyman in the middle-class American's fevered imagination. This version of the Wobbly died hard.

It died hard because violence and bloodshed *did* follow Wobblies wherever they fought for free speech or higher wages. It died hard because IWW rhetoric and songs fed the myth of the Wobbly as a wild and woolly warrior, a man who contemptuously scorned the conventional morality of what he characterized as "bushwa" society. While organizers like James P. Thompson were boasting that only *"red-blooded"* revolutionaries belonged to the IWW, Wobbly bards like Joe Hill were deriding voting machines and suggesting that workers "may find out that the only 'machine' worth while is the one which the capitalists use on us when we ask for more bread for ourselves and our families. *The one that works with a trigger.*"[2]

146

With the IWW, as with other radical organizations that have been romanticized and mythologized, the legend is several removes from reality. Wobblies did not carry bombs, nor burn harvest fields, nor destroy timber, nor depend upon the machine that works with a trigger. Instead they tried in their own ways to comprehend the nature and dynamics of capitalist society, and through increased knowledge, as well as through revolutionary activism, to develop a better system for the organization and functioning of the American economy.

The IWW, it is true, produced no intellectual giants. It did not spawn a Karl Marx or a Georges Sorel, a Lenin or a Jean Jaurès, or even an Edward Bellamy or a Henry George. It offered no genuinely original ideas, no sweeping explanations of social change, no fundamental theories of revolution. Wobblies instead took their basic concepts from others: from Marx the concepts of labor value, commodity value, surplus value, and class struggle; from Darwin the idea of organic evolution and the struggle for survival as a paradigm for social evolution and the survival of the fittest class; from Bakunin and the anarchists the "propaganda of the deed" and the idea of "direct action"; and from Sorel the notion of the "militant minority." Hence, IWW beliefs became a peculiar amalgam of Marxism and Darwinism, anarchism and syndicalism—all overlaid with a singularly American patina.

True, they did read books—IWW libraries included works by Marx, Engels, Kautsky, Sorel, Jaurès, Bellamy, George, and others; IWW publications advertised complete bibliographies of socialist literature—but they read to understand better what they already knew from life. For above all else, Wobblies derived their beliefs from their own experiences in America. The Coeur d'Alenes, Leadville, and Cripple Creek taught them that society was divided into contending classes; that American business had evolved from small-scale endeavors to giant corporations; that labor was divided, not united; and that a "militant minority" could surmount the resistance of a complacent majority. In other words, European theoreticians explained in coherent, analytical, and learned terms what most Wobblies grasped instinctively.

As early as 1912 William E. Bohn, an astute journalist and observer of the American scene, could declare that the IWW "did not come into being as the result of any foreign influence. It is distinctly an American product." Ben Williams agreed. For seven years, as editor of *Solidarity*, he vigorously criticized those who associated the IWW with foreign ideologies. "Whatever it may have in common with European labor movements," he insisted, the IWW

is a distinct product of America and American conditions. . . . Neither "in aim and methods" is the I.W.W. European. . . . Whatever terms or phrases we may borrow from the French or other language to denote our methods cut no figure: the methods conform to American conditions. . . . The form of structure of the I.W.W. is also distinctly American, and differs materially from the less developed forms of European labor organization . . .[3]

IWW beliefs must be understood in terms of those whom the organization tried to organize. After the defection of the Western Federation of Miners in 1907, Wobblies concentrated upon those workers neglected by the mainstream of the labor movement: timber beasts, hobo harvesters, itinerant construction workers, exploited eastern and southern European immigrants, racially excluded Negroes, Mexicans, and Asian Americans.

Contemporaries frequently remarked the IWW's unique following. Rexford Tugwell poignantly described the timber beast attracted to the IWW: "His eyes are dull and reddened; his joints are stiff with the rheumatism almost universal in the wettest climate in the world; his teeth are rotting; he is wracked with strange diseases and tortured by unrealized dreams that haunt his soul. . . . The blanket-stiff is a man without a home. . . . The void of his atrophied affections is filled with a resentful despair and a bitterness against the society that self-righteously cast him out." The same could be said of the IWW harvest worker and construction hand. After a careful study based upon personal interviews with West Coast Wobblies, Carleton Parker concluded that they were floaters, men without homes, wives, women, or "normal" sex; the men who appear in his case studies shared lives of brutality, degradation, and violence, "starting with the long hours and dreary winters of the farms they ran away from, or the sour-smelling bunkhouse in a coal village, through their character-debasing experience with the drifting 'hire and fire' life in the industries, on to the vicious social and economic life of the winter unemployed . . ."[4]

Wobbly recruits thus shared aspects of what cultural anthropologist Oscar Lewis has only recently labeled the "culture of poverty." Like Lewis' more recent case-study families in Mexico, Puerto Rico, and New York City, America's Wobblies had life histories revealing "family disruption, violence, brutality, cheapness of life, lack of love, lack of education, lack of medical facilities . . ." [5]

Lewis also contends that the "culture of poverty" emerges within a society that possesses the following dominant characteristics: (1) a cash economy, wage labor, and production for profit; (2) a persistently high rate of unemployment and underemployment for unskilled labor; (3) low wages; (4) a paucity of social, political, and economic organization, whether on a voluntary basis or by government imposition, for the low-income population; and (5) a pervasive set of values, imposed by the dominant class, which stresses the accumulation of wealth and property and the possibility of upward mobility through thrift, and explains low economic status as the result of personal inadequacy or inferiority.[6]

Although Lewis' loosely drawn characteristics might apply to almost any society in the process of industrialization, they are particularly relevant to the America of 1877–1917. Unencumbered by a feudal-aristocratic tradition and the paternalistic anti-capitalism associated with it, America's dominant business class could impose its values on society with relative ease. This was singularly true in the American West, where, in less than a generation, industrialization and urbanization tamed a wilderness. There, where social structure was fluid and government relatively weak, the spirit of rugged individualism reigned supreme and the strong prevailed. Those who failed to rise were pushed into society's backwaters to endure, as best they could, the stigmata associated with failure in a competitive industrial society.

Wobbly members, like Marx's proletariat and Lewis' poverty-stricken, were "people . . . from the lower strata of a rapidly changing society and . . . already partially alienated from it." The men who associated with the IWW in its heyday were largely first-generation citizens of an industrial society. As is frequently noted, immigrants from the south and east of Europe often first experienced urban-industrial life upon their arrival in the new world. But dispossessed native Americans were equally newcomers to industrial society; like E. J. Hobsbawm's first-generation English industrial workers, such native Americans may be considered internal immigrants who also made the frightening journey from a preindustrial to an industrial

149

society.[7] Caught between two systems and two modes of existence, these immigrants—internal and external—were indeed uprooted. Torn from an old, ordered, and comprehensible way of life, they found themselves unable to replace it with an integrated and meaningful mode of existence, and soon became the human flotsam and jetsam of early industrial capitalism's frequent shipwrecks.

Feeling impotent and alienated, these men harbored deep grievances against the essential institutions of the ruling classes: police, government, and church. Hence, Wobblies, like Lewis' Latin Americans living in a "culture of poverty," exhibited a high susceptibility to unrest and to radical movements aimed at destroying the established social order.[8]

This is what IWW leaders sensed, though they themselves did not come out of the "culture of poverty." The leadership consisted largely of two types: skilled workers and formerly successful trade-union officials such as Haywood, St. John, Ettor, and Little; and restless intellectuals such as Williams, Ebert, and the Swedish immigrant syndicalist John Sandgren. These men shared a common desire to effect a nonpolitical revolution in America and a common alienation from the AFL and from reformist American socialists. Eager to make a revolution which would destroy the existing system root and branch, they naturally turned to those most alienated from the American dream—and located them in the lower strata of a rapidly changing society.

The IWW clearly shaped its doctrines and its tactics to attract such recruits. That is why it maintained low initiation fees and still lower dues, why it allowed universal transfer of union cards, why it belittled union leaders as the labor lieutenants of capitalism, and why, finally, it derogated business unionism as pork-chop unionism and trade-union welfare systems as "coffin benefits." IWW members simply could not afford the initiation fees and dues required to sustain business unionism; partly because of their feelings of impotence and partly because they moved from industry to industry, Wobblies also needed self-leadership and self-discipline more than the counsel of professional, bureaucratic union officials. Thus, only by implementing policies sure to keep its treasury bare and its bureaucracy immobilized could the IWW attract the followers it sought. Accordingly, the IWW's formal defense of its nonbenefit system should be understood more as a rationalization of what existed than as a hard-core belief in what should exist. The same kind of rationalization, or ambivalence, as we shall see, permeated many other Wobbly beliefs and practices.

Basically, the IWW did what other American unions refused to do. It opened its doors to all: Negro and Asian, Jew and Catholic, immigrant and native. Wobbly locals had no closed membership rolls, no apprenticeship regulations. As West Coast organizer George Speed put it: ". . . One man is as good as another to me; I don't care whether he is black, blue, green, or yellow, as long as he acts the man and acts true to his economic interests as a worker." [9]

The disinherited joined the IWW by the thousands because it offered them "a ready made dream of a new world where there is a new touch with sweetness and light and where for a while they can escape the torture of forever being indecently kicked about." Or, as Carleton Parker discovered of his wandering rank and file, the IWW offered "the only social break in the harsh search for work that they have ever had; its headquarters the only competitor of the saloon in which they are welcome. They listen stolidly to their frequent lecturers with an obvious and sustained interest . . . the concrete details of industrial renovation find eager interest." [10]

Most important of all, the IWW promised its members a way out of their respective "cultures of poverty." "When the poor become class-conscious or active members of trade-union organizations," Lewis notes, "they are no longer part of the culture of poverty." He adds: "Any movement . . . which organizes and gives hope to the poor and effectively promotes solidarity and a sense of identification with larger groups, destroys the psychological and social core of the culture of poverty." That is just what the IWW attempted to do, as it sought to improve the self-image and self-respect of its members. Wobblies instilled among their alienated following what Lewis found Castro offering the Cuban peasants: ". . . a new sense of power and importance. They were armed and were given a doctrine which glorified the lower class as the hope of humanity." [11]

But, as Rexford Tugwell perceptively noted in 1920, the revolutionary potential of the poor in America is limited. "No world regenerating philosophy comes out of them and they are not going to inherit the earth. When we are a bit more orderly they will disappear." [12] When Tugwell wrote those lines, the IWW had been fatally weakened by federal and state repression. Yet for a time, from 1909 to 1917, the IWW seemed well on the way to organizing the revolutionary potential of the poor.

The IWW's ideologues, as suggested earlier, had few original thoughts about the nature of society, the place of workers within it, or the manner by which society changes. For social theory and its economic foundations they turned, as we have seen, to the writings of others, particularly Marx and Darwin. Yet they also drew upon an older American tradition, dating back to the era of Jefferson and Jackson, which divided society into producers and nonproducers, productive classes and parasites.

Wobblies never questioned the labor theory of value, or the other basic tenets of Marxian economics. Indeed, since labor created all value, the worker was robbed when (as under capitalism) he did not receive the money equivalent of his full product. Capitalism and thievery were thus synonymous: profits represented the capitalist's seizure of his worker's surplus value. This robbery could end only with the abolition of capitalism.[13]

Like Marx, the Wobblies also believed that the working class, or proletariat, would rise up in wrath and destroy the capitalists. Like Marx, they asserted that capitalism carried the seeds of its own destruction, and that workers would create "the new society within the shell of the old." Like Marx, again, they saw in the class struggle "the relentless logic of history," which would roll on until, as the IWW proclaimed in its preamble, ". . . the workers of the world organize as a class, take possession of the earth and the machinery of production and abolish the wage system."

The IWW was never precise in its definition of class. Sometimes Wobblies divided society into two classes: capitalists and workers; sometimes they perceived distinct and separate sub-classes within the two major categories; and sometimes they followed Haywood's example of dividing "all the world into three parts: the capitalists, who are the employing class that makes money out of money; the skilled laborers; and the masses." [14] The IWW, of course, represented the masses who would act as the agents of the new and better social order.

Wobblies also reversed common American assumptions about the applicability of Darwinian evolution to social change. Carrying the theory of biological evolution over into social analysis enabled many Americans to conclude that the wealthy had risen to the top of the economic heap solely as a result of their fitness in the struggle for business survival; conversely, failure, poverty, and dependence were signs of unfitness. Eric Goldman has called this ideology conservative Darwinism, in contradistinction to reform Darwinism, the ideology which used the theory of biological evolution to promote reform and attack the status quo.[15] If Goldman's concept of conservative versus reform Darwinism has any validity, then Wobblies may properly be termed radical, or revolutionary, Darwinists. For IWW ideology began with the belief that "social evolution differs in no essential respect from organic evolution." "The central fact or principle which we cannot ignore except at our own peril," wrote Ben Williams, "is the fact of social evolution, which is not always a direct or simple process, but often a slow, painful, and tortuous course of human development with the wrecks of social experiments scattered along the way." Whatever the perils along the way, the IWW sought to ride the evolutionary wave of the future. In the IWW's amalgam of Marxism and Darwinism, capitalism was the stage preceding the establishment of the workers' paradise. As Ben Williams expressed it: "Trustified American Capital leads the world. The I.W.W. aims to trustify American labor." In the IWW's view, since the working class was most fit, its mode of organization would be superior to that of the capitalists, and thus would enable the IWW to build its new order within the shell of the old.[16] Thus was social Darwinism stood on its head; thus would the beaten become the fit; thus would the slaves become the masters.

Wobblies glorified themselves as the saviors of society. The IWW perceived in America's disinherited the raw material for the transformation of a basically sick society. Writing to the *Industrial Worker* from a Louisiana jail, the organizer E. F. Doree was moved to poetry: "Arise like lions after slumber / In unvanquishable number. / Shake your chains to earth like dew / Which in sleep have fallen on you. / Ye are many, they are few." John Sandgren added: "The world is gone mad. We are the only sane people on earth. The future belongs to us." [17] IWW ideology, in essence, saw America's downtrodden masses, no longer satisfied with mere crumbs from their masters' abundant tables, emerging from the abyss of society to seize for themselves the world of industry. "We are many," proclaimed *Solidarity*. "We are resourceful; we are animated by the most glorious vision of the ages; we cannot be conquered, and *we shall conquer the world for the working class.*" Listen to our song, urged the paper, printing the IWW's own version of the "Internationale":

> Arise, ye prisoners of starvation!
> Arise, ye wretched of the earth!
> For Justice thunders condemnation.
> A better world's in birth.
> No more tradition's chains shall bind us;
> Arise, ye slaves! No more in thrall!
> The earth shall stand on new foundations;
> We have been *naught*—We shall be *All!*
> 'Tis the final conflict!
> Let each stand in his place.
> The Industrial Union
> Shall be the Human Race.[18]

The song epitomizes the IWW's ultimate objectives: a combination of primitive millennarianism and modern revolutionary goals. "The essence of millennnarianism," Eric Hobsbawm writes, "is the hope of a complete and radical change in the world which will be reflected in the millennium, a world shorn of all its present deficiencies . . ."[19] It seems clear that the IWW shared with primitive millennarians an instinctive distaste for the world as it was, as well as hope for the creation of a completely new world. But the Wobblies had rejected the apocalyptic Judeo-Christian vision of the way in which the millennial society would be established. In its place they substituted more earth-bound ideas about how to topple the old order and create the new one. Modern revolutionary movements—Marxism and syndicalism especially—would be the means to achieve what Hobsbawm calls "the transfer of power." Yet Wobblies always remained more vague about the processes of revolution than the Marxists, and never abandoned primitive millennarian dreams of a final conflict, a Judgment Day when the exploiters would be turned out and the banner of Industrial Freedom raised over the workshops of the world "in a free society of men and women . . ."[20]

Notwithstanding this belief in ultimate revolution, the IWW constantly sought opportunities to improve the immediate circumstances

154

of its members. Speakers and publications emphasized a twofold purpose: "First, to improve conditions for the working class day by day. Second, to build up an organization that can take possession of the industries and run them for the benefit of the workers when capitalism shall have been overthrown." Or as William D. Haywood phrased it in testimony before the Commission on Industrial Relations: "I don't think that I presented any Utopian ideas. I talked for the necessities of life, food, clothing, shelter, and amusement. We can talk of Utopia afterwards." [21] For, as St. John insisted, before it could have utopia the IWW must necessarily handle the workers' everyday problems: shorter hours, better wages, and improved shop conditions. A Wobbly organizer said simply: "The final aim . . . is revolution. But for the present *let's see if we can get a bed to sleep in, water enough to take a bath and decent food to eat . . .*" [22]

But utopia and revolution always lurked just beneath the surface. To the convinced Wobbly, each battle, whether for higher wages or shorter hours, better food or better bedding, prepared the participant for the final struggle with the master class. Only by daily fights with the employer could a strong revolutionary organization be formed. ". . . The very fights themselves, like the drill of an army, prepare the workers for ever greater tasks and victories." [23]

IWW leaders made no bones about their quarrel with other labor leaders who contented themselves with wringing short-term concessions from employers. Joe Ettor proudly proclaimed the IWW's unwillingness to subvert its ideas, make peace with employers, or sign protocols and contracts. Like Marx, he said, "we disdain to conceal our views, we openly declare that our ends can be attained only by the forcible overthrow of all existing conditions." "Big Jim" Larkin, émigré Irish labor leader and in 1914 a new recruit to the IWW, gloried in the IWW's refusal to endorse the palliatives and outworn nostrums (arbitration, time agreements, and protocols) proposed by the "sycophants masquerading as labor leaders, whose sole purpose in life seems to be apologizing for and defending the capitalist system of exploitation." The IWW, Larkin averred, "true to its mission as the pioneer movement of the newer time . . . advocates perpetual war, and the total abolition of wage slavery that blights humanity." Organizer James Thompson reminded government investigators that "the I.W.W. is aiming not only to better our condition now but to prepare for the revolution." He warned businessmen: "You are doomed. The best thing you can do is to look for a soft place to fall." [24]

Only the revolution could produce the dream which inspired Haywood:

. . . I have had a dream that I have in the morning and at night and during the day, that is that there will be a new society sometime in which there will be no battle between capitalist and wage earner . . . there will be no political government . . . but . . . experts will come together for the purpose of discussing the welfare of all the people and discussing the means by which the machinery can be made the slave of the people instead of a part of the people being made the slave of machinery . . .

Haywood's dream also included a day when no child would labor, when all men would work—either with brain or with muscle—when women would be fully emancipated from bondage to men, and when every aged man and woman would have at least the assurance of dying in peace.[25]

Unlike primitive millennarians, Wobblies did not expect their revolution to come about through "a divine revelation . . . an announcement from on high [or] . . . a miracle." Furthermore, they expected neither the inevitable Marxist class struggle nor the ineluctable Darwinian evolution of society alone to make their revolution. Inevitable it was, but they could assist the course of history. "Our organization is not content with merely making the prophecy," asserted *Solidarity*, "but acts upon industrial and social conditions with a view to shaping them in accord with the general tendency." [26]

To make history, as Marx advised all good radicals to do, the Wobblies followed the pattern of modern revolutionaries: they proposed a program, developed a doctrine concerning the transfer of power, and elaborated a system of organization. But unlike most other modern revolutionaries, with the exception of the anarcho-syndicalists whom they resembled, Wobblies excluded politics from any role in their struggle for utopia.

The Wobblies believed they could best make history by seizing power. He who held power ruled society. The IWW proposed to transfer power from the capitalists, who used it for anti-social purposes, to the proletariat, who, they fondly believed, would exercise it for the benefit of humanity.

In *The Iron Heel*, a novel well known to Wobblies, Jack London expressed better than any IWW pamphlet the organization's notions about power. Ernest Everhardt, London's fictional Haywood, responds to a capitalist adversary who has just given him a lesson in *realpolitik:* "Power. It is what we of the working class preach. We know and well we know by bitter experience, that no appeal for the right, for justice, can ever touch you. . . . So we have preached power." "Power will be the arbiter," Everhardt proceeds, "as it has always been the arbiter. . . . We of the labor hosts have conned that word over till our minds are all a-tingle with it. Power. It is a kingly word." [27]

The IWW's gospelers with their doctrine of power made a great deal of sense to men in the social jungle who saw naked force—by employers, police, and courts—constantly used against them. When an IWW pamphlet proclaimed, "It is the law of nature that the strong rule and the weak are enslaved," Wobblies simply recognized the reality of their own lives writ large. George Speed, an admired IWW organizer, expressed their emotions tersely. "Power," he said, "is the thing that determines everything today . . . it stands to reason that the fellow that has got the big club swings it over the balance. That is life as it exists today." When Speed asserted that neither socialism nor politics nor legislation could aid the Wobblies, and that they would suffer until they learned the uses of power, he made sense to those he represented.[28]

The IWW's antipathy toward political action also made sense to its members. Migratory workers moved too often to establish legal voting residences. Millions of immigrants lacked the franchise, as did the Negroes, the women, and the child workers to whom the IWW appealed. Even those immigrants and natives in the IWW ranks who had the right to vote nourished a deep suspicion of government. To them the policeman's club and the magistrate's edict symbolized the state's alliance with entrenched privilege. Who knew the injustices of the state better than a Wobbly imprisoned for exercising his right of free speech, or clubbed by bullying policemen while picketing peacefully for higher wages? Daily experience demonstrated the truth of Elizabeth Gurley Flynn's comment that the state was simply the slugging agency of the capitalists. Or, as *Solidarity* phrased it: all governments in history "have become cruel, corrupt, decayed and perished by reason of their own internal defects. To this rule the government of the United States is no exception." [29] Hence, Wobblies refused to believe that stuffing pieces of paper—even socialist ones—into a box would transform the basically repressive institution of the state into a humane one.

Even the wonderful list of reform legislation enacted during the Progressive years did not impress Wobblies. When IWW members were reminded of marvelous labor reforms newly placed on the statute books, their reply was: "How are they *enforced?*" To Wobblies, as to most other trade unionists, labor legislation was worthless without the organized power to enforce it on the job. Wobblies were as perceptive as AFL members in realizing that American workers were more concerned with what went on at the plant than with what transpired in the state capitol, that they cared more about a higher wage and a more secure job than about a Democratic or a Republican—or even a Socialist—victory.

By thus refusing to endorse political parties, the IWW did not, as Philip Foner asserts, divorce itself from the mainstream of the American labor movement. Quite the contrary. The IWW's political position brought the organization closer to the masses to whom it appealed and more in harmony with the attitude of AFL members—those to whom the political party and the state always remained a distant and fearful enemy.

Representing workers who could not conceive of political power as a means to alter the rules of the game, Wobblies had to offer an alternative. This they discovered in economic power. Naively believing themselves better Marxists than their socialist critics, Wobblies insisted that political power was but a reflex of economic power, and that without economic organization behind it, labor politics was "like a house without a foundation or a dream without substance." [30] IWW leaders concentrated on teaching their followers how to obtain economic power. To quote some of their favorite aphorisms: "Get it through industrial organization"; "Organize the workers to control the use of their labor power"; "The secret of power is organization"; "The only force that can break . . . tyrannical rule . . . is the one big union of all the workers." [31]

From the IWW point of view, direct action was the essential means for bringing its new society into existence. As defined by Wobblies, direct action included any step taken by workers at the point of production which improved wages, reduced hours, and bettered conditions. It encompassed conventional strikes, intermittent strikes, silent strikes, passive resistance, sabotage, and the ultimate direct-action measure: the general strike which would displace the capitalists from power and place the means of production in working-class hands.[32] "Shall I tell you what direct action really means?" an IWW manifesto asked. "The worker on the job shall tell the boss when and where he shall work, how long, and for what wages and under what conditions." Direct action, according to Haywood, would eventually reach the point at which workers would be strong enough to say: "Here, Mr. Stockholder, we won't work for you any longer. You have drawn dividends out of our hides long enough; we propose that you shall go to work now and under the same opportunities that we have had." [33]

The emphasis on direct action in preference to parliamentary politics or socialist dialectics represented a profound insight by IWW leaders into the minds of industrial workers and inhabitants of the "culture of poverty." Abstract doctrine meant nothing to the disinherited; specific grievances meant everything! Justus Ebert expressed this idea for the IWW:

Workingmen on the job don't care a whoop in hell for free love . . . they are not interested in why Bakunin was fired from the International by Marx . . . nor do they care about the co-operative commonwealth; they want practical organization first, all else after. They want to know how they can win out against the trusts and the bosses. . . . Give us specific shop methods. We plead for them.[34]

Richard Brazier on the West Coast echoed Ebert's plea. He asked fellow Wobblies to stop telling men to stay away from bum jobs; instead, Brazier urged workers to take such jobs and fight. The Philadelphia Longshoremen, an IWW affiliate which successfully used direct action and actually controlled job conditions, urged: "We have work to do. We function as a job organization and have no time to split hairs. Job control is the thing." [35] How much like the AFL!

But while the IWW's emphasis on direct action, job control, and economic power resembled the AFL's line, the Wobblies' rhetoric was of an entirely different order. Restrained in action, Wobblies were considerably less restrained in utterance. Where the AFL spoke cautiously of law and order, the IWW exuberantly discussed the law of the jungle. Where the AFL pleaded for contracts and protocols, the IWW hymned clubs and brute force. Where the AFL sought industrial harmony, the IWW praised perpetual industrial war.

Consequently, it became easy for critics of the IWW, whether on the right or the left, to listen to Wobbly speakers, to read Wobbly propaganda, and to conclude that the IWW actually *preferred* bullets to ballots, dynamite to mediation. After all, Wobblies constantly announced that their organization respected neither the property rights of capitalists nor the laws they made. *"I despise the law,"* Haywood defiantly informed a Socialist party audience, "and I am not a law-abiding citizen. And more than that, no Socialist *can* be a law-abiding citizen." Equally defiant, he told the Commission on Industrial Relations: ". . . I have been plastered up with injunctions until I do not need a suit of clothes, and I have treated them with contempt." He warned Socialist party members fearful of breaking the law and going to prison: "Those of us who are in jail—those of us who have been in jail—all of us who are willing to go to jail care not what you say or what you do! We despise your hypocrisy. . . . We are the Revolution!" [36]

Wobblies even enjoyed comparing themselves to antebellum abolitionists, who also had defied laws which sanctioned human bondage, and who had publicly burned the Constitution. As James Thompson boasted: "We are the modern abolitionists fighting against wage slavery." [37] Some Wobblies may indeed have considered unsheathing the Lord's terrible swift sword. St. John, for one, admitted under questioning that he would counsel destruction of property and violence against persons if it accomplished improvement for the workers and brought the revolution closer. Other IWW leaders conceded they would be willing to dynamite factories and mills in order to win a strike. All of them hurled their defiance at "bushwa" law.[38]

Such talk led most Americans to conclude, as did Harris Weinstock of the Federal Commission on Industrial Relations, that "it is the organized and deliberate purpose of the I.W.W. to teach and preach and to burn into the hearts and minds of its followers that they are justified in lying; that they are justified in stealing and in trampling under foot their own agreements and in confiscating the property of others . . . that it would make a Nation of thieves and liars and scoundrels." [39]

Having created this image of itself, the IWW simultaneously tried to dispel it. To the convinced Wobbly, Weinstock's words better described the practices and attitudes of the American capitalist. Although the IWW employed the vocabulary of violence, more often than not it practiced passive resistance, and was itself the victim of violence instigated by law-enforcement officials and condoned by the law-abiding. In fact, even the Wobblies' vocabulary was ambivalent, the language of nonviolence being employed at least as frequently as that of violence. Big Bill Haywood, for example, whose career with the WFM had been associated with labor violence, told a reporter during the 1912 Lawrence textile strike: "I should never think of conducting a strike in the old way. . . . I, for one, have turned my back on violence. It wins nothing. When we strike now, we strike with our hands in our pockets. We have a new kind of violence—the havoc we raise with money by laying down our tools. Pure strength lies in the overwhelming power of numbers." [40]

Any careful investigator of the IWW soon becomes aware that the organization regularly proclaimed the superiority of passive resistance over the use of dynamite or guns. Vincent St. John, while conceding the possible usefulness of violence under certain circumstances, nevertheless insisted: "We do not . . . want to be understood as saying that we expect to achieve our aims through violence and through the destruction of human life, because in my judgment, that is impossible." Joe Ettor similarly commented: ". . . We are organized against violence, and our war cry is 'War against war.'" Haywood remarked in 1912 that he regarded hunger strikes as "action more violent than the discharge of bombs in St. Patrick's Cathedral." [41] Big Bill now looked forward to a "bloodless revolution."

Solidarity, the *Industrial Worker*, and IWW pamphlets all preached the same nonviolent message. The *Industrial Worker* cautioned members against being misled by *agents provocateurs* into resorting to violent means of economic action. *Solidarity* noted: "The revolutionary industrial union promises the only possible safeguard against violence in industrial warfare." Sometimes it puts its position another way: "Our dynamite is mental and our force is in organization at the point of production." Again and again IWW publications advised members: "*We do not advocate violence;* it is to be discouraged." [42]

In actuality, Wobblies looked to *nonviolent* tactics in order to throw into sharper relief the brutality of their enemy, and to win sympathy for their sufferings. Passive resistance, *Solidarity* editorialized, "has a tremendous moral effect; it puts the enemy on record; it exposes the police and city authorities as a bunch of law breakers; it drives the masters to the last ditch of resistance. 'Passive resistance' by the workers results in laying bare the inner workings and purposes of the capitalist mind. It also reveals the self-control, the fortitude, the courage, the inherent sense of order, of the workers' mind. As such, 'passive resistance' is of immense educational value." [43]

But IWW passive resistance should not be confused with pacifism. Nonviolence was only a means, never an end. If passive resistance resulted only in beatings and deaths, then the IWW threatened to respond in kind. Arturo Giovannitti, sometime poet and Wobbly, put the IWW's position bluntly: "The generally accepted notion seems to be that to kill is a great crime, but to be killed is the greatest." Haywood cited Abraham Lincoln's alleged advice to citizens suffering from hunger as a result of wartime food speculation: "Take your pickaxes and crowbars and go to the granaries and warehouses and help yourselves . . ." That, said Haywood, "is good I.W.W. doctrine." [44]

In most cases the IWW hoped to gain its ends through nonviolent measures, through what it described as "Force of education, force of organization, force of a growing class-consciousness and force of working class aspirations for freedom." [45] One forceful method explicitly advocated by the Wobblies—indeed, the tactic with which they are most indelibly associated—was sabotage. To most Americans, sabotage implied the needless destruction of property, the senseless adulteration of products, and, possibly, the inexcusable injuring of persons. Wobblies did not always dispel such images. The *Industrial Worker* suggested to harvest hands in 1910: "Grain sacks come loose and rip, nuts come off wagon wheels and loads are dumped on the way to the barn, machinery breaks down, nobody to blame, everybody innocent . . . boss decides to furnish a little inspiration in the shape of more money and shorter hours . . . just try a little sabotage on the kind hearted, benevolent boss . . . and see how it works." For the next three years the paper continued to urge this method upon its readers, telling them: "Sabotage is an awakening of labor. It is the spirit of revolt." This campaign culminated in 1913 with a series of twelve editorials fully explaining the methods of sabotage and when they should be utilized.[46]

Eastern Wobblies proved no less restrained in their emphasis on sabotage. Haywood informed the same Socialist party audience mentioned above, which he had encouraged to break the law: "I don't know of anything that can be applied that will bring as much anguish to the boss as a little sabotage in the right place at the proper time. Find out what it means. It won't hurt you, and it will cripple the boss." To help Wobblies find out what sabotage meant, Elizabeth Gurley Flynn prepared a new translation of Emile Pouget's classic, *Sabotage,* which the IWW published and distributed in 1915. Even Ben Williams, generally unenthusiastic about the effectiveness of sabotage, felt constrained to recommend its use. "Sabotage has great possibilities as a means of defense and aggression," he explained. "It is useless to try to argue it out of existence. We need not 'advocate it,' we need only explain it. The organized workers will do the acting." [47]

What was actually meant by all this talk? Some Wobblies might have agreed with James Thompson, who said, ". . . I not only believe in destruction of property, but I believe in the destruction of human life if it will save human life." But most stressed sabotage's nonviolent characteristics. Repeatedly, IWW speakers asserted that sabotage simply implied soldiering on the job, playing dumb, tampering with machines without destroying them—in short, simply harassing the employer to the point of granting his workers' demands. Sometimes, it was claimed, the workers could even effect sabotage through exceptional obedience: Williams and Haywood were fond of noting that Italian and French workers had on occasion tied up the national railroads simply by observing every operating rule in their work regulations. They suggested that laborers refuse to cooperate in the adulteration of products, and that labor unions warn consumers against purchasing inferior goods. That, the Wobblies argued, was benevolent sabotage: *"sabotage not aimed at the consumer but at the heart and soul of the employing class—the pocketbook."* [48]

One might scarcely expect the typical Wobbly to comprehend the subtleties of nonviolent as compared to violent sabotage. Sabotage, after all, is a weapon of the disorganized, the defeated, the dejected, and, as such, it must have had great appeal to workers drawn from the "culture of poverty." What better way to strike back against one's enemy than to destroy what he most worships—in this case, private property! Yet, hard as they tried, state and federal authorities could never establish legal proof of IWW-instigated sabotage. Rudolph Katz, a DeLeonite who had followed his leader out of the St. John IWW in 1908, was perhaps close to the truth when he informed federal investigators: ". . . The American Federation of Labor does not preach sabotage, but it practices sabotage; and the . . . I.W.W. preaches sabotage, but does not practice it." [49]

Wobbly ideology and tactics explained why Katz was right. In revealing testimony before the Commission on Industrial Relations, Jim Thompson declared: "The greatest weapon in the hands of the working class is economic power. . . . All we have to do is fold our arms and industry is paralyzed. . . . I would much prefer as a lesson to . . . other workers . . . instead of destroying the street car in times of a street car strike that they should stop that car by shutting off the juice at the power house. That would be a lesson." Ben Williams phrased this attitude simply: "Organized a little we control a little; organized more we control more; organized as a class we control everything." [50]

Until the IWW succeeded in organizing all workers into industrial unions which combined to form the celebrated "One Big Union" which would eventually seize control of industry, it had to employ practices and tactics much like those of any labor union. Accordingly, the IWW encouraged strikes to win immediate improvements in working conditions, for such strikes served a dual purpose: they offered the men involved valuable experience in the class struggle and developed their sense of *power*, and they weakened the capitalist's power. When conventional strikes failed, the IWW recommended the on-the-job strike—essentially a form of nonviolent sabotage—and the intermittent or short strike begun when the boss least expected it and ended before the strikers could be starved or beaten. [51]

The IWW never lost its vision of the ultimate revolution. Thus, many demands associated with AFL industrial conflicts were absent from those of the IWW. With improvements in working conditions, the AFL unions demanded recognition and ironclad contracts. The IWW spurned both. It would achieve its closed shop "by having an 'open union' for everybody who toils." In other words, collective action and voluntary cooperation by the exploited, not capitalist concessions, would bring the true closed shop. Wobblies were convinced that employer benevolence only lessened working-class solidarity. For somewhat similar reasons, the IWW refused to sign contracts which restricted the right to strike for stated periods of time. All workers had to retain the right to strike simultaneously, the IWW reasoned, or employers could play one group of workers off against another, as had happened time and again in the AFL's history. No agreement could be allowed to impinge upon the IWW's governing principle: "An injury to one is the concern of all." Workers, moreover, had to be free to strike when employers were weakest, but time contracts provided employers with the option to choose the moment of conflict and

164

to prepare for it in advance. Finally, without the unreserved right to strike, the IWW could not wage the class war, and without the on-going class struggle there could be no revolution and no cooperative commonwealth.[52]

But even on the issue of time contracts the IWW could be ambivalent, conceding the possibility that it might sign agreements which concerned only wages, hours, and conditions of work. Nevertheless, it regularly reiterated its belief that employers had no rights that workers were obliged to respect. "The contract between an employer and a workman is no more binding than the title deed to a negro slave is just." [53]

The organization's refusal to sign contracts raised problems that the IWW never resolved. American employers were never particularly happy dealing with labor unions, and certainly under no circumstances would they negotiate with a labor organization that refused to sign contracts and insisted that capitalists had no rights worthy of respect. Hence, employers constantly used the IWW's no-contract principle to rationalize their own resistance to any form of collective bargaining. If the IWW could not negotiate with employers, how could it raise wages or improve working conditions? If it could offer its members nothing but perpetual industrial warfare, how could it maintain its membership, let alone increase its ranks? On the other hand, if the IWW did sanction contracts, win recognition, and improve its members' lives, what would keep them from forsaking revolutionary goals and adhering to the well-established AFL pattern? If the IWW began to declare truces in the class war, how could it bring about the ultimate revolution? In the end, IWW leaders usually subordinated reform opportunities to revolutionary necessities, while the rank and file, when it could, took the reforms and neglected the revolution.

Even for those Wobblies who cherished the hope of revolution, the means of achieving their dream remained vague. Politics or working-class violence would not accomplish it. What, then, remained? "In a word," wrote Haywood and Ettor, "the general strike is the measure by which the capitalistic system will be overthrown." [54]

Neither Haywood nor any other Wobbly ever precisely defined the general strike. Haywood described it as the stoppage of all work and the destruction of the capitalists through a peaceful paralysis of industry. Ben Williams insisted that it was not a strike at all, simply "a 'general lockout of the employing class' leaving the workers in possession of the machinery of distribution and production." Whatever the exact definition of the general strike, Haywood wrote, when its day comes ". . . control of industry will pass from the capitalists to the masses and capitalists will vanish from the face of the earth." [55] That utopian day would come peaceably if workers had their way, violently if capitalists attempted to postpone it with "roar of shell and whine of machine-guns."

The precise date of the general strike which would usher in the arrival of the IWW's utopia remained as vague for Wobblies as the millennium, or Judgment Day, does for Christians. But the *prospect* of such a Judgment Day was intended to stir among the toiling masses the same ecstatic belief and fanaticism that anticipation of the Second Coming arouses among evangelical Christians. Only with such true believers could the IWW build its One Big Union which would, when fully organized, ring the death knell for American capitalism. In other words, in IWW ideology workers represented a chosen people who, through faith and works—faith in the One Big Union and such works as peaceful sabotage—would attain salvation and enter the Kingdom of Heaven here on earth.

In a jail cell in Aberdeen, Washington, John Pancner dreamed the pleasures of an IWW utopia, where there would be no poverty, jails, police, army, or marines; no Christians, no churches, no heaven or hell. The cities would be clean and beautiful, filled with wide streets, parks, flowers, and fine homes; the workers would be "no longer stoop shouldered and consumptive looking . . ." Prudery would have vanished, and naked children would frisk on the grass and bask in the sun. Economic freedom, plus an abundance of food, shelter, clothing, leisure, and education, would lead "all hearts and minds . . . [to] turn . . . towards solving the mysteries of the Universe." [56]

Wobblies never quite explained how their terrestrial paradise would be governed. They did agree that the state, as most Americans knew it, would be nonexistent. "There will be no such thing as the State or States," Haywood said. "The industries will take the place of what are now existing States." "Whenever the workers are organized in the industry, whenever they have a sufficient organization in the industry," added St. John, "they will have all the government they need right there." Somehow each industrial union would possess and manage its own industry. Union members would elect superintendents, foremen, secretaries, and all the managers of modern industry. The separate industrial unions would also meet jointly to plan for the welfare of the entire society. This system, "in which each worker will have a share in the ownership and a voice in the control of industry, and in which each shall receive the full product of his labor," was variously called the "Cooperative Commonwealth," the "Workers' Commonwealth," the "Industrial Commonwealth," "Industrial Democracy," and "Industrial Communism." [57] Unsure of what their system was, the Wobblies could not label it.

Perhaps Ben Williams came closest to describing how the IWW commonwealth would function. Writing primarily about city government, Williams suggested that every aspect of urban life would be managed by different groups of municipal workers, "their efforts being correlated by whatever central body they may find necessary. The members of that central body will not be 'placemen' or 'politicians,' but *technical experts*, trained for that special service" [italics added]. Haywood also foresaw a future society molded and managed by experts in the different branches of industry, "brain workers" who directed the activities of scientifically organized laborers.[58]

A future society based upon "brain workers," technical experts, and scientific controls resembled St. Simon's ideal state or Bellamy's society of the year 2000 more than it did the Marxian "dictatorship of the proletariat," or the revisionist socialist's equalitarian parliamentary society. It was this aspect of the IWW, combined with its abiding distrust of political parties and the state, which made the American Industrial Workers so much like the continental European syndicalists of the same era.

It was in their views about the general strike and the governance of utopia that Wobblies diverged farthest from the modern revolutionary spirit, for these two vital matters were indeed left as vague as the primitive millennarians' eschatology. How the IWW expected to displace capitalism from power peaceably, when the masters of "The Iron Heel" couched their answer in "roar of shell and whine of machine-guns," advocates of the general strike failed to explain. How the IWW would defend its utopia from counterrevolutionary terror, supporters of its syndicalist commonwealth never clarified. Like primitive millennarians, but unlike modern revolutionaries, Wobblies almost expected their revolution to make itself, if not by divine revelation, at least by a miracle (secular, of course). Some Wobblies even saw the roots of their doctrine in the works of the "Hobo Carpenter from Nazareth," whose call, "stripped of the mystical and mythical veil of Constantine and his successors, and clothed in the original garb of communism and brotherhood, continues to sound intermittently across the ages." [59]

While IWW ideology derived much of its spirit from Socialist party doctrine, the two maintained only an uneasy harmony. Both Wobblies and Socialists drew their inspiration from similar ideological sources, both opposed the capitalist order, and both demanded the establishment of a just and equalitarian new order. Beyond that, they conflicted more often than they agreed.

Industrial unionism, Haywood once said, was socialism with its working clothes on. But after 1913, when Haywood was recalled from the Socialist party's National Executive Committee, IWW industrial unionists and American Socialists had little in common. When Socialists talked of capturing control of existing government through the ballot box and transforming the capitalist state into the Cooperative Commonwealth, the IWW responded with a proverb: "A wise tailor does not put stitches into rotten cloth." To American Socialists who prided themselves on their intellectual abilities, Haywood asserted: "Socialism is so plain, so clear, so simple that when a person becomes an intellectual he doesn't understand socialism." [60]

In short, American Socialists, optimistic about their future prospects and eager to widen the popular base of their party, subordinated revolutionary fervor to the cause of immediate reform and popular acceptance. Wobblies, more pessimistic about the future and more respectful of capitalism's staying power, tried to instill revolutionary fervor in their adherents. The Socialist party, unlike the IWW, had no room for men who counseled defiance of the law, neglect of the ballot box, and "real" revolution. Hence Haywood's recall from the National

Executive Committee in 1913. After that date, though some "left-wing" Socialists still looked to the IWW as the hope of the working class and the vanguard of revolution, most Socialists and Wobblies went their own separate ways—ideologically as well as organizationally.[61]

Actually, as Will Herberg perceptively pointed out more than fifteen years ago, the IWW was much more the left wing of the American labor movement than of the socialist movement. Herberg emphasized that the AFL's early approach, "with its stress on proletarian direct action and its marked distrust of government and politics, shows definite affinity to basic syndicalism. It differs from the more familiar radical variety of syndicalism in very much the same way as the gradualistic socialism of Eduard Bernstein differed from the revolutionary socialism of his orthodox opponents." [62] What Bernstein and evolutionary socialism were to Marx and revolutionary socialism, Gompers and the AFL were to St. John, Haywood, and radical syndicalism.

Indeed, the IWW *was* the American variety of the syndicalism which at that time was sweeping across the Italian, French, and Scandinavian labor movements. There is no escaping the similarities. Even when the IWW denied its syndicalist nature, it would simultaneously counsel syndicalist principles. One editorialist, for example, while maintaining that the IWW was not a syndicalist organization but an industrial union, went on to assert: "Industrial unionism accepts all of the syndicalist tactics that experience has shown to be available for present purposes." Despite the fuzzy-mindedness of some Wobbly thinkers, there was absolutely no incompatibility between industrial unionism and syndicalism. The IWW even took over George Sorel's syndicalist concept of the militant minority, claiming in the words of the *Industrial Worker:* "Our task is to develop the conscious, intelligent minority to the point where they will be capable of carrying out the imperfectly expressed desires of the toiling millions," who were still "hopelessly stupid and stupidly hopeless." [63] Whenever some Wobblies attempted to dispute their organization's syndicalist tendencies, other more perceptive members stressed the IWW's basic similarity to European syndicalism. John Sandgren, a Swedish immigrant and IWW theorist who maintained close contact with the labor movement of his native land, tried to impress upon Wobblies their obvious likeness to Scandinavian syndicalists. The Socialist Robert Rives LaMonte, while acknowledging that "because Revolutionary Unionism is the child of economic and political conditions, it differs in different countries," nevertheless firmly asserted: "In spite of superficial differences this living spirit of revolutionary purpose unifies French and British syndicalism and American Industrial Unionism. To forget or even make light of this underlying identity can but substitute muddle-headed confusion for clear thinking." [64] Finally, John Spargo's 1913 definition of syndicalism clearly encompasses the IWW's mode of operation. Syndicalism, he wrote,

is a form of labor unionism which aims at the abolition of the capitalist system. . . . Its distinctive principle as a practical movement is that these ends are to be attained by the direct action of the unions, without parliamentary action or the intervention of the State. The distinctive feature of its ideal is that in the new social order the political state will not exist, the only form of government being the administration of industry directly by the workers themselves.[65]

Certainly nobody should expect American syndicalism to be precisely like that of France or Italy; also, nobody should seek to explain the emergence of syndicalism in America, as does Philip Foner, by tracing its roots to Europe and then treating it as a foreign import transplanted to fertile native soil.

In the final analysis, ideological disputation remained a form of academic nitpicking to most Wobblies, for the organization always appealed to the activist rather than the intellectual. It sought to motivate the disinherited, not to satisfy the ideologue. As an IWW member, reviewing John Graham Brooks's *American Syndicalism*, noted: "It is not the Sorels . . . the Wallings, LaMontes and such figures who count the most—it is the obscure Bill Jones on the firing line, with stink in his clothes, rebellion in his brain, hope in his heart, determination in his eye and direct action in his gnarled fist." [66] To such as "Bill Jones" the IWW carried its gospel from 1909 to 1917.

PART THREE

Free Speech and
Free Men,
1909–1917

CHAPTER

8

The Fight for Free Speech,
1909–1912

"Quit your job. Go to Missoula. Fight with the Lumber Jacks for Free Speech," the *Industrial Worker* encouraged its readers on September 30, 1909. "Are you game? Are you afraid? Do you love the police? Have you been robbed, skinned, grafted on? If so, then go to Missoula, and defy the police, the courts and the people who live off the wages of prostitution." Thus did the IWW proclaim the first of its many fights for free speech.

Many years after the IWW's free-speech fights had faded from public memory, Roger Baldwin, founding father of the American Civil Liberties Union, recalled that the Wobblies "wrote a chapter in the history of American liberties like that of the struggle of the Quakers for freedom to meet and worship, of the militant suffragists to carry their propaganda to the seats of government, and of the Abolitionists to be heard. . . . The little minority of the working class represented in the I.W.W. blazed the trail in those ten years of fighting for free speech [1908-1918] which the entire American working class must in some fashion follow." [1]

For Wobblies free-speech fights involved nothing so abstract as defending the Constitution, preserving the Bill of Rights, or protecting the civil liberties of American citizens. They were instigated primarily to overcome resistance to IWW organizing tactics and also to demonstrate that America's dispossessed could, through direct action, challenge established authority. To workers dubious about the results

173

achieved by legal action and the reforms won through political action, the IWW taught the effectiveness of victories gained through a strategy of open, yet nonviolent confrontations with public officials. Roger Baldwin perceived as much when, writing long before the post-1954 civil rights movement had made the strategy of confrontation a commonplace of American protest movements, he commented about the IWW's approach: "Far more effective is this direct action of open conflict than all the legal maneuvers in the courts to get rights that no government willingly grants. Power wins rights—the power of determination, backed by ·willingness to suffer jail or violence, to get them." [2]

The IWW and its members did challenge the law and endure violence and imprisonment to win free speech—that is, the right for their soapboxers to stand on street corners, or in front of employment offices, and harangue working-class crowds about the iniquities of capitalism and the decay of American society. But behind the right to speak freely lay more important IWW goals. Many Wobblies considered street speaking the most effective means of carrying their gospel to Western workers. They had solid evidence for this belief. Experience had demonstrated that it was almost impossible for organizers to reach timber workers, construction hands, and harvesters out on the job where watchful employers harassed "labor agitators" and where workers were scattered over a vast geographical area. Only in the city did Western workers concentrate in sufficiently large numbers to be reached effectively by the handful of organizers proselytizing for the IWW, and only in the city did the "agitator" have a measure of freedom to recruit without interference by employers. Many an IWW recruit—among them, Richard Brazier, who later became a leader in the Northwest and also a member of the general executive board—testified to how urban soapboxers such as Joe Ettor aroused his initial interest in the IWW. The IWW and the Western workers also had a common enemy in the city: the employment agent or "shark." These "sharks," against whom the IWW directed most of its street-corner harangues, controlled employment in agriculture and lumber. With anti-union employers they maintained the heavy labor turnover among the unskilled workers—one on the way, one on the job, one leaving—that kept labor organization out of the fields and forests, wages low, and working conditions primitive. The heavy labor turnover guaranteed substantial commissions to the employment agencies that located jobs for the unemployed, as well as large payoffs to cooperating managers and foremen. If the IWW could break the links connecting the "shark," the employer, and the transient laborer, it could loosen the heavy chain of economic circumstances that kept the Western worker in semi-bondage.

Breaking the hold of the employment agencies on the job market would be the initial step in improving working conditions and raising wages, results which would themselves insure a sharp rise in IWW membership. With this in mind, IWW organizers, conceding that industrial conflict belonged in the *shop*, not on the street, stressed: ". . . To carry the war into the shop we must first get into the shop—in this case the camp. To control the source of supply in the industrial cities by forcing the employers to hire men through the I.W.W. is a great step in the direction of industrial control." [3] Put differently, this meant that Western migratories had to be organized before going out on the job, which might last only a few days; and this, in turn, could be accomplished only by controlling the employment agencies, or abolishing them and replacing them with IWW hiring halls. Here is the primary reason the IWW demanded free speech in Spokane, Fresno, Missoula, Aberdeen, Minot, Kansas City, and scores of other Western cities where migratories laid over between jobs, or patronized employment agencies to find new jobs. Three of these many free-speech struggles reveal the pattern of IWW confrontations and their role in the history and development of the organization: Spokane, 1909–1910; Fresno, 1910–1911; and San Diego, 1912.

The first significant IWW struggle for free speech erupted in Spokane, Washington, the hub of the Inland Empire's agricultural, mining, and lumber industries and the central metropolis for all of western Washington, western Oregon, and northern Idaho. Here employers came to locate labor for the mines of the Coeur d'Alenes, the woods of the interior, and the farms of the Palouse and other inland valleys. Migratory workers came to rest up in Spokane during the winter after a long hard harvest summer or an equally arduous season of railroad construction work. In Spokane workers discovered cheap skid-row hotels and cheaper whisky and women to spend their skimpy savings on. When spring approached and savings dwindled, the migratories could turn to the "sharks," who for a price offered another season of employment out in the countryside or forest.

What the IWW accomplished in Spokane was in some·respects truly remarkable. Recruiting largely among workers whose lives were often brutal and violent and who had a view of masculinity somewhat akin to the Latin idea of *machismo,* the IWW channeled working-class hostility toward employment agencies into constructive courses. Soapboxers warned angry workers that broken heads and shattered windows would not put the "sharks out of business." No! they thundered. "There is only one way you can get out of their hold. That is by joining the I.W.W. and refusing to go to them for jobs." [4]

The IWW's message was heard. Overalls Brigade "General" J. H. Walsh had come to Spokane after the 1908 convention, and within six months rejuvenated a previously moribund IWW local. The re-vitalized union leased expensive new headquarters which included a large library and reading room, ample office space, and an assembly hall seating several hundred. It held inside propaganda meetings four nights a week, operated its own cigar and newsstand, and even fea-tured regular movies: from conventional one-reelers to illustrated rebel songs and dry economic lectures. When local authorities restricted street speaking, the Spokane local published its own newspaper, the *Industrial Worker,* which reached a wide local working-class audience. Walsh's local even retained a Spokane law firm on a yearly retainer, as well as maintaining a voluntary hospital plan for members. All this was supported from March to April 1909 by the dues of twelve hundred to fifteen hundred members in good standing and double that number on the local's books.[5] For the first time, or so it now seemed, a labor organization had succeeded in reaching the Inland Empire's migratory workers.

IWW growth brought an immediate and inevitable reaction from Spokane's employers, "sharks," and officials. In March 1909 the city council, acting on complaints from the chamber of commerce, pro-hibited street-corner orations by closing Spokane's streets to Wobblies and all other "revolutionists." It did so partly because the soapboxers castigated organized religion and partly because IWW oratory had a greater effect than "respectable" citizens realized upon "the army of the unemployed and poorly paid workers." Spokane's city council's action was in accord with the observation made by a later federal investigator that the IWW's right to speak should be restricted when the organization denounced "everything we have been taught to respect from our earliest days . . . all kinds of religions and religious sects . . ." 6 Christianity and patriotism thus became the employment agents' first line of defense against the IWW onslaught. Thus, Spokane's initial street-speaking ordinance allowed religious groups, most notably the Salvation Army, the IWW's major competitor, the right to speak on the city's streets.

The IWW maintained that its organizers would continue speaking until the ordinance was repealed or made binding upon all organizations. On March 4 the city council placed religious groups under the ban, but the IWW remained unsatisfied. That very day J. H. Walsh himself mounted a soapbox and addressed his "fellow workers and friends," only to be hauled off to jail by local police. Later he was tried, convicted, and fined for violating the local street-speaking ordinance. For the next several days, as Walsh's legal appeals moved through the various courts, Wobblies spoke on Spokane's streets—and were promptly arrested and jailed. As the number of those arrested rose, so did the fines and the length of imprisonment. In March 1909 Spokane's jail filled with Wobblies, ten to twelve men crammed in cells built to accommodate only four. The free-speech prisoners, fed a diet of bread and water twice daily, could neither lie nor sit down. One Wobbly later recalled: "The misery in those cells was something never to be forgotten . . ." 7

But the Wobblies refused to give up the struggle. Instead, they sang revolutionary songs, refused to work on the jail rock pile, held daily business meetings, made speeches, and preserved their militancy even within the prison walls. Those who passed by Spokane's jail during those March days must have thought it an odd prison, when they heard the words of the "Red Flag" or the "Marseillaise" filtering out from behind the bars.

As spring approached, the migratories began to leave Spokane for the countryside. Under these circumstances, city authorities released the imprisoned Wobblies, while state courts considered the constitutionality of Spokane's street-speaking ordinance. Spring and summer were not the time for the IWW to contend for free speech: it had to wait for its members to return for another winter in the city.

With the bulk of the migratories temporarily away, Spokane's officials acted to avert another winter of discontent and tumult. On August 10 the city council enacted a revised law that allowed religious groups to hold street meetings but required all other organizations to obtain permits before doing so. The *Industrial Worker* promptly warned the city fathers that the IWW would not ask permission to speak on streets its members had built. "The toad-eaters who make up the Spokane city council are afraid of the I.W.W.," a Wobbly rhetorician noted in an editorial. "Even the devil is not afraid of the Starvation Army." [8] Thus a renewed clash between Wobblies and public authorities awaited summer's end.

Summer ended, the migratories returned to Spokane, and IWW soapboxers again took to the streets. The inevitable followed. On Monday, October 25, the police arrested Jim Thompson for street speaking without a permit. The IWW promptly demanded the inalienable right of free speech and also declared that it would send as many men to Spokane as were needed to win its struggle. Despite the IWW's threat and a legal ruling declaring the revised street-speaking ordinance discriminatory and unconstitutional, the battle continued to rage. On November 1, the day of the legal decision ruling the ban on speaking unconstitutional, the IWW initiated round-the-clock street meetings. Spokane's police promptly arrested each speaker who mounted a soapbox. Before long the city jail held every local IWW leader: Walter Nef, Jim Thompson, James Wilson, C. L. Filigno, and A. C. Cousins. Those not hauled off a soapbox were picked up in a police raid on IWW headquarters, which also netted three female sympathizers. The arrested Wobblies went to jail peaceably, for, as the *Industrial Worker* advised its readers, "it must be understood that any person, at any time, who would try to incite disorder or 'rioting' is an enemy of the I.W.W. Nothing of the kind will be tolerated at this time." [9] Passive resistance and confrontation tactics as a form of direct action were being put to the test in Spokane.

The city fathers used every instrument of power they controlled to thwart the IWW. Before the battle ended almost four hundred Wobblies had been jailed. For a time, public officials reasoned that if they could incapacitate the IWW's leaders, the fight would dissipate. Such reasoning lay behind the city's decision to raid IWW headquarters on November 3, and to arrest local Wobblies on criminal conspiracy charges; it was also behind the move to arrest the editors of the *Industrial Worker*. None of this decisively stifled the Wobblies, however, for as one policeman remarked: "Hell! we got the leaders, but damned if it don't look like they are all leaders." [10]

After their arrest Wobblies received a further taste of Spokane justice. When Frank Little appeared in court, the presiding magistrate asked him what he had been doing at the time of his arrest. "Reading the Declaration of Independence," Little answered. "Thirty days," said the magistrate. The prosecuting attorney demanded that the IWW "feel the mailed fist of the law," which for those leaders charged with criminal conspiracy meant four to six months in jail. For most Wobblies arrested for disorderly conduct the sentence was thirty days, then release, followed by further street speaking and another thirty-day sentence. This legal treatment, most Wobblies thought, justified their definition of government "as the slugging committee of the capitalist class." [11]

In Spokane, indeed, slugging soon became more than merely rhetorical. Arresting police officers used their clubs liberally. Jail life proved even worse: twenty-eight to thirty Wobblies would be tossed into an eight-by-six-foot sweatbox, where they would steam for a full day while staring at bloodstained walls.[12] After that they would be moved into an ice-cold cell without cots or blankets. Those who did not weaken from the heat of the first cell often collapsed from the chill of the second. Because Spokane's regular jails could not accommodate the hordes of IWW prisoners, the city converted an unheated, abandoned schoolhouse into a temporary prison. There in mid-winter jailers offered scantily clad prisoners two ounces of bread daily, soft pine for a pillow, and hardwood for a bed. Inside the schoolhouse guards woke the inmates at all hours of the night and then chased them from room to room. Under these conditions some Wobblies fell ill; others, no longer able to stand the strain, collapsed in the middle of the floor; still others maintained their spirits by walking around in a circle singing the "Red Flag." Once a week the school's jailers marched the prisoners out in order to have them bathe for allegedly sanitary reasons. Taken to the city jail, the Wobblies were stripped, thrust under an ice-cold shower, and then, frequently in frigid weather, marched back to their unheated prison.

The IWW estimated that, as a result of this treatment, 334 of the 400 men in prison for 110 days (from November through March) were treated in the emergency hospital a total of 1,600 times. Many left prison with permanent scars and missing teeth; the more fortunate walked away with weakened constitutions.

When police repression and prison brutality failed to weaken the Wobblies' resistance, the authorities resorted to different tactics. After raiding and closing IWW headquarters, they denied every hall in Spokane, except Turner Hall, to the Wobblies. Police seized copies of the *Industrial Worker* and arrested the men—even the boys—who peddled the paper. Unable to function in Spokane, the IWW moved its headquarters and all its defense activities to Coeur d'Alene City under the direction of Fred Heslewood, and published the *Industrial Worker* in Seattle. In the face of relentless repression, the IWW resisted.

The IWW ultimately triumphed because of the spirit and determination of its members. When IWW headquarters pleaded for volunteers to fight for free speech, scores of Wobblies descended upon Spokane. One Wobbly left Minneapolis on November 10, traveling across North Dakota and Montana atop a Pullman car despite subzero temperatures. Arriving in Spokane on November 21, somewhat chilled but ready to fight, he was arrested by police two days later. He was not alone: hundreds like him came to Spokane, and hundreds more were ready to come. All intended to make the free-speech fight an expensive and difficult proposition for Spokane's taxpayers. "Let them cry quits to their Mayor and police force if they do not relish it," threatened the Wobblies. "We can keep up the fight all winter." [13]

No one better exemplified this IWW spirit than the "Rebel Girl," Elizabeth Gurley Flynn.[14] Only nineteen years old and recently released from a Missoula jail (where another free-speech battle had ended), she was several months pregnant when she arrived in Spokane in November 1909. Local papers described her at that time as a "frail, slender girl, pretty and graceful, with a resonant voice and a fiery eloquence that attracted huge crowds." Another observer pictured her as a little woman, Irish all over, with "the Celt in her grey-blue eyes and almost black hair and in the way she clenches her small hands into fists when she's speaking." To Woodrow Wilson, she described herself in 1918 as "an humble and obscure citizen who has struggled for democracy as her vision glimpsed it and who has suffered for espousing an unpopular and much misrepresented point of view. . . . For seven years I have supported my child, and helped to educate two sisters . . . and a brother . . . This . . . has been a labor of love, but it is rather incompatible with the popular conception of a 'labor agitator.' " [15]

Elizabeth Gurley Flynn, however, was all agitator. Daughter of immigrant Irish parents, at fifteen or sixteen she made her first speech as a "materialistic socialist" before her father's radical club in Harlem; at seventeen she had been arrested for street speaking in New York; and at nineteen she was jailed, first in Missoula, then in Spokane. So adept an agitator was she that the Spokane authorities considered her the most dangerous and effective of Wobbly soapboxers. When a young attorney suggested to the city fathers that she not be tried along with the men on charges of criminal conspiracy, the local officials responded: "Hell, no! You just don't understand. She's the one we are after. She makes all the trouble. She puts fight into the men, gets them the publicity they enjoy. As it is, they're having the time of their lives." [16]

Spokane brought Elizabeth Gurley Flynn to trial on charges of criminal conspiracy with a young Italian Wobbly named Charley Filigno. Not unexpectedly, the jury declared on February 24, 1910: "Filigno, guilty. Elizabeth Gurley Flynn, not guilty." An enraged prosecutor demanded of the jury foreman, "What in hell do you fellows mean by acquitting the most guilty, and convicting the man, far less guilty." To which the foreman calmly replied: "She ain't a criminal, Fred, an' you know it! If you think this jury, or any jury, is goin' to send that pretty Irish girl to jail merely for bein' bighearted and idealistic, to mix with all those whores and crooks down at the pen, you've got another guess comin'." [17]

But looks can be deceiving, and in Elizabeth Gurley Flynn's case they certainly were. After the fight in Spokane she proceeded to bigger and better battles. She was with the IWW at Lawrence, Paterson, and Everett. Still later, with Roger Baldwin, she helped found the American Civil Liberties Union, and fought to defend the rights of the poor and the exploited. Her vision of democracy as she glimpsed it took her from the Socialist party to the IWW to the ACLU and ultimately in the 1930's to the Communist party. During the forties and fifties she became American communism's leading female advocate as well as the only woman ever sentenced to a prison term under the Smith Act. While in Moscow attending a Soviet party congress in her capacity as chairman of the American Communist party, she died on September 5, 1964, at the age of seventy-four. From her first speech before the Harlem Socialist Club as a teen-ager to her last talk as a Communist, Elizabeth Gurley Flynn remained true to what she allegedly told theatrical producer David Belasco, upon turning down a part in a Broadway play: "I don't want to be an actress! I'm in the labor movement and I speak my own piece." [18]

The piece she spoke in Spokane in the winter of 1909–1910 aided the IWW immeasurably. She won national attention and sympathy that no male agitator could. Her clash with local authorities, her arrest, and the despicable treatment she received in jail made nationwide headlines. She exemplified the IWW's determination to win free speech in Spokane. If repression could not break the spirit of a pregnant, slightly built, teen-age girl, how could it crush the Wobblies' free-speech fighters flooding into Spokane in an unending stream?

Yet the Spokane struggle continued through the winter of 1910, as public officials resorted to further repressive measures. On February 22 Spokane officials crossed the state line into Idaho, raided IWW defense headquarters in Coeur d'Alene City, and arrested Fred Heslewood on a fugitive warrant. In response the IWW advised its members: "Let us go to Spokane, fill their jails and overthrow the whole tottering edifice of corruption misnamed the Spokane City Government." Five thousand volunteers were asked to demonstrate their contempt for the "slugging committee of the capitalist class." [19]

Faced with this unrelenting nonviolent resistance, city officials finally weakened. From the IWW's point of view, Spokane's authorities chose a propitious moment for compromise, for by the end of February the Wobblies also were weakening in their resolve. St. John and other IWW officials found it harder and harder to recruit volunteers for the Spokane fight. When spring came it would be even more difficult. Acting the part of realists, not visionary revolutionaries, a three-man IWW committee, including William Z. Foster, a new member, approached Spokane's mayor to discuss peace terms. The mayor at first proved unresponsive. He approved the IWW's defense of free speech, yet stressed that street speaking would not be tolerated when it interefered with the normal flow of traffic or the business of citizens —a decision that would be made by responsible public officials. The mayor further reminded the IWW committee that only the city council and the courts could determine the constitutionality of city restrictions on street speaking. Somewhat ominously, he warned that continued IWW free-speech activities would be more stringently repressed. The Wobblies, in turn, threatened that the "IWW is going to use the streets of Spokane or go down fighting." In truth, neither side had much stomach for continued warfare. For one thing, the city could not stand the expense of several hundred individual legal trials, including the ensuing appeals; for another, the IWW had exhausted campaigners and it lacked new recruits to take up the slack. Thus, on March 3, 1910, after a series of conferences between IWW representatives and various city officials, peace came to Spokane.[20]

The IWW won its major demands. Indoor meeting places would no longer be denied to the organization, and it could also hold peaceful outdoor meetings without police interference. Spokane agreed to respect the IWW's right to publish the *Industrial Worker* and to sell it on the city's streets. Complicated terms were also devised to secure the release of those Wobblies still in prison. Significantly, the authorities assured the IWW that free speech would be allowed on city streets in the near future. Until the council enacted new speaking ordinances, it barred street corners to religious groups: the Salvation Army as well as the IWW would have to await the passage of a free-speech statute later that year.

Wobblies also won the secondary demands which had undergirded their fight for free speech. In the midst of the battle, Spokane officials had initiated reforms in the employment agency system, rescinding the licenses of the worst of the "sharks." After the battle, public officials throughout the Northwest attempted to regulate private employment agencies more closely.[21]

As viewed by the Wobblies, the Spokane free-speech fight had been an impressive triumph for the twin principles of direct action and passive resistance. The discipline maintained by the free-speech fighters and the passivity with which they endured brutalities won the respect of many parties usually critical of or hostile to the IWW. During the struggle local socialists, Spokane's AFL members, and WFM miners in the Coeur d'Alenes, as well as "respectable" townspeople, contributed money, food, or just plain sympathy to the Wobbly cause. Passive resistance also showed what migratory workers who lacked the franchise might accomplish by more direct means. *Solidarity* grasped the lesson of Spokane when it observed: "By use of its weakest weapon—passive resistance—labor forced civic authorities to recognize a power equal to the state." If labor can gain so much through its crudest weapon, it asked, "what will the result be when an industrially organized working class stands forth prepared to seize, operate, and control the machinery of production and distribution?" [22]

But free speech on the streets of Spokane did not guarantee successful labor organization among the workers of the fields, woods, and construction camps of the Inland Empire. In 1910 the IWW had only learned how to attract migratory workers during their winter layovers in town; it had not yet hit upon the secret of maintaining an everyday, effective labor organization out on the job among workers who moved freely. It had not yet discovered how to survive when employers set armed gunmen upon "labor agitators" and summarily discharged union members. Victory in Spokane did, however, inspire the soapboxers and organizer-agitators so prominent within the IWW to carry their campaigns for free speech to other Western cities where migratories gathered to rest or to seek employment.

One such city was Fresno, California, where ranchers from the lush San Joaquin Valley came to acquire labor for their vegetable and fruit farms. In Fresno, as in Spokane, lonely men recently returned from a season of fruit picking or construction work spent their hard-earned funds on whisky and women. Here Wobbly soapboxers found an audience ready for the IWW's gospel.

Fresno had become the most active IWW center in California, and no other local in the state could compare to Fresno Local 66 in size of membership or in militancy of spirit. Late in 1909 and early the following year, Local 66 had unexpected success in organizing Mexican-American railroad laborers and migratory farm hands—a development not at all to the liking of city officials, the management of the Santa Fe Railroad, or the ranchers. As Wobblies continued to hold open street meetings and to win more recruits for their organization, minor skirmishes with the police rose in number—so much so that by May 1910 the local IWW forecast a full-scale free-speech fight. Fresno, indeed, was ready for the challenge. Its police chief had revoked the IWW's permit to hold street meetings and had threatened to jail on vagrancy charges any man without a job (serving as an IWW official was not considered employment). This led Frank Little, the leading local Wobbly, to predict that when the summer harvest ended, Wobblies would invade Fresno to battle for free speech.[23]

That fall a struggle similar in all basic respects to the one recently terminated in Spokane erupted in Fresno. In this case no money would be wasted on lawyers and defense funds; whatever funds the Fresno local obtained would be used to keep Wobblies on the streets, the local court docket crowded, and Fresno's pocketbook empty. "All aboard for Fresno," announced the *Industrial Worker* on September 10, "Free Speech Fight On."

Fresno's town fathers responded to the IWW invasion just as their civic neighbors to the north had done. First, they closed every hall in the city to the Wobblies, who were thus compelled to re-establish headquarters in a large rented tent outside the city limits. Fresno police followed up with a series of wholesale arrests which, by mid-November, temporarily broke IWW resistance. By the end of the month, though, the Wobblies were back on the streets in increasing numbers, and the more men Fresno arrested, the more Wobblies seemed to materialize. Fresno learned the hard way that arrests did not subdue militant Wobblies. Worse yet, the city discovered that it had no statute forbidding street speaking, thus invalidating the charges upon which the bulk of the arrests had been made. With the city thus deterred from legal action, mob action resulted. On the evening of December 9 a large mob gathered outside the city jail, where it severely beat a number of Wobblies who had come to visit imprisoned fellow workers. Its martial spirit duly aroused, the mob promptly marched out to the IWW's tent camp and put it to the torch. That evening, St. John wired Fresno's mayor: "Action of 'respectable mob' will not deter this organization . . . Free speech will be established in Fresno if it takes twenty years." [24]

Met by mob violence, the IWW counseled passive resistance, advising its fighters: ". . . Remember despite police brutality, don't retaliate in kind." So disciplined did the Wobblies remain that the *Sacramento Bee*, itself a bitter and sometimes unrestrained critic of the IWW, commented: ". . . When the good citizens and the authorities of any city countenance such outrages as those committed by the Fresno mob, the I.W.W. may be said to shine by comparison." [25]

Despite legal and extra-legal repression (Fresno on December 20 had enacted an ordinance banning street speaking), Wobblies continued to arrive in town in increasing numbers. Moving in and out of Fresno, and also in and out of jail, they encountered repression and brutality. What kept them coming and going was the same spirit and determination that motivated their leader in Fresno—Frank H. Little.

If Elizabeth Gurley Flynn was the "Rebel Girl," Frank Little was the "hobo agitator." More than any other individual he personified the IWW's rebelliousness and its strange compound of violent rhetoric, pride in physical courage (the *machismo* element), and its seemingly contradictory resort to nonviolent resistance. Part American Indian, part hard-rock miner, part hobo, he was all Wobbly. A tall, spare, muscular man with a weatherbeaten yet ruggedly handsome face, Little looked the complete proletarian rebel. As James P. Cannon, an old friend who fought with Little in Peoria and Duluth, remembered him: "He was always for the revolt, for the struggle, for the fight. Wherever he went he 'stirred up trouble' and organized the workers to rebel. . . . He was a blood brother to all insurgents . . . the world over." [26]

This one-eyed rebel * never occupied a comfortable union office or kept books like his close associates, St. John and Haywood; instead, he always went where the action was. From 1900 to 1905 he fought in the major WFM industrial conflicts, joining with that union's militants and following them into the IWW, where he remained when the WFM withdrew. In 1909 he was in Spokane, the following year in Fresno. In later years Little would turn up in San Diego, Duluth, Butte—anywhere Wobblies fought for a better world. Whenever miners, harvesters, or construction workers needed a leader, Little was available. When fear immobilized workers, he set an example for others to follow. His utter fearlessness brought him to Butte in 1917 to aid rebellious copper miners. By this time he was an ailing rheumatic, bearing the vestiges of too many beatings and too many jailings, and hobbling about on crutches as the result of a recently broken leg. Yet Little remained the active agitator—an agitator apparently so terrifying to the "respectable" that on August 1, 1917, Montana vigi-

---

* W. D. Haywood and Charles Lambert, who served with Little on the IWW's last pre-war general executive board, were also prominent one-eyed Wobblies.

lantes lynched him and left his body dangling from a railroad trestle on Butte's outskirts.

In 1910–1911 he was still a reasonably healthy man. He demonstrated in Fresno how a man unafraid, a man whose life had already taken him, and would later take him again, from one violent incident to another, could also lead a struggle based entirely on the moral suasion of passive resistance. Little proved in Fresno, as the IWW proved in so many other places, that even the potentially violent, given a good cause and a compelling ideology, could set an example of peaceful direct action.

Frank Little instilled his own rebelliousness in those who fought for free speech with him in Fresno. Only dedication and courage approximating Little's can account for teen-age Herbert Minderman's ability to withstand the tortures endured by Wobbly prisoners in Fresno's jail. Minderman kept a daily diary which described in some detail the course of the Fresno struggle and the punishments inflicted upon IWW prisoners.[27] As Minderman described it, imprisonment had no appreciable effect on the Wobbly spirit. In jail Wobblies sang rebel songs, held propaganda meetings, and transacted the somewhat irregular business of Local 66. They talked so cantankerously and sang so loudly that their jailers took unusual steps to silence the noisy ones. A guard gagged one Wobbly with his own sock, causing a government investigator to comment: "The severity of this punishment can be understood only by one who is familiar with the rank and file of I.W.W.'s and knows how rarely they bathe." [28] Wobblies responded to repression within the jail by mounting what they labeled a "battleship," which meant continuous yelling, jeering, and pounding on cell bars and floors until the guards felt compelled to use more forceful measures.

The sheriff thus denied his prisoners adequate sleeping gear, tobacco, reading materials, and decent food. When this failed to still the tumult, he resorted to physical force. Firemen appeared at the city jail with a 150-pound pressure hose, which was turned upon the cell holding the Wobblies. Prisoners tried to protect themselves by erecting a barricade of mattresses. But the pressure of the water swept the mattresses away and drove the Wobblies against the cell wall. Some Wobblies sought refuge by lying flat on the floor, but the hose was aimed down upon them, the stream of water then thrusting them up into the air like toothpicks. Even the most rebellious soon had enough of this treatment. Yet the firemen maintained the water pressure for fully a half-hour, and before they left almost every prisoner found his clothes in shreds and his body black and blue. The Wobblies spent the remainder of that chill December night up to their knees in water.

Some Wobblies broke under these tactics, promising to leave town if released. But most refused to compromise. They served out their time and then returned to Fresno's streets to soapbox.

The IWW's refusal to terminate its struggle had the same effect in Fresno as it had had earlier in Spokane. Each prisoner demanded a jury trial, managed his own defense, and challenged as many prospective jurors as possible. Wobblies used every delaying tactic their limited legal knowledge made available. On a good day Fresno's courts might try two or three men; however many Wobblies they sentenced, it seemed more were always on the docket. To make matters worse, still more Wobblies were always on the road to Fresno. Although the IWW found it harder to attract volunteers than it had been in Spokane, nevertheless many Wobblies shared the militancy of Little and young Herbert Minderman and set off to join their fellow workers in Fresno.[29] This eventually became too great a burden for the city's taxpayers, its judges, and its businessmen.

Fresno's officials finally weakened in their resolve to repress their antagonists. Again, IWW leaders proved realistic and able negotiators. Well aware that local authorities hated to compromise while under pressure, the Wobblies allowed secret and informal talks to proceed. These conferences began on February 25 when a local citizens' committee visited the Fresno jail in order to ascertain the IWW's truce terms. In less than two weeks the citizens' committee and city officials consented to the release of all IWW prisoners and to a guarantee of the organization's right to speak on Fresno's streets. Finally, on March 6 Local 66 wired IWW headquarters: "The Free Speech Fight is over, and won. . . . Complete victory." [30]

What the IWW won in Fresno was not precisely clear. No public settlement terms were announced, either by the local IWW or by Fresno's citizens' committee. Moreover, for the next several years Local 66 and Fresno disappeared from mention in the IWW press; Frank

Little left the area to fight IWW wars elsewhere, and the San Joaquin Valley's fruit pickers remained unorganized, overworked, and underpaid. In brief, an inglorious and inconclusive climax. In Fresno as in Spokane, the IWW had learned how to contact the migratories in town but not how to organize them on the job. Local 66 had succeeded in making its headquarters a community center for the West's dispossessed, yet it failed to carry the organization into the surrounding countryside where it was most needed.

As propaganda, however, the IWW may have gained something from the Fresno struggle. In a conflict which lasted over six months but cost less than $1,000, the IWW received enormous national publicity. Although the Fresno conflict did not attract quite the nationwide attention that Elizabeth Gurley Flynn had focused on Spokane, it did reinforce the image of the IWW as an organization that used passive resistance to defend clear constitutional rights. It demonstrated once again that the most exploited and dependent groups in American society could act for themselves—and act peaceably at that—as well as that they also had the power—nonpolitical power, of course—to alter the prevailing arrangements of the local community. Yet the Fresno fight left behind no effective labor organization to capitalize upon the IWW's apparent "victory," and no immediate membership growth followed this new triumph for free speech.[31]

The Spokane and Fresno victories led Wobblies to contend for free speech elsewhere, though with uneven success. Almost always these fights were associated with efforts to organize lumber workers and migratory harvesters. In one tragic case the IWW's campaign for free speech was entirely unrelated to the objectives of labor organization. In San Diego in 1912 the IWW learned the limits of passive resistance, as well as the folly of concentrating its limited power on tangential causes.

In 1912 San Diego was a comfortable city of fifty thousand, mostly well-to-do devotees of the area's ideal climate. It had a small and contented working class and no important or large industries threatened by labor difficulties. No migratories drifted into town *en masse* to spend the winter, and no ground seemed less fertile for IWW efforts.

As IWW martyr-bard Joe Hill noted: "A town like San Diego for instance where the main 'industry' consists of 'catching suckers' [tourists] is not worth a whoop in Hell from a rebel's point of view." [32] Indeed, never did the number of Wobblies in San Diego exceed a few hundred. Yet those few, as a contemporary journalist commented, "goaded the authorities and the populace into a hysterical frenzy, into an epidemic of unreasoning fear and brutal rage, into a condition of lawlessness so pronounced that travelers feared to visit the city." [33]

For years E Street between Fifth and Sixth Avenues in the heart of downtown San Diego had served as a sort of Hyde Park Speakers' Corner. Every evening socialists and anarchists, savers and atheists, suffragists and Wobblies, harangued the faithful from their accustomed spots on the corner. But in December 1911 San Diego's city council, acting upon a grand jury recommendation, closed the downtown area, the so-called "congested district," to street meetings. In response, Wobblies, socialists, single-taxers, and even the local AFL men created a broad coalition called the Free Speech League. From the day the anti-street-speaking ordinance took effect, February 8, 1912, police and league members clashed over the right of free speech. By February 12, ninety men and women had been arrested, and by February 15, 150 prisoners languished in city and county jails. Day and night for the next several weeks, the League held free-speech meetings and the police arrested speakers, until the county as well as the city jails were crowded beyond normal capacity.[34]

Before long, what began as a common struggle by a broad coalition of anti-establishment organizations became a largely IWW-led struggle. Although the non-Wobbly groups continued to participate in the San Diego struggle, the public, locally and nationally, associated the conflict with the IWW. The battle did, in fact, feature the tactics the IWW had tested successfully in Spokane and Fresno. Again Wobblies threatened to fill the jails and crowd the court dockets until a financially drained city surrendered. Again the Wobblies looked to passive resistance to accomplish their aims. One IWW bard, an early, perhaps premature version of Dr. Seuss, advised: "Come on the cushions; Ride up on top; Stick to the brakebeams; Let nothing stop. Come in great numbers; This we beseech; Help San Diego to win *Free Speech!*" [35]

Although San Diego had less to fear from the Wobblies than either Spokane or Fresno, it nevertheless acted more savagely to repress free speech. No brutality proved beyond the imagination of San Diego's "good" citizens. What the police could not accomplish by stretching the local law's elastic fabric, private citizens, acting as vigilantes, did. Even discounting the predictable exaggeration of the reports in the *Industrial Worker* and *Solidarity*, repression proved the rule in San Diego. The city's citizens learned from the mistakes previously revealed in Spokane and Fresno. San Diego would not be invaded by armies of Wobblies, nor bankrupted by scores of prisoners who resided in jail as beneficiaries of the public purse and who demanded costly individual trials. San Diego devised just the remedy for these IWW tactics. Several nights a week vigilantes visited the jails, seized a group of free-speech prisoners, and escorted them beyond the county line. To any Wobbly who dared to return, and to those who attempted to join the fight, the vigilantes promised worse treatment.[36]

San Diego's brand of vigilante justice has been described best by some of the Wobblies who experienced it. On the night of either April 4 or 5,* 1912, Albert Tucker and 140 other men, half of whom were under twenty-one years of age, hopped a freight train out of Los Angeles bound for San Diego. About one o'clock that morning the train slowed down and Tucker noticed on either side of the freight cars about four hundred men armed with rifles, pistols, and clubs of every variety. Tucker has vividly portrayed what ensued.[37]

The moon was shining dimly through the clouds and I could see pick handles, ax handles, wagon spokes and every kind of club imaginable swinging from the wrists of all of them while they also had their rifles leveled at us . . . the only sign of civilization was a cattle corral. . . . We were ordered to unload and we refused. Then they closed in around the flat car which we were on and began clubbing and knocking and pulling men off by their heels, so inside of a half hour they had us all off the train and then bruised and bleeding we were lined up and marched into the cattle corral, where they made us hold our hands up and march around in the crowd for more than an hour. . . . They marched us several times, now

* Tucker was not certain of the precise date when he wrote his account of these events two years later.

and then picking out a man they thought was a leader and giving him an extra beating. Several men were carried out unconscious . . . afterwards there was a lot of our men unaccounted for and never have been heard from since. The vigilantes all wore constable badges and a white handkerchief around their left arms. They were drunk and hollering and cursing the rest of the night. In the morning they took us out four or five at a time and marched us up the track to the county line . . . where we were forced to kiss the flag and then run a gauntlet of 106 men, every one of which was striking at us as hard as they could with their pick axe handles. They broke one man's leg, and everyone was beaten black and blue, and was bleeding from a dozen wounds.

The man with the broken leg, Chris Hansen, himself a veteran of other IWW free-speech fights, also described what happened that night:

As I was lying there I saw other fellows running the gauntlet. Some were bleeding freely from cracked heads, others were knocked down to be made to get up and run again. Some tried to break the line only to be beaten back. It was the most cowardly and inhuman cracking of heads I ever witnessed . . .[38]

"Thus did San Diego," in the words of anti-IWW journalist Walter Woehlke, "having given its money to mark the historic highway [El Camino Real] with the symbols of love and charity, teach patriotism and reverence for the law to the travelers thereon." [39]

That all of this vigilante violence had occurred with the connivance of local public officials soon became known to the entire nation. Governor Hiram Johnson, Progressive politician extraordinary, under pressure from the AFL, the Socialist party, the IWW, and many influential Californians, some of whom had played a prominent role in his election, dispatched special investigator Harris Weinstock to San Diego. Weinstock's investigation corroborated all the Free Speech League's charges of police and vigilante brutality. A thoroughly outraged Weinstock compared San Diego's behavior to the worst excesses of the tsarist Russian regime.[40]

This public condemnation notwithstanding, San Diego vigilantes continued their previous activities. Early in May 1912 police fatally wounded an IWW member. On May 15 anarchist Emma Goldman and her manager-lover, Ben Reitman, arrived in town to lend their voices to the struggle. When they debarked at the railroad station they found a howling mob, including many women, screaming: "Give us that anarchist; we will strip her naked; we will tear out her guts." That evening vigilantes abducted Reitman from his hotel room. Placing him in the back seat of a speeding auto, they tortured him as they sped out of town. About twenty miles beyond San Diego's limits the vigilantes stopped the car, got out, and proceeded to a second round of torture. As later described by Reitman, this is what happened: "With tar taken from a can [they] traced I.W.W. on my back and a doctor burned the letters in with a lighted cigar . . ." Afterward, Reitman ran the gauntlet, and then he kissed the American flag and sang the "Star Spangled Banner." Beaten, bruised, and degraded, he dragged himself away clad only in his underwear, "because the Christian gentlemen thought that I might meet some ladies and shock them." [41]

Despite their militancy and the sympathy they received as a result of the kind of treatment described above, Wobblies lacked the power to alter conditions in San Diego. The state had the power, but it used it to condemn, not to reform. The federal government also had the power, but in 1912, unlike a half-century later, its power was not at the disposal of peaceful protesters being abused by local or state authorities.

In 1912 it was San Diego's public officials, not the beaten and intimidated Wobblies, who turned to the federal Justice Department for support. Early in May city police superintendent John Sehon asked Attorney General George Wickersham for federal assistance in local efforts to repress the subversive, un-American IWW. Well before that date Sehon had been cooperating with the federal attorney for southern California (John McCormick) and with private detectives appointed by a citizens' committee controlled by sugar king John Spreckels and anti-union Los Angeles newspaper magnate Harrison Grey Otis. Sehon, the federal attorney, and the private detectives searched for evidence linking the IWW to an alleged plot to overthrow the constituted authorities in San Diego and Washington, D.C., and also to join the Mexican Revolution, the aim here being to capture Lower California for the IWW. Where these diligent investigators could not find evidence, they manufactured it. On May 4 Sehon informed the Justice Department that Wobblies were congregating across the nation—275 in Los Angeles, 140 outside San Diego, 1,060 at various points in the state, and other bands in Chicago, Kansas City, and Oklahoma City—preparing "to overthrow the Government

193

and take possession of all things . . ." Armed with guns and dynamite and led personally by St. John and Haywood, the Wobblies, according to Sehon and United States Attorney McCormick, had organized "a criminally treasonous" conspiracy which had to be nipped in the bud by federal authorities.[42]

Fortunately, Attorney General Wickersham remained calm and collected. Despite strong pressure from one of California's senators and from San Diego's congressman, Wickersham realized that the IWW posed no threat to American stability or security. What little disorder had occurred in San Diego, local authorities could manage, and the Attorney General certainly knew that San Diego had not been hesitant in its use of repression. But as a Republican politician with a presidential election upcoming, Wickersham mollified southern California Republicans by allowing McCormick to continue his federal investigation for evidence of IWW subversion.[43]

Throughout the summer of 1912, San Diego officials tried unsuccessfully to involve the Justice Department in the local conflict. McCormick even impaneled a Los Angeles grand jury to take evidence in an attempt to indict Wobblies for criminal conspiracy. In the opinion of a Justice Department official in Washington, McCormick's grand jury proved no more than that Wobblies "are apparently self-confessed liars and law-breakers, but there is nothing indicating a specific attack upon the Government of the United States." After having allowed McCormick and his Republican supporters to have their fun, Wickersham ordered federal proceedings against the IWW dropped.[44]

At this juncture southern California's "reactionary" Republicans went over the Attorney General's head, carrying their case for federal repression of the IWW directly to President William Howard Taft. F. W. Estabrook, a prominent member of the Republican National Committee and an industrialist whose own factory had earlier been struck by the IWW, compared the California labor situation to that in Chicago in 1894 when Cleveland dispatched troops to crush the Pullman strike. He suggested to the President "that this matter [the San Diego conflict] is of the greatest importance, not only in a political way . . . but . . . it is time that vigorous action, whenever opportunity occurs, should be taken to stamp out the revolutionary methods of this anarchistic organization." More to the point, Estabrook assured Charles Hilles, Taft's secretary, that vigorous anti-IWW action would guarantee California's votes for Taft in the November election; furthermore, he added, such action would weaken the cause of the Hiram Johnson Progressive Republicans, who supported Theodore Roosevelt and the Progressive party in the 1912 election.[45]

Taft was receptive to Estabrook's suggestions. Political intrigue and his desire to be re-elected apparently clouded his usually clear mind, for Taft wrote as follows to Wickersham on September 7: "There is not any doubt that that corner of the country is a basis for most of the anarchists and the industrial world workers [sic], and for all the lawless flotsam and jetsam that proximity to the Mexican border thrusts into those two cities. . . . We ought to take decided action. The State of California is under an utterly unscrupulous boss [Hiram Johnson], who does not hesitate . . . to do with these people and cultivate their good will, and it is our business to go in and show the strong hand of the United States in a marked way so that they shall understand that we are on the job."[46] In other words, Taft expected repression of the IWW to win California's electoral votes.

Lacking presidential ambitions himself, Wickersham remained calm. Acceding to Taft's desire to investigate IWW subversion, the Attorney General nevertheless discounted the overblown reports and rumors emanating from southern California. Indeed, he maintained at the very end of the San Diego affair just as he had at the beginning: "I know of no reason why the [Justice] Department should take any further action."[47]

Although the federal government refused to intervene in San Diego, and Taft won neither California's votes nor re-election, the IWW continued to suffer at the hands of police and also private citizens. No agency of government was prepared in 1912 to defend the civil liberties of citizens who flaunted the traditions and rules of America's dominant classes.

Still, the IWW and its free-speech allies fought on. Pleading for funds and volunteers, they obtained money but precious few men. Even with a diminishing supply of manpower and close to defeat, the Wobblies remained defiant. Upon being sentenced to prison, one Wobbly, Jack White, proclaimed: "To hell with your courts; I know what justice is."[48]

Courtroom defiance was no substitute for victory. By October 1912, nine months after the inauguration of the free-speech fight, downtown San Diego remained vacant and lonely at night. "The sacred spot where so many I.W.W.'s were clubbed and arrested last winter," wrote Laura Payne Emerson, "lies safe and secure from the unhallowed tread of the hated anarchist, and in fact, from all other human beings." And she lamented: "They have the courts, the jails and funds. What are we going to do about it?" [49]

Some Wobblies still counseled passive resistance, "the trump card that we hold and the vigilantes cannot use." Other Wobblies had their doubts. A crippled Chris Hansen vowed from his hospital bed: "My lesson is passive resistance no more." Albert Tucker, another survivor of the vigilantes' gauntlet, declaimed: "If I ever take part in another [free-speech fight] it will be with machine guns and aerial bombs." There must be, Tucker reasoned, "a better way of fighting and better results . . ." [50] Similar frustration with nonviolent tactics appeared in a warning the *Industrial Worker* delivered to San Diego's public officials on April 4, 1912. "Take warning! Sehon, Wilson, Utley, Keno—take heed members of the 'vigilance committee'—Your names will be spread broadcast! Reparation will be exacted! He laughs best who laughs last!"

Yet IWW threats and violence always remained rhetorical; the beatings suffered by nonviolent Wobblies, on the other hand, were very real. They hardly seemed worth it when the object to be gained, free speech, of and by itself brought no improvement in working conditions and added few members to the IWW. It seemed worth even less when, as Joe Hill remarked, San Diego was "not worth a whoop in Hell from a rebel's point of view."

If the battles in Spokane and Fresno demonstrated the effectiveness of nonviolence, San Diego starkly revealed the weakness of passive resistance as a tactic when the opposition refused to respect common decency and when no higher authority would intervene on behalf of the oppressed. Well before their defeat in San Diego, however, many Wobblies had had second thoughts about their organization's involvement in free-speech fights. At the time of the Spokane conflict, W. I. Fisher wrote to the *Industrial Worker:* "If we are to have a strong union we have to go to the job where the workers are and begin our agitation. . . . It is only where we control or are seeking control of the job that we can build up a lasting economic power." In 1911, during the Fresno struggle, Pacific Coast IWW representatives meeting in Portland voiced their opposition to unnecessary free-speech campaigns when more effective work remained to be accomplished in organizing and educating "wage slaves" on the job.[51]

But the IWW could not avert further free-speech fights. In the Far West and in other regions where migratory workers congregated, street speaking continued to be the most effective means for spreading the IWW gospel and for winning new recruits to the organization. After all, the migratories attracted to the IWW as a result of the 1909–1912 free-speech fights would become the dedicated Wobblies who later spearheaded the IWW's successful penetration of the woods and the wheat fields during the World War I years. Other motives also kept Wobblies on their soapboxes. They were, to be sure, as much agitators as organizers, as much propagandists as labor leaders, and they needed their street corners and soapboxes in order to denounce capitalist society and "bushwa" morality. Wobblies also felt compelled to compete with the Salvation Army's street-corner preachers, who counseled the oppressed to be humble and content while awaiting their reward in heaven. In response to this advice, the IWW gospelers preached "a little less hell on earth" for exploited workers.

CHAPTER

9

Steel, Southern Lumber, and Internal Decay, 1909–1912

As the IWW fought for free speech in the Far West, it also struggled to bring labor organization to Eastern industrial workers and Southern woodsmen. As in the West it appealed to those workers Carleton Parker described as social outcasts and outlaws, so in the East and the South it agitated among frustrated new immigrants, exploited black men, and poor Southern whites.

In 1909 no industry seemed less open and yet more attractive to the believer in militant industrial unionism than steel. That year the United States Steel Company had dealt the final blow to the existence of the Amalgamated Association of Iron and Steel Workers—an AFL affiliate composed largely of skilled American-born workers—which had been declining since its defeat in the 1901 steel strike. Thus, in 1909 neither skilled nor unskilled steel workers had an organization to defend their rights. Moreover, most steel companies, and United States Steel in particular, had established rudimentary welfare-capitalism schemes in order to keep employees content. By skillfully mixing their labor force ethnically, promoting American-born workers, and dominating the steel towns' power structures (including police, courts, schools, and churches), employers created what David Brody has defined as "a situation of labor stability." [1]

Certainly, the companies' control of the mill towns and artful manipulation of the skilled workers in the industry boded ill for any uprising by the unskilled. Yet the newer immigrant workers—Hungarians, Croats, Slovenians, Austrians, and Serbs, to name but a few of the diverse ethnic groups—were outside steel's labor consensus. They represented the instability inherent in the labor force. The companies exploited them; the skilled workers denigrated them; the mill towns ostracized them. Getting only the most backbreaking and lowest-paying jobs, the new immigrants lived in their noisome "Hunky towns" and "Dago villages." A Pittsburgh reporter who claimed to be a sympathizer conveyed how the mill-town communities felt about the mass of steel-industry workers when he referred to the new immigrants as an "undisciplined horde . . . Slavs, Poles, Russians, Croats, and Italians, most of them of less than ordinary intelligence or opportunity, unable to understand any language but their own." [2]

To these immigrant industrial workers, then, the IWW hoped to bring its program of direct action and its principle of industrial unionism.

Quite unexpectedly, an opportunity to reach the steel industry's unskilled workers soon presented itself to the IWW. On Saturday, July 10, 1909, workers at the Pressed Steel Car Company in McKees Rocks, Pennsylvania, received their biweekly paychecks.[3] All day Sunday they reflected bitterly upon their skimpy earnings, and on returning to work on Monday morning complained about their wages to foremen and timekeepers. In one department about forty workers refused to work until they received more explicit information about the company's method of calculating wage rates. That same evening employees met in a group to discuss their grievances before lodging a formal demand for redress with plant officials. On Wednesday morning, July 14, company officials declined to see them. At that juncture, six hundred men in the riveting department spontaneously put down their tools and walked out the factory door. By mid-morning only about five hundred men, out of a total work force estimated at thirty-five hundred, remained on the job. These skilled workers soon faced a hostile and threatening force of strikers. The next morning the unskilled immigrants formed mass picket lines at all points of entry to the plant and kept the skilled men from reporting to work. At noon, company officials, announcing that no strike existed, nevertheless closed the plant, ostensibly to protect it from the "violent" immigrants milling about outside the gates. By mid-afternoon on Thursday, July 15, 1909, the steel industry's carefully constructed "situation of labor stability" was under attack in McKees Rocks by an industrial conflict that involved the entire local labor force. Why?

McKees Rocks was much like the other steel towns in the Pittsburgh area. Situated on the left bank of the Ohio River six miles below Pittsburgh, in 1910 it had a population of 14,702, well over half of whom were foreign born. As in other steel towns, its workers were segregated ethnically. The immigrants lived in dreary ghettos lining the river "bottoms," while the Americans lived on higher ground in town, or across the river in Pittsburgh. Little contact existed outside the factory between these two major components of the labor force.

As in other steel towns a single company dominated the community—in this instance the Pressed Steel Car Company, formed in 1899 as a merger of the two leading American railroad car building firms. Long noted for its anti-labor policies—by no means unique in the industry, but simply more stringently applied—the company, under the direction of President Frank Hoffstot, had by 1909 followed the trend set by United States Steel in using assembly-line techniques of mass production combined with the principles of scientific management. The new techniques, in line with the best thought of the Progressive era about industrial efficiency, raised profits to new heights. But these same methods stimulated labor discontent.

The Pressed Steel Car Company had never been known for good working conditions or high wages, and in both respects things seemed worse than usual in 1909. The Panic of 1907 and the ensuing business recession drastically reduced orders for new railroad cars, causing the company to lay off workers and to cut wages. Wages had not yet been restored to pre-depression levels in 1909, the plant still operated at less than full capacity, and between two thousand and three thousand immigrants composed a reserve labor army anxious to work at almost any wage. Hoffstot freely admitted to an inquiring reporter during the strike the reason behind low wages: "When all's said and done, it's supply and demand that fixed wages, the same as everything else. . . . We buy labor in the cheapest market." [4]

Before he reduced wage rates in 1907, Hoffstot had also introduced a new assembly-line production method which accelerated the pace of work through a piece-rate system. At the same time he devised a technique for pooling wages which penalized all members of a labor pool for time and production lost by any single slow worker. This new production system also penalized workers for delays caused by company failure to repair machinery, or for breakdowns caused by vague instructions issued by plant superintendents. Although compelled to work at a feverish pace in order to satisfy the pool's production target, the men on the assembly line never knew what their actual piece rates would be and, in fact, usually found their weekly earnings well below expectations. Frank Kellogg, the professional social worker who directed the famous Pittsburgh Survey (a study of that city's economic and social structure), discovered wage slips among McKees Rocks' workers which showed that some men received as little as $6.50 for ten days and two nights' work as riveters, $1 for three days, $3.50 for four days, and $15 for two weeks on the job (low even for the Pittsburgh area).

Working and living conditions added to the general discontent. Minimal plant safety precautions could not be relied upon. Contemporary newspaper accounts may have exaggerated the extent of industrial mayhem within the factory, but a *Pittsburgh Leader* reporter conveyed company attitudes when he noted: "A human life is worth less than a rivet. Rivets cost money." That same journalist described the town's immigrant quarters:

They are all alike both without and within. Situated in what is known as the Dump of Schoenville, runs a narrow dirt road. Frequently strewn with tin cans and debris, it is bereft of trees and the glaring sun shines pitilessly down on hundreds of ragged, unkempt and poorly fed children. They seem too young to leave their mothers' sides, but in spite of their youth, their faces wan . . . are peculiarly aged in expression, and their eyes gleam with premature knowledge, which is the result of a daily struggle, not for life, but for existence.[5]

Many of these immigrants dwelled in the two hundred company-owned double houses. Renting for $12 monthly for four rooms, they lacked indoor plumbing and other amenities. Moreover, many working-class families had to take in lodgers in order to meet their monthly rent. What appeared on the surface as "model" company homes became, in fact, the overcrowded slums described by the Pittsburgh reporter. Everywhere the immigrant turned in McKees Rocks, he encountered company agents who exploited him: boarding-bosses who covertly raised his rent for company housing if he took in boarders; foremen who charged him for a job; special company police who tyrannized him.

Thus, despite the immigrants' lack of organization, the reserve labor army available locally, and the company's domination of the community, the men struck on July 15. They walked out of the factory in order to abolish the pooling system, to restore wages to pre-1907 levels, to demand a posted statement of wage rates and a written record of their earnings, and to obtain machinery through which to present future grievances. At the moment of the walkout, a union, let alone membership in the radical IWW, seemed the farthest thing from the immigrants' minds. Yet circumstances would soon draw Wobblies and immigrants into a marriage of convenience.

It was one thing for unorganized workers to strike, quite another to achieve their demands. McKees Rocks' strikers had more to contend with than most. Many lived in company houses from which they could be evicted—and eventually were. Community leaders rejected and despised them as aliens. The immigrants could not even rely upon the complete support of their fellow workers, especially the skilled Americans. The Pressed Steel Car Company had its own Coal and Iron Police to disperse pickets and harass strikers; when private police proved deficient, Hoffstot could call upon the local sheriff, or better still, the state police.

Pennsylvania's state police had been created at the behest of reformers anxious to abolish the use of private police forces during industrial conflicts. In theory, a state constabulary would serve neither employers nor strikers; it would, instead, protect the community's stability and preserve the public peace. Yet in practice Pennsylvania's state troopers, or "Cossacks," as striking workers labeled them, worked to the advantage of employers. In the McKees Rocks dispute the state police protected the strikebreakers Hoffstot had obtained from New York's Pearl Berghoff Agency, a specialist in supplying scabs. State troopers proved effective in guaranteeing the "poor worker's" right to labor on his own freely chosen terms, which, in the case of Berghoff Agency employees, meant the right to break strikes.

Despite the strength of the opposition, the strikers at first had considerable leverage. Ethnic solidarity impelled the community's unemployed men to join strikers on the picket lines rather than to take their places in the plant. Accustomed to a hard life in the Old World and to deprivation in the new, immigrants were better prepared than many American workers to endure the privations of a protracted conflict. Able to survive on less, they could fight longer. During the strike's initial stages, the American workers joined with the immigrants. Although unaffected by the pooling system, skilled American workers shared the general employee distaste for the company's autocratic labor policies. Moreover, the skilled workers could not labor full-time with more than half the work force out on strike; some of the Americans also honestly feared they would be the victims of violence if they remained on the job. In the last analysis, however, Hoffstot's refusal to deal with any group of workers for a time kept immigrants and Americans united. Company arrogance also led influential sectors of the Pittsburgh community to sympathize with the strikers and to provide them with funds, as long as the industrial conflict in McKees Rocks could be kept within the limits defined by the skilled workers.

Under these circumstances, a skilled worker, C. A. Wise, an engineer in the axle department, emerged as the strike leader. Working with a Pittsburgh attorney named William McNair, Wise amalgamated the immigrants and the Americans into a joint committee led by the so-called "Big Six," which Wise dominated. Only four days after the walkout began (July 19), Wise and the skilled workers, much to the relief of the Pittsburgh press and the city's reformers, seemed in firm control of the conflict. When immigrants complained about Wise's conservative, self-serving leadership, he responded brusquely: "If we [native Americans] step down and out, contributions will cease and you will starve." [6] Wise and his faction, unlike the unskilled immigrants, simply wanted to return to work as soon as possible.

Hoffstot soon realized that his skilled employees would compromise the very issues basic to the immigrants' walkout. Indeed, as more and more Berghoff strikebreakers entered the community and violence became a distinct possibility, the skilled workers groped about for a settlement on almost any terms.

Not so the immigrant workers. Within their ranks were several men who had had some experience in European labor and radical movements.[7] These men established the "unknown committee": a new executive body offering the kind of leadership the "Big Six" refused to provide. The "unknown committee" used tactics designed to limit the importation of strikebreakers. It formed mass picketing corps and special signal and watch groups to sound the alert when strikebreakers approached the community. These new, more radical leaders also issued threats to the state police; according to one reporter, they swore to "get" a trooper in retaliation for every striker injured or murdered.

When the conflict suddenly heated up, with violence flaring between immigrants and strikebreakers, Wise and the skilled workers rushed into Hoffstot's arms, announcing settlement terms on July 31. The unskilled immigrants saw no gain in the unexpected settlement, and so instead of returning to work they repudiated Wise and sought new leadership elsewhere. Enter the IWW.

Exactly how and when the IWW became involved in the McKees Rocks conflict remains unclear. During the strike's first weeks no mention of the IWW appeared in the commercial press, the *Survey,* or in any other news sources; even the *Industrial Worker,* the Wobblies' own sheet, contained no reference to the dispute. Then, on August 5, 1909, the following message from General Organizer William Trautmann appeared in the *Industrial Worker:* ". . . We have at last arrived at the turning point here in the East. . . . I am off for McKees Rocks, perhaps to face the bullets of the foe." [8] What is clear about the timing is that Trautmann and the IWW appeared on the scene just when the differences between immigrants and Americans became irreconcilable. On August 4, the day before the *Industrial Worker* printed Trautmann's message, the immigrants had unanimously rejected the compromise settlement arranged by Wise and the "Big Six." Subsequently, the gap between immigrants and Americans widened. When the company evicted strikers from their homes to make room for strikebreakers, violence threatened the community. Immigrant strikers were even planning to dynamite a river steamer carrying scabs to the factory. But Wise and his followers foiled that scheme, thus permitting the strikebreakers to arrive unmolested. From this juncture on, immigrants and Americans proceeded in separate ways.

It appears that the "unknown committee," influenced by its handful of European revolutionaries in exile, invited Trautmann and the IWW to McKees Rocks. But it is also possible that Trautmann, sensing the split within the strikers' ranks, simply saw an opportunity to promote the IWW's brand of radical industrial unionism. Whatever the case, by mid-August Trautmann and the IWW had assumed leadership of the immigrant strikers. On August 15 a crowd estimated at eight thousand gathered on Indian Mound, a hill overlooking the Ohio River where strikers met regularly, to hear Trautmann and other speakers. Trautmann addressed the audience in English and German; others spoke in nine different foreign tongues. All speakers sounded the same tocsin: solidarity and resistance. All emphasized the IWW slogan: "An injury to one is an injury to all." Yet the IWW had not assumed formal control among the strikers, effective power still being exercised by the radicals among the immigrants, though they accepted aid and advice from Wobblies.

Neither IWW assistance nor strike solidarity curtailed the importation of strikebreakers. The presence of rising numbers of Berghoff's men could have but one result: violence. On Sunday, August 22, immigrant strikers decided to act. They had been without jobs and income for more than a month; other men had now taken their jobs and in some cases their homes. So early Sunday evening, as Berghoff's men returned to work, strikers sought to deter them from entering the plant. Words failing to impress the strikebreakers, fists and rocks followed. As fight after fight erupted, Coal and Iron Police, local sheriff's deputies, and state troopers became involved. When Sunday's battle ended, McKees Rocks counted six dead, six dying, and forty to fifty injured—mostly strikers. Within three days state troopers, acting under limited martial law, searched every immigrant's home, confiscating guns, knives, and weapons under terms of a state law which prohibited possession of weapons by aliens.

That strike violence occurred cannot be denied. To associate the IWW with violent outbreaks and to imply that IWW leadership instigated the slaughter of August 22, as has been done, is both unfair and naive.[9] First, a handful of Wobblies was in no position to control five thousand cantankerous immigrant strikers who saw their jobs being threatened by scabs. Second, Wobblies never counseled violent tactics.

One observer at the IWW-sponsored Indian Mound mass meetings reported that the keynote struck by all orators was for strikers to abstain from violence.[10] Third, granted the bitterness engendered during the conflict, the strike was as remarkable for the absence of violence as for the August 22 riot. "The reports of violence have been . . . greatly exaggerated . . ." Paul Kellogg noted at the time. Another observer concluded that for a strike which had lasted eight weeks, the McKees Rocks dispute had been unusually quiet and orderly.[11] Finally, as generally occurred in IWW conflicts, when violence finally erupted, Wobblies usually suffered most.

Notwithstanding the IWW's pacific counsel and the strikers' orderliness, fear of violence enveloped the Pittsburgh area. Immediately after the August 22 bloodletting, the *Survey* reported: ". . . The strikers are sullen and nothing more is needed to precipitate further rioting and bloodshed than a leader and another spark." [12] Many feared that the IWW's Trautmann would be the leader who would provide the spark.

Wise and the skilled Americans saw in these anxieties the opportunity they had been seeking to terminate the strike. Everyone concerned—Wise, Hoffstot, and the reformers—feared the IWW-immigrant alliance. Only a prompt strike settlement, they now reasoned, would remove the cancerous Wobbly influence from the region. Hence Wise and Hoffstot agreed upon a second compromise agreement early in September. On September 8 a selected group of strikers, carefully screened by Wise and the local chamber of commerce, voted on the proposed settlement terms. Overwhelming approval resulted, and that day St. John wired the *Industrial Worker*: "McKees Rocks strike settled. Company beat on all points. Strikers all members of I.W.W. and in control." To which the IWW paper added: "Western Pennsylvania bids fair to be the storm center for the I.W.W. and the working class of the country from now on." [13]

At the time of the settlement, most observers and participants hailed the terms, as did St. John, as a great victory for the strikers. Wise maintained that the men had won all their demands, and the *Survey* concluded that the "company practically agrees to the strikers'

terms." [14] Supposedly, Hoffstot agreed to restore the pre-1907 wage scale, to modify the pooling system to the workers' satisfaction, to establish minimum wages, to post wage rates clearly, to abolish all favoritism and graft in employment, and to rehire all strikers without prejudice.

Careful scrutiny of the terms leads to a different conclusion. The company refused to raise wages immediately, and it did not agree to abandon the pooling system. Pressed Steel simply offered the strikers the *status quo ante*, which was what Wise and the skilled Americans had desired all along. The immigrants and the Wobblies, as they later painfully realized, had been had. [15]

Upon perceiving what had really happened, Trautmann attempted to keep out the more than one thousand strikers not yet rehired. Again he planned to schedule mass meetings at Indian Mound in order to impress upon the immigrants the need for solidarity. Now, however, the gap between immigrants and native Americans had become so wide that, upon a complaint filed by Wise, local police arrested and jailed Trautmann. As usual, imprisonment of its leaders did not stop the IWW. No sooner was Trautmann settled in jail than Joe Ettor appeared in McKees Rocks to take the imprisoned general organizer's place. Industrial warfare seemed about to resume when over four thousand workers walked out again on September 15.

Now Pressed Steel employed its skilled workers to break the strike. Wise and his followers heckled and disrupted IWW strike meetings, demanded that the immigrants act like American citizens, and offered to lead the strikers back to work behind the American flag. In fact, on September 16 Wise's men, carrying a huge American flag at their head, led some two thousand workers toward the plant gate and the massed IWW pickets. As the procession approached the plant, the picket line parted, allowing the marchers to enter the factory unmolested. Thus ended the second walkout. The demoralized strikers returned to work, while Wise, in conjunction with company officials, dropped immigrant strike leaders from the payroll.

Hoffstot learned his lesson well. Instead of opposing all labor organizations and treating his entire labor force autocratically, he now distinguished between the skilled and the unskilled, the native and the foreign. The strike over, Pressed Steel officials agreed to confer with the skilled workers' organization in order to save their company "from dealing with the radical and socialistic organization of the I.W.W." Before long Pressed Steel had the makings of a full-fledged company union.[16] Thereafter immigrant workers, with few allies inside the plant and fewer still in the community, had only the little offered them by the IWW.

The immigrant workers undoubtedly realized the extent of their loss before the IWW did. Once again IWW leaders believed their organization had fully demonstrated the primacy of economic over political action, and the elemental advantages of direct action at the point of production. Some members of the Socialist party, elated by the IWW "victory" in the steel industry, viewed the IWW as the best available rallying point for radical activity on the economic field. Other reformers and radicals thought that for the first time a revolutionary industrial union had won a foothold in America's most basic industry. The Wobblies themselves looked forward to a bright future in the Pittsburgh area. At McKees Rocks, as late as September 23, they claimed five thousand members in Car Builders Industrial Union No. 229, which represented "a case of an open union and a closed shop." [17] Ettor and several IWW organizers were already at work organizing among workers in other district steel mills, and by late October Ettor waxed enthusiastic about the prospects for direct action. He reported success in organizing among Poles, Slovenians, Germans, Czechs, Hungarians, Croatians, and other nationalities. An IWW district convention held on October 10, Ettor noted, had established a Pittsburgh–New Castle District Industrial Council, which planned to issue an official publication known as *Solidarity*. (Whatever the McKees Rocks strike may have failed to accomplish, it did give birth to the IWW's official newspaper.) "From now on," concluded Ettor, "if I am not mistaken, things and men will move around here. History will be made, and, let us hope, so fast that we shall have no time to write about it." [18]

Ettor was not entirely mistaken. Several weeks after he published his report from the "war zone," *Solidarity* hit the newsstands and the IWW became involved in steel-industry labor conflicts at New Castle and at Butler, Pennsylvania. Wobblies lacked the time to write about their new activities, for local officials, disturbed by the outbreak of Wobbly-agitated labor unrest, had jailed the entire editorial and production staff of *Solidarity*. Management and public officials proved equally effective in squelching the strikes undertaken by new IWW recruits. If the McKees Rocks dispute had ended in partial success, those at New Castle and Butler ended in total failure.[19]

Although *Solidarity* remained as a going concern for several years in New Castle, the same could not be said for the IWW as a labor organization within the steel industry. Try as they might, Wobblies never recaptured the spirit, or even the limited success, that was theirs at McKees Rocks. Opposed by employers, public officials, and skilled American workers, the IWW could not keep the immigrants organized. Heaven knows it tried. But given the IWW's limited funds and small staff, effort and will were not enough. In October 1909 the IWW had had six thousand members of every nationality on its books at McKees Rocks; less than three years later, on August 26, 1912, when Trautmann attempted to reorganize the local there, he could claim only twenty signatures on the charter application.[20]

What, then, had the IWW foray into the steel industry accomplished? It certainly demonstrated that the immigrant workers, so long neglected by craft unions, were good strikers, and that they could be organized. Ethnic diversity and language barriers had proved no obstacle to IWW organizers, who did not patronize the foreigners the way the typical AFL organizer did. But McKees Rocks also illustrated that the division between immigrants and Americans was close to irreconcilable. The skilled Americans apparently despised the immigrants as dirty aliens and detested the Wobblies as dangerous subversives. They preferred, if possible, to collaborate with management. Given the anti-union structure of the steel industry and its mill towns, any labor union would have found it difficult to maintain stable organization among the immigrants. McKees Rocks proved that the IWW was not the union to do it, for it lacked the money, the men, and the administrative ability. Yet the IWW left an idea as its legacy. In the future steel workers would strive for the goal of industrial unionism that cut across the lines of nationality and skill. But they would have to wait for a more opportune time and better labor leadership to achieve that elusive ideal.

From 1910 to 1912 the IWW proved that other neglected workers could be organized and that racial as well as nationality differences might be surmounted by championing the cause of white and black workers in the South.

Southern labor history has always been something of a puzzle.

Few studies have been written about labor organizations or of working-class discontent below the Mason and Dixon Line. Although the region has generally been considered an agrarian monolith, it is well known that even the antebellum South had an urban-industrial working class, and that after the Civil War this class increased in size and importance. It is equally well known that Southern workers received lower wages and labored under more difficult conditions than their Northern cousins. Yet Southern poverty and exploitation apparently resulted in little labor organization and less industrial conflict. Some students of Southern labor history believe that the existence of a large Negro labor surplus degraded the white laborer, keeping all workers divided and hence unorganized. It has only recently been perceived that labor organization and class conflict existed within the race-ridden, agrarian American South. One of the strangest and most interesting of Southern labor conflicts occurred in the cypress and pine forests and mill towns of Louisiana and east Texas between 1910 and 1913, and it involved the IWW.

Few Southern workers were more abominably treated than those who toiled in the damp, isolated woods and mill towns of the Louisiana-Texas timber belt. Black or white, they led a miserable existence. Many resided in company towns where they were paid in scrip and required to buy necessities in a company store at inflated prices. Writing in *Harper's* about Texas sawmill towns, George Creel observed: "The lumber communities of the Lone Star State are as far removed from freedom and democracy as though time had rolled back to the days of Ivanhoe." A labor newspaper added:

He [the lumber worker] is born in a Company house; wrapped in Company swaddling clothes, rocked in a Company cradle. At two years of age he toddles out on the Company street and takes his first infantile look at the Company mill. At five years of age he goes to the Company school. At eleven he graduates and goes to the Company woods. At 16 he goes to work in the Company mill. At 21 he gets married in a Company church. . . . At 40 he sickens with Company malaria, lies down on a Company bed, is attended by a Company doctor who doses him with Company drugs, and then he draws his last Company breath, while the undertaker is paid by the widow in Company scrip for the Company coffin in which he is buried on Company ground.

That the labor paper exaggerated only in part was substantiated by the findings of the United States Commission on Industrial Relations, whose investigators reported: "We find that many communities exist under arbitrary economic control of corporation officials charged with the management of an industry . . . and we find that in such communities, political liberty does not exist and its forms are hollow mockery. . . . Free speech, free assembly, and a free press may be denied as they have been denied time and again . . ." [21] This report was made three years after labor conflict erupted in the woods!

Naturally, these communities had almost no history of labor organization. In a painstaking study of Texas timber workers, Ruth Allen could find only one official mention of a strike before 1911. Interestingly enough, that strike, which occurred in 1904, had been instigated by the American Labor Union, an organizational parent of the IWW. (Miss Allen's evidence also indicated that the ALU had two organizers in the field recruiting Southern timber beasts.) [22] But between 1904 and 1910 neither industrial conflict nor labor agitators disturbed the region's labor scene. Workers remained exploited, leaderless, and quiescent.

Sometime late in 1909 or possibly early in 1910, however, a "messiah" appeared in the region in the person of young Arthur Lee Emerson. A Southern-born Protestant, Emerson looked too gentle to be a labor organizer, let alone a Wobbly. Tall, thin, almost effeminately handsome, he carried the union gospel into the woods of Louisiana. Emerson apparently derived his faith in unionism from a brief experience lumberjacking in the Pacific Northwest, where he met dedicated Wobblies. Upon his return to the South, he immediately turned to labor organizing in order to raise Gulf Coast wages and working conditions up to the none-too-high Pacific Coast standards. After finding a job in a Fullerton, Louisiana, mill, he signed up 85 to 125 employees in his new union. Buoyed by this initial success, he traveled from place to place, signing on for a few days' employment—time enough to use the Wobbly tactic of organizing on the job. [23]

Emerson soon discovered an ally in Jay Smith, another native-born Southern white Protestant, and the two roamed the woods of Louisiana and Texas signing up union members during the winter of 1910–1911. They soon had enough members and sufficient locals to create a larger regional labor organization, and in June 1911 they founded the Brotherhood of Timber Workers. From headquarters in Alexandria, Louisiana, the BTW dispatched organizers and propaganda throughout the region. Membership soared. At one point in the BTW's brief history its membership ranged between 18,000 and 35,000. [24]

At its birth, the BTW's link with the IWW was at best tenuous.

Aside from the ALU's 1904 attempt to organize the lumber industry and Emerson's experiences in the Northwest, only one other possible thread connected the BTW to the IWW. Covington Hall, Wobbly poet, songwriter, and essayist, a native Southerner of distinctly patrician ancestry, then resided in New Orleans, and from the first he volunteered his pen and typewriter in the timber workers' cause. Beyond this, the BTW differed drastically from the IWW.

Possibly bearing in mind the Southern environment, the BTW adopted a distinctly conservative constitution—so conservative in fact that many an AFL affiliate would have been shocked by its relatively stolid tone. The constitution specifically ruled out violence as a tactic, it de-emphasized the role of class conflict, and it proclaimed the BTW's desire to collaborate with employers. It also beseeched employers to cooperate with the union in the achievement of "equal rights, a living wage, a just consideration of abuses, exact and equal justice to those who work with their hands, and who contribute so much to the comforts of mankind, and who get so little in return." The union abided by the Southern code of race relations and segregated Negro members in separate lodges. It also provided in its constitution for rituals derived from the rural Protestant church (union meetings sometimes resembled revivals) and from America's popular fraternal orders.[25] Only in the composition and nature of its membership did the character of the BTW diverge from that of the AFL.

Southern lumber operators wanted no part of this ostensibly conservative, even pragmatic, labor organization. When the Southern Lumber Operators' Association met in New Orleans in 1910, its Texas and Louisiana constituents decided to combat the emerging union movement. John H. Kirby, a man well suited for command in the struggle, assumed the lead in the fight against organized labor. Kirby's companies dominated the entire Southern lumber industry during those years. Incorporated in 1901, the Kirby Lumber Company controlled twenty-five plants with a total capitalization of $21 million; according to the 1906 *Southwest* magazine, "The Kirby Lumber Company is not only the largest enterprise of its kind in the State [Texas], but also in the South and possibly in the U.S." At various times in his busy life, Kirby served as president of the National Lumber Manufacturers Association, the Southern Pine Association, and the Southern Tariff Association; twice a member of the Texas House of Representatives and a member of the University of Texas Board of Regents, he also served as president of the National Association of Manufacturers, in which capacity he directed that organization's anti-union campaign. Kirby's official biography notes: "There is no way of estimating the number of millions of dollars earned by him during a busy lifetime, but his life and all of his earnings were given to his friends." [26] Workers, it may safely be said, were not among his friends!

Kirby directed a many-faceted offensive against the BTW in Texas and Louisiana. Whenever they had the power to do so, employers compelled workers to sign anti-union pledges. Employees of the Long-Bell Company in Longville, Louisiana, pledged themselves "to use our best efforts and influence to discourage any and all attempts of labor organizers representing the so-called Timber Workers' Union to disturb the good will which exists between the company and its employees." [27] Lumber companies also resorted to an anti-union blacklist, although this violated Louisiana law. All lumber workers had to renounce allegiance to the BTW, for refusal to do so would result in denial of employment and in blacklisting. Operators simultaneously played Negro and white workers off against each other. Employers replaced white workers with Negro strikebreakers; when Negroes joined the union, however, employers suggested to their white workers that the Brotherhood, by admitting Negro members, threatened the Southern pattern of race relations. Management also retained scores of hired gunmen and transformed many company towns into armed baronies. (In one such Louisiana town, the United States Post Office, situated within a company barricade, compelled outsiders to get their mail through a back window.) [28]

As the BTW continued to recruit new members in 1910 and 1911, employers decided upon a more forceful approach. In mid-May 1911 owners announced a decision to reduce all mills to four days' operation a week beginning June 1. If that failed to curtail union organizing and the union's demands for an eight-hour day and higher wages, the companies threatened to close all their mills for an indefinite period. The Operators' Association thus considered putting more than twenty thousand men out of work. When showdowns and threats of a lockout brought no end to union agitation, in August 1911 the Operators' Association shut eleven Louisiana mills employing three thousand men and empowered a special committee to order the closing of any of three hundred other properties in Texas, Louisiana, and Arkansas.

Kirby publicly maintained that his association fought socialism and anarchy, not organized labor. He even publicized his willingness to deal with the AFL, which, he claimed, recognized and respected private property. Kirby emphasized that his association would never bargain with the IWW, an organization which "would destroy the Constitution, plunge all the states into anarchy, and bring disorder and the rule of brute force into every community in America." [29]

Kirby's reference to the IWW at this particular time was in fact a red herring, for no formal link then existed between the BTW and the Wobblies. Nor had IWW organizers yet been sent south. Not until April 20, 1911, almost two full years after Emerson and Smith began their organizing efforts, did mention of the BTW appear in the IWW press. Even then, all the IWW did for several months was to appeal to Southern lumber workers—who, by the way, did not read Wobbly publications—cautioning them to be moderate. "Try and withhold the battle until we have *Power* to win," advised the *Industrial Worker*.[30]

Kirby's favorable references to the AFL and his personal overtures to Sam Gompers were equally disingenuous. Employers liked to speak about negotiations with conservative, respectable American labor organizations when those organizations did not have the power to press labor-management bargaining. Yet rumors spread to the effect that Kirby and Gompers had united to drive the BTW from the woods and to organize in its place a lily-white union of skilled workers.[31] The most likely explanation behind the rumors and also behind Kirby's apparently warm approval of the AFL is not overly complicated. Lumber operators at that time had to deal with the BTW, not the AFL. By intimating to the higher-paid, more skilled lumber workers that the BTW was linked to the IWW, which endorsed union integration, socialism, and violence, Kirby hoped to turn skilled men away from the union. Since the AFL had never had any influence or members in the industry, lumber workers would then return to the job without a union.

The association's strikebreakers, gunmen, blacklists, and lockouts meanwhile took their toll upon the BTW. As early as September 1911, association investigators reported that membership had fallen off sharply and that not over 50 per cent of Brotherhood members were then mill workers.* The investigators also pointed out that the considerable number of Negro union members (estimated at 50 per cent) created a general undercurrent of dissatisfaction among white Brotherhood members. "It would therefore appear from a general summary," an Operators' Association investigator concluded, "that this Association has but to adhere strictly to the policy adopted and its members to give their full cooperation in order to ultimately clear the territory of socialistic agitators and to resume operations free and unhampered." [32]

These association tactics, more than any other factors, drove the BTW's leaders to preach integration with Negroes and affiliation with the IWW. Emerson and Smith realized that if Negroes remained outside the union, they would tend to scab. Hence, they advised the black worker: "The BTW . . . takes the Negro and protects him and his family along with the white wage worker and his family on an industrial basis." To the white worker they proclaimed: "As far as we, the workers of the South, are concerned, the only 'supremacy' and 'equality' they [the employers] have ever granted us is the supremacy of misery and the equality of rags. . . . No longer will we allow the Southern oligarchy to divide and weaken us on lines of race, craft, religion, and nationality." Having as great a need for financial support as it had for racial integration, the BTW moved closer to the IWW, the only outside labor organization willing to offer aid. Although not yet prepared to ally itself fully with the Wobblies, the Brotherhood sent three fraternal delegates to the 1911 IWW convention.[33]

Southern workers also had a firm local basis for their resistance to the employer counteroffensive. Unlike the despised immigrant workers of the North or the unattached migratories of the West, Southern lumber workers belonged to a tightly knit local community. Small local farmers, lacking markets, often worked in the mills as family units. What most impressed two IWW organizers sent south in 1912 was the alliance between local farmers and laborers based upon kinship, marriage, settled conditions, and mutual hostility to the company store system. (Farmers often had to sell their produce to these stores at low prices, while they paid high prices for their purchases.) This

---

* Many lumber workers were also part-time farmers, who, unable to find work, returned to farming. Many of their relatives were full-time farmers who joined the Brotherhood partly as a gesture of sympathy and partly as an anti-employer strategy.

community of sentiment and of blood led several Louisiana lumber towns to elect socialist administrations, which protected union organizers and strikers from the worst excesses of company repression.[34] It also encouraged union members to resist their enemies with force and mob action.

Union resistance nevertheless weakened. In February 1912 the Operators' Association ended its lockout and resumed operations with a largely nonunion work force bound by yellow-dog contracts. At this juncture the IWW actually entered the conflict. Seeking to instill new life into the BTW's ebbing spirit, Big Bill Haywood himself went south in the spring of 1912 to attend the BTW's second regional convention in Alexandria (May 6–9). Covington Hall joined him as an IWW representative. They pleaded with the disillusioned and dejected Brotherhood delegates to maintain the struggle, and promised IWW assistance if the BTW affiliated with the Wobblies. Haywood, in particular, pleaded with union members to transcend racial animosities, achieve real union integration, and meet employers with a black-white united front. Carried away by Haywood's enthusiasm, convention delegates voted to affiliate with the IWW and to move more firmly toward an integrated organization. In return, IWW national headquarters sent two veteran organizers, George Speed and E. F. Doree, south early in the summer of 1912. For a time IWW assistance increased the Brotherhood's waning militancy.[35]

Revitalized by its new alliance, the BTW once again struck to obtain higher wages and improved working conditions from Southern lumber operators. Again employers responded with a lockout and a lengthening blacklist. An army of strikebreakers went to work in the woods and mills accompanied by gunmen, whose function was to intimidate union organizers. One eager local businessman even attempted to assassinate a socialist newspaper reporter then covering the labor dispute for the *National Ripsaw*.[36] Although the reporter, a man named H. G. Creel, escaped with his life, the assassination attempt was an indication of things to come.

On Sunday afternoon, July 7, A. L. Emerson and several other BTW organizers held an unscheduled meeting near the premises of the nonunion Galloway Lumber Company in Grabow, Louisiana. Shortly before dusk a crowd began to gather, and Emerson climbed on the back of a wagon to address the farmer-laborers. Suddenly, three shots punctuated the heavy evening air. The crowd broke and ran for cover. Armed union men turned to defend their unarmed

comrades and kin from the fire of guards shooting at them from concealed spots on company premises. Ten minutes and roughly three
hundred rounds later, the shooting stopped. That evening saw three
men dead, a fourth dying, and more than forty wounded. Three of
the dead were union men, the fourth a company guard; the vast
majority of the injured belonged to the Brotherhood.

Immediately after the incident Emerson and sixty-four union
members, with the mill owner and three of his armed guards, were
arrested. Grand jury proceedings began promptly, and on July 23 Jay
Smith wired IWW headquarters: "Three true bills for murder against
Emerson and sixty-four other union men and one true bill against
each of them for assault with willful shooting. No true bill found
against mill owners." [37] The "Iron Heel," bemoaned BTW leaders, had
stamped on Dixie.

When IWW organizers Speed and Doree arrived in Alexandria,
which they claimed to be 137 degrees "hotter than Hell," they found
the "Iron Heel" very effective indeed. Expecting to witness an area-
wide strike, they discovered a shattered labor organization. The
Grabow incident had stifled labor militancy. The BTW now concentrated its slender funds and its diminished strength upon defending
imprisoned members. Speed and Doree soon learned why the strike
had collapsed. Touring the timber belt to stir up union sentiment,
they were tailed by company detectives and threatened by local
citizens of anti-union sentiments. They brushed up against the "Iron
Heel" in one Texas town where a member of the local elite dispersed a meeting addressed by Doree, warning the Wobbly organizer:
"We built this town, and we're going to keep it just as it is." [38]

While Doree and Speed agitated and eluded law officers and
vigilantes, the indicted BTW members waited in prison before being
brought to trial for murder. Not until October 8, three months after
their indictment, did the state of Louisiana, with ample financial and
legal assistance donated by the Lumber Operators' Association, bring
to court the case of Emerson and eight other BTW members. A month
later a local jury, apparently sympathetic to the union and unim-
pressed with the prosecution's evidence, acquitted Emerson and his
co-defendants.

The "Iron Heel" was not yet lifted from Dixie. As Emerson and
his co-defendants walked out of prison, IWW organizers Doree and
C. L. Filigno, as well as Brotherhood leader Clarence Edwards,
marched in on charges of jury tampering. Now it was Emerson's turn

to come to their defense. "I am going to enter into the fight again and fight harder than ever before," he pledged. "I leave in an hour for Lake Charles to see what can be done for those . . . men still in jail. They will either be turned out of there or, by God, they'll have to turn me back in." As a matter of fact, Emerson wasn't much longer for the battle. Nor was the BTW-IWW alliance.[39]

Just before the Grabow defendants went to trial, Negro and white BTW delegates to the 1912 IWW convention had installed their organization as the Southern District of the National Industrial Union of Forest and Lumber Workers. BTW delegates then returned south to resume their labor struggle under IWW auspices.

On November 11, 1912, thirteen hundred members of the union, now officially known as the NIUF&LW, struck the American Lumber Company, once a union concern but now a Santa Fe Railroad open-shop subsidiary at Merryville, Louisiana. The strikers demanded that fifteen men blacklisted because they had appeared as defense witnesses on Emerson's behalf be rehired. White and black Merryville workers presented a united front. Company agents who sought to turn Negroes against the union met unexpected resistance. When company men inquired of the black workers, "What in hell do you niggers expect to get out of this damn union?" Negroes answered that they expected nothing out of the union, for they had joined the union in order to obtain something out of the bosses.[40]

But racial solidarity proved of little value against determined company opposition. American Lumber employed the usual anti-union tactics: blacklists, strikebreakers, gunmen, and vigilante justice. More and more reports began to reach IWW headquarters concerning armed attacks upon strikers as company gunmen and detectives resorted to a campaign of open intimidation. They kidnaped strike leaders, beating one and shooting another. Mob law enveloped Merryville as vigilantes sacked union headquarters and confiscated records and equipment. They also deported all union men, threatening them with death if any dared return to Merryville.[41]

By the spring of 1913 the Southern lumber workers' cause seemed doomed. Not even the IWW could offer hope or help. Little wonder, then, that at the first convention of the NIUF&LW, which met in Alexandria on May 19, 1913, not a single delegate from the Northwest arrived and only twenty-four Southerners appeared. Worse yet, A. L. Emerson, pleading poor health, resigned as general organizer for the Southern district. His health was actually no worse than that of the organization he had founded: both were finished as militant fighters. The Lake Charles murder trial and the Merryville strike coming so close on its heels had exhausted the Southern union financially and spiritually. Organized labor simply could not survive on pleas for solidarity or on the reiteration of the cliché that "an injury to one is the concern of all," which was all the IWW could offer Southern workers. Denied financial sustenance and lacking a stable bureaucratic nucleus, the Southern lumber workers' union, like many an earlier and a later IWW affiliate, shriveled and died.[42]

Yet to blame the failure and death of the BTW partly upon its decision to ally with the IWW, as some students of Southern labor history have done, would be a mistake.[43] The Brotherhood, as has been seen, decided to join the IWW only after its efforts to organize workers and to improve conditions were verging on failure. Even before the Brotherhood officially affiliated with the IWW, Kirby and other employers had accused it of "anarchistic IWW'ism." The IWW's anti-religious attitude, its "addiction to violence," and its uncompromising anti-segregationism may have alienated it from Southern workers. That assertion, however, rests on some dubious assumptions. To begin with, IWW organizers and the literature they aimed at Southern workers never mentioned religion; it is also unlikely that the workers involved knew anything of the IWW's religious philosophy, which in fact contained an element of evangelical, revivalistic Protestantism. They knew, however, that the IWW endorsed their cause. As for the issue of race, what alternative existed to the IWW-BTW's anti-segregationism? Lily-white unions implied a surplus of Negro strikebreakers; skilled lily-white unions on the model of the AFL offered nothing to the mass of poorly paid white and black workers. Whatever the union did on the Negro question, employers stood to gain, for labor had to appeal to both races while the employer merely had to play one off against the other. Finally, as far as Southern workers were concerned, the IWW preached nonviolent industrial action; the companies practiced violence and inflicted murder and mayhem upon union members. To put it bluntly, violence initiated by employers destroyed Southern unionism. In the last analysis, Southern timber workers turned to the IWW out of desperation. The Wobblies alone promised assistance to America's most despised and degraded workers. But in 1911 the IWW was a very frail reed upon which to have to lean for survival.

Since its reorganization at the 1908 convention under Vincent St. John's leadership, the IWW, despite a record of militant industrial activity, had made few substantial gains in membership. Nor had it achieved anything approaching internal stability. Wobblies had fought for free speech in Missoula, Spokane, and Fresno; they had struggled for improved working conditions at McKees Rocks and in Southern forests. But the IWW had failed to construct effective labor organizations in any of those places. Although the *Industrial Worker* reported on April 30, 1910, that sixty-six locals had been chartered since the 1908 convention, the IWW could not even hold a national convention in 1909, and one finally convened in June 1910 transacted no business of importance. At that 1910 Chicago convention, National Organizer Trautmann offered few specific data on IWW membership. *Solidarity* sought to demonstrate organizational achievements by enumerating the IWW's sanctioned newspapers—by 1910, seven in number, including journals in Spanish, Polish, French, and even Japanese. Placing a bright but false façade over the IWW's dim interior, Ben Williams commented: "A movement is judged not only by what it does itself, but also by what it compels the opposition to do." [44] To be sure, the IWW had certainly met more than its share of opposition. St. John, in a letter to Paul Brissenden just after the 1911 convention, put the IWW's actual status into perspective. St. John noted that the general office had in an eighteen-month period issued sixty thousand dues books, but of that number only about one in ten, or roughly six thousand, represented members in good standing. The pattern of Wobblies' work, St. John added, "means that they are out of touch with the organization the greater part of the year either on the job or moving about the country looking for work . . . but as they drift into town they pay up. In passing," St. John concluded, "it may be stated that the above number is the largest membership the IWW has had since its inception, except when the WFM was supposed to be a part of the organization." As of October 1911 he claimed ten thousand IWW members in good standing.[45]

This dismal growth pattern led left-wing socialist and erstwhile Wobbly Frank Bohn to title a July 11 article in the *International Socialist Review*, "Is the I.W.W. to Grow?" [46] The essay opened by asking readers whether the IWW had a future, or only a past—and an inglorious one at that. A pessimist, Bohn held the triumph within the IWW of an anti-political faction—the so-called philosophical anarchists, who made a fetish of attacking the Socialist party—responsible for the organization's lack of success. He accused the IWW's mixed locals and its propaganda locals of alienating "real" industrial unionists and thereby becoming solely cells for "hot-air social revolutionaries." If the anti-political element remained dominant in the organization, wrote Bohn, "the I.W.W. is not dying. It is dead."

Justus Ebert attempted to answer Bohn on behalf of the IWW. Writing in the *New York Call*, Ebert reminded his readers of how poorly the AFL had fared during its first decade, having a total annual income less than that of the IWW during its initial five years. Conceding that the IWW was not "likely to grow with the speed of a prairie fire," Ebert pointed to the organization's manifold militant activities from 1909 to 1911, and concluded: "We submit that an organization that can show such results as the I.W.W. has shown in the past three years is not a moribund but a healthy body that is going to grow." [47]

On the eve of the 1911 IWW convention, however, rumors seemed to substantiate Bohn's gloomy prophecy. One set of rumors contended that the convention majority would purge all advocates and practitioners of political action from the organization, thus converting the IWW once and for all into an anarcho-syndicalist cell composed of pristine believers. Another set of rumors implied that Western delegates, DeLeon's old "Bum Brigade," would dominate the convention, dismantle what little bureaucratic administration the IWW possessed, abolish the general executive board, as well as all national officials, and create in their place a form of "participatory union democracy." [48]

One man even came to Chicago intent on burying the IWW as a labor organization. That man, William Z. Foster, had joined the IWW during the Spokane free-speech fight. A child of Philadelphia's slums, from which he had fled as a teen-ager, Foster had worked his way over and around the Western hemisphere as a sailor, ditchdigger, harvester, and general roustabout. A slight, earnest, intense individual, he demonstrated at an early age his penchant for radicalism and his flair for labor agitation and political polemics. Soon after his experience in Spokane and his enlistment in the IWW, Foster went to France. Traveling about Europe in 1910, he closely observed the tactics of the French labor movement (the Confédération Générale du Travail, or CGT) as well as European socialism. Six months in France deeply impressed the young American with what he called the tactic of boring from within, "the policy of militant workers penetrating conservative unions, rather than trying to construct new, ideal industrial unions on the outside." Foster resolved to return to the United States in order to propose using a militant minority to bore from within the established labor movement instead of building dual industrial unions outside the AFL.[49]

Not Foster, or the decentralizers, or the anti-political fanatics disrupted the 1911 convention. Delegates never raised the political question, and the convention voted down an amendment asserting the futility of parliamentary action. Western proposals to abolish or to minimize the power of the general executive board were roundly defeated, and the delegates managed, at least temporarily, to harmonize Western demands for increased autonomy and rotation in office with Eastern insistence upon tighter organization and more bureaucratic, professional leadership.[50] Thus far, no clear geographical divisions existed within the IWW. Opposition to centralized administration and to "autocratic" leadership usually came from those Wobblies dissatisfied with what the administration was doing, not those who came from a particular geographical area. Westerners such as St. John, Haywood, Little, and Brazier, to name only a few, struggled to create within the organization a more professional central leadership supported by higher dues; while Easterners such as Elizabeth Gurley Flynn, Ettor, and Giovannitti chafed at orders from general headquarters. Westerners seemed more in favor of decentralization and rotation in office, partly because the physical distance from central headquarters allowed them even more autonomy in practice than was provided in theory, and partly because the very nature of their work—migratory and isolated—compelled them to change local leaders often and to function just as often without a well-established local headquarters. Had the Westerners truly wished to dismantle the IWW's administrative machinery and put "participatory democracy" into practice, they certainly could have done so given their numerical preponderance within the organization.

Foster, not the so-called Western anarchists, had the most complete and well-thought-out proposals for dismantling the IWW as it existed in 1911. He proposed that the IWW relinquish its attempt to build a new labor movement, transform itself into a propaganda league, and then revolutionize the old unions by boring from within them. In his autobiography, Foster later claimed to have persuaded two Wobblies, Earl Ford and Frank Little, to his view of American labor's future. But the IWW's top officials—St. John, Trautmann, and Haywood— opposed Foster's plan, which would have started with the organization dissolving its own dual unions in mining, building, metals, printing, and railroads. Rather than bring his resolution to the convention floor, where he realized he would suffer a resounding defeat, Foster resolved to agitate among the rank and file. Initially, even he applauded the 1911 convention's outcome. Writing in the *Industrial Worker* of October 2, 1911, he praised the Chicago sessions as the most successful IWW convention yet held. Foster apparently agreed with Ben Williams, who noted "that from now on the I.W.W. should move forward with increasing numbers and power." [51]

But Foster had only beat a strategic retreat, for he declined to concede either the deficiencies or the unpopularity of his belief in the principle of boring from within. The chance to carry the organization with him came when a small faction of Western decentralizers nominated Foster for editor of the *Industrial Worker*. On November 2, 1911, he proclaimed his policy publicly in an editorial announcing his candidacy for editorship of the Western paper. Foster reminded the rank and file that, after seven years of struggle, the IWW still had only a minuscule membership, like other radical dual labor movements in England and Germany, and unlike the old unions in France, which had been captured by the syndicalists. He called upon Wobblies to learn from the French workers' example, as Tom Mann, the radical British labor leader, was now learning in England, where he had recently declared against dual unionism and was "boring from within" the Trades Union Congress. Foster concluded his polemic by asserting: "I am satisfied that the only way for the I.W.W. to have the workers adopt and practice the principles of revolutionary unionism . . . is to give up its attempt to create a new labor movement . . . get into the organized labor movement and by building up better fighting machines within the old unions . . . revolutionize those unions . . ." [52]

The debate was soon on in earnest. Both the *Industrial Worker* and *Solidarity* filled their columns in November–December 1911 with "boring from within" articles and correspondence, mostly anti-Foster in substance. J. S. Biscay offered the most thoughtful and complete rebuttal of Foster's position in the *Industrial Worker*. Like other Wobblies, Biscay pointed out that no exact analogy existed between the AFL and its European counterparts. What might be accomplished in Europe, in other words, could not so easily be achieved in America. Biscay made lucid the problems facing American, especially Wobbly, borers from within. "To start boring from within with all the craft unionists prejudiced already would mean the disbanding of the I.W.W., and hardly causing a ripple in the crafts. Their overwhelming membership would soon dispose of the few capable men who would begin their 'boring.' The rest of the rank and file of the I.W.W. being of the floating element to a large extent, can't even get into the crafts to 'bore.' To change our ideas at this time," Biscay reasoned, "would only spell defeat. . . . By building from without we will demonstrate to the crafts that we are right." [53]

He might also have added that the European analogy broke down at other points. The established French, German, and English labor movements already contained a significant proportion of socialists and radicals in positions of influence ready to cooperate with the "borer," whereas the AFL, dominated by ardent foes of any form of labor radicalism, was prepared to rid the Federation of such radicals at the first opportunity. The European syndicalists, whatever their country, did not advocate a form of trade unionism at odds with the prevailing structure of their nations' labor movements. By 1910 England had had over two decades' experience with general unions (their counterparts of industrial unions). In France, syndicalists did not take exception to the craft basis of the French labor movement; indeed, they supported it, and often favored craft unionism. But in America the industrial unionism proposed by the IWW, politics and ideology excluded, was unacceptable to a dominant majority within the AFL, and even to some of the Federation's socialist craft-oriented affiliates. That European developments did not in fact carry obvious lessons for American radicals was demonstrated by the experience of Bill Haywood, who visited Europe at the same time as Foster. Also impressed by European radicals, syndicalists, and labor leaders, Haywood decided, while in France, that he would rededicate himself to working for the IWW upon his return to the States. The Wobblies reminded Haywood of the allegedly successful European syndicalists.

Despite the strength and the logic of his opponents, Foster carried his fight to the membership. Organizing his own militant minority groups, of which he appointed himself national secretary, he began a six-thousand-mile hobo trip across the West in the dead of winter in order to carry his message to IWW locals. At some places he claimed victory and the establishment of syndicalist cells within the IWW. During this whirlwind campaign Foster and his adversaries even resorted to poetry. The Foster faction recited:

> "The proper way," said Jay the Fox,
> "To start the revolution
> Is just to bore a hole or two
> In existing institutions."

> "Agreed," cried Mr. Foster.
> "I have my gimlet ready,
> My arm is long, my hand is strong,
> My nerves are cool and steady."[54]

To which Walker C. Smith responded in a poem signed O. U. Gimlet:

> Within craft unions we are told to bore;
> To form an apple from a rotten core;
> Yet boring till we find ourselves outside,
> We will have built a hole—but nothing more.[55]

Foster's efforts were doomed to failure. Lacking support from any national IWW leader, he could scarcely carry his proposals effectively to the small but scattered organization membership. He could not even win the referendum vote for the editorship of the *Industrial Worker*. On December 16, 1911, Ben Williams closed *Solidarity's* columns to discussion of Foster's proposition. "Why . . . waste time trying to capture a corpse?" Williams noted.

Admitting defeat, Foster resigned from the IWW in February 1912, joined the Brotherhood of Railway Carmen, a craft union, and with Earl Ford founded the short-lived Syndicalist League of North America.[56] Foster, of course, never captured the railroad brotherhoods for revolutionary unionism. Yet in 1919 Gompers allowed him to direct that year's steelworkers' organizing drive, an effort that craft-union jealousies partially subverted. Soon thereafter Foster had enough of boring from within the AFL, which he left for the Communist party, becoming that party's major trade-union figure. In the 1920's he tried initially to attack the AFL from outside; failing in that approach, he again sought to bore from within unsuccessfully. Foster's fondest hopes notwithstanding, the AFL proved so resistant to decisive structural change that, as late as the 1930's, nonrevolutionary industrial unionists were compelled to build their new industrial unions outside the AFL. What the Committee for Industrial Organization failed to accomplish within the AFL in 1935, the IWW could scarcely have achieved in 1911.

But early in 1912, both Frank Bohn's question "Is the IWW to Grow?" and William Z. Foster's challenge became purely academic. Events in Lawrence, Massachusetts, revived the IWW and made it appear for a time a real competitor to the AFL as well as a distinct threat to American society. Industrial conflict in Lawrence catapulted the Wobblies to national prominence.

CHAPTER

10

Satan's Dark Mills: Lawrence, 1912

THURSDAY, January 11, 1912, dawned cold and grey in the Massachusetts textile city of Lawrence. The city's woolen mills, huddled along the Merrimac River like ugly pearls on a filthy string, appeared forbidding as the first rays of light accentuated the grimy snow and ice accumulated along the river banks and beside the plant gates. Soon thousands of men, women, and children would leave their congested tenements and form a stream flowing slowly but steadily toward the mills. Many of these workers would arrive at the factories in a mood as sullen as the sky above them and as bleak as the landscape around them.

January 11 would be the first payday at Lawrence's textile mills since the state of Massachusetts' new fifty-four-hour law had gone into effect.* The last time state legislation had reduced hours (from fifty-eight to fifty-six) employers had maintained prevailing wage rates. Now, however, workers seemed confused and anxious. Most mills had posted notices warning of the required reduction in hours, yet many failed to mention wages, while others treated the issue in

---

* Although the new law limited the hours of only female and child workers, they composed a majority of the work force; reducing their hours of labor in effect also set a new maximum for skilled adult men omitted from the law's coverage.

vague if not misleading terms. In fact, all posted notices, specific or not, were difficult for the poorly educated immigrants to understand. Employers arrogantly rebuffed employees who came to see them in order to clarify the status of wage rates under the fifty-four-hour law. In short, neither the owners nor the managers of Lawrence's mills had prepared their employees for reductions in an already low wage scale.

In one mill a group of Polish women, upon opening their pay envelopes, cried, "Short pay!" left their looms, and walked out. That evening the *Lawrence Sun* reported: "Italian Mill Workers Vote to Go Out on Strike Friday—In Noisy Meeting 900 Men Voice Dissatisfaction Over Reduced Pay Because of 54 Hour Law." The next morning, which was payday at most mills, employees arrived for work more sullen than they had been the previous day. About 9 A.M. an angry mob of Italians in the Wood Mill of the American Woolen Company, Lawrence's largest employer, deserted their machinery and ran through the mill demanding that other workers march out. As the Italians moved from one department to another they disassembled machinery, cut wires, blew fuses, and intimidated noncooperating workers into joining their walkout. The mob surged out of the Wood Mill and down Canal Street along the Merrimac River. The Italians rushed from mill to mill, heaving stones and chunks of ice at factory windows, beseeching the men and women inside to come out. By evening the original few hundred strikers had increased their number to roughly ten thousand men, women, and children. The day of machine wrecking, ice throwing, and window smashing came to a spasmodic end. Friday, January 12, would long be remembered in Lawrence history.[1]

On Saturday those still at work accepted their pay envelopes without a murmur of protest. No violence flared. Some Boston papers reported: "Peace seems assured." Yet industrial warfare was close at hand, for on Saturday evening, January 13, the IWW's Joseph Ettor arrived in Lawrence.

For some years a small Italian IWW local had been functioning in Lawrence. At its meeting on January 10, the local decided, at the insistence of young Angelo Rocco, to invite Ettor to assist it in organizing mill workers and protesting low wages. No sooner was he in Lawrence than Ettor infused the immigrants with his own militancy. All night Saturday and all day Sunday, at meeting after meeting, he urged mill workers to strike for higher wages. By Monday he had them in an aggressive mood, and that morning, the start of a new work week, an immense crowd fired up by Ettor stormed City Hall. There a frightened mayor responded by calling out 250 local militiamen to disperse the mob and to patrol the mill district. Thus had peace ended in Lawrence, as its citizens began to choose sides in what would later become known as the great Lawrence textile strike.

The last thing Lawrence's employers had expected was that a wage reduction would result in labor troubles. At worst, as one mill agent suggested, there might be a strike in a single mill. His impression of local conditions amply demonstrated how impervious employers, city officials, and old-line craft-union leaders were to the conditions of life among Lawrence's unskilled immigrant workers.[2]

A product of New England's industrial revolution, Lawrence was built on cotton and woolens. In 1845 the eminently successful business group known as the Boston Associates had selected one of the few remaining water-power sites along the Merrimac River, some thirty-five miles north of Boston, as an ideal location for a textile establishment. Here they decided to erect a model community—one that would make the famous textile town of Lowell appear backward. For the welfare of their workers the Boston Associates envisioned elaborate paternalistic plans, which included housing, schools, literature, and religion. They decided to name their capitalist utopia after one of the most successful and wealthy Boston businessmen of the era: Abbott Lawrence.

In some ways the Boston Associates built better than they knew; in other ways, far worse. By 1912 Lawrence led the nation in the production of woolen worsteds, and in the American Woolen Company housed the largest, most profitable firm in the field. The city had a labor force of more than 35,000, and approximately 60,000 of 85,892 people living there depended directly upon textile mill payrolls. But Lawrence was no paternalistic capitalist utopia. Perhaps, at first, when its employees were mostly native New Englanders, Lawrence could boast of excellent living conditions and a healthy, well-clothed working class. But from its origins, Lawrence, unlike the older textile cities in the region, attracted large numbers of immigrants. Its creation came roughly at the time of the potato blight which forced poor peasant farmers by the millions off the land in Ireland and Germany, thus providing the Boston Associates with an excellent source of cheap labor.

For starving peasants, Lawrence represented an opportunity to work and to eat. The Irish and the Germans worked hard, ate skimpily, lived frugally, and some of them thrived. Soon new immigrants arrived. From Lancashire and Yorkshire came skilled English textile workers; from the north came unskilled French-Canadians. They, too, worked hard, lived frugally, and sometimes thrived. Lawrence apparently had little trouble assimilating these immigrants. By the 1880's, according to one historian, Lawrence seemed a prosperous textile center; its Americanized immigrants were ascending the economic ladder, and the years ahead seemed full of promise.[3]

Europe's poor continued to look to America for opportunity. Lawrence's mills still demanded cheap labor. So, at the turn of the century, the poor began to arrive from Italy, Austria, Russia, and Turkey. Few of these new immigrants had had any experience in industry. Fewer still spoke English. By 1911, 74,000 of the city's 86,000 inhabitants were first- or second-generation Americans; southeast Europeans represented one-third of Lawrence's immigrant population, and for them room existed only at the bottom of the economic ladder and Lawrence was no utopia.

Indeed, these new immigrants found life hard. Most worked in the textile industry, where wages had always been notoriously low. Although no truly accurate wage figures exist, the Massachusetts Bureau of Labor Statistics and the United States Commissioner of Labor made some reasonably valid estimates. Both estimates agreed that in December 1911 the peak weekly wage for workers was about $8.76, which meant an average annual income of $400 for heads of families, well below that needed for a minimal health and welfare budget. Yet women and children, who formed over half the labor force, received well below the average; in addition, the average wage for the unskilled, a large majority of the mill hands, seems to have been closer to $6 a week than to $8.76. During slack periods, which were quite frequent in the seasonal textile industry, wages fell even lower. The State Bureau of Labor Statistics reported: "It is obvious . . . that the full-time earnings of a large number of adult employees are entirely inadequate to maintain a family." The plain fact was, the report continued, that the textile industry "is in large part a 'family industry.' It gives employment to men, women, and children. The normal family of five, unless the father is employed in one of the comparatively few better-paying occupations, is compelled to supply two wage-earners in order to secure the necessities of life." [4]

Hence, whatever economic and social security immigrants had in 1912 was based upon sending wives, mothers, and children over fourteen into the mills. (Many parents falsified their children's ages and sent them into the mills at an even younger age.) Children of preschool age would often have to be left in the care of neighboring women or go untended. At the age of fourteen, Lawrence's typical immigrant child would leave school, no matter what his grade or academic standing, and substitute a 6:45 A.M. to 5:30 P.M. mill day for his 9 to 3 school day.[5] Lawrence's leading citizens saw nothing wrong in this. A local minister and charity-society official (who lived in Andover to escape the noise and dirt of the mills) testified publicly that he saw no difference between ball playing and bobbin tending, schoolwork and millwork, as long as the child was occupied.[6]

Admittedly, Lawrence employers paid low wages and sought the cheap labor of women and children because of competitive difficulties. Hours were shorter and wages higher in Massachusetts than in most other American textile centers, especially those in the cheap-labor South. But poor conditions elsewhere did not make the misery in Lawrence any easier to bear. Nor did the views of the leading Boston citizen and company stockholder who justified Lawrence's low wage scale thus to Harry Emerson Fosdick: "There is no question of right and wrong. . . . The whole matter is a case of supply and demand. Any man who pays more for labor than the lowest sum he can get men for is robbing his stockholders. If he can secure men for $6 and pays more, he is stealing from the company." [7]

Closer examination of the economic realities of the industry shows that competitive difficulties were not as severe as Lawrence employers claimed. For years local employers had maintained that they required protection against low-wage English competition. Yet a statistician who compared real wages in England to those in Massachusetts found that "the adult males among these cotton mill workers [in Lawrence] are scarcely as well paid as the adult males employed in English cotton mills." Another economist discovered precisely what Lawrence's sacrosanct tariff walls meant for its mill hands:

The recent development at Lawrence . . . has disclosed the fact that the so-called American wage-earner, whose standard of living, it is claimed, must be upheld by the tariff, is largely a myth, and that in reality the

American woolen mill operatives are made up of "pauper workmen" of almost half-a-hundred of the immigrant races from the south and east of Europe and Asia.[8]

Any careful observer could prove that Lawrence's living standards were low. Indeed, by 1912 four-story wooden tenements, erected with scarcely any open space separating one from another, had become Lawrence's most notable feature. Contractors jammed buildings so close together that people in adjacent houses used opposing walls for kitchen shelves. Lawrence, in fact, could claim some of the most densely populated blocks in the nation—blocks where frequent fires, filth, and vermin bore down heavily on the residents.[9] Nor were Lawrence's immigrant families well nourished or well clothed. Margaret Sanger, a registered nurse as well as the Progressive era's most militant birth-control advocate, arrived in Lawrence on a cold winter day in 1912 in order to take a group of strikers' children to New York City, where sympathizers had volunteered to care for them. Of the 119 children she chaperoned, only four wore underwear beneath their ragged outer clothing. "I have been brought up in a factory town where there are glassblowers and children of glassblowers," Miss Sanger observed, "and I must say that I have never seen in any place children so ragged and so deplorable as these children were." Walter Weyl, another prominent reformer of the Progressive era and a co-founder of the *New Republic,* added: "I have rarely seen in any American city so many shivering men without overcoats as I have seen in the cloth-producing town of Lawrence." [10]

Mortality statistics reflected abysmal working and living conditions. Lawrence, with several other textile cities, led the nation in death rate per one thousand population. Like other textile towns, Lawrence had a shockingly high infant-mortality rate. In 1909, the last year before 1912 for which figures are available, for every thousand births in Lawrence 172 infants did not survive their first year. Tuberculosis, pneumonia, and other respiratory ailments stalked the adult mill workers, often cutting them down in the prime of life. Respiratory infections proved fatal to almost 70 per cent of the mill hands but to only 4 per cent of Massachusetts farmers, "who consequently lived to be sixty while the textile workers could not reach forty." [11]

Such was immigrant life in Lawrence, Massachusetts, during the peak of Progressivism. Reform legislation had several times reduced the hours of labor for women and children; factory inspection acts had somewhat improved mill conditions. But working and living conditions remained otherwise virtually unchanged. Lawrence's immigrants would have been the last to know they were living in a "progressive" era. Is it any wonder they rebelled, and that in their rebellion they turned to the IWW for leadership?

Trade unions had never been a smashing success in Lawrence. Mill superintendents had effectively crushed all trade unions which emerged in their plants. At one time the Lawrence Central Labor Union had invited the United Textile Workers of America to organize the skilled workers. But the union president, John Golden, later remarked: "For years every beginning we have made in Lawrence has been instantly stamped upon by the mill superintendents and their subordinates." [12] The shifting tides of immigration and the consequent changing complexion of the labor force created imposing obstacles to the process of union organization. Many immigrants resisted unionization, preferring semi-formal nationality associations or church groups, while such craft unions as the United Textile Workers showed little desire to organize "foreigners."

From its birth in 1905 the IWW had tried to organize workers neglected by the craft unions, though the Wobblies could hardly claim greater success than John Golden. Unlike Golden and his union, however, they never ceased in their attempts to organize the immigrant masses of Lawrence. By 1910 the IWW had begun to build a dedicated following in Lawrence. In April of that year Local No. 20 of the National Industrial Union of Textile Workers publicly boasted about its rising membership and its new headquarters, which included a five-hundred-seat auditorium, meeting rooms, a gym, and a game room. In January 1911, Louis Picavet, a local French-Canadian Wobbly, reported that Local 20 had joined with other Lawrence labor organizations to establish an Alliance of Textile Workers Unions. This alliance adopted the IWW's statement of principles, which emphasized the abolition of the wage system and social revolution. Lawrence Wobblies, according to Picavet, were doing some "boring from within." "The idea of meeting with the unions, even the conservative ones," he wrote, "can only result in good, because through our contact with them we can lead them first of all in a more progressive direction, and finally to the revolutionary conception." [13]

Shortly thereafter, Local 20 initiated an active organizing campaign among textile workers. Members held street meetings featuring speakers adept in Lawrence's diverse languages; Wobblies also distributed literature and even sparked several wildcat strikes. Local 20 organized an Italian branch, intending to invite Ettor to Lawrence to proselyte among Italians. Ettor arrived in Lawrence in May 1911, and he left convinced that the IWW would grow rapidly among the immigrant textile workers. Later that same month the French branches of the NIUTW met at Lawrence's IWW headquarters, where they planned to establish the French IWW paper *L'Emancipation* upon a firmer foundation and to increase agitation among French-speaking workers. In June, Elizabeth Gurley Flynn joined the Massachusetts organizing campaign. "If the boys in Lawrence keep up their work," an NIUTW official named Francis Miller wrote, "they will have one of the largest local unions in the I.W.W. The agitation carried on by Ettor and Miss Flynn should make things hum." [14]

In August 1911, Local 20 began to lead Lawrence workers in a series of slowdowns and wildcat walkouts, which aimed to ease the work pace and to increase wages. Although few of these conflicts affected more than one mill, or more than a handful of weavers, Miss Flynn pleaded with Lawrence's workers "to weave the shroud of capitalism." [15] Despite the IWW's small total membership in Lawrence, by January 1912 most local workers knew of the organization's existence, its aims, and its local activities.

Still, on the eve of the 1912 strike no stable labor organization existed in Lawrence. The English-speaking skilled workers in the United Textile Workers' crafts claimed a membership of 2,500, but their somnolent locals scarcely disturbed employers. At best the IWW could lay claim to only 300 paid-up members. Thus, out of a work force of 30,000 to 35,000 in January 1912, only about 2,800 workers definitely belonged to trade unions.[16]

By December 1911, however, the IWW had laid the basis for action in Lawrence, and the new fifty-four-hour law and the subsequent wage reduction offered Wobblies an opportunity for action which they did not hesitate to seize. When Ettor returned to Lawrence for the third time on January 13 to lead a spontaneous strike, he was no stranger to the town's textile workers; nor, for that matter, was the IWW an alien institution. The 1912 strike did not, as most students of the subject have asserted, represent the first IWW conflict in New England's textile mills. In 1907 the Wobblies had led a walkout from the mills of Skowhegan, Maine; a few years later they hit New Bedford's factories; and, as we have seen, during the autumn of 1911 Local 20 had led walkouts in Lawrence itself. Moreover, when Lawrence's immigrants walked out of the mills, they were neither as secure nor as moderate nor as nonradical as Donald Cole asserts. They may, as Cole contends, have been "miserably poor people who wanted a better life." [17] But they were also a good deal more than that. IWW agitation had affected them; they were not immune to socialist literature; they detested the conditions under which they labored and lived; and they despised the foremen and supervisors who treated them like cattle. Of course the immigrants wanted better wages, improved working conditions, and decent homes; yet they also sought a social system better than the one they had—which was what the IWW and socialism promised them. Most importantly, the immigrants had begun to see that the system under which they labored treated them as less than human, and that only by acting directly and defiantly under IWW leadership could they establish their claim to be treated as human beings. "Whether all the members hold the theories of the I.W.W. or not, a more important thing is true," Harry Emerson Fosdick wrote of Lawrence's immigrant workers, "they have all caught its spirit." [18]

In the winter of 1912 Lawrence, Massachusetts, was America in microcosm. The textile workers represented both the new and the old immigrants, the skilled and unskilled; William Wood (president of the American Woolen Company) and the other mill directors typified one segment of the nation's industrial leaders; Governor John Foss and the state legislature embodied the hopes of the Progressive era; John Golden and the United Textile Workers acted as surrogates for the "conservative" American labor movement, ever willing to accommodate the established order; and the IWW typified the radicalism of many Americans who felt that only revolutionary changes could correct the abuses of industrial capitalism.

Divided by nationality, craft, and religion, the textile workers seemed a weak adversary to pit against united employers. The older immigrants—Germans, Irish, French-Canadians, and most of the English—opposed the strike. Reflecting the sentiments of the more established skilled workers, John Golden did all in his limited power to break the IWW-led strike, exceeding some manufacturers in his condemnation of the immigrants' union tactics. Even Samuel Gompers had to apologize before a congressional committee for some of Golden's more egregious anti-strike, anti-worker statements.[19] Golden consistently sought to vitiate the IWW strike by offering himself and his union to the mill owners, the city officials, and the state authorities. For a price—company recognition of the skilled workers—Golden practically offered to break the strike.

In reality, Golden had precious little to offer anyone. For by the end of the first week of the dispute the IWW had brought unity out of diversity, order out of chaos. It was now to the IWW, and to it alone, that the mass of immigrant workers looked for advice and hope.

No man did more to unify and inspire the strikers than Joseph Ettor.[20] Only twenty-six years old in 1912, he was already an experienced orator, organizer, and labor agitator. Born of Italian immigrant parents in Brooklyn in 1886, Ettor grew up in Chicago. From his father he heard tales of industrial warfare and revolutionary sentiments, and this early education directed him toward radicalism. As a young man in San Francisco he impressed Jane Roulston, the model for Jack London's "Red Virgin" of *The Iron Heel,* as "hardly more than a child, a big boy, member of the socialist party . . ." A San Francisco iron worker by trade, Ettor soon became a Wobbly agitator by vocation, traveling up and down the West Coast visiting mining, lumber, and construction camps to organize for the IWW. During this period (1905–1908) he became an adept soapboxer and one of the most popular Wobbly propagandists. The 1909 McKees Rocks strike brought him east, where he put to good use his command of the English, Italian, Polish, Yiddish, and Hungarian languages. After organizing among Pennsylvania's immigrant steel workers and coal miners, he turned up in Brooklyn to lead a strike by Italian IWW shoemakers. From Brooklyn he went to Lawrence.

The young but experienced Wobbly who arrived in Lawrence in the winter of 1912 was short and stocky, running a little to fat, though nonetheless uncommonly attractive. He had flowing black hair, dark brown eyes, and high color; by no means handsome, his face yet seemed candid and youthful. Typically wearing a big, soft hat to one side of his head, a flowing Windsor tie, and a natty blue suit, Ettor had a touch of the artistic bohemian. Looking anything but a wage worker, he nevertheless magnetized laboring groups.

Arturo Giovannitti, poet, mystic, dreamer, and syndicalist, accompanied Ettor to Lawrence. Born of upper-middle-class parents in 1884 in Campobasso, Abruzzi, Italy, Giovannitti rejected his parents and his native land at the age of sixteen.[21] Emigrating to America in 1900, he mined, kept books, and taught school in the New World. Not one for steady work, he knew what it was like to sleep in New York's doorways and starve in its streets. Born and raised an Italian Catholic, he flirted with Protestantism in America, and for a time trained at a seminary. But he found his true ministry not with Jesus and Christianity but with Marx and socialism. In time he became a leader in the Italian Socialist Federation of New York. From Marxism he converted to romantic syndicalism and thence to "pure" revolutionary action (the propaganda of the deed), which he promoted in the pages of *Il Proletario,* an Italian syndicalist sheet. When the Lawrence strike erupted and the Italian IWW branch wired New York for assistance, Giovannitti saw his chance to engage in the propaganda of the deed, which previously he had only preached. Able to speak fluent English, Italian, and French, he hoped to become as popular among the strikers as his friend Ettor. Tall, robust, with a powerful voice, he played the mature intellectual to Ettor's boyish radical; where Ettor impressed audiences with his childlike enthusiasm, Giovannitti did it with a romantic, mystical intensity.

Even more important to the future of the IWW was the return of Big Bill Haywood to its front ranks during the Lawrence strike. Arriving in town on January 24, 1912, Haywood received the wildest demonstration ever accorded a visitor to Lawrence, as thousands of strikers jammed the railroad station to welcome him. It was a moment fraught with great consequence for the Lawrence strikers as well as for the IWW, which welcomed back a lost son.

A dominant figure at the IWW's 1905 founding convention, Haywood shortly thereafter was lost to the organization.[22] In prison from 1906 through 1907 because of the Steunenberg case, he left prison a labor leader without a union, a radical without an organization, and a revolutionary in an overwhelmingly conservative society. Rejected by his old union (the WFM) and unwilling to throw in with a divided IWW, from 1908 to 1910 Haywood crisscrossed the country propagandizing for socialism and keeping only a minimal connection to the labor movement. In 1910 Haywood was a Socialist party delegate to the International Socialist Congress in Copenhagen. He traveled the radical speakers' circuit in Europe at the same time that William Z. Foster made his grand tour. Both American radicals reported their impressions of European socialism and labor to the IWW press. But whereas Foster returned to America dedicated to burying the IWW and "boring from within" the AFL, Haywood came home convinced that his future lay as much (perhaps more) with the Wobblies as with the political socialists.

Haywood's life, his personality, and his beliefs always had an enigmatic touch about them. To President Theodore Roosevelt, Haywood was an undesirable citizen; but to Frank P. Walsh, chairman of the Commission on Industrial Relations, he was the "rugged intellectual, with his facility of phrasing, his marvelous memory and his singularly clear and apt method of illustration." To conservatives, Haywood's was the voice of anarchy; to friends and admirers, he was the epitome of sweet reason. To such trade-union foes as Samuel Gompers, he was an inept propagandizer and a smasher of trade unions; while to his supporters he seemed to be an effective administrator and a talented labor organizer. To Mary Gallagher, a fellow radical, he was in every way a great leader; to Ramsay MacDonald, the British socialist leader, he was a rough-hewn agitator, splendid with crowds though ineffectual as an administrator.[23]

The fact is that Haywood's life offers sufficient evidence to support any of these views. Haywood's own efforts to mythologize his childhood, adolescence, and early manhood along the lines of the typical Western frontiersman portrayed him as a believer in the homemade justice of the Colt .45, a homesteader, and the organizer of a cowboys' union. (All of this appears in his autobiography, a book composed with the help of American communist ghost-writers while he was in exile in Moscow and dying.) His life, at least as much of it as can be reconstructed accurately, developed in five distinct phases, which appear to have flowed smoothly one into the other. Beginning with few advantages in the way of family, education, or wealth, Haywood had to earn his own keep at an early age. Born in Salt Lake City in 1869, left fatherless as a child, and never thereafter enjoying a secure home, he sustained himself by picking up the various marginal jobs then open to a child worker. By the age of fifteen he had become a hard-rock miner, and for the next twelve years he worked in mining camps, seldom remaining in one place very long. From these early experiences in an industry unusual for its labor solidarity as well as its labor violence he probably derived his beliefs about the worker's place in American society and the irrepressibility of conflict between capital and labor.

During the next decade (1896–1905), after marrying, raising a family, and settling down in Silver City, Idaho, Haywood served as a local union official and then as an officer in his International union. Service in the cause of trade unionism taught him the limitations as well as the advantages of the American labor movement. Aware of the movement's inadequacies, he became a crusader for industrial union- ism and for the socialization of American society. Before long the importance of his role as a labor leader diminished in comparison with his activities as a Socialist party politician. But seven years (1906– 1913) of Socialist party struggles left Haywood disillusioned with the ability of American Marxists to make a revolution in his native land. Recalled from the party's national executive committee in 1913, he began a new phase in his career: national leader of the apolitical, syndicalist, and revolutionary IWW. At last finding full satisfaction in his work, Haywood now joined diligent and efficient union adminis- tration to the fire-eating, spellbinding rhetoric of revolution. But his success with the IWW would end in federal repression of the organi- zation, which would bring Haywood's life to its final phase: a political exile which left him unable to promote radicalism in the land of his birth, or to build the new society in the land of his exile. Such, in brief outline, are the various phases through which Haywood's life passed.

The only comment one can make with any certainty about Hay- wood is that, like most Wobblies, he was neither an original thinker nor a thorough theoretician. Beyond that, his life was a tale of match- less inconsistency. During his early years with the WFM he displayed outstanding ability as an administrator and as an organizer. Willing to work long hours and to drive himself furiously, Haywood mastered the intricacies of trade unionism. In 1914–1917, this time in a vastly different environment, he again proved to be the industrious union official. During these years—years in which the IWW experienced its most rapid growth—Haywood strove to give Wobblies their first taste of effective administration under a rationalized central office. But in between his tours of duty as a union official he devoted himself to agitation and to free-wheeling revolutionary oratory, impressing many observers with his anti-disciplinarian, anti-organizational, anarchistic personality. His life was shadowed by violence, but few radicals ever expressed the doctrine of passive resistance so forcefully, or played so prominent a part in nonviolent labor demonstrations. An enemy of effete intellectualism, Haywood nonetheless had intellectual pretensions of his own. Although he might harangue strikers in working-class vernacular, he read widely (and deeply) and wrote with considerable skill. Beginning his writing career as temporary editor of the *Miners' Magazine*—he was later a contributing editor to the *International Socialist Review* and a regular commentator in the IWW press—Haywood developed from an immature awkward stylist into a master of the caustic comment and the cutting phrase. In his writings and speeches on economics, politics, sex, and religion, he stood midway between romanticism and realism, Victorianism and modernism. If he never wrote graceful and closely reasoned economic or social treatises, Haywood nevertheless unfailingly appealed to immigrant workers in the East and migrant workers in the West as well as to such intellectuals as John Reed and Max Eastman.

Unlike the more typical labor leader who opens his career as a radical, finds success, and becomes more conservative, Haywood began his union career conservatively, discovered success, and became radical. A man of many talents—administrator, organizer, agitator, speaker, writer—he developed none fully, which was perhaps his gravest deficiency. A labor leader who was at home with both wage workers and intellectuals (an unusual combination in America), he led a labor organization of scant membership and frustrated many intellectuals by his refusal to accept martyrdom in 1921, preferring instead to flee to Russia.

But when Bill Haywood came to Lawrence in 1912, what most people saw was a giant of a man who was able to inspire solidarity among a cantankerous assortment of ethnic groups. Tall and broad-shouldered, with a pockmarked and scarred face set off by a patch over his right eye (which he had lost in a childhood accident), Haywood bore ample physical witness to the battles he had waged and the sufferings he had endured. With only his eye patch and soft Western hat to distinguish him from thousands of other workmen who wore the same blue shirt, plain tie, dull suit and overcoat, Haywood would carry his immense frame to the speaker's platform, and, without stamping, pounding, bellowing, or bullying, use plain workingman's language to carry his audience along with him. After watching Big Bill perform numerous times before strikers, one sympathetic observer commented: "Stripping Haywood of all the attributes which usually enable labor leaders to lead, we end by finding in him two qualities, rare ones: genuine power and genuine simplicity." Or as the *Nation* remembered him years later in a poignant obituary: "Standing up before a mass of unskilled workers, preaching the eternal irreconcilability of employer and employed with one breath and the brotherhood of man with the next, denouncing craft unionism and race distinctions, he was at home." [24]

In Lawrence, Haywood, Ettor, and Giovannitti had ample assistance from local Wobblies in leading the strike and organizing the workers. William Yates and Thomas Holliday, for example, provided what the two imported Italian agitators could not: knowledge of the textile industry, its workers, and its ways. A long-time official of the NIUTW, Yates was born in Lancashire, England, where at the age of ten he entered the cotton mills. For the next thirty-three years he labored in every branch of the textile industry. A union member at fourteen, he became a socialist at sixteen and secretary of his local branch of the English Social Democratic Federation. Arriving in the United States in 1900, he immediately joined the Socialist Labor party and the Socialist Trades and Labor Alliance and moved with them into the IWW. After its founding in 1908, Yates had worked constantly to keep the NIUTW, of which he became secretary in 1910, a going concern. Thomas Holliday was also born in Lancashire. Like Yates, Holliday went to work in the mills at an early age, but in his case it was an American mill, his family having emigrated to America in 1887 when he was only five. He was one of the first IWW members in Lawrence and one of its few links to the skilled, English-speaking community of workers. [25]

Lawrence's new immigrants, similarly, provided their share of strike leaders. Nineteen-year-old Angelo Rocco, who first sent for Ettor, gave the Italians unstinting service. Samuel Lipson did the same for Jewish strikers, Joseph Bedard and Louis Picavet for the French-Canadians, Cyrille De Tollenaere for the Franco-Belgians, and many an unknown leader for the Poles and Syrians.

The national IWW figures and the local strike leaders together produced organizational order out of anarchy. Enlisting men capable of speaking the native language of every striker and drawing representatives from every ethnic group involved, they created unified strike committees and relief committees. Structured upon nationality lines and though led by men already in the IWW or soon to join, these committees existed independently of the IWW. They operated on Haywood's advice: "There is no foreigner here except the capitalists. . . . Do not let them divide you by sex, color, creed, or nationality. . . . 'Billy' Wood can lick one Pole, in fact he can lick all the Poles, but he cannot lick all the nationalities put together." [26]

Led by Ettor, the strike committee promptly drew up its basic demands, which were few and limited in objective. The strikers asked for a 15 per cent wage increase based on the fifty-four-hour week; double pay for overtime; elimination of the premium system (a system of bonus wage payments based upon a speed-up in production, which workers considered to be exploitative); and assurance that no discriminatory action would be taken against any worker who had walked out during the strike. In other words, no demands for union recognition or a closed shop, nor any mention of revolution.

Ettor, an IWW veteran, taught the inexperienced immigrants the nature of industrial warfare. He devised special tactics to achieve the strikers' main immediate objective, which was to keep nonstrikers out of the mills. The strike committee organized mass picket squads, which, forming near the mill gates, would march around them without stopping, without slowing down, without resorting to open force or violence, and thus offering the police or militia no occasion to intervene. Any worker who desired to enter the mills had to endure the verbal insults shouted by thousands of fellow workers, many of whom were his neighbors. Social intimidation of this kind proved much more effective than physical violence. The strike committee also arranged regular parades during which thousands of workers would march through Lawrence's streets to music, singing the "Marsellaise" and the "Internationale." These parades served to convince the non-union, nonstriking workers of their opponents' solidarity and strength. Again, strikers substituted social and psychological intimidation for the cruder and usually less effective tactic of violence.

Peaceful picketing, musical parading, and nonviolent coercion worked. The strike grew. By January 20, less than a week after it began, more than fourteen thousand workers had left the mills, which were now crippled. At first the mill owners declined to deal with the strikers. Lawrence's employers remained certain that, with the assistance of city and state authorities and given the workers' own ethnic and craft divisions, they could break the strike. So convinced of their chances for absolute victory were the mill owners that, unlike other employers with whom the IWW had contended, they had not bothered to make any provisions for the introduction of strikebreakers.

William Wood directed the anti-strike coalition. Expressing complete surprise at the course of events, he called the strikers ignorant and irresponsible men who were unaware of the hard economic fact that employers could not pay employees for fifty-six hours' work when they labored only fifty-four hours. "I have consulted long and anxiously with the directors and those associated with me in the management," Wood said. "Regretfully and reluctantly, we have come to the conclusion that it is impossible, with a proper regard for the interests of the company, to grant at this time any increase in wages." Wood and the other mill owners pleaded poverty. With Southern textile workers toiling longer hours for less pay, with textile imports increasing, and with tariff agitation in Washington causing business depression, how could Lawrence's wage rates be increased? "There is no cause for striking," Wood advised his workers, "and when the employees find that justice is not on their side, the strike cannot possibly be long lived. I look for an early resumption of work." [27]

Wood's imperviousness to the strikers' grievances was shared by Lawrence's dominant classes. Nothing better illustrated the existence in Lawrence of two separate nations—haves and have-nots—than the attitudes and policies of the city's elite. City Judge Wilbur Rowell, attempting to answer what he deemed slanders on the city's reputation, reflected Lawrence's pervasive social myopia when he remarked: "It is a typical New England industrial city, with all the equipment and resources that are found in such a city for generous and noble life, and for the sympathetic relief of weakness and suffering." The generous and noble life apparently included the one-penny school lunches of molasses and bread that Lawrence granted the children of its working classes. Local leaders did not even bother to deny that the immigrants lived abysmally. As John N. Cole, former Speaker of the Massachusetts House, put it: "Living conditions in Lawrence are exactly what the different kinds of people in Lawrence wish them to be." To clarify his point, he added: ". . . Not until the present generation has passed away will the European methods of 'herding' . . . be changed." Cole and his fellows could also prove, or so they asserted, that immigrant workers had grown prosperous in Lawrence. Judge Rowell located a sure sign of prosperity in the frequent appearance of immigrants in court as litigants, "a luxury of which they are very fond." Savings accounts seemed an ever surer sign of working-class prosperity. Wood, Rowell, Cole, and other Lawrenceites boasted about the immense savings amassed by the city's poorer folk. To this a reporter responded: "Of course the poorest workers save money. They save if they have to sleep ten in a room and half starve in the attempt." [28] As Rowell and his class surveyed the strike scene, given their deeply ingrained prejudices, they necessarily concluded that industrial conflict had been imported into a peaceful New England town by outside agitators—the age-old rationalization of exploiters shocked by the rebellion of the natives. Rowell beseeched the misguided strikers to see that what their employers "desire for the good of their employees is a thousand times deeper than that of either social students or strike leaders who are here to-day and (we sincerely hope) will be gone to-morrow." As the strike wore on, the good judge could only lament: "We had thought we were living on pleasant terms with the strangers [the working-class population]. We told ourselves and others that they were in a way our guests and that we owed them the duty of hospitality." But, Rowell dejectedly concluded: "We must exercise some patience about their regeneration." [29]

Other Lawrence leaders were less solicitous. Mayor Scanlon had called out the local police and militia immediately upon the strike and soon thereafter requested state militia. He also purportedly hired Sherman Agency private detectives to keep the strikers and Wobblies under surveillance. In his magistrate's court, Judge Mahoney treated the strikers with harsh justice, declaring, ". . . The only way we can teach them is to deal out the severest sentences." Local priests joined the anti-strike coalition. Father O'Reilly, the leading Irish-American cleric, condemned the IWW in his parish calendar for misleading "ignorant" immigrants, and a French-Canadian priest advised a jeering crowd of seven thousand strikers to return to work. Catholic priests also visited their East European immigrant flock to warn them that continued disobedience to employers and to public authorities would lead to damnation.[30] Some of Lawrence's better citizens even engaged in criminal conspiracies to break the strike.

State authorities, though less concerned than Lawrence's officials with the textile manufacturers' interests, proved equally anxious to end the strike and remove the IWW's influence from the city. Governor Foss and the state legislature sought to bring strikers and employers together in mutual negotiations which would end the conflict on the basis of a compromise that altogether excluded the IWW. Foss, for example, publicly professed his desire to cooperate with John Golden and the craft unionists. But that proved impossible, for Golden had no influence with the strikers, and the manufacturers disliked the craft unionists as much as the Wobblies. Unable to mediate the dispute himself, the Governor asked strikers and employers to submit their respective cases to the State Board of Conciliation and Arbitration. Lawrence's employers declined to do so, while the strikers agreed to mediation but not to arbitration—a clear indication they were weakening and felt the need of outside aid. Finally, on January 29 Foss beseeched the disputants to accept a thirty-day truce during which the employers would pay the fifty-six-hour wage and the workers would return to the mills, while he, Foss, adjudicated the outstanding grievances. The owners leaped at this opportunity to resume full production. Golden and the United Textile Workers proved equally anxious to end the strike before the IWW's inroads among the workers deepened. But the strike committee firmly and flatly rejected the Governor's offer. How could it resume a strike after a month-long truce if Foss failed to arrange a settlement satisfying the workers' demands? Ettor and several strikers had already presented their demands directly to Wood, who had rejected them out of hand.[31]

Walter Weyl discovered why the state's efforts to mediate the industrial dispute failed. He overheard the strikers ask the following questions at a conference between strike leaders and state legislators: "What can your state do? If you find one party wrong, can your state force it to do right? Can you legislators be impartial as arbitrators, when you have not lived the bitter life of the workers? Would you arbitrate a question of life and death, and are the worst wages paid in these mills anything short of death? Do you investigate because conditions are bad, or because the workers broke loose and struck? Why did you not come before the strike?"[32] The immigrants had indeed learned their catechism well from Ettor, Giovannitti, Haywood, and the IWW gospels: Workers must look to themselves for relief, not to the state!

Although the state did little to assist the strikers, it did a great deal to aid employers. It sent militia to Lawrence, and Massachusetts soldiers proved no different from those Wobblies had encountered in other states during other strikes. Ostensibly sent to protect lives and property, the militia usually interfered with the strikers' civil rights. One Boston Brahmin on militia duty in Lawrence informed a reporter: "Most of them [militia] had to leave Harvard for it, but they *rather enjoyed going down there and having their fling at those people!"* Owen R. Lovejoy, of the National Child Labor Committee, interviewed and observed the militia in action. "We learned that in Lawrence today," he wrote, "three peaceable citizens are not permitted to stand at a corner long enough to say, 'Shall we turn up or down the street?'" Lovejoy asked a soldier, "Don't you allow any picketing if they are quiet and orderly and peaceable?" and the soldier replied sneeringly, "Not a damned one; not if we see 'em." After the strike ended, a militiaman recounting his experiences in Lawrence noted: "There was too much feeling that we were fighting on the side of the mill owners. . . . Nothing was said to us about their [the workers'] rights, and no suggestion was handed down that we should treat both sides fairly." [33]

Despite the nature of the opposition, the strikers held firm. For a time, at least, they had caught the Wobbly spirit, the same spirit that had carried the IWW through the battles at Spokane and Fresno and was even then carrying it through the brutal San Diego struggle. Walter Weyl noted "a new halting self-confidence breaking through the mists of apathy [among the strikers]. The souls behind these white faces were beginning to stir." "We are a new people," said one striker to another observer. "We have hope. We never will stand again what we stood before." [34] Such faith enabled the strikers to surmount all the tactics used against them—including the manufacture of stories of violence.

The Lawrence strike began with violence. On Friday, January 12, Italian workers had undeniably run amok through the Wood Mill. Later that same day strikers had shattered factory windows. By Monday, January 15, strikers had already clashed openly with local police and militia, leading the *New York Times* to report, "Bayonet Charge on Lawrence Strikers," and the *New York Call* to assert that several workers had been shot and fifty to one hundred had been wounded. As usual, the newspapers exaggerated the actual events. All that in fact had happened was that as a group of strikers had marched toward the Pacific Mill to call upon the operatives inside to join the walkout, the militia, assisted by Lawrence firemen, had met the marchers with blasts of icy water from a high-pressure hose. During the ensuing turmoil, the mob scattered, flinging ice at the enemy as it retreated. That, in brief, was the first "bloody" battle of Lawrence.

Violence was certainly not among the objectives of Ettor, the Wobblies, and the strike committee. Indeed, as the Wobblies and the members of the strike committee asserted firmer influence among the strikers, violence diminished. But reporters and their publishers, eager to sell copy, did their best to manufacture stories and headlines about clashes between strikers and soldiers. Some of Lawrence's "better" citizens added to the rumors of violence. On Saturday, January 20, the police, acting upon an anonymous tip, found dynamite at several locations, including a cache next to the printing office where Ettor received his mail. The newspapers immediately proclaimed the strikers guilty of a conspiracy to blow up Lawrence, implying to boot an imminent Wobbly plot for revolution. Much to the dismay of the IWW's critics, it turned out that John Breen, a successful local businessman and school board member, had planted the dynamite in order to turn sentiment against the strikers. In May 1912 a local court tried, convicted, and fined Breen $500. Not long after this conviction, a contractor for the American Woolen Company admitted that the dynamite scheme had been arranged at company president Wood's suggestion. But the second confessed dynamiter committed suicide before Wood could be brought to trial, and the eminent Bostonian eluded justice.[35]

Employers, local officials, and newspapers continued to seek out or to create strike violence. Stories spread to the effect that Italian strikers threatened nonstrikers with "Black Hand" * retribution. One Italian-language strike circular, purported to be the work of Ettor, advised the following treatment of nonstrikers: "Throw them down the stairs. Break their bones; and leave them a remembrance for life." [36] Yet law officials never uncovered any solid evidence to prove physical intimidation by Wobblies or by ordinary strikers.

Nevertheless, a *New York Times* headline proclaimed on January 30, 1912: "Real Labor War Now in Lawrence." Behind the headline was the first outbreak of strike violence in two weeks. On the morning of January 29, irate strikers had spontaneously thrown ice and rocks at streetcars carrying nonstrikers to work. Local authorities now sought to make the most of a minor disturbance. That evening, as the IWW led one of its regular parades down Lawrence's streets, the police were in an ugly mood. Parading, singing strikers soon found themselves

* A Mafia organization supposedly brought to America by Sicilian immigrants.

confronted by determined and barricaded policemen. Both sides began to push and shove, and in the resulting turmoil one officer was stabbed and a young Italian striker, Annie LoPezzi, was shot and killed. Unhesitatingly, yet without evidence, the police accused the strikers of both deeds. The workers, in turn, accused the police of having shot Annie. But the police, not the strikers, could make their accusations carry weight. A few days after the incident the police had captured an alleged murderer, a man named Joseph Caruso, and his alleged accomplices and co-conspirators, Ettor and Giovannitti, who were accused of inciting, procuring, counseling, and commanding an *unknown* person to commit murder. Despite the flimsiness of their evidence the police accomplished their primary objective: the imprisonment of Ettor and Giovannitti, who, from their arrest in late January until their trial the following autumn, remained in prison and hence unable to lead the strike.

With the strikers' leaders in jail, Lawrence's employers expected the walkout to collapse. But city officials and mill owners could not have been more wrong. Haywood, Trautmann, and Elizabeth Gurley Flynn more than adequately replaced the imprisoned leaders, and with the conflict then more than three weeks old, the strikers had had time to produce spokesmen from their own ranks.

All the headlines and rumors of violence meanwhile operated to the advantage of the strikers and the IWW. Strikers, not soldiers, had died. Innocent men had been imprisoned for a crime they apparently had not committed, and in jail Ettor and Giovannitti could play the roles their dramatic personalities craved to fill: the roles, that is, of martyrs sacrificed to the cause of human justice and equality. It would not be an exaggeration to assert that these two Wobblies did more for the strikers inside prison walls than they could have done on the outside. From all sides and all classes, sympathy and words of encouragement rained down upon the "persecuted" strikers, who suddenly discovered allies they never knew they had.

By stressing nonviolent strike tactics, the Wobblies did their best to preserve the loyalty of their newfound allies. Even before blood had been shed in Lawrence, Ettor had advised the strikers: "By all means make this strike as peaceful as possible. In the last analysis, all the blood spilled will be your own." From prison he continued to stress caution and peaceful persuasion. Victory for the cause, he said, would be retribution enough for himself and Giovannitti. When Haywood assumed leadership of the strike, he sounded a similar note.

Only a short time before Lawrence, Haywood had lectured New York Socialists on the need for sabotage and the imbecility of obeying capitalist laws and bourgeois courts. In Lawrence, faced with actual industrial conflict, he offered quite different counsel. "Can you weave cloth with the bayonets of your militia, or spin with the clubs of your policemen?" he asked employers. The workers, he said, would simply keep their hands in their pockets, weave no more, and let the soldiers go naked. Friendly observers sensed the nonviolent spirit inculcated among the strikers. "Almost everywhere," Weyl commented, "I meet this same objective attitude, this same aversion from violence and the threat of violence." Another commentator, making light of the whole issue of strike violence, asked sarcastically ". . . whether the police with their billies or the girls with their muffs, the militia with their bayonets or the boys with their tin horns and snow balls, had been guilty of more violence." Even an enemy of the IWW concluded that "in the end the violence was mostly talk and murders did not occur." The State Bureau of Labor summed it all up in conceding that "few strikes involving so large a number of employees, unorganized, and many of them unfamiliar with our language and methods of government, have continued as long as the Lawrence strike and with so little actual violence or riot." [37]

In Lawrence IWW propagandists did not have to emphasize the inevitability of class conflict or the hostility of the state. The facts spoke for themselves, and the strikers could draw their own lessons. The actions of employers, city officials, and the militia demonstrated better than any IWW speaker or pamphlet the realities of class warfare.

The IWW's main problem in Lawrence was to obtain strike funds. With about 23,000 men, women, and children out of work for nine weeks, and another 30,coo or more dependent upon their earnings, strike relief posed no small problem. The IWW itself lacked a substantial treasury, and neither the Lawrence Central Labor Union, which was hostile to the IWW, nor the usual local charitable agencies could be expected to contribute generously. The fraternal, religious, and mutual-aid societies established by the city's various ethnic groups assumed some of the relief burden, for these ethnic organizations, regardless of their views on the strike, could not refuse aid to fellow nationals. But throughout the protracted conflict the IWW shouldered the main burden of relief.

It did so masterfully. The strike committee organized an elaborate system directed by a relief committee composed of representatives of all the nationalities caught up in the struggle. Each ethnic group also had its own special relief committee. These committees investigated the needs of applicants, provided soup kitchens for single men, and furnished food or store orders for families. The committees provided for fuel, shoes, medical assistance, and, in some cases, even rent. Although loosely organized and administered by uneducated immigrants, the committees operated with remarkable efficiency. As a result of their effective operation, no worker or his family starved during the strike; none went without the necessities of life; and none, certainly, lived any more poorly than he would have done during ordinary periods of unemployment.[38] The hardships and privations they normally endured prepared Lawrence's immigrants, as they had the strikers at McKees Rocks, for the tribulations of industrial warfare.

But the strike committee's well-conceived and well-organized relief operation relied almost entirely on financial contributions from outside Lawrence. Here the IWW's organizers and its general headquarters proved most useful. Using every contact they had with other labor organizations, socialist groups, and radicals, the Wobblies solicited funds. Solicitation was made all the easier by the arrogance of the mill owners and the obstinacy of city officials. Every time Wood or another employer rejected negotiations, contributions to the strikers' cause increased. Every time the police, the militia, and the judiciary harassed strikers, more financial angels appeared to finance the strike. When Ettor and Giovannitti were charged with murder and jailed, thousands of dollars poured into the strike committee's treasury.

The IWW also hit upon a perfect scheme to increase newspaper publicity and to lessen the local relief burden. At the end of January, Italian socialists in New York suggested that the strikers' children be cared for by families outside the strike zone, as had been done on occasion in France, Italy, and Belgium. The *New York Call* publicized the idea, and within three days four hundred New Yorkers offered to take one or more of Lawrence's strike children. In response, the strike committee came to New York to investigate the homes of prospective foster parents, while in Lawrence the committee accepted applications from parents who wanted to send their children to New York. Strike leaders carefully selected the children, who were given new clothes and a medical examination. On February 11, Margaret Sanger and three other New York reformers arrived in Lawrence to pick up the first group of 119 children, aged five to fifteen, for distribution to foster parents. When the refugees' train arrived later that day at New York's Grand Central Station, a huge crowd, composed mostly of immigrant working people, greeted the children. "The children marched down the platform," wrote an observer, "four in a row, holding hands, all dressed much alike in their new cloaks and caps. First, there was silence, then a curious emotional wave passed through the crowd. . . . The silence was followed by a steady roar of cheers, and to its accompaniment the children were led to the elevated station, a black-draped red flag in front of them. . . . Another crowd awaited them in the Labor Temple. It turned out that many had come to offer a home to any child who might be 'left over.' There was no one left over, and at the headquarters of the committee it is stated that there are still some thousands of homes of working people eager to receive one or more of the strikers' children." [39]

No one could have dreamed that this new tactic would work so well. Not only did the removal of the children ease the relief problem in Lawrence; it also gained the most remarkable national publicity. Nothing, after all, was more calculated to increase sympathy for the strikers' cause than the sight of undernourished children removed from their parents' homes because of industrial warfare. To take advantage of this publicity and sympathy, the IWW organized more children's pilgrimages. They sent strike orphans to New York, Jersey City, Philadelphia, and Barre, Vermont. In each case the strike committee planned its operation carefully. Investigators checked the prospective foster parents' homes, others secured written permission from Lawrence families, still others provided medical assistance, food, and clothing for the children upon their arrival at their new homes.

The children's crusade worked much *too* well in the view of Lawrence's mill owners and public officials. When children quit school to work in the mills, or when immigrant parents left very young children at home untended while they worked in the mills, no city official or local employer cried neglect. But now that the IWW sent these same children out of Lawrence to good homes with the guarantee of ample food, medical care, and supervision, the owners and the officials screamed neglect. They decided to halt the children's exodus at almost any cost. The militia commander posted an order on February 17 to the effect that no child could leave town without his parents' written consent. When the strike committee obtained the necessary written statements, the city marshal announced on February 22 that no more children would be allowed to leave Lawrence —period.[40] These officials meant to keep their word.

This ruling led to what proved to be the strike's turning point, for on February 24 a group of Philadelphia socialists arrived in Lawrence to pick up some two hundred children for transport back to Philadelphia. Well aware of the marshal's February 22 edict, the Philadelphians intended to challenge and defeat it. Eager to stand on solid legal ground, they obtained the written permission of the parents involved and even took some of the children's mothers to the train station. As the socialists, the children, and their mothers proceeded toward the special car obtained from the Boston and Maine Railroad, the local police acted. Two members of the Philadelphia Women's Committee described what followed: ". . . The police . . . closed in on us with clubs, beating right and left, with no thought of children, who were in the most desperate danger of being trampled to death. The mothers and children were thus hurled in a mass and bodily dragged to a military truck, and even then clubbed, irrespective of the cries of the panic-stricken women and children." [41]

Newspapers and magazines made the entire nation witness to the arrogance, stupidity, and brutality of Lawrence's employers and public officials. Governor Foss ordered an immediate investigation of the incident, and his secretary apologized publicly for the brutal behavior of Lawrence's officials. Socialist Congressman Victor Berger demanded a congressional investigation, which resulted in hearings in Washington at which the strikers obtained still wider publicity. Progressive senators initiated a Bureau of Labor investigation of the strike, and Senator R. F. Pettigrew, Mrs. William Howard Taft, and Mrs. Gifford Pinchot traveled to Lawrence to see the strikers' plight for themselves. Nor were they alone. Reporters, free-lance writers, and social reformers by the score came to Lawrence to investigate conditions, their reports becoming grist for the IWW's publicity mill. The relief committees no longer had to worry about outside contributions.[42]

Eight weeks of industrial conflict had brought no break in the strikers' ranks. In early March they appeared stronger than ever. Their relief organization handled all needs satisfactorily, and nation-wide support and sympathy almost inundated the strikers. Unable to operate at capacity, Lawrence's mills could not fill spring orders. Meanwhile, a Democratic Congress had begun to investigate a strike that involved staunch Republican mill owners.

Given these circumstances, the employers beat a strategic retreat. On March 1 the American Woolen Company offered a 5 per cent wage increase to all its workers. Several AFL craft unions, which had belatedly and unethusiastically joined the walkout, accepted the offer and returned to work, but the strike committee rejected it absolutely. For ten days, from March 3 through March 12, delegates chosen by the strike committee negotiated with a delegation of employers. Finally, on Saturday, March 12, the strike committee obtained a satisfactory settlement proposal from the American Woolen Company. The agreement provided a flat 5 per cent wage hike for all piece-workers; 5 to 25 per cent increases for all hourly rated employees, with the highest percentage going to the lowest-paid workers; time and a quarter for overtime; no discrimination against any striker; and reforms in the premium or bonus system, with premiums to be distributed every two, instead of every four, weeks. Two days later at an excited mass meeting the strikers voted to end their walkout and to accept the proposed settlement.[43]

The workers had thus achieved their four original demands. As Haywood gloatingly remarked: "Passive, with folded arms, the strikers won." He later said to the even more gleeful immigrants: "I want to say . . . that the strikers of Lawrence have won the most signal victory of any organized body of workers in the world. You have demonstrated, as has been shown nowhere else, the common interest of the working class in bringing all nationalities together." [44] Indeed they had, for they returned to the mills not only united ethnically but also, in the majority of cases, as members of the IWW.

For Lawrence and for the New England textile industry, however, the settlement failed to bring peace or a sense of security. An uneasy fear lingered. The IWW remained in Lawrence, and to mill owners, public officials, and federal investigators that labor organization seemed to be the spearhead of a threatened social revolution. So claimed William Wood, Charles P. Neill, United States Commissioner of Labor, and even Walter Weyl, who had been sympathetic to the strike. Textile industry employers throughout New England raised wages—partly in fear of the IWW, partly to arrest further industrial conflict, and partly to remove the possibility of social revolution.

The legal proceedings arising out of the Lawrence strike, especially the Ettor-Giovannitti case, also aroused anxiety in New England. Who knew what the IWW would use as a pretext for beginning the revolution? What would happen if a jury convicted the two Wobblies of murder? Would the IWW-led mill hands take to the streets, destroying property and attacking people? Would New England ever again have industrial peace and quiet? As the state prepared its case against Ettor and Giovannitti, such anxieties troubled New Englanders through the spring and summer of 1912.[45]

All that spring and summer the IWW organized its Ettor-Giovannitti defense campaign. Every available Eastern organizer, and some from the West, were put to work on it. Some of the effort which should have been devoted to solidification of the organizational gains achieved in Lawrence went instead into legal-defense activities, which brought no new members to the organization.[46] The closer the trial came, the more energy the IWW expended on it. On September 15, 1912, 35,000 workers, including 13,500 who traveled from Lawrence to Boston on two Red Specials, assembled on the Boston Common to protest the scheduled trial and to threaten an industry-wide general strike. Later in the month, on September 28, Lawrence textile workers spontaneously walked out of the mills. The rank and file continued to advocate a general strike, despite the opposition of Local 20's officials and of the imprisoned Ettor and Giovannitti. But on September 27, Vincent St. John and Haywood wired Lawrence IWW leaders to inform them that the IWW convention, then in session in Chicago, as well as the general executive board, had endorsed a general protest strike, which would "make the mill owners open the jail doors." [47]

On September 30 the two accused Wobblies were brought before the bar of justice at—of all places—the site of America's earliest witch-hunt, Salem. Witches, however, were no longer in vogue; anarcho-syndicalists had replaced them in the demonology of the defenders of the commonweal. For fifty-eight days the trial dragged on, ending on November 26, when Ettor and Giovannitti made their final impressive speeches. Ettor informed the jury: "I neither offer apology nor excuse; I ask no favors; I ask for nothing but justice in this matter." Giovannitti proved even more eloquent, closing with these words:

And if it be that these hearts of ours must be stilled on the same death chair and by the same current of fire that has destroyed the life of the wife murderer and the patricide and parricide, then I say that tomorrow we shall pass into a greater judgment, that tomorrow we shall go from your presence where history shall give its last word to us.

The IWW thought so highly of these two speeches that it put them together in a little pamphlet edited by Justus Ebert and widely distributed under the title *The Trial of New Society*. The jury thought so highly of the defendants' closing arguments and so lightly of the state's evidence that it acquitted Ettor and Giovannitti.[48]

At first the IWW seemed to have achieved an even more remarkable triumph in its hold upon Lawrence's immigrants and in the establishment of a stable, effective industrial union. As late as mid-September 1912 the IWW claimed about sixteen thousand paid-up members in Lawrence's mills—an impressive achievement in a formerly anti-union city. In August an IWW leader had gleefully compared the aftermath of the Lawrence strike to what had followed victory in McKees Rocks, where organizational strength had melted away; and he noted how wrong were the commentators who had said "that the workers [in Lawrence] would be satisfied with butter instead of molasses on their bread and the revolutionary movement would be at a standstill. . . . Nothing could be farther from the truth," he went on. "The unions are growing by leaps and bounds . . . and the work of adding recruits goes merrily on." [49] Yet in the last analysis the pessimists proved correct in their impressions of the immigrant workers' basic desires and in their forecast of an IWW decline. Why?

Most analysts of the IWW and of the Lawrence strike have found a simple explanation for the organization's failure to preserve the gains it had achieved during the heat of the battle. The traditional version asserts that the IWW "was more interested in winning converts for the revolution than in building a day-to-day collective bargaining agency." Its leaders, being "crusaders for times of crisis" rather than builders of realistic trade unions, thus never left behind a solid and permanent oganization. If Wobblies had to compromise with employers and sign contracts in order to preserve their local unions, they preferred to wage the class war and to destroy their own organizations. After a successful strike, the traditional explanation of IWW failure continues, Wobbly leaders packed their bags, left town, and allowed inexperienced and ineffectual rank-and-filers to administer union affairs. In Lawrence, for example, when strike and legal defense operations ended, Ettor, Giovannitti, Haywood, Elizabeth Gurley Flynn, and Trautmann all left town, never to return. Finally, Wobblies allegedly committed some tactical error, some stupid outrage upon community sentiment, during every conflict in which they participated. In the case of Lawrence it was the spontaneous strike and demonstration of September 30, 1912, during which a marcher carried a placard reading, "No God! No Master!" This allegedly gave the anti-union forces a chance to drive a wedge between immigrant Catholic workers, loyal to their God and to their adopted country, and the atheistic, unpatriotic IWW leaders. By initiating a God-and-Country crusade, conservatives supposedly vitiated working-class support for the IWW's Local 20.[50]

All of these assertions misjudge the IWW's activities in Lawrence. Thât the IWW preached the irrepressible class war is certainly true; that it preferred revolution to bread-and-butter gains is less true. Haywood and other IWW leaders advised strikers to accept the March 13 strike settlement, and it was Ettor and Giovannitti who, in September 1912, counseled Lawrence's rank and file against protest strikes. That IWW leaders like Haywood, Flynn, and Trautmann left Lawrence is equally true; that the IWW left Local 20 without experienced leadership is untrue. Louis Picavet, Joseph Bedard, Cyrille De Tollenaere, William Yates, Thomas Holliday, Samuel Lipson, and all the veterans of the strike and relief committees remained in Lawrence, and they were well able to manage the affairs of Local 20.

That God-and-country crusades won workers away from the IWW may be true, but it is unlikely. Throughout the course of the strike, public officials and priests had tried, without any great success, to sway the immigrants' emotions by accusing the IWW of anti-patriotism and atheism.[51]

Other reasons must be sought for the IWW's eventual failure in Lawrence, and they are not all that hard to find. Late in 1913 Selig Perlman, then working for the Commission on Industrial Relations, investigated labor conditions in Lawrence, specifically as they related to the IWW. He had no problem locating the causes of the organization's difficulties. Perlman discovered that employers regularly infiltrated spies into the union, and that local newspapers just as regularly printed false and unfavorable articles about the IWW. Manufacturers also manipulated the labor market to the union's disadvantage: in periods of unemployment the mills continued to advertise for labor outside Lawrence in order to flood the local labor market. The multi-plant companies operating in Lawrence would shut down their local mills, while running similar operations elsewhere full-time. Employers, Perlman also found, consciously played one nationality off against another, and with considerable success. The favored nationalities, for example, received higher wages, rapid promotions, and a share in municipal patronage and power. Father O'Reilly, alleged by Perlman to be Lawrence's uncrowned king, kept the Irish workers, who had opposed the IWW from the first, loyal to the employers. In conclusion, Perlman noted that perhaps the most important clue to why the IWW in particular and unions in general stagnated in Lawrence would be found in answer to the question ". . . why some nationalities are loyal to the employer and others are not." [52]

A report presented to the IWW by Thomas Holliday of Local 20 in March 1913 indicates that Perlman's assessment was remarkably accurate. Holliday reported that Lawrence's employers had initiated a temporary depression—the closing of local mills to which Perlman had referred—which threw thousands of immigrants out of work. This move, Holliday asserted, had three objectives: (1) to embarrass the local IWW union and drive its members back into a state of submissiveness and disorganization; (2) to warn the Democratic national administration not to toy with the tariff schedule; and (3) to force militant workers to desert Lawrence, leaving the labor force in the control of more conservative elements. (In fact, within two years not a single local strike leader remained at work in Lawrence's mills.) A year later, in 1914, conditions appeared still worse. A nationwide recession had developed, and Lawrence Wobblies suffered considerably. A local union official reported sadly: ". . . Reaction . . . has been busily at work within the ranks of Local Union No. 20 . . . sowing the seeds of dissension and despair." [53]

One final factor militated against IWW success in Lawrence. Out of a sense of despair caused partly by their exploitation by employers and partly by their total rejection by Lawrence's elite, the new immigrants had turned to the IWW. When the IWW could not resist exploitation or alter the attitudes of the local ruling class, for reasons Perlman enumerated, the immigrants drifted out of the organization. Membership in the IWW only threatened the immigrants' already insecure employment as well as what little chance they might have for promotion within the mill. Although the new immigrants may never have had complete economic security, they did possess a sense of social and psychological community which derived from their membership in tightly knit family groups, ethnic societies, and religious bodies brought over from the old country. Hence, for them, the IWW did not provide "the only social break in the harsh search for work that they have ever had; its headquarters the only competitor of the saloon in which they are welcome." Since the IWW alone could not (and did not) make life meaningful for the immigrant industrial worker in Lawrence, in time of adversity he deserted it.

But in the early spring of 1912 no one, either inside or outside the IWW, could foresee how few members the organization would have in Lawrence only a year later, or how completely paralyzed the IWW would be at the time in the industrial Northeast. After the well-publicized events in Lawrence, outsiders still feared and exaggerated the IWW's power. And the Wobblies, gloating over their victory, also exaggerated the effects of the Lawrence conflict.

American newspapers, magazines, and commentators had alerted citizens to the "rising tide of socialism" in 1911. But, as the socialist tide receded in 1912, Americans discovered a new and graver menace: the rising tide of syndicalism. Decent citizens seemed to have been left stranded on a lonely beach, where wave after wave of immigrant industrial workers beat in upon them, and where tidal waves of sabotage, direct action, and revolution inundated them. Throughout 1912 and 1913 many Americans wondered whether the IWW tide would recede, or whether, instead, it would surge on and submerge forever the America they knew.

Every commentator on the Lawrence strike agreed that it had been a conflict without precedent in America. To William English Walling, at that time a Socialist party sympathizer of the IWW, "All the world saw that the new movement had a revolutionary aspect." Quoting the *New York Times*, he observed that the IWW "declares war on capital—war to the death, and intends to tear down the whole social structure and build it anew." Only since the Lawrence strike, Walling pointed out, had the public been fully aware of the significance of a movement that had been developing steadily. Federal investigators of the Lawrence conflict, the city's employers, officials, and its clergymen, as well as Gompers and John Golden, viewed the strike as the social revolution in microcosm. Lincoln Steffens declared that the mill owners now lay awake at night worrying about sabotage. In an IWW strike, unlike an AFL conflict, Steffens noted, "the labor leaders are intent upon spreading revolutionary doctrines . . ." "Haywood makes Gompers look like an angel," he concluded. "The I.W.W. makes the mill men sigh for the A.F.L." Even those who had been sympathetic to the IWW's cause during the strike feared for the future. Profoundly fearful of another such outbreak of industrial warfare, Walter Weyl said of the arrogant mill owners who had precipitated the struggle: "*Neither may we allow men, however wealthy or respectable, to scatter explosives upon the ground.*" And the *Survey*, which had given the strikers all the favorable publicity they wanted and more, nervously asked after the strike had ended:

Are we to expect that instead of playing the game respectably, or else frankly breaking out into lawless riot which we know well enough how to deal with, the laborers are to listen to a subtle anarchistic philosophy which challenges the fundamental idea of law and order, inculcating such strange doctrines as those of "direct action," "sabotage," "syndicalism," "the general strike," and "violence"? . . . We think that our whole current morality as to the sacredness of property and even of life is involved.[54]

Out of such fears were IWW dreams made. What turned most Americans off turned Wobblies on. To the convinced Wobbly, 1912 seemed like the dawn of a new, freer era. The IWW, indeed, conducted more strikes and free-speech fights from 1912 to 1913 than at any other time in its pre–World War I history. In the midst of the San Diego struggle and only two weeks after the triumph in Lawrence, the *Industrial Worker* boasted: "The revolutionary pot seems to be boiling in all quarters. The day of transformation is now at hand." [55]

Wobblies had suddenly discovered that their tactics worked. In the past they had preached but not practiced industrial organization and direct action at the point of production; now that they had started, as in Lawrence, "to practice what we preached, the growth surprised even the most enthusiastic industrialist." "The question of 'Will the I.W.W. Grow?'" commented another Wobbly, "is now answered in the affirmative by the masters who add, 'and damn it, *Can it be stopped?*'" [56]

Wherever Wobblies chose to look in the summer of 1912 they could see organizational activity. E. F. Doree boasted of four thousand Wobblies out on the Grand Trunk Pacific in Canada, fifteen thousand in eleven New Bedford textile mills, fifteen thousand timber workers in Louisiana and Texas, and two thousand auto workers in Cleveland. He told John Pancner to expect a boom in Spokane in mid-September when things closed down and the mob looked for "something that is not, i.e. a job." To Doree the day did not then seem far off when employers and public officials "will be glad to eat out of our hands." An IWW organizer in Vancouver, Canada, reported with equal enthusiasm that the organization had established five new locals in Vancouver and that the impact of IWW agitation was being felt all over British Columbia and elsewhere in Canada. "Vancouver and vicinity," he noted, "are busy as h-ll taking in members. Seattle is very much alive . . ." In Canada, unlike the States, the AFL and the socialists, "who talk nothing but straight industrial unionism to the boys," cooperated with the IWW.[57]

This euphoric optimism carried right on through to the seventh IWW national convention, which met at Brand's Hall in Chicago September 16–26, 1912. Forty-five delegates from all over the United States and from Canada attended. Although some signs of decentralist sentiment appeared, no ideological or sectional lines divided the delegates. Some Westerners spoke in favor of limiting the general executive board's power to control strikes and free-speech fights, but other Westerners insisted upon the need for stricter organization and for firmer control of the rank and file. Moreover, many of those Westerners who criticized the general executive board lacked an ideological commitment to decentralization; instead, for perfectly understandable reasons, they believed that general headquarters in Chicago was too far from the Northwest (two thousand miles) to react promptly and wisely to distant events. It was, after all, the Western IWW newspaper which remarked: "To deny leadership is to fall back on the utopian theory that all men are equal in ability and enterprise." A lumber workers' delegate from Seattle even introduced a resolution recommending that the IWW devise a more systematic means of organization, and concluded by asserting: "We are convinced that the evil of leaving so much to chance . . . should as thoroughly as possible be done away with, and certainly, scientific agitation and organization be substituted in its place. . . . Hoping that fellow workers will . . . begin the active work of substituting system and order in agitating, organizing, and carrying on industrial conflicts instead of the largely chaotic lack of methods that now prevail." Delegates from Portland, Oregon, came to the Chicago convention with similar proposals for tightening and centralizing the IWW's methods and structure. So much for the alleged commitment of Western Wobblies to primitive frontier individualism and to rank-and-file participatory democracy. From his prison cell in Massachusetts, Ettor agreed: "Centralization of energies and abilities can be no stone barring the path and progress of the organization but loose, irresponsible, free hand methods are surely bound to impede the work of education, organization, and emancipation." So advised, the convention voted to encourage the appointment of more professional organizers who would recruit out on the job and maintain accurate and complete membership records.[58]

Most Wobblies returned home from the seventh convention enraptured about their organization's future. James P. Cannon, one of the younger Wobblies then rising to prominence in American radical circles, thought the organization's rapid growth had ended internal strife and dissension forever. Yet the harmony Cannon witnessed at the 1912 convention had failed in his view to diminish the revolutionary ardor of the Wobblies. Organizational success, he averred, had not resulted in opportunism. No delegate had wished to modify the IWW's uncompromising revolutionary ideology. "Nor was there any reaching out for respectability," Cannon wrote. "Every man was a 'Red,' most of them with jail records, too. . . . Here was an assemblage which, to a man, rejected the moral and ethical teachings of the existing order, and had formulated a creed of their own which begins with Solidarity and ends with Freedom."[59]

But in 1912 freedom and solidarity were farther away than most Wobblies suspected. Still transfixed by their success at Lawrence, they forgot the relative paucity of the IWW's total membership and the bankruptcy of its treasury. Swept away by the growth and successes of 1912, they would be ill prepared to meet the decline and defeats to come their way in 1913.

CHAPTER

I I

Satan's Dark Mills: Paterson and After

 HISTORY never repeats itself precisely. To paraphrase Hegel's famous aphorism: Similar historical events occur first as success, next as failure. This, much to its regret, the IWW learned in 1913.

The 1912 victory at Lawrence had brought the IWW thousands of new recruits (although, in fact, paid-up membership at its 1912 peak numbered only a little over eighteen thousand), nationwide publicity, and visions of imminent revolution. Throughout the remainder of the year Wobblies acted as if the industrial millennium was near at hand. But events the next year initiated another period of paralyzing internal dissension and organizational decline.

In 1913 IWW organizers directed a walkout begun by rebellious textile workers in Paterson, New Jersey, just as they had done the previous year in Lawrence. In Paterson, however, the industrial conflict ended in defeat, and the IWW's failure there presaged its bleak future among the immigrant workers of the industrial Northeast.

Like Lawrence, Paterson in 1913 was a relatively old, established industrial city. In fact, when during the 1790's Alexander Hamilton

263

first dreamed of industrializing America, he selected Paterson as an ideal site for his Society for the Encouragement of Manufacturing. Although Hamilton's dreams came to naught in his own lifetime, Paterson was indeed an ideal industrial location. About twenty miles from New York City and less than a hundred from Philadelphia, it sat astride the most compact domestic market in nineteenth-century America. The Passaic River, which bisected the city, provided ample water power to run its mills, while the region's fine canals, railroads, and public highways provided a convenient and efficient means for transporting raw materials into Paterson and finished manufactures out. The region also abounded in capital and labor. New York was the nation's prime money market, with Boston and Philadelphia not far behind. Moreover, by the mid-nineteenth century New York was the major port of entry for the cheap immigrant labor beginning to flood the domestic labor market. By the second half of the nineteenth century, Paterson, taking advantage of all its geographical attractions, had become one of the Northeast's more significant small industrial centers.

By 1913 Paterson led the nation in silk production. More than three hundred mills and dyehouses employing about 25,000 men, women, and children (out of a total of about 73,000 working men, women, and children in the city) dyed and wove the fine as well as the cheap silks demanded by New York's garment industry. Once a producer of only the finest high-grade and high-cost silks, Paterson, compelled by changes in the structure of the market, had turned to the manufacture of cheaper silks, which could be produced on larger, more efficient looms operated by women and children.

Like other industrial cities of its size, Paterson had a polyglot population. At first its people consisted largely of native Americans of British and Dutch stock. Then, in the 1840's and 1850's, the first waves of Irish and German immigrants reached the city. Even after the Civil War the Irish, the Germans, and some Englishmen continued to settle in Paterson. Toward the end of the century East European Jews and southern Italians started to arrive in significant numbers, and they continued to do so right up to the strike year of 1913.

Working conditions in Paterson did not differ materially from those in Lawrence. Work was hard—ten hours daily—and the mills were dirty, stuffy, and noisy. The people who toiled inside were much like the laborers of Lawrence: adult males and females worked alongside adolescent boys and girls (over fourteen).

Wages conformed to the pattern prevalent elsewhere in the textile industry. Paterson's average wage for skilled workers in 1913 was $11.69 a week. The unskilled, of course, received much less—closer to $6 or $7 a week. The number of unskilled, especially women and children, at work in the industry was rising rapidly in proportion to the total number of employees. Striking exceptions to the average could of course be found. Elizabeth Gurley Flynn discovered one of the smaller mills, the Bamford Ribbon Company, where girls fourteen to seventeen years old received only half their wages weekly—less fines. The boss kept the other half until the end of the year, returning it then without interest to the girls still in the company's employ. Miss Flynn knew of one girl whose pay vouchers showed an average weekly wage of $1.42 for forty-two weeks, and another whose slips showed $1.85 for thirty-two weeks. Bamford Mills, said Elizabeth Gurley Flynn, had discovered easy money in Paterson's children: "Kept in perpetual motion, a crowd working, a crowd quitting, and a crowd coming from school, his mill can profit as long as childhood lasts." On the other hand, a manufacturer's spokesman could point to a quite different small mill where a female weaver averaged more than $75 every two weeks.[1] Exceptions aside, most skilled workers earned adequate wages, but the unskilled, who comprised a large majority of the total labor force, received little enough for their arduous work; and as in Lawrence, most immigrant workers sent their sons and daughters into the mills as soon as possible in order to provide the family with a "decent" standard of living.

But even family labor failed to provide Paterson's immigrants with comfort or security. Although the city's slums did not match the worst in Lawrence, the housing of many workers was still, in the words of Paterson's leading rabbi, "distinctly bad." It was nevertheless true that most skilled workers and those among the unskilled whose entire families worked could probably afford the comfortable and sanitary housing that social investigator John Fitch claimed to be more general in Paterson "than is the rule among industrial cities." Housing aside, the unskilled immigrants lived on the margin of economic security: seasonal and technological shifts frequently left them jobless; competition from low-wage mills in Pennsylvania threatened their wage scale; and the abundant supply of cheap immigrant labor exercised relentless downward pressure on their wage rates.[2]

There were, too, important differences between Lawrence and Paterson. In Paterson, unlike Lawrence, no single company dominated the city's economy, and numerous small mills ruthlessly competed with the larger manufacturers. Paterson also had fewer significant nationality groups among its new immigrants. In both textile towns, however, wages were low and immigrant families sent their children into the mills in order to supplement income. In short, Paterson, like Lawrence, contained within itself the social dynamite which, given the spark, could explode into industrial warfare.

Paterson had long been a favorite target for IWW agitators. From the IWW's founding in 1905, not a year passed without some organizational activity in Paterson. The 1908 convention which established the NIUTW met there. But over the years IWW efforts to penetrate the silk industry met with little success, for Paterson's employers were as hostile to trade unions as were Lawrence's, and they had been equally successful in beating back trade-union threats. Although silk workers belonged to several craft unions affiliated with the United Textile Workers, these unions were neither active nor effective. On the eve of the 1913 strike Paterson was relatively unorganized.

At one time Paterson's silk manufacturers had faced little competition. This was no longer so in 1913. Technological innovation and changing demands brought an intensive competition to the silk industry, much more bitter than that faced by Lawrence's American Woolen Company. In the mid-1890's engineers had perfected a high-speed loom which could be operated by women. Simultaneously, demand increased for the cheap silk turned out by the new looms, thereby providing manufacturers of cheap-grade silks with larger profits on their investments than could be had by Paterson's producers of fine silks. The cheap-silk industry also moved to the coal-mining communities of eastern Pennsylvania, where a large female labor force sought work at low wages. Paterson's weavers had traditionally worked only one or two Jacquard looms, which turned out fine silk. The Pennsylvania women, however, tended four looms and produced considerably more silk per unit of labor than their higher-paid Paterson competitors. Paterson's manufacturers used several approaches in fighting competitors. Some with large capital reserves established their own branch operations in Pennsylvania. Others introduced women workers and multiple looms into Paterson's mills and shifted to the production of cheap silks. Still others limited themselves to the production of only those high-quality silks with which Pennsylvania mills could not compete.[3]

The ensuing technological innovations destroyed traditional working patterns in Paterson. An industry once composed largely of well-paid skilled weavers fast became one with more and more low-paid women workers. Weavers who once tended two looms now worked three or four. As a pieceworker, any weaver who preferred to tend two looms could continue to do so provided he accepted the lower four-loom piece rate. In addition, his piece rate depended upon the number of threads in a pattern; since the cheaper silks contained fewer threads per piece, employers paid a lower rate for their production. Under the new four-loom system, the weaver's total wages nevertheless rose: four looms produced more silk than two in the same time, and cheaper silks with fewer threads could be turned out more rapidly than fine silks.

Considerations other than wages made weavers discontented with the four-loom system. Many weavers considered the obligation to tend four looms in poorly illuminated mills to be too much of a strain on their eyes and nerves. Others feared that the general introduction of the four-loom system would engender rising unemployment, create a reserve labor army anxious for work at any price, and thus ultimately undermine prevailing wage rates. When one man or woman could do the work formerly done by two or three hands, how could Paterson provide jobs enough for all its workers? Still other workers asserted that although their wages rose with increased productivity, employers took an inordinate share of the enlarged profits. As one unhappy worker put it: ". . . We don't object to improved machinery. We welcome improved machinery, if we can get some benefit out of it . . . but as a rule we never receive any benefit from any improved machinery they put into the mills. . . . the benefit is really taken away from us and the manufacturer gets the benefit instead of the worker. . . . improved machinery only antagonizes the workers the more, because they can see themselves that they can produce more under the improved machinery; still they get less wages." [4]

When silk workers asked for shorter hours or higher wages, employers pleaded poverty. Paterson's manufacturers claimed, and with some justice, that their wages were higher than those paid in any other American silk-making community. Moreover, New Jersey state law limited the workers to a fifty-five-hour week, while out-of-state competitors worked their employees from fifty-seven to sixty hours. How, in short, asked Paterson's employers, could they meet their workers' demands when concessions would place them at the mercy of competitors in other states with lower wage rates and weaker labor laws? [5]

Paterson's workers refused to accept their employers' case for the status quo. Early in 1912, when several local mills introduced the four-loom system, the weavers rebelled. They demanded either increased piece rates or the elimination of the multiple-loom system. At first only the skilled workers allied to the AFL craft unions protested. The United Textile Workers, however, instead of supporting the protest, placed itself at the mercy of the employers' sense of justice. Nothing coming of UTW efforts to improve working conditions—the employers' sense of justice being, to say the least, narrow—Paterson's workers looked elsewhere for union leadership.

At that particular time the IWW was fully occupied in Lawrence. Not so Daniel DeLeon's then insignificant organization, the so-called Detroit IWW. DeLeon's right-hand man, Rudolph Katz, rushed to Paterson to lead the rebellious local workers. Under Katz's leadership more than five thousand workers came out on strike. Coming during the peak production season, the walkout caused several mills to settle on union terms—largely an increase in wages and limited recognition of the union.

These gains proved short-lived. The larger mills never negotiated with the strikers; instead, they used their influence to have Katz jailed for six months, and then proceeded to smash the leaderless strike. The smaller manufacturers, who had settled with the union, broke their contracts as soon as the busy season ended. DeLeon's IWW never, in fact, had a chance in Paterson. Not only was it fought by employers, but both the AFL craft unions and the Chicago IWW opposed it as well. [6]

As 1912 ended, Paterson's basic industrial relations problem remained unresolved. Employers continued to introduce four looms, hire women, and slash piece rates. ". . . There was deepseated grievance in the minds and hearts of the strikers," one veteran silk worker recalled in 1914, "produced or caused by the manner in which employers had been treating them for the four or five years previous." [7]

Finally, in January 1913, the decision by Doherty and Company, the largest mill in Paterson, to introduce the four-loom system in a plant traditionally run on the two-loom pattern brought the city's festering discontent to a head. At once Doherty's skilled weavers protested. Yet when Doherty responded by asserting that external competition dictated the introduction of the four-loom system, the protesting craft unionists did nothing more.[8]

With Lawrence out of the way, the IWW was now ready to move in. Early in January an IWW leader reported to *Solidarity* that Paterson Local 152 had been doing good work agitating for an eight-hour day and for the abolition of the four-loom system. The IWW, he added, should be able to make Paterson's bosses sit up and take notice. Local 152 appealed to workers by arguing that the eight-hour day would compel employers to hire more workers, and that once the reserve labor army shrunk in size, workers could compel employers to grant "more wages, better treatment, better light . . ." Refuse to run more than two looms on broadsilk, more than one loom on silk, the IWW agitators advised, but "organize your forces. Act together. When we get ready we will set the date and refuse to work longer than 8 hours." After years of agitation, IWW propaganda finally appeared to be taking effect in Paterson. As one worker who became an IWW recruit later remembered: ". . . There was a fruitful and fertile soil when the I.W.W. dropped its seed here in . . . Paterson which rapidly took root and spread." [9]

As the IWW sent its message throughout the city, it stimulated further discontent among Doherty employees, who, late in January, walked out spontaneously. This time, however, they did not lack for leadership or organization. Local 152 immediately offered help and set about widening the original walkout initiated by only a handful of workers. By February 1 the IWW succeeded in making the Doherty walkout plant-wide. Strike leaders now reasoned that unless Paterson's other mill hands came out and shut down all the city's mills, the Doherty strike would collapse. The occasion seemed ripe for such a movement, for there was, as one participant recalled, "a general desire among the workers . . . of Paterson for an improvement in their conditions that seemed to center on a shorter workday." For three weeks, Local 152's officials struggled to organize union committees in each of the city's mills, preparatory to declaring a general strike in the silk industry. Calling upon the workers in every mill and dyehouse to strike on Tuesday morning, February 25, Wobbly organizers advised: "It is far better to starve fighting than to starve working." On the morning of the 25th workers began to walk out of Paterson's silk mills;

and in the days that followed more and more workers came out. First, they came from the broadsilk mills, then the ribbon mills, and finally the dyehouses; they left at the rate of almost 1,200 a day, until 25,000 workers were out and Paterson's silk industry had been shut down tight. At this point the strikers made only two specific demands: an eight-hour day, and a $12 minimum weekly wage for dyehouse workers (the filthiest and least desirable employment in the industry).[10]

In Paterson, as in Lawrence, the strikers were divided by nationality and by craft. Again, the previously unorganized and less skilled new immigrants walked out first, followed, though somewhat reluctantly, by the skilled English-speaking workers. Throughout what was to prove a protracted conflict, the two groups of strikers maintained a shaky alliance of convenience, ready to crumble at the first shock. In the past the English-speaking workers had never shown any inclination to cooperate with the immigrants who labored alongside them in the mills. Secure in their established craft unions with their higher wages, the skilled workers were patronizing to their foreign colleagues. One veteran AFL craft unionist told the Commission on Industrial Relations that the trouble in Paterson "was too many immigrants coming into the silk trade that did not thoroughly understand the working of our organizations, or had not become Americanized." He contended that the AFL could not organize Paterson's "unAmerican" immigrants partly because they were too anxious to strike and partly because they were too radical to accept the fundamentally moderate tactics associated with American craft unions. Or as a fellow craft unionist commented regarding the Russian Jews and Italians in the silk industry: "If an organization is formed today, they want to strike tomorrow. They don't seem willing to stick to any organization any length of time unless they have a strike. We have tried time and again to form locals for the American Federation of Labor . . . and every one of them has seemed to fail . . . and *if there is any fault it is with the workers themselves.*" [11]

Elizabeth Gurley Flynn, one of the most active IWW agitators during the Paterson struggle, clearly recalled the city's tenacious ethnic divisions. She found the immigrant broadsilk weavers and dyers, though largely unorganized and unfamiliar with unionism, easy to stimulate to aggressive activity. But the English-speaking ribbon weavers, with thirty years of craft-union traditions behind them, responded to the IWW-led walkout only after three weeks of actual conflict. Even then they continued to exert a conservative influence upon the mass of immigrant strikers. John Reed, then a young reporter fresh out of Harvard and making his first contact with the realities of the class struggle in America, carried away from Paterson the same impressions as Miss Flynn. Upon asking a young Jew which nationalities were united in the strike, Reed obtained the following reply: " 'Tree great nations stick togedder like dis.' He made a fist. 'Tree great nations—Italians, Hebrews, and Germans." How about Americans? Reed inquired. "The Jew shrugged his shoulders, grinned scornfully, and answered: 'English peoples not go on picket line. Mericans no lika fight!' " "It is the English speaking contingent that remains passive at Paterson," Reed concluded, "while the 'wops,' the 'kikes,' the 'hunkies'—the 'degraded and ignorant races from Southern Europe'—go out and get clubbed on the picket-line and gaily take their medicine in Paterson jail." [12]

"The degraded and ignorant races" went out on Paterson's picket lines and got clubbed partly because they rebelled against miserable working conditions and partly because the IWW organized their rebellion. The AFL never came forward, at least not to organize the immigrants. "Instead," wrote John Fitch, "came Haywood . . . Flynn, [Patrick] Quinlan, [Carlo] Tresca*—empty handed, with neither money nor credit nor with the prestige of a 2,000,000 membership, but willing to work and to go to jail. They have put into the 25,000 strikers a spirit that has made them stand together with a united determination for a period that 'must have tried the souls of the strongest." [13]

When the IWW organizers and agitators arrived in Paterson, Silk Workers Local 152 had only about nine hundred members. Two weeks after the strike began, the union had more than ten thousand new members.[14] The IWW immediately set about organizing the silk strikers into an effective force. First, it created a strike committee comprised of two delegates from each shop (six hundred members at

---

* The Italian syndicalist, romantic radical, lover of Elizabeth Gurley Flynn, and anti-fascist purportedly assassinated by Mussolini's agents in America in 1943.

full strength) to administer the conflict. As in Lawrence, the majority of committee members at first were nonunion, non-IWW. Although IWW personnel arranged the regular meetings and conducted the basic strike agitation, the non-IWW-dominated committee determined and dictated all tactics and strategy. When inquiring journalists asked the strikers who their leaders were, the workers shot back: "We are all leaders." The IWW organizers—Haywood, Flynn, Quinlan—served in a purely advisory capacity. Miss Flynn described the relationship between the IWW and the actual strikers this way: ". . . The preparation and declaration as well as the stimulation of the strike was all done by the I.W.W., by the militant minority among the silk workers; the administering of the strike was done democratically by the silk workers themselves." And, she added ruefully: "Our plan of battle was very often nullified by the democratic administration of the strike committee." [15]

With the strikers organized, Wobbly agitators could go about their work more effectively. Precisely what they did has been described by Miss Flynn, according to whom the agitators' primary goal was to educate the strikers. Sounding almost like John Dewey, she noted that "education is not a conversion, it is a process." IWW speakers, she observed, sought to transcend the prejudices of a lifetime: prejudices on national issues, prejudices between crafts, prejudices between men and women, prejudices between ethnic and religious groups. The Wobblies attempted to convert the immigrants from their diverse Old World religions to a new single-minded faith in the class struggle, to make the strikers forget that their walkout was over a few cents more or a few hours less, "but to make them feel it is a 'religious duty' for them to win that strike." One overriding goal underly the IWW's work in Paterson, Miss Flynn declared: "To create in them [the strikers] a feeling of solidarity" as part of the long process of instilling "class spirit, class respect, class consciousness." [16]

Neither the IWW organizers nor the strike committee ever lost sight of the walkout's immediate objectives. From the first, the strike committee offered to confer with employers in order to settle the dispute. Similarly, the separate shop committees approached their respective employers to probe the possibilities of reaching an equitable accord. Within the larger strike committee, a smaller executive body of twenty—all IWW members, but also all local Paterson men— handled the preliminary negotiations. The various shop committees' most basic demand was the eight-hour day. One strike leader afterward remarked: ". . . I know positively had the manufacturers at the time of the strike granted an eight-hour day the strikers would have thrown all other grievances aside." But once the strike had erupted they asked for more. They demanded time and a half for overtime, minimum-wage levels for the less skilled (particularly the dyehouse workers), increases in the general piece rates, abolition of the three- and four-loom system in broadsilk, and several minor items. As in all IWW-led strikes, the workers did not insist on union recognition or on the closed shop.[17]

The IWW's administration of the Paterson struggle differed in no basic respect from what it had been in Lawrence. Picket squads assigned to each of the mills marched continuously up and down the sidewalks in front of the factory gates with every intention of psychologically intimidating men and women who might have considered breaking the united front by re-entering the mills. (Physical violence, however, always remained a possibility.) Every day for seven months, in the face of policemen's clubs, detectives' pistols, and rough weather, the pickets performed their function. While some men and women fought the class war on Paterson's streets, others waged it indoors by visiting working-class families to deliver dire warnings against potential scabs, or by administering relief funds and providing the needy with food, clothes, medical care and drugs.

IWW agitators insured that the strikers' ranks remained united. Miss Flynn explained how this was done. Sunday was the crucial day: "If on Sunday," she said, "you let these people stay at home, sit around the stove without any fire in it, sit down at the table where there isn't very much food, see the feet of the children with shoes getting thin, and the bodies of the children where the clothes are getting ragged, they begin to think in terms of 'myself' and lose the spirit of the mass and the realization that all are suffering as they are suffering. You have got to keep them busy every day in the week, and particularly on Sunday, in order to keep that spirit from going down to zero." Which was why the IWW held constant meetings that were more in the character of high school pep rallies than serious war councils. This was why every Sunday the IWW would lead a march to Haledon, a small socialist-administered township just outside Paterson's city limits, where strikers could picnic, listen to radical oratory, and sing without fear and without police interference. The novelty and group spirit of Sunday mass picnics, Miss Flynn thought, stimulated the strikers for the coming week of industrial warfare.[18]

The IWW once more pledged to wage a nonviolent struggle. In Paterson, as in Lawrence, it insisted that the strikers could gain victory simply by keeping their hands in their pockets. Again, it advised its followers that bayonets and clubs could not weave silk. "We believe the most violent thing the worker can do," local IWW leader Adolph Lessig said, "is when they quit work." "Your power is your folded arms," counseled other Wobblies. "You have killed the mills; you have stopped production; you have broken off profits. Any other violence you may commit is less than this . . ." Although physical violence was dramatic, Miss Flynn noted, "it's especially dramatic when you talk about it and don't resort to it." Actual violence she considered an anachronistic method of industrial conflict; mass action, nonviolent but tenacious, she believed to be a modern "and a much more feared method" of battle.[19]

Numerous witnesses testified to the effectiveness of the IWW's peaceful methods. Paterson's Rabbi Leo Mannheimer paid tribute to the leadership of Haywood, Flynn, Tresca, *et al.*, who held in check an army of 25,000 for thirteen weeks. "Had they been preaching anarchism and violence," the rabbi wrote, "there would have been anarchism and violence." Instead, excepting a few broken windows, there had been no destruction of property, and certainly no destruction of lives. Passive resistance had been the strikers' weapon, Rabbi Mannheimer concluded. Even Paterson's police chief informed John Fitch on May 22 that no silk worker desiring to return to work had ever needed police protection against the pickets, "and there has not been a single case of assault on a 'scab' by a striker that has come to the knowledge of the police." [20]

From the attitudes, policies, and actions of Paterson's employers and its leading citizens, one would never have known that nonviolent industrial conflict was being waged. Paterson's manufacturers and local elite made Lawrence's appear almost benevolently enlightened. From the start of the strike to its finish, Paterson employers refused to deal with any organized group of workers. One employer, refusing even to accept a note from a strike committee, declared: "I'll receive no paper with the stamp of the I.W.W. on it." He added emphatically, ". . . The I.W.W. I don't consider an American organization." Another equally adamant manufacturer explained his hostility to unions this way: "We'd rather go to the wall at once than yield everything we own to them by degrees." Paterson's employers developed a "domino theory" of industrial warfare, as explained by one local manufacturer:

"The silk manufacturers of the country are watching our fight and praying for our success for they realize that if we are beaten it will be their turn next." "The IWW must go" became Paterson's battle cry. Employers did all they could to make the Wobblies leave. They stubbornly refused to participate in any meetings, negotiations, or mediation sessions with strikers. They hired armed private detectives to patrol the mills and to intimidate the strikers. Manufacturers had one overriding aim, according to Rabbi Mannheimer, and that was "to starve the strikers into submission, so that they will return to the mills disheartened." [21]

Following what had by then become a time-honored American practice, Paterson's employers proclaimed their belief in decent, honest, God-fearing American trade unions, and their desire to protect decent men and women from intimidation by hoodlum, radical, un-American unionists. But any reasonably astute observer saw through employer propaganda. If pinned down, John Fitch observed, "the employers admit that they are opposed to unionism as such, and not to the I.W.W. alone." Or as Rabbi Mannheimer more tersely put it, *"No form of labor organization among the silk employees would be tolerated in Paterson."* [22] If unionism could not be resisted, however, employers preferred the AFL to the Wobblies.

Paterson's dominant groups agreed with the employers' anti-union sentiments. Mayor Andrew McBride claimed the conflict had been caused by out-of-town agitators who preached "unAmerican" doctrines to gullible and confused immigrants. Most strikers, the Mayor declared, stayed at home out of fear. The Black Hand appeared in Paterson's newspapers as regularly as it had in Lawrence's: a bomb threat here, property destroyed there, honest workers intimidated or beaten everywhere. The editor of the *Paterson Press* suggested the city handle the IWW with the same dispatch San Diego had demonstrated in the previous year's free-speech fight. ". . . The sooner the I.W.W. outfit leave town," he informed his readers, "the better it will be for all concerned, *no matter how it is accomplished*" (italics added). A Civil War veteran, taking the *Press*'s advice to heart, suggested: ". . . If we are to have new cemeteries . . . they be filled with just such people as those who are now making the disturbance—the first graves to be filled with Haywood and his crowd . . ." [23]

The city authorities thus decided to drive the "outside" agitators out of Paterson—subtly if possible, forcibly if necessary. A specially established group of local clergymen (excluding Rabbi Mannheimer), founded with the blessings of the board of aldermen, sought to bring employers and employees together on an individual, nonunion basis. But because the IWW refused to recognize the clergymen's version of the Golden Rule, most Paterson preachers came to agree with laymen that the Wobblies should never have been permitted into town, "but having come they should be driven out." [24]

Perhaps one way of driving the Wobblies out was to invite the AFL in. Although manufacturers made no direct overtures to an AFL union, Paterson's press, pulpit, and municipal officials invited Gompers' organization in to help stymie the Wobblies. The Paterson central labor organization, an AFL affiliate, tried to arrange a peace conference between employers and strikers. Just as local AFL men had almost completed their arrangements, however, Elizabeth Gurley Flynn warned the strikers against following AFL "fakirs and grafters." She proposed instead that the strikers cooperate with the central labor council if that body would endorse a twenty-four-hour sympathy strike—a demand no AFL affiliate could possibly accept. The first AFL peacemaking venture proving a failure, the town fathers invited John Golden and the United Textile Workers to organize the strikers. At a time when every meeting hall in Paterson had been denied the IWW, John Golden, Sarah Conboy, and their AFL associates obtained the local armory to plead their case. On the evening of April 16, and with the conflict now two months old, thousands of Paterson strikers flocked to the armory to hear what the UTW-AFL had to offer. When Mrs. Conboy and Golden stepped to the platform, boos, hisses, and catcalls echoed across the cavernous building for fully forty-five minutes. Then Ewald Koettgen, raising his hand for quiet, said: "I have been informed by the Committee that the I.W.W. will not be permitted to speak here tonight. Let's go home." Mrs. Conboy immediately hoisted the American flag; the hissing changed to cheers, and suddenly thousands of IWW red cards flashed above the armory floor, turning it into a sea of crimson. The local police finally drove the strikers out of the armory, leaving the UTW-AFL, in the words of one observer, "in possession of a vast emptiness." [25]

Having accused outsiders of fomenting discord in their industrial Eden, Paterson public officials brought in their own outsiders— Gompers, Golden, and Conboy—in order to restore the lost harmony. But Haywood warned: "As in Lawrence, so also in Paterson, Golden . . . will be unable to make any success as a strikebreaker. . . . The employers indeed would like to 'settle' with Mr. Golden, but the

Paterson strike will not be settled by outsiders, but by the workers themselves who have the strike in their own hands." [26] The charge of alien influence in Paterson could be made to cut both ways.

Another way of driving the IWW out seemed simpler and more expedient. Rudolph Katz once said, "The IWW preaches sabotage; the AFL practices it." It could also be said with some truth that the IWW preached defiance of bourgeois law and capitalist justice; but "law-abiding" American citizens practiced it. This was certainly the case in Paterson. John Fitch witnessed Paterson's leaders denouncing Wobblies for preaching violence, lawlessness, and anarchy, then themselves proposing that "methods frankly violent, lawless and anarchistic be used against the IWW." John Reed saw it the same way. "There's war in Paterson," he reported hyperbolically in *The Masses*. "But it's a curious kind of war. All the violence is the work of one side—the Mill Owners." [27]

Reed was very nearly right. The day after the general strike began, Paterson's police arrested Miss Flynn, Tresca, and Quinlan, and closed every hall in town to the strikers. The following evening police arrested a socialist named Frederick Sumner Boyd for having read at a strike meeting the free-speech clause of the New Jersey state constitution. Later, at the station house, Police Chief Bimson asked the socialist what strange law he had been reading. Boyd replied: "Why, chief, that was the constitution of New Jersey. Never hear of it before? I thought not." Day after day the police interfered with strike meetings, confiscated socialist newspapers and strike literature, and arrested strikers by the score. Any Wobbly who dared speak in Paterson courted arrest and imprisonment. Paterson's police, trying to learn from Lawrence's mistakes, arrested not two men but every leader it could lay its "legal" hands on and 1,850 of the strikers.[28]

On March 30 Big Bill Haywood arrived in Paterson. Scheduled to speak at LaFayette Oval, a public meeting place, he found himself denied the right to speak by the police. Someone then suggested that his audience walk to Haledon. About eight hundred to a thousand men and women eager to go on to Haledon formed behind Haywood and Lessig, who marched in the van. After arriving at a point just a few feet short of the Haledon line, the marchers encountered a police patrol. Paterson's police stepped from the patrol wagon, approached Haywood and Lessig, and peremptorily placed them under arrest, allegedly for disturbing the peace, acting disorderly, and holding an unlawful assembly. As Police Recorder Carroll interpreted the local law, those offenses cost the defendants six months in jail. An appellate court, however, overturned these convictions, demonstrating that outside of Paterson and Recorder Carroll's court, Wobblies and strikers sometimes obtained justice.[29]

Inside Paterson, strikers continued to face repressive justice. The arrests went on, as did the beatings and clubbings. On April 19, company detectives shot and killed Modestino Valentino, an innocent bystander to a scuffle between pickets and scabs. Justice never visited the silk manufacturers' gunmen. A week later local prosecutors indicted Tresca, Flynn, Quinlan, and Lessig on insubstantial charges, and on May 10 a Paterson jury convicted the socialist editor Alexander Scott of sedition—that is, of criticizing the city police—and sentenced him to one to fifteen years in prison. Shortly thereafter, Frederick Sumner Boyd found himself in prison on sedition charges. On July 13 a strikebreaker shot and killed Vincenzo Madonna, an IWW striker; and murder again went unpunished. IWW leaders shuttled back and forth between court and prison. There seemed to be no end to the injustices committed by Paterson's lawfully constituted authorities. Unhappy about the IWW meetings in Haledon, on July 19 Paterson's police instigated a riot there in order to arrest Haledon's socialist mayor on the pretext of "unlawful assemblage and malfeasance in office." [30]

John Reed had first arrived in Paterson one morning at sunrise to find the city's streets grey, cold, and deserted. The police soon appeared, and a little later the pickets came out. Then came the rain, compelling Reed to seek shelter on a nearby porch, whereupon the police attempted to drive him off the porch and back again out into the downpour. When Reed refused to desert his shelter, a policeman —whom Reed was later to describe as "doubtless a good, stupid Irishman in time of peace [but] . . . almost helpless in a situation that requires thinking"—promptly placed him under arrest. The young reporter found himself in a jail cell, about four feet wide by seven feet long, with an iron bunk hung from one side, "and an open toilet of disgusting dirtiness in the corner." Here, in jail, Reed learned how the strikers endured Paterson-style justice. While he paced nervously in his tiny cell, forty pickets joined him in the lockup, two to a cell. Joking and laughing, the forty new arrivals lifted and slammed heavy iron beds against metal walls, causing a commotion which to Reed sounded "like a cannon battery in action." For Wobblies it was simply another jail battleship. The prisoners also cheered the IWW, Haywood, Flynn, and Tresca, the Italians among them singing constantly right up until their release. As Reed left the jail later that week, he said goodbye "to all those gentle, alert, brave men, ennobled by something greater than themselves. *They* were the strike—not Bill Haywood, not Gurley Flynn, not any other individual." [31] For a time the Wobblies had made true believers out of Paterson's silk workers and John Reed as well.

But the strikers could not exist solely on true belief. As the conflict wore on, through spring and early summer, the strikers grew hungrier. As always, the IWW's own resources were limited. Socialists, craft unionists, social reformers, and sympathizers had to provide the bulk of material assistance for the conflict. Fortunately, in Paterson, as in Lawrence, every repressive measure taken by the IWW's enemies brought increased aid to the strikers. Still they needed that *cause célèbre* which Lawrence had had in the "Children's Crusade," and which Paterson, after three months of industrial warfare, still lacked.

John Reed and New York's Greenwich Village intellectuals intended to provide this essential ingredient for Paterson's silk workers. During a gathering at the home of Mabel Dodge Luhan, the salon hostess and radical dilettante, Big Bill Haywood complained bitterly about the lack of publicity the Paterson strikers were getting in New York. Not to be outdone in radical rhetoric by her special guest, Mrs. Luhan suggested, "Why don't you bring the strike to New York and *show* it to the workers?" "Well, by God! There's an idea!" Haywood responded. "But how? What hall?" Then, as Mrs. Luhan recalled in her memoirs, a young man in the salon burst out: "I'll do it! My name is Reed . . . we'll make a Pageant of the strike! The first in the world." [32]

Thus did John Reed hope simultaneously to save the strikers from certain defeat and to make the IWW the link between New York's radical "new" intellectuals and the "new" working-class revolutionaries, who together, in Nietzschean fashion, would leap out of their times, transcend the prevailing structure of society, and transform

279

the values of bourgeois America. Reed's militant minority of intellectuals would unite with the IWW's militant minority of workers to make a new and revolutionary America!

Reed worked day and night to bring off his dream. He recruited other intellectuals, artists, designers, stage directors, voice experts, and anyone else he could make use of. Together they drilled Paterson's conglomerate strikers into a unified theatrical company which could sing with one voice and act with some feeling. Finally, June 7, the day of the pageant, arrived. Thousands of strikers marched out from Paterson, crossed the Hudson River, and paraded through Manhattan to the old Madison Square Garden, where an immense sign blazed the letters "IWW" across New York's skyline. Inside thousands of spectators looked down upon a flaming red stage set. Waiting for the pageant to open, the expectant audience chanted strike slogans and thundered out IWW songs to "fan the flames of discontent." Silence finally settled on the Garden as the silk workers came on stage to re-enact Reed's version of industrial warfare. Whistles blew, pickets marched, cheered, and sang; police harassed the innocent; the strikers held fast. Even murder reappeared on the stage, as the strikers dramatized the gratuitous slaying of Modestino Valentino and the mass funeral which followed. At the pageant's close, Haywood, Flynn, Tresca, and Quinlan ended the strike drama with a re-enactment of their standard Paterson oratory. As the striker-actors left the stage, a band struck up the "Marseillaise" and the "Internationale"— which the audience bellowed out in a swelling chorus.[33] So ended Reed's strike pageant, the first and last such event the world has seen.

From the next morning on, the strike went downhill; the pageant proved to be its climax, the rest was anti-climax. Reed had promised money for the strikers—thousands of dollars to feed, clothe, and shelter them—and now he couldn't deliver on his promise. Miss Flynn vividly recalled the aftermath: "This thing that had been heralded as the salvation of the strike, this thing that was going to bring thousands of dollars to the strike—$150 came to Paterson, and all kinds of explanations. . . . It did not in any way placate the workers of Paterson to tell them that people in New York had made sacrifices, in view of the long time that they had been making sacrifices. And so with the pageant as a climax, with the papers claiming that tens of thousands of dollars had been made, and with the committee explaining what was very simple, that nothing *could* have been made with one performance on such a gigantic scale, there came trouble, dissatisfaction . . ." "Bread was the need of the hour," lamented Miss Flynn, "and bread was not forthcoming even from the most beautiful and realistic example of art that has been put on the stage in the last half century."

Preparations for the pageant had meanwhile distracted strikers from the more important job of picketing. While they turned away from the field of life to the fantasy of the theatre, the first significant numbers of strikebreakers entered Paterson's mills. The pageant provoked jealousy as well. Only a thousand strikers could go to New York, leaving 24,000 others behind. Women demanded to know, "Why did she go? Why couldn't I go?" Men, emphasizing their individual arrest records, asked why others went in their places. Discord grew, and all for nothing: cheers, tears, publicity—but no money! [34]

After the financial fiasco of the pageant, cracks appeared in the strikers' previously solid wall. As June passed into July and July into August, the cracks widened into gaping holes. First, the skilled English-speaking workers, always more moderate than the mass of immigrant strikers, tried to exert their power on the strike committee to arrange a compromise shop-by-shop settlement. Next the Socialists and the Wobblies, previously united in support of the strike, began to tear at each other's throats. All the while the strikers contended with hunger—"hunger gnawing at their vitals; hunger tearing them down . . ." [35] Men with empty stomachs proved easy prey for every variety of dissension.

When employers proposed a shop-by-shop settlement in early July, the skilled ribbon weavers leaped at the opportunity of returning to work. The IWW leaders, however, insisted that the great majority of strikers must receive some concessions before the walkout ended. But now the more conservative workers turned IWW principles against the Wobblies. "We are the silk workers," the ribbon weavers said. "You are simply outside agitators. You can't talk to this strike committee even." Miss Flynn remembered having a committee room door virtually slammed in her face until the Italian and Jewish strikers present forced the English-speaking workers to allow the "Rebel Girl" a hearing. Although most of the strikers followed her and the other IWW organizers in rejecting a shop-by-shop settlement in a referendum vote, employers realized that the workers were divided—not only split but also weakening—and now they refused to take the workers back except under pre-strike conditions. [36]

During the conflict's first months Socialists and Wobblies had displayed almost perfect harmony. Wobblies did most of the agitating and organizing; Socialists provided most of the publicity, sympathy, and money. Paterson's strikers had no better friend than the Socialist *New York Call*. To some American radicals Paterson demonstrated beautifully the need for both kinds of working-class action—direct and political. "Let us have unity," the Socialist Alexander Scott proclaimed, ". . . let the revolutionary labor movement use both its arms —and its feet, if necessary." [37]

Cooperation faltered as hunger and pessimism spread. The old submerged grievances and conflicts separating IWW syndicalists from Socialist politicians soon rose to the surface. By July, Socialists joined the more moderate English-speaking strikers (some of whom were themselves Socialists) in supporting compromise shop-by-shop agreements. The local Socialist paper began to advise strikers: "Industrial action has failed; now try political action." At the very beginning of the Paterson strike, the campaign to recall Haywood from the Socialist party's national executive committee for advocating sabotage had succeeded. Explaining why his group refused to treat with IWW-led strikers, a silk manufacturer's spokesman pointed out: "The Socialists as you know have repudiated Haywood." When the Socialist Boyd was sentenced to five years in prison for sedition, Socialists had no grounds for complaint, for Boyd had advocated sabotage, and the 1912 Socialist party convention had made such advocacy grounds for expulsion from the party. As the strike weakened, the earlier Socialist support of IWW leadership turned to criticism. The *New York Call*, originally a leading advocate of the strikers' cause, became its most outspoken critic. When confused strikers asked John Reed why Socialists no longer supported them, he had no answer. "All I could say," Reed later wrote, "was that a good share of the Socialist Party and the American Federation of Labor have forgotten all about the Class Struggle, and seem to be playing a little game with Capitalistic rules, called 'Button, button, who's got the vote!'" [38]

By mid-July, with Quinlan and Boyd in prison, Miss Flynn finally released after a jury deadlock, Haywood and Tresca awaiting trial in the fall, and hundreds of other strikers either in jail or out on bond, the silk workers held on only by the skin of their teeth. Although the manufacturers had also begun to weaken by July, finding themselves unable to fill profitable orders for the coming fall fashion season, they remained united. United the employers could take advantage of the breaks developing in the strikers' ranks.

The strike collapsed in a fashion that was all too predictable. The English-speaking skilled workers cut their less-skilled comrades adrift. On July 18 the ribbon weavers notified the strike committee: "We have drawn out of your committee. We are going to settle our strike to suit ourselves. We are going to settle it shop by shop." With the ribbon weavers' secession, the strike committee decided, without taking a referendum vote, to allow the remaining strikers to return to work on the basis of individual shop agreements, whatever the terms. The weaker strikers stampeded back to the mills on the employers' terms; the stronger strikers, the true recalcitrants, ultimately faced either the blacklist or surrender. In either event, they lost. By July 28 everybody was back at work, and nobody had obtained much of an improvement in either wages or working conditions.[39]

Elizabeth Gurley Flynn later asserted, ". . . If the strikers had been able to hold out a little longer by any means, by money if possible . . . we could have won the Paterson strike." But, as she argued, the Socialists who had the funds offered only criticism and complained about Wobbly ingratitude. They berated the IWW for not having allowed individual shop settlements earlier in July. Miss Flynn was quick to point out that it was precisely these individual shop settlements that had cost them the strike. "Every general knows," she observed, "it is far better for an army to retreat en masse than it is to scatter and be shot to pieces." [40] In Paterson, as Miss Flynn and other Wobblies had to concede, the strikers fled like a disorganized rabble, and the employers shot them to pieces.

After the strike some local IWW leaders still claimed: "The fight will be on until the workers get what they came out for originally. The union is in good shape and Paterson will be heard from again in the near future." [41] But Paterson was not heard from again.

Elizabeth Gurley Flynn, in a postmortem on Paterson, explained why the IWW could achieve short-run coalitions with immigrant industrial workers, yet could not maintain their commitment over the long haul. To Miss Flynn a labor victory in order to be meaningful had to be two-sided: workers must gain economic advantage but they must also achieve the revolutionary spirit. If a strike could achieve only one objective, she argued, better to gain in spirit than in economic advantage. But even Miss Flynn perceived that if the IWW offered strikers only revolutionary spirit and no bread, its appeal would be too circumscribed. Consequently, the IWW conducted its strikes, like the one in Paterson, pragmatically. It followed no hard and fast rules. Wobblies realized, to quote Miss Flynn again, "that we are dealing with human beings and not with chemicals." Or as she also put it: "People are not material, you can't lay them down on the table and cut them according to a pattern. You may have the best principles, but you can't always fit the people to the best principles." The IWW let its strikers learn industrial warfare and union tactics in the manner prescribed by Karl Marx and John Dewey: by doing. If the strikers wanted higher wages, shorter hours, and better conditions, IWW organizers let them fight for them. If they wanted agreements (not time contracts) with their employers, IWW leaders let them negotiate for them. The IWW organized, agitated, advised; but the strikers, most of whom in Paterson and elsewhere in the East did not understand or accept hard-core IWW doctrine, finally made the decisions. Wobblies hoped that simple ideas would lead to action, and that action, in turn, would transform the strikers' originally simple concepts into more complicated revolutionary principles. In other words, the simple concept that employers mistreated workers would result in a strike, the nature of which would teach the strikers about the realities of class, the viciousness of employers, and the depravity of the capitalist state, and from this the strikers would derive a sense of class consciousness and revolutionary principles. If the strikers failed to learn from action, or if they decided wrongly, there was nothing IWW leaders could do. After the IWW's experience in Paterson, Miss Flynn suggested that in the future when the IWW "assumes the responsibility of a strike the I.W.W. should control the strike absolutely through a union strike committee . . . there should be no outside interference." Direct action and solidarity under tight IWW control, she asserted, "are the only keys to a worker's success." [42]

Now, had the IWW organizers in Paterson been prepared to offer the correct advice and to exert the proper control, the result for both the strikers and for the IWW might have been different. Unfortunately, Wobblies did not necessarily give strikers wise counsel. Paterson's workers had sought to earn a few cents more and work a few minutes less each day. But to Miss Flynn and Haywood, among others, if the strikers returned to the job with material gains but "with the same psychology, the same attitude toward society . . ." they would have won only a temporary triumph, not a lasting victory. In Miss Flynn's words, "For workers to go back with a class-conscious spirit, with an organized and a determined attitude toward society, means that even if they have made no economic gain they have the possibility of gaining in the future." In this sense, Wobblies could even discover a triumph in the ruins at Paterson, where the silk workers received no wage increases, no reduction of hours, but where, according to the IWW, they obtained "a class feeling, a trust in themselves and a distrust for everybody else." [43] This IWW commitment to larger revolutionary principles and goals, this desire to inculcate Marxist ideology among immigrant workers, made it difficult, if not impossible, for Wobblies to maintain permanent organization among workers whose needs were short run and whose ideological commitment was minimal.

Only an IWW true believer could perceive a victory in Paterson. During the peak of the strike more than ten thousand silk workers had enrolled in the IWW; less than six months later the most optimistic estimate was fifteen hundred members in good standing; and in the following months that fifteen hundred steadily shrank.[44] The National Industrial Union of Textile Workers took sick after Lawrence; after Paterson it died.

When the IWW failed to deliver improved working and living conditions to Paterson's immigrants, they, like Lawrence's immigrants, found security in their families, their ethnic associations, their religious groups. For them, the IWW was never a home, never a true belief, never the kind of cause which merited absolute sacrifice. For a time the IWW had simply offered Paterson's workers hope for an immediate improvement in their wretched lives. Then the unyielding structure of American society and capitalism, which caused the AFL to concentrate its efforts upon the skilled workers and to ignore the less skilled, made it impossible for the IWW, which promised the immigrants so much, to give them anything at all.

Paterson was not the sole IWW failure in 1913. Its pattern was repeated elsewhere with similarly dismal results.

During the summer of 1912 the IWW had begun to agitate among the unskilled workers in the thriving rubber factories of Akron, Ohio. At first it made little progress in organizing among the industry's twenty thousand workers, many of whom were native Americans from the hills of West Virginia, Kentucky, and Tennessee. Early in February 1913, however, just as the Paterson strike was beginning, the IWW announced a meeting for those Akron rubber workers interested in more of the good things in life. Promising Akron's immigrant workers speakers in four languages—English, Serbian, Italian, and Hungarian—Wobblies sent the rubber workers "A Message from Hell," which proclaimed: "You don't have to die to get to hell. Just come to Akron, Ohio, and get a pass to enter any one of the many rubber shops." Shortly after the IWW released its message from hell, 300 men walked out of the Firestone plant, demanding higher wages. At that point the IWW could claim no more than 150 members in Akron; indeed, the 300 Firestone strikers knew almost nothing about the IWW as a radical labor organization. In Akron, as in Lawrence and Paterson, the Wobblies quickly promised to provide strikers with leadership and aid. By February 15 the more than 3,500 men and women who had by then walked out of work gladly accepted IWW leadership. As usual the strikers demanded not revolution but bread, a sentiment which an IWW leaflet turned into the slogan: "Less booze for the bosses! More bread for the workers!" By February 18 IWW agitation had increased the strikers' ranks to 14,000, mass picketing had shut down the city's major rubber plants, and the Wobblies proclaimed complete control of the walkout.[45]

Only a week later, Akron's employers and public authorities responded to the IWW threat with outright repression. Police broke the picket lines and escorted strikebreakers to work. They arrested IWW leaders and clubbed protesting strikers into submission. Riots erupted across the city. These police-precipitated outbursts of violence became an excuse for further repression. Local businessmen, sanctioned by public officials, organized vigilante committees to drive IWW organizers from Akron. They stimulated a back-to-work movement which pleaded with the rubber workers to endorse God and Country.[46]

After the repression began in earnest, the strikers' ranks began to splinter, and local AFL affiliates joined the crusade against the IWW. Finally, on March 31 the strike committee, making no mention of higher wages, shorter hours, or better conditions, reported that the walkout had been terminated. The strike committee nevertheless boasted that seven weeks of industrial conflict had resulted in the creation of a splendid IWW local.[47] Such was the splendor of this Akron rubber workers' local that within the IWW it was never heard from again.

At least one IWW organizer learned something from Akron. Writing in *Solidarity*, Frank Donovan commented: "A spontaneous strike is a spontaneous tragedy unless there is a strong local organization on the spot or unless a strong force of outside experienced men are thrown into town immediately. The strikers drifted back to work," he explained, "because there was nothing doing, because there was no permanent headquarters, no co-ordination of activities . . ." [48] This was precisely what Elizabeth Gurley Flynn discovered at the same time in Paterson: ". . . When the I.W.W. assumes the responsibility of a strike the I.W.W. should control the strike absolutely . . ."

Yet the lesson did not sink into the IWW's consciousness immediately, for that June Wobblies conducted a poorly coordinated strike of six thousand workers at the Studebaker auto plant in Detroit. Again the IWW simply assumed leadership of a spontaneous rebellion. After framing the usual material demands and advising the strikers regarding tactics, the Wobblies directed a strike as unsuccessful as the others it led in 1913, and even shorter in duration.[49]

Successive defeats at Akron, Detroit, and Paterson made the IWW's future appear so dim that the editor of *Solidarity* suggested that perhaps the organization had better forget about leading large-scale, protracted industrial conflicts. Instead, he recommended the use of short, sharp fights "which require little financial aid . . . as more effective in dealing with the powerful forces of organized capital." [50]

Only one bright spot illuminated an otherwise bleak IWW landscape. In April 1913 the Marine Firemen, Oilers, and Water Tenders' Union, claiming 25,000 members and effective control of ships on the Atlantic and Gulf coasts, voted to affiliate with the IWW.[51] It would remain the one stable and effective IWW organization outside the Western states.

Apart from this, in the summer of 1913 the IWW seemed on the verge of disintegration. That year's membership referendum on the election of national officers and the adoption of constitutional amendments counted only 2,800 votes. Open dissension broke out among Wobblies on the West Coast, where civil war threatened the future of the *Industrial Worker*. Things became so bad that at a July meeting the general executive board, by a unanimous vote, suspended Walker C. Smith as editor of the Pacific Coast paper. No reason was given for the decision. Most likely, board members had decided that Smith's editorial series endorsing sabotage and his attacks on the IWW's national administration, combined with his demands for organizational decentralization, injured the IWW's image and its stability.[52] That September the *Industrial Worker* ceased publication, which was not to be resumed until April 1916.

On the eve of the September 1913 national convention even Ben Williams questioned the IWW's future as a labor organization. "At present we are to the labor movement," wrote Williams,

. . . what the highdiver is to the circus. A sensation, marvelous and ever thrilling. We attract the crowds. We give them thrills, we do hair-raising stunts and send the crowd home to wait impatiently for the next sensationalist to come along. As far as making Industrial Unionism fit the everyday life of the workers we have failed miserably.

For the future he suggested that the IWW provide less of the sensational and more of the quietly effectual in the way of organization, administered by leaders whom the members would allow to work without the distraction of a brass band. "Unless we organize the workers without doing the spectacular," he concluded, "we are doomed." [53]

The 1913 convention did nothing to quiet Williams' fears. After it was over, he saw an organization rent by conflict between those who advocated industrial organization and competent leadership and those who argued for complete local autonomy (decentralizers) and rank-and-file plebiscite democracy. Williams feared that this latter faction, which neglected industrial unionism to concentrate upon mixed propaganda locals, might yet triumph. "I can scarcely say that it has been a huge success," he commented about the convention. "A great deal of time has been taken up in wrangling over forms of organization." [54]

What to Williams was scarcely a huge success was to other non-IWW observers an unmitigated failure. Anarchist Ben Reitman sat in the hot, stuffy Chicago convention hall watching the IWW delegates, most of whom, he claimed, "knew as much about the real labor

movement as they did about psychology . . . [which was nothing]."
Marveling at the things the IWW had done, Reitman remarked to
himself: "God! Is it possible that this bunch of porkchop philosophers,
agitators who have no real, great organizing ability or creative brain
power, are able to frighten the capitalistic class more than any other
labor movement organized in America?" To the labor economist
Robert Hoxie, who also attended the 1913 convention, the sessions
revealed the IWW as pathetically weak. After eight years in existence
it could not claim more than fourteen thousand members, nor could
it pretend to have founded a stable organization in any large industry,
he observed. The IWW, Hoxie contended, "instead of being the grim,
brooding power which it is pictured in popular imagination, is a body
utterly incapable of strong, efficient, united action and the attainment
of results of a permanent character; a body capable of local and
spasmodic effort only . . . it has no present power . . . of constructive
action." As a directly effective social force, Hoxie found the IWW
useless.[55]

Critics once again prepared obituaries for the IWW. The Socialist
Algernon Lee claimed that the Paterson defeat had sent the IWW to
its deathbed. Tom Mann, the English labor leader and syndicalist who
had come to America on a speaking tour in 1913 (partially under-
written by the IWW), recommended that the IWW follow William Z.
Foster's 1911 advice "to bore from within." Mann counseled the IWW
to do in America what the syndicalists had done in England—surrender their dual unions in order to permeate the Trades Union
Congress (TUC). After observing American workers for twenty weeks,
the English labor leader asserted that their psychology did not differ
from that of the English workers. Just as the future of British labor
was with the TUC, so, in America, the labor movement's future remained totally with the AFL. In order for them to ride the wave of
the future, Mann called upon Wobblies to board the good ship
Gompers.[56]

IWW leaders answered Mann precisely as they had responded to
Foster's earlier advice. Ettor informed the English labor leader that
those radicals who had tried to bore from within the AFL, the Socialist
party, and the parliamentary state had all in the end been captured by
the institutions they had sought to penetrate. In other words, those
who tried boring from within "became the greatest supporters of the
old and the most serious enemies of the new." Haywood reminded
Mann, as he had earlier reminded Foster, that the American environ-

ment differed from that of Europe, that the AFL could not be compared to the TUC or the Confédération Générale du Travail (CGT), and that American industrial unionism was not synonymous with European syndicalism.[57] In essence Ettor and Haywood told Mann to pack up and take his advice home.

The IWW, Ettor declared, was a damned lively corpse, which would yet build the new society within the shell of the old. Instead of dissolving their organization, IWW leaders sought to improve it. They demanded less agitation and more organization, fewer mixed locals and more real industrial unions. Build, build, build, declaimed the IWW's many publications. "Don't worry overmuch about the 'top.' Begin at the bottom," suggested *Solidarity*.[58]

But building was not easy for the IWW. In May 1914, a year after the Paterson strike, Vincent St. John estimated that the IWW had a membership in good standing of 30,157, of whom 75 per cent were engaged in seasonal work. Insisting that his figures were conservative, he asserted that the IWW probably had twice as many members. When Paul Brissenden attended the 1914 convention in Chicago (September 22–24), however, he observed only twenty-five delegates during the course of the convention, and no more than seventeen delegates and ten spectators at any one time. So unstable did the IWW seem that the convention kept no stenographic record, printed no full proceedings; only a brief *Solidarity* account described the proceedings, which transacted no important business.[59]

At the end of 1914 the IWW appeared about to wither on its own radical vine. A frail plant, it had originally taken root and bloomed in the arid soil of the American West. Transplanted to the East, its roots never took firm hold; its blossoms withered in Lawrence and died in Paterson and Akron. After its failure in the industrial East, all that seemed left for the IWW was to return to the Western environment that had spawned it. This is what the Wobblies began to do in 1913 and 1914. Within three years the IWW's radicalism would once again be an effective social force, "a grim, brooding power capable of strong, efficient united action . . ."

CHAPTER

12

Back to the West,
1913–1916

1913 and 1914 were not good years for the American worker. Nor were they any better for organized labor, and least of all for the IWW. The legislative reforms of President Woodrow Wilson's New Freedom, which passed Congress in the summer of 1913, coincided with the onset of what had by then become a typical American cyclical depression (as in 1873 and 1893). As business inventories rose, capital investment slackened, and production declined, union membership fell partly because unemployment increased sharply and partly because workers could not pay union dues. For the IWW, depression only aggravated the internal disorders wrought by industrial defeats in Paterson and Akron, the collapse of the *Industrial Worker,* and the sectarian schisms always ready to fragment the organization's shaky structure. Not until European war orders reached America late in 1915 would the economic environment improve for business, organized labor, and simultaneously for the IWW.

Even in the bleak years 1913 and 1914, however, the IWW sowed the seeds of discontent which it would harvest in the bumper years to follow. A labor riot in Wheatland, California (1913), a union explosion in Butte (1914), and the execution of an IWW martyr in Salt Lake City (1915) cultivated the soil of the American West for a harvest of hate—one in which Wobblies would not be the only harvesters.

Few workers in America were better adapted to the doctrines and tactics of the IWW than the migrants who followed the harvest on the West Coast, from the fruit and hop fields of Washington and Oregon to the ranches of California's San Joaquin, Central, and Imperial valleys. No workers were more mistreated by their employers, and none so lacked the elementary amenities of a decent life: a home, a family, an adequate diet. Those with wives and children—probably a minority at this time—had to send them out into the fields to do long and arduous stoop labor for a pittance. Family men undoubtedly had a tougher time than bachelors, for the single migrant unencumbered by familial responsibilities could always walk off an unsatisfactory job. But single or married, the migrant workers, mistreated, over-worked, and underpaid, formed one of the largest pockets in prewar America's "culture of poverty."

They also displayed all the wretchedness of life within such a culture. To men, women, and children who received little from the society that spawned them, used them, and discarded them, country, flag, and loyalty were all meaningless terms. Investigating migrants for California, Carleton Parker found them sullenly hostile, and "ever . . . ready to take up political or legal war against the employing class." A federal investigator discovered similar characteristics among the casual workers of the West Coast, whose pervading belief in the One Big Union of all workingmen, skilled and unskilled, steady and casual, caused them to belittle the "aristocratic" notions and practices of the AFL. The workers he interviewed indicated deep resentment against established institutions yet little interest in political move-ments.[1] In short, they were fine recruits for the IWW's total war upon capitalism, the American system, and "bushwa" law and morality.

Yet labor organizers, including those from the IWW, found the migrants difficult to organize. Moving from place to place and from job to job, the casuals were hard to contact and harder still to keep in a stable labor organization. Often unemployed and always poorly paid, they could seldom pay dues regularly enough to maintain union membership in good standing. Thus before 1913 all efforts to organize West Coast migrants, whether by the AFL or the IWW, failed.[2]

Not that the IWW did not seek to recruit the casuals. From headquarters in Spokane, Seattle, Fresno, and other West Coast cities,
Wobblies vigorously propagandized among the migrants. Soapboxers
lectured farm workers on city street corners, IWW organizers went out
on the job with them, and Wobbly headquarters offered them rest,
recreation, and even education, providing migrants with the only
welcome they received outside the saloon and the Salvation Army's
soup line. Ben Williams even fit the organization of the migrants into
the IWW's larger revolutionary framework: "The revolution in the
cities must be fed and clothed and fortified against possible reaction
from the rural districts." [3] Despite the West Coast free-speech fights
and incessant propaganda, however, no significant increase in IWW
membership among migrants could be discerned before 1913.

But Western Wobblies persisted and eventually found an organizing technique which seemed to work. From such IWW locals as those
in Redding, Sacramento, Fresno, Bakersfield, Los Angeles, and San
Diego, they sent a continual stream of literature and what came to be
known as "camp delegates" into the countryside. The camp delegate
took the IWW local directly out onto the job. He would find work
among the migrants, talk up the IWW to them, sign up those interested in the organization, and then send the names, initiation fees,
and dues to permanent local headquarters in the nearest town. Each
of the central, or permanent, California locals dispatched job delegates
out into the field, where they continually agitated and organized on
the job, carrying IWW dues books and stamps, red cards, songbooks,
and leaflets. The camp or job delegates literally carried a union local
under their hats. As they wandered through California's farmlands in
search of work, they spread the propaganda of industrial unionism.
Although by 1913 the camp delegates had not organized large numbers of California's casuals, they had nonetheless permeated the mass
of migrants with IWW doctrines.[4] This provided the backdrop for an
incident at Wheatland, California, in August 1913 which gave the
IWW the publicity it so desperately sought and the increased influence among the migrants it so ardently desired.

The Durst Ranch at Wheatland, described by IWW attorney Austin Lewis as "an open air factory," was in 1913 the largest single employer of agricultural labor in California. In the summer of 1913, as he had done every year just before harvest time, Durst advertised extensively for hop pickers, promising them ample work and high wages. The workers came: footloose, native-born migrants; immigrant families uprooted from communities in Europe and Asia; and even some middle-class boys and girls out from California's cities for a summer of "fun" and to earn some money in the healthful countryside. By the end of July, some 2,800 men, women, and children had reached Durst's ranch.[5]

What they found was not what Durst had promised. Work was not ample, wages were anything but high. Working and living conditions were even worse. As usual, in order to keep wages down Durst had advertised for more pickers than he needed. Never posting a flat piece rate for picking, he altered it daily. When the pickers were abundant, the rate declined; when they were scarce, it rose. Regardless of the piece rate, Durst withheld 10 per cent of the day's wages from every picker, to be distributed at the end of the harvest. Supposedly, the loyal and diligent workers who lasted the entire season would share among themselves the 10 per cent withheld from the disloyal or lazy. But Durst, not the pickers, decided who lasted the full season. Aside from field work, there was little to occupy the pickers' time. More than two thousand of them camped on a barren hillside—some in tents (which Durst rented at $2.75 per week), some in topless canvas squares, some on straw pallets. Men, women, and children shared eight small, unkempt toilets, which in the course of an average day overflowed with human waste and insects. Durst failed to provide regular sanitary measures. The flies which infested the toilets also visited the tents, the pallets, and the dinner "tables." Filth, germs, and disease abounded. Out in the hop fields, conditions were no better, probably worse. Work began on July 30, and for the next week the temperature hovered near 105 degrees. Drinking wells were a mile from the harvest site, and Durst refused to provide his pickers with water. During the harvest's first week a lemonade wagon, operated by Durst's cousin, sold an acidy drink to the harvesters. Even local Wheatland stores could not deliver supplies to the camp, because Durst maintained a half-interest in an allegedly independent grocery.

Against this background, on Friday, August 1, a handful of pickers began to agitate among the great mass to demand an improvement in working and living conditions. Mostly Wobblies, these agitators found a ready audience for their message, which stressed direct action to redress the pickers' primary grievances. In Richard "Blackie" Ford, a veteran Wobbly, the migrants discovered an able leader. Ford and the other Wobblies persuaded the pickers to agree upon a list of demands to be presented to Durst. The migrants called for uniform minimum wages, free water in the fields, and decent camp conditions. Durst, however, chose not to listen to his employees, who, in turn, became more discontented and more militant. Wobblies circulated throughout the camp stirring that discontent, holding irregular small meetings on Saturday, August 2, to demonstrate the migrants' solidarity, and planning to culminate their agitation at a mass meeting scheduled for late Sunday afternoon.

At 5 P.M. Sunday, August 3, as a hot sun beat down on Durst's ranch, the IWW-sponsored mass meeting opened peacefully. "Blackie" Ford suggested that the pickers consider a general strike, which, granted worker solidarity, would compel Durst to meet the migrants' demands. In the midst of his oration he dashed into the crowd, lifted a sick baby from the arms of its mother, and, holding it before the assembled pickers, cried out: "It's for the life of the kids we're doing this."

While Ford thus dramatized the pickers' plight, Durst panicked. Unsure about what two thousand agitated migrants might do, and unsurer still of what was actually being done at the mass meeting, Durst did precisely what other employers threatened by the IWW had done in the past and would do in the future: he turned to the law, calling in the Yuba County district attorney, the sheriff, his deputies, and a special posse. As the agents of the law sped to the scene of the meeting (some of them traveling in Durst's private car), the migrants were in the middle of a rollicking IWW song, "Mr. Block," written by Joe Hill. Coming closer to the meeting ground, the authorities could pick up the words of the song, which derided the nonunion worker who accepted the American success myth. "Poor Block," the last verse ran,

he died one evening, I'm very glad to state:
He climbed the golden ladder up to the pearly gate.
He said, "Oh, Mr. Peter, one word I'd like to tell,
I'd like to meet the Astorbilts and John D. Rockefell."
Old Pete said, "Is that so?
You'll meet them down below."

Oh, Mr. Block, you were born by mistake,
    You take the cake,
    You make me ache.
Tie a rock on your block and then jump in the lake,
Kindly do that for liberty's sake.

As the law officers arrived at the meeting ground, what followed was perhaps inevitable. Durst expected the outnumbered authorities to disperse the crowd. Carrying out his wishes, a group of deputies approached the speaker's platform to arrest Ford, while another deputy, in an effort to intimidate the crowd, fired his shotgun in the air. The simultaneous attempt to seize Ford and the unwarranted warning shot transformed an orderly audience into an unruly mob, one which vented its anger on the poorly disciplined deputies, who themselves now resembled nothing so much as a mob. Before the violence subsided four men—District Attorney Manwell, a deputy sheriff, a Puerto Rican worker, and an English boy—lay dead; many more were wounded or beaten. The exhausted mobs, both workers and posse, fled the field of battle, leaving it in possession of the dead, the wounded, the vermin, the flies, and the filth. Jack London, who encountered a large group of fleeing hop pickers, was reminded "of nothing so much as the refugees after the earthquake. When I did get one of them to tell about the affair they all spoke of it as an accident, a spontaneous, unpremeditated explosion." [6] That was the end of the Wheatland "strike." As in an earthquake, those affected by it—migrants, Wobblies, and public officials—felt the subsidiary tremors it set off long after the initial shock had subsided.

Although public officials and California's newspapers declared the IWW responsible for the bloodshed at Wheatland, Austin Lewis rightly pointed out that the labor discontent at the Durst Ranch had grown spontaneously. The extent of planned, systematic agitation was, after all, limited by circumstances. The pickers spoke twenty-seven different languages or dialects; yet Ford was fluent only in English. Harvesting had begun on Wednesday, agitation on Friday, and the first public meetings were held on Saturday. Three days was not much time to agitate effectively among 2,800 workers of diverse nationalities, religions, and languages. The violence could not be ascribed to the IWW. It was instead, as Lewis claimed, the natural emotional result "of the nervous impact of the exceedingly irritating and intolerable conditions under which those people worked." [7]

Yuba County's public officials and the press nevertheless charged the IWW with responsibility for the bloodshed. As a result, deputies and Burns detectives traveled up and down California with John Doe warrants charging anonymous individuals with assorted crimes, including inciting to riot and first-degree murder. Wherever the deputies or Burns men discovered a suspicious migrant or an IWW suspect, they served process and locked him in jail. All over the state's agricultural communities the dragnet proceeded. In one small town after another migrants were locked up beyond the reach or discovery of defense counsel. "Blackie" Ford's jail location, for instance, was discovered only by accident. When Austin Lewis assumed defense work for the IWW in September 1913, he "found the whole course of justice thoroughly obstructed . . . found every impediment placed in our way to the discovery of the whereabouts of prisoners and to giving them a fair, full, impartial hearing at an early date." His experiences after the Wheatland incident led Lewis to conclude:

. . . I think that migratory laborers in the State of California are treated with a calloused indifference both to the law and to ordinary elemental justice. They are incontinently arrested, thrown into filthy, fetid jails without any power of recourse, and illy treated while in jail, and kicked out of jail. [8]

Because someone had to be punished for the August 3 bloodshed at Durst's ranch, and because no official agency would dare reprimand the public officials most responsible, California decided to punish the IWW. Yuba County officials indicted Ford and Herman D. Suhr, a mentally retarded Wobbly also active at Wheatland, for the murder of District Attorney Manwell and the deputy sheriff. Except that Ford and Suhr were physically present at the time and place of the alleged murders, their role did not differ materially from that played by Ettor and Giovannitti in Lawrence a year earlier. Both had consistently advised the hop pickers to refrain from violence, and neither man had been observed by witnesses to have attacked or killed any person. Their guilt consisted, or so at any rate it was argued in court, of having instigated a strike that resulted in a riot and four deaths. From the day of their arrest until their trial in Maryville * on January 24, 1914, California's newspapers featured stories connecting the IWW with crop destruction, sabotage, violence, and even murder. To be sure, IWW agitators' hyperbolic rhetoric of class warfare did little to counteract the organization's negative public image; indeed, it worsened it. All this made the jury's verdict of guilty as charged in the Ford-Suhr case inevitable. The two Wobblies were sentenced to life imprisonment in Folsom State Penitentiary.

The conviction and imprisonment of Ford and Suhr did not end the tumult caused by the Wheatland incident. The Wobblies promptly organized a movement to secure from Governor Hiram Johnson a pardon for the two prisoners. Wobblies ran their pardon campaign with their typical combination of aplomb and confusion. On the one hand, the IWW secured support from respectable Californians, who petitioned Governor Johnson for a pardon, appealing to the chief executive's sense of justice and fair play. On the other hand, the IWW *demanded* a pardon and threatened to tie up California's fields in a general strike of hop pickers. One Wobbly even sent the Governor a scatalogical missive, while others threatened the state's ranchers with sabotage. F. H. Esmond warned in *Solidarity:* "Unless Ford and Suhr are freed outright by the Appellate Court, the cat and his kittens are coming to enjoy a merry picnic in the hop fields of California." [9] The pardon campaign backfired. Although Johnson agreed that justice had been less than perfect during the Maryville trial, he could not readily pardon individuals who belonged to an organization which counseled direct action, encouraged sabotage, and waged unremitting class war.

Johnson and the California Progressives who had placed him in office realized that more than legal repression would be needed to rid their state of the IWW menace. So did ranchers like Durst, who attempted to remove the Wobbly threat to their interests by hiring private detectives and watchmen to guard their fields during the harvest. The Progressives sought to restrict IWW influence among the migrants by reforming work conditions on California's ranches. Governor Johnson initiated a special investigation of migrant labor conditions by the State Immigration and Housing Commission, which the labor economist Carleton Parker directed and brought to completion in 1914. Parker's investigations at Wheatland and elsewhere in

---

* A city in an adjoining county selected on a change-of-venue proceeding by the defense in order to avoid the anti-IWW hysteria rampant in the Wheatland area.

the state led him to sympathize with the plight of the migrants, though he remained hostile to the IWW. The commission thus proposed that the state regulate conditions more effectively, using the power it already had to set sanitary and living standards for California's migrant labor camps. It also suggested that employers could best combat the IWW by improving working conditions, and it warned migrants that strikes, sabotage, and violent demonstrations would bring no improvement to their lives.[10]

But commission-instigated reforms and suggestions did not liberate California from the IWW. Migrants drew their own lessons from Wheatland. When they had been peaceful and tolerated exploitation, the state and its Progressives had neglected them. When they turned to the IWW and confronted employers as an organized force, public neglect changed to public concern. Deaths and injuries at Wheatland brought an immediate reaction from the state and the beginnings of labor reforms which did much to clean up the worst conditions in California's labor camps. A little violence, after all, must have seemed a good thing!

If anything, Wheatland increased the IWW's attraction to California's migrants. When Paul Brissenden investigated California labor conditions for the Commission on Industrial Relations in August 1914, he discovered forty IWW locals and a total membership of about five thousand, of whom half were "missionary revolutionists" who passed the message on and organized on the job. Brissenden also suggested that paid-up membership figures failed to measure the IWW's influence in California, which, he claimed, thousands of nonmembers respected. Although the IWW usually captured public attention as a result of its sanguinary free-speech and industrial conflicts, Brissenden stressed that the real-life record of California's forty locals consisted of quiet, persistent education, propaganda, and job organization. He also predicted that, after the conviction of Ford and Suhr, the IWW would become more aggressive, devoting additional effort and manpower to agitation and organization among migrant agricultural workers, principally by expansion of the camp delegate system. One California Wobbly proudly informed Brissenden: "Three or four years ago I had a hard time to get those scissorsbills working stiffs to even listen to the I.W.W. dope. Now it's easy. They come around and ask for it." [11]

That was precisely what California's public officials and private employers feared. The Commission on Immigration and Housing, led in 1914–1915 by the Progressive reformer Simon Lubin, sought by further improving conditions in California's "factories in the fields" to limit the IWW's influence among migrants. Failing in that, the commission thought in terms of using federal penal power to suppress the IWW. By the summer of 1915 California officials had already succeeded, in cooperation with officials of the states of Washington, Oregon, and Utah, in obtaining a special agent from the Department of Justice to assist them in an investigation of the IWW's activities in the West. Lubin later reported to United States Attorney General Thomas Gregory that the West Coast investigation had established, among other findings, that the Wobblies preached and practiced sabotage, property destruction, arson, violation of federal laws, and even threatened public officials with assassination. Moreover, Lubin added, the IWW's "reign of terror" in the West encompassed anti-patriotism and open revolution, which Wobblies promoted through the United States mail and public speeches. "The existence within our midst of such a band . . . is a distinct menace to the public welfare; particularly dangerous at a time when we require the unquestioned loyalty of all who live within our borders" (because of the European war and diplomatic difficulties with Mexico), Lubin reminded the Attorney General. The California reformers thus pleaded for federal action against the IWW, arguing that the Wobbly "conspiracy" was interstate in character and beyond the reach of any single state. Lubin suggested that if no existing federal statutes could be used to crush the IWW, then, in the interest of the general welfare, the nation should modify its federal laws. Unable to prove a single specific violation of federal law by the IWW, Lubin nevertheless maintained that a well-conceived Justice Department investigation would clearly demonstrate the IWW's lawlessness.[12]

But Gregory and the Justice Department read Lubin's 1915 report skeptically, taking it as simply another neurotic local reaction to a limited radical threat. Only two years later, however, with the United States involved in a bloody war, the Justice Department would treat Western accounts of an IWW-posed threat to national security more seriously. In 1917, Westerners like Lubin would obtain the federal suppression of the Wobblies that they had unsuccessfully demanded in 1915.

Only a year after the Wheatland incident the IWW returned to Butte, Montana. In 1914 Butte was one of the most solid labor union cities in America. The unionism which dominated there bore slight resemblance to the radical miners' unionism of the late nineteenth century, or to the IWW's original impact on the city's labor movement from 1905 to 1907. By 1914 the more moderate form of trade unionism associated with AFL affiliates had come to prevail among Butte's workers, the miners included.[13] This would make the IWW's return to the city more surprising—and also more disruptive.

Local 1 of the Western Federation of Miners had long controlled Butte's labor world. With eight thousand members it was the largest local in the WFM as well as in the city. Impressive in its economic power before 1905, it had begun to atrophy afterward as the Anaconda Copper Company established its own economic hegemony. Once Anaconda emerged triumphant over its business rivals, the union's ability to influence working conditions diminished. Wages stabilized, hours of work grew longer—in some cases the seven-day week prevailed in the mines and smelters—and safety conditions deteriorated. In the three-year period from 1910 to 1913 almost six hundred miners suffered serious injuries, and over 160 died in mine "accidents." Those not injured or killed often fell victims to the workers' white plague: tuberculosis. "Along at the years when a man is struggling, raising a family, building a home, or acquiring something," a member of Montana's Industrial Commission observed, "it is at that time when he is doing his very best that the tuberculosis seizes him." [14]

Conservative though the unions and their members seemed in 1914, Butte nevertheless had a long and deep radical tradition. The city's voters, in fact, had elected a Socialist administration in 1913, and the Socialists controlled the strongest party organization in Butte. Although the WFM's secession from the IWW in 1907 had undermined the Wobblies' influence in Butte, the miners retained an abiding faith in the principle of industrial unionism, which gave the IWW a prestige it lacked in some other industrial communities.[15] It was only a matter of time before Butte's radical past would reassert itself.

The IWW, of course, did not willingly relinquish its influence in Butte after its break with the WFM. Indeed, Wobblies founded a local propaganda league and circulated IWW literature and newspapers throughout the district. Propaganda, however, brought few paid-up members into the organization; late in 1910, for example, an IWW organizer reported that the AFL held full sway over the city's unions, even those once affiliated with the IWW. Unable to contact the so-called radical wing of the WFM's Local 1, this organizer concluded that Butte radicals had either disappeared or were lying low. "Butte, at present," he noted, "can not be classified with the revolutionary towns. The labor movement there has become sane, sanctified and rotten." [16]

But the radicals had not vanished. One of them, Thomas Campbell, who would play a key role in Butte's tangled labor history from 1914 to 1920, attended the 1911 WFM convention as a delegate from Butte Local 1. He departed from the convention convinced that the AFL and the incumbent WFM administration were treacherous, and he hoped that Butte's miners would soon find "that the organization known as the IWW have got the key to the situation . . . in spite of the treachery and trickery of the labor fakers of today." The "treachery and trickery" to which Campbell alluded made him and his fellow radicals cautious. This became especially apparent after 1912 when company-influenced (if not -dominated) conservatives seized effective control of Local 1, which was by then completely permeated with agents working for Anaconda and Con F. Kelley, manager of Anaconda's Butte mines. Even those who were not actually labor spies received special benefits from the company if they voted and behaved properly. As "company" men they received special leasing arrangements and better working areas in the mines.

With conservatives in the union saddle, the mine operators rode roughshod over their more militant employees. Local 1, for example, failed to protest the company's discharge of two hundred to three hundred Socialist Finnish miners. Any miner or union member who complained about company influence was apt to be labeled a Socialist, a Wobbly, or an anarchist, and thrown out the window of the union's hall. [17]

Company domination of Local 1, however, caused increasing numbers of union members to become dissatisfied with the lack of union democracy and with the heavy assessments placed upon Butte's miners to support strikers elsewhere. Most important, the miners grew disenchanted with their organization's inability to improve working conditions in Butte. But Local 1 checked this discontent by cooperating with company officials in blacklisting workers disliked by management through use of the rustling card, a theoretically innocuous employment application, which Anaconda in effect used as a blacklisting device. Miners who refused to keep their union dues current, or who opposed local union leaders, were thus denied employment in Butte's mines. In other words, by 1914, Local 1 had become a company union.[18]

How the mass of miners felt about these developments became apparent on June 13, 1914, which was Miners' Union Day and a legal holiday in Butte. Traditionally, *all* the city's miners paraded through the downtown area, after which they celebrated with an orgy of oratory, machine-drilling contests, boxing exhibitions, and drinking bouts. But on June 13, 1914, only four hundred of the eight thousand local miners came to the parade; even the police, who usually accompanied the paraders, refused to march. The nonparticipating miners lined the streets along the parade route prepared to attack the company men who controlled Local 1. Before the paraders could proceed very far, a mob of angry onlookers surged in upon them and forced the marchers to flee for shelter. Suddenly, a member of the mob yelled, "Let's destroy the Hall!" (Local 1's headquarters). Seconding that sentiment, the crowd headed toward the union headquarters, where it unleashed its emotions. Storming the building, the enraged miners destroyed everything in sight, throwing a piano out the window, followed by books, furniture, and two safes. "When the crowd was through," a special federal investigator reported, "there was not a whole article left in the place." Butte's Socialist city officials did not lift a finger to stop the demonstrations; the mayor, in fact, had conveniently left town the previous night.[19]

The destruction accomplished, the rebellious miners turned to the task of construction. Insurgent leaders decided to establish a new union entirely independent of Local 1, and they planned an early referendum on the question open to all miners. While the leaders made constructive plans, their unopposed followers rampaged through the town. On Sunday, June 14, a mob blasted open the old union's safes, and $1,600 in cash and all the local's official papers disappeared. The referendum, nevertheless, went off peacefully as scheduled, with 6,348 miners declaring against the old union and only 243 voting in favor of it. The new organization, called the Butte Mine Workers' Union, was unaffiliated with the WFM, AFL, or IWW.[20]

The creation of the independent union only worsened Butte's labor turmoil. Anaconda officials and the officers of Local 1 were naturally displeased. So, too, were Charles Moyer, president of the WFM, and Samuel Gompers. Company officials, Local 1's leaders, Moyer, and Gompers all blamed the IWW for Butte's labor problems. Instead of seeking to appease the miners in the new union or trying to reform and rebuild Local 1, Moyer joined the discredited local union officials in combating the insurgents. On June 19, before he had clearly ascertained what had occurred in Butte, Moyer wired Gompers: "Situation here serious. Influences at work to destroy organized labor. Wire me at once pledging support of American labor movement in defense of unionism in Butte. . . ." That same day Gompers pledged the AFL's support to Moyer, though he remained unconvinced of the reliability of·reports blaming the IWW for these labor troubles. Two days later an informant in Butte told Gompers: "I.W.W. elements active and in control of main situation." Convinced now of the IWW's role in Butte, Gompers advised all international unions with affiliates in the Montana city to send representatives there to join Moyer in fighting Wobbly influence.[21]

Apparently unaware of the depth of local hostility to himself and to his organization, Moyer arrived in Butte on June 23 hopeful of converting the miners to his view and of regaining their loyalty to Local 1. Instead, he met hate: deep, unreasoning, and violent. Few miners showed up for his talk that evening at the old union hall. Most miners instead gathered on the sidewalk outside to shout imprecations and threats at the WFM president. Nevertheless, Moyer tried to speak—that is, until a shot rang out somewhere in the hall. Shooting suddenly erupted on all sides; as one man fell dead outside on the street, the anti-Moyer mob grew infuriated and attacked the union hall, placing it under total siege. Moyer and his supporters fled for their lives out a back exit, while an armed crowd, estimated at 150, blazed away at the hall from the front sidewalk. After Moyer and his group completed their escape via the rear fire escape, the mob entered the hall, placed dynamite charges in it, and blew it sky-high. Haywood later described these events in miners' parlance: "The miners got in two splendid shifts' work. They picked down, mucked back, set up, drilled a full round and blasted. Every hole broke bottom." [22]

Again, no local officials opposed the miners' destructive wrath. That whole evening the anti-Moyer miners had Butte to themselves, while non-working-class residents, expecting the worst, barricaded themselves at home. Throughout that explosive day and evening Butte's Socialist Mayor Duncan advised Montana's governor that all would be well if only the authorities left the miners alone. Duncan later reminded the governor that, with an angry mob estimated at seven thousand roaming Butte's streets, only one man was killed, one was injured, one building was destroyed, and a number of houses received minor damage.[23]

Once again, Moyer, Gompers, and Anaconda officials blamed the IWW for Butte's troubles. It was true, particularly after the June 23 dynamiting of the union hall, that IWW agitators had taken to the streets with increased vigor. It was also true that several of the local insurgent leaders, notably Tom Campbell and Joe Shannon, were by then probably IWW members, and militant ones at that. But to contend that two hundred Wobblies in a propaganda league, the only official organization maintained by the IWW in Butte in 1914, were responsible for all the city's turmoil and tension is to stretch a point. After all, the new independent miners' union claimed 5,400 members, and even IWW sympathizers agreed that no more than a hundred of these were Wobblies. In fact, some of the demonstrators Moyer took for Wobblies were probably private detectives who had infiltrated either Local 1, the independent Mine Workers' Union, or the IWW propaganda league in order to provide Con Kelley with information about his employees and also to serve as *agents provocateurs* for the company. A miner with thirty years' labor in Butte's mines behind him put Moyer's charges about IWW influence into perspective: ". . . Industrial unionists, of course, would naturally take advantage of any trouble that might come up. . . . But I don't believe the IWW are very strong in Butte." [24]

After the violence of June subsided, the Butte Mine Workers' Union exercised firm control over mine labor. It denied work to nonmembers, it summarily deported or tried its opponents, and it applied for and won membership in Silver Bow County's central labor organization.[25]

Neither Moyer, Gompers, nor Anaconda officials enjoyed these new developments. Gompers considered labor conditions in Butte deplorable, and on August 30 he suggested to Moyer that Montana's governor might well exercise his power to repress the insurgent miners. The AFL president attacked Butte's insurgents simultaneously on several fronts. He ordered Butte's central labor organization to deny the rebels a seat; he advised various international union presidents to weed troublemakers out of their locals in Butte; and he even agreed to sanction the governor's use of military police power. Not until the morning of August 31, however, when insurgent unionists dynamited the "rustling" shack at a local mine, did the rebels' opponents have an opportunity to retaliate. Even before the smoke cleared from the area of the shack, the county sheriff had issued warrants for the arrest of miners' union officials, and he had also wired the governor requesting troops. The next day, September 1, militia arrived in Butte to place the city and the county under martial law as directed by the governor.[26]

Before a state supreme court decision finally lifted martial law several months later, the troops had crushed the Mine Workers' Union as an effective labor organization. No sooner had they arrived in Butte than their commander prohibited all street meetings (except those of the Salvation Army), censored local papers, closed the Socialist press, and arrested insurgent union leaders. The arrested men were held incommunicado, without bail, and were tried by military courts without a hint of due process. The military's treatment of some of the arrestees, who were hurriedly transported out of the district and released, leads one to conclude that they were probably the *agents provocateurs* who had infiltrated the union for the company. With Butte under martial law, union leaders incarcerated, and the troops claiming evidence to prove an IWW conspiracy, the Anaconda Company severed all relationships with any union faction. It would thereafter employ only men with valid rustling cards, and it would bargain with no organization of miners, including WFM affiliates. To enforce these new company policies, Con Kelley hired three hundred "gunmen" to protect company properties.[27] When the militia finally withdrew from Butte at the end of 1914, what had once been the strongest miners' union in the West was no more. Indeed, union domination of Butte had been completely terminated.

Moyer and Gompers proved their own worst enemies, and the IWW's best allies. Not only had they failed to end the IWW's influence in Butte; they inadvertently destroyed the remainder of Local 1's strength and also undermined the power of other local AFL affiliates. Their hysterical charges of IWW influence and conspiracy presented Kelley and the governor with a firm foundation upon which to erect their repressive anti-union policies. Moreover, Moyer's and Gompers' endorsement of corrupt local union officials, and even of military repression, turned Butte's miners completely away from both the WFM and the AFL. When unionism returned to Butte full strength during the First World War, it would come in the form of a large independent miners' union and a smaller IWW local, which, because of their antagonism toward the WFM-AFL, cooperated closely. After 1914 the outstanding miners' union leaders in Butte would be either IWW members or fellow travelers. During the first days of martial law, *Solidarity* had gloated: "Martial law is making rebels faster than anything that has ever happened in this town, and in many cases out of material that we had given up as hopeless." [28] The developments in Butte would have even larger implications for the IWW's future among Western miners. Moyer's mistakes there, soon compounded elsewhere, opened the entire Western nonferrous mining industry to IWW influence and penetration, which would reach its peak in the war years.

On Saturday evening, January 10, 1914, two armed, masked men entered the small Salt Lake City grocery of John G. Morrison. Morrison was alone in the store with his two teen-age sons, Arling and Merlin, who were helping their father close shop for the evening. One of the masked men shouted at the eldest Morrison: "We've got you now," and then one of them shot directly at the grocer. A frightened Merlin rushed into hiding as his father fell and his older brother Arling seized a gun and returned the fire. At this point, the two gunmen turned their revolvers on Arling and pumped three bullets into his body, killing him almost instantly. Leaving one dead youth, one dying man, and one terrified boy, the assailants fled from the grocery without taking money or merchandise. Later that same evening, John Morrison died, leaving behind no clue to his murderers.[29]

Three days later, on January 13, Salt Lake police claimed to have a prime suspect in custody. The same night that the two Morrisons had been killed an itinerant worker had appeared in a local doctor's office, asking to be treated for a gunshot wound in the chest, which he claimed to have received in a quarrel over a woman. Just three days later, the doctor, named McHugh, reported this case to the police, who, with the doctor's cooperation, seized the suspect at his boarding house, where he was still in bed recovering from the January 10 gunshot wound. (During the arrest the police shot the wounded man in the hand.) On January 22 the suspect, now identified as Joseph Hillstrom, alias Joe Hill, pleaded "not guilty" to murder charges. Six days later, at a preliminary court hearing, witnesses in the neighborhood of the murder identified Hill as one of the masked murderers whom they had seen flee from the grocery. The court bound him over for trial on June 10.

Up to that point there was nothing unusual about the case. A brutal pair of murders had occurred and the police were naturally eager to locate a suspect in order to satisfy the public's clamor for vengeance. Just such a prime suspect had appeared in the person of Joe Hill, an unemployed itinerant worker, who had also been shot the evening of January 10 (as had one of the murderers) and who refused to provide himself with an alibi, insisting that he could not do so when a woman's honor was at stake. Ordinarily, an unimportant man like Hill might have been promptly tried, convicted, and executed without a whisper of protest. After all, who was Joe Hill?

In January 1914 few Salt Lake residents could have answered that question. At first, even Salt Lake's police had little information regarding their suspect. Perhaps a few Wobblies knew something about Hill, but even in their case knowledge about him was limited. Many Wobblies claimed to know Hill but, as a matter of fact, they knew his songs, not the man. As the first IWW account of Hill's arrest commented: ". . . Wherever rebels meet, the name of Fellow Worker *Joe Hill* is known. Though we may not know him personally, who among us can say he is not on speaking terms with 'Scissor Bill,' 'Mr. Block' . . . the famous 'Casey Jones' . . . and many others in the little red song book." [30] The police soon learned this much. San Diego and Los Angeles authorities informed those in Salt Lake of Hill's activities as a California Wobbly; indeed, his membership in the IWW only served to make him an even better murder suspect. Still, beyond his links to the IWW, who was Joe Hill?

Answers to that question were soon forthcoming. Born in Sweden, October 7, 1879, Joel Hägglund, the man who became famous as Joe Hill, emigrated to the United States in 1902. For ten years he worked itinerantly, stacking wheat, laying pipe, digging copper, and at sea. As he worked and traveled his way across the United States, he composed songs, poems, and idle verse. His name was changed to Joseph Hillstrom, and then to plain Joe Hill. These name changes reflected his changing interests. Sometime in 1910 Hill became interested in labor affairs and radicalism, taking out a membership card in the San Pedro local of the IWW and becoming, later that year, an active agitator in the Portland area. In 1912 he participated in the San Diego free-speech fight, flirted with joining the Mexican revolutionaries active in Lower California, and, by then apparently convinced of the uselessness of politics and the need for violent revolution, he derided the introduction of voting machines and suggested instead that workers "may find out that the only 'machine' worthwhile is the one which capitalists use on us when we ask for more bread. . . . The one that works with a trigger. All aboard for Mexico!" * But Hill never departed for Mexico. Instead, like many other Wobblies, he drifted from job to job, probably as often as not being delinquent in his union dues. But unlike most of his fellow Wobblies, Hill continued to write songs that inspired men on picket lines, around soapboxes, in union halls, and in jail cells. His wandering eventually took him to Utah, where, at some time in 1913, he labored in the Bingham Canyon copper mines and also for a local construction company. Joe Hill agitated and organized, possibly participating in two IWW-linked strikes which occurred in the Salt Lake City vicinity.[31] At the time of his arrest and indictment he was unemployed and not representing the IWW in any capacity.

Whatever they may have been, the exact circumstances that brought Joe Hill to Utah and kept him there transformed him from an obscure Wobbly bard into a legendary martyr. In April 1914, more than three months after Hill's arrest, the IWW first became interested in his case, forming defense committees, soliciting funds, and all the while asserting that Hill was being prosecuted not for having murdered the Morrisons but simply because he was a Wobbly. IWW defense efforts turned the Hill case from an ordinary murder trial into the prospective lynching of a radical labor agitator. The prosecution's tactics and the stories which appeared regularly in the Salt Lake press gave credence to IWW assertions. Prosecution and press constantly stressed Hill's link to the IWW, the IWW's commitment to direct action, sabotage, violence, and anarchy—arguing, in effect, that the dual murders had been a demonstration of Wobbly anarchy at work.[32]

Even before his case came to trial, Joe Hill had been convicted in the court of public hysteria. The pre-trial proceedings and the ensuing trial violated many of the basic principles of due process. From

---

* A reference to the abortive 1912 Baja California revolution in which twenty or so Wobblies participated.

the time of his arrest until the trial began, Hill lacked legal assistance. Police and press created a hostile environment which reduced the already minimal prospects for a fair trial. Later the trial judge repeatedly favored the prosecution and hampered the defense. No witness ever absolutely identified Hill as the murderer; no motive was ever introduced to account for the crime; no bullet could be found to link Hill to the killer allegedly wounded in the grocery; and no gun could be located to connect Hill with the murder of either the grocer or his son. Yet on June 26, 1914, a jury found Joe Hill guilty, and on July 8 a judge sentenced him to death.

Verdict and sentence merely served as an introduction to the Joe Hill case. For the next year and a half a defense campaign of international proportions rallied support for Hill. From Salt Lake City to San Francisco, from New York to Washington, D.C., from Stockholm to Berlin, his sympathizers protested the verdict and demanded a pardon. Thousands of letters and telegrams of protest reached Utah's Governor Spry. The Swedish ambassador interceded with President Wilson, who also appealed to the Governor for clemency. Non-IWW Americans sympathetic to his cause obtained outstanding legal assistance for Hill's appeals and pardon hearings. But the best the defense campaign could do was to stay the execution, expend considerable time in the appeal process, and obtain a hearing before Utah's Board of Pardons, all of which, in the end, brought no relief.[33] On November 19, 1915, the state of Utah prepared to execute Joe Hill.

Although the defense campaign finally failed to save Hill's life, it did produce a myth and a martyr. Stories spread concerning Hill's incredibly exemplary character. Three reform-minded upper-class women, who tried to interest Frank Walsh in the case, called the radical attorney's attention to Hill's "coolness, courage, and quiet determination under all circumstances." The women added that this near perfect specimen of a Christlike labor agitator neither smoked, drank, nor had a prison record, even during labor troubles.[34] To them, his virtues did not stop at purity and goodness; he was also strikingly handsome, with sharply sculptured and well-proportioned features, a tall man of remarkable strength, whose every facet and movement demonstrated impeccable character.

Hill himself added to the martyr myth by writing a series of letters while in prison awaiting his execution. They reveal a man and a mind warmly human and willing to face death with wry humor and pathos. They also reveal the mind of a man who knew how to play the role of martyr. To Elizabeth Gurley Flynn, he emphasized his own insignificance: "We cannot afford to drain the resources of the whole organization and weaken its fighting strength just on account of one individual—common sense will tell you that. . . . There will be plenty of new rebels come to 'fill the gaps,' as the war news puts it, and one more or less does not count any more than it does in the European War." To a close West Coast friend, he wrote in the same vein but added a touch of humor:

Well, Van this is Sept. 4 [1914] which was supposed to be my last day on earth,—but I am still wriggling my old lead pencil and I might live a long time yet, if I don't die from 'Beanasitis.' . . .°

Well, Van, all joking aside, I guess I have a long wait ahead of me and I think the best you all can do is to forget me for awhile. . . . the best you boys can do is to forget me and use your energies and your financial resources for the One Big Union.

I think some of you are making too much of a fuss about me anyway. I wish you would tell those who are writing poems about me that there is no poetry about my personality. I am just one of the rank and file—just a common Pacific Coast wharfrat—that's all. I have always tried to be true to my friends and to my class. What any outsider may think about me is no concern of mine.

Hill played his role to the very end. On November 18, the eve of his execution, he wired Haywood: "Good-bye, Bill. I will die like a true blue rebel. Don't waste any time in mourning. *Organize.*" Then he wrote his last will:

> My will is easy to decide,
> For there is nothing to divide.
> My kin don't need to fuss and moan—
> "Moss does not cling to a rolling stone."
> My body? Ah, if I could choose,
> I would to ashes it reduce,
> And let the merry breezes blow
> My dust to where some flowers grow.
> Perhaps some fading flower then
> Would come to life and bloom again.
> This is my last and final will,
> Good luck to all of you.[35]

Hill's wry humor and dramatic qualities notwithstanding, the state of Utah decided to transform him into what the upper-class women who had appealed on his behalf considered to be "one of the martyrs

° A reference to his prison diet of beans.

for whom we of the human race seem to lust." On November 19, 1915, a Utah firing squad executed Joe Hill.

Hill received a martyr's funeral. Taken to Chicago, his body was buried at Waldheim Cemetery alongside the graves of the Haymarket anarchists. Haywood, an American labor radical, and Big Jim Larkin, an Irish labor radical, spoke the last words over his grave. Larkin declaimed: "Let his blood cement the many divided sections of our movement, and our slogan for the future be: Joe Hill's body lies mouldering in the grave, but the cause goes marching on." [36]

Joe Hill arrived in Utah an insignificant migrant worker; when his corpse departed the state two years later, he was internationally proclaimed as a martyr to labor's cause. He was, according to the later song of Alfred Hayes and Earl Robinson, the Joe Hill "who had never died." For the next fifty years Wobblies, novelists, playwrights, and poets kept the memory of the rebel Swedish immigrant alive. In that period many Wobblies tried to emulate Hill's appeal for self-sacrifice, and several met comparable fates.

Several students of the Hill case, most notably the labor economist Vernon Jensen and the novelist Wallace Stegner, have maintained that Hill's martyrdom is undeserved. Other scholars and novelists have continued to plead Hill's cause. We shall probably never have definitive proof as to whether Hill was guilty or innocent of the crime for which he was executed. Suffice it to say, his guilt cannot be proved beyond a reasonable doubt; nor can his innocence be positively established. Both his prosecutors and his defenders must fall back on circumstantial evidence. Too many riddles still plague the case. Without answers to them we will never know what brought Joe Hill to Salt Lake City, where he was on the night of January 10, 1914, how he received his gunshot wound, and whether he was indeed sent to his death for a crime he never committed. It is difficult to agree with Stegner, whose own investigation led him to think of Hill as a "Wobbly more dedicated and more violent than most . . ." who had a Robin Hood streak and "took from society because he hated the system, and stole company money . . ." Yet Stegner's preference for Frank Little and Wesley Everest (two Wobblies later killed by vigilante mobs) as martyrs is clearly just: "They," he notes, "at least died on workers' business." [37]

Early twentieth-century Utah justice rendered questions about Hill's innocence and martyrdom purely academic. The action of Utah's officials and Hill's felicitous phrasemaking earned for him a martyr's fate. What he had once done or believed in became unimportant after his arrest, trial, and execution. What became important was how Wobblies, radicals, and others felt about him; and for all Wobblies, most radicals, and many other Americans, Hill became symbolic of the individual sacrifice that made a revolutionary new society possible. In death, Joe Hill became a symbol, and, as a symbol, he assumed more importance than he had ever had as a living man.

Much more important to the future of the IWW than the exciting and explosive incidents in Wheatland, Butte, and Salt Lake City was the tedious agitating and organizing the Wobblies had begun among the migratory harvesters in the plains states. Every summer thousands of men and boys would fan out from Chicago, Kansas City, Sioux City, and the twin cities of Minneapolis and St. Paul to follow the wheat harvest from Texas north across the plains to southern Canada. Like migratory farm workers everywhere, they worked long hours for minimal pay and execrable room and board. Most of them traveled by riding the rods or side-door coach, which subjected them to the extortions and the brutalities of trainmen and railroad detectives. On the freights they rode and in the jungles they infested, the wheat harvesters fell prey to holdup men and professional gamblers, who, as E. F. Doree put it, harvested the harvesters. After a summer in the fields these migratories often returned to the city for the winter as poor as when they had left.[38]

Like the migratories of the West Coast, those of the plains states lacked wives, families, homes, roots; nothing tied them to society; their alienation, if frequently unconscious, was nevertheless complete. They seemed perfect recruits for the IWW's gospel, as one Wobbly, who saw in them the last, best chance for establishing the One Big Union, asserted:

The nomadic worker of the West embodies the very spirit of the I.W.W. His cheerful cynicism, his frank and outspoken contemp' for most of the conventions of bourgeois society . . . make him an admirable exemplar of the iconoclastic doctrines of revolutionary unionism. His anomalous position, half industrial slave, half vagabond adventurer, leaves him infinitely less servile than his fellow worker of the East. . . .

Nowhere else can a section of the working class be found so admirably fitted to serve as scouts and advance guards of the labor army. Rather, they may become the guerrillas of the revolution—the *franc tireurs* of the class struggle.[39]

Yet the migratories of the plains were as hard to organize on a stable basis as their counterparts on the West Coast, and for the same reasons. Their geographical mobility made them hard to reach, and, once they were reached, the seasonal nature of their employment and their continuing mobility caused them to neglect regular dues payment and to be out of touch with any union headquarters. Beginning in the summer of 1914 the IWW decided to organize them, and within two years the Wobblies had developed effective methods to reach the wheat harvesters.

After experimenting with new methods of recruitment during the 1914 summer harvest, Wobblies planned to make this issue the major order of business at their approaching national convention.[40] At a convention otherwise marked by pessimism and failure, IWW delegates adopted a motion presented by Frank Little to call a conference early in 1915 bringing together members from different locals bordering the harvest district in order to determine ways and means to combine the organization's previously spasmodic efforts to organize the harvesters. The IWW press continued the discussion, as numerous Midwestern Wobblies offered suggestions on how best to organize the harvest hands. All the pleas and advice stressed job organization. Revolutionary pronouncements, one editorial concluded, were useless without organization at the point of production. "Around the 'job,' distasteful, monotonous, and gruesome as it actually is in many instances, center all our revolutionary aspirations. . . . The I.W.W. . . . aims to unionize the migratory workers," the editorial went on, "with an eye first to improve conditions in industry. . . . This . . . accomplished will mean immediate alleviation of miserable conditions of life and labor . . . from now on the I.W.W. slogan should be, 'The control of the job by the working class.'"[41] Haywood, elected general secretary at the 1914 convention upon St. John's retirement from office, made organization of the migratories his first order of business. He announced the formation of a Bureau of Migratory Workers to assist the harvesters in improving their working conditions, and he scheduled two organizational meetings for IWW leaders and migratories to be held in Kansas City in April and May 1915. Even the retiring St. John gave his blessing to the new organizing campaign.[42]

On April 15, 1915, harvest workers and Wobblies from points as far apart as Des Moines, Fresno, San Francisco, Portland (Oregon), Salt Lake City, and Minneapolis descended on Kansas City to found an IWW harvest workers' organization. These delegates promptly created the Agricultural Workers' Organization (AWO Local 400),* composed of all local unions whose members worked in the agricultural districts of the United States and Canada. That done, the delegates provided for a general secretary-treasurer as the AWO's presiding official, and for field delegates, counterparts to the West Coast's job delegates. Significantly, the Kansas City meeting resolved to ban street speaking and soapboxing as methods of organization; delegates seemed more interested in members and dues than in propaganda and revolutionary rhetoric. Before adjourning the delegates chose Walter T. Nef as general secretary-treasurer, and elected a five-man executive board to assist him. Haywood promised Nef, his executive advisers, and the delegates adequate financial support to launch their venture, and they left Kansas City with high hopes.[43]

Those hopes were soon to be justified, for the destiny of the AWO lay in able hands. Nef was an experienced, dedicated, no-nonsense Wobbly. He had already organized on both coasts, as well as in the wheat belt. He had worked in construction, lumber, longshoring, and mining, as well as in agriculture. He was a builder, not a booster; an organizer, not a propagandist. He promptly established a $2 initiation fee, high by IWW standards, but necessary to the creation of a stable organization. If the union was sufficiently important, Nef argued, the worker would pay to belong to it and to make it function effectively.[44]

Nef's immediate objectives were limited. The AWO entered the harvest fields to demand a better deal today—not revolution tomorrow. A ten-hour day, a minimum wage, premium pay for overtime, good board, and clean beds with ample bedding: this is what the AWO sought in the summer of 1915. By August, during the Kansas harvest, the AWO had achieved many of its demands, and with some optimism it began to draw up stronger demands for the approaching Northern harvest. Rising membership rosters and increasing revenue made it possible for Nef to announce on August 7 the opening of a permanent AWO central office in Minneapolis. From that office Nef sent one hundred job delegates out into the field, who brought in at least one hundred new members a week. By September the AWO counted fifteen hundred members in North Dakota alone, and another

* A sardonic IWW comment on New York City "high society's" famous "400."

three hundred to five hundred in South Dakota. As the harvest season moved toward its close, the AWO reported weekly membership increases. At the end of the harvest, when it held a second convention in Minneapolis (November 15–16), the AWO claimed a minimum of three thousand members.[45]

Optimism spread from the AWO to the remainder of the IWW. Ben Williams later recalled 1915 as the first time in his ten years with the organization that the IWW had ample funds: sufficient money to rent a large general office on Madison Street in Chicago, where it also established a printing plant and editorial offices for foreign-language sheets, while planning future consolidations of IWW operations within the expanded and suddenly affluent general headquarters.[46]

Nef and the AWO meanwhile proposed grander projects for the immediate future, suggesting, among other things, the establishment of permanent AWO branch headquarters in Omaha, Sioux City, and Kansas City, from which job delegates could more efficiently organize the 1916 harvest. Nef now planned to organize corn harvesters and loggers as well. On December 12–13, 1915, fifty-five IWW delegates, meeting in Sacramento, founded a California branch of the AWO, patterned exactly after its Minneapolis parent. Before long, Minnesota lumberjacks as well as the entire Spokane lumber workers' local had taken out membership in Nef's organization. With an adequate surplus in its treasury and with more than two thousand paid-up members, the AWO's future looked bright.[47]

Nef's lieutenants moved into the wheat fields in 1916 with the same tactics they had taken in 1915: organization on the job and immediate improvements in working conditions. Business was never better for them. In July the AWO took in four thousand new members, with the expectation of another six thousand in August. By late August it claimed over twelve thousand members and job control over many harvesting machines and farm districts, where wages and hours met AWO standards. As the money and the members rolled in, IWW general headquarters grew ecstatic over its harvest campaign. On September 30, 1916, *Solidarity* devoted an entire issue to the activities of the harvest hands. The AWO closed the 1916 harvest season twenty thousand strong, apparently having proven that given the proper tactics and the necessary leadership, migratory workers could be organized.[48]

How had the AWO succeeded where other labor organizations

had always failed? To begin with, it made the effort, the first earnest attempt to organize harvesters. It offered the migratories what they most needed: protection on the freights they rode and in the hobo jungles they called home; higher wages and better treatment on the job; and, in IWW headquarters, a place to meet friends, lounge, rest, and even read while in town between jobs. The IWW red card became a sign of status in the grain belt, the pass that offered the holder a railroad ride free from extortions and beatings, the symbol that provided him with friends and protection throughout the harvest states. The worker who did not hold a card had ample reasons to take one out. Not only did the IWW card protect him against railroad bulls and holdup men, it secured him against physical attacks by harvesters already enrolled in the IWW and firm believers in the AWO. The migratories flocked to the AWO, which provided them with organizers who worked beside the rank and file in the fields and who spoke their language and shared their needs and aspirations.

In the last analysis, the AWO's accomplishments might have been impossible had not the First World War erupted and provided the American farmer with prosperity. The AWO's membership surge came in 1916, or only after European war orders had showered upon America's agrarians. With production rising, profits increasing, and labor scarce, wheat raisers, anxious to turn a quick buck, did not relish a fight with their workers. As long as the AWO moderated its demands, farmers could concede higher wages and better conditions. As long as the AWO improved working conditions, it could count upon increases in membership and a flood of funds in its treasury. Finally, as long as the war continued, the IWW could look forward to boom times, to the best days of its stormy history.

Nef and Haywood dreamed of using the AWO's successes as a basis from which to penetrate other industries, though they differed sharply about what should be the AWO's precise role. His differences of opinion with Haywood led Nef to resign as AWO general secretary-treasurer in November 1916, and to move to Philadelphia, where he established an IWW office patterned after the AWO. Nef proposed to recruit Philadelphia workers regardless of their particular industry for his organization, until the IWW had established stable industrial unions in all areas. He did not choose Philadelphia by accident. In April 1916 the IWW had over three thousand members in good standing in a local branch of the Marine Transport Workers' Union,

317

which had full job control on the city's waterfront—the kind of closed-shop and wage agreements the AFL unions prided themselves upon achieving.[49]

Everywhere a Wobbly looked in 1916 he saw revived organizational life—in the wheat fields of the Midwest, the orange groves of southern California, the Douglas fir forests of the Pacific Northwest, the north woods of Minnesota, Philadelphia's waterfront, Chicago general headquarters, and most spectacularly of all in the vast Mesabi Iron Range of northern Minnesota, where, in the summer of 1916, the IWW waged its most spectacular strike since Lawrence and Paterson.

CHAPTER

13

Miners, Lumberjacks, and a Reorganized IWW, 1916

THE year 1916 found the IWW's fortunes at floodtide. Fresh from their triumphs in the wheat fields and with funds to support their activities, Wobbly organizers inundated the mining and lumber regions of northern Minnesota, the forests of the Inland Empire and the Cascades, and the wheat, fruit, and hop fields of Washington and Oregon.

Some seventy-five miles north of Duluth, Minnesota, in one of that state's most isolated regions, lies a group of low hills, surrounded by great wastes of land, covered only with the charred, blackened stumps of a once magnificent pine forest. The hills extend for fifty miles, east and west, hiding an immense mineral treasure beneath their blackened bosoms. From steep shafts driven a thousand feet below the earth's surface, miners with dynamite, drill, pick, and shovel labored to bring forth two million tons of hard iron ores annually; above ground, giant steam shovels tore at the earth's crust, stripping away over twenty million tons of soft iron ore each year. These underground and open-pit mines of Minnesota's Mesabi Range fed the insatiable steel mills in Gary, Cleveland, Youngstown, and Pittsburgh.[1]

As mineral wealth poured out of the Mesabi Range, large corporations entered. The nation's leading steel companies took possession of the range's primary ore bodies; by 1902 the Oliver Mining Company, a subsidiary of United States Steel, was the largest single operator on the range.

Unlike other isolated mining districts, the range was never blighted by company towns. Instead, small independent frontier communities grew and flourished, keeping pace with the mining industry's own expansion. By 1916 over sixty thousand people lived in the five range towns, which together formed an integrated community. (Virginia and Hibbing, the two largest towns, claimed populations of fifteen thousand each.) Although not controlled by the mining corporations, the cities heavily depended upon company prosperity. Local merchants and professionals catered to working-class families; municipal governments, using taxes wrested from protesting mining companies, provided their residents with paved, brightly lit streets, gracious public buildings, and fine schools.[2]

Behind the carefully constructed façade of white ways and public edifices, however, the commonplace sores of life in urban America festered. Although local wages and earnings appeared relatively high, the cost of living in these isolated mining communities was equally high. Owing to the short local growing season, most food had to be transported to the range, raising food prices 50 to 100 per cent above those in other sections of the Midwest. A rapid increase in local population, compounded by the difficulty in clearing and improving land, caused high rentals. Severe winters—with two to four weeks of temperatures from 20 to 40 degrees below zero—inflated the cost of household fuel and family clothing. "It becomes apparent," an impartial observer wrote in 1916, "that the majority of workmen on the Mesabi Range are not earning sufficient to maintain a desirable family standard of living [causing them to live in] . . . ugly-looking houses, with dilapidated fences and outbuildings, and a general appearance of wretchedness that is comparable only to the slums of our great cities." [3]

Ethnic diversity added to the miners' problems. Always short of labor, employers had introduced successive immigrant groups into the range's labor force. First came the Irish, Cornish, and Scandinavians, many of whom brought previous mining experience to their work in the deep shafts. After 1905, as open-pit mining expanded and the demand for unskilled labor increased, Finns, followed by eastern and southern European immigrants, entered the labor force. By 1912 over thirty different tongues could be heard in the range's cities, and the diverse ethnic groups had fallen into distinct camps. The earliest arrivals had become mine captains, shift bosses, skilled, highly paid workers, and, on occasion, successful local businessmen. The late-comers did the dirty work, earned low wages, lived in shacks, and were exploited by those who had preceded them to the range. It was a recent arrival who in 1916 complained: "If our women go to church the priest they say 'What the matter with Austrian women. They stink in church.' Rest of people have better jobs than we do, and we couldn't support our family like these Americans." Another newcomer added: "If we eat we can't dress, and if we dress we don't eat." [4]

The IWW had sporadically sought to organize the Mesabi Range's immigrant miners. One of Elizabeth Gurley Flynn's first lecture tours in 1907 had taken her to Duluth and then north to the range towns, where she had propagandized for industrial unionism. From the defeat of a WFM-led strike in 1907 until 1916, however, the range's mines remained completely open shop, though many of the local Finns retained links to radicalism and to Marxian socialism. Wobbly agitators nevertheless continued to dream of winning converts on the range. On occasion they tried to act out their dreams. In 1913, for example, Frank Little, James Cannon, and E. F. Doree carried the Wobbly gospel north. Starting in Duluth among dock wallopers and ore handlers, they planned to move north and west to the range communities. But in August local Duluth businessmen kidnaped Little, and though other Wobblies later rescued him, such repressive tactics kept the IWW from gaining recruits in the district. [5]

During the next three years, as AWO triumphs pumped new life and fresh money into the IWW, Wobblies carefully watched labor developments on the range. On February 7, 1916, an AWO report concluded: "The Finnish organizer is up on the Range, and expects good results as soon as the weather gets a little better." Several days later, Walter Nef noted that the Metal Mine Workers' Industrial Union of the IWW had just been established as Local 490, and that it included within its jurisdiction the iron miners of northern Minnesota. That same spring Miss Flynn again appeared on the range, carrying the IWW's message to the miners. Her timing was now better: increased production, as a result of European war orders, made local labor scarce. Worker discontent could no longer be easily repressed, and, unlike 1907, European immigrants could not be imported for strike-breaking duty, leading an IWW organizer to report in May 1916: "I have recently been on a lecture tour on the Range, through Virginia, Kinney, and Chisolm, and the Finnish boys told me that the 'blacks' [eastern and southern Europeans] . . . everywhere and all the time talk about strike." At about the same time, radical Finns contacted Nef to request south Slav and Italian organizers to work among the range's miners. Unless Italian and Slav organizers came, they warned, self-defeating, spontaneous strikes would erupt. But Nef rejected their request, lamenting that he had no such organizers available, though as of May 2, 1916, an English-speaking organizer had reported to AWO headquarters: "I have never before found the time so ripe for organization and action as just now." [6] Almost one month later to the day, a spontaneous miners' revolt erupted.

Throughout the month of May, as underground miners watched production rise and the cost of living soar, they expected a wage increase. But on June 2 the workers at the St. James, an underground mine near Aurora, were sorely disappointed as their monthly paychecks showed no increase. The next morning, as these miners congregated in the dry room to change into working clothes, they discussed their low wages. Led by Joe Greeni, an Italian miner, the others agreed not to work until the contract system* was abolished and they received a $3 daily minimum. That evening the members of the day shift returned to the mine shaft and brought the night-shift miners out with them, closing the St. James tight. Both shifts, some eighty men, then paraded toward a meeting hall in Aurora. On their way, more and more miners joined the parade, until four hundred men in all entered the hall. A spirit of solidarity surged through the miners, who, without any labor organization or outside leadership then available, voted to strike.[7]

The initial walkout spread rapidly. Aurora's miners, with their wives and children, marched to other range communities, where they added thousands of recruits to the strike. By the end of June, two-thirds of the range's working force, or ten thousand out of fifteen

---

* Foremen acted as hiring agents and set the wages based upon the quantity of ore dug, not the number of hours worked. Desirable mining locations were thus placed at a premium.

thousand miners, had walked out, including fully 85 per cent of the underground workers. The conflict indirectly affected another fifteen thousand district workers, as it spread to the adjacent and subsidiary Vermillion Range.[8]

Underground miners had walked out first because their grievances were deeply felt and because they outnumbered the surface workers. Complaining that the contract system of wage payments exploited them, the underground miners accused the mine captains of giving the most productive locations to workers who paid off in money, cigars, and women. Some miners even asserted that the captains had, in return for good working positions in the mines, demanded sexual liberties from the workers' wives and daughters. Most miners, unable to pay the expected bribes, worked to exhaustion simply to earn a bare subsistence wage. Insisting that the contract system devoured the miners' blood, a strike leader declared: "I challenge anybody to say that any miner who works in these mines at contract for ten years . . . is entirely fit for any labor after he gets to be 35 or 40 years. . . . He is absolutely physically unfit for labor after that." A Virginia miner with thirteen years' experience put it more succinctly: "The contract system just kill the man." [9]

Exploitation under the contract system wore many faces. Workers never knew how much they had earned until they received their monthly paychecks. Piece rates fluctuated constantly, while the charges levied upon the miners for supplies rose regularly. A worker expecting to average $3 or $4 a day might end the month with as little as $1.60. Two Department of Labor mediators who investigated the conflict were appalled by the absence of uniform wage rates, especially among the employees of the Oliver Mining Company. "Is it not liable to create the impression," they asked, "that district superintendents are allowed to control the wage scale on the theory of 'all that the workmen can be made to bear'?" The mediators also noted that, though mining companies had advanced wages before the 1916 strike, the cost of living had risen twice as rapidly as wage rates. Which led an immigrant miner with a wife and seven children to complain: "Children go to church and priest like to see wife dressed nice like American ladies, and children like American children. I like too but can't. Maybe single man can get by on wages like mine, but we are nine. I pay rent, no longer get free wood, pay coal, insurance, taxes, light, water, how can I live. The house and property I now have, which I got from school board not U.S. Steel, I am about to lose. I don't get enough working to clothe and care for 7 children . . . . the mining captains give all the good places to single men who can go to the saloon with them and buy cigars . . . but we married men can't do that and so we don't get $4 places." [10]

To abolish the contract system, to secure a minimum wage, and to liberate themselves from company exploitation, the miners struck. Aware that they lacked organization and leadership, the strikers turned first to the AFL and the WFM, but both failed to respond to the miners' overtures. Only at this point did the strikers request assistance from AWO headquarters in Minneapolis. Now Walter Nef officially placed the IWW in the dispute by dispatching organizers to the range.[11]

The IWW's role in the strike has long been the subject of misunderstanding and controversy. The miners who first walked out, the federal mediators who later investigated the dispute, and most contemporary observers believed that the IWW played no part in the initial walkout. Most scholars have accepted this version of events. The companies, however, charged that the conflict was largely the result of IWW agitation among miners contented with their lot. The strike may have started spontaneously, employers conceded, but it was kept going by the IWW, which coerced frightened workers into staying away from the mines.[12]

What was the actual role of the IWW? On one point the evidence is incontrovertible: the original walkout at the St. James mine occurred without IWW intervention. But from that point on, considerable evidence supports the company's version of events: the IWW kept the strike going, and indeed helped it spread. The IWW achieved its aims not by coercion but by giving the striking miners leadership, funds, and publicity. As had already been the case in Lawrence and in Paterson, Wobblies transformed a spontaneous revolt into a full-scale industrial conflict. In all three instances, IWW headquarters had been advised of employee discontent on the eve of the strikes, and in all three instances the IWW instantly had organizers on the spot. Although the federal mediators alleged, in their official report on the 1916 strike, that the IWW responded to it tardily, sending only one or two organizers into the field several days after the walkout at Aurora, and not sending its leaders to the range until late June or early July when the strike was already in full force, the mediators were wrong. The IWW had six to eight organizers (not one or two) on the Mesabi Range by June 6, and thereafter Nef and Haywood recruited further assistance for the strikers, especially among Wobblies who could speak Italian, Polish, and other East European languages. Miss Flynn and Ettor, the leaders referred to in the mediators' report, arrived later because they were *not* strike leaders; they had come north to conduct a legal-defense campaign for imprisoned Wobblies and strikers. Miss Flynn, in fact, had been on the range earlier in the spring of 1916 to agitate among the immigrant miners, and Arthur Boose, one of the first Wobblies to arrive on the strike scene, later wrote to her: "Yes, Gurley, the seed you sowed here on the Range this spring is now ready for harvesting. The harvest is great but the harvesters are few." [13]

Few as the IWW harvesters may have been, they nevertheless reaped a bumper crop of union members. Before the strike was a week old, the miners had established the first range local of Metal Mine Workers' Union No. 490; by July 1, Nef counted four thousand IWW members on the range. As IWW prospects brightened, Haywood and Nef pleaded for more organizers to work the Mesabi Range. By mid-July the IWW had sent thirty-four organizers, the most it had ever employed in any single conflict. By then the IWW had also helped the local miners to print a *Strike Bulletin* to present their viewpoint, which never appeared in the region's newspapers, and also to establish a central strike committee composed entirely of local miners, which had ultimate responsibility for all negotiations with employers. [14]

The IWW's role in the Mesabi Range strike was not the only similarity with the conflicts at Lawrence and Paterson. Minnesota employers used familiar tactics to break the strike. The mining companies controlled the local sheriff's office, the range police chiefs, and the St. Louis County authorities (situated in Duluth), and they maintained significant influence with Governor J. A. Burnquist. Not satisfied with the ability of public authorities to control the strikers, the companies also hired more than 550 private armed police of their own, whom they made available to the local sheriff. Sheriff Meining appointed the company police as deputies, thus investing private gunmen with public authority. Firm in their resolve and in their preparations, employers intended to waste no sentiment on the strikers. "Such men," the *Duluth News Tribune* (a company mouthpiece) editorialized, "can never be amalgamated, Americanized nor harmlessly absorbed. They are a virulent poison." [15]

The mining companies and their local supporters regularly accused the miners of plotting property destruction, the subversion of middle-class morality, and violent political revolution. To prevent this alleged insurrection, local police practiced savage repression. When strikers marched on a public highway accompanied by a band, Sheriff Meining dispersed them for disturbing the peace, and jailed six IWW organizers on unspecified charges. The sheriff, so disturbed by parade noises, showed no such concern when company gunmen disrupted peaceful union meetings and placid picketers. From the isolated range down into Duluth, officials denied the strikers access to any public communication, while the private company guards established a veritable reign of terror. George P. West, representing the Committee on Industrial Relations, a private outgrowth of the federal government's Commission on Industrial Relations, called the campaign waged against the strikers "a story of tyrannical abuse, cruelty and persecution involving a hundred cases and a thousand details." Investigators from Minnesota's Department of Labor concluded: "Such violence as has occurred has been more chargeable to the mine guards and police than to the strikers." [16]

Repression reached its climax on July 3 when a posse, consisting largely of company guards deputized by Sheriff Meining, forcibly entered the Biwabik home of striker Philip Masanovitch, to search for an illegal still. The "deputies" treated their suspects, including Masanovitch's wife, roughly. An altercation ensued during which two men, one of whom was a deputy, were killed. Easily subduing their enraged antagonists, the armed guards immediately arrested five occupants of Masanovitch's home on first-degree murder charges. Later that same day seven IWW organizers, including James Gilday, Joseph Schmidt, Carlo Tresca, and Sam Scarlett, charged with being accessories to the murder, were arrested in the town of Virginia, miles from the scene of the incident. It was the Ettor-Giovannitti affair all over again: the same senseless violence engendered by callous public officials; the same charges leveled against men lacking a direct connection to the violence; and the same purpose in mind, "to put all the strike leaders out of action." [17]

In Minnesota, as in Massachusetts and New Jersey, repression, murder indictments, and arrests failed to disrupt the strike. The IWW sent new organizers to replace those in prison; it taught local miners to manage their own union and their strike committees; and it used the repressive incidents to win publicity, sympathy, and funds for the strikers' cause. The strikers, though opposed by the companies, the county authorities, the Duluth press, and even the Governor, now found they had important allies of their own.

The most important of the strikers' allies were the mayors and businessmen of the range communities. As the conflict dragged on and violence increased, elected town officials decided to intercede. On July 7 they called a public meeting at Virginia to discuss the tense local situation. At that meeting, which was attended by the strikers' committees, local officials, and range businessmen, one miner after another testified about his exploitation by mine captains and about the low wages that made a decent life impossible for most immigrant families. A union spokesman pleaded with the mayors: "You may break this strike with police; you may drive some of these men back like rats in a hole, but I tell you you will lose thousands and thousands of good miners here." Every request the strikers placed before the meeting sought to redress a specific grievance: an eight-hour day (portal to portal), abolition of the contract system, a $3 minimum for underground work and $2.75 for surface labor, and so on. At no time did the strikers demand union recognition, let alone revolution. Indeed, Tony Shragal, a union leader, and John Keyes, a union attorney, emphasized that the IWW was quite willing to leave the range and to allow the local miners' own representatives to negotiate with the companies. "We don't want to use force," they said. "What we want to do is to get a decent, living, American wage here in Minnesota."

Aware of the moderate nature of the strikers' demands, local businessmen and public officials sympathized with the miners' cause. One

3 2 7

Hibbing businessman, himself a former immigrant workingman who had made good, told the miners that every man at the Virginia meeting supported them. He observed that local officials and businessmen had also been fighting the mine companies "for the rights of individuals and of people . . ." Every laborer, this man proclaimed, "should have sufficient money to clothe his family well, so he can feed them, so he can educate the children, and so he can have a comfortable home, and sufficient to save for his old age." [18]

The range mayors tried to negotiate with the companies on behalf of the strikers to obtain a decent living for every local miner. Mayors Boylan of Virginia and Power of Hibbing hoped at first that, by persuading the strikers to return to work pending arbitration, they could inveigle the employers to bargain. But the strike leaders, their attorney, and the rank and file rejected arbitration on the mayors' terms. When Boylan argued the case for arbitration, a strike leader shouted at him: "Here is the truth. I couldn't go back and report this to the men waiting for this report. I know there are sixty per cent of them that will die before they will go back to work under the same conditions. If I told them that they would kill me in the hall." Every striker present agreed. With arbitration eliminated as a means of settlement, the municipal officials decided to form a special committee which would then approach the employers in an effort to terminate the strike on a just basis. On July 8 the mayors contacted the mining companies; and in order to assure the employers of the moderateness of the miners' demands, the mayors stressed that "the miners do not require recognition of any union . . . [they] will not require the participation of any union, or of the organizers or officials of any union in the deliberations that may be had to reach a settlement of this strike." [19]

The companies, however, rejected all peace overtures. They preferred victory to negotiation. Thus, employers refused to meet municipal officials, and, in order to justify their own repressive tactics, they continued to accuse the strikers of being IWW anarchists and dangerous revolutionaries. But company intransigence only gained the strikers additional support. The Minnesota State Federation of Labor, though hostile to the IWW, now endorsed the strike. Frank P. Walsh, former chairman of the Commission on Industrial Relations, and his close friends George West and Dante Barton, used their special creation, the Committee on Industrial Relations, to flood the metropolitan press and middlebrow journals with pro-strike literature.[20] The IWW, of course, continued to send funds and organizers.

Unable to bring employers to the bargaining table, the strikers and their allies finally turned to the federal government. On July 19 four local mayors and Fluvio Pellinelli, representing the strike committee, sent identical telegrams to Secretary of Labor William Wilson requesting federal mediation. Simultaneously, Dante Barton, George West, and Louis F. Post urged Wilson to accede to the request, and, more particularly, to appoint Hywel Davies, a former Tennessee coal miner, as a federal mediator. Only two days later, on July 21, Secretary Wilson ordered Davies and W. R. Fairley, an Alabaman with mining experience, to the range to attempt federal mediation.[21]

Davies and Fairley reached the range on July 27 and immediately conferred with the local mayors and with the strikers' central committee. Afterward they contacted company officials. Although the mediators complained that the absence of real organization among the strikers made it difficult to derive the facts in dispute, they soon had their desired information. Davies and Fairley proved, at least to their own satisfaction, that the strikers' grievances were legitimate, that the strike had erupted spontaneously, that the IWW had agreed to peaceful, pragmatic negotiations (even without IWW participation), and that the companies in conjunction with county officials had violated wholesale the strikers' constitutional rights and indeed had established brutal repression across the range.[22]

Although the mediators, unlike some others who would later investigate IWW-associated conflicts, sympathized with the strikers and favored their cause, they, too, failed to bring the companies to the bargaining table, let alone to terms. When the mediators produced hundreds of affidavits to substantiate the miners' charges about exploitation by mine captains, the companies demanded public hearings on the issue. Davies and Fairley then discovered that about 50 per cent of the strikers had left the area to work in the woods or on the wheat harvest; that most of the remainder feared to testify publicly owing to their anxieties about what would happen to them after the strike ended; and, finally, that when the more courageous did testify, the captains and their employers steadfastly denied the existence of exploitation.[23]

So ineffectual was federal mediation that on September 9, Pellinelli and Shragal, speaking for the strike committee, proclaimed: "We consider it a crime . . . that up to the present time no attempt has been made thru the mediators . . . to bring about a conference between the men and the companies . . ." At which point Davies and Fairley could only bicker about the strikers' unwillingness to make sworn statements or to face publicly the accused foremen and captains.[24]

With winter approaching and with federal mediation a failure, the strikers' resistance weakened. The IWW had begun to worry more about the future of its imprisoned leaders charged with murder than about the result of the conflict. Not unexpectedly, on September 17 the range branches of the Metal Mine Workers' Industrial Union voted, without even notifying Davies and Fairley, to call off their strike. Joe Ettor wired the *Industrial Worker:* "Strike declared off that the fight for the freedom of the prisoners may proceed with renewed vigor." Haywood reminded Wobblies: "It is, now, the defense of the organizers and strikers that is all-important." Somewhat bitterly, Fairley reported to Davies that the strike had been ended without any improvement in wages or working conditions, and that the IWW leaders, of course, placed the blame for failure upon the federal mediators. "It is not at all unexpected," Fairley wrote, "as men of this kind always seek to make goats for their lack of success." [25]

Yet the strikers' failure was more apparent than real. By mid-October even the Labor Department agents perceived that the strike had frightened employers into granting concessions. On October 17 Davies informed Labor Secretary Wilson that his final report would show material improvements in miners' wages and positive company policy statements which guaranteed elimination of the strikers' primary grievances. Afterward the federal mediators urged the employers to make further improvements in the contract system, the method and regularity of wage payments, and the elimination of exploitation by captains. By January 8, 1917, Davies and Fairley boasted that, with the exception of the Oliver Company and several smaller ones, most of the employers had advanced wages for a second time on December 15, and had also consented to comply with the mediators' recommendations concerning rationalization of the contract system and the elimination of exploitation in employment.[26]

330

With the end of the strike and the companies' ensuing improvements in wages and working conditions, the IWW's locals on the range atrophied. Wobblies nevertheless took pride in the improved conditions they had helped win for the miners and in the spirit of solidarity they believed they had inculcated among the range's workers. A solid core of Finnish and Slovenian Wobblies remained active, the Finnish-language paper *Socialisti* transformed itself into an IWW sheet, local Wobblies produced a Slovenian IWW paper, and Haywood even provided two permanent paid organizers to work on the range.[27] The IWW expectantly awaited the spring and summer of 1917, when the miners, with better weather, would once again be ready to fight their employers under IWW auspices. Content that it had planted the seeds of industrial unionism and syndicalism on the Mesabi Range, the IWW devoted itself to securing the freedom of its imprisoned leaders and the poor immigrants incarcerated with them in a Duluth jail.

The IWW spared no effort and no expense in defending the indicted prisoners. At first, Haywood, Miss Flynn, and Ettor beseeched Frank Walsh to act as defense attorney. When Walsh begged off, they obtained O. N. Hilton, a Salt Lake City attorney who had made a reputation defending radicals by his handling of the Joe Hill case and other labor trials involving the WFM. Miss Flynn and Ettor, however, continued to plead with Walsh and other influential reformers to aid the Duluth defense.[28]

Luckily, the IWW needed no additional legal talent. On December 15, five days before the Minnesota murder trial was scheduled to open, IWW Chicago headquarters learned that Tresca, Scarlett, Schmidt, Mrs. Masanovitch, and another immigrant worker had been freed; that the cases against James Gilday and Joe Greeni had been dismissed; and that Phil Masanovitch and two other immigrants had received indeterminate sentences, with eligibility for parole at the end of a year. A week later Harrison George explained to *Solidarity*'s readers precisely what had happened in Duluth. On December 8 State's Attorney Warren Green had suggested a pre-trial settlement, which, with both sides fearing the expense and uncertainties involved in any trial, promptly won approval. Green acceded to an IWW demand that the organization would never consent to a pre-trial settlement that restricted its activities on the range or infringed upon its basic principles. Speaking for the IWW, Hilton agreed that Masanovitch and two other immigrants would plead guilty to manslaughter, with the other prisoners to be released. But before the settlement could be sealed, the IWW attorneys and leaders maintained that the defendants, who had the most to gain or lose from a trial, should decide for themselves whether or not to accept the prosecution's offer. For understandable reasons, the eight defendants accepted the compromise. Five naturally had nothing to lose, only their freedom to gain, and their decision needs no further explication. What about the other three? Phil Masanovitch certainly gained by having his wife released; in addition, he and his two co-defendants, who pleaded guilty to manslaughter, received relatively light sentences. Certainly to immigrant workers facing trial for murder in a heated and prejudiced community, with a long prison term or death a distinct possibility, Green's proposal must have seemed attractive. In December 1916 neither the defendants, Ettor, Miss Flynn, nor Haywood complained about the legal compromise. Harrison George, who presented the official IWW version, thought the agreement of "incalculable value to the organization." [29]

Many years after the event, rumors and recriminations spread concerning the pre-trial deal at Duluth. In his ghost-written autobiography, Haywood claimed that Miss Flynn and Joe Ettor had betrayed ignorant, illiterate immigrants in order to secure the freedom of four IWW organizers. Miss Flynn, in her own autobiography (published after Haywood's), accused Haywood of refusing to send legal-defense funds to the range because he disliked her and Ettor. Moreover, she accused Haywood of establishing a dangerous form of bureaucratic centralism within the IWW, which caused her, Ettor, and Tresca to break away from the Wobblies. Philip Foner, in his heavily factual 1964 history of the IWW, reiterated Miss Flynn's version of the Duluth affair.[30]

Yet no solid evidence buttresses either Miss Flynn's or Haywood's later account of the Minnesota legal incident. Possibly the true facts could have been found in the official IWW papers destroyed by federal authorities in 1923. However that may be, all the available evidence suggests that organizational unity prevailed within the IWW in December 1916. No IWW publication carried any criticism of Miss

Flynn, Ettor, or Haywood. Nor did Miss Flynn or Ettor castigate Haywood publicly. Dissension had indeed developed between Ettor and general headquarters, but not as a result of legal-defense proceedings. John Pancner had complained to Haywood and Chicago headquarters about Ettor's interference with organizing activities on the range, which the entire Wobbly general executive board agreed to investigate. Moreover, at the 1916 IWW convention, Haywood and the general executive board made $5,000 available to the defense campaign, and thus could hardly be said to have starved the cause financially, as Miss Flynn asserted. Dissatisfaction had developed within the IWW's highest echelons, but it was entirely personal and had nothing to do with legal deals in Minnesota. Miss Flynn, Ettor, Tresca, Nef, and several other Wobblies had obviously grown jealous of Haywood's increasing prominence within the organization and of his success at establishing a more centralized and efficient general headquarters in Chicago. Pushed into the background by Big Bill, these other Wobblies, who were not immune to the glories of publicity, vented their frustrations: Ettor and Nef by resigning their positions in the IWW, Tresca by dissociating himself from the IWW, Elizabeth Gurley Flynn by divorcing herself from the Haywood faction within the organization.[31]

Nevertheless, in December 1916 all IWW leaders were satisfied by the outcome of the Mesabi Range legal-defense effort. Indeed, they were glad to have the Minnesota cases out of the way so they could devote the organization's resources to defense of another large group of Wobblies about to be tried for murder in Everett, Washington. Many of those who had just been involved in the Duluth proceedings, including Haywood, Miss Flynn, and Harrison George, would also work together to secure the acquittal of the Everett defendants, under indictment in a case which derived from the IWW's renewed organization work among the lumberjacks of the Pacific Northwest.

The Pacific Northwest's lumber industry had undergone few changes since 1907, when the IWW first attempted to penetrate it in that year's unsuccessful walkout by Portland mill workers. Familyless, womanless, overworked, underpaid, poorly treated, the timber beasts, as they were called, still seemed to be perfect IWW material. Employers in the lumber industry were still fiercely competitive, practicing classic nineteenth-century capitalism in a twentieth-century world and continuing to misuse their employees and combat labor unions.

In the years following the 1907 Portland strike the IWW struggled, without success, to organize the Northwest's lumber workers. Street-corner meetings, soapbox orations, and free-speech fights—all city-centered activities—accomplished precious little in the way of reaching lumber workers who toiled in the region's isolated logging camps. Unable to improve the lumberjack's working conditions through free-speech fights, the Wobblies went out on the job as camp delegates to carry their gospel directly into the logging camps, where they could wage the economic struggle at the point of production. John Pancner and Walter Nef, who until 1914 worked as organizers in the Northwest, realized that the only way to recruit the lumber worker was "by showing him the immediate necessity of the union and its ability, not to display to him a picture of an ideal state in the dim, distant future, but to produce the 'goods' here and now." Yet new organizing tactics could not surmount an old IWW dilemma. E. J. Foote, a Seattle Wobbly ideologue, stated this dilemma succinctly: "We feel that we have yet to learn the secret of reaching the lumber workers in a way that will make revolutionists out of them and at the same time give them power in the industry." [32] As usual, if the IWW made revolutionists, it gained few recruits and less power in industry; if it gained members and industrial power, it lost its revolutionary fervor. Initially, in the lumber industry it possessed neither industrial power nor revolutionary recruits.

Employers nevertheless took seriously the IWW threat to their interests, and kept themselves well informed about Wobbly plans and progress. "A concerted effort should be made to thwart the efforts of this organization," one employer warned, "for if they are allowed to continue, and increase in numbers, sooner or later it means serious trouble." The Puget Mill Company's manager simply instructed his foremen that "when any man shows up in our works that is affiliated with this Order or a *sympathizer* with it, no excuse is given but he is quietly handed his time check and requested to leave our road" (italics added). Even so, the Puget Mill never entirely eliminated the IWW influence from its own properties.[33]

That employers meant to eliminate the IWW from the Northwest was demonstrated by three events. First, the employers established the West Coast Lumbermen's Association in the summer of 1911, merging three regional trade associations. Originally organized to combat business insecurity and competitive malpractices, the new association united most effectively on anti-union measures. Second, most of the West Coast lumber companies now began to employ private detectives on a regular basis, and also often stationed sheriff's deputies on company premises. Third, in 1912 employers persuaded local federal officials to investigate the IWW for alleged illegal activities, though businessmen were dubious that any federal official "can be found with nerve to press proceedings." [34] (Six years later such doubts would seem quite mistaken.)

Hard as employers combated the IWW from 1910 to 1912, they could not entirely stymie the Wobblies, particularly after the IWW's victory in Lawrence resurrected the organization. The spring of 1912 saw the Wobblies lead mill workers in the Puget Sound region in a strike for higher wages and the eight-hour day. Defeated in the mill towns by the combined opposition of AFL-affiliated central labor councils and vigilante justice (organized by private citizens and endorsed by public officials), the IWW hoped for better luck out in the woods.

Logging camps, however, were as well prepared as mill towns to fight the Wobblies. When word of urban labor disturbances reached the interior, camp foremen began to screen new workers more carefully. Private detectives again found plentiful employment in the industry, and the Lumbermen's Association, in conjunction with the Employers' Association of Washington State, influenced public officials to hound Wobblies, both in and out of town. By mid-May 1912 employers had completely repulsed the IWW's invasion.[35] By July Wobblies had become so leery of spies and detectives that Captain W. S. Seavey, the Thiel Agency's labor spy supreme, reported that they neither wore IWW buttons nor carried red cards. Seavey estimated that the IWW retained about 1,060 members in the Puget Sound area, and that it had begun to concentrate upon the organization of Finns, Greeks, and Scandinavians, now more numerous in the industry and concentrated in the less-skilled, lower-paying, more transient jobs.[36]

From 1913 to 1915 the IWW declined in the Northwest as it did elsewhere in the nation. More secure from labor discontent than ever, West Coast lumbermen sounded a common note. "So far as the I.W.W.'s are concerned," the Puget Mill's manager wrote in April

1913, "I do not think they are getting along very well, as they do not seem to have public opinion with them." Two months later he informed his San Francisco superiors of further IWW failures, owing to the Wobblies' complete lack of public sympathy. Another mill manager agreed with this estimate, writing in the summer of 1913: "The I.W.W.'s do not seem to be causing any inconvenience. . . . So far as the I.W.W. is concerned . . . they . . . are not in a position to do any harm at this time." [37]

West Coast employers took further precautions to insure that the IWW would do no harm in the future. The Employers' Association of Washington prepared an elaborate reference file on lumber workers, which could serve as an effective anti-union blacklist. Lumber companies still employed detectives and summarily discharged all suspected Wobblies and "agitators." As unemployment increased with the onset of an economic recession in late 1913, employers became more aggressively anti-labor; their trade associations forged common anti-union policies which led one businessman to observe: ". . . Manufacturers and merchants are better organized today than ever they were." [38]

The IWW could do little to combat economic recession, vigilant employers, private detectives, and vindictive vigilantes. But war orders ended economic stagnation in 1915 and 1916, the labor market tightened, and the IWW, fresh from its wheat-belt victories, its treasury replenished with the AWO's funds, resumed its aggressive organizing tactics in the Northwest. 1916 saw the class struggle in the Northwest enter a more virulent and ominous phase.

The Spokane Lumber Workers' Local formally affiliated with the AWO in February 1916 and—suddenly obtaining money for its usually empty treasury—initiated an intensive organizing campaign among the Inland Empire's workers. That summer the organizing impulse also reached the West Coast, when several hundred IWW lumber workers met in Seattle on July 3 to plan for "a vigorous and aggressive campaign of organization in the lumber industry," which would emphasize job organization and concrete material demands. Wobblies hoped to inaugurate what they called a new era in the history of the lumber industry.[39]

As the IWW pressed its organizing drive, employers counterattacked. As early as January 11, 1916, the Washington Employers' Association brought district lumbermen together in Seattle to discuss the threat raised by unionism. By June employers had welded a united front up and down the West Coast to fight not just the IWW but all organized labor. Oregon and Washington fir manufacturers met in San Francisco in July "for the sole purpose of dealing with the labor question." Employers put aside whatever business differences they may have had in order to establish the open shop. At a July 18 meeting in Portland, lumbermen unanimously decided to commit themselves to the open shop and to found the Lumbermen's Open Shop Association.[40]

Employers may have honestly believed, as they asserted in public propaganda and even in private correspondence, that they were not fighting unions. "According to my idea," Manager Ames of the Puget Mill wrote, "that is not the way we are fighting; we are fighting for the open shop principle, and the right to hire whoever we please." In practice, however, winning the open shop meant, as always, breaking the unions—in this case not only the IWW but also the AFL-organized sailors and longshoremen who shipped and handled the coast's lumber. By November 1916 the employers' offensive had prevailed even in San Francisco, a union stronghold, and the Puget Mill's San Francisco office informed its men in the field in Washington State: ". . . The principal thing to look out for now is to see that we keep a goodly *number* of *non-union* men always on the job, so that the unions will not have a chance to again get control."[41]

Yet by 1916 lumbermen came to understand that it took more than blacklists and repression to defeat unions. "This bringing men in at night and putting them into a cabin in a dark hole, with no bed, no bed clothes, no light, no heat, no anything of that kind, is altogether played out," the Puget Mill's manager wrote, and then added: "Men expect different things altogether nowadays . . ." His company decided to give its employees those "different things," primarily better bunks, bedding, and board, partly because they reduced labor discontent and partly because they decreased accidents, production delays, and operating expenses. The Merrill Ring Company was even more solicitous of its employees, causing a Wobbly organizer to observe: "The bunk house is perhaps the best on the coast. . . . The cooks are instructed to feed the men an abundance of clean, wholesome food, and there is a long list of good rules. . . . With a few improvements, such as furnishing bed clothes, these camps would even be tolerated by an I.W.W."[42]

Organized labor in the Northwest could find solace only in its strength in Everett, Washington, a booming mill town at the mouth of the Snohomish River on the northern part of Puget Sound. There, even during the dark recession days of 1913–1915, unions had retained some power, the shingle weavers' ° local, for instance, obtaining union-shop contracts from Everett's manufacturers. "We understand that Everett is the only union town in the State," a lumberman commented in 1916. "Everett has been classed as thoroughly unionized." "It is about time," a lumber industry executive suggested, ". . . that conditions are changed." [43] This employer determination to alter conditions in Everett would soon bring the city's businessmen and the IWW into a bloody confrontation.

The 1916 employers' open-shop drive had not bypassed Everett; it simply took a different form there: brutal, violent, and ultimately fatal. On May Day, 1916, the city's unionized shingle weavers (affiliated with the AFL, not the IWW) walked out to protest their employers' refusal to increase wages, which had been cut eighteen months earlier during the recession. Easily identifiable by the fingers they had lost to mill saws, Everett's shingle weavers demanded a share of the lumber industry's new prosperity. Although during earlier labor struggles in Everett the city's employers had been internally divided and unaligned with management interests outside the city, now, in 1916, Everett's mill owners presented a united front and drew upon support from both the state employers' association and the lumbermen's association. This new alignment of forces encouraged Everett's employers to smash the union and to establish the open shop in the city. Resolute mill owners thus hired armed, professional strike-breakers to assist them in reopening the mills, and as smokestacks once again darkened the city's sky, resistance among the strikers ebbed. By mid-summer many shingle weavers had returned to work without their union. Those who held out—the most bitter, militant, and sometimes violent of the men—engaged in desultory battles with strikebreakers, who usually got the better of these fights. By mid-August the shingle weavers' strike was a shambles (the AFL during this time had done almost nothing to save the life of a weak affiliate),

° Mill workers who produced building shingles.

and one more Northwest labor front had succumbed before the open-shop drive.[44]

With the AFL shingle weavers beaten, the IWW intervened to see what it could salvage from the wreckage. Already well known and widely feared by Everett's employers and citizens, Wobblies for several years had maintained a small local headquarters which provided the city with soapboxers and radical literature. Haywood himself had addressed a large Everett audience in 1913, and Seattle, an IWW hotbed, was just down the Sound from Everett. In the summer of 1916, Seattle came to Everett in the person of James H. Rowan and other IWW agitators. When city officials arrested the agitators, the IWW threatened Everett with "a drastic dose of direct action." [45]

Already triumphant in their conflict with the AFL shingle weavers, Everett employers were not about to open their industry to the IWW. They thus decided to test San Diego's anti-IWW tactics in the Northwest. The local Commercial Club, dominated by the mill owners, organized a vigilante group, which, when denied city cooperation, called upon Donald McRae, the county sheriff, who promised to deputize five hundred volunteers to protect Everett against invasion by outside agitators. Under McRae's leadership, the city's soldier citizens—junior executives, white-collar workers, petty bureaucrats—harassed the Wobblies, breaking up street meetings, pulling Wobs off trains and trolleys, beating them and deporting them.[46]

The battle between Wobblies and vigilantes continued at varying intensity through late August and early September. For a time the IWW thought it had won another triumph for free speech, but then the vigilantes resumed the struggle with a vengeance. As more and more Wobblies came north to Everett, the Commercial Club and Sheriff McRae resorted to San Diego–style measures. On October 30 forty Wobblies arrived on a boat from Seattle prepared to talk their way into Everett's jail. They never even had a chance to begin: McRae and his armed deputies met the Wobs at the boat dock, clubbed them, and escorted them directly to the city jail. That night deputies removed the prisoners from jail and took them to Beverly Park, a local forest preserve, where they stripped their captives and made the Wobblies run a gauntlet of several hundred vigilantes, who delighted in beating the naked prisoners with guns, clubs, and whips.[47] To Wobblies the events of October 30 soon became known as the Everett Massacre. But the "massacre" would pale into insignificance compared to events of the following week.

As reports of the Beverly Park incident trickled back to IWW headquarters in Seattle, Wobbly leaders there decided to stage a mass invasion of Everett in order to confront the vigilantes with the power of numbers. Taking its call for action into isolated logging camps, skid-row hotels, and radical clubs, the IWW pleaded for invaders. Before long, several hundred loggers, itinerants, unemployed workers, radicals, and even a few young students had volunteered to fight in Everett for free speech and for the right to organize unions. Sunday, November 5, was set aside as the day to challenge Everett.

As Sunday approached Wobblies made their way to Everett, the main body, about 250 strong, chartering a small steamer, the *Verona*, to carry them up Puget Sound. On the morning of November 5, a boisterous, happy bunch of workers, who might well have been out on a Sunday pleasure cruise, sang merrily as their boat glided up the Sound.[48]

Everett's employers and vigilantes meanwhile had decided to accept the IWW's challenge and to meet force with force. Informed by private detectives of all the IWW's plans, the Commercial Club knew in advance about the voyage of the *Verona*. Down to Everett's docks marched the vigilantes, deputized by McRae, and armed with rifles, shotguns, and pistols. Fortified with whiskey and motivated by self-righteous notions of civic pride and respect for the law, McRae's deputies concealed themselves in a warehouse and in several small tugboats, forming a semi-circle around the dock where the *Verona* was expected to land. Soon the concealed deputies, as well as a large crowd which had gathered high on a hilltop above the harbor, heard the strains of song drift across the harbor. "Hold the fort for we are coming, Union men, be strong," the Wobblies sang. As the *Verona* slipped into its dock and sailors made fast the ship's lines, McRae and two other deputies exchanged heated words with the "invaders." Suddenly a shot rang out, and then the sound of gunfire burst out in all directions. Caught in a deadly crossfire, the men aboard the *Verona* panicked, almost capsizing the boat, some of the Wobblies indeed falling overboard and probably drowning. With the men on the tightly snubbed boat providing helpless and inviting targets, deputies rushed out from cover to draw better beads on their intended victims. McRae's men ran around the dock, shooting every which way, never really knowing at whom they were firing. McRae, shot in the leg, fell victim to an unidentified assailant. Behind him other deputies fell, possibly victims of their undisciplined fellows. Finally, at least one Wobbly aboard the ship had the good sense to order the boat's lines cast loose and its engines reversed. Still under constant fire, the *Verona* steamed out into the bay, and as it glided away from Everett, four men lay dead on its decks, one man was dying, and thirty-one others were wounded. An unknown number of passengers had also fallen into the water, their bodies washed away, unknown, unidentified, and unmourned. On the dock, one deputy lay dead, another lay dying, and twenty were wounded. Thus ended Everett's "Bloody Sunday."

To this day no one knows with any certainty who fired the first shot. Nor does anyone know whether the wounded deputies were shot by Wobblies who had come armed, or by their own allies. One lumberman even suspected that members of McRae's army sympathized with the IWW, and that the sheriff "expected trouble from the rear as well as from dead ahead . . ." [49]

Who fired the first shot is really unimportant. What is significant is that public authorities and private citizens had attempted to deny Wobblies their constitutional right to land at a public dock and to speak in Everett. Even more significant, Everett's leaders decided to deny those rights through the use of force, even at the cost of violence, bloodshed, and death. Of further significance was the refusal of federal authorities, despite appeals from Haywood, the AFL, and influential West Coast citizens and reformers, to intervene on behalf of the rights of American citizens, who happened to be powerless workingmen.[50] The federal government's refusal to intervene on the IWW's behalf in 1916 would take on added import only a year later, when, at the instigation of businessmen and politicians, federal officials would actively repress the IWW.

The only sane note in a chorus of public insanity was struck by Seattle's Mayor Robert S. Gill, who accused Everett's officials of the worst of all crimes: acting illegally in the name of the law. Yet Seattle's press, area businessmen, and scores of political enemies publicly condemned and slandered the Mayor. Not even Gill could save the Wobblies who had returned to Seattle on the *Verona* from being arrested and imprisoned on murder indictments issued by Everett authorities.

This genuine "Everett Massacre," however, proved a blessing in disguise for the IWW. Already the beneficiary of national publicity resulting from the Mesabi Range strike and the murder trials there, the IWW now received the same treatment on the West Coast. Washington State's workers learned that the IWW was willing to fight and die for the principle of labor organization, and that it was willing to go where AFL affiliates feared to tread. Repression in Everett, instead of capping the employers' open-shop drive, only served to make businessmen more anxious about labor problems. Vexed by the IWW's rapid increase in membership and its support from sympathetic preachers and "scheming politicians," one lumberman lamented: ". . . All in all the situation does not look any too good for me." [51] For the Wobblies, however, the situation looked very good indeed. From December 1916 through March 1917 the IWW amassed pre-trial publicity; Elizabeth Gurley Flynn and other effective agitators came west to lead the defense campaign; local reformers, like Anna Louise Strong, daughter of a Seattle minister, pleaded the IWW's case. During this time the IWW also founded a new industrial union of lumber workers, added thousands of members to its ranks, and laid the basis for an intensive organizing and strike campaign in the lumber industry planned for the spring and summer of 1917.

Legal matters also progressed well; and so they should have, for no solid evidence linked any Wobbly directly to the murders of November 5; no eyewitness could identify an IWW gunman or murderer It was probably the inherent weakness of the state's case that caused defense attorney Anton Johannsen to write on March 10, 1917: "From all I am able to learn the jury . . . is of a character that gives hope for an acquittal and a reasonable certainty of a hung jury at the worst." [52] Two months later he was proved correct. On May 5 the jury acquitted Thomas Tracy, the first Wobbly brought to trial. Defeated in this case and with no better evidence to present against any other defendant, the state released the remaining seventy-three prisoners, after having confined them for six months.

For Wobblies and their sympathizers, the Tracy verdict seemed at the time a great victory. Perhaps they were right; yet, like so many other IWW triumphs, the acquittal had little connection with organizing workers, improving working conditions, or hastening the revolution. In fact, Tracy's acquittal was a victory only in terms of the "bushwa" law Wobblies purportedly despised and defied. Perhaps the lesson Anna Louise Strong drew from the trial was the most important: ". . . The fruit of war is war and yet more war."

Within the year the Wobblies also realized the truth of Miss Strong's lesson. The United States entered the First World War in the spring of 1917, just as the Wobblies accelerated their own domestic class war. One conflict would feed on the other, and there would be no real victors among the contestants, abroad or at home, though the Wobblies would suffer the gravest defeat.

In late 1916 and early 1917, however, the IWW viewed its future with unabated optimism. Exhilarated by the struggle on the Mesabi Range, united in adversity by the Everett Massacre, and revived financially by the AWO's growth, the IWW proposed at its 1916 convention to create for migratories and mass-production workers the structure of an effective labor organization. Indeed that convention would be the most important held by the IWW since 1908, when the "direct-actionists" had seized control of the organization.

As the IWW general executive board began to plan for the coming national convention in the spring of 1916, a new sense of purpose prevailed among its members. At its April sessions the general executive board concluded that the IWW had completed its preliminary phases of agitation and education; now it could embark upon its final phase: organization and control of American industry. General executive board members decided that the chaotic, mass mixed unions should become relics of the past, that the AWO should become an industrial organization for agricultural workers, and that nonagricultural workers recruited by the AWO should be organized as soon as feasible into industrial unions in their respective industries. Moreover, in order to limit the AWO's recruitment of nonfarm workers, the general executive board proposed to establish separate recruiting unions which would organize workers in all industries lacking separate locals.[53]

The first thing that impressed Ben Williams, editor of *Solidarity,* when the 1916 convention opened on November 20 at Bush Temple in Chicago, was the absence of the soapboxer. "The I.W.W.," Williams commented, quoting a delegate, "is passing out of the purely propaganda stage and is entering the stage of constructive organization." The important convention role played by delegates representing the AWO, an organization which had built its reputation through constructive recruiting and negotiating in the harvest fields, offered further proof of the IWW's changing character.[54]

But despite the voting strength of AWO delegates at the convention, Haywood and the general executive board in fact dominated the proceedings. Gratified by the accomplishments of the AWO but determined to reassert firmly the authority of general headquarters, Haywood proposed to use the success of the AWO to nurture well-endowed industrial unions. In a burst of exuberance, Haywood prophesied that "the rest of the world will soon be asking the Industrial Workers of the World, What are we going to have for breakfast in the morning?" To achieve the industrial control and discipline necessary to dictate the world's breakfast menu, Haywood recommended, first, that all IWW administrative, printing, and publishing operations be consolidated in Chicago; second, that a general recruiting union, responsible to and controlled by general headquarters, be created to serve as a clearing house which would later refer new recruits to their proper industrial unions. The general executive board accepted his recommendations and added some of its own, including a proposal to abolish the office of general organizer—then held by Joe Ettor, who had just resigned after several years in that position—and leave its functions in the hands of the general secretary-treasurer (Haywood). It also suggested that national industrial unions, relatively autonomous institutions in theory but impotent in practice, be replaced by simple industrial unions, which like all other subordinate bodies would then become subject to direct control by general headquarters.[55] All the proposed internal reforms aimed at a single objective: to centralize the IWW's operations and to make field work subject to discipline by the elected administrators and their staff functioning out of national headquarters. The IWW's unexpected affluence also enabled the proponents of organizational centralization to offer, for the first time in the IWW's history, decent salaries to national organizers and officers. No longer dependent upon income from sales of literature or upon donations from the widely scattered locals, nationally selected organizers and elected officials could serve as a potent centralizing influence within the IWW.

The 1916 convention also put Haywood firmly in the saddle, ceding him the power, as it were, to ride where he wanted when he wanted. Without a single dissent, delegates accepted Ettor's resignation as general organizer and then abolished that office; they then abolished the propaganda leagues and the national industrial unions, replacing them with a general recruiting union and separate industrial unions under Haywood's personal direction. Finally, the delegates

344

voted IWW officials the precise salaries demanded by Haywood.[56]

When the convention adjourned *sine die* on December 1, Haywood found himself commander-in-chief of an expanding empire. No other figure remained within the organization to challenge his power. St. John still followed the lure of gold in New Mexico. Joe Ettor, now resigned, was destined to find a new career as a small-time entrepreneur. Elizabeth Gurley Flynn, then occupied full time with the defense of the Mesabi and Everett defendants, was on the verge of an irreparable rupture with Haywood and with the IWW; Carlo Tresca, Miss Flynn's ardent lover, would follow her example. Under intense criticism, though for ill-defined reasons, Ben Williams had just resigned as editor of *Solidarity*, and was soon to be replaced by Ralph Chaplin, Haywood's hand-picked candidate. Walter Nef, the creator and guiding genius of the AWO, had previously been forced out of that organization, even before the 1916 convention limited its power, and he was now laboring obscurely as an organizer on the Philadelphia waterfront.

What had happened was simple, if not at first clear: The flamboyant agitators, strike leaders, and propagandists of the past had been replaced by less well-known but more effective labor organizers—all under Haywood's control. Even Ben Williams, no friend of Haywood, conceded in January 1917 that the changes wrought by the 1916 convention were "designed to promote a better system and more efficiency in the work of the organization. If the tendency towards centralization does not become extreme, the I.W.W. . . . took a long step forward toward the formation of the new society within the structure of the old." [57]

On the eve of America's entry into the First World War the IWW stood poised to open a new and more successful chapter in its history. It appeared ready to generate a sense of solidarity and a spirit of organization among workers long neglected by the trade unions: Minnesota loggers; Western hop and fruit pickers; harvest hands following wheat crops from Texas to Canada; Negro dockworkers in Philadelphia and Baltimore; white and black American as well as Spanish-speaking seamen, sailing the Great Lakes and the seven seas;

hard-rock miners in Arizona's company towns and the anti-union bastion of Butte; riggers and day laborers in the oil fields of Kansas, Oklahoma, and California. The IWW hoped to accomplish what no other American labor organization had ever done, or even attempted: effectively organize America's disinherited and dispossessed, including some of the *lumpenproletariat* whom even Marxists found unlikely recruits for unions or for revolutionary objectives.

The IWW proposed to organize the disinherited not by offering pie in the sky, or revolution in the sweet by-and-by, but by winning for them *more now!* The IWW increasingly addressed itself to higher wages and shorter workdays, to improved conditions of life and job security; and it said less and less about revolutions to come and utopias to be.

This change in tone notwithstanding, IWW leaders and theorists declined to discount the need for revolution, even violent revolution if necessary; and they still dreamed about a utopia to come, a new society born from the womb of the old. Haywood, Chaplin, and Frank Little, among others, had no intention of making peace with the American system; they did not plan to convert themselves into labor lieutenants for the captains of industry. Indeed, still personally dedicated to the concept of revolution, they probably would have been ultimately incapable of transforming the unions they organized into institutions that would exist amicably with employers, public officials, and society at large. But the chance to do so would never be theirs.

The surge in the American economy induced by European war orders had made possible labor triumphs the IWW itself scarcely thought conceivable. America's belated intervention in the war promised to stimulate the domestic economy further and to make the labor market even tighter. Yet despite the promise of success which the war presented to the IWW, the war would, in the final analysis, insure the IWW's repression and ultimate decline.

PART FOUR

Trials
and Tribulations,
1917–1924

CHAPTER

14

The Class War at Home and Abroad, 1914–1917

SITTING behind his large rolltop desk at IWW headquarters on Chicago's West Madison Street early in 1917, William D. Haywood was a happy man. To Ralph Chaplin, then editor of *Solidarity,* Haywood seemed more self-assured than ever, more firm in voice, and more youthful in appearance as he worked amidst busy clerks and harried secretaries. Big Bill, Chaplin later recalled, suddenly seemed to be "a revolutionary tycoon whose dream had come true." Haywood's exuberant, boyish enthusiasm infected everyone at IWW headquarters, an office teeming with activities as its occupants prepared to "build their new society within the shell of the old." [1]

A war-generated economic boom had produced the resurgence of both Haywood and the IWW. With production rising and labor increasingly scarce, employers hesitated to sacrifice profits to anti-union principles. The IWW now not only organized successfully but won material improvements for its members. Although statistics concerning the organization's membership growth between 1916 and late 1917 are at best imprecise, it seems likely that during this brief period the IWW more than doubled its membership—from roughly 40,000 in 1916 to 100,000 or more at one point in 1917. (Federal authorities at

349

the 1918 Chicago trial even estimated a peak membership that year of 250,000, undoubtedly a gross exaggeration.) Whatever the precise figures, the IWW was indeed on the upswing.

America's entry into the war in April 1917 further tightened the labor market, opening attractive opportunities for assertive IWW organizers. As Woodrow Wilson brought the nation into war, the IWW marshaled its labor armies for another round in the irrepressible class war between labor and capital. Yet at the same time other Americans viewed the emergency as an opportunity to destroy the IWW.

The IWW had always preached revolution, anti-militarism, and anti-patriotism. Neither the war in Europe nor American intervention in that war caused the Wobblies to alter their ideology. Aware that workers and their families received a steady diet of patriotic shibboleths in school, factory, and community, IWW journals did their best to counteract the rhetoric of Americanism. "Love of Country?" asked the *Industrial Worker*. "They [the workers] have no country. Love of flag? None floats for them. Love of birthplace? No one loves the slums. Love of the spot where they were reared? Not when it is a mill and necessity cries ever 'move on.' Love of mother tongue? They know but the slave driver's jargon whose every word spells wearisome toil followed by enforced idleness. Love of Race? Capitalism has forced them to work with all manner of men and under all climes and the worker has become cosmopolite." A leaflet by Walker C. Smith piquantly advised Wobblies: "General Sherman said: 'War is Hell!' Don't go to Hell in order to give the capitalists a bigger slice of heaven." Let those who own the country fight for it, Wobbly soapboxers declaimed. "Put the wealthiest in the front ranks," another Walker Smith appeal suggested, "the middle class next; follow those with judges, lawyers, preachers and politicians." [2]

Instead of going abroad to slay capitalist-created dragons, Wobblies were advised to remain at home in order to fight their bosses in the only worthwhile war: the class war. When American forces threatened to invade Mexico in 1914, Haywood told a New York City protest meeting: ". . . It is better to be a traitor to your country than to your class." Let the bankers, the interest takers, and the dividend takers go to Sherman's Hell, Haywood implied.[3]

While the IWW criticized patriotism and opposed war as an instrument of national policy, it offered no program to end war or to keep its members out of military service. About all it could do, and ever did do, was grind out anti-war propaganda and bar membership in the organization to any worker who enlisted voluntarily in any branch of the military service.

The IWW's lack of a specific strategy to oppose war did not mean that the organization substituted anti-war propaganda for realistic policies. It reflected instead the IWW's own estimate of the strengths —or, more accurately, the weaknesses—of American anti-war factions. Wobblies spread their anti-war propaganda so profusely because they perceived how patriotic, even jingoistic, most workers were. The IWW also criticized the anti-war crusades of American pacifists and socialists as ineffectual movements lacking economic and social substance. Pacifists, in their view, engaged in wishful thinking, substituting pious platitudes for realistic policies, Christian beatitudes for real power. More Marxist in their interpretation of war than many socialists—or so they thought—the Wobblies believed wars to be inevitable as long as profit-hungry, monopoly capitalist societies dominated the globe.

The outbreak of world war in the summer of 1914 revealed both the IWW's realism and its utter inability to devise an effective response. "We had no reason to expect a different turn of events," *Solidarity* commented when it heard the war news. European workers had acted much as the IWW feared they would: nationalism transcended class, patriotism blighted politics. Before the war European workers had preached the international solidarity of labor and voted for the party of internationalism. With the onset of the war, these same workers answered the call to arms, treated fellow workers of different nationalities as enemies, and applauded their party of internationalism, which shamelessly voted the funds to pursue the conflict. Watching the sorry example of European labor, *Solidarity*'s editor ruefully remarked: "The European working class is still under the control of their capitalist masters." [4] Though condemning the European war, the IWW did nothing to change American foreign policies. While the nation remained at peace, the IWW pursued its customary business of organizing workers, leaving peace crusades in other hands.

Explaining to an enraged reader of *Solidarity* why the IWW refused to take anti-war pledges or to join peace crusades, Ben Williams argued that pledges, resolutions, and crusades, unsupported by economic control and power, would not stop war if war was what the masters wanted.[5]

As early as 1914 some Wobblies realized that American intervention was inevitable. Harrison George, commenting on the European tragedy in a special six-page war issue of *Solidarity,* asked: "Can America Keep Out of the War?" Basing his answer upon the Marxist-Leninist analysis of surplus value and imperialism, he answered with a resounding No! Committed to peace, however, George suggested that the IWW speak out against militarism and war, and, if need be, even declare a general strike. But like most IWW leaders he realized that the Wobblies lacked the power to influence national policy.[6]

Not only did the IWW sense that America would eventually enter the war, but Ben Williams prophesied what in 1914 seemed even more fantastic. While European and American radicals, as well as liberals and conservatives, regarded tsarist Russia as a major threat to the progressive forces of the Western world, Williams hailed Russia as a revolutionary force. "At the risk of shocking some of our readers," he wrote, "we are offering to bet on Russia as *the hope of Europe.*" [7]

For the next three years, as Wilsonian diplomacy drew America into the maelstrom and Williams awaited a Russian revolution, the IWW pursued its organizing campaigns and its struggle for material improvements in working conditions. Other anti-war Americans might petition Congress, write letters to the President, or organize protest meetings in their communities, but not the Wobblies. They thought they had more important battles to wage; protesting the world war abroad had to wait upon winning the class war at home.

But even Wobblies followed the accepted rituals of radical protest against war at their 1916 convention. "We condemn all wars," the delegates resolved, "and, for the prevention of such, we proclaim anti-militarist propaganda in time of peace, thus promoting Class Solidarity among the workers . . . and, in time of war, the General Strike in all industries." [8] That, however, was before America intervened.

During the pre-war period Wobblies discussed what the IWW should do when war came. These discussions reached a peak on the eve of American intervention. Anxious for action, a Spokane IWW official suggested that the organization emulate the example of its Australian fellow workers who went to prison rather than wage a capitalistic war. Specifically, he recommended a vigorous anti-war campaign and a twenty-four-hour protest general strike. Speaking for majority sentiment, Ben Williams opposed "meaningless" anti-war gestures. "In case of war," he advised, "we want the One Big Union . . . to come out of the conflict stronger and with more industrial control than previously. Why should we," he asked, "sacrifice working class interests for the sake of a few noisy and impotent parades or antiwar demonstrations? Let us rather get on the job of organizing the working class to take over the industries, war or no war, and stop all future capitalist aggression that leads to war and other forms of barbarism." [9]

In February 1917 James M. Slovick, secretary of the Marine Transport Workers' Industrial Union, glimpsed the IWW's future. Writing to Haywood for advice, Slovick recommended that the IWW declare a general strike if a declaration of war against Germany passed Congress. He granted all the usual objections to his recommendation. Yes, he agreed, the IWW lacked strength; American workers did not have a fully developed sense of class consciousness; and, indeed, they were too patriotic. Yet Slovick reminded Haywood: "In case war is declared and the war lasts any length of time as it most assuredly will, the capitalists of this country must have recourse to conscription and if that happens we have to fight such a measure, and in consequence our organization will stand in danger of being completely destroyed." Fearing destruction of the IWW in any event, Slovick saw no sound reason for the organization to equivocate its anti-war position or to disclaim a protest general strike, particularly when German-, Austrian-, Hungarian-, and Irish-Americans were not anxious to fight on the Allied side. Certain that the war emergency would be used as a pretext to crush the IWW, he further maintained that an anti-war general strike would demonstrate, for the present and for posterity, that the IWW was the only labor organization in the world that took positive action to end bloodshed. In conclusion, Slovick pleaded with Haywood to call a special IWW convention to consider an anti-war general strike.[10]

Haywood spurned Slovick's suggestion, advising the Marine Workers' official that the general executive board could not constitutionally act upon the request of a single member. Haywood thus placed Slovick's letter on "file for future reference," where Justice Department agents found it when they raided IWW headquarters later that same year.[11]

Between February 1917 and America's declaration of war on April 4, the IWW followed a course midway between that recommended by Slovick and that suggested by Ben Williams. In line with Williams' advice, the IWW concentrated upon organizing harvest hands, copper miners, and lumber workers. Yet on March 24 *Solidarity* did what Slovick had demanded: it distinguished the IWW from those labor organizations that sanctioned war. In a box on page one, the paper published "The Deadly Parallel," placing side by side in bold-face type the IWW's 1916 declaration against war and the AFL's pledge to offer devoted and patriotic service to the American nation in case of war. Then, beneath an estimate of the war's casualties, *Solidarity* commented: "Ten million human lives stand as a monument to the national patriotic stupidity of the working class of Europe! Who will be to blame if the workers of America are betrayed and led into the bloodiest slaughter of history? Who?" [12] The question answered itself.

On April 4, however, academic discussions and rhetorical questions ended for the IWW. America was now at war. What, indeed, would the IWW do? Wobblies themselves wondered. Members all over the country turned to their regional headquarters or to Chicago for guidance. IWW leaders, of course, sought to enlighten their followers. At first, they counseled and followed a consistent course. Playing down anti-war propaganda and putting away their "Deadly Parallels" and their sabotage stickers for the duration, they concentrated upon what *Solidarity* called "the great work of ORGANIZATION." Even Frank Little, later to become notorious as the IWW's most bitter foe of war, limited his comments to advice that workers "stay at home and fight their own battles with their own enemy—the boss." In Kansas City, Forrest Edwards, leader of the Agricultural Workers' Industrial Union (the new name for the AWO), took anti-war and anti-military soap-boxers off the streets. On the West Coast, J. A. MacDonald, the *Industrial Worker's* editor, explained why he soft-pedaled anti-war talk. "My reason," he wrote, "is that if we came out strong there are hundreds of the boys who would pull stunts that would do the movement no good and land them on the inside of a jail, when they could be doing effective work on the inside of industry." MacDonald hinted at another reason for the IWW's refusal to join anti-war protest movements. "Attended a peace meeting at which one of the strongest advocates of anti-militarism was a pudgy parasite waving a hand with diamonds," MacDonald wrote to a friend. "I said to myself, 'I am an anti-militarist because I am an internationalist, but, you, damn you, peace or no peace, I am against you!' " [13]

Although the IWW took no specific anti-war actions, it refused, unlike the AFL and most other labor organizations, to sanction Wilson's crusade. At the time this took courage, courage enough to justify Harrison George's comment to Frank Walsh that the IWW "is one of the few sane spots in a world of universal lunacy." [14] (The Socialist party also adopted an anti-war resolution in 1917, causing an influential group of intellectuals to secede from the party and become Wilsonians.)

Soon, however, the IWW faced an issue more difficult to resolve than that of war or peace. As Slovick had predicted, the war dragged on, and as America settled in for the long haul, it resorted to conscription. Forced to adopt a position on the draft question, IWW leaders equivocated. On May 3, Haywood, writing to Frank Walsh, noted that the IWW, though opposed to the war, had established no precise anti-war program. "What our steps will be in the event of members . . . being conscripted," wrote Haywood, "has not yet been determined. While being opposed to the Imperial Government of Germany, we are likewise opposed to the Industrial Oligarchy of this country, and instead of fighting to continue it, we will always be found fighting in our small way for the restitution of the rights of the working people." [15] That, however, did not amount to a policy on conscription.

Before the enactment of the draft law, the *Industrial Worker* had offered a poetic solution:

> I love my flag, I do, I do,
> Which floats upon the breeze,
> I also love my arms and legs,
> And neck, and 'nose and knees.
> One little shell might spoil them all
> Or give them such a twist,
> They would be of no use to me;
> I guess I won't enlist.

I love my country, yes I do
I hope her folks do well.
Without our arms, and legs, and things,
I think we'd look like hell.
Young men with faces half shot off
Are unfit to be kissed,
I've read in books it spoils their looks,
    I guess I won't enlist.[16]

Yet anti-enlistment poetry provided an inadequate guide for Wobblies who wanted to know what to do when their draft boards beckoned. Members asked whether they were entitled to exemptions as conscientious objectors since anti-militarism was a principle as sacred to a Wobbly as pacifism was to a Quaker. Would a member lose his red card if he obeyed his draft board? Did the IWW have an official policy?

Several influential Wobblies thought the organization should oppose conscription. Most militant and outspoken of these was Frank Little, who traveled across the West organizing workers and criticizing the draft. Richard Brazier, West Coast organizer and a new general executive board member, also suggested to Haywood on May 26 that the board take a definite stand on the issue; Brazier advised Wobblies to declare their conscientious objection to war and their willingness to resist conscription. He even prepared an open letter to President Wilson proclaiming the IWW's intentions and concluding: "We hope you will realize that in the name of liberty you are destroying every vestige of liberty the American people ever had. . . . Mr. President, the gods are laughing." These anti-war militants apparently forced a special general executive board meeting in mid-July that considered anti-conscription tactics. What happened at that meeting is unclear, the only record of it being a Justice Department report edited by Department agents for use in court against the IWW. This report stressed the subversive, anti-war nature of the July meeting, claiming that the IWW board decided to violate the conscription act. Yet other less tendentious evidence indicates that the militants were defeated at the session, and that Haywood won majority approval for the IWW's equivocal war policies. But Chaplin, one of the defeated militants at the general executive board session, continued to publish anti-war pleas in *Solidarity*, including a July 28 special anti-conscription feature that concluded: "All members of the I.W.W. who have been drafted should mark their claims for exemption, 'I.W.W.; opposed to war.'" [17]

Still, the militants failed to force the organization's hand. The IWW proved more cautious than Little, Brazier, and Chaplin would have liked. Regional officials, Haywood among them, left conscription a matter of individual conscience and choice. Haywood reported to one correspondent that no union in the IWW had taken a definitive position. "It is an individual proposition," the West Coast militant James Rowan insisted, "and the fellows ought to have the guts to make a stand themselves without getting advice about it." IWW leaders refused to take what Rowan declared to be "foolish chances." [18]

Yet roughly 95 per cent of the eligible Wobblies registered with their draft boards, and most of those served when called. Some apparently entered the service in the hope that they could foment antimilitarism from within. On the other hand, most of those who resisted conscription did so for ethnic reasons: primarily the Finns on the Mesabi Range and the Scandinavians in Rockford, Illinois.[19]

In accepting conscription without endorsing it, the IWW acted in a manner it deemed realistic. As Rowan commented about the draft: "If we do not have the economic power, it is of little use to raise a ruction about." He cautioned that the IWW must wait "until we are strong enough to make ourselves felt on the field of production as that is the only place that the workers have any power." J. A. Mac-Donald summarized the official position thus: "Talk against conscription will get us nowhere; Power is what counts. . . . A kick to be effective must have power behind it. Power can only be developed on the job." [20]

The IWW's cautious reaction to war and to conscription failed to protect the organization from the waves of wartime hysteria that swept across America. As the IWW increased its economic power during the first months of American involvement in the war, employers, faced with an increasingly assertive labor force, struck back against the Wobblies. Using the war emergency as a pretext and accusing the Wobblies of sedition and treason, businessmen enlisted public opinion and government power to repress the IWW.

Wobblies had premonitions of the threat war posed to their organization. Since the IWW's birth in 1905 public authorities had sought to proscribe or repress it, and since the 1912 San Diego free-speech fight the federal government had been drawn intermittently into the struggle to outlaw the Wobblies. World War I, as far as businessmen and public officials were concerned, quite obviously transformed the IWW's subversive potentialities into living realities. Many Wobblies realized this.

They also realized that never had things looked so propitious for a successful organizing drive among harvesters, copper miners, and loggers. Profit-conscious employers would think twice about stimulating employee dissatisfaction by interfering with labor organizers or by discharging IWW members summarily. Federal officials, eager to achieve full war production, would urge private employers to improve working conditions and to avoid anti-union crusades. Indeed, as both union membership and wages rose, the IWW could take credit for these improvements, further heightening its appeal to prospective members.

IWW publications and private correspondence among Wobblies reflected their perceptions of the war as both a threat and an opportunity. A Washington State member, for instance, wrote just a few days after the American declaration of war: "I hope this damn war business is not going to set us back, as the prospect for the I.W.W. looks very bright." Herbert Mahler, who had directed the Everett defense effort and was in 1917 active in organizing lumber workers, also saw a glowing future for the IWW; nevertheless he expressed anxieties to a friend: "The masters are undoubtedly looking for an opportunity to close down some of our halls, and if we do give them an excuse we should be sure to give them a damn good one." [21]

Which was just what Haywood and the IWW intended. If the IWW was to be repressed during the war, it would not be for offering rhetorical opposition to America's involvement. Nor would it be for encouraging sabotage, sedition, and subversion. Repression, if it came, would be a result of IWW struggles to organize workers and to improve working conditions. Rather than squandering precious resources in fighting against United States involvement in the war, the IWW intended to use all its strength to fight what Haywood labeled America's "industrial oligarchy."

Planning to hit its enemy where it hurt most—in the pocketbook—the IWW concentrated upon industries where it had already demonstrated some strength. Quite fortuitously, those industries happened to be vital to the nation's war effort. American and Allied soldiers could not fight without food; without lumber, the military could not house recruits, transport them across the ocean, or challenge German pilots for control of the skies; without copper, production of military-related hardware was hampered and wire essential to battlefield communication lines was impossible to obtain. It is most significant, then, that in the spring and summer of 1917 IWW strikes affected the wheat fields, the forests, and the copper mines.

The IWW's resurgence as a labor organization had begun in the summer of 1915, it will be recalled, with the AWO's triumphs in the wheat belt. As war increased the demand for wheat, and conscription diminished the available labor supply, the Agricultural Workers' Industrial Union looked forward to 1917 as its best year. At its annual convention in May 1917, the AWIU heard reports that the Farmers' Nonpartisan League of North Dakota° was anxious to meet with IWW representatives. A. C. Townley, president of the Nonpartisan League, had proposed that five League delegates confer with an identical number from the IWW to decide upon wages, hours, and working conditions for the approaching harvest season. The League's attorney, Arthur LeSeur, a veteran radical who had participated in the Populist crusade and then become a socialist, presented his group's offer to the IWW. He stressed the League's good faith, and as a symbol of it offered the League's political influence to help obtain free transportation for IWW members to the fields of North Dakota. Because LeSeur, Townley, and the League did not request a signed agreement from the IWW, the AWIU convention elected five men to confer with League representatives at the union's Minneapolis office.

Two months later, in July 1917, just before the Dakota harvest season began, the IWW announced a tentative agreement with the Nonpartisan League. For the first time, IWW headquarters promised, a uniform wage scale (unspecified) had been established for the harvest hands, which the League voted to recommend for adoption by North Dakota's farmers. In order not to upset traditional IWW sanctions against signed agreements or customary agrarian, anti-labor individualism, the agreement between the AWIU and the League remained verbal and tentative.[22]

° A radical agrarian group committed to public ownership of grain elevators and railroads, among other reforms, and a potent political force in the Dakotas.

Tentative though the agreement was, and though honored as much in the breach as in the practice, it nevertheless benefited the IWW. The following year (1918), when Thorstein Veblen investigated the farm labor situation at the behest of the federal government's Food Administration, he was impressed by the IWW's hold on the harvest workers at a time when the organization had been shattered by legal and extralegal attacks. Veblen estimated that a large majority of the migratory workers belonged to the union, and that an increasing percentage of the settled, permanent farm hands had affiliated with the IWW. In fact, he refused to dispute the AWIU's own (probably grossly exaggerated) claim to fifty thousand members as of April 1918. Moreover, Veblen discovered no sharp hostility between grain farmers and Wobblies; nor did he uncover any IWW disloyalty or opposition to the government's war efforts. The IWW, in his view, sought improved working conditions by peaceful means, and farmers generally united with their hired hands in improving conditions and raising worker efficiency and agricultural productivity. Whatever violence and labor conflict affected the grain belt, Veblen continued, was introduced by urban-based commercial clubs, bankers, editors, and politicians.[23]

Although the IWW encountered no bitter-end employer opposition in the wheat fields, it faced an entirely different situation in its attempts to organize the harvesters and loggers of the Pacific Northwest. In the Northwest the IWW never enjoyed the success that had marked its initial efforts in the Midwest, and employers, farmers, and lumbermen fought ferociously against union organization.

The IWW's appeal to labor in the Northwest resulted from the refusal of employers in that region either to alter unacceptable working conditions or to bargain with moderate AFL affiliates. As President Woodrow Wilson's Mediation Commission reported in 1918, the IWW filled the vacuum created by the employers' obdurate anti-labor policies. Seizing upon the loggers' desire to be treated with dignity, which in the lumber industry meant largely the eight-hour day, decent bedding, and wholesome board, the IWW made its red card common throughout the Pacific Northwest.

Even before America entered the war the IWW had initiated an organizing drive in the Northwest patterned after the AWO's successful tactics. First organized as a branch of the AWO, the lumber workers were, by March 1917, strong enough to go their own way. At a special convention held in Spokane on March 4–6, 1917, the lumber workers established a six-thousand-member IWW industrial union: Lumber Workers' Industrial Union No. 500. To its Spokane central headquarters this union soon added branch offices in Seattle and Duluth. From all three locations it sent job delegates into the woods to organize the unorganized. Like the AWO delegates in the wheat belt, the lumber workers' job delegates had little difficulty recruiting members.[24]

That spring, as the ice in the rivers and lakes of the short-log region of northern Idaho and eastern Washington thawed, the IWW wisely chose to take its members off the job, leaving Idaho's rivers clogged with logs and its mills starved for fresh supplies of raw material. Rather than combat this unexpected strike, and thus lose a favorable market opportunity, employers conceded the union's demands, giving Wobblies higher wages and an eight-hour day.[25]

The IWW success in the Inland Empire proved infectious. From headquarters in Spokane, the IWW moved against the fruit, vegetable, and wheat farmers of eastern Washington; and from its Seattle headquarters, the lumber workers' union planned to organize the Douglas fir industry west of the Cascades. Not to be outdone, the West Coast's AFL affiliate in the lumber industry formulated its own strike plans.

Employers and public officials in the Northwest became so fearful of the IWW that by mid-June 1917 panic pervaded the region. As a result of IWW pressure in his state's farm and logging districts, Washington Governor Ernest Lister had already appointed a special committee, including the president of the state Federation of Labor, to investigate local labor conditions. On June 19 the United States attorney for the eastern district of Washington asserted that the IWW had made preposterous demands upon the region's farmers, which could not possibly be granted. Although he filled his report with warnings about impending violence and property destruction, the U.S. attorney admitted that when he asked an IWW leader with what weapon the Wobblies intended to win their fight, the Wobbly "merely folded his arms . . ."[26]

Less panicky than public officials, lumbermen also worried about the IWW. The Puget Mill Company's manager instituted wage increases in order to avert labor discontent, yet he still found the IWW active—more active, indeed, than the AFL. By late May, company officials conceded that the area's labor situation had deteriorated further and that it promised to get much worse. Soon, they, too, began to comment about IWW threats to burn mills, destroy property, and beat noncooperating workers, who, in the employers' view, were the decent, law-abiding majority of the labor force.[27]

The labor situation in the Northwest continued to deteriorate. Reports filled the IWW press describing region-wide walkouts by lumber workers aimed at securing the eight-hour day and wages in line with the prevailing inflationary trend. Federal attorneys in Washington and Idaho noted a rising tide of IWW threats to the peace and security of the Northwest. The AFL joined in the clamor for action, reviving its long-defunct Brotherhood of Timber Workers and laying plans for a sweeping strike in the Douglas fir industry.[28] Such scholars as Vernon Jensen have even implied that the AFL, not the IWW, initiated the revived labor movement in the lumber industry, and that the IWW merely reacted to AFL initiatives. Employers, however, perceived the situation quite differently, for they believed the AFL had reacted to IWW triumphs, and that as the Wobblies weakened employer resistance to unionism, AFL leaders planned to offer their organization to desperate employers as a moderate alternative to the IWW. Although the AFL's Brotherhood of Timber Workers issued strike proclamations, made demands upon employers, and set a general strike for July 16, the IWW in fact controlled the bulk of the forest workers. Since IWW crews had been striking intermittently since mid-June, Wobbly leaders decided that, rather than allow AFL officials to assume credit for any future walkouts, the IWW should declare its own industry-wide walkout, effective July 17. It was in response to the IWW's strike call that thousands of men left their jobs and partially paralyzed the lumber industry.[29]

Although the IWW's critics stressed the violent, anarchic aspects of the ensuing strike, Wobblies themselves insisted upon absolutely passive resistance. Strike leader James Rowan advised his followers "to avoid any one or any actions that may tend to breed violence or disorder. . . . Realize that our organized economic power is our greatest and *only* weapon . . ." He warned Wobblies to be leery of men who advocated violence and who infiltrated the organization in order to serve as *agents provocateurs*.[30]

As the IWW's strike for the eight-hour day gathered momentum, employers had important decisions to make. They could choose voluntarily to go on an eight-hour day and thus avert employee discontent, or they could remain on minimum ten-hour shifts. They could fight or woo labor jointly, or each employer could go his own way, as had been traditional in the lumber industry. Yet even before the IWW general strike began on July 17, lumbermen had made cooperative plans to cope with their labor problems. At a July 17 Seattle meeting, the industry's top executives decided, despite some dissent, to refuse to grant the eight-hour day. What prompted their decision is unclear. Employers maintained they could not afford a shorter day while their primary Southern competitors enjoyed ten- and twelve-hour work schedules. Although this claim contained a large element of truth, it seems likely that West Coast employers were motivated more by custom than by fear of external competition for markets. With war orders increasing and prices rising, an eight-hour day might have reduced total profits; it would not have spelled competitive defeat. Most district lumbermen believed in the traditional Calvinist ethos: work, however miserable, was a blessing, not an exaction; the longer a man toiled, the better he was for it. Rather than see their employees labor fewer hours in the woods and mills and squander their extra leisure on books or drink, lumbermen preferred to work their hands longer, and in the process make them better men.[31]

To maintain the customary ten-hour day, employers established the Lumbermen's Protective Association on July 9, 1917. The association's leaders threatened firms which refused to join with business boycotts, and pledged to penalize any member company that granted the eight-hour day. Companies joined the association—sixty of them the day it was formed, including Weyerhaeuser, the industry's giant—because they suddenly realized that the IWW had established an effective organization among the loggers. More firms promptly joined the association, leading one lumber executive to conclude that the new group "has more nearly brought all of the lumbermen, shingle men, and loggers together than anything that has ever been attempted in the State." The IWW had achieved the nearly impossible; it had united businessmen known more for their primitive economic instincts than for their economic planning. As Alex Polson, one of the most individualistic and difficult of lumbermen, explained it: "If it were not for the I.W.W. menace to our country . . . I never would have attended the meeting [July 9] . . . nor permitted them to use my name on the committee. . . . It is to beat this organization [the IWW] that I think our company should stay with them [Protective League] right down the line to the last ditch." [32]

Neither the Protective League nor employer-hired detectives and deputies repulsed the IWW eight-hour movement. Reports reached the Department of Labor on July 19–20 describing widespread strike activity in the Northwest. E. G. Ames of the Puget Mill Company declared that the lumber and logging business of the Grays Harbor district was practically paralyzed. A Labor Department official estimated that more than twenty thousand men were on strike in the lumber and shingle industries. At the end of July a federal attorney estimated that 75 per cent of the lumber industry west of the Cascades had been tied up by the IWW. In his report, attorney Clay Allen appended accounts of labor troubles prepared by state prosecutors, demonstrating that wherever the IWW had followers, harvesting crops and cutting logs had been brought nearly to a standstill. Alex Polson, among others, could see no break in the lumber strike. Carleton Parker, a more objective observer than Polson, used similar terms to describe the labor situation. Writing to Walter Lippmann on August 15, Parker noted: "Labor conditions here hysterical and strikes are cropping up everywhere. . . . IWW problem throughout the West is complicated badly by general refusal to grant dignity or respect to any IWW demands though many have a real basis and justification." [33]

How could workers be granted dignity or respect when their employers denied the existence of their grievances? Most lumbermen considered wages, up sharply over the past year, more than adequate, and thought working conditions little short of ideal. To employers, strikes resulted from intimidation and violence instigated by subversive IWW agitators, perhaps in the employ of the Imperial German government. "It is the thugs from Everett, Montana, and elsewhere," Polson complained, "who have terrified the men in the woods and brought them out." Like Polson, most lumbermen honestly believed that their industry had been paralyzed by the activities of thugs, foreigners, and pro-Germans. [34]

AFL tactics made the lumbermen even unhappier. While employers attempted to protect the "loyal" majority of their workers against subversive labor agitators, AFL affiliates tried to use the crisis to enroll lumber workers in the Brotherhood of Timber Workers. Labor Department agents, AFL leaders in the Northwest, and Samuel Gompers himself thought lumbermen might recognize an AFL affiliate in order to end the IWW threat. But employers showed as little love for the "patriotic" AFL as for the "subversive" IWW. According to one lumberman: "About the only entertainments we have out here . . . are those in which the I.W.W.'s and the American Federation of Labor are the chief actors, and there is not very much fun in it; in fact, we do not like their style of music." [35]

Unwilling to grant their employees an eight-hour day, even more unwilling to deal with unions, including AFL unions, lumbermen had no choice but to fight the strike to the bitter end. Using Pinkertons, local sheriffs, state officials, federal attorneys, and ultimately the federal government, employers could partially offset the effectiveness of the IWW-led strike. In a tactical response the IWW, in late August, sent its members back to work with orders to strike on the job. Thereafter when workers malingered, soldiered, or walked off the job without warning, employers found themselves impotent. Once they would simply have replaced unsatisfactory men with a new work crew; in wartime this could not be done. Labor was scarce in the Northwest, and efforts to recruit men in the South failed. Northwest lumbermen refused to hire Negro workers, and Southern businessmen placed legal and extralegal obstacles in the way of emigrating white workers. Northwest employers thus had no recourse but to hire many workers who carried the red card.[36]

Even with the IWW general strike an apparent failure, the Washington State Council of Defense nevertheless reported gloomily in late September that logging camps were operating at only 50 per cent of capacity and mills at 60 to 65 per cent, scarcely sufficient in either case to satisfy wartime demands. The council found more workers joining the IWW and the AFL, and it warned that if operators maintained their unyielding opposition to a shorter workday, costly strikes and labor inefficiency would worsen.[37]

In the lumber industry, at least, the IWW appeared to be waging its class war effectively. But Wobblies, like the Allies and the Central Powers, fought their war on more than a single front. While clashing with lumber operators in the Pacific Northwest, the IWW simultaneously carried the struggle to copper barons in Montana and Arizona.

If lumber workers had legitimate grievances, so too did copper miners. If employers had refused to redress grievances in the lumber industry and AFL affiliates had proved unable to organize workers, the same could be said of the hard-rock mining industry. If employer intransigence had opened the lumber industry to the "destructive" radicalism of the IWW, a similar situation threatened the copper industry.

Nowhere was this clearer than in Butte, Montana, once a miners' union stronghold, but in April 1917 an open-shop city for miners. No copper miner could get work without his rustling card, and none received his card if he participated in union affairs. According to mine owners' libertarian employment policies, men were free to join unions but not to work. Since the labor explosion that rocked Butte in 1914, few miners looked to the International Union of Mine, Mill and Smelter Workers (the IUMMSW—Charles Moyer's organization) or to its parent AFL for assistance. In addition, the local miners most prominent in labor affairs had affiliated with the IWW, which, in turn, promised Butte's miners the aid denied them by Moyer and the AFL.

For three years the rustling card, Pinkertons, company gunmen, and union rivalries closed Butte's mines to organized labor. Then the war came, and in Butte, as elsewhere, prices rose, profits increased, and the labor market tightened. Now even the smallest spark could set off the city's highly combustible labor force.

That spark flashed literally on June 8, 1917, when a fire broke out at the shaft bottom on the 2,400-foot level in the North Butte Mining Company's Speculator mine. Flames roared through the shaft and tongues of fire seared its crevices and crannies, turning the whole mine into an inferno. Men fled in all directions. A few fortunate ones succeeded in breaking through heavy concrete bulkheads designed to limit trespass; most miners were trapped by these unbreakable barriers. Wherever they fled in the shaft, the miners were pursued by the flames and the poisonous gases released by the intense heat. In the end, 164 men roasted to death in the hell known as the Speculator mine. "Butte for some time had been a volcano on the point of eruption," Montana's Commissioner of Labor and Industry later com-

366

mented. "The heavy toll of life in the Speculator catastrophe proved to be the flaming torch." [38]

Seething with indignation, Butte's miners reacted to the tragedy. Led by IWW men, notably Tom Campbell and Joe Shannon, the only leaders the miners now trusted, the workers organized a new independent union, the Metal Mine Workers' Union (MMWU), in order to transcend traditional IUMMSW-AFL-IWW rivalries. Its nominal independence notwithstanding, the MMWU was dominated by the Campbells and the Shannons (IWW militants), and many among its rank and file promptly obtained red cards. IWW headquarters meanwhile wasted no time in dispatching organizers to Butte. The simmering labor pot boiled over on June 11, when ten thousand to twelve thousand independently organized miners led by Wobblies walked off the job to demand better working conditions, a $6 minimum daily wage, union recognition, and abolition of the rustling card.[39]

Even before the formation of the new union and the ensuing walkout, Butte's mine owners ridiculed their workers' grievances. Asserting that local wages and living conditions were unsurpassed, the owners refused to bargain with any miners' union. W. A. Clark, former United States senator and Heinze's old ally in the losing struggle with Anaconda, announced: "As far as I am concerned, and the Clark mines, I will close them down, flood them and not raise a pound of copper before I will recognize the anarchistic leaders of the Union." [40] Thus did one Butte employer respond to Washington's emergency war production program.

Miners answered their employers' recalcitrance not with violence, sabotage, or anarchy, but with moderation. On June 20 an official of the Metal Mine Workers' Union asked Labor Secretary Wilson to initiate a federal investigation of Butte's labor problems. Three days later, the union communicated its specific demands to Secretary Wilson, adding three mine-safety items to its original list and suggesting to Wilson that the union would abide by a federal determination concerning the practicability and reasonableness of its demands.[41]

Assistant Attorney General William C. Fitts simultaneously warned Secretary Wilson of the seriousness of the labor situation in Butte, as well as the likelihood that it would interfere with the war effort. Fitts also mentioned that the Justice Department was searching for possible violations of federal law. At this juncture Secretary Wilson learned that Butte's AFL craft unions had suddenly walked off the job, further disrupting copper and zinc production. To find a way out of this confusion, Wilson sent W. H. Rogers, a federal mediator and a former United Mine Workers official, to Butte.[42]

Upon his arrival in Butte, Rogers found the labor situation unusually threatening. Immediately declaring settlement of the miners' strike impossible, he urged a concerted effort on the part of Gompers and the AFL to compel the craft unionists to return to work. In concert with Anaconda officials, Rogers worked out a scheme to undermine the miners' strike. First, they enticed the skilled workers in the craft unions back to the job with an attractive offer, endorsed by Gompers, international union officials, and Rogers. They then offered less determined and more hard-pressed individual miners an illusory wage increase. As a result of these maneuvers, Rogers proved so satisfactory to copper interests that John D. Ryan, president of the Amalgamated (parent company of the Anaconda) and now prominent in directing the national war effort for the federal government, and Bernard Baruch, President Wilson's appointee to administer the total industrial war effort, urged the Labor Secretary not to send any other mediators to Butte. Baruch made clear what he and Ryan sought: "While I am in favor of making every possible concession, at the same time we certainly should preserve the *status quo* and not permit anything to be used as a leverage to change conditions from the standpoint either of the employer or the employees." [43] Thus did an eminent corporation official, an influential federal administrator, and a Labor Department mediator demonstrate their disinterested patriotism.

Although all the craft unionists had returned to work by mid-July, the vast majority of miners rejected the limited concessions that Rogers had arranged with the mine owners. Despite charges of subversion, anti-patriotism, and anarchy leveled against them by employers and newspapers, the miners maintained their nonviolent walkout. According to an informant of Montana Congresswoman Jeannette Rankin, they still looked to President Wilson and the federal government to settle the dispute equitably. The same informant reported that the miners would suspend their strike if President Wilson commissioned Miss Rankin to effect a permanent settlement.[44] Washington, of course, had no such plans in mind.

Throughout September the strike crippled copper and zinc production in Montana. Pleading with federal authorities to enforce a strike settlement based upon abolition of the rustling card, the miners got nowhere. In Montana, as in Washington State, employers could break the outward manifestations of an IWW strike. Yet they failed to restore production to pre-strike levels. Dissatisfied miners returned to the mines only to malinger.

Mine owners, like lumbermen, rejected the sage advice offered them by a Montana county attorney, who explained the Northwest's labor difficulties this way: ". . . The only way to eliminate the I.W.W. is to destroy the cause that produces the discontent of the laborers. . . . I think that if the employing class of the West would meet the I.W.W.'s and other . . . employees of theirs half way on a common ground that there would be no general discontent and that the I.W.W. agitation would die." [45] That, of course, is precisely what the West's employers refused to contemplate. Instead of meeting their workers halfway, they fought them all the way: in Washington State, Idaho, Montana—and in Arizona.

Arizona's wartime labor situation proved even more confused and complicated than Montana's. Equally essential to the war effort, Arizona's copper mines produced 28 per cent of the nation's total supply. Unlike Montana's mines, Arizona's were scattered about the state in four widely separated and geographically isolated districts. Except for the Warren district in the Bisbee area, Arizona's mining regions had a notoriously polyglot work force: Americans, East Europeans, Mexicans of American and foreign birth, Spanish-born workers, and even some American Indians, who were mixed together in a cantankerous, divided, and discontented labor army. Miners' unions, moreover, had never had the success in Arizona they once had in Butte. The state's boom mining years began just as the Western Federation of Miners decayed, and when the war came in 1917 Arizona miners lacked any effective means of redressing basic job grievances.[46]

Arizona was thus an ideal breeding ground for the IWW, which had just the leaders to organize there: Charles MacKinnon, Big Bill Haywood's brother-in-law, who carried both an IUMMSW card and a red card, a veteran of the 1906–1907 Goldfield conflict, and a hard-rock miner with considerable influence in Arizona's mining camps; Frank Little, the one-eyed, part-Indian organizer-agitator, respected by the state's hard-rock miners for his courage and unyielding principles; and Grover H. Perry, secretary-treasurer of Metal Mine Workers' Industrial Union No. 800, an experienced IWW official who had already done notable organizing work among maritime workers on the Great Lakes and in Baltimore, and who was now anxious to organize copper mines from his union headquarters in Phoenix. In addition, at its 1916 convention the IWW had allotted several thousand dollars to a special fund for organizing Arizona's miners.[47]

The IWW moved ahead in Arizona in two ways. Where Moyer's union (the IUMMSW) was largely ineffective—as in Bisbee—Wobblies easily captured the old IUMMSW local from within, transforming it into a branch of the Metal Mine Workers' Industrial Union (in Bisbee the IWW even took over the IUMMSW's hall). Elsewhere in the state where Moyer's union retained influence, the IWW formed dual local unions and also infiltrated the IUMMSW locals—planning first to disrupt them and then to capture them from within.[48]

In its organizing campaign the IWW made a simple, direct economic appeal to Arizona's miners. Emphasizing the IUMMSW's inability to raise wages as wartime prices soared, IWW leaflets demanded "shorter hours, more wages, and better conditions *today*, while tomorrow we will be satisfied with no less than the complete ownership of the mills, mines, and smelters" (italics added). Organizers called for the six-hour day, two men to each mining drill machine in order to reduce technological unemployment, the end of the speed-up, and the abolition of autocratic company labor policies. They reminded miners that these demands were only starters. "When we get to making and getting our demands in earnest we will make the boss squirm. In fact, he is squirming now with anticipation." Aware of the polyglot composition of the miners, IWW organizers stressed that their union "provides for the admittance . . . of every person working in the mining industry, regardless of creed, color, or nationality." Metal Mine Workers' Union No. 800 promised workers a solidarity never before achieved in the hard-rock mining industry; it also offered Arizona's miners support from their fellow workers in Montana, Utah, Nevada, and even Alaska.[49]

The IWW's appeal worked well in Arizona. Helped along by the IUMMSW's inability to act, the IWW grew by leaps and bounds in Bisbee and added members in Arizona's other mining districts. Organized on January 29, 1917, Metal Mine Workers' Union No. 800 had over six thousand members by April, and 125 paid organizers at work, mostly in Arizona, including Spanish-speaking organizers who distributed copies of *El Rebelde*, the Spanish-language IWW paper.

The organizing drive went so well that Perry planned to hold a conference of union officials in Phoenix in mid-June in order to formulate industry-wide demands and devise tactics to achieve them.[50]

Yet in Arizona, as had often been the case elsewhere in the nation, working-class discontent outran IWW plans. After April 1917, wages simply could not keep pace with price inflation, and neither IWW leaders nor IUMMSW officials could restrain Arizona's miners in their demand for higher wages. Spontaneous labor disputes thus erupted in the Jerome and the Clifton-Morenci districts in May 1917. Federal mediation and expedient concessions by the affected mine owners, however, terminated these walkouts.[51] For the moment, at least, Arizona's labor scene appeared placid.

Yet the state's labor problems had become too twisted to unravel. It was impossible without a scorecard to distinguish Wobblies, AFL men, and labor spies. Where employers thought that the IUMMSW was strong, they tried to use IWW locals to disrupt the stronger union. Where the IWW was strong, as in Bisbee, mine owners instigated the IUMMSW and the state Federation of Labor to act against the Wobblies. Throughout the state, Wobblies joined the IUMMSW, spies infiltrated the IWW, Justice Department agents hunted subversives, and mine owners and local businessmen formed loyalty leagues in order to suppress all trade unions. Only two constants prevailed: the employers' absolute refusal to deal with organized labor, and the miners' unheard demands for a redress of their grievances through collective bargaining. Such a situation could only worsen before it improved.

Worsen it did, as Walter Douglas, president of the Phelps Dodge Corporation, found in the first week of June when he surveyed labor conditions at his Arizona mining properties. In a letter to Secretary of the Interior Franklin Lane, Douglas blamed his company's labor difficulties upon IWW propaganda and the unpatriotic attempt of the president of the state Federation of Labor to unionize the mining industry at a time of national peril. Warning Lane about the violence he expected from the Spanish and Mexican elements at Clifton-Morenci, Douglas castigated the unions' attempt "to take advantage of the country's extremity to force conditions which heretofore had not met with the approval of the majority of the working men."[52] Like so many other employers, he equated labor's desire to share in wartime profits with treason and exaggerated the IWW threat, finding Wobblies dominant in the districts where they were in fact weakest.

Until the Speculator disaster precipitated labor conflict in Butte, it appeared that employers might manage to control Arizona's tense labor situation. But after the Butte disaster, Arizona's copper miners could not be contained. Encouraged by events in Montana, Arizona's Wobblies decided to accelerate their drive in the Southwest. On June 26 the IWW called out its members working the mines in Bisbee, Globe, Miami, Swansea, and Jerome, Arizona. The next day Bisbee leader A. D. Kimball wired Haywood to inform him that the strike movement had spread statewide and that prospects were for 80 per cent effectiveness. Asserting that Arizona's miners toiled for the same copper trust as Butte's, the IWW demanded from Arizona employers exactly what it had already insisted upon in Montana.[53]

Not to be outdone, IUMMSW locals initiated their own strikes for higher wages, shorter hours, and union recognition. By July 1, ten thousand men were out in the Clifton-Morenci district, where all large producers had been shut down; a day later eight thousand miners walked off their jobs in the Globe-Miami district. Spreading rapidly from one area to another, the strike movement by July 6 included 25,000 men and had succeeded in tying up every mining camp in the state. By then, the walkout was 90 per cent effective in Bisbee, where the IWW controlled it, and was 100 per cent effective in Clifton-Morenci, where the IWW and the IUMMSW joined in an uncomfortable and unholy alliance. Regardless of the ethnic composition of the miners in a given district, the comparative strength of the IUMMSW and the IWW, the stability of the labor force, or the relationship between employers and workers, the copper strikes spread across Arizona.[54]

In an investigation of the causes of these labor disturbances, a mediation commission appointed by Woodrow Wilson placed responsibility on the copper industry's heterogeneous, un-Americanized labor force, its heavy labor turnover, its anti-union policies, and its insistence upon maintaining autocratic patterns of work discipline. Yet in Bisbee, where the commission had to account not only for industrial conflict but also for IWW dominance, the workers were largely American and almost all English-speaking; they were by and large settled family men; and they worked for Phelps Dodge, which, though autocratic and anti-union, provided the towns of Bisbee and Douglas with numerous company-sponsored and -financed advantages. The mediation commission simply blamed the IWW's rise in Bisbee upon Phelps Dodge's destruction of the IUMMSW local there. Yet, as the commission's own evidence proved, in Clifton-Morenci and Globe-

Miami, where less Americanized miners were more transient and the operators seemed just as anti-union and provided fewer company benefits, the IWW never achieved dominance. Despite the Wilson Commission's conclusions, the IWW's success or failure in Arizona often depended more upon the errors and weaknesses of its union opponents than it did upon the Wobblies' own tactics and strength or, for that matter, upon employer policies. After all, most of Arizona's miners, IWW or not, shared similar grievances and desired similar improvements in their conditions. Except for disagreement over the union-shop issue and the dues check-off system, which the IWW opposed, IWW and non-IWW strikers made the same demands. Joe Cannon, an IUMMSW organizer, speaking to miners at Globe, spoke in a manner Frank Little, Grover Perry, and Bill Haywood would have applauded. No one could have damned American participation in a capitalist war more vehemently; no one could have indicted the autocratic practices of American capitalists more stringently.[55]

It made little difference in fact whether or not the strikes were inspired by the IWW. Regardless of which union initiated conflicts, the strikers asserted that if Americans could wage war abroad to spread democracy, they could also struggle at home to win the industrial democracy so long denied them by capitalist "autocrats," whose tyrannies were more real to the miners than those charged to Kaiser Wilhelm. As a matter of fact, the mine owners themselves drew no distinctions between the IWW and the AFL. Wrapping themselves in the American flag, Arizona's employers declared total war in defense of the status quo.

No labor understanding could be reached with Arizona's mine operators, who adamantly refused any concession to their employees. Phelps Dodge executives maintained that "any sign of weakness at this time will probably mean prolonged labor trouble . . ." John D. Ryan, of Wall Street and the Amalgamated Copper Company (Anaconda), then chairman of the federal government's Council of National Defense's Committee on Copper, informed Baruch on July 3 that Arizona's labor troubles resulted from IWW subversion and German agents. Ryan also asserted that the strikers lacked substantial grievances or rational demands, and, in his words, ". . . these fellows who are striking are not looking for better conditions—they are simply trying to keep the mines closed."[56]

Labor Secretary Wilson's mediators consequently found the mine owners far from conciliatory or cooperative. They failed to obtain any

373

substantial labor concessions from the copper companies, which insisted upon handling labor relations in their customary autocratic spirit; as one company informed the Globe IUMMSW local: "First and foremost, we reserve the right and privilege to conduct our own affairs." Or, as Walter Douglas stated publicly: "There will be no compromise because you cannot compromise with a rattlesnake. That goes for both the International Union and the I.W.W.'s." Wherever federal mediators went they heard the same complaints. Miners refused to moderate their demands; owners declined to compromise or even to treat with unions; and local citizens' committees proclaimed their business to be "driving the IWW from this district." The mediators thus had no option but to withdraw from the dispute in order to allow the main contenders to fight it out.[57]

The Arizona labor conflict seemed to defeat everyone involved in it. Mine owners begged federal authorities for assistance; yet when Labor Department mediators offered it, employers refused to cooperate. Unable to defeat the copper companies, the IWW found itself also attacked by state officials, AFL affiliates, and federal agents. The AFL and the IUMMSW seemed equally impotent. Opposed by the IWW, though supported by the federal government, the AFL could not force employers to the bargaining table. Charles Moyer practically surrendered the struggle, writing to Gompers on August 30: "Personally, I am doing everything I can to carry out the policy of the American Federation of Labor, but with the combined opposition of the Industrial Workers of the World and many of the employing companies, it is a herculean task, and I feel at times that I must withdraw from the contest." [58]

Arizona's mine operators, like the businessmen in Montana and Washington State, could neither break the IWW strikes nor restore full production. When President Wilson's mediation commission arrived in Arizona in the fall of 1917, it discovered that the state's copper mines had been totally or partially shut down for over three months, with a production loss of more than one hundred million pounds of copper.[59]

In the summer of 1917, from the Douglas fir forests of Puget Sound to the "richest hill on earth" at Butte, from the isolated mining towns of Arizona to the golden wheat fields of the Midwest, the IWW threatened the nation's war-making capacity. Many Americans thus wondered precisely what the IWW wanted before it would declare a truce in its class war. To find an answer to that question, the editor

374

of the *Spokane Press* asked Haywood what the IWW would do if the federal government commandeered the nation's basic industries and established a shorter workday and humane working conditions. "Were these demands granted by the private owners or by the government if the industries were commandeered," replied Haywood, "it is my opinion the men would immediately return to work." Nevertheless, the IWW leader added: "This . . . is not the ultimate solution of the wage system." [60]

No ultimate solution was available to the IWW in 1917, but in any event private employers had no intention of granting the IWW's immediate demands and federal authorities had even less intention of seizing the nation's basic industries. As a consequence, while American boys sailed across the Atlantic in the summer of 1917 to fight and to die in Wilson's crusade for democracy, employers and employees waged their own private industrial war at home.

CHAPTER

15

Employers Strike Back

O N August 17, 1917, United States Senator Henry Ashurst of Arizona arose on the Senate floor to denounce the Industrial Workers of the World. "I have frequently been asked what 'IWW' means," he informed fellow senators, then added: "It means simply, solely, and only 'Imperial Wilhelm's Warriors.'" That same month a cartoon on the *St. Louis Republic*'s editorial page titled "Birds of a Feather" depicted Uncle Sam, shotgun in hand, stalking the woods in search of strange game. Perched on a bare tree limb sat Uncle Sam's prey: three sinister-looking birds, one labeled "draft dodgers," the second "spies," and the third "I.W.W." [1]

War ordinarily engenders hatred for the enemy. This was particularly true in the America of 1917–1918, when public authorities sought to inoculate against unpatriotic backsliding the millions of citizens who had emigrated from nations fighting on the enemy side. From printing press, pulpit, and President Wilson's war propaganda creation, George Creel's Committee on Public Information, propaganda flowed charging that the German nation was synonymous with evil, that the Kaiser was the devil incarnate, and that the German people were less than human. Small wonder, then, that in a flurry of patriotism Americans renamed sauerkraut "liberty cabbage," and dachshunds "liberty hounds."

The anti-German propaganda, which Creel's committee distributed in every community, equated disagreement with Wilson's war policies with incipient treason and saw evidence of German espionage in every action that hampered the American war effort. Since the IWW opposed the war in theory and took action in practice—namely, the lumber and copper strikes—which threatened war production, the nation's communications media declared the IWW *ipso facto* guilty of treason and espionage. In the spring and summer of 1917 America's press stimulated a new form of gold rush: the frantic search to discover German gold clinking in Bill Haywood's pockets.

From coast to coast—and most virulently in communities disturbed by IWW strikes—the tocsin sounded for repression of the Wobblies. Well after repression had become a fact, the *San Francisco Chronicle* commented on February 6, 1918: "The I.W.W. are worse than the Germans . . . the I.W.W. will never cease until persistently imprisoned or put out of existence." Across the nation, the *Wall Street Journal* noted: "The nation is at war, and treason must be met with preventive as well as punitive measures. When you hear the copperhead [i.e., IWW] hissing in the grass why wait until it strikes before stamping on it? Instead of waiting to see if their bite is poisonous, the heel of the Government should stamp them at once." In Everett, Washington, the editor of the *Herald* tersely commented on IWW activities in the Northwest. "Treason," he observed, "is treason." [2]

More thoughtful journals proved as frantic as the daily press in their denunciations of the IWW. The *Outlook* asserted that, whether or not German gold financed IWW intrigues, the Wobblies' industrial conflicts aided the enemy. "If the fullest military preparations are needed against an external enemy," the magazine advised, "they are no less needed against this internal enemy." The *Independent* was even more denunciatory toward the IWW. It declared that the issue of a German-IWW conspiracy was beside the point, suggesting coldly: "The organization is a public nuisance. . . . Its moving spirits are temperamentally lawless, and anarchists by profession. . . . It is time for the American public to take them in hand, put them behind bars and break their organization." Even the usually objective, unemotional *Nation*, not known for its warlike enthusiasm, advised: ". . . It seems likely that [IWW] leaders can here and there be arrested on substantial grounds of sedition or disorderly intent; and their arrest and summary punishment would give a salutary lesson to prospective lawbreakers." [3]

Throughout the American West, the Wobblies' enemies shared the sentiments addressed to Helena's chamber of commerce by L. O. Evans, an attorney for the Anaconda Company. Comparing the IWW to a cancerous growth, Evans suggested prompt and effective surgical treatment. No surgery would be too drastic for the organization, which, in the corporation attorney's words, was the Kaiser's best ally. Even the pastor of Seattle's First Presbyterian Church joined the anti-IWW outcry in a most un-Christian manner. Discovering in the IWW "America's most damnable enemy," the Reverend Mark Mathews declared: "By the power of Almighty God, universal democracy shall be established, and the damnable enemies, like the I.W.W., at home and abroad shall be forever chained." [4]

In 1917 the halls of Congress echoed to denunciations of the IWW. Senators and congressmen from the Western states most affected by IWW strikes instigated the oratory. Miles Poindexter, a progressive senator from Washington whom the lumber barons once claimed had been elected by IWW votes, declared Wobbly leaders to be outlaws who should be handled firmly by public officials even in the absence of specific infractions of federal law. As anti-IWW talk heated up in Congress, Senator Smoot of Utah demanded action rather than words, and he found ready allies in, among others, Senators Borah and Ashurst. Only two congressional voices disputed the slanders and calumnies heaped upon the IWW. Jeannette Rankin, who had voted against America's declaration of war and who was a political ally of Butte's mine workers, including the IWW element, and Senator George Norris of Nebraska, another anti-war advocate who asked about the grievances which had provoked IWW strikes, alone sought unsuccessfully to reason with their colleagues.[5]

This mass wartime hysteria, which affected every class, sector, and region of the country, primed the employers' counterattack against the IWW. Although the bulk of anti-IWW propaganda may have been well intended and motivated by unselfish patriotic beliefs, this was only partially the case with Western employers, who used the rhetoric of patriotism to thwart the IWW menace to their wartime profits. Portraying themselves as loyal American citizens simply doing their duty to defeat a militaristic enemy and to preserve America's liberties (which they indeed thought was the case), employers also plotted to smash the IWW's unprecedented organizing activities among harvesters, miners, loggers, and migratories, as well as to limit the growth of AFL affiliates. Western businessmen missed no opportunity to make profits compatible with patriotism and organized labor synonymous with treason.

Whichever the Western state involved, employers used similar tactics in stymieing the IWW's labor offensive. Pledging their wholehearted cooperation in the nation's moment of need, businessmen offered to do anything feasible to serve their country—except bargaining with or making concessions to traitors. In return for their loyalty, businessmen expected local, state, and federal authorities to repress the IWW.

Before the IWW general strike hit the Northwest's lumber industry, employers believed they could deflect trade-union penetration by obtaining government war contracts which would insure federal protection for their economic interests. When the lumber strike began in Idaho in June, employers demanded federal secret service agents to protect their loyal employees from IWW intimidation. Early in July, before the beginning of the general strike, an association of Western lumbermen pleaded with their congressmen for federal protection in Idaho, Washington, and Montana. Later that month, with the IWW walkout fully effective, E. G. Griggs, of the St. Paul and Tacoma Lumber Company, demanded federal aid to defend Grays Harbor against what he deemed to be an "enemy invasion." In addition, scores of Northwest lumbermen wired panicky reports to Washington in which they stressed IWW interference with the government's supply of spruce for airplanes and shipbuilding, the desire of loyal employees to work if troops defended them against labor agitators, and the obvious links between the IWW and German espionage. Alex Polson was explicit in his prescription for the IWW: ". . . The state or federal authorities will have to take a strong hand in suppressing the I.W.W.'s. It seems from every indication that they are backed by German influence. . . . If the government will close, and keep closed, every I.W.W. hall and meeting place in the United States . . . the strike will soon settle itself." [6]

Mine owners perceived their labor problems in much the same way. "We feel," a group of Arizona mine owners wrote on June 28, "that without the protection of federal troops . . . it is impossible to reopen our mines and works." Round up the Wobblies and the labor problem will disappear, the director of Arizona's council of defense suggested. [7]

Unable to gain strikebreaking assistance from the Labor Department, Western businessmen found the Justice Department much more amenable to pressure.* From their contacts with local United States attorneys, which were close and warm, employers learned that the Justice Department's local officials despised the IWW, disliked all branches of organized labor, and demonstrated scant sympathy for the worker's cause. Employers thus resorted to United States attorneys as the best channel through which to carry business suggestions to the highest echelons of the federal government.

These local attorneys faithfully conveyed to their Washington superiors the Western case against the IWW. On July 19, for instance, U.S. Attorney Francis Garrecht of Spokane, after conferring with local bankers and businessmen, advised Washington that "there is a feeling that the power of the Federal Government alone is capable of meeting the exigencies of the situation." He added: ". . . It is the general opinion . . . that the sending of one or more military companies into the Valley [Yakima] is the only thing that will correct existing conditions." Similar advice reached the Justice Department from its attorney in Idaho, as well as from local officials in other Western states plagued by IWW strikes.[8]

In their pleas for federal action against the IWW, these local Justice Department officials exhibited—considering their profession—a striking disregard for the law. Representing the Department in Seattle, Clay Allen simply advised that all IWW agitators and organizers be interned for the duration of the war, or, if aliens, that they be deported. He was not alone in this suggestion. Garrecht reported ecstatically about the success of an internment policy implemented by military authorities in eastern Washington. Rather than turn IWW prisoners over to civilian officials as required by law, the military detained them in order to avoid *habeas corpus* proceedings and the release of their prisoners on bond. "While it would scarcely be expected that this system would be satisfactory to those interned," Garrecht commented, "I give it as my unqualified opinion that in reality it is best for them too." Conceding that this practice might have exceeded the power of the military and violated the letter of the law, he concluded: " . . . The plan meets with public approval and covers the situation as nothing else can, and every effort should be made to continue in effect the arrangement here outlined."[9]

* See Chapter Sixteen for the interdepartmental clashes within the federal bureaucracy.

While United States attorneys recommended stretching the law up to and beyond its breaking point, they also took delight in reporting elaborate "German plots." Their lack of evidence did not diminish the enthusiasm with which Justice Department attorneys in the West regularly informed Attorney General Thomas Gregory of sinister German-IWW conspiracies.[10] Clay Allen even urged the establishment of concentration-work camps in which to place IWW-German agents. Further illustrating his true beliefs, which were as much anti-labor as anti-IWW, Allen asserted that the presence of federal troops in the Northwest served to quiet the legitimate (AFL) labor movement in Seattle, which, in his judgment, was "in the hands of men whose loyalty might properly be questioned." [11]

That United States attorneys known for their intimate contacts with businessmen demanded repression of the IWW will occasion no surprise when it is realized that during these same years more moderate voices counseled similar action. Carleton Parker, a veteran West Coast labor reformer despised for his "radicalism" by some of the region's most prominent employers, proposed policies remarkably like those of attorneys Garrecht and Allen. Responsible lumbermen, Parker advised, in order to meet war production requirements, "need to have IWW propaganda and leadership outlawed by federal government." [12]

The Western businessman's battle against the IWW won other unexpected allies. Not only did federal attorneys and local labor reformers join the fight; so did AFL affiliates. Wherever the IWW struck, AFL leaders such as Charles Moyer of the IUMMSW and J. G. Brown of the Brotherhood of Timber Workers endorsed the action of workers who crossed picket lines or accepted jobs vacated by IWW strikers.[13]

Employers not only pleaded for federal intervention; they also beseeched local and state officials to repress the IWW. At those levels business pleas received a more prompt reaction. In state after state, sheriffs, mayors, governors, committees of national defense, and other public organizations allied with employers to fight the IWW's threat to business prosperity. The states of Minnesota and Idaho, to cite but two examples, enacted so-called criminal syndicalism laws, which in effect outlawed IWW membership. This legislation defined almost every fundamental tenet of IWW ideology as a crime against the state, and hence anyone who advocated the Wobbly creed by speech, writing, publication, or display became *ipso facto* a criminal. Just such a law, Washington lumberman Alex Polson thought, would enable his state to manage the IWW expeditiously. Criminal syndicalism laws, however, failed to disrupt the IWW's offensive, even in Minnesota and Idaho.[14]

State and public officials thus resorted to different tactics to quell the IWW. In Minnesota, a committee of public safety, directed by ex-Governor John Lind, initiated a secret investigation of the IWW aimed at uncovering enough evidence of German involvement to enable the Justice Department to prosecute the Wobblies for espionage or treason. California's State Commission on Immigration and Housing, a product of the 1913 Wheatland incident, kept a close eye on the Wobblies, while it also encouraged employers to improve wages and working conditions in order to reduce labor discontent. Washington State's council of defense, representing business, organized labor (meaning the AFL), and the public (whatever that meant), waged a multi-faceted struggle against the IWW. It searched the state for evidence of disloyalty, it took into custody "irresponsible," "seditious," and "disloyal" IWW ringleaders, and it investigated the causes of labor disturbances. Where the state's power proved insufficient to the occasion, it unhesitatingly called for federal troops.[15]

In wartime, state power generally proved incapable of coping with IWW activity. State militias, never noted for their efficiency, became unavailable in the summer of 1917, as they were federalized. Thus those governors planning to resort to military repression had to turn to Washington for aid. Montana's governor was the first to request and to use federal troops to break an IWW strike, doing so on April 21 in the case of a labor dispute on the Great Northern Railroad at Eureka, Montana. Soon thereafter Arizona's chief executive requested similar assistance in order to control the strikes in his state's copper mines, and early in June Washington Governor Ernest Lister asked the War Department for troops to patrol the Yakima Valley's farms and irrigation systems.[16] In the end, state officials agreed with businessmen and United States attorneys that only federal power was capable of suppressing the IWW.

Until the federal government could be persuaded to act decisively against the IWW, many employers and private citizens preferred to act on their own. Loyalty leagues, citizens' alliances, and vigilante organizations cropped up in every Western community blighted by labor conflict. In communities threatened by the IWW, one either became a Wobbly or joined a group dedicated to destroying the IWW by extralegal and illegal means. No unoccupied middle ground remained available for the law-abiding citizen.

Before America formally entered the war, the IWW felt the sting of this new generation of vigilantes. State militiamen and "off-duty" United States Marines raided IWW headquarters in Kansas City on April 3, 1917, destroying organization papers and office furnishings, as Kansas City's police placidly watched and then departed in company with the soldiers.[17]

Kansas City marked only the beginning of vigilante activity. On May 30, IWW headquarters in Detroit had a similar visitation; on June 16, soldiers and sailors attacked Seattle headquarters, and police arrested forty-one Wobblies; a week later it was Duluth. No Wobbly knew where or when vigilantes would strike next. Chicago headquarters had even been invaded secretly the night of May 24, and a number of dictaphone records, rolls of correspondence, and other items stolen. Citing the above events as well as others, in late June, Haywood predicted that a coordinated campaign of repression would be directed against the IWW.

In order to protect itself from vigilante "justice," the IWW itself turned for assistance to federal authorities. Haywood sent two general executive board members and IWW attorney Fred Moore to Washington to lay the IWW's claim for justice before the President and the Justice Department.[18] This was another of the Wobblies' wartime decisions that staggers the imagination. Already slandered by Democratic (and Republican) congressmen for its "treasonable" actions, how could the IWW have expected relief from the Justice Department, which was then seeking evidence of Wobbly-instigated subversion? Having declared the war a capitalist bloodbath caused by businessmen eager to create an American empire, how could the IWW have expected sympathy from Woodrow Wilson, who had decided to sacrifice American lives to make the world safe for democracy, a goal Wobblies looked upon with derision? Certainly, the IWW could not have expected the hands it bit—businessmen's, public officials', and the President's—to protect, if not feed, it. Why, then, did Haywood turn to Washington to secure the IWW against virulent vigilantism? Only one explanation seems plausible: Wobblies obviously had more faith in American society's commitment to fair play and to due process than their own rhetoric allowed. Believing themselves innocent of sedition, subversion, and espionage, Wobblies sought protection from the capitalist laws they condemned, the public officials they ridiculed, and the President they despised. Such faith would ultimately prove misplaced. The more traditional IWW analyses of the nature and dynamics of the American system would have offered a better guide to action in 1917–1918 than an emotional, almost intuitive, belief in the nation's sense of fairness. Paradoxically, expecting the best from a society whose structure it considered plutocratic and exploitative, the IWW received the worst treatment America had to offer to radicals.

Left defenseless by public officials, Wobblies fell easy victim to vigilante justice. In the Midwestern wheat belt, commercial clubs provided Wobblies foolish enough to enter town a warm welcome. Beaten, arrested, jailed, tarred and feathered, the Wobbly harvester found refuge only at work among farmers more sympathetic to him than town dwellers.[19]

Most grain-belt terrorism was spontaneous and sporadic, but that which occurred in the copper regions of Arizona and Montana was organized, continuous, and brutal. Unable at first to win quick federal repression of the IWW, copper interests decided, in the words of an Arizona vigilante: ". . . The citizens will have to handle the situation if the government will not." [20] How Western citizens planned to handle the situation soon became evident.

Jerome, Arizona, had been one of the first areas in the state affected by IWW and IUMMSW strikes. There Wobblies fought AFL men, private detectives infiltrated the IWW local, and Justice Department agents observed everybody. Predictably, copper production lagged. Complicated by inter-union rivalry, the labor problem in Jerome seemed beyond repair. Mine owners and local businessmen thus decided to alter the situation. On July 3, 1917, they organized the Jerome Loyalty League, which armed its members and threatened to arrest any individual who interfered with copper production. A week later the League went into action. "There was a picturesque occurrence at Jerome on July 10," the *Outlook* commented, "when hundreds of miners and other citizens, some with rifles and others with pick handles, cleared the town of the agitators whom they considered undesirable." So thorough indeed was this deportation of Jerome's "undesirables" that several private detectives were caught in the dragnet and banished to the California desert with the Wobblies.[21]

The IWW, of course, protested. Its spokesmen in Jerome demanded that the federal government protect the constitutional right of copper miners to work and live where they desired. Instead of investigating the Loyalty League's action, however, the Justice Department probed the IWW deportees, seeking evidence to indict them on criminal charges.

Having forcibly rid the area of Wobblies, the Jerome Loyalty League now turned to the IUMMSW. AFL members were threatened with deportation unless they obeyed the edicts promulgated by League members and local mine owners. Even the loyal AFL failed to obtain relief from Washington. Only Secretary Wilson spoke out on behalf of the IUMMSW, and he was curtly informed by Arizona's governor that Jerome's Loyalty League favored patriotism, loyalty, high wages, and organized labor.[22]

Given the green light by a favorable public response to the Jerome deportations and the unwillingness of federal authorities to intervene on behalf of the deportees, Arizona's vigilantes attacked elsewhere. The town of Bisbee, like Jerome, had had its copper production tied up by industrial conflict. Again like Jerome, Bisbee had its share of private detectives and Justice Department agents. But in Bisbee, *unlike* Jerome, the copper miners, almost to a man, belonged to an IWW local, thus compounding the industrial impasse.

Since Bisbee's miners had walked out on June 28, County Sheriff Harry Wheeler, an ex–Rough Rider, and Governor Thomas Campbell had requested federal troops to break the strike. The War Department, however, offered only an observer, Lieutenant Colonel James J. Hornbrook, who reported "no violence or disorder" in Bisbee. Mine operators, local businessmen, and county officials assessed the problem quite differently. They saw violence, German gold, and treason everywhere. No one represented the local attitude better than Sheriff Wheeler, who found force the easiest solution to difficult problems. In his view, the strikers were inferior Mexicans, aliens, and enemies of the state, who kept Bisbee's mines shut through intimidation and violence. Think of it, the sheriff informed Arizona's attorney general, "white women in an American town so terrorized by foreigners that they were compelled to quit work in terror of their lives."

To preserve the virtue of Bisbee's white women and to defend national security from what he took to be a clear and present danger, on the night of July 11 Wheeler set into operation a carefully contrived conspiracy.[23] The sheriff imposed military discipline upon a select group of so-called posse captains, and deputized almost two thousand other anti-IWW townsmen. Late that evening and into the next morning, Wheeler, his captains and deputies, the mayor and the county council, the Phelps Dodge Company's top local executives (supported by their president, Walter Douglas), and leading railroad, telephone, and telegraph company officials met together secretly to plot their course of action. In the words of one participant at that meeting: "We worked our plans out thoroughly and had a thorough organization." So thorough was the organization that, with the cooperation of the telephone, telegraph, and railroad companies, the conspirators shut Bisbee off from the outside world. No messages could reach or leave the city without the permission of Wheeler or one of his confidants. Thus prepared, at dawn on July 12 Wheeler's two thousand deputies, wearing white armbands to distinguish them from their intended victims, began a vast Wobbly hunt. By 6:30 A.M. the deputies had corralled more than twelve hundred men, the majority of whom were allegedly Mexicans, enemy aliens, and IWW, German-financed subversives. The armed posse marched its captives to a central distribution point at the Warren ball park. There, with rifles and bayonets gleaming in the early morning sun, the vigilantes placed their prisoners on cattle cars (obligingly provided by the El Paso and Southwestern Railroad) for transportation beyond Arizona's borders. With well-dressed women cheering the vigilantes and little children jeering the captives, the locomotive worked up steam. With the last prisoner crammed into a cattle car, the train pulled out of Bisbee with its strange cargo, and a minimal supply of water, bread, and crackers.

Several days later Sheriff Wheeler, neither disclaiming responsibility nor making any excuse for his actions of July 12, piquantly described the results of Bisbee's deportation: on July 11, he said, the IWW's defied the mayor and marshal of Bisbee; on July 12 he got rid of them; and on July 14 Bisbee had more men working in the mines than it had had on July 1. Not in the least penitent about the mass deportation—in fact, rather elated at its success—Wheeler advised Arizona's attorney general: "If we are guilty of taking the law into our own hands, I can only cite to you the Universal Law that necessity makes . . . and I can only add now and here . . . I would repeat the operation any time I find my own people endangered by a mob composed of eighty per cent aliens and enemies of my Government."

While the sheriff gloated, his victims found themselves stranded on the desert at Hermanas, New Mexico, unable to return to their homes and families in Bisbee, where armed vigilantes still threatened their lives. As involuntary refugees from America's class war, the Bisbee deportees located temporary refuge in an Army camp at Columbus, New Mexico. There Army officers, under orders from Washington, provided the refugees with bare rations and a few feet of desert ground upon which to lay their heads.

At the New Mexico camp Army officers also took a careful census of the deportees. Instead of uncovering an army of Mexicans, Germans, and subversives, they discovered that almost half the deportees were American citizens, most of whom had registered for the draft; only a handful were technically enemy aliens (that is, German- or Austrian-born); Mexicans were an insignificant minority; and a substantial number of the refugees had wives, children, property, bank accounts, and even Liberty Bonds in Bisbee. Among the deportees were also businessmen, AFL members, and a Bisbee lawyer. The census never determined the precise percentage of Wobblies in the camp; all investigators agreed that the deportation had increased the number of IWW sympathizers among the refugees. Throughout their ordeal, which lasted into September, the refugees were led by IWW militants A. S. Embree, A. D. Kimball, and Sam Brooks.[24]

Protestors immediately appealed to Governor Campbell, the Justice Department, and President Wilson to restore the refugees' rights. Haywood was not alone in wiring President Wilson on July 13 to demand that Bisbee's "Prussianized" methods be curbed, and that the deportees be supported adequately until they could be restored to their homes and families. Two Labor Department mediators, Cochise County's state representative, Arizona's AFL officials, and countless private citizens united in the plea for federal action against Bisbee's vigilantes, who remained unrepentant and who, with the sanction of Colonel Hornbrook, continued to hold kangaroo court, deport suspected subversives, and keep "undesirables" out of the Warren district.[25]

Federal officials soon disabused the refugees and their sympathizers of any confidence in constitutional guarantees. Every request from the deportees for federal action was brushed aside. Except for perfunctory condemnations of Bisbee vigilantism by President Wilson and Governor Campbell, public officials did nothing to restore the refugees' basic civil rights. The Justice Department simply denied them federal relief, and Assistant Attorney General William Fitts contended that the refugees had absolute freedom of action: they could subsist on military rations or, unprotected by federal power, they could return to Arizona. But the Army thought otherwise. Both Colonel Hornbrook and the commanding general of the Southwest District opposed permitting the deportees to return to Bisbee, where they might instigate further labor conflict. Finally, even if the refugees exercised their putative right to leave Columbus, they had no way to re-enter a Bisbee guarded by armed vigilantes.[26]

At the end of July, then, Bisbee remained as remote from constitutional guarantees as it had been on the morning of July 12. An IWW attorney sent there to look after the interests of the deportees' wives and children was arrested by vigilantes, hauled before a kangaroo court, and, despite protests from the Governor, run out of town. AFL investigators enjoyed a similar reception. No one, in fact, could enter Bisbee—unless willing to dig copper on company terms or serve the vigilante cause.[27]

Failing to obtain relief by citing constitutional rights, the IWW resorted to rhetorical intimidation. On July 31 the deportees' leaders wired Haywood that "if action is not taken by Federal Government forthwith in sending deported men back to homes in Bisbee, men themselves will take action in returning with arms if necessary." Actually, on the preceding day Haywood had wired President Wilson to threaten a general strike of metal miners and harvest workers if the government did not return the deportees to their homes and families. In a final effort to gain relief, the deportees promised the President that they would dig copper if the federal government operated the nation's mines and smelters.[28]

Protests, threats, and demands for nationalization of the copper industry availed the IWW naught. Haywood's July 30 telegram and the deportees' demand for government ownership of the mines only confirmed President Wilson's suspicion that Wobblies were dangerous, un-American subversives: an abomination in peacetime, a clear and present danger to national security in wartime. From the President the IWW could expect neither sympathy nor aid. Nor could it expect more from the Justice Department, which continued to deny that federal laws or constitutional rights had been contravened by

Bisbee's vigilantes. The Army, of course, advised against federal interference with vigilantism, and as the desert nights grew colder, Army officers cut the deportees' rations and denied them extra blankets. Forced out of Columbus by these cuts in rations, and failing to obtain relief from the Justice Department, the IWW militants at Columbus informed President Wilson on September 12 that "Common American citizens here are now convinced that they have no constitutional rights." [29]

The deportees finally deserted Columbus in mid-September. Most avoided Bisbee, but a few, such as A. S. Embree, tried to return home, where the vigilantes expected him. They wasted no time in jailing the militant Wobbly, who from prison continued to demand his constitutional right to live with his wife and children where he chose —only to be told by the Justice Department that the federal government was impotent to act.[30]

Yet federal officials at this time—it was now mid-September 1917 —had indeed acted in the matter of the IWW. Not, to be sure, in defense of the Wobblies' basic constitutional rights. Federal officials had instead initiated an intensive nationwide effort to suppress the IWW and break its strikes in the lumber, copper, and harvest districts.

The Bisbee deportation precipitated two major decisions by the Wilson administration. First, Haywood's threats of a general strike convinced Wilson and the Justice Department that "IWW-ism," not vigilantism, must be repressed. Second, the blatantly unconstitutional actions taken by Bisbee's vigilantes provoked protests from Gompers and other prominent American patriots that Wilson could not ignore. In order to mollify the protestants and to establish the federal government's commitment to harmonious industrial relations, Wilson appointed a special mediation commission to investigate wartime industrial conflicts and to suggest equitable remedies. The President's first decision would demonstrate the effectiveness of federal power when it determined to crush radical labor organizations; the second decision would illustrate the government's weakness when it attempted to protect the basic rights of powerless workers.[31]

Among the matters Wilson's mediation commission chose to investigate was the Bisbee deportation. It found this inquiry no easy task, for as late as the last week in October 1917, when the commissioners planned to open their Bisbee inquiry, the city remained under vigilante law. Sheriff Wheeler refused to cooperate with the federal investigators, whose witnesses the sheriff's men intimidated or stopped from appearing at the hearings. Even after the commission concluded its hearings and recommended that American citizens be allowed to enter and to leave Bisbee freely, Wheeler and his local vigilantes refused to heed the requests of federal authorities.[32]

Yet the federal government wanted to demonstrate publicly its impartiality in the Bisbee affair After all, it could scarcely arrest, indict, and prosecute Wobblies for violating federal laws, as it was then doing, without meting out similar justice to Bisbee's vigilantes, who publicly confessed their "crimes." President Wilson thus urged the Justice Department to institute criminal proceedings against the vigilantes on the dubious ground that they had violated the conscription act by deporting men legally registered for the draft.

The Justice Department lacked the enthusiasm to prosecute a patriotic sheriff, reputable local businessmen, and prominent corporation officials. Although the political appointees in the Department— the Attorney General and his assistant, William C. Fitts, for example— sensitive to the realities of party politics, agreed with the President's desire to prosecute, the Department's career officials did not. To a man they argued that no legal ground existed on which the federal government could prosecute the vigilantes. In the words of one career official: "The deportations were of course a serious invasion of the liberties of the parties . . . but nothing is better settled than that the rights of life and personal liberty are natural rights of men and as such under our system of Government come properly within the sovereignty and jurisdiction of the States." [33]

For political reasons the Justice Department nevertheless proceeded in 1918 with its prosecution of the vigilantes, whom it proved had been armed and financed by the Phelps Dodge Company. (The company's attorney even served as the vigilantes' defense counsel.) Without enthusiasm for the case, however, the Justice Department refused to indict the man most responsible for the deportations: Walter Douglas, president of Phelps Dodge. William Fitts also railed against Arizona's new governor, G. W. P. Hunt, who wanted further prosecutions, and who, because of lack of balance, "mistakes those who merely masquerade as legitimate labor agitators [to Fitts even the legitimate labor leader was an agitator] for the real article." Fitts and his colleagues thus were probably not displeased when in December 1918 the Arizona federal district court quashed the Bisbee indictments, asserting that the deportations violated no federally guaranteed rights. Yet, once again for exigent political reasons, the

Department appealed the district court's decision to the Supreme Court, which in December 1920 upheld the lower court's ruling.[34] The nation's highest court ruled that vigilantes, who had denied American citizens the right to live and work where they chose and who had interfered with interstate railroad, telephone, and telegraph communications, were not subject to federal prosecution. That, ironically, illustrated the odder aspects of American law and society during the Progressive and World War I years.

If Bisbee's citizens played fast and loose with the rights of Americans, Butte's would do them one better. In the Montana city, too, an IWW-endorsed strike had curtailed copper production, and Butte's mine owners, like those of Bisbee, had thus far unsuccessfully sought federal repression of the IWW.

Immediately after news of the Bisbee deportations reached Butte, Montana copper miners, fearing similar treatment at the hands of local vigilantes, asked Congresswoman Jeannette Rankin to obtain federal protection for them. While she pleaded the miners' case in Washington, Thomas Walsh, Montana's junior senator, informed federal authorities that Montana would definitely not resort to vigilante violence in order to smash the copper strike. During the last two weeks in July, Walsh's evaluation of local conditions seemed more realistic than Miss Rankin's: Butte remained placid and no deportations occurred. But on July 30 Miss Rankin received disturbing information. A Butte informant reported to her that the mine operators intended, with the help of private gunmen and United States soldiers, to deport the strike's leaders.[35] In fact, the employers had only one leader in mind.

Frank Little had arrived in Butte just a few days earlier to promote IWW activities. Hobbling about on crutches as the result of a leg broken in an accident and enduring constant pain from a rupture sustained in a beating he received during an Arizona labor conflict, Little brought his own personal anti-war crusade to Montana. Heedless of his own comfort and safety, the one-eyed, part-Indian IWW agitator advised his supporters to continue their strike for improved conditions of life and work and to join him in refusing to

391

endorse an imperialistic, capitalistic war. Previously, most local Wobblies had avoided the use of anti-war propaganda, but Little, much to the disgust of Butte's establishment, espoused his anti-war gospel wherever an audience congregated. Little's prominence within the IWW, his wide following among hard-rock miners, and his blatantly "unpatriotic" speeches made him a choice target for vigilante justice.

On the night of July 31 Butte's vigilantes paid Frank Little an unexpected visit. Asleep in his room next door to the Independent Miners' Union hall, he awoke to find his bed surrounded by armed masked men. Not yet fully awake and still undressed, he was seized by six men and carried from his room. At 3 A.M. on August 1, after an auto ride during which they tortured Little, the vigilantes brought him to his destination: a railroad trestle on Butte's outskirts. Wasting neither sympathy nor time, the masked men placed a rope around Little's neck, fastened the rope end to the trestle, and sent the crippled, tortured Wobbly swinging off to eternity. Five hours later, Butte's sheriff found Little's limp body still dangling from the trestle with the sign of the original Montana vigilantes * pinned to the dead man.[36]

State and local authorities did nothing to apprehend Little's murderers, and federal officials lacked any basis for action, for in this case, at least, no federal law had been violated. Even if the federal government had had a basis for intervention, it seems unlikely that Butte's vigilantes would have suffered any more than their Bisbee counterparts. In fact, the lynchers won sympathy from prominent politicians and from much of the nation's press. Many Americans seconded the verdict of Montana's senior senator, H. L. Myers, who blamed Washington, not Butte, for Little's murder. "Had he been arrested and put in jail for his seditious and incendiary talks," the Senator wrote, "he would not have been lynched." [37]

That the IWW should simultaneously suffer from public condemnation as well as from vigilante "justice" was doubly ironic. While vigilantes usurped the law, local officials looked the other way, and federal authorities maintained they could not punish lynchers or deporters, the IWW miners in Butte, as had those in Arizona, stressed that they had consistently sought to avert disturbances and riots. "We are going to the bottom of this thing," an IWW attorney commented about the lynching of Little, "but in a legal way." From the morning of the lynching until Little's solemnly impressive funeral on August 5

* "3/7/77"—the symbol of Alder Gulch's 1870's generation of vigilantes. Also appended were initials said to signify other intended IWW victims.

(the largest ever held in Butte), Butte remained absolutely peaceful. Instead of retaliating against the vigilantes by taking up arms or accelerating its strike activities, the IWW simply proclaimed Sunday, August 19, as a day of protest. Beseeching other labor organizations to join the IWW protest, Haywood announced his organization's new motto: *"We never forget. Organize and act."* 38

While Haywood called upon his followers to organize and act, other Americans prepared to end once and for all the IWW's menace to industrial peace and to the status quo. Throughout July 1917, as vigilantes hunted Wobblies, Western businessmen, congressmen, and governors insistently hammered upon the theme that only federal action could stamp out the IWW. The Westerners maintained that local legal repression and private vigilantism had proved ineffective in coping with subversion that was interstate in scope and directed from the IWW's Chicago headquarters. Whether in the halls of Congress, statehouses in Montana, Nevada, California, and elsewhere, or simply in letters to the Departments of Labor, Justice, and Interior, Westerners demanded a federal solution to the IWW problem.

By mid-July 1917 these efforts to thwart the IWW had reached a new level of organization and intensity. On July 13, after numerous private meetings, the governors of California, Arizona, Utah, Nevada, Idaho, Colorado, Oregon, and Wyoming adopted a common plan of action to control the Wobblies, which they communicated to President Wilson. The President, in turn, referred the Western governors' representative, George Bell, chairman of the California Commission on Immigration and Housing, to the Secretaries of Labor, Justice, and Interior, and to the Council of National Defense, the last of which heard Bell's plea for federal suppression of the IWW.39 At a July 18 session of the Council of National Defense, Bell presented the Western governors' anti-IWW scheme. Stressing the nationwide extent of IWW subversion, the interstate essence of the Wobby conspiracy, and the dangerous growth of vigilantism, Bell urged Washington officials to act decisively. No riots had yet erupted, he conceded, and no conspiracy had yet struck; yet he demanded preventive action: punish Wobblies for what they planned to do, not for what they actually had done. By a singular form of reasoning, Bell suggested that the federal government should itself break the law before private citizens justly usurped it. In other words, Bell advised that, since the IWW had to be suppressed at all costs, better that responsible public officials accomplish it than irregular private citizens' "committees." In accordance with this sort of logic, Bell and the Western governors recommended that the federal government intern "subversive" Wobblies in concentration camps for the duration of the war, to be held incommunicado without recourse to the law and without publicity; that federal censorship remove all mention of the IWW, whatever the circumstances, from newspapers and magazines; and that after IWW leaders had been interned and censorship established, the federal government compel employers to improve working conditions during the war emergency. If Washington adopted their plan, Bell and his gubernatorial backers promised further coordinated planning behind a federal effort to crush the IWW.[40]

When Washington failed to implement this program promptly, Bell and the governors flooded the White House with telegrams demanding immediate repression of the IWW and full censorship of all news dealing with labor affairs. Throughout July and August the President, the Labor Department, and the Justice Department came under increasing pressures from Western businessmen and politicians. At the end of August the governor of Montana appeared in Washington personally to present the case for suppression of the IWW. Arizona Senator Ashurst warned President Wilson on August 30: "Unless prompt and courageous action looking toward the efficiency and firmness of the Government is taken, no man can foretell what may occur." [41]

Well before the end of August, however, federal officials were indeed planning "prompt and courageous" action against the IWW. Where Bell's proposals for concentration camps and national censorship won little favor in Washington, a lower-key campaign for repression of the IWW initiated in Minnesota received a warm response from Justice Department officials. Like the states to its west, Minnesota had been plagued by IWW threats to its three primary industries: iron mining, lumber, and agriculture. Although its Commission of Public Safety, directed by former Governor John Lind, had largely stifled IWW agitation in the lumber and mining regions, it had failed to curb IWW activities in the widely scattered and sparsely populated agricultural districts. To achieve this last goal,

Lind worked with Hinton Clabaugh, head of the Justice Department's Chicago investigation office, in an effort to obtain evidence proving that the IWW had violated federal wartime statutes. Finally convinced that they had uncovered the necessary evidence, Lind, Clabaugh, and several of their associates met secretly in Chicago on July 26 to plan future action against the IWW. Like other IWW opponents, they would resort to federal power. Unlike Bell and the Western governors, Lind and Clabaugh recommended no illegal or extralegal procedures; indeed, they discovered adequate grounds for repression in the existing legal structure. Lind advised Attorney General Gregory that if the Justice, Labor, and Postal Departments coordinated their actions, the IWW could be destroyed easily. Justice could prosecute Wobblies for violations of wartime statutes; Labor's immigration service could detain and then deport alien IWW's; and the Post Office could deny mailing privileges to the IWW. Lind thus promised to achieve the same results sought by Bell in strict accordance with the letter of the law and supported by legal evidence amassed by the Minnesota Commission of Public Safety and the Federal Bureau of Investigation.[42]

Few public figures of any influence pleaded the IWW's cause in Washington, or sought to enlighten the Justice Department about the motives behind the drive to repress the IWW. Among the handful of dissenters, two stand out: George W. Anderson, United States attorney for Massachusetts, a sensible New England Yankee representing a state relatively untouched by the IWW in 1917; and Burton K. Wheeler, then a young Montana U.S. attorney and aspiring politician, who would later become nationally famous as a progressive senator, vice-presidential candidate of the 1924 Progressive party, and isolationist critic of Franklin Roosevelt's foreign policies. Untroubled by the IWW threat, Anderson warned the Justice Department: "I think the Federal Government should be critically careful not only to keep within the law . . . but to see to it that it is not made an unwilling and perhaps unconscionable partner in one of the lowest and meanest mercenary tricks ever played in any aspect of the class struggle." Responding to popular demands for severe repression of labor agitators, Anderson remarked: "If I were prepared to commit myself to that as a reasonable course in our world contest, I should begin with shooting private detectives." More to the point was Wheeler's dissent. Already the proud possessor of a reputation as a maverick and opponent of Western mine owners, Wheeler throughout the spring and summer of 1917 had been struggling to preserve the spirit of the law and to protect Western workers against violations of their civil liberties. When he learned about the proposals of Bell and the eight governors, Wheeler immediately contacted Attorney General Gregory. "At this time," he wrote, "I consider it proper to call to your attention that the requests [for press censorship] contained in the telegrams to the President are fathered by a desire of the interests, employing labor that may be more or less involved with the general unrest among their employees, to keep the true condition of affairs from the public at large." Wheeler asserted that Butte's miners were not dangerous subversives seeking to betray their country and ruin the war effort; rather, he pointed out, they were workers engaged in a peaceful and orderly struggle to improve their conditions of life. If any group was interfering with the war effort, Wheeler observed, it was the mine owners, who refused to raise wages, improve working conditions, or deal with unions at a time when profits were higher than ever and when inflation had reduced many miners' families to penury. "That portion of the press in Montana which is subsidized and under the control of the large employers of labor has been continuously criticizing all government officials for failure to control the IWW situation . . . whereas in fact," Wheeler concluded, "the situation has consisted merely of an agitation among the laboring classes urging them to better their conditions and this agitation has been done wholly by word of mouth and not by violent means." [43]

Neither sensible suggestions nor reasoned reports about the IWW received much attention in Washington during the hysterical summer of 1917. Too busy battling the Kaiser's forces overseas, President Wilson and his closest advisers could not trouble themselves to probe deeply into the roots of Western labor conflict. Aware that IWW strikes interfered with war production, Wilson found it easy to believe reports which stressed that the IWW had struck the lumber and copper industries not to raise wages or improve working conditions but to obtain German gold and subvert the war effort. Hence the Wilson administration succumbed to the Western businessmen's anti-IWW crusade. In August 1917 the President appointed Federal Judge J. Harry Covington to undertake a special investigation of the IWW that might acquire evidence to be used to prosecute the Wobblies. Almost simultaneously, Assistant Attorney General Fitts assuaged New Mexico Senator Albert Fall's anxieties about the

IWW. "I must say to you," Fitts wrote, "that under the direction of the Attorney General something quite effective is under way with respect to the I.W.W. situation. This is as far as it would be prudent to go at present. . . . I do not think you or any of your western friends will be disappointed if the results which we hope to obtain are achieved." [44]

CHAPTER

16

Decision in Washington,
1917–1918

I n July 1917, Ralph Chaplin, editor of *Solidarity*, warned the IWW's critics: " . . . Unless our enemies are desirous of stirring up something they cannot finish, we advise them to handle the I.W.W. with extreme care." [1] His warning did not fall on deaf ears, for at precisely that moment federal officials were in fact formulating careful plans to eliminate the IWW's threat to war production.

No irate lumber baron, no apoplectic copper mine owner, and no outraged state official had to convince the federal government of the seriousness of the IWW menace to national security. Wartime production statistics indicated that IWW strikes had curtailed lumber and copper production and made it necessary for the federal government to act decisively against the Wobblies. Yet the *form* of that action divided the three federal departments most responsible for coping with the Wobblies. Although the Labor, War, and Justice Departments each had its own exclusive policy for restraining the Wobblies, all three eventually learned to work in harness. By the fall of 1917 they cooperated closely enough to deprive rank-and-file Wobblies of their leaders, to separate the leaders from their followers, and to supply Western employers with an ample and malleable labor force.

It is not surprising that no concrete policy for handling the IWW emerged in Washington in the spring of 1917. Although a firm, even domineering President when necessary, Woodrow Wilson had lost interest in domestic affairs. Preoccupied with waging an international war to make the world safe for democracy, busily involved in forging a diplomacy to preserve the peace after the war ended, he by and large left the home front in the hands of industrious subordinates.

The departments involved in the formulation of wartime labor policy were governed by their own particular requirements. The War Department's interest was clearest: to speed up the production of supplies for its troops in the field. Except for its secretary, Newton Baker, the War Department—staffed largely by professional military men or by amateurs sympathetic to the military—proved most responsive to Western pressures to repress the IWW. The Labor Department's objectives were more complicated: also desirous of breaking production bottlenecks caused by labor discontent, it was not noticeably amenable to the suggestions of Western employers. Unlike War, Labor intended that strikers return to the job only after employers improved working conditions and allowed their employees to join loyal, government-sanctioned AFL unions. The Justice Department's concern with wartime industrial conflict was more ambiguous than that of the War or Labor Department. Having no soldiers to supply, lacking any desire to promote the cause of strikers or of AFL unions, but empowered to investigate violations of federal law, Justice served, at least in theory, as handmaiden to War and Labor. But partly because of the links between United States attorneys and local businessmen, and partly because officials high in the Justice Department had intimate connections with the corporate business world, it often served the needs of American soldiers and Western employers more faithfully than it subscribed to the goals of federal labor mediators.

Even within the three departments, disunity and disagreement prevailed. Secretary of War Baker, for example, was much more objective than his underlings about the IWW menace, which sometimes caused military commanders stationed in the States to disregard War Department orders. A somewhat comparable situation prevailed in the Justice Department, where Attorney General Gregory and his closest advisers restrained those federal attorneys who served Western employers more scrupulously than they served the law. In this case, while Gregory concentrated upon maintaining the letter of the law, his subordinates sometimes stretched, when not actually violating, it. On the surface, Labor seemed to be the most united of the three departments; from Secretary of Labor William B. Wilson on down, department officials promoted the cause of labor and of the AFL. But here, too, some officials proved amenable to employers, and some department agents were more irrationally and bitterly hostile to the IWW than the worst of businessmen and generals.

For a time the moderating influence exerted by Baker, Gregory, and William B. Wilson contained the groups in Washington that sought outright repression of the IWW. When Walter Douglas of Phelps Dodge demanded that federal troops be sent to Arizona to control the IWW, Baker balked at the idea. "This is clearly *not* a case for troops," Baker informed Secretory of the Interior Franklin K. Lane, "but for justice and good sense." A week later, William B. Wilson thanked Baker and Gregory for their broad views of the labor situation and for referring all requests for federal intervention in labor disputes to the Labor Department. The Labor Secretary proposed to handle these disturbances in the customary manner, providing conciliators instead of troops or Justice Department agents. In June 1917 Secretaries Baker and Gregory seemed to agree with their Cabinet colleague's approach.[2]

But the pressures for more forceful federal intervention against the IWW proved irresistible. Walter Douglas and other businessmen were not alone in their call for troops; Bernard Baruch, the federal official most responsible for organizing the industrial war effort, endorsed Douglas' suggestion, and implied that Labor Secretary Wilson and the AFL's leaders also conceded the need for military action against the IWW.[3]

Although it is true that business pressures from the West prompted the formulation of wartime national labor policy, as William Preston asserts in his study of the federal repression of radicals, it is equally true that the federal government had a vital stake in labor relations. Not employers' demands but Washington's own estimate of war requirements determined the extent and nature of federal involvement in labor disputes. Federal intervention against the IWW followed a singular and ultimately repressive course not because of the existence of an anti-IWW conspiracy, nor because of discriminatory action by federal officials.[4] Of course, troops seldom broke AFL strikes; and federal agents did not imprison or intern AFL leaders. There was simply no reason to do so, for the AFL pledged to support the war effort and to respect government-established labor standards. Not so the IWW. Unsure of what Wobblies in fact wanted, aware that the IWW's propaganda called for revolution, and fearful that the IWW, whatever its actual motives, might actually sabotage the war effort, federal officials honestly believed they had only one recourse—to restrain the Wobblies from interfering with national security. Perhaps the best way of doing so was to call in troops as a preventive force.

By 1917 the War Department already had had considerable experience in using soldiers to quell domestic labor disturbances. In 1877 federal troops had repressed strikes, riots, and demonstrations arising from that year's railroad labor conflicts. Fifteen years later federal soldiers went to northern Idaho to break a miners' strike; and in 1894, despite opposition from Illinois Governor John Peter Altgeld, President Cleveland dispatched federal troops to the Chicago area to crush the American Railway Union's Pullman boycott. When the occasion demanded, federal authorities could always justify the employment of troops to preserve the domestic peace. The First World War seemed such an occasion.

Almost as soon as America entered the conflict, and before IWW strikes affected war production, federal troops were assigned to protect railroads and other "public utilities" (initially defined as dams, water works, and gas and electric plants) from enemy espionage. Not entirely by coincidence, the first railroads and utilities so protected were in Montana and Washington State—states farthest removed from the area of German espionage and closest to the scene of IWW activity.[5] Little rationalization was required to broaden Washington's 1917 definition of public utilities, or to define certain other Western industries as vital to the war effort. Legal niceties aside, the government needed immediate solutions to pressing problems. With the military effort on Europe's western front not proceeding as well as desired, copper and lumber production had to be increased; this, in turn, could not wait upon new legislation authorizing military intervention in peaceful labor disputes or upon the validation of such action by constitutional law experts.

To serve American military objectives, not to guarantee employers war-inflated profits, by July 1917 federal troops patrolled the mining regions of Arizona and Montana, the farms of eastern Washington, and the timber districts of western Washington and Oregon. No labor violence had occurred in any of these districts, and no evidence of German espionage or intrigue could be uncovered. Nevertheless, federal officials acted to prevent what. they thought *might* be done by Wobblies active in the West. In other words, in a time of crisis the federal government refused to trust its survival to chance: troops acted as a guarantee that labor disputes would not interrupt production or undermine the war effort.

Although federal troops broke AFL strikes as well as those of the IWW in the course of military intervention, this was never Washington's intention. Yet professional military men frankly did not know how to react to labor disputes. Accustomed to strict discipline among their men and to obedience to their orders, they expected labor unionists and strikers to behave with the regularity and good order exhibited by troops. When workers instead proved unruly and disobedient, when they picketed, protested, and demonstrated, soldiers intervened. In Arizona, for instance, an Army officer, in violation of the state's own laws, forbade picketing, encouraged strikebreaking, and offered troop protection to all scabs. At home among fellow disciplinarians, Army officers found them among Western mine managers and county sheriffs. Ordered by Washington to serve the national interest impartially, military men preferred to work most closely with local businessmen. Consequently, instructions from Washington to observe the law brought no changes in military behavior in Arizona, where soldiers continued to break strikes, to persecute suspected Wobblies, and to assist local authorities in making unlawful searches and seizures.[6]

With Washington two thousand miles away, those on the firing line—soldiers, employers, United States attorneys, and state and local officials—claimed to have knowledge of the real situation, indeed to understand, as Washington apparently could not, the danger the IWW posed to national security. Western attitudes seemed to permeate federal agents in the region, and were used in many districts to rationalize the unsanctioned establishment of martial law, under which alleged Wobblies were apprehended, questioned, and interned by military authorities who removed them from the jurisdiction of federal courts. Although the Justice Department and the Secretary of War disowned responsibility for these tactics, their disclaimers did imprisoned Wobblies scant good.[7]

On one occasion in that troubled summer of 1917, the IWW threatened to retaliate against military harassment. James Rowan, representing Western loggers and harvesters, called for a general strike to begin in Washington State on Monday, August 20, with the walkout to continue until the military released its class-war prisoners. The Army wasted no time in answering Rowan's threat. On Sunday, August 19, federal troops moved into Spokane and raided the local IWW headquarters, where they seized Rowan and twenty-six other Wobblies—all of whom were later interned. Although the IWW then canceled its general strike, the soldiers continued to guard IWW headquarters and to arrest other Wobblies.[8]

With military intervention thus hampering the IWW, strikes in the copper and lumber industries weakened. The IWW was put on the defensive, now devoting as much energy to eluding capture as to waging the class war. Military reports concurred that relative labor peace and quiet had returned to the West.

Despite the restoration of apparent stability, troops remained on duty from 1917 to 1919, and in Butte till 1920. They had proved so effective in preserving the peace that Western governors, United States attorneys, and local employers hated to see them withdrawn. Every Westerner committed to smashing the IWW pleaded with the War Department to maintain some of its soldiers on stateside duty. Even Burton K. Wheeler, no irrational or vindictive foe of the IWW, advised Attorney General Gregory on December 8, 1917: "I am of the opinion that the presence of, say, a company of soldiers, would be the best deterrent upon lawlessness and prevent outbreaks of any kind." [9] But merely assuring labor peace did not in itself eliminate the IWW's influence among Western workers; nor did it ensure that workers would be content. That responsibility fell to the Justice and Labor Departments.

By 1917 Wobblies were familiar problem children to the Justice Department. Since the IWW's creation in 1905, department officials had unsuccessfully sought to establish a basis for federal action against the Wobblies. This became particularly clear in 1912 when President Taft said he believed that firm repression of the IWW would carry California for the Republican ticket and return him to the presidency. Taft's successor, Woodrow Wilson, also ordered an investigation of the Wobblies in 1915, when, in response to urgent pleas from the California Commission on Immigration and Housing, he dispatched a special agent to the West Coast to seek evidence of IWW violations of federal law. Before 1917, however, federal investigators failed to uncover evidence of a kind sufficient to justify criminal prosecution of the Wobblies.

The war crisis presented the Justice Department with the legal basis upon which to prosecute the IWW. A presidential proclamation of April 6 authorized the detention of enemy aliens, and federal officials believed that a considerable number of IWW leaders fit that category. Congressional legislation made interference with conscription and with war-related industrial production a statutory crime. Rumors circulated in the nation's capital that German agents financed the IWW—ample grounds for prosecution even under pre-war statutes. By July 11, 1917, Attorney General Gregory, himself now a believer in the allegations that German gold was subsidizing the IWW's labor offensive, decided to amass the evidence necessary to prosecute the Wobblies.[10]

For several days Justice Department officials carefully weighed their options, determining precisely what evidence United States attorneys and special agents should accumulate against the Wobblies. Finally, on July 16 Assistant Attorney General Charles Warren, the well-known historian of the Supreme Court, prepared a circular for distribution to all United States attorneys, which Gregory then moderated in tone in order to shield the department from public criticism. On the following day the department mailed Warren's circular to all its attorneys and special agents. In this circular the department recommended that an extraordinary effort be undertaken to ascertain the future plans of all Wobblies, as well as the names, descriptions, and history of the IWW's leaders, the sources of its income, the nature of its expenses, copies of all IWW publications, and any data that might possibly incriminate the Wobblies. The circular also suggested that alien Germans belonging to the IWW and participating in unlawful acts be promptly apprehended, so that the department could obtain warrants for their detention under the President's April proclamation. To help the attorneys and agents get the evidence Washington desired, the circular directed their attention to Section 3 of Titles I and IV of the Espionage Act of June 15, 1917. It then concluded with a fair-minded plea to federal officials that they exert their utmost influence to discourage oppressive and illegal actions against the IWW.[11]

An intensive nationwide investigation of the IWW failed to disclose German gold in Wobbly pockets or to provide evidence that either the IWW as an organization or its members individually had violated either the 1917 conscription or espionage acts. "So far as this Department has been able to discover, after the most careful and painstaking investigation," William C. Fitts informed the United States attorney for Oregon on July 28, "the I.W.W. organization is a matter for the States themselves to control under such laws as they deem proper to enact and to enforce."[12] Yet in closing his letter, Fitts in fact held out the glimmer of hope for future federal action against the IWW.

The summer of 1917 saw the optimistic hope for revolution that had exhilarated Wobblies at Chicago headquarters during the first part of the year turn to fear and foreboding. Looking out of the IWW office onto West Madison Street that July, Chaplin, Haywood, and other officer workers watched detectives daily change guard. Whether going to a restaurant for a snack or walking home after a day at the office, Chaplin and Haywood were constantly trailed by supposedly unobtrusive secret agents. Early in August IWW headquarters learned of a Post Office Department ruling that declared the organization's Italian- and Hungarian-language newspapers, for unspecified reasons, unmailable. Only a month before, Haywood had learned that President Wilson had appointed Judge J. Harry Covington to initiate a special investigation of the IWW. Fearing the worst, yet unwilling to show it, the Wobblies managed to put up a brave façade. After a July break-in at IWW headquarters, for instance, Haywood and Chaplin visited Hinton Clabaugh at the

Justice Department's Chicago office of the Bureau of Investigation to offer him any information or papers he might desire concerning the IWW. Haywood made the same offer to Judge Covington. Neither responded to these overtures, however, and as August drew to a close the officials at Chicago IWW headquarters continued to pursue their usual business—keenly aware of imminent danger.[13]

Yet not even the most astute Wobbly realized the extent of the danger about to befall the IWW. Nor did they have to wait long to discover it. Less than a month after the Justice Department found no incriminating evidence against the IWW, the federal government satisfied the fondest wishes of Western employers and public officials. Without informing any Western governors of a change in Justice Department policy toward the IWW, Attorney General Gregory notified President Wilson on August 21, 1917, that his department, acting through the usual channels, planned to strike against the IWW. Only three days later, the Justice Department's investigators discovered what had eluded them since the war began: "evidence" that the Wobblies' objective was to cripple the national war effort. Still deceiving Western officials about its intentions, by August 30 the Justice Department had formulated its final response to the IWW threat.[14] On the morning of September 5, 1917, Justice Department agents and local police officers in Chicago, in Fresno, in Seattle, in Spokane, indeed in every city where the IWW had an office and where influential Wobblies congregated, invaded local IWW headquarters and the homes of Wobbly officials. Operating under perhaps the broadest search warrants ever issued by the American judiciary, federal agents seized everything they could find: minute books, correspondence, typewriters, desks, rubber bands, paper clips, and (in Chicago) even Ralph Chaplin's love letters. From Chicago headquarters alone the federal authorities confiscated over five tons of material. Weeks after the raids had occurred, IWW officials were still unable to carry on ordinary organization business because they lacked the equipment with which to handle bookkeeping and correspondence.

"The expected has happened," Haywood reported two days later, adding: "The situation . . . is not serious yet. . . . No one is under arrest at the present time and we expect to have the office open for our usual transactions of business very soon." Knowing full well that the Justice Department had failed to locate German gold or IWW-associated espionage in June or July, Haywood and other

Wobblies believed that their organization's papers, then being avidly scanned by federal agents and attorneys, would serve only to establish more fully the IWW's innocence. Maintaining its customary cheerful front, *Solidarity* prophesied: "The books of the General Office will prove beyond a shadow of a doubt, that the foolish and vicious charge of 'German gold' is a huge and malicious slander. After the investigation it will no longer be possible for the prostituted press to continue spreading this misleading and venomous lie broadcast over the nation." [15]

Unfortunately, Haywood and *Solidarity*'s editors were indulging in wishful thinking. On the very day that Haywood labeled the situation less than grave, the United States attorney for Philadelphia, writing to Gregory about what his agents had confiscated from local Wobbly offices, noted: ". . . our purpose being, as I understand it, very largely to put the I.W.W. out of business." [16]

Which is precisely what the Justice Department intended. Federal investigators had a field day sorting through IWW papers. For thirteen years the Wobblies had been publishing and distributing radical, sometimes revolutionary, literature; its officers corresponded luridly with each other about sab-cats, firebombs, and emery dust in machines; anti-war and anti-government tirades filled the organization's newspapers, pamphlets, and correspondence. Like the Bible, the IWW's basic gospels provided ample support for almost any position one might wish to adopt; they preached violence and nonviolence, sabotage destructive and constructive, anti-patriotism and patriotism, war and peace. Not overly concerned about when the items might have been written or about their complete context, the Justice Department could prove through the Wobblies' own words that: (1) they interfered with eleven different congressional acts and presidential proclamations involving the war effort; (2) their strikes constituted a criminal conspiracy to interfere with the constitutional rights of employers executing government contracts; (3) they influenced other Wobblies to refuse to register for conscription and others to desert the armed forces; (4) they conspired to cause insubordination in the armed forces; and (5) they conspired to defraud certain employers. The Justice Department easily succeeded in persuading a Chicago federal grand jury to indict 166 IWW members on the five above counts, and also for conspiring with Frank Little (a dead man) and "diverse other persons" (unknown, thus unnamed) to violate federal law. Other federal grand juries returned similar indictments in

Fresno, Sacramento, Wichita, and Omaha. By prosecuting the IWW's national leaders as well as its primary regional officials, the Justice Department obviously intended to put the IWW out of business.[17]

Curiously enough, the indicted Wobblies did not flee into exile, nor did they go into hiding. No secret cells were established, no conspiratorial plans were laid. Instead, on September 29, only a day after the Chicago grand jury handed down its indictments, IWW attorney George Vanderveer and General Secretary-Treasurer Haywood advised all indicted Wobblies to surrender themselves for arrest. Even Vincent St. John and Ben Williams, both of whom had left the organization before America went to war, turned themselves in. In a California construction camp one Wobbly did not discover until December that he was among the 166 indicted leaders. Learning the news from an IWW publication, he immediately notified the Justice Department: "Have a U.S. marshal call and I will be here as I have committed no crime and I do not care to be a fugitive."[18]

Only an overwhelming belief in their own innocence and an unquestioning faith that the laws they denigrated would protect them could explain the behavior of IWW leaders in September 1917. Perhaps they felt that a fair public trial proving the IWW's innocence would end forever the threat of legal repression and lend the IWW respectability as a labor organization. Perhaps, as some historians have suggested, they had an irresistible desire for martyrdom, or a masochistic streak in their personalities. The available evidence does lead one to believe that, IWW propaganda aside, most Wobblies naively trusted to the fundamental decency of their fellow Americans and the justness of legal due process. They had previously won courtroom victories in Boise, Salem, Duluth, and Everett. Why not an even greater legal triumph now? Whatever their individual reasons, Haywood, his associates, and their followers meekly surrendered to federal authorities in order to await their day in court.

What Ralph Chaplin observed as the IWW prisoners left the federal building in Chicago before being transported to Cook County Jail should have served as a precursor of the future and as a warning about the course a wartime trial of labor radicals would take. Across the street from the federal building a cheap North Clark Street movie theater's marquee proclaimed: "Special Feature —The Menace of the I.W.W.," and it announced in big, bright red letters, "The Red Viper."[19] The marquee simply reflected what the nation's press, politicians, and many of its citizens had already established in their own minds: that the IWW was guilty not of dissent in wartime or of revolutionary propaganda-making, but of crime and treason.

The Justice Department's action against the IWW flowed from a split departmental personality. On the one hand, locating no German gold in IWW coffers and no concrete proof of IWW sabotage, local attorneys manufactured it, continuously supplying Washington with unsubstantiated evidence. After the Bolshevik Revolution in October–November 1917, West Coast Justice Department officials, in league with a crackpot colonel in military intelligence, even linked the IWW to Kerensky's overthrow in Russia. Rebuffed in their attempts to imprison Wobblies on federal charges, local officials suggested that alien Wobblies be interned and deported solely on the basis of their IWW membership. On the other hand, Washington officials scrupulously sought to observe due process and to provide Wobblies with the justice that Haywood naively expected as his due. When Mark Matthews, minister of Seattle's First Presbyterian Church, suggested a dictatorship for America and execution for the Wobblies, Gregory ruefully responded: "This is still a land of laws and it is my business to enforce the law and not to violate it. . . . Really, my dear doctor, I might find some difficulty in choosing between the rule of the Hohenzollerns and a rule by you as a dictator enforcing the ideas expressed in your letter." To pleas for the detention and deportation of alien Wobblies, Gregory endorsed the policy of Louis Post and William B. Wilson of the Labor Department, who maintained that aliens should not be detained solely on the basis of organizational affiliations, but should be judged by their individual actions.[20]

But even in Washington, justice was to be a rare commodity for the IWW. The men who insisted that America remained "a land of laws" and who were charged with enforcing those laws considered Wobblies to be degenerate and, in fact, beyond the pale of the law. William Fitts, on loan to the Justice Department from a Wall Street law office, was notorious for his anti-IWW prejudices. Convinced at first that Germany subsidized the IWW (though he later conceded this to be false), Fitts considered all the IWW's activities to be nefarious. He cooperated in 1918 with Gompers and with Ralph Easley, former National Civic Federation leader, to mount a nationwide propaganda campaign among organized workers to enlighten them about the IWW's un-American, immoral, and illegitimate be-

409

havior. Nine months after the Justice Department began to repress the IWW firmly, Fitts thought further suppression in order. Writing to a former Washington State congressman, he commented: ". . . I think that it is measurably time that the [Wobblies] have had the fear of the law instilled in them. . . . Fear is the only force that will keep the wretches in order." [21]

Had putting the IWW out of business and "keeping the wretches in order" been the only aim of federal authorities in 1917, their job would have been manageable. It took no great skill to imprison organization leaders, close down IWW presses, deny use of the mail to Wobblies, detain and deport aliens, or keep radical labor under control. That, however, was not Washington's essential objective. Repression had ultimately been resorted to not to smash the IWW—though that may have been a goal desired by many, including Gompers and the AFL—but to break the bottlenecks in the production of spruce and copper. This, however, the indictment of IWW leaders failed to do. Suppression of an organization could not transform discontented workers into efficient laborers. While military and legal repression of the IWW stifled the outward manifestations of labor discontent, it failed to overcome deep-seated working-class frustration and basic dissatisfaction with wages and working conditions. In order to end labor discontent in the West, the federal government ultimately turned to the Labor Department, the American Federation of Labor, and a special presidential mediation commission.

From the start of the wartime labor troubles, the Labor Department had approached the IWW problem with caution and common sense. Though as hostile to IWW influence and gains as any other federal agency, Labor personnel sensibly took the view that discontent among the workers arose from economic and social exploitation—and not from Wobbly agitation. The labor revolt in the West as seen by the Labor Department, *Survey* magazine reported in August 1917, "is an expression primarily of social unrest, of revolt at low wages and hard conditions in industry and impatience with the slow evolution of economic democracy through the organized labor movement." [22]

Cooperating closely with Gompers and the leadership of the AFL, Secretary of Labor Wilson and his colleagues sought to reach the roots of labor discontent. On August 10, 1917, Gompers stated the problem bluntly for President Wilson: either the government and Western employers would bargain with representatives of the bona fide organized, constructive labor movement, or they would have to confront the "so-called" IWW. If lumbermen and mine operators negotiated with the AFL, Gompers and the Labor Department promised that the IWW would disappear.[23]

Throughout July 1917 the Labor Department unsuccessfully attempted to bring together Western lumbermen and AFL officials. Secretary of War Baker tried to edge the AFL into the lumber industry, suggesting to Secretary Wilson on August 1, 1917: "Would it not be a wise thing to send able organizers representing the American Federation to this section [Northwest] and let them actually organize these men under the banner of the Federation so that we will have responsible agencies to deal with?" To which Wilson could only reply by noting the lumbermen's unyielding refusal to negotiate, concluding: "I know of nothing further that we can do in this matter, as everything that this Department can do is being done to secure an adjustment." [24]

The Labor Department, however, had influential allies. The Washington State Council of National Defense shared its assessment of the IWW problem. Shaped largely by reformer Carleton Parker, Council labor policies aimed at separating rank-and-file lumber workers from their IWW leaders. This could be done, the Council's members reasoned, by establishing the eight-hour day and greater job security in the lumber industry. When employers refused to go along with its recommendations, the Council urged President Wilson to pressure lumbermen in the interest of patriotism to offer an equitable settlement to their employees.[25]

Although the President remained aloof from domestic labor conflict, the Council of National Defense on August 10 authorized Secretaries Baker and Wilson to urge lumbermen to do their nation a patriotic service by operating their industry at peak efficiency, a condition that could only be reached by bargaining with legitimate (read: AFL) labor unions and by granting employees the eight-hour day. But the lumbermen were unable to conceive of the eight-hour day as a patriotic obligation, particularly when the Southern lumber industry continued to operate on a longer workday. Destroy the IWW, lumbermen countered, and spruce production would reach, indeed surpass, normal levels.[26]

Yet when the IWW leaders were indicted and imprisoned, spruce production still failed to satisfy wartime needs. By late September 1917, desperate federal authorities considered employing soldiers to fell trees, a policy long favored by some military men. Only the Labor Department opposed this new idea; it continued to point out that if working conditions and industrial relations improved in the lumber industry, spruce production would become more than adequate.[27]

By October, however, the lumber production problem was passing out of the hands of the Labor Department and into those of the military. As early as May 1917 General John "Black Jack" Pershing, sharing the lumbermen's assumption that Western labor discontent had been fomented by the Kaiser's agents within the IWW, had delegated a junior officer to survey labor conditions in the spruce industry. That officer, Lieutenant Colonel Brice P. Disque, was to play a singular role in the fall of 1917 and the following spring in winning the eight-hour day for lumber workers. Not a career officer, Disque at first acted like a typical Progressive-era social reformer, one perceptibly influenced by Carleton Parker and Samuel Gompers. The colonel proved so satisfactory to Gompers that the AFL president informed his West Coast associates that Disque would be sympathetic to organizing mill and forest workers into AFL affiliates.[28] On October 16, when Gompers wrote this, he had good reason for his optimism.

Before departing for the West Coast to meet with lumbermen, Disque had obtained most of his knowledge about labor affairs from Parker, Gompers, Walter Lippmann, and Felix Frankfurter. These influential reformers reinforced the colonel's own belief that the IWW could best be curbed by improving working conditions in the lumber industry. Playing his military role, however, Disque schemed to gain approval in Washington for the creation of a special Army division composed primarily of former lumberjacks, who would serve in the Western woods instead of on the Western front. Disque eventually obtained sanction from the Department of Labor and from Gompers himself for what would in time become the Army's spruce production division: soldiers who wore civilian clothes and who did civilian labor at prevailing civilian wages (minus their regular Army pay) but who nevertheless remained under military discipline.[29]

Once on the West Coast among the lumbermen whom he was supposed to cajole into granting improved working conditions, Disque underwent a slight but significant transformation. Dealing on a day-to-day basis with employers, Disque discovered that the lumber barons could be charming hosts. More and more he came to share employers' prejudices against organized labor, AFL as well as IWW. Away from Gompers' influence, Disque lost interest in assisting the AFL to organize the lumber industry in order to preserve labor peace and increase production. As a result of this change in his attitude, the labor situation in the Northwest remained tense and unsatisfactory.[30]

Like the IWW, the AFL, the Labor Department, and the War Department before him, it appeared Disque had failed to win the eight-hour day or restore labor tranquillity. But he had succeeded, unlike the others, in allaying the fears of lumbermen, who distrusted most federal officials, whom they accused of being reformers and radicals. The same employers who steadfastly protested Washington's establishment of an eight-hour day consented to allow the colonel leeway to resolve all labor issues, including the eight-hour day.[31]

With this newly acquired authority, Disque accomplished the goal which had eluded every other government official who had entered what one historian has since labeled the "graveyard of reputations." At the end of February 1918 Disque won the lumbermen's consent to establish an industry-wide eight-hour day, a victory heartily applauded by President Wilson. The colonel achieved his particular triumph because he was more attuned to the lumbermen's mentality and personality than the "academics," "schoolteachers," and "do-gooders" regularly deplored by the employers.[32]

Disque also proved his business acumen by granting lumbermen something substantial in return for their concession of the eight-hour day and improved working conditions. When Disque finished rationalizing lumber industry labor practices, neither the AFL nor the IWW theatened employers' economic power. In recompense for giving their employees the eight-hour day, uniform wages, and decent bed and board, employers obtained a more docile labor force. Disque closed the woods to labor organizers and to trade-union members by organizing a company union—the Loyal Legion of Loggers and Lumbermen (or, as it was called, the 4L's)—with practically compulsory membership and a no-strike policy. Meanwhile, his junior

413

officers and the troops in his spruce production division acted as
recruiters for the 4L's and as military police empowered to harry
Wobblies and AFL organizers out of the forests.[33]

What originated in wartime as an emergency program formulated
by the Labor Department and the social reformers within its orbit
to improve conditions in the lumber industry and to supplant the IWW
with the AFL became, in the hands of an Army officer, a plain,
old-fashioned union-busting arrangement. Disque taught employers
a valuable lesson some had been unable to learn by themselves:
that granting workers the shadow of industrial democracy without
the substance kept them contented and productive.[34] Tutored by a
soldier, lumbermen learned how to tame the Wobblies; never again,
after 1918, would the IWW represent a substantial threat to the
lumber industry. What Disque began and employers imitated, postwar technological changes would finish, finally converting West
Coast Wobblies into an aging and vanishing breed.

Forced in the end to defer to the military in coping with the
IWW in the Northwest, the Labor Department and its reform allies
intended to do better in the Southwest. Since the eruption of the
copper strikes in Arizona, the Labor Department had fought to root
the IWW out of the region by winning higher wages and union
(AFL) recognition for the copper miners. Mine operators, of course,
were no more amenable than lumbermen to federal labor conciliation.
To every Labor Department attempt to meliorate the copper industry's labor strife, employers asserted that "we must have a free
hand in the employment of our men and authority in the direction
of work." [35]

A free hand for management had already brought deportations
in Jerome and Bisbee, the rude repression of AFL as well as IWW
affiliates, and the failure of copper mines to produce at peak levels.
Waging a war abroad to defeat military autocracy, President Wilson
refused to allow mine owners to rape democracy at home. Committed
to improving working conditions and to protecting the AFL against
repression, the Labor Department necessarily had to challenge the
policies implemented by Arizona mine owners. Desperately in need

of copper for the war effort, Baruch and his War Industries Board clearly could not allow employer obstinacy to interfere with production.

Gompers planned to rescue federal officials from their predicament. He devised a scheme which, so he thought, would spread industrial democracy domestically and simultaneously increase copper production. On August 22, responding to a query from Newton Baker, Gompers suggested that the Council of National Defense eliminate the IWW by providing new federally sanctioned labor agencies to study and adjust industrial disputes. At the end of the month the Council of National Defense, under intense pressure from Gompers, Baker, and President Wilson, resolved to appoint a special commission to investigate the deportation of workers from their homes. In fact, this commission would seek to reform labor-management relations and to promote AFL-type unionism.[36]

As the first hints of this new proposal reached the West, governors and businessmen protested its implementation. Fearful that an impartial investigation of Western labor conditions would establish the justice of labor's demands and place state officials and employers in an unfavorable light, Western interests warned Washington once again that the publicity engendered by a federal commission would only benefit the IWW and worsen the problems that such a federal survey was intended to ameliorate.[37]

By now inured to Western protests, Labor Secretary Wilson pursued Gompers' proposal to create a presidential commission that would study the wartime labor situation. What ostensibly began as an investigation of illegal deportations became under Secretary Wilson's astute management an opportunity to mediate the substantive issues causing labor discontent in the West, particularly in industries threatened by the IWW. To cloak the true purpose of the commission, which was primarily to curb the Wobblies, Secretary Wilson suggested that it also investigate disputes not related to the IWW. Moving ahead rapidly on his own, on August 31 the Labor Secretary presented President Wilson with recommended appointees to a five-man commission. He suggested two businessmen: J. L. Spangler, a Pennsylvania-Dutch coal-mine operator with a reputation for fair dealing with the United Mine Workers, and Verner Z. Reed, a Colorado entrepreneur of unusually liberal and catholic leanings (he was also a liberal Catholic); two trade unionists: John H. Walker, a former United Mine Workers' official, then president of the Illinois

Federation of Labor and a moderate socialist, and E. P. Marsh, a more conservative unionist and president of the Washington State Federation of Labor; Secretary Wilson himself would be the fifth commission member, and he would serve as chairman. More important than any of the commission members, however, was the man Wilson selected as his secretary: Felix Frankfurter.[38]

Then a young Harvard Law School professor serving his first tour of duty in Washington as a junior Labor Department official, Frankfurter lost no time in establishing his own pre-eminence among the commission appointees. Just as thirty years later he would lecture his colleagues on the Supreme Court and lesser lawyers about the subtleties of the American Constitution and the Supreme's Court role in interpreting it, in October 1917 Frankfurter taught President Wilson's mediators, including the Secretary of Labor, the refinements of industrial conciliation and the means of destroying the IWW. He defined the mediation commission's purposes, pressured Western employers into accepting government-mandated settlement terms, and stood prepared to crush any opposition to his wartime labor program.

Frankfurter accepted the Gompers–William B. Wilson–Newton Baker assessment of wartime industrial conflicts involving the IWW. Like them, he believed that labor conflict arose from tangible grievances, not from German or IWW intrigues; like others, he, too, maintained that the IWW must be curbed. Consequently, Frankfurter urged the five presidential mediators to undertake an in-depth investigation of Arizona copper miners' grievances, to establish conciliation machinery to abolish the actual grievances, to impress upon employers their responsibility to compromise with employees in the interest of national security, and to devote particular attention to convincing anti-war workers that their labor could play an essential part not only in winning the war and spreading democracy abroad but also in establishing industrial justice at home.[39]

Officially appointed by the President on September 19, 1917, the mediation commission operated on the basis of Frankfurter's guidelines. Because it intended to eliminate IWW spokesmen as partners in any ensuing labor agreements with the mine owners, AFL and IUMMSW affiliates in Arizona readily accepted commission recommendations. At the commission's first formal hearing in Arizona on October 6, its labor members explained precisely which strikers and unions they proposed to aid. In the words of the ex-coal miner John Walker: "The organization that would be considered a legitimate organization is the one that accepts the present status and tries to accept that in the right way. The organization that is willing to do that is the place we are going to help the workingmen . . ." To which Secretary Wilson added: "It would be folly to deal with any organization that does not believe in negotiating collectively or otherwise." [40]

Although the President's mediators declared Wobblies to be illegitimate and un-American trade-unionists, employers remained as recalcitrant as ever about bargaining with workers. Even though the commission now offered them the opportunity to settle disputes with government-sanctioned AFL unions, operators still declined to negotiate with labor.

Frankfurter, however, came to his elders' rescue. The young attorney's influential contacts proved remarkable in their variety and power. Not only did he have entry to the world of labor and social reform, but his connections extended to Wall Street financiers, War Department bureaucrats, foreign diplomats, and Bernard Baruch, director of the war production effort. When Arizona's mine managers balked at commission proposals, Frankfurter used his personal influence to the fullest extent. Writing to a Wall Street friend, Sam Lewisohn, an owner of considerable mining property in Arizona, Frankfurter urged Lewisohn to instruct his mine managers to abide by commission recommendations concerning the labor question. To his friends in the British Embassy, Frankfurter suggested pressure on Scottish capitalists with copper-mine interests in America to compromise on the labor issue. He resorted to acquaintances in the Justice and War departments for authority to threaten recalcitrant mine operators and owners with the seizure of their properties. All this he did, as he informed Lewisohn, "entirely on my own personal responsibility without either authority or knowledge of the Commission." [41]

As a result of Frankfurter's private initiatives, on October 20 the commission succeeded in settling the labor dispute in the Globe-Miami district; subsequently it arranged similar settlements for the Clifton-Morenci and the Warren districts. All three settlements disposed of the IWW by establishing the principle that industrial conflict must be suspended for the duration of the war and that copper production must assume priority over workers' wages or employers' profits. Employers consented to deal with miners' grievance committees elected secretly, and to bargain with union representatives when local grievance procedures failed to settle disputes. Employers nevertheless retained open-shop conditions and won federal support for their wage policies which previously had been endorsed by the War Industries Board. Both parties to the commission's settlement consented to binding arbitration by Department of Labor agents if labor grievances could not now be adjusted locally. A simple procedure eliminated the Wobblies from the terms of the agreement: any employee who since the copper strike had uttered comments disloyal to the United States or who belonged to an organization that refused to recognize contractual obligations (meaning the IWW) was declared ineligible for re-employment in the mines. IWW members thus either had to resign from their organization or had to seek employment elsewhere.[42]

This agreement should have occasioned considerable rejoicing among mine owners and managers, for it terminated the IWW menace to copper production, supplied the mines with a government-certified labor force, and maintained wages at the current level— a level which had not risen as rapidly as wartime prices. Yet operators balked at accepting even this settlement. Too long free to do as they had pleased, they sought to treat federal officials as cavalierly as they handled trade unionists. Frankfurter once again had to resort to his Wall Street and British Embassy contacts for help. Only pressure from their out-of-state superiors—men cajoled and charmed by Frankfurter—caused Arizona's resident mine managers to cooperate with the federal government.[43]

But employer cooperation proved more apparent than real. Labor Department mediators promptly discovered that an immense number of miners had been designated either as disloyal or as Wobblies, which in either event rendered them ineligible for re-employment. In addition, wherever possible the mine operators purged AFL members as well as Wobblies, rejected out of hand consideration of their employees' grievances, subverted the elected grievance committees, and refused to adjust wages to the cost of living.[44]

In response to this continued employer autocracy, the IWW re-emerged in Arizona. If AFL membership and federally sanctioned grievance procedures failed to protect miners from exploitation, why not join the IWW? Perhaps the Wobblies had been correct: perhaps the AFL was indeed a fraud, its leaders serving as the lieutenants of capitalism and representing a federal government that acted as the "slugging agency of the capitalists." After all, federal troops patrolled Arizona mine districts, federal jails held imprisoned labor leaders, and federal mediators had arranged a strike settlement in Arizona that returned workers to the mines without any material improvement in wages or working conditions.

Believing that its commission had eliminated the IWW from Arizona in October–November 1917, early the next year the federal government suddenly found itself face to face with another Wobbly labor offensive. Reporting on the Arizona labor situation in March 1918, Labor Department conciliator Hywel Davies sensed imminent danger. Although he discovered that employers discriminated against IUMMSW members, subverted the existing grievance machinery, and rejected necessary wage increases, Davies found no fault with employers' continued anti-labor position; instead, he indicted Wobbly agitators for the rising labor discontent. Davies, in fact, warned the Labor Department that a spirit of disloyalty and anarchy was festering in Arizona, awaiting only the proper psychological moment to erupt. "The industrial mass is not disloyal," he reported, "but idleness furnishes the . . . opportunity for the anarchist to develop his deviltry." Hence, a Labor Department official sent to Arizona to mediate and to conciliate advised his Washington superiors to allow the Justice Department to deport alien Wobblies and to prosecute "disloyal" citizens. After the IWW had been totally suppressed, Davies suggested, then the Labor Department together with Gompers could flood Arizona with AFL organizers and Labor Department agents, who would recruit workers into loyal trade unions that were satisfactory to employers. Davies, in other words, recommended that the AFL and the Labor Department unite to promote a sort of loyal legion of miners and operators. He suggested a whole new breed of labor organizers for Arizona, ". . . strong men; men that can tactfully emphasize the loyalty and just claims of the men to the managers— men free from local prejudice or past contributors to local hate." [45] So intense was federal fear of the IWW that Labor Department officials and national AFL leaders actually considered subverting accredited AFL affiliates (the IUMMSW) in order to eliminate the *possible* danger of a Wobbly insurrection. *

---

* Davies even suggested that the IUMMSW and the Arizona Federation of Labor—the former of which he suspected of disloyalty—be entirely bypassed.

Events in Butte demonstrated abundantly that federal labor policies were governed as much by anxiety about the IWW as by an objective interest in improving working conditions and in establishing industrial justice. Montana's labor problems differed in no essential respect from Arizona's: in Butte, too, an IWW-associated strike had crippled copper production and triggered the vigilantism and military intervention that culminated in the lynching of Frank Little. Thus the factors that had brought Frankfurter and his commission associates to Arizona's copper districts should have led them to Butte, where the Metal Mine Workers' Union and Congresswoman Jeannette Rankin pleaded for a mediation commission investigation of labor conditions. But the Butte strike had been broken by the time the mediation commission began its operation. Copper production in Montana was fast returning to normal, and a Labor Department conciliator reported on November 20, 1917: ". . . There is not much left of the Butte Metal Miners' Union . . ." By December, Frankfurter learned from Eugene Meyer of the War Industries Board that Butte's operating capacity seemed satisfactory. Even Charles Moyer offered his "humble opinion" that the commission should not visit Butte, for such a step would only publicize the IWW and hence extend its life. Supporting the IUMMSW president, Gompers advised Labor Secretary Wilson on December 13 that ". . . it seems to me that the Commission might well omit Butte." Unable to interest the federal government in an investigation of labor conditions once production had returned to normal, the Metal Mine Workers' Union on December 20, 1917, officially ended its walkout.[46]

The IWW thus proved an excellent barometer of federal interest in Western working conditions. When IWW membership flourished and IWW strikes crippled full production, federal concern with decent working conditions and industrial justice rose sharply. When IWW membership declined and its ability to strike collapsed, federal interest in decent treatment for workers fell precipitously.

It was to be expected, then, that when the IWW reawakened in Butte in the spring of 1918, federal concern about the city's working conditions also came to life. Immediately upon news that a reorganized

Metal Mine Workers' Independent Union, dominated by Wobblies and their fellow travelers, in June 1918 had petitioned the National War Labor Board for a hearing on working and union conditions in Butte, Frankfurter, the Labor Department, and Hywel Davies went to work. At Frankfurter's suggestion, Davies traveled to Montana. Before arriving in Butte, he wired Frankfurter: "The imperative need of the hour is action by the A. F. of L. President Gompers understands the whole trouble." [47] Once in Montana, Davies discovered conditions much as he had just left them in Arizona. Employer autocracy and the IUMMSW's debilitated condition had opened the breach for an IWW resurgence. Montana's Wobblies, according to Davies, also spread disloyalty and anarchy, causing the conciliator to offer his customary prescription for curing the IWW disease: avoid all contacts with "radical" elements in the labor movement; go over the heads of local labor leaders; work closely with Gompers; and defer to the sensibilities of company officials. He boiled the Butte problem down to a single question: "*Shall the legitimate or the illegitimate labor unions dominate?*" His preferences were clear. "An outlaw organization, camouflaging under another name [i.e., the IWW in Butte], can be eliminated," Davies prescribed, "only when the opportunity for a more decent relationship is provided, and it is in this particular case the joint duty of the Employers to join hands with the A. F. of L." He again urged Frankfurter to obtain Gompers' consent to put into effect a strategy that would bypass the IUMMSW as well as the IWW. "To continue to sleep at the switch is to court disaster," Davies warned. "The miners must be provided with an A. F. of L. affiliation, but the A. F. of L. must conduct a campaign of education in legitimate trade unionism." [48]

Working with Gompers, accommodating Butte's mine owners, and maintaining federal troops on duty in Montana enabled federal authorities to hold the IWW on a tight rein. Wherever and whenever the IWW threatened war production in 1917 and 1918, the federal government reacted with a combination of military repression, judicial prosecution, and industrial conciliation.

By the end of 1917 rank-and-file Wobblies as well as their leaders were in an unenviable predicament. Remaining loyal to their organization and its objectives, they courted deportation or arrest. Walking out on strike, even without a commitment to revolutionary rhetoric or unmotivated by opposition to the war effort, they found themselves declared illegitimate trade unionists and thus ineligible for re-employment under improved working conditions. Surrendering their red cards and enrolling in the AFL, rank-and-file Wobblies learned that Federation membership conferred few tangible benefits and weak federal guardianship, except when IWW activities increased. Knowing neither which way to go nor precisely what to do, Wobblies no longer could turn to experienced leaders for guidance. By December 1917 every first-line IWW leader was behind bars and restricted, by Post Office Department regulations and Justice Department surveillance, from communication with members on the outside.

No wonder at the beginning of 1918 the IWW faced extinction. Wobblies had always expected to meet resistance from employers and from the AFL; they had learned to live with it, and, in the end, to survive it. A full-scale federal anti-IWW crusade was something else, especially when it offered carrots as it struck with sticks. Even the Supreme Court entered the struggle: in a case brought by a West Virginia coal company against the United Mine Workers, *Hitchman Coal Company v. Mitchell* (1917), the Court upheld yellow-dog contracts and ruled that labor organizers who approached miners working under such contracts were guilty of encouraging a breach of contract. Federal labor policy, as described in 1918 by Robert Bruere, could only cause a typical Wobbly to lose his bearings. "Here were three branches of the Federal Government," Bruere wrote in February, "pursuing three radically divergent and hopelessly conflicting policies towards the wage-workers at the very moment when the nation was making a patriotic appeal to the workers to get out a maximum production of copper. The United States Department of Justice was arresting them, the President's Mediation Commission was telling them that they must organize into unions, and the United States Supreme Court was announcing that if they attempted to organize under certain conditions they would be guilty of contempt of court." [49]

CHAPTER

17

Courtroom Charades,
1918–1919

O N April 1, 1918, in an impressive white marble federal courthouse in Chicago, Judge Kenesaw Mountain Landis, who would later become famous in the aftermath of the 1919 Black Sox scandal as baseball's first commissioner, ascended the bench to inaugurate the initial wartime trial of the Wobblies. In the courtroom that day was a young reporter and radical who had just returned from Russia, where he had witnessed the Bolshevik Revolution and written *Ten Days That Shook the World,* the classic journalistic account of that shattering event. In 1918 John Reed was no stranger to American courtrooms, to class conflict, or to the IWW. Since his participation in the 1913 Paterson strike shortly after his graduation from Harvard College, Reed had grown increasingly radical, until he crowned his intellectual journey to the left with firsthand reports of the Bolshevik Revolution and with membership in the newly established American Communist party (1919). In Chicago to report the IWW trial for left-wing American publications, Reed hoped to do as well by the Wobblies as he had done by the Bolsheviks.

Reed's dispatches from Chicago transformed the impending courtroom struggle into an American folk myth. He described Judge Landis thus: "Small on the huge bench sits a wasted man with untidy white hair, an emaciated face in which two burning eyes are set like jewels, parchment-like skin split by a crack for a mouth;

the face of Andrew Jackson three years dead." Turning to the defendants, Reed wrote: "I doubt if ever in history there has been a sight just like them. One hundred and one lumberjacks, harvest hands, miners, editors . . . who believe the wealth of the world belongs to him who creates it . . . the outdoor men, hard-rock blasters, tree-fellers, wheat-binders, longshoremen, the boys who do the strong work of the world. . . . To me, fresh from Russia, the scene was strangely familiar. . . . The IWW trial . . . looked like a meeting of the Central Executive Committee of the All-Russian Soviet of Workers and Deputies in Petrograd!" [1]

Reed's likening of the Wobblies to Russia's successful revolutionaries only worsened their public image. For, as the *Outlook*'s man in Chicago reported, "Regardless of their [jury] verdict, it has been made clear . . . that we have in the United States a full-fledged revolutionary organization under a leadership as radical as any that existed in Russia prior to the overthrow of the autocracy." [2] Given Americans' increasing paranoia about bolshevism, the Wobblies on trial in Chicago would become the first victims of the Great Red Scare that began with the repression of the IWW in 1917 and culminated in Attorney General A. Mitchell Palmer's 1919 raids.

Because Americans tend to place such confidence in the justice dispensed by their adversary system, a favorable decision in the Chicago trials—an outcome that each of the adversaries expected—promised immense benefits to the victor. In the case of the federal government and those private citizens who had instigated the prosecution, conviction of the defendants would still uneasy consciences. If a jury convicted the Wobblies of disloyalty, sabotage, and sedition after a fair and open hearing, the repression instituted to curb the IWW, much of which certainly violated due process, would seem in retrospect to have been necessary. For the defendants, acquittal would prove capitalists to have been guilty of a conspiracy against the working class, and establish the IWW once and for all as a legal organization free to promulgate its doctrines and recruit members.

The Chicago adversaries thus expected the impossible. Even if a jury convicted the defendants, federal officials acknowledged privately —though they would never admit it publicly—that conviction would come more as a result of public hysteria than of hard evidence indisputably proving the Wobblies' guilt. Even if tangible evidence had been found against individual defendants, the more conscientious public officials recognized that it would provide no valid justification for the outrageous crimes committed against the IWW in the names of patriotism and Americanism. As for the defendants, their hopes for an acquittal were simply pipe dreams. How could they expect to receive justice at the hands of citizens who applauded vigilantes and lynchers? Yet the prosecution and the defense pursued their mutual legal charades in Judge Landis' courtroom, though the outcome of the trial had been largely predetermined by the ubiquitous environment of public hysteria and by the pre-trial strategies of the contenders.

Almost six months elapsed between the September 1917 raids on IWW headquarters and the actual trial, which opened on April 1, 1918. During that period the defenders and the prosecutors devised the tactics and the strategy that shaped the course of the entire legal struggle not only in Chicago but also in courtrooms in Sacramento, Wichita, and Omaha.

Not all the indicted Wobblies agreed upon a course of legal action. Most outspoken among the dissenters was Elizabeth Gurley Flynn, who, sometime between the September raids and her indictment, severed her connection with the IWW. Miss Flynn maintained that since the federal government insisted upon observing the mechanics of due process, the IWW should take advantage of the prosecution's fairness. She asserted that the government could not substantiate its blanket indictment of 166 Wobblies; after all, she noted, it was incredible that the prosecution had ample evidence to present against each defendant charged with having committed a hundred separate crimes. Miss Flynn suggested that each defendant move for a severance of his case (i.e., request a separate trial), thus, through a nationwide series of pre-trial proceedings, stymieing the prosecution. Indeed Miss Flynn herself, with Tresca, Giovannitti, and Ettor, moved for severance.[3]

Logic buttressed Miss Flynn's recommendations. At least twenty-two of the defendants originally indicted in Chicago were either dead, no longer members of the IWW (some had never formally belonged in the first place), inactive, or in military service. Each of these (or their attorneys) certainly had adequate grounds to demand a dismissal or, at a minimum, a severance.[4] For the remaining defendants separate trials might have increased the likelihood they would be judged on their own individual guilt or innocence, and not on the basis of guilt by association with the feared Haywood and the dead Frank Little.

Although logic favored Elizabeth Gurley Flynn's legal strategy, certain inescapable realities suggested a different course. First, the IWW lacked the legal and financial resources to conduct a battery of individual cases, whereas the federal government had unlimited resources. Second, most Wobblies lacked the influential and respectable friends whom Miss Flynn and her associates claimed as sympathizers. Third, the defendants saw their trial as a matter of conscience, not crime; certain that they had committed no criminal acts and that they had been indicted for their beliefs, which they refused to recant, they chose to stand together on a matter of principle. Most Wobblies simply could not dissemble as Miss Flynn had done in a personal letter to President Wilson in which she claimed to have ceased all activity in the IWW before April 1917 (that is, before America declared war), and in which she emphasized her loyalty to the nation and her commitment to the defeat of German imperialism. Dissembling is, in fact, a euphemistic description of Miss Flynn's behavior at this time, for as late as August 25, 1917, she had written to *Solidarity:* "I am a member of the I.W.W. at this writing and have never stated otherwise anywhere. . . . I would not have my friends believe me a quitter in a crisis. We have enough 'slackers' in the class war already." [5] What were her friends to think of her letter to the President, or of her behavior during the IWW's legal crisis? In addition, Miss Flynn misinterpreted what was happening in federal government circles, as will be seen. Finally, the indicted Wobblies thought their strategy superior to hers: expecting to be acquitted, they saw more propaganda value in one great legal victory than in numerous smaller ones.

Miss Flynn's recommendations deserve further scrutiny, however, for they were later implicitly endorsed by the historians Philip Taft and Patrick Renshaw.[6] Miss Flynn's version of the circumstances and decisions surrounding the legal maneuvers from October 1917 to April 1918 were not made public until the publication of her autobiography almost forty years later. How much her evidence represents the inevitable distortions wrought by time and age, how much it reflects wishful thinking, and how much it includes deliberate slanting of the facts may never be known. But certain points are clear. She claimed that federal officials were at first divided over the wisdom of a mass prosecution. Precisely whom she had in mind it is impossible to ascertain; perhaps Labor Secretary Wilson or War Secretary Baker, neither of whom was enthusiastic about the prosecutions, but neither of whom actively opposed the Justice Department's approach. Moreover, within the Justice Department and the White House consensus prevailed; no evidence has been located in departmental archives or in presidential papers to indicate that any prominent officials hesitated at the thought of a mass trial. Both the President and his attorney general were under unrelenting pressure from congressmen and businessmen to proceed with the prosecution. Miss Flynn, however, alleged to have in her possession telegrams that IWW attorney Fred Moore gave her in 1919, which indicated that a "deal" could have been arranged between the IWW and the federal government in January 1918. According to this story—related in telegrams which George Vanderveer, defense attorney, allegedly sent to Haywood on January 29 and 30, 1918—the federal government would agree to dismiss all cases pending against the Wobblies and halt all anti-IWW raids provided the defendants renounced their beliefs for the duration of the war and made no propaganda over their liberation. Supposedly, these charitable terms resulted from pressures brought upon federal officials by Roger Baldwin of the National Civil Liberties Bureau, Carleton Parker, John Graham Brooks, and other influential reformers. In Miss Flynn's account, Haywood ended all negotiations by insisting that "we cannot compromise." [7]

It is hard to believe that the telegrams Miss Flynn cited ever existed, for her account of what transpired is wrong on almost every count. Vanderveer did suggest a bargain in letters to President Wilson and to George Creel, but this elicited no response. Indeed, Wilson had firmly resolved that the IWW must be repressed; as William Preston has clearly shown, the President's political and economic philosophy left him unmoved by the IWW's sufferings, leading him to write to his attorney general that "the I.W.W.'s . . . certainly are worthy of being suppressed." All the correspondence and supporting materials in the Justice Department's voluminous file on the Haywood case indicate a firm federal determination to press the prosecution to a successful conclusion. Finally, reformers like Baldwin and Brooks had minimal influence in Washington, especially among certain prominent Justice Department officials who dismissed them as naive humanitarians.[8]

Elizabeth Gurley Flynn's history of the period is further flawed by the actual events surrounding her move for a severance. As early as October 1 the government realized that it lacked evidence against Miss Flynn, and that, moreover, Tresca and Giovannitti were not IWW members. Yet the Justice Department proceeded to take action against the three defendants and opposed severances. The Attorney General even asserted that their current status of nonmembership in the IWW should not spare Giovannitti and Tresca from standing trial. When Gregory eventually granted Miss Flynn and the rest their severances, he did so as a strategy of *realpolitik*, and not out of an interest in abstract justice. Afraid that the government lacked the evidence to convict Flynn, Ettor, Giovannitti, or Tresca, he feared the impact of acquittals upon the prosecution's remaining cases. By voluntarily abandoning the prosecution of these four in December 1917, the government would inspire public confidence in its fairness and would also convince interested citizens that the prosecution had a strong case against the bulk of the defendants. In other words, Miss Flynn's severance would only make it easier for the government to convict her former friends and associates, some of whom were less "guilty" than she. But Gregory's subordinates opposed Miss Flynn's severance, not granting it until February 1918 when her attorney promised to advise his client to be patriotic and not in any way to retard the prosecution of the other Wobblies. To ensure that Miss Flynn and her friends respected the February 1918 understanding, the Justice Department allowed the original indictments against them to stand until March 15, 1919, when it finally authorized the charges dismissed.[9] Thus, Miss Flynn's path out of the legal maze was blocked for other Wobblies, whom the government was determined to convict. In the end, Miss Flynn's version of events can only be understood as a belated effort to rationalize her betrayal of comrades and of principles to which she swore allegiance as late as August 25, 1917.

Lacking the options available to Miss Flynn, the remaining IWW defendants pursued what had for them become customary legal defense procedures. Before the Chicago federal grand jury returned indictments against the arrested Wobblies, Haywood's office formed a general defense committee composed of members with previous experience in managing legal matters. The general office also proposed a voluntary fifty-cent membership assessment for defense work, as well as the establishment of local defense committees to operate in conjunction with the national one. In November 1917 the general executive board replaced *Solidarity* with the *Defense News Bulletin,* a journal devoted primarily to the IWW's legal campaign, which was published regularly until July 1918, when it was suspended. Haywood lost no time in obtaining competent legal assistance. Fortunately, he did not have far to seek; George Vanderveer, famous among Wobblies for his defense of the Everett prisoners and for his efforts on behalf of Seattle's disinherited (which gained him his reputation as "Counsel for the Damned"), willingly took charge of the legal defense.[10]

Although intensified wartime hysteria boded ill for the Wobblies, they retained several important friends. Most influential, though least useful, among the IWW's allies was Frank Walsh, who, with William Howard Taft, was shortly to become co-chairman of the National War Labor Board. Early in November Haywood had asked Walsh for assistance in creating a nonpartisan defense league to work in conjunction with the IWW's own committees. However sympathetic Walsh was to the Wobblies—and that he was sympathetic there can be no doubt—his official ties to the Wilson administration and his desire to maintain them militated against his cooperating publicly with the IWW. But Walsh offered Haywood and Vanderveer confidential advice and put them in contact with helpful sympathizers. Foremost among this latter group was Roger Baldwin, founder of the National Civil Liberties Bureau, who, throughout February 1918, pleaded with President Wilson, Labor Secretary Wilson, and War Secretary Baker to drop the prosecutions of the Wobblies as a matter of expediency as well as in the interests of civil liberties. Baldwin maintained that labor unrest could best be contained through the administrative machinery of the Labor Department and that "it cannot be successfully solved by prosecutions." Louis F. Post, an official in the Labor Department's Immigration and Naturalization Service and also publisher of *The Public,* a reformist journal, defended the Wobblies' civil liberties both in the pages of his publication and in Washington. Alexander Lanier, a captain in military intelligence, shared Baldwin's and Post's reservations about the prosecutions. In a long, carefully reasoned letter to President Wilson (later published in *The New Republic*), Lanier point by point destroyed the government's entire legal case against the IWW.[11]

Defense efforts notwithstanding, many Wobblies expected the worst. Writing from his jail cell in Tombstone, Arizona, A. S. Embree acknowledged that "our men can be killed and jailed." Writing to a Wobbly friend from Chicago's Cook County Jail, James Rowan confessed: "Of course we expect nothing else than to be jailed for taking part in a strike . . . for we know that a rebellious slave is the worst criminal in the eyes of the master." At the same time, these men were not altogether without optimism. Finding solace in the successful November Revolution in Russia, Rowan remarked: "What they can do in Russia, we can do in this 'Land of the Free.'" More philosophically, Embree noted: "The end in view is well worth striving for, but in the struggle itself lies the happiness of the fighter." [12] Wobblies indeed acted upon the prescription of the Italian communist Antonio Gramsci: "Pessimism of the Intelligence. Optimism of the Will."

Although the defendants themselves were pessimistic about their legal fate, Vanderveer labored with unabated optimism to defend them. Fully expecting to win dismissal of the Chicago indictments before the trial opened, during arraignment in December he argued that the Justice Department's evidence had been seized illegally in violation of the First and Fourth Amendments to the Constitution, and hence that the indictments should be quashed. His legal points overruled, Vanderveer resorted to different arguments with George Creel and President Wilson. He reminded both men that several of the Chicago defendants had previously severed their connections with the IWW, while others had never been members in the first place. He suggested that the government's prosecution of the IWW was assumed throughout the world of labor to be an attack on labor's right to organize, and that unless the defendants were released and working conditions improved, industrial unrest would intensify. This line of argument, however, proved equally unrewarding. Nevertheless, Vanderveer still expected victory when the case came to trial. Investigation had convinced him that none of the four counts in the indictment would stand up in court, for never had the IWW as an organization opposed conscription; and neither had any Wobblies refused conscription on organizational grounds, nor been found guilty of insubordination while in the armed services. The industrial counts seemed even more ludicrous to Vanderveer, who felt certain that he could prove to a jury's satisfaction that IWW strikes were undertaken solely to improve working conditions, never to interfere with the war effort. Hence Vanderveer boastfully informed Frank Walsh: "Our record on the strike issue presented in the first and second counts, and on the issue of violence and destruction of property, is absolutely clean, and I have not the slightest doubt about our ability to make the position which the government has outlined in the indictment look ridiculous." [13]

But Vanderveer's optimistic assessment ignored the intense pressures to destroy the IWW generated by Western businessmen and the mass popular war hysteria. It was unlikely that a jury composed of ordinary American citizens—the type even then sanctioning vigilante action against the Wobblies—would acquit alleged traitors. The facts of life in wartime America simply made Vanderveer's optimism baseless.[14]

In preparing its case against the IWW, the Justice Department left little to chance. Ostensibly, Charles F. Clyne, federal attorney for the Northern Illinois District, was handling the prosecution; but in fact the department turned the case over to three special prosecutors. Of the three, two—Frank K. Nebeker and William C. Fitts—had been prominent corporation attorneys in peacetime; Nebeker for mining and smelting enterprises in the Mountain States, and Fitts as a partner in an influential Wall Street law firm. Claude Porter, the third member of the special team, was a Justice Department professional who had forged an outstanding record in the Iowa District. When Clyne eventually proved unable to cope with Vanderveer in open court, the department took the prosecution entirely out of his hands, and Nebeker was put in command of the trial.

The Justice Department placed every conceivable roadblock in the IWW's path. While pressing the case against the Chicago defendants, the government made further IWW arrests in Wichita, Omaha, and Sacramento, as we shall see. This effectively immobilized the defense operations of second- and third-line IWW leaders and added to the newspaper coverage that reinforced the popular conviction that the Wobblies were disloyal. Those Wobblies fortunate enough to escape arrest felt the heavy hand of federal repression. Federal raids disrupted the IWW attempt to organize and to rationalize its defense activities. On Monday, December 20, three days after the Chicago defendants had been arraigned, federal agents invaded general defense headquarters in Chicago, seizing literature, subscription lists, and mailing lists. Long after the original warrant upon which the agents had acted expired, federal officials continued to occupy Chicago defense headquarters. Simultaneous raids interfered with defense activities in Seattle, Sacramento, and other cities.[15] Meanwhile, the Justice Department, in conjunction with postal authorities, barred IWW literature from the mails. Not even private correspondence completely escaped federal censorship or control. Nebeker at times even sought to interfere with newspapers and magazines that published stories possibly favorable to the IWW's defense.[16] Congress, too, assisted the Justice Department's prosecution, for as the Chicago trial began in the spring of 1918, several congressmen introduced bills to declare the IWW illegal and to make membership in it a crime.[17] Unsuccessful though they were, the bills' backers did succeed in further poisoning the public atmosphere against the IWW.

Just how polluted that atmosphere had become is shown in the private correspondence of two otherwise sensible and decent citizens, both of whom had by 1918 earned reputations as reformers. Ralph M. Easley, one-time secretary of the National Civic Federation, an organization of businessmen and labor leaders devoted to improving labor-management relations, wrote to Creel in February 1918 concerning the indicted Wobblies as follows: "I do not think you can go through it [the indictment] without concluding with me that Haywood and all that bunch should be 'hanged as high as Haman' if it were possible to erect a gibbet of that character." In the midst of the actual trial, Professor Richard T. Ely of the University of Wisconsin, a long-time advocate of the social gospel, reform economics, and labor unions, asked the Justice Department for assistance with a book he was completing on treason in America, in which he planned to use "the utterances of these traitors" on trial.[18]

The Justice Department was indeed fortunate that public hysteria had convicted the Wobblies before the jury heard the prosecution's evidence, for the prosecution, in fact, had no evidence. This became obvious as Nebeker, Fitts, and Porter prepared their case. Although for public consumption the Justice Department had consistently held that the IWW as an organization was not on trial, its case clearly hinged on the organization's record rather than on specific crimes committed by individual Wobblies. From the beginning of its investigation, the prosecution had based its case against the defendants largely on the existence of an anti-capitalist and anti-war conspiracy by the IWW, the evidence for which derived from the Wobblies' own publications. In March, on the eve of the trial, the prosecution still could do no better. In a twenty-three-page summary of the IWW's criminal record Fitts prepared for the Attorney General, for example, he could not cite a single instance of a specific crime committed by a Wobbly. Instead, Fitts restricted his legal brief to quotations and citations from IWW newspapers and pamphlets on sabotage, all of which led him to conclude that "the seditious and disloyal *character and teachings* of the organization necessarily brought it into conflict with other federal laws" (italics added).[19] The evidence amassed by the prosecution proved, if anything, the innocence of individual Wobblies. Expected to present evidence of IWW sabotage in the forests, federal forestry officials instead offered examples of IWW cooperation in fighting fires.[20] The Justice Department failed to locate Army and Navy officers able to present substantial evidence in court against the IWW. And a West Coast AFL official sought desperately to avoid a courtroom appearance, for he could only produce facts favorable to the defense.[21]

Perhaps it was his certainty that the government had no tangible evidence against the Chicago defendants that caused Vanderveer to conclude in mid-March 1918: "Every day now furnishes some new reason for believing that the Chicago case will shortly be disposed of, probably on our motion to quash the indictment. In large part no doubt this is because the Government . . . are afraid to take chances on the outcome of so public a trial."[22] Vanderveer could not have been more wrong. A public trial—the more public the better —offered the Justice Department its best opportunity for legally wrecking the IWW. Lacking the evidence it thought necessary to convince a federal judge, or perhaps a judicious elite, of the Wobblies' guilt, the department realized that a jury composed of twelve randomly chosen citizens would probably reflect the nation's war hysteria. What abstract justice could not accomplish for the prosecution, flesh and blood Americans would.

On April 1, 1918, 113 Wobblies were brought before Judge Landis, and each was charged with over one hundred separate crimes, for a grand total of well over ten thousand violations. Before the prosecution could present its evidence, or the defense could rebut it, however, a jury had to be selected. At this juncture the trial almost collapsed. Partly out of dissatisfaction with the veniremen initially chosen, partly out of discontent with Clyne's mismanagement of the jury selection, the Justice Department moved that the jury be dismissed because the defense had improperly investigated prospective jurors. Landis granted the government's motion, and once again a jury had to be selected. This time Nebeker directed the prosecution—with Clyne retiring to the background—and after almost a full month of examination he chose a jury eminently satisfactory to the Justice Department. Exactly a month to the day—April 1 to May 1 —after the defendants initially came before the bench, formal presentation of the government's case began.[23] The irony of the dates that separated the two primary phases of the IWW trial should not pass unremarked. How fitting that a trial that was to become a judicial farce, if not a circus, should commence on April Fool's Day, and that formal presentation of evidence against a radical, allegedly revolutionary labor organization should begin on May Day!

The setting of the trial was a strange mixture of incongruities. The stern and dignified Judge Landis presided over a courtroom in which spittoons were prominently in evidence. The Justice Department's legal celebrities competed for attention with a motley assortment of journalists—among them, Carl Sandburg, Art Young, David Karsner, and John Reed. Some of these men were eager to grind out lurid copy about the dangerous Wobbly traitors, while others were more interested in exploring the implications of such a trial for free speech, dissent, and labor activities in a wartime democracy.

Yet despite the drama of the personalities and the setting, the trial proved a disappointing anti-climax to the hysterical propaganda and the massive federal raids that preceded it. Nothing original or startling came to light during the trial. Evidence that the prosecution had been unable to secure previously was not suddenly introduced from the witness stand, nor in Nebeker's opening and closing arguments. For every instance of alleged sabotage, sedition, and subversion introduced by the prosecution—and these were exceedingly few—Vanderveer produced numerous witnesses to testify to the loyalty of individual Wobblies. For every strike that Nebeker alleged deliberately interfered with the war effort, the defense, using federal publications and reports, demonstrated that economic factors, not political objectives, were behind the strike. For every anti-conscription or anti-war Wobbly that Nebeker cited, Vanderveer produced others, larger in number, loyally serving in the armed forces. In fact, one of the original 113 defenders, A. C. Christ, appeared in court in military uniform on April 1; the government, however, wisely dismissed Christ's case along with that of eleven other defendants.[24]

The Chicago trial was Boise, Paterson, and Everett all over again—but on a larger and grander scale. Previous prosecutors had promised to prove the guilt of individual Wobblies, and, unable to do so, had instead indicted the organization on the basis of its philosophy and its publications; this was Nebeker's gambit in 1918. Failing to prove specific individual crimes, he read to the jury from the IWW preamble, from *Solidarity*, from Elizabeth Gurley Flynn's translation of Pouget's *Sabotage*, and from the private correspondence of various Wobblies. Most of this had been written before the period covered in the indictment, and none of it related to specific alleged "crimes." For a month and a half the jury listened—sometimes raptly, other times openly bored—as Nebeker and his staff lectured them about the subversive nature and the criminal, atheistic essence of the IWW's ideology. In the last analysis the Justice Department asked the jury, as representatives for an entire nation, to condemn a philosophy, an attitude toward life, and, most important, an organization.

The defense, for its part, followed established precedent. Easily surmounting a court ruling that declared evidence concerning exploitative working conditions inadmissible, Vanderveer brought IWW soapboxers to the witness stand to testify about their life experiences; and they inevitably focused upon just such exploitative working conditions. Big Jim Thompson gave the same speech in the Chicago courtroom that he had given in hundreds of lumber camps, hobo jungles, and on city street corners. "Red" Doran presented his famous illustrated chalk talk—a crudely metaphorical analysis and indictment of capitalism—which may have excited working-class audiences but only bored the jury and the courtroom. The trial's high point was Haywood's testimony, which extended through two days of repetitive questioning. As Carl Sandburg had observed several months earlier, Haywood was inclined to discuss the alleged ten thousand crimes "with the massive leisure of Hippo Vaughn pitching a shutout." [25] Anyone familiar with Haywood's testimony from the witness stand in Boise in 1907, or before the Commission on Industrial

Relations in 1915, would have discovered nothing new in his 1918 rendition of his life, his philosophy, and his version of IWW history.

The only surprise in the defense's strategy came when Vanderveer declined to offer a closing argument to the jury. No adequate explanation has ever been suggested for that decision, and, given the lack of sources, any explanation must remain highly conjectural. Nevertheless, it does not seem improbable that Vanderveer had nothing to say in a summation that he had not already said or established more effectively during his examination and cross-examination of witnesses. Moreover, it appears likely that Vanderveer honestly believed the prosecution had failed to adduce evidence that would lead a jury to convict any individual defendant; since the organization, in theory, was not on trial, the defense had no reason to present a final rebuttal. In other words, Vanderveer probably assumed that whatever decision the jury reached, it could hardly be based upon the evidence offered by the government.

Be that as it may, in mid-August, after nearly four months of testimony, Landis instructed the jury on the intricacies of determining the guilt or innocence of one hundred defendants charged on four separate counts with having committed more than ten thousand crimes. The jurymen thus had to make four hundred distinct determinations. Difficult as that may have seemed, it apparently proved astonishingly easy, for in less than one hour the jury returned with a verdict of "guilty" for every defendant on each and every count. The speed and the substance of the verdict shocked the Wobblies. "I did not think," Vincent St. John wrote to Frank Walsh, "that mob justice would prevail in a U.S. court." [26] But St. John should not have been surprised. After all, before the jury announced its verdict, the *Outlook* had informed its middle-class readers that "regardless of their verdict, it has been made clear during the . . . trial that we have . . . a full-fledged revolutionary organization . . . as bad as any that existed in Russia prior to the overthrow of the autocracy." And *World's Work* advised its subscribers: "We should show as little mercy to internal agitators caught committing these acts as the Huns who destroy women and children and who seek to annihilate democratic civilization." [27]

After having demonstrated judicial objectivity and restraint for five long months, Judge Landis revealed his real emotions on August 31, when he sentenced most of the defendants with as little mercy as possible. Seventeen defendants received some measure of clemency, but their connection to the IWW was at best debatable. Landis meanwhile sentenced thirty-five Wobblies to five years in prison; thirty-three to ten years; and fifteen, including Haywood, St. John, and Chaplin, to twenty years, or the legal maximum. Total fines levied in the case exceeded $2 million. Among those sent to the federal prison at Leavenworth, Kansas, was Ray Fanning, a nineteen-year-old Harvard sophomore who was not even an IWW member.[28] As the sentences were announced, Ben Fletcher, a Baltimore and Philadelphia waterfront organizer and the only Negro among the defendants, added some strained gallows humor to the somber proceedings as he observed: "Judge Landis is using poor English today. His sentences are too long." (Earlier in the proceedings Fletcher had sardonically informed Haywood: "If it wasn't for me, there'd be no color in this trial at all.") [29]

Landis' harsh sentences sat well with the press and with popular opinion in an emotional climate that was soon to nourish A. Mitchell Palmer's Red Scare. In the past, more conservative American labor factions had usually united with more radical ones in time of legal peril; this had been the case in Boise, Lawrence, Paterson, and Everett. But not in Chicago. Although scores of British labor organizations made formal protests, not a single AFL affiliate opposed the Justice Department concerning the IWW verdict.[30]

Deserted by press, public, and organized labor, the convicted Wobblies could turn for support only to the small body of civil libertarians clustered around Roger Baldwin and the National Civil Liberties Bureau; to such former "comrades" as Elizabeth Gurley Flynn; to isolated sympathizers such as Captain Lanier and Louis F. Post; and to their old friend Frank P. Walsh. Yet none of these sympathizers could rescue the Wobblies from the substantial terms at Leavenworth inflicted on them by Landis.[31]

But the Chicago Wobblies were not alone in their tribulations and prison sentences. While they sat in court awaiting their fate, other Wobblies languished in jail in California, Kansas, and Nebraska, awaiting trial when the main show in Chicago concluded. As long as the Justice Department subordinated all else to convicting the Chicago defendants, public attention focused on the Haywood case. With Haywood and the others convicted, the Justice Department, its boosters, its camp followers, and its lonely opponents turned their full attention to the West.

Although the IWW cases in the West were directly related to the federal crackdown on the organization and to the specific needs of the prosecution in the Chicago trial, local pressures and passions, particularly in California, added an extra fillip to the repressive legal campaign. Most of the Wobblies held prisoners in the Western states had been arrested during the September–November 1917 raids. The more important among them, however, had been transferred to Chicago to stand trial there with other first-line IWW leaders; some of the evidence confiscated in the West was used in Chicago. Now in August 1918, its main trial successfully completed, the Justice Department could cater to Western businessmen, politicians, and inflamed citizens by prosecuting local Wobblies. (Politics was never far beneath the surface: administration Democrats were keenly conscious of the importance of Western votes to their national success.)

By far the most interesting and revealing of the secondary IWW trials opened in Sacramento in December 1918. Sacramento demonstrated more clearly than Chicago the lengths to which the Justice Department went in order to "get" Wobblies and their sympathizers. Approximately half of the forty-six defendants in the Sacramento case had been arrested during a federal raid on IWW headquarters in Fresno in September 1917, at which time the government had been mainly interested in securing evidence for Chicago.[32] As a result, the prisoners seized at Fresno remained in jail for more than a year while the Justice Department was preoccupied elsewhere. Meanwhile, on December 17, 1917, an alleged assassination attempt had been made upon California Governor-elect William D. Stephens at the executive mansion in Sacramento. Almost immediately local officials, newspaper editors, and California congressmen implicated the IWW. State authorities lost no time in apprehending two additional Wobblies, whom they accused of shipping dynamite illegally through the mails and charged with the alleged assassination attempt. At this juncture, several prominent Californians urged the Justice Department to undertake a full-scale investigation of the IWW's role in the attempt upon the Governor's life. Washington yielded to these pressures from the West, but the Bureau of Investigation agent assigned to the case discovered no evidence connecting the IWW to the crime; nor did he find evidence against the two arrested Wobblies. (Much later, federal officials learned that the entire assassination affair had been arranged by a corrupt San Francisco district attorney, who was desperately seeking an issue upon which to secure re-election to office.) Yet, its own agent's report notwithstanding, the Justice Department arrested a large group of Bay Area–Sacramento Wobblies, whom it then put with the prisoners seized in Fresno the previous September.[33]

By January 1918 the government thus held some fifty to sixty Wobblies in a Sacramento jail. There they suffered from the flu epidemic then sweeping the nation; flu eventually took the life of several IWW inmates and permanently impaired the health of others. An epidemic of a different but no less virulent nature was simultaneously poisoning the California atmosphere. Editorials in the *Sacramento Bee* advocated lynching the prisoners, and rumors of wholesale lynchings filled the air.

IWW defense efforts in California encountered the more customary obstacles. Federal agents raided local defense headquarters seven times in six months, seizing all IWW records and papers; agents arrested the defense committee's secretaries, one of whom they held incommunicado for eight months.[34] No Wobbly or IWW sympathizer altogether evaded the authorities. When Theodora Pollok, a young lady with the best family connections, appeared at the Sacramento police station to arrange bail for several prisoners, police arrested her, confiscated her funds, and subjected her to a medical examination intended for prostitutes. (When President Wilson later protested this treatment, United States Attorney John Preston replied that Wobblies, like prostitutes, were notoriously promiscuous sexually, only in their case love was *not for sale*.) [35]

Theodora Pollok's links to the IWW are interesting to trace. The daughter of a prominent Baltimore family whose influential friends in Washington could plead her case before the highest federal officials, including Woodrow Wilson, Miss Pollok, like so many other well-bred and well-educated young women of her generation, despised the restraints imposed by society upon the Victorian (American) woman, and she sought release in a life of strenuous social reform. Asthmatic and tubercular, she was compelled to move to California for her health. Theodora became active first in the Mooney-Billings defense campaign and then in IWW legal defense work, which resulted in her taking out a red card and later being arrested in

Sacramento. Although she could scarcely be classified a saboteur, a subversive, or an assassin, the prosecution refused to dismiss its charges against her, despite the remonstrations of President Wilson, Attorney General Gregory, Labor Secretary Wilson, and lesser federal officials.[36]

The prosecution had good reason for refusing to dismiss its case against Miss Pollok. As attorney Preston admitted in one of his franker moments, the government's evidence against the other Sacramento defendants was barely more substantial than what it had against Miss Pollok. In other words, to liberate her would automatically throw into doubt the validity of the prosecution's entire case, something the government could not risk even in California's intensely anti-IWW atmosphere. Better, Preston's reasoning went, try and convict an innocent woman than weaken the case against fifty-four dangerous Wobblies.[37]

Despite his lack of evidence, Preston secured grand jury indictments in February 1918. He had to postpone the trial of the Sacramento defendants until after the Chicago trial ended, however, for an acquittal in Sacramento would naturally have undermined the government's chances for conviction in Chicago. From February until December 1918, when the Sacramento trial finally began, the Bureau of Investigation sought to build a case against the California defendants. It did, but only of the most circumstantial kind. Using IWW publications and the private correspondence of several Wobblies, the Bureau proved that members of the organization advocated sabotage. Inveigling Elbert Coutts and John Dymond, two Wobblies of dubious reputation, into becoming informers (later, in the 1920's, both men earned their living as paid informers during a series of California IWW prosecutions under the state's criminal syndicalism statute), the Bureau claimed to have evidence to prove acts of sabotage committed by Wobblies in California's fruit fields. Producing what the *Nation* described as "ol' rags an' bottles," the Bureau reconstructed the ingredients of bombs allegedly used by the IWW's saboteurs.[38]

The Sacramento prosecution thus came into court with what it apparently thought was incriminating evidence; at least it cited specific instances of criminal acts alleged to have been committed by individual defendants. Yet, as in Chicago, the bulk of the correspondence cited by the prosecutors, as well as the alleged use of the "ol rags an' bottles" to destroy crops, dated from the years 1913–

1915, before the period covered by the indictment. The evidence of IWW crimes for the war years proved even more circumstantial than that for the pre-war period, and it was founded in large degree upon the testimony of the two paid informants. In a sense the prosecution admitted the weakness of its case when it tried Miss Pollok along with the other defendants, though she obviously had not joined in the so-called sabotage conspiracy. As usual, the prosecution relied upon the IWW's philosophy, its publications, and its ideological opposition to the war to win its case; and on those grounds, Miss Pollok was equally guilty, for she sympathized with the IWW's philosophy and she ideologically opposed the war.[39]

Most of the Sacramento Wobblies, unlike those in Chicago who had expected to win justice in a capitalist court, remained true to their IWW faith. Asserting that judges and courts were purely institutions designed to place a legal veneer upon the exploitation of the ruling American capitalist class, all but three of the Sacramento Wobblies declined to hire an attorney or to defend themselves in court. Only Miss Pollok and two other less notable defendants dissented from the strategy of a "silent defense" and chose to be represented by counsel and offer a defense in court.[40]

Whether they elected counsel or not, whether they defended themselves before the jury or not, the Sacramento defendants met similar fates: conviction by a jury that deliberated less than an hour before handing down its verdict on January 16, 1919. All of the "silent defenders" were sentenced to prison terms, ranging from one to ten years. The three vocal defendants had to wait until June 18, 1919, before being sentenced. During this period, further unsuccessful pleas for pardon were made on behalf of Miss Pollok, but neither her innocence of the crimes charged against her nor President Wilson's intercession rescued her from "justice." Only a medical report by a Stanford University physician, concluding that imprisonment would kill Miss Pollok, and the trial judge's own conscience, if not that of the Justice Department, saved her from a term in prison. Instead, the judge fined her $100, while he sentenced her two co-defendants to two months in jail.[41]

Just before the end of the Sacramento trial, another twenty-seven Wobblies received prison terms in Wichita, Kansas. Arrested during a federal raid in November 1917, possibly at the instigation of the Carter Oil Company, the Kansas Wobblies were imprisoned for over a year before their case came to trial in December 1918. In Kansas, as elsewhere, the evidence amassed against the Wobblies consisted entirely of organization publications and private correspondence, not overt illegal acts. As usual, after a trial lasting less than three weeks, a local jury found all the defendants guilty; the judge then sentenced twenty-six of them to prison terms ranging from one to nine years.[42]

More fortunate but equally maltreated was a group of sixty-four Wobblies arrested in Omaha, Nebraska, on November 13, 1917. Arriving in Omaha to attend a special convention called by the Agricultural Workers' Industrial Union, the Wobblies instead met federal agents. United States Attorney Thomas Allen realized at once that he had no legitimate case against the arrested men. Turning to Attorney General Gregory for advice, he was counseled to delay legal action until after the trial in Chicago; at the same time Gregory ordered him to hold the Wobblies till the next regular session of the Omaha federal grand jury. In June 1918, eight months after their arrest, these Wobblies were still in jail, awaiting presentment before a grand jury. Certain that he had no case against his prisoners, whom he conceded were innocent, Allen offered the Wobblies a "compromise": they could plead guilty and be sentenced to the length of time they had already served in jail. The Wobblies, of course, rejected the "compromise," and Allen, despite the considered opinion of high-level Justice Department officials that "there is not evidence sufficient to warrant a prosecution," pushed ahead with plans for a trial. Given Nebraska's anti-radical and anti-Wobbly environment, Allen felt positive that a jury would convict; moreover, as he informed the Attorney General: "If these men are not tried and indicted the Council of Defense and many well meaning citizens may be dissatisfied and disappointed."[43]

But in the Omaha case for the first time Washington officials equivocated. Perhaps some of them had pangs of conscience about the propriety of sentencing another large group of probably innocent men to prison. Federal indecision nevertheless brought few immediate benefits to the jailed Wobblies, who, unable to raise bail, remained incarcerated while the Justice Department slowly made up its mind. Not until April 1919 did the department reach a decision; after having kept the Wobblies locked up for a year and a half, it decided to dismiss all charges, since, in the words of Allen: ". . . In view of the fact that the case is not a strong one, it occurs to me that if it is to be dropped, the I.W.W. . . . or other similar organizations cannot say that the Department is prosecuting them simply because of their membership in the organizations." [44] Yet Allen and the department were in fact less generous than his suggestion implies, for none of the sixty-four Wobblies arrested in Omaha had been prominent in the IWW (quite apart from the fact that none had committed crimes). By April 1919 almost all the first- and second-line IWW leaders were in federal prison; those still at large were either free on bail, fugitives from justice, victims of the immigration authorities, or on the verge of being tried on criminal-syndicalism charges in various state courts.

The law had clearly proved to be an effective instrument of repression. When vigilantes had deported miners from Bisbee or had lynched Little in Butte, the American conscience had been troubled. But when the Justice Department arrested suspected criminals, indicted them before grand juries, tried them before impartial judges and randomly selected petit juries—that is, when the formal requirements of legal due process were observed—the American conscience rested easier. As long as most Americans deemed membership in the IWW to be tantamount to treason, there was little danger that due process would release an army of Wobbly bandits upon a helpless community. Where the federal government doubted the effectiveness of the courtroom as an instrument of repression, it could remit alien or naturalized Wobblies to immigration authorities, who were not compelled to observe due process in their deportation proceedings. Whatever the method chosen—be it legal trial or administrative deportation—the government accomplished its essential objective: repression of the IWW.

Although the federal trials and deportations did not force the IWW out of existence, the whole basis of its existence changed. Before September 1917 it had been a flourishing labor organization, daily gaining new recruits and funds; afterward its leaders were imprisoned, its ranks decimated, and its treasury depleted by legal expenses. Before 1917 it had been a fighting labor organization, waging industrial war against lumber barons, mine owners, and wheat farmers; afterward it became primarily a legal-defense organization, combating writs, government lawyers, and judges. From this latter struggle the IWW had no surcease, for though federal repression finally subsided after the war with the collapse of Palmer's discredited Red Scare, state governments, especially California's, used the legal techniques perfected by the Justice Department to harass and repress the IWW in the early 1920's. Constantly threatened by legal attack, during much of its postwar life the IWW remained a legal organization concerned as much with the defense of civil liberties as it was with winning higher wages, shorter hours, or a new and better world.

Yet before fading from public consciousness the IWW retained sufficient vigor to present employers, state governments, and federal authorities with many a tormented moment from 1919 to 1921. In commenting on the concerted federal-state effort to eradicate the organization, one United States attorney observed in April 1919: " . . . The germ of discontent, destruction and outlawry has not yet been exterminated from the I.W.W." [45] The nation was just then recovering from a threatened IWW general strike in the Northwest; still in the future were other labor disturbances stimulated by the Wobblies, as well as the Centralia, Washington, tragedy of Armistice Day, 1919.

CHAPTER

18

Disorder and Decline,
1918–1924

I N 1917-1918 the IWW seemed to pose a distinct threat to the established order in America. Claiming from 100,000 to 250,000 members, it had tied up the woods of the Northwest and paralyzed the copper mines of Montana and Arizona. The IWW's threat to national security had appeared so grave that Western governors, the United States Army, at least three federal cabinet departments, and the President himself had sought to cope with the menace it posed.

Having decided to suppress the IWW, the United States government in 1918 in effect told the Wobblies what Leon Trotsky had told Martov and the Mensheviks after the Bolshevik Revolution: "You are miserable isolated individuals. You are bankrupt. You have played out your role. Go where you belong, to the dustheap of history." Three years later, in 1921, Ben H. Williams, who had briefly returned to the IWW as editor of *Solidarity*, observed in a valedictory editorial announcing his absolute divorce from the IWW: " 'Isolation' is a word that aptly describes the present position of the I.W.W. in the labor movement of the United States." [1]

The IWW's failure to adapt to the realities of life in postwar America insured its continued isolation from the mainstream of the labor movement as well as from the "new" radicalism. After the war a more sophisticated breed of American employer erected an antiunion dam composed in equal parts of welfare capitalism and an

"American Plan" that channeled the labor movement away from a swift running course into a languid backwater. Simultaneously the course of radicalism flowed away from pre-war reform socialism into the more turbulent riverbed of revolutionary communism, ultimately leaving the Wobblies and the socialists cut off not only from the radical current but also from the mainstream of American history, which, in the 1920's, flowed swiftly with the capitalist current.

Before and during the First World War the IWW had flourished in the copper and lumber industries partly as a result of obstinate employers and partly as a consequence of abominable working conditions. Although the war effort revolutionized neither employer attitudes nor working conditions, it nevertheless wrought perceptible —and, from the IWW's point of view, decisive—changes in both. This was particularly true in the case of the lumbermen, who before 1916 had been among the most combative and anti-labor of American businessmen. Long accustomed to fighting among themselves as well as against trade unions, lumbermen united in 1916 in reaction to the IWW's labor offensive. Traditionally callous in labor relations, lumbermen had been compelled by federal wartime policies to give a new look to their relationship with employees. Under pressure from Washington and from the Army, they had inaugurated the eight-hour day, increased daily wages, and improved living and working conditions. In response to federal initiatives, the employers acquiesced in the creation of the Loyal Legion of Loggers and Lumbermen (4L's), a company union that offered lumber workers the shadow of industrial democracy. For the first time in the industry's history, its workers were granted, if not actual power, a voice in decisions affecting their lives. When the war ended in November 1918 the lumbermen did not forget what they had learned under duress: that accommodation was more effective than opposition in averting labor unrest. Hence in 1919 most employers retained the 4L's as a civilian organization; still others considered adopting the company union scheme that the Rockefeller interests had instituted successfully at the Colorado Fuel and Iron Company in the aftermath of the 1914 Ludlow massacre. Several lumbermen who refused to accommodate their employees brought strikes upon their companies, only to conclude that, had they organized their workers under the 4L's, labor unrest might have been stifled. So well did lumbermen finally learn their lesson that in 1919 they established an industrial relations bureau in the West Coast Lumbermen's Association, charged with offering labor a "square deal." This "square deal" included higher wages and better housing for family men who would form a less transient labor force—also, one less attracted to the IWW. Not only did these tactics reduce the IWW's success among lumber workers; the AFL timber workers' union, strenuous as were its efforts in many districts, could not sign up enough members to charter a local.[2]

Similar though somewhat less substantial improvements in labor-management relations took place in the copper industry. Here employers remained obdurately anti-labor, yet after the war they continued to cooperate with Labor Department mediators, who still tried to foist AFL affiliates upon recalcitrant employers as an alternative to the IWW. Although the copper companies declined to deal with AFL unions—except where powerful skilled unions of machinists, engineers, and building tradesmen left them no choice—they maintained the grievance machinery created during the war. In some cases—Phelps Dodge most notable among them—they expanded what had already been an elaborate paternalistic welfare labor policy.[3]

After 1918 the Wobblies found their appeal to migratory harvesters circumscribed. Here, however, the causes were different. Federal officials had not had to intervene during the war in order to insure efficient production in agriculture; nor had farmer-employers altered their basic attitudes toward labor. Midwestern farmers remained as tolerant toward their hired hands as they had been in 1918, when Thorstein Veblen completed his famous report on the "Farm Labor Problem" for the Department of Labor. California's ranchers remained truculently, sometimes violently, anti-labor. But the labor force itself began to change. The Ford "flivver" was already working its wonders among migratory harvest hands. Where once migratory workers had been mostly unattached men who beat their way from job to job on "sidedoor coach," they were fast becoming more and more family units that traveled as far and as often as their battered secondhand cars carried them. For the migratory who rode the rods and camped in the jungles, an IWW red card had been a necessity of life: his insurance policy against coercion by detectives, brakemen, gamblers, and thugs. For the family of harvesters which traveled by auto as a self-contained unit, the red card was much less important. As the years passed and more migratories took to automobiles and more families joined the annual migrations of harvest hands, the IWW's appeal to agricultural workers diminished proportionately. Meanwhile, in the wheat fields the widespread use of the combine reduced the total demand for labor, and hence the size of the migratory army among whom the IWW had traditionally recruited.[4]

Even where objective conditions remained the same—as on the Philadelphia waterfront—the postwar IWW isolated itself from the labor movement. Since 1913 an IWW local of longshoremen affiliated with the Marine Transport Workers' Industrial Union had maintained job control on the Philadelphia waterfront. Ably led, first by Ben Fletcher and then by Walter Nef, in effect the longshoremen achieved a closed shop and union-determined wages. After having loyally loaded ammunition and troop ships during the war, the longshoremen's local entered the postwar world more powerful than ever. With its closed shop and its $25 initiation fee (which was well above the IWW's constitutionally sanctioned maximum) intended to restrict entry into the union, it was the second largest postwar affiliate of the IWW. As such, it inevitably came into conflict with the putative leaders of the IWW, who, having no strong following of their own, clung to outdated revolutionary precepts that dated back to the organization's earliest and least successful days. These leaders asserted that the longshoremen's initiation fee contravened the IWW constitution and that the local's regular, orderly negotiations with employers subverted the IWW's revolutionary spirit. They thus presented an ultimatum to the longshoremen: either reduce the union initiation fee to the constitutionally sanctioned $2 maximum or be suspended from IWW membership. Ben Fletcher, who had gone to prison for his principles and who, upon his release from Leavenworth, returned to Philadelphia to lead his fellow black workers, accepted the 1922 challenge of the IWW's general executive board and in 1924 led his longshoremen out of the IWW and into the AFL.[5]

If changing economic realities and self-defeating organizational policies had not weakened the IWW, further government repression would have done so. Public surveillance of the Wobblies did not end with the conclusion of the wartime trials. Well after the close of the war, federal troops stayed on duty in Arizona and Montana, where they cooperated with mine owners and local authorities in curbing IWW activities. Naval and Army intelligence infiltrated spies into IWW locals and sent agents to the 1919 IWW convention in Chicago. Meanwhile, the Western states that had enacted criminal-syndicalism statutes inaugurated their own prosecutions against Wobblies as federal prosecution abated.[6]

This combination of economic change, government repression, and internal inadequacies rendered the IWW largely inactive and ineffective in the spring and summer of 1918. The organization had not held a national convention since 1916, and it would not convene another until May 1919. Its newspapers, journals, and pamphlets were censored and denied use of the mails; its basic records remained impounded in a Chicago warehouse. There is no way of ascertaining how large, or how small, IWW membership was from 1917 to 1919.* With all its most capable and experienced leaders in prison, administratively the organization was in chaos. No expert officials coordinated the activities of the various affiliates, which more than ever were left to go their own haphazard ways; indeed, on some occasions, federal agents rather than IWW couriers carried important messages from temporary headquarters in Chicago to affiliates in the Northwest. Only legal defense work was administered with some aplomb or efficiency; but concentration on legal endeavors diverted scarce manpower from industrial activities and nearly bankrupted the IWW. The IWW's pre-trial hearings, its ensuing appeals, and its subsequent pardon campaign probably cost the organization more than $1 million.[7] (This does not include what was spent by the National Civil Liberties Bureau and other legal defense organizations.) Yet never had the IWW spent so much money to so little effect.

At a time when the Wobblies needed leaders as never before, and when the organization had to cope with new social and economic realities, there was no one with sufficient experience or talent to refashion the IWW in the radical manner required. Whether Haywood, Brazier, Lambert, Fletcher, and almost two hundred other Wobblies serving time in federal prison could have saved the IWW from decline is at best debatable. Clearly, their years in prison insulated these men from the changes transforming America, just as those changes further isolated the IWW from the labor movement. Wobblies went into prison as representatives of America's most radical

---

* John S. Gambs, citing the *American Labor Yearbook* for 1919–1920, estimates membership at seventy thousand.

social movement; they would come out into a world in which communists had replaced them on the revolutionary left. The world that had been and the world that was diverged so greatly that few of the imprisoned IWW leaders ever again assumed prominence in the organization they had helped establish. One after another the old-time Wobblies left the country (either voluntarily or forcibly) or abandoned the IWW for communism, the AFL, "Americanism," or, in some cases, the church. Given the number of problems that plagued the IWW in 1917 and 1918, it is remarkable that the organization survived at all. Yet survive it did. Indeed, it remained virile enough to frighten military men, Western employers, and local officials, though closer observers of the labor scene knew better.

Events of the fall of 1918 form one of the most confused strands in the tangled web of IWW history. Most of that spring and summer the Wobblies had been quiescent, fearing that any action they took might prejudice the case of their leaders standing trial in Chicago. Once the verdict was in, however, the Wobblies swung into action. From provisional headquarters in Chicago orders went out West for members to inaugurate a general strike of timber workers and copper miners for October 1. According to the version provided by military intelligence, the decision to call the strike had been relayed from Haywood in Leavenworth to A. S. Embree in Chicago, and thence to lesser officials in Butte, Spokane, and Seattle. The same account has it that the purpose of the strike was to compel the government to release all its IWW prisoners, as well as Eugene Debs and Tom Mooney, two other victims of wartime jingoism. Strike leaflets to this effect, at any rate, were printed in Butte, though they were not widely distributed.[8]

Many of the circumstances surrounding the 1918 "general strike" incident are now lost beyond recall. That Haywood should have ordered such an action seems ludicrous. In 1917, when the IWW had a mass membership and actual power in the Northwest, Haywood had been reluctant to call a general strike as an anti-war measure. Yet the federal government had tried him, convicted him, and imprisoned him for interfering with the war effort. He had no reason to expect that in September–October 1918, with war still raging on the western front, Washington would be more gentle in its treatment of labor leaders if he suggested a step that could only disrupt war production. What is more, a strike intended to liberate political prisoners—i.e., a political strike—was clearly illegal under the terms of the 1918 federal Espionage Act, a fact Haywood certainly was not likely to have forgotten. That any significant number of copper miners or loggers was willing to strike in order to free imprisoned Wobblies seems equally dubious. Although military intelligence reported that general-strike plans were well advanced in Butte and Spokane, an FBI agent and Labor Department conciliators there saw no indications of revolutionary working-class sentiment, however discontented the miners were about wages and working conditions. Burton K. Wheeler relayed similar observations to Washington.[9]

Some facts about the general-strike incident, however, are quite clear. For one, Army intelligence and Anaconda Copper Company agents were in close contact with every move the IWW made; they had also infiltrated the IWW's top echelons. These spies apparently spread the rumors of the general walkout scheduled to disrupt Butte in early September. It was, indeed, upon their own secret agents' advice that the military authorities in Montana, honestly perceiving a threat to the nation's war effort, embarked upon a course of military repression. Under the command of Major Omar Bradley, [*] federal troops joined with local police and Anaconda gunmen in raiding Butte IWW headquarters, closing down union newspapers—in particular, the *Butte Bulletin*—arresting workers without cause, and beating workers on the city's streets. The military instituted what one later student of the Butte situation termed "an unfair, unrestrained, vicious . . . veritable reign of terror . . . " So reprehensible was the military's behavior that Burton Wheeler, the FBI agent on duty in Butte, the Justice Department, and Secretary of War Baker spoke out against the soldiers. But such criticism had little impact on professional military men, who prepared their own version of the Butte "general strike." [10]

In fact, a general strike never occurred in the Northwest. The IWW leaders, who had originally allowed themselves to be provoked into declaring a general walkout, soon realized that political strikes

[*] Later to become famous as one of the outstanding American generals in Europe during World War II.

451

violated the Espionage Act, and withdrew leaflets they had circulated demanding release of political prisoners; these were replaced with new ones demanding the eight-hour day, a $6 minimum wage, and abolition of the rustling card. When September 13, the day set for the general walkout, finally arrived, only five hundred men out of a total work force estimated at sixteen to twenty thousand miners left work.

It is evident that two of the most prominent and militant of the advocates of a general strike were *agents provocateurs* associated with Anaconda and with military intelligence. It was these two men who had framed the demands that violated the Espionage Act. Constructing a highly incriminating chain of circumstantial evidence that linked the United States Army to Anaconda and the copper company to labor espionage, a New Deal Justice Department official who made an official study of the Butte affair was later to inquire: ". . . Is it going too far to infer . . . that the Anaconda men and the Army operatives were the same? And that therefore the Army was guilty of a strike against the Army which the Army very dutifully crushed?" [11] From available evidence these inferences seem correct.

The Anaconda Company and the Army thus duped the inexperienced men leading the IWW. By inducing gullible Wobblies to sponsor an illegal walkout in strategic war industries, Anaconda and the Army could achieve long-sought objectives: the Army could crush what it deemed a threat to national security; the company could root out from among its employees an extremely irritating influence. Yet by the time the Army achieved its goal the original motive for its action scarcely existed, for the war had ended in November 1918. The company, however, still looked forward to a future free from Wobblies; and by the spring of 1920 most Wobblies had been effectively weeded out of the copper mines of Montana and Arizona.[12]

If the events in the Northwest in the autumn of 1918 seem peculiar, the year of 1919 was strange indeed. It was one of those years, like 1789, or 1848, or 1871, when rumors of impending revolution haunted conservatives and elated radicals. In Russia the Bolsheviks had held power for two years despite domestic chaos, civil war, and external invaders; led by Béla Kun, a communist faction had risen to power in Hungary; and the Bolsheviks also threatened to capture control of postwar Germany. In England an ambitious and growing Labour party proclaimed a postwar reconstruction program that called for the total socialization of British society. In 1919, too, left-wing socialists had broken with the Socialist Party of America in order to found an American Communist party. Though America's communists split into three factions and were compelled by federal action to go underground, not to emerge as a united party until 1922, many citizens took the Bolshevik threat to America seriously. More frightening to most Americans than bolshevism was labor unrest, which was sometimes equated with revolution in the public, as well as the business, mind. In America the year opened with a general strike that paralyzed Seattle for five days in January and ended with the September Boston police strike and the massive nationwide steel strike that lasted into the winter of 1919–1920. In between, over 300,000 coal miners, under the leadership of John L. Lewis, walked out of the mines. More ominous still, that spring and summer bombs were sent to prominent businessmen and public figures, including John D. Rockefeller, Ole Hanson, the anti-Red mayor of Seattle, and Attorney General A. Mitchell Palmer.[13]

Fred Thompson, who was later to become the IWW's last official historian, still recalls 1919 with a special relish. That year he had just come to America from his native Newfoundland, where he had been an ardent teen-age Marxist. In the United States he joined the IWW. Today he remembers 1919 as a time when the IWW membership was at a peak and the revolution seemed close at hand. He has since thought about writing a history of that year, demonstrating how, but for a few unexpected and fortuitous setbacks, the revolution might have come to America. Such romantic notions shared by men who belonged to an organization that had only a past and no future led them to assume major credit for the Seattle general strike and some credit for other labor disturbances that rent America in 1919.[14]

In reality, the IWW was in no position to take credit for major strikes, let alone to lead them. This was demonstrated at its 1919 convention, which met in Chicago in May. Thirteen unions and forty-six delegates representing an undetermined number of members attended the sessions. Among the delegates, hardly a link to the IWW's substantial past could be discovered, excepting perhaps John

Pancner's wife. The names of the secretary-treasurer and the members of the general executive board were unfamiliar. The decisions rendered by the convention seemed still less familiar. Delegates from the AWIU, a body that had once prided itself on its realism and on its experienced, skilled leadership, introduced a resolution forbidding national officials, except for editors, to hold office for two consecutive terms. The convention adopted this resolution. Other delegates proposed a referendum to decide whether legal-defense efforts should be continued—clearly a slap in the face to pre-war IWW leaders then serving prison terms. Despite the organization's lamentable experience with the general strike in the Northwest in 1918, the convention resolved unanimously in favor of a nationwide general strike in the summer of 1919 aimed at liberating all prisoners of the class war. The convention also dismantled the general recruiting union, an institution Haywood had worked so hard to perfect, and it threatened to deny all IWW members then in prison, or even under indictment—virtually the entire prewar leadership—the right to hold office. In a letter sent from his Leavenworth cell to Secretary-Treasurer Thomas Whitehead, Haywood protested these actions. But the 1919 convention seemed unconscious of the IWW's past. It nominated another group of new and inexperienced men for membership on the general executive board. Haywood, who volunteered to serve as editor of the *One Big Union Monthly,* failed to receive enough votes to have his name placed on the ballot; he fared little better as a nominee for the editorship of *Solidarity,* receiving just enough votes to qualify as the third of three candidates for the job, only to have the convention remove his name from candidacy (though after he left prison on appeal bond the general executive board sent him on the road to speak for the *One Big Union Monthly*). Strong leadership had never been the IWW's long suit; now its new leaders made weak leadership a certainty, partly by restricting tenure in office to one term and partly by isolating the organization from most of its former leaders.[15]

The convention decisions came at a particularly inopportune time, for the IWW was in no position to endure another wave of repression such as had almost decimated it during the war. Yet the industrial conflicts and the bomb scares of 1919 set the stage for A. Mitchell Palmer's repressive raids and the beginning of the great Red Scare.[16] Wobblies, it must be said, did their own little bit to bring on the scare. Their flirtations with Russian Bolsheviks, as well as with American communists, and the 1919 convention's mindless general-strike pronunciamento gave worried Americans additional reasons for anxiety.

Before the year ended, Wobblies engaged in armed conflict. Centralia, Washington, was a lumber town in a region with a long history of IWW activity. Like most towns in the area, it had a small IWW hall downtown where Wobblies congregated to chat about old times, read radical literature, and discuss when the revolution would come. That particular hall soon became famous. Centralia's American Legionnaires planned to celebrate Armistice Day, 1919, with a parade; a parade, however, that included an unusual touch of patriotic fervor: destruction of the local IWW hall. Knowing what was coming and acting upon legal advice, the Wobblies prepared to defend their hall against attack. When the Legionnaires' line of march approached IWW headquarters, its participants met an unexpected welcome, for inside, as well as on adjoining rooftops, armed Wobblies prepared to fire upon them. A brief and bloody gunfight followed, during which the more numerous Legionnaires stormed the hall and drove the Wobblies into flight. Bloodied and enraged, the Legionnaires pursued the fleeing Wobblies, cornering one of them on the town's outskirts. Wesley Everest, the trapped Wobbly and a distinguished war veteran, attempted to hold off his pursuers in a gun battle that John Dos Passos was later to describe in his novel *1919*. Outnumbered and encircled, Everest had no choice but to surrender to the Legionnaires, who promptly and unceremoniously castrated and then lynched him. (Another group of local Wobblies was later arrested, charged with the murder of two marchers slain during the attack on the hall, and then tried, convicted, and sentenced to long prison terms.) [17]

Its dramatic element aside, the Centralia incident was of little intrinsic importance to the IWW. It affected no strike, involved no important leaders, destroyed no affiliate, and brought about no real change in IWW attitudes or policies. What it did do was to reveal the lengths to which public authorities and private citizens would go to destroy an already enfeebled organization.

It also coincided with the initiation of Palmer's Red Hunt, a sport in which Wobblies were frequently found to be favorite prey. Shortly after the Centralia affair, a prominent Washington State lumberman wrote to a business associate: "Ordinarily I do not believe in mob law but the action taken by the citizens of Centralia in hanging the leader of the 'Reds' [Everest] was the only right and proper thing. . . . I sincerely trust that . . . the people of the State . . . will take such action as will result in the wiping out of the entire Red gang." Fearing Wobbly-induced violence in his state also, the governor of California wired Palmer: "Will you please at once take all steps possible to the end that America may be kept wholly American." Palmer agreed to do so, and indeed he tried. So did his eager young associate in the Red Hunt, J. Edgar Hoover. Hoover, in fact, sought to make deportation of alien Wobblies an automatic and mandatory procedure, and proposed the selective arrest of Wobblies in groups of five hundred in order to cripple the organization permanently.[18]

In Washington and other states, the IWW had to go underground to survive. "The Wobblies being unable to function legally, that is, they can't speak, write or even run a dance," a former IWW attorney in Washington observed, "are organizing underground." A year later the Supreme Court of Washington declared its state's criminal-syndicalism law to be constitutional, thereby outlawing all Wobblies, and causing their former attorney to comment: "The Wobs are nearly extinct, the Supreme Court decisions, the one handed by the State outlawing them, and the refusal of the U.S. to give them a hearing [a reference to an appeal in the Haywood case] have put them out of existence."[19] Outlawed and forced underground in most Western states, the Wobblies came into close touch with many communists, and many came to believe that the IWW was the radicalism of the past and communism the wave of the future.

The Red Scare and the legal decisions unfavorable to the IWW rendered the organization's ineffectual and inexperienced national officials impotent. Certainly they were in no position to undertake major organizing campaigns or to stimulate industrial conflict. Unable to recruit new members, incapable of improving wages or working conditions for existing members, IWW leaders had become supernumeraries in the labor movement. As such, they began to quarrel about tangential issues, thereby raising problems that effectively drained what little strength the IWW had left at the end of 1919.

From 1920 to 1924 three issues divided the IWW: the status of its political prisoners; its relationship with the Communist party at home and the Comintern abroad; and the distribution of power within the organization between centralists and decentralists, industrial unionists and anarchists. The first issue determined what role the old leadership would play in the post-war IWW; the second decided whether the Wobblies would continue to function as an independent radical entity; and the third irreparably split the organization.

Few organizations could have survived the leadership drain the IWW suffered almost from the day of its birth. Early in its history it had lost Debs, Simons, DeLeon, and Moyer; later, Trautmann, William Z. Foster, and others dropped out; and on the eve of as well as throughout the First World War, Elizabeth Gurley Flynn, Joe Ettor, Carlo Tresca, Arturo Giovannitti, and James P. Cannon, among others, bade the organization farewell. To this small but select group of voluntary dropouts was added the mass of leaders sentenced to federal penitentiary terms. A cursory look at the delegates in attendance at IWW conventions from 1919 through 1924, and at the men nominated for office at these conventions, illustrates the magnitude of the leadership lost to the organization. Such a drain was simply too great a handicap for an organization as inherently weak as the IWW.

Had most of the IWW officials imprisoned in 1918 returned to assume control of the organization when their jail terms ended, there might have been a slim chance for a resurgence of the IWW in the 1920's. From the first, however, imprisonment frayed the nerves of the already edgy Wobbly inmates and vitiated the little solidarity they had brought into prison with them. At Leavenworth the Wobblies quarreled often and bitterly over how they should behave: one faction counseled acquiescence to prison authorities in order to abet the efforts of the general defense committee; another faction advised resistance and even a "general strike" against prison work assignments.[20] These differences over tactics would soon widen into substantial disagreements about the nature of the legal-defense campaign.

While the prisoners quarreled on the inside, on the outside the general defense committee, the American Civil Liberties Union (the renamed National Civil Liberties Bureau), and the Workers' Defense League (directed by Elizabeth Gurley Flynn) waged a legal struggle on two fronts. On one front, attorneys appealed the Chicago, Sacramento, and Wichita verdicts, planning, if necessary, to carry their appeals to the Supreme Court. On the other, the general defense committee, in alliance with a wide variety of middle- and working-class reformers, lobbied within the Justice Department and the White House for pardons. Since the war had ended and patriotic passions had cooled, these groups urged the federal government to commute the sentences of all wartime political prisoners—socialists, Wobblies, and pacifists alike. The IWW meanwhile scraped its slender financial resources together and raised cash collateral sufficient to bring forty-six Wobblies, including Haywood, out of Leavenworth on bond pending the appeals. Coming out in August 1919, these men promptly went to work for the general defense committee, now directed by Haywood, speaking throughout the country in an effort to raise defense funds.[21]

These legal-defense endeavors all ended in failure, which further exacerbated differences within the IWW. As long as Woodrow Wilson sat in the White House and A. Mitchell Palmer controlled the Justice Department, the commutation campaign met a stone wall. In Wilson's view, to pardon or commute the sentences of Debs and the Wobblies would be to concede that they had been imprisoned in the first place for political reasons; moreover, to release them from prison would be tantamount to certifying them as loyal, patriotic Americans, a concession the self-righteous Wilson could never make. The Justice Department fully supported the President in these views. It recommended against commutation, observing that "these persons are all against government in any form and have no respect for law. . . . There is little doubt that if they were released they would immediately return to their former activities."[22]

Warren Harding's election to the presidency, however, promised relief and a new look at the clemency petitions. Harding did prove more flexible than Wilson, but his willingness to bend ironically proved more destructive to the IWW than Wilson's obduracy. At first the Justice Department continued to oppose clemency for the

Wobblies, advising the new President: "The defendants . . . apparently voice the same contempt for the law that they did when they fought for Germany . . . and they would probably again turn to sowing seeds of discontent and preaching revolution . . . if their sentences were commuted." [23]

Judicial appeals had proved equally fruitless. In October 1920 the United States Court of Appeals upheld the decision in the Chicago case on the third and fourth counts, though disallowing the first two (the industrial) counts in the indictment. (In the case of the Sacramento "silent" defenders, all four counts were upheld.) Finally, on April 11, 1921, the Supreme Court refused to review the lower courts' decisions, thereby ending the IWW's legal defense.

When the Supreme Court declined to review the IWW cases, the Wobblies were confronted with yet another crisis. Only thirty-seven of the forty-six Wobblies then out on appeal bond surrendered for confinement; among the nine who disappeared, and hence jumped bond, were Haywood, Vladimir Lossief, and George Andreytchine— all of whom later showed up in Soviet Russia. Haywood's flight, in particular, stunned the Wobblies. For more years than they would have cared to admit, Haywood had symbolized the IWW's cause and spirit in the public mind; Big Bill had seemed the prototypical Wobbly, the rebel ideal type, ever ready to throw down the gauntlet to capitalist injustice. Now unexpectedly refusing to be martyred for the cause he personified, Haywood had betrayed friends and fellow workers (those who had provided collateral for his bond), and deserted the IWW and the United States for communism and exile. As the secretary of the general defense committee sorrowfully informed the 1921 IWW convention: "His reasons for leaving the United States are unknown to me as I had not the least knowledge of his departure, nor even of his intention of taking such a step, until the day I was informed by a Federated Press reporter that he was in Russia." [24] Some Wobblies could not believe that Haywood had fled, and they were certain he would return. Others simply reacted with deep disappointment. One IWW fellow traveler, Mary Gallagher, who was chairman of the Mooney-Billings legal defense organization, was convinced that Haywood's flight had a catastrophic impact on the IWW; it gave Wobblies, she observed, "the same feeling that they always had; that you can't trust your leaders, you can only trust the rank and file. To that extent it weakened their confidence in their own organization." [25] In fact, the bond of confidence between Haywood and other Wobblies had already been broken before he fled to Russia, and this in itself may have been one of the major reasons for his flight into exile.

Like most of Haywood's friends and acquaintances, most historians of the IWW have found his decision to jump bail inexplicable. By and large, they maintain that he naively saw in Soviet Russia the revolution and the new society he had so much wanted to create in America; hence he leaped at the opportunity to help the Russian communists build a workers' state.[26] Actually, the reasons for his decision are much more prosaic. The time Haywood served at the Cook County Jail and at Leavenworth in 1917–1919 undermined his failing health. By the time he left prison on bail he was probably suffering from ulcers and diabetes.[27] Soon he would suffer psychological setbacks as well. Both his advice and his offers to serve the IWW rejected at the 1919 convention, Haywood came out of Leavenworth a physically sick and psychically wounded man. This was evident in his tenure as secretary of the general defense committee. Apparently drinking heavily, Haywood let the defense office fall apart. So chaotic did its operations become that the IWW's general executive board felt compelled to remove Haywood from office. Thus, before he fled to Russia, Haywood had been practically disowned by the IWW. To that degree, at least, it would seem that he fled into exile more as a result of physical illness and psychological depression than as a consequence of his attraction to Soviet communism. Added support for this interpretation arises from Haywood's offer to return to the United States in July 1921 if the Justice Department would agree not to forfeit his bond. For reasons unknown, however, the Justice Department refused to cancel the forfeiture. Had Haywood returned, he would have had to make good his $15,000 bond, as well as to serve a twenty-year prison sentence. Perhaps the federal government preferred to have Haywood an exile in Moscow rather than a political prisoner in Leavenworth.[28]

Haywood's experiences in Russia suggest that exile hurt him at least as much as it did the IWW. Scarcely a Bolshevik, he did not fit into Lenin's or Trotsky's schemes. Expecting to find the Wobblies' utopian workers' state—or a nonpolitical, anarcho-syndicalist society —Haywood instead found revolutionaries busily constructing their own political and industrial bureaucracy. The IWW's anti-organizational approach proved as unacceptable to Russia's new rulers as it had been to America's. For a time Haywood directed a labor project in the Kuznets district, but it is clear that by 1923 his dream of building a Wobbly-style utopia in Russia had soured. Tired and sick, he retired to Moscow's Lux Hotel. Some time later he married a Russian national, a liaison about which there is very little real information. When the American communist leader Alexander Trachtenberg made his pilgrimages to Russia in the 1920's, he usually found Haywood in his Moscow hotel. Much later, Trachtenberg remembered Haywood as having been a desperately lonely man, an alien in Moscow's new society, who found solace in whisky and in the old Wobbly associates who, somehow or other, occasionally drifted into his hotel room. They would join their former chief in drink and song, going interminably through the *Little Red Song Book* until they collapsed in a drunken stupor. These were apparently the high points of Haywood's quiet Moscow exile. Frequently hospitalized, he tried to keep abreast of labor developments at home, and found time to complete his unsatisfactory and distorted autobiography. Finally, on May 28, 1928, Haywood died unmourned in a Moscow hospital. Soviet officials placed part of his ashes beneath a plaque in the Kremlin wall alongside those of John Reed. The remainder were shipped to Chicago's Waldheim Cemetery and placed next to the graves of the Haymarket Riot martyrs.[29]

The Wobblies who returned to prison to join their fellow workers in Leavenworth faced their own crises. In 1922 the clemency campaign had finally achieved some success with President Harding, who in December pardoned Debs and commuted the sentences of eleven Wobblies who agreed to withdraw from the IWW. Then, in June 1923, Harding offered to commute the sentences of the remaining IWW prisoners, except for the Sacramento defendants, if they would agree to remain law-abiding and in no way to encourage law-breaking. By implication, Harding's proposal assumed that the Wobblies had broken the law and had been justly convicted. This caused eleven of the eligible Wobblies to decline the offer and to harass those Wobblies who accepted Harding's proposal. The split between the Leavenworth prisoners on this issue was reflected in IWW convention discussions and in organization journals. Those on the outside favored the recalcitrants and castigated the other prisoners as traitors to the organization. Ralph Chaplin, who accepted commutation in 1923, rationalized his decision and that of the others who acted with him, telling a newspaper reporter that "others among us feel that refusal to accept the formality of President Harding's conditions is tantamount to insisting on our right to break the law at will. To us that appears to be the real admission of guilt. Our friends have supported us in the claim that we are law-abiding. Why should we be afraid to prove it?" But Chaplin was not being entirely honest with himself or with the reporter, for he had written to his father in February 1922: "As I have told you before I have quit the I.W.W. and quit for good . . ." [30] How many other Wobblies had made that same decision is hard to say, but at least one other prisoner, writing to the pardon attorney of his decision to leave the IWW, said: "Sometimes it requires a great experience to see things in their true light and I can frankly say I had mine." [31] Even the recalcitrants did not have much longer to wait for relief, for on December 15, 1923, President Coolidge commuted the sentences of all the remaining wartime prisoners.

The Wobblies who left prison in 1923 returned to an organization that no longer particularly desired them. For understandable reasons, the Wobblies distrusted Chaplin and the others who had accepted commutation in June 1923; for inexplicable reasons, they also distrusted the prisoners who came out in December. Unwanted in positions of leadership by the organization for which they had gone to prison, the freed Wobblies devoted much of their time to internecine battles which disrupted annual conventions and further weakened the organization.[32] It is impossible to determine how many of the prisoners, like Chaplin, returned to the IWW apparently from habit, and not conviction. It seems altogether likely that while in prison other Wobblies, consciously or unconsciously, severed their links to the IWW, thereafter remaining in the organization solely because they had no place else to go.

Some of the leading pre-war Wobblies did indeed have somewhere else to go: the Communist party. As early as 1920 three men well known and admired by many Wobblies had moved toward communism: William Z. Foster, James P. Cannon, and John Reed. Furthermore, Moscow's re-established Third International (Comintern) as well as its newly created Red International of Labor

Unions (RILU, or Profintern) pleaded with IWW leaders to join the common world-wide revolutionary front represented by the Bolsheviks. Several Wobblies found the Bolshevik invitation appealing. Chaplin claimed that Haywood had told him in 1919: "Ralph, here is what we have been dreaming about; here is the I.W.W. all feathered out." Under the imprimatur of the IWW, Harrison George published *The Red Dawn*, a little paean to bolshevism. George Hardy, who served as general secretary-treasurer for a short time in 1921, went to Berlin that year to attend an anti-Bolshevik convention of syndicalist organizations. He stayed only briefly, and then traveled on to Moscow for a longer visit, falling in love with the "future" he saw embodied in the Soviet Union. Returning to America, he called upon the IWW to endorse the dictatorship of the proletariat and to sanction the violent revolutionary seizure of power. Other influential Wobblies followed Haywood, George, and Hardy on their pilgrimage to Moscow.[33]

For many other Wobblies, however, communism offered few attractions. Still dedicated to syndicalism and to nonviolent direct action, they found repugnant a movement based upon control of the state and the violent seizure of power. Committed to the concept of industrial democracy, they found alien the Bolshevik principles of the dictatorship of the proletariat and democratic centralism. Opposed to all forms of coercion and bureaucracy, they looked upon the Soviet system with deep suspicion.

Disagreements over communism further aggravated the IWW's internal disorders. Communism became topic number one in the IWW; when Wobblies weren't fighting over it in their halls or in the streets, they debated the issue in their newspapers and conventions. John Sandgren, in the *One Big Union Monthly*, and C. E. Payne, in the *Industrial Worker*, waged often slanderous rhetorical warfare against communism. At the same time, the editor of *Solidarity* unleashed his heaviest editorial guns in defense of communism. So violent and divisive did these editorial battles become that the 1921 convention removed the editors of both *Solidarity* and the *One Big Union Monthly*, changing the latter's name to the *Industrial Pioneer*. But the verbal battle continued, for the new joint editor of the *Industrial Pioneer* and *Solidarity* advocated communism, and thus continued to clash with Payne of the *Industrial Worker*. At annual conventions IWW delegates debated whether to send delegates to RILU conferences, their decisions usually coming only after extremely close votes.[34] George Williams, the IWW delegate dispatched to Moscow in 1921, was repelled by what he observed in the Soviet Union and, in a report to the IWW, asserted that the Bolsheviks intended to capture the IWW for communism. He also charged that a communist takeover would leave the Wobblies with neither an organization nor principles.[35]

Acting on Williams' report, in 1922 the IWW's general executive board rejected IWW participation in the Profintern. Restating traditional IWW syndicalist doctrines (which the 1922 leaders believed to be industrial unionism), the general executive board explained why Wobblies and communists had nothing in common. "The history of American unionism testifies to the destructive influence of labor politics and politicians," the IWW statement asserted. "Experience has proven that when politics moves into a union economic effectiveness moves out, and hope for the workers moves out with it." To insure that its point was understood, the general executive board emphasized the following: "We believe that the character of the state will not permit that institution to aid the proletariat in its class struggle. Therefore, we teach the workers that . . . through economic class organization . . . they will be enabled to protect themselves against the hostility of the capitalist state." Moreover, most Wobblies held that workers could not make a successful revolution through the violent seizure of power; instead, they could create the new society only through the slow and tedious process of constructing industrial unions which would parallel the giant corporations in structure and function and thus train the workers eventually to seize control of industry peacefully and to operate it in the interest of the proletariat.[36] To most Wobblies, who remained loyal to the faith as it had been handed down to them in 1908 and after, coalition or compromise with the communists remained impossible.[37]

In fact, no matter what the IWW did on the issue of communism it stood to lose. Had it entered the Profintern and formed a coalition with the American communists, it would undoubtedly have been subverted as a distinct organization and swallowed up by the more organized, more industrious, and better-financed communists. Choosing, as it did eventually, to oppose communism, and in language even more violent than that later used by post–World War II "cold warriors," it only succeeded in isolating itself from the center of revolutionary ferment in the 1920's and 1930's without entering the mainstream of American society. In other words, in the end Wobblies were forced to decide whether to remain ideologically pure and organizationally impotent, or ideologically corrupted and organizationally nonexistent.

By the time of its 1924 convention, then, the IWW stood on the verge of collapse, needing only the slightest nudge to push it over into the abyss of nonexistence. Its decline can be traced in the annual convention proceedings, in the factional struggles between prisoners and free Wobblies, in its debates between pro- and anti-communists. Where the IWW had once been a lustily militant labor organization famous for its leadership in free-speech fights and industrial conflicts, it now began to look more like an amateur debating society. From 1920 to 1924 the reports of the annual conventions show an amazing turnover in leadership. Each year a new generation rose to power in the IWW, each more inexperienced and inept than its predecessor. The 1919 convention delegates insured that the IWW would never have mature, experienced leaders when they amended the constitution to forbid officers to serve consecutive terms. Despite annual general executive board recommendations that this amendment be repealed, the delegates refused to abandon it. Finally, at the 1923 convention the delegates voted to abolish the entire existing general office structure, including the office of general secretary-treasurer, though a year later another IWW convention restored the abolished positions.

The sterility of the IWW during the 1920's can also be charted in other aspects of the annual conventions. Instead of spending time with proposals for organizing workers, delegates emphasized education and propaganda, devoting more discussion to IWW newspapers than to IWW organizers. This new emphasis on education in place of industrial conflict enabled an industrial engineer named Howard Scott in 1920–1921 to gull Ralph Chaplin into promoting a Bureau of Research within the IWW, which would supply the Wobblies with the scientific information about industry necessary to organize brain-workers—scientists, technicians, and professionals, the new "expert" class—and thus to establish the perfect worker-controlled technocracy. Taking $3,500 from the IWW, Scott gave the organization nothing substantial in return.[38] The IWW's finances and membership tumbled downhill in the 1920's; by 1924 Secretary-Treasurer Tom Doyle, speaking for a leadership that laid claim to an almost invisible membership, reported an absolutely bankrupt treasury. During the period 1920–1924 the number of affiliated unions and delegates in attendance at annual IWW conventions declined steadily. Even at the crucial 1924 convention, which decided the IWW's future, only nine unions and twenty-six delegates were seated.[39]

The 1924 convention completed the disruption of the IWW. Delegates arrived in Chicago to find two separate sessions scheduled —one called by the existing officials, the other announced by James Rowan and the West Coast lumber workers' union. On the fifth day of the regularly scheduled convention, delegates voted to suspend the IWW's entire national leadership, including the bulk of the general executive board and the Lumber Workers' Industrial Union No. 120, the IWW's largest affiliate. After the convention, the contending factions, in a fashion reminiscent of 1906, struggled in the streets and in the courts for control of IWW headquarters at 1001 West Madison Street. When the new leaders enthroned by the 1924 convention secured title to headquarters, they insured their own future impotence by denying Richard Brazier and Forrest Edwards, two prominent and outstanding pre-war Wobblies, roles in reconstructing the IWW.[40]

It is nearly impossible to fathom the issues dividing the two main IWW factions in 1924. The reasons for the split usually cited by historians—centralization versus decentralization, and the prison commutation questions—clearly were *not* vital. Convention debates indicate that Wobblies split not about centralism and decentralism, anarcho-syndicalism and industrial unionism, as most historians have asserted; rather, they were divided over tactics, and particularly over what constituted the most effective type of centralized organization. Those who are generally characterized as anarcho-syndicalists (or decentralists) were in fact advocates of the type of autonomous industrial unionism later favored by the CIO unions; the so-called centralists (the industrial unionists of 1924) advocated the "One Big Union" concept, a belief that usually insured organizational chaos. The question of conditional pardons and commutations never figured significantly during the 1924 convention, which dragged on for almost a month. The factional strife which surfaced in that year thus appears to be more a result of organizational failure and frustration than it was of internal divisions over vital substantive issues of policy. Lacking flourishing affiliates or major industrial conflicts in which they could sublimate their hostilities, the frustrated delegates released their aggressions on each other. In the process, they wrecked the organization to which they proclaimed undying loyalty.[41]

Reflecting years later on the impact of the 1924 schism, Mary Gallagher surmised: "My personal opinion has been that the whole split was engineered to break up the I.W.W. as completely as possible." [42]

Contrary to her notion, the IWW division did not occur as the result of a conspiracy, though the end was the same as if it had: total collapse. In California, where for a brief time the IWW had increased its membership, scores of Wobblies dropped away, never to return. Rowan went back to Washington State in 1925 to resume his fight against the IWW leadership by calling upon timber workers and other Wobblies to join his Emergency Program to save the IWW. By 1926, however, Rowan's movement was almost bankrupt, and in 1930 it claimed at best two hundred followers.[43] Old-time Wobblies, who had remained loyal out of habit or conviction, silently slipped away from the IWW. At the 1925 convention only eleven delegates representing seven unions met. Another convention would not be held until 1928, when seven unions would send a total of eight delegates; then there would be another three-year hiatus until seven Wobblies representing eight unions convened in 1931. By then, IWW conventions seemed more like college homecomings in which alumni exaggerated the good old days than like the sessions of a radical labor organization.

Unable to maintain a vital role in American radicalism in the 1920's (a decade during which radicalism in general reached its nadir), deserted by many of their former leaders and sympathizers, irrevocably divided among themselves, those Wobblies who kept the faith disappeared into what the journalist Dan Wakefield has characterized as "haunted halls." [44] In seedy little store-front head-quarters in Seattle, San Pedro, Houston, New York—anywhere a few Wobblies could maintain a local—the old-timers would get together to scan dog-eared IWW tracts and fresh copies of the *Industrial Worker,* and to chat amiably about the revolution that had not been but that might yet be. The most loyal of the old breed maintained a national headquarters in Chicago. There on North Halsted Street, above a rundown Syrian restaurant which occupied the first floor of a two-story brick building, a dwindling staff edited the *Industrial Worker,* produced leaflets and tracts for the times, collected dues, counted members, and kept the books on battered adding machines and typewriters. Everything in the office, from the literature and the furniture to the portraits of martyrs Joe Hill and Frank Little, had the smell of the past. Yet on occasion, even after 1924, the IWW's ghostly spirit emerged from its haunted halls to trouble America's conscience.

Epilogue

CHAPTER

19

Remembrance of Things Past: The IWW Legacy

A s recently as December 1967 the IWW convened a district meeting at Chicago national headquarters on North Halsted Street. A small group of delegates and their wives met on a quiet Saturday afternoon to discuss the iniquities of the war in Vietnam and the unlikely prospects of interesting American workers in the IWW. None represented a legitimate trade union, none had been a Wobbly during the organization's heyday. Like Carl Keller and Walter Westman, who were in their seventies, or like Fred Thompson, who was near retirement, they were mostly old men who could still dream about revolutions that might have been, great times that had been, fellow workers that had passed away, and the IWW martyrs under whose portraits they now sat and reminisced. After three hours of discussion, these remnants of a once-feared and militant breed of labor radicals adjourned, taking home their memories and dreams.[1] What had once been an impressive set of beliefs had become little more than insignificant private fantasies. Soon even the last physical reminder of the original IWW would disappear, for the city of Chicago planned to demolish Wobbly headquarters as part of its urban renewal program.

So completely had the old Wobblies withdrawn to their private world that several were almost completely unaware that the young rebels and radicals who during the 1960's criticized society did so in terms reminiscent of the IWW in its youth. In the face of long-haired college students and members of the "New Left" who castigated America's power structure; reviled the symbols of authority, among them the police, the state, and the church; rejected "bourgeois morality"; and demanded direct action and "participatory democracy," old Wobblies like Fred Thompson sometimes reacted much as Joe Hill had once responded to the "long-haired preachers [who] come out every night, try to tell you what's wrong and what's right . . ." Thompson on occasion felt like saying to the militant students—mostly children of privilege who had neither worked for their living nor endured exploitation—what Hill had advised the Salvation Army's preachers:

> You will eat, bye and bye
> When you've learned how to cook and to fry;
> Chop some wood, 'twill do you good,
> And you'll eat in the sweet bye and bye.[2]

At the twenty-eighth "national" convention, held in Chicago in September 1968, twenty-three delegates did spend some time considering whether the IWW should admit students and housewives as full-fledged members, but little came of the discussion. One member proposed that housewives be admitted to the food-handlers' union.

If the IWW lost touch with the radical realities of American life and society in the 1960's, its commitment to industrial unionism had long since been appropriated by the AFL-CIO. The tide of new immigrants had diminished to a trickle, and the children and grandchildren of the old immigrants had made a satisfactory accommodation to American society. Mechanization had displaced the harvesters of wheat. California's remaining migratories had finally found in Cesar Chavez a new, effective, and indigenous leader. Other voices and other groups now offered black Americans hope for today and promise for the future. There was nowhere for the lonely survivors of the IWW to go.

Yet those Wobblies who retained the faith continued to publish the *Industrial Worker,* to peddle *The Little Red Song Book,* and to collect dues and issue membership cards. When they pass away, the IWW will die, for, unlike the neighborhood surrounding its Chicago headquarters, it cannot be renewed.[3]

Perhaps the most remarkable feature about the IWW has been its extended old age. After a ten-year period of infancy and adolescence extending from 1905 to 1915, it enjoyed three years of maturity, followed by almost half a century of declining virility and approaching senility. No longer a vital presence on the American radical scene after 1919, only a shell of its former self after 1924, the IWW could on occasion still momentarily recapture the essence of its remarkable past.

One fact should be made clear: IWW influence and effectiveness cannot be measured in terms of organization membership. If one believed the published membership records and the reminiscences of old Wobblies, the organization was most powerful from 1919 to 1923, when it maintained a membership that fluctuated between 58,000 and 100,000, the best five-year record in the organization's history.[4] Yet employers and government officials seemed less threatened by the "large" postwar IWW than they had been by the "small" pre-war IWW. Even if the IWW had thousands of members in the post-war period, it had lost relevance as a working-class organization, and it lacked the power to tie up the woods of the Northwest or to paralyze copper mining.[5] In fact, many members probably paid dues for old times' sake, given the minimal sum necessary to maintain their membership in good standing. Granting the haphazardness of IWW bookkeeping methods, it is also conceivable that many, if not most, of its new recruits during those years were simply former members renewing lapsed memberships—sometimes even more than once in the same year. Even in the IWW's heyday, during Haywood's tenure as general secretary-treasurer, what one Wobbly, the seaman Bob Willock, told Dan Wakefield in 1956 had to some extent been true: "The fellows who still belong, it's mostly an ideal with them. You can't keep paying dues on two unions, and the one that gets you a job is the one you take." But for a time some workers probably continued to pay double dues: minimal ones to the IWW, which had once offered them the promise of a better society free from exploitation; high dues to AFL affiliates, which did something tangible about exploitation.[6] In that sense, the IWW from 1919 to 1923 was a radical fellowship and not a functioning labor organization. The internal disputes that plagued Wobblies during those years, culminating in the 1924 split, diminished the fellowship aspects of membership and thus accounted to a considerable extent for the precipitous decline in membership after 1924. Thereafter no concrete membership statistics were published or revealed, and by 1930 the IWW could at best claim seven thousand to eight thousand members. By 1949, when the federal government included it on the Attorney General's list of "subversive" organizations, the IWW was credited with having fourteen hundred members. Since then, owing to death, illness, and loss of faith, membership has dwindled much further.[7]

But even in decline the IWW waged several major industrial conflicts significant enough to attract public attention and to recall its pre-war struggles. For a brief time in 1923–1924 the IWW experienced a resurgence in California, particularly among maritime workers, who were long a prime source of Wobbly recruits.[8] Since the end of World War I, Andrew Furuseth's West Coast Seamen's Union, an AFL affiliate, had been torn by internal dissension and weakened by an employer anti-union drive fostered by recessions. Compelled in 1921 by shrinking membership and aggressive employers to accept a contract that cut wages and in other ways benefited management, Furuseth's union splintered as he drove all so-called "reds" from his organization. Wobblies picked up the pieces of the shattered AFL affiliate by promising California's maritime workers militancy, solidarity, and bitter-end opposition to wage cuts. Many dissatisfied seamen and ousted AFL unionists consequently drifted into the IWW's Marine Transport Workers' Industrial Union. Before long an old ritual repeated itself: as the IWW and AFL affiliates fought each other, employers played one union off against the other. Wobblies had unusual success in San Pedro (the port of Los Angeles), where they often pulled sailors off a ship just before its departure and, through such unexpected "quickie" strikes, won improved conditions. Elated by rising membership and instant success, the Marine Transport Workers decided to call a general strike for April 25, 1923.[9]

As so often in the past, the general strike proved both the zenith and the nadir of the IWW's activities among marine workers. When longshoremen joined the sailors' strike on April 25, San Pedro's shipping was nearly paralyzed, and shipping in San Francisco harbor was also seriously crippled, though longshoremen there remained on the job. But the Wobblies as usual had too many enemies. Not only did they have to combat employers and Furuseth's union (which provided strikebreakers); they also had to contend with public authorities who made wholesale arrests of union organizers and speakers. When Upton Sinclair, the novelist and socialist reformer, attempted to read the preamble to the United States Constitution at a meeting of strikers and sympathizers, the police arrested him and held him in detention for twenty-four hours. In the end the IWW's opponents proved too strong, and on May 24, 1923, waterfront workers ended their walkout at San Pedro (it had long since petered out in San Francisco), voting to malinger.[10]

Despite its defeat, the IWW's Marine Transport Workers' Union temporarily retained the support of San Pedro's workers. The organization held regular and well-attended meetings in both English and Spanish, as well as Sunday classes and Saturday evening forums. The continued life of the IWW apparently threatened San Pedro's employers and authorities, for they encouraged Ku Klux Klanners and vigilantes to harass the Wobblies. In his study of the IWW, John S. Gambs cites the alleged statement of a Los Angeles police captain, who remarked about a local businessman: "He told me to take a bunch of my men, arm them with clubs, go up on Liberty Hill [an IWW meeting place in San Pedro] and break the heads of the Wobblies."[11] Vigilante attacks on the IWW culminated on June 14, 1924. That day San Pedro's Wobblies, with their wives and children, attended a benefit show at the IWW's hall in memory of two dead fellow workers. While children danced and sang before an audience of some three hundred people, 150 men armed with guns, blackjacks, and axes waited outside the hall for a signal. Receiving their prearranged sign, they attacked the people inside, beating men and women, destroying furniture, and taking sadistic delight in scalding the children with an urn of boiling coffee. Nine Wobblies earned an added dose of vigilante justice: thrown into a pickup truck, they were transported forty-one miles to Santa Ana Canyon, there to be stripped naked, beaten, tarred and feathered, and made to walk back to city limits. The police, later finishing what the vigilantes had started, systematically drove the Wobblies from the waterfront.[12]

Three years later an industrial conflict in Colorado once again returned the IWW to national attention. Just as AFL unionism in the maritime industry had declined in the 1920's as a result of economic recession and intra-union dissension, so unionism among soft-coal miners collapsed in those same years. Throughout the country the once-powerful United Mine Workers decayed, as employers, facing a shrinking market for coal yet benefiting from rising labor productivity, fought the unions; meanwhile, within the unions, factions for and against John L. Lewis fought one another. In Colorado, as elsewhere, UMW locals approved contracts which included wage cuts and other infringements on union rights. As wages tumbled in the state's soft-coal districts, miners, frustrated by their union's conservatism, turned in increasing numbers to a recently founded local of the IWW: Industrial Union 210-220. The IWW made rapid progress in recruiting Colorado coal miners, particularly after A. S. Embree, a leading pre-war organizer just released from prison in Montana, arrived to direct the effort. Again, despite opposition from employers, AFL affiliates, and public officials, the IWW planned to lead its followers out on strike.[13]

After failing to win limited economic objectives from mine owners —most notably from the Colorado Fuel and Iron Company *—or to gain assistance from the state industrial commission in improving working conditions, IWW members walked out of the mines in October 1927. Everything associated with the struggle in Colorado bore the distinctive traits of an IWW conflict. Although Embree and other Wobbly leaders agitated and organized, the coal miners themselves made the final decisions about tactics, objectives, and actual negotiations. Strike relief efforts demonstrated the IWW's old flair for publicity and color: car caravans from as far away as California brought fresh leaders, food supplies, and money to the strike district.[14] The IWW's opponents also reacted as expected: ignoring the miners' tangible economic grievances and their actual demands, employers, newspapers, and AFL leaders focused upon the IWW's alleged subversive character. Vigilantes, local police, state police, and finally national guardsmen harassed, arrested, beat, and shot miners and their sympathizers. Against this opposition the strikers could not resist beyond February 1928. They returned to the mines, advised by Embree: "Do not mistakenly make . . . sacrifices of no avail by refusing to return to work now. . . . Vote for your organization. Vote to return to work at once. Take your splendid solidarity with

---

* The Rockefeller subsidiary made infamous as a result of the 1914 Ludlow "Massacre," an unprovoked militia attack on striking miners and their families at a Colorado tent camp.

you to your jobs." On their return to work the miners received a dollar-a-day increase in wages and a corresponding rise in the tonnage rates—the only such increase reported between 1928 and 1930 in any American coal field.[15]

This strike has been described by one scholar as a gem of tactical perfection, a struggle in which "the IWW projected . . . leadership that was at once democratic, peaceful, conservative, and selectively law-abiding . . . and . . . calculated to give the widest and freest opportunity for the expression of the strikers' views."[16] Yet when it was over, what did the Wobblies have to show for their genius? Very little indeed! The only Colorado coal miners to win union recognition as a result of the IWW-led strike were UMWA members; moreover, the residue of unionism left behind among unorganized miners later redounded to the benefit of a revitalized United Mine Workers. As an IWW leader informed Mary Gallagher in the summer of 1928: "We are anything but prosperous and the strike in Colorado last winter . . . put us in hock for some time."[17]

Bankrupt and decrepit at the peak of prosperity, the IWW could scarcely be expected to withstand the severe depression about to grip the nation. In 1928 Wobblies devoted more thought to reorganizing their general-defense committee than to organizing workers.[18] Not much could be expected of such a labor organization when bad times came and millions of American workers clamored for an escape from the industrial wilderness in which they felt themselves trapped.

With the depression, the IWW floundered. Apart from minor involvements on the fringes of the labor warfare of the 1930's in bloody Harlan County, Kentucky, among coal miners, and in Washington State's Yakima Valley among hop pickers,[19] where Wobblies endured their usual indignities, the IWW was more isolated than ever from the mainstream of radicalism and the labor movement. Communists, not Wobblies, now led unemployed workers in protest demonstrations and hunger marches. Symbolically, Ralph Chaplin was silenced at a Chicago street-corner meeting by young communists who drowned out his voice by loudly singing *Solidarity Forever,* Chaplin's most famous song.[20] When Franklin Roosevelt became President and for the first time in American history the federal government actively encouraged the emergence of independent unionism, the IWW was too weak to benefit. In fact, it criticized both Section 7a of the National Industrial Recovery Act and the 1935

Wagner (National Labor Relations) Act for placing the government in an area where it did not belong: labor-management relations. The IWW's critique of the Wagner Act was in fact remarkably like that issued by the National Association of Manufacturers!

Incapable of competing with communism's variety of revolution, the IWW was equally unable to contend with the CIO's variety of industrial unionism. In steel, in autos, in rubber, lumber, textiles, and on the high seas, CIO unions gained those areas of potential industrial unionism long since relinquished by the Wobblies. CIO leaders and organizers did not have to resort to IWW guidelines, nor to Wobbly precedents, in order to attract the loyalty of mass-production workers and to organize them in stable, effective industrial unions. Mostly refugees from the AFL, CIO leaders found adequate precedents for industrial unionism in the AFL's own history; AFL miners, brewery workers, and garment workers had consistently advocated and practiced versions of industrial unionism; with its own hallowed tradition of conservative syndicalism, the AFL had also consistently stressed the primacy of working-class direct action over the more indirect and more compromising strategy of political action.

Some Wobblies realized that times had changed and that their former organization had lost its purpose, as John Pancner's personal decision in the 1930's indicated. No member had stayed with the IWW longer, nor suffered more frequent imprisonments, than Pancner (he had been one of the 1918 federal prisoners), yet during the labor crisis of the 1930's he joined the CIO, affiliating with a United Auto Workers' local in Detroit and remaining a loyal UAW-CIO man.[21] While Pancner was not alone among Wobblies in making that decision, the prominence of his role in the IWW and his loyal twenty-five-year commitment to that organization gave his action a special significance.

The CIO's success diminished any prospects Wobblies might have had for a rebirth of their organization. With skilled workers firmly committed to the AFL, the mass-production workers enthralled and rewarded by the CIO, and most of the unorganized laborers hostile to any form of unionism, the Wobblies had no place to go except back into their "haunted halls."

When the Second World War ended in 1945 and the Cold War began the following year, the IWW was little more than a historical relic. *Time* magazine sarcastically described its 1946 convention as a family reunion of thirty-nine men and a grandmotherly-looking woman, who met in an office building on the North Side of Chicago to pass resolutions that denounced capitalism, fascism, Nazism, the CIO, and the AFL. "With that off their chests, the Industrial Workers of the World went home." [22]

Even at home old Wobblies could not rest in peace. Revisionist writers like the novelist Wallace Stegner and the economist Vernon Jensen suggested, in 1948 and 1951 respectively, that perhaps Joe Hill had been a thug, a gunman, and a murderer, and had deserved the conviction handed down by a Utah jury and the punishment inflicted by a firing squad. Fred Thompson and the friends of the IWW, of course, responded with a perfervid defense of Hill published in the *New Republic* and at greater length in the *Industrial Worker*.[23] The federal government meanwhile had not entirely forgotten the Wobblies. Victimized by an earlier red scare, Wobblies again fell prey to the anti-radical hysteria ignited by the Cold War and fanned by Senator Joseph McCarthy. After doing battle with American and foreign communists for three decades, the remaining Wobblies in 1949 found themselves included on Attorney General Tom Clark's list of subversive organizations. Unable to hire a lawyer or to send a member to appear before the Subversive Activities Control Board in Washington to challenge the Attorney General's decision, the IWW was shorn of the right to act as a collective-bargaining agency for American workers under the terms of the Taft-Hartley Act. (In addition, Wobblies refused, on principle, to sign loyalty oaths.) Ostracized by organized labor and by the government, the IWW had become an organization of charming but tired old men and a handful of alienated college students who were unsure about where to take their dissatisfaction with American society.

In their analyses of the IWW's eventful history, several scholars have concluded that had it not been for America's entry into World War I and the repression of the organization that ensued, the IWW might well have usurped the CIO's subsequent role in organizing mass-production workers. These scholars believe that the base established by the IWW among harvesters, loggers, and copper miners would have become sufficiently stable, had war not intervened, for the Wobblies later to have penetrated other unorganized sectors of the economy.[24] This rendering of history leads one to conclude that the IWW's ultimate failure was more a result of external repression than of internal inadequacies.

Nothing, of course, need be inevitable. Yet given the internal deficiencies of the IWW, the aspirations of most of its members during the organization's heyday, and the dynamics of American capitalism—what might better be called the "American system"—the Wobblies' attempt to transform American workers into a revolutionary vanguard was doomed to failure. Wobbly doctrine taught workers how to gain short-range goals indistinguishable from those sought by ordinary, non-revolutionary trade unions. Able to rally exploited workers behind crusades to abolish specific grievances, the IWW failed to transform its followers' concrete grievances into a higher consciousness of class, ultimate purpose, and necessary revolution; to create, in short, a revolutionary working class in the Marxist sense. This was so because the IWW never explained precisely how it would achieve its new society —apart from vague allusions to the social general strike and to "building the new society within the shell of the old"—or how, once established, it would be governed. Wobblies simply suggested that the state, at least as most Americans knew it, would disappear. Hence, at their best IWW ideologues offered only warmed-over versions of St.-Simon's technocratic society, with gleanings from Edward Bellamy's *Looking Backward*—scarcely a workable prescription for revolution in the modern world. In their imprecise ideology and vague doctrine, the Wobblies too often substituted romantic anarcho-utopianism for hard analysis of social and economic realities.

Even had the IWW had a more palatable prescription for revolution, it is far from likely that its followers would have taken it. In fact, IWW members had limited revolutionary potential. At the IWW's founding convention Haywood had alluded to lifting impoverished Americans up from the gutter. But those lying in Haywood's metaphorical gutters thought only of rising to the sidewalk, and once there of entering the house. Individuals locked in the subculture of poverty share narrow perspectives on life and society; as Oscar Lewis has observed, the main blight of the "culture of poverty is the poverty of its culture." [25] Struggling just to maintain body, such men lacked the time or comfort to worry much about their souls; they could think only of the moment, not the future, only of a better job or more food, not of a distant utopian society.

This placed the IWW in an impossible dilemma. On the one hand, it was committed to ultimate revolution; on the other, it sought immediate improvements for its members. Like all men who truly care about humanity, the Wobblies always accepted betterment for their members today at the expense of achieving utopia tomorrow. This had been true at Lawrence, McKees Rocks, and Paterson, among other places, where the IWW allowed workers to fight for immediate improvements, a result which, if achieved, inevitably diminished their discontent and hence their revolutionary potential. Even at Paterson, where IWW-led strikers failed to win concessions, some Wobblies discerned the dilemma of their position—the leaders' desire for revolution coming up against their members' desire for palpable gains.

Internally, the Wobblies never made up their minds about precisely what kind of structure their organization should adopt. By far the most capable IWW leaders favored an industrial union structure under which largely independent, though not entirely autonomous, affiliates organized by specific industry would cooperate closely with each other under the supervision of an active general executive board. But many lesser leaders, and more among the rank and file, were captivated with the concept of the One Big Union (the mythical OBU) in which workers, regardless of skill, industry, nationality, or color, would be amalgamated into a single unit. Incapable of negotiating union-management agreements owing to its protean character, the OBU would be solely the vessel of revolution. Considering the inherent difficulties involved in organizing unskilled workers on a stable basis, organizational form and structure was an issue of the utmost importance. Yet it remained a problem that the Wobblies never resolved satisfactorily.

This was not the only issue the IWW failed to resolve. Operating in industries traditionally hostile to unionism, Wobblies aggravated hard-core employer prejudices. To employers who rejected negotiations with AFL affiliates that offered to sign and to respect binding legal contracts, the IWW offered unremitting industrial war, for it refused to sign time agreements reached through collective bargaining, and declined to respect labor-management contracts. Hesitant to recognize unions on any basis, management thus had less reason to acknowledge the IWW. If the IWW had had the raw economic power to win concessions without time agreements and written contracts, its policies might have made some sense. But time and again it challenged powerful employers from behind union fortifications erected on sand.

Its mythology concerning rank-and-file democracy—comprising what today is known as "participatory democracy"—further compounded the IWW's internal deficiencies. The IWW had been most successful when led by strong individuals like Haywood, who centralized general headquarters in 1916, or Walter Nef, who constructed a tightly knit and carefully administered Agricultural Workers' Organization. Too often, however, jealous and frustrated Wobblies, lacking the abilities of a Haywood or a Nef, but desiring their power and positions, used the concept of "participatory democracy" to snipe at the IWW's leaders on behalf of an idealized rank and file. And without firm leadership the organization drifted aimlessly.

Even had the IWW combined the necessary structure, the proper tactics, and experienced, capable leaders, as it did for a time from 1915 to 1917, its difficulties might still have proved insurmountable. There is no reason to believe that before the 1930's any of America's basic mass-production industries could have been organized. Not until World War II was the CIO, an organization with immense financial resources, millions of members, and federal encouragement, able to solidify its hold on the nation's mass-production industries. And even then the CIO made no headway among migratory workers or Southern mill hands.[26] What reason, then, is there to think that the IWW could have succeeded in the 1920's or earlier, when it lacked funds, counted its members by the thousands, not the millions, and could scarcely expect government assistance? To ask the question is to answer it.

Yet had the IWW done everything its academic critics ask of it—established true industrial unions, accepted long-term officials and a permanent union bureaucracy, signed collective agreements with employers and agreed to respect them—done, in other words, what the CIO did, what would have remained of its original purpose?[27] Had the founders of the IWW been interested in simply constructing industrial unions on the model of the CIO, the advice of their scholarly critics would be well taken. But the IWW was created by radicals eager to revolutionize American society, and to have asked them to deny their primary values and goals would have been to ask too much.

Whatever the IWW's internal dilemmas, the dynamics of American history unquestionably compounded them. Unlike radicals in other societies who contended with established orders unresponsive to lower-class discontent and impervious to change from within, the Wobblies struggled against flexible and sophisticated adversaries. The years of IWW growth and success coincided with the era when welfare capitalism spread among American businesses, when all levels of government began to exhibit solicitude for the workingman, and when the catalyst of reform altered all aspects of national society. This process became even more pronounced during World War I, when the federal government used its vast power and influence to hasten the growth of welfare capitalism and conservative unionism. Whatever success the Wobblies achieved only stimulated the reform process, for employers who were threatened by the IWW paid greater attention to labor relations, and government agencies, initially called upon to repress labor strife, encouraged employers to improve working conditions. While IWW leaders felt federal repression during World War I, their followers enjoyed eight-hour days, grievance boards, and company unions. Put more simply, reform finally proved a better method than repression for weakening the IWW's appeal to workers.

Although the IWW ultimately failed to achieve its major objectives, it nevertheless bequeathed Americans an invaluable legacy. Those young Americans who practice direct action, passive resistance, and civil disobedience, and who seek an authentic "radical tradition," should find much to ponder in the Wobblies' past. Those who distrust establishment politics, deride bureaucracies, favor community action, and preach "participatory democracy" would also do well to remember the history of the IWW. Indeed, all who prefer a society based upon community to one founded on coercion cannot afford to neglect the tragic history of the IWW.

In this history, two lessons stand out. The first underscores the harsh truth of Antonio Gramsci's comment, quoted earlier, that in advanced industrial nations revolutionaries should take as their slogan: "Pessimism of the Intelligence; Optimism of the Will." The second lesson emphasizes the irony of the radical experience in America, and elsewhere in the Western industrial world. As a result of their commitment to ultimate revolution as well as to immediate improvements in the existence of the working class, radicals the world over quickened the emergence of strong labor unions and acted as midwives at the birth of the "welfare state." But success, instead of breeding more success, only produced a new working class enthralled with a consumer society and only too willing, even eager, to trade working-class consciousness for a middle-class style of life. The ultimate tragedy, then, for all radicals, the American Wobblies included, has been that the brighter they have helped make life for the masses, the dimmer has grown the prospect for revolution in the advanced societies.

Yet no better epitaph could be written for the American Wobbly than A. S. Embree's comment from his prison cell in 1917: "The end in view is well worth striving for, but in the struggle itself lies the happiness of the fighter."

NOTES

Preface

1. The origin of the descriptive term "Wobbly" for IWW members is uncertain. The most common and accepted version has been offered by Stewart Holbrook, who suggested that it derived from a Chinese restaurant owner in Alberta, Canada, who served IWW's and responded to criticism by saying, "Eye Like Eye Wobbly Wobbly." "Wobbly Talk," *American Mercury*, VII (January 1926), 62.

2. John Dos Passos, *The 42nd Parallel* (New York, 1930), pp. 89–93, 100–109; James Jones, *From Here to Eternity* (New York, 1951), pp. 640–642; Wallace Stegner, *The Preacher and the Slave* (Boston, 1950); Barrie Stavis, *The Man Who Would Not Die* (New York, 1954).

3. Thomas R. Brooks, *Toil and Trouble: A History of American Labor* (New York, 1964), Ch. 9.

4. Richard Brazier, "The Story of the I.W.W.'s 'Little Red Song Book,'" *Labor History*, IX (Winter 1968), 91–105.

5. "The IWW in California," Commission on Industrial Relations Papers, Department of Labor, Record Group 174, National Archives.

Chapter 1: A Setting for Radicalism, 1877–1917

1. Sigmund Diamond, ed., *The Nation Transformed* (New York, 1963), p. 6.

2. U.S. Bureau of the Census, *Historical Statistics of the United States* (Washington, 1960), p. 44.

3. John Moody, *The Truth About Trusts* (New York, 1904), p. xi and *passim;* Edward C. Kirkland, *Industry Comes of Age* (New York, 1961), Ch. 8 and 10; Alfred D. Chandler, Jr., *Strategy and Structure* (New York, 1966 ed.), Ch. 1.

4. Robert Hunter, *Poverty: Social Conscience in the Progressive Era* (New York, 1965 ed.), pp. 24–27, 31–32. Hunter's estimates and extrapolations are based largely on charity applications and unemployment statistics. His estimates, though imprecise, seem conservative.

5. Mary Van Kleeck, "Working Hours of Women in Factories," *Charities and the Commons*, XVII (October 6, 1906), 13–16.

6. C. Vann Woodward, *Origins of the New South* (Baton Rouge, 1951), p. 206.

7. U.S. Immigration Commission, *Abstract: Report on Immigrants in Manufacturing and Mining* (Washington, 1911), p. 143; Marcus E. Ravage, *An American in the Making* (New York, 1917), pp. 66–67.

8. Fred A. Shannon, *The Farmer's Last Frontier: Agriculture, 1860–1897* (New York, 1945), pp. 159, 367; Carey McWilliams, *Factories in the Field* (Boston, 1939), Ch. 1–9.

9. Herbert Gutman, "The Tompkins Square Riot in New York City on January 13, 1874," *Labor History*, VI (Winter 1965), 70.

10. John Roche, "Entrepreneurial Liberty and the 14th Amendment," *Labor History*, IV (Winter 1963), 3–31.

11. Norman Ware, *The Labor Movement in the United States, 1860–1895* (New York, 1929), p. xviii.

12. *Ibid.*, p. xii; Philip S. Foner, *History of the Labor Movement in the United States: From the Founding of the American Federation of Labor to the Emergence of American Imperialism* (New York, 1955), II, 132–144.

13. See Norman Pollack, *The Populist Response to Industrial America: Midwestern Populist Thought* (Cambridge, Mass., 1962), on the theme of Populism's radical social critique.

14. DeLeon is quoted in *ibid.*, p. 88; John D. Hicks, *The Populist Revolt* (Lincoln, Nebr., 1959 ed.), *passim;* Richard Hofstadter, *The Age of Reform* (New York, 1955), pp. 58–59, 104–107.

15. Hofstadter, *Age of Reform*, pp. 213–224; George E. Mowry, *The Era of Theodore Roosevelt* (New York, 1958), pp. 85–105.

16. Gabriel Kolko, *The Triumph of American Conservatism* (New York, 1963), p. 2.

17. Charles Sprague Smith to Hillquit, May 18, 1908, Morris Hillquit Papers, State Historical Society of Wisconsin, Madison.

18. Howard H. Quint, *The Forging of American Socialism: Origins of the Modern Movement* (Indianapolis, 1964 ed.), Ch. 10–11 and *passim;* David A. Shannon, *The Socialist Party of America* (New York, 1952), Ch. 1.

19. Robert F. Hoxie, "The Rising Tide of Socialism," *Journal of Political Economy*, XIX (October 1911), 609–631, and "The Socialist Party in the November Elections," *ibid.*, XX (March 1912), 205–223.

20. Shannon, *Socialist Party*, p. 5; James Weinstein, *The Decline of Socialism in America, 1912–1925* (New York, 1967), Ch. 1 and 2, pp. 93–118.

21. See Ira Kipnis, *The American Socialist Movement, 1897–1912* (New York, 1952) for a tendentious account of the left-right split. Cf. Marc Karson, *American Labor Unions and Politics, 1900–1918* (Carbondale, Ill., 1958), pp. 212–284.

Chapter 2: The Urban-Industrial Frontier, 1890–1905

1. Rodman W. Paul, *Mining Frontiers of the Far West, 1848–1880* (New York, 1963), pp. 9–10, 137–138, 195–196.

2. 47th Cong., 1st sess., House of Representatives, *Miscellaneous Document 64, Part I*, "Compendium of the 10th Census" (Washington, 1883), I, 452, 492; Vernon Jensen, *Heritage of Conflict* (Ithaca, N.Y., 1950), pp. 19–24; Percy S. Fritz, *Colorado: The Centennial State* (New York, 1941), p. 304.

3. Sources cited in note above.

4. Fritz, *Colorado*, pp. 311–312, 367; Marshall Sprague, *Money Mountain: The Story of Cripple Creek Gold* (Boston, 1953).

5. *The Works of Hubert Howe Bancroft*, XXXI, "History of Washington, Idaho, and Montana, 1845-1889" (San Francisco, 1890), pp. 752n, 755n, 763–764, 769; Joseph K. Howard, *Montana: High, Wide and Handsome* (New Haven, 1943), pp. 83–84.

6. *The Works of Hubert Howe Bancroft*, XXXI, 572; Merrill D. Beal and Merle W. Wells, *History of Idaho* (New York, 1959), I; Robert Cleland, *A History of Phelps Dodge, 1834–1950* (New York, 1952), pp. 107–108, 117.

7. Fritz, *Colorado*, p. 312; Clark C. Spence, *British Investment and the American Mining Frontier* (Ithaca, N.Y., 1958), Ch. 1 and *passim*.

8. T. A. Rickard, *A History of American Mining* (New York, 1932), Ch. 11–15; Isaac Marcosson, *Anaconda* (New York, 1957), Ch. 4–6; Kirkland, *Industry Comes of Age*, pp. 154–157, 161–162.

9. Cleland, *Phelps Dodge*, pp. 107–108.

10. *Ibid.*, p. 117.

11. Jensen, *Heritage of Conflict*, p. 17.

12. U.S. Census Office, *Compendium of the 11th Census, 1890*, Part I: Population (Washington, 1892), pp. 478, 481, 496, 541, 559; *Compendium of the 12th Census, 1900*, Part I: Population (Washington, 1901), pp. 495–496, 499, 511, 648, 664, 739–741, 744, 768; *Compendium of the 13th Census, 1910*, Part II: Population (Washington, 1914), pp. 216–217, 228 430, 432, 1156, 1158–1159; Paul, *Mining Frontiers*, pp. 22, 182; Emma F. Langdon, *The Cripple Creek Strike* (Denver, 1904–1905), p. 34; 56th Cong., 1st sess., *Senate Document No. 24*, "Coeur d'Alene Mining Troubles," p. 13; *Report of the Industrial Commission on the Relations and Conditions of Capital and Labor Employed in the Mining Industry* (Washington, 1901), XII, 313, 377, 485, 572, 588, 595.

13. Paul, *Mining Frontiers*, pp. 69–70, 94–95, 122, 182.

14. Stewart Holbrook, *The Rocky Mountain Revolution* (New York, 1956), p. 74; Western Federation of Miners, *Proceedings of the 11th Convention* (Denver, 1903), p. 17; May A. Hutton, *The Coeur d'Alenes* (Denver, 1900), pp. 53–54; *Final Report and Testimony of the U.S. Commission on Industrial Relations* (Washington, 1915), XI, 10, 569–570, 573; *Evidence and Cross-Examination in the Case of U.S.A. v. W. D. Haywood, et al.* (n.p., n.d.).

15. Fred Thompson to author, September 5, 1966.

16. Secret Reports of Operative L.C. during the 1896–1897 Leadville, Colorado, strike in the Official Papers of Governors Albert A. McIntyre and Alva Adams, Colorado State Archives, Denver, Record Group No. A-69, Boxes 9-10, 1895–1899; similar references were found in the papers of Governor James H. Peabody, also in Colorado State Archives, R.G. A-69, 1903–1905.

17. *Capital and Labor in Mining*, XII, 389–546; Robert W. Smith, *The Coeur d'Alene Mining War of 1892: A Case Study of an Industrial Dispute* (Corvallis, Ore., 1961), pp. 38–40; Hutton, *Coeur d'Alenes, passim;* James H. Hawley to H. F. Brinton, November 1, 1892; to George A. Pettibone, November 15, 1892, January 3, 1893; to Patrick F. Reddy, March 20, 1893; to J. F. Poynton, April 29, 1893; to Pettibone, May 4, 1893; to Poynton, October 17, 1893; to Reddy, February 5, 1894, all in James H. Hawley Letterbooks, Idaho State Historical Society, Boise.

18. *Butte Reveille*, May 23, 1904, p. 8; June 6, 1904, p. 5.

19. *Bill Haywood's Book: The Autobiography of Big Bill Haywood* (New York, 1958 ed.), pp. 117–128; Stenographic Report of the Advisory Board Appointed by Governor James H. Peabody to Investigate and Report upon Labor Difficulties in the State of Colorado and More Particularly at Colorado City, James H. Hawley Papers, Idaho State Historical Society.

20. *Haywood's Book*, pp. 80–81; Job Harriman, "The Class War in Idaho," *Miners' Magazine*, V (October 8, 1903), 8; Smith, *Mining War*, pp. 24–35.

21. *The Labor World*, April 28, 1902; *Butte Reveille*, June 14, 1907, p. 1.

22. *Miners' Magazine*, II (June 1901), 20–24.

23. Henry L. Day, "Mining Highlights of the Coeur d'Alene District," *Idaho Yesterdays*, VII (Winter 1964), 2–9.

24. *Ibid.*

25. B. Goldsmith to Simeon G. Reed, June 6, 1887, Simeon G. Reed Papers, Idaho State Historical Society (microfilm copy).

26. Victor Clement to Reed, November 23, 1889, Reed Papers.

27. Charlie Siringo, *Riata and Spurs* (Boston, 1927), pp. 158–159; cf. John Hays Hammond, *Autobiography of John Hays Hammond* (New York, 1935), pp. 181–191; Smith, *Mining War*, pp. 18–30; Job Harriman, "Class War," *Miners' Magazine*, V (November 5, 1903), 13; October 8, 1903, 8; October 22, 1903, 9–12.

28. Smith, *Mining War*, pp. 31–37.

29. *Ibid.*, pp. 38–40.

30. *Ibid.*, pp. 40, 44–46.

31. *Ibid.*, pp. 41–43.

32. Governor Norman Willey to Senator George L. Shoup, May 23, 1892; Willey to W. H. Frazier, *et al.*, June 10, 1892; Willey to President Benjamin Harrison, June 24, 1892; Harrison to Willey, July 4, 1892, all in Norman H. Willey Papers, Idaho State Historical Society (microfilm copy).

33. Esler and Finch to Shoup and Dubois, July 11, 1892; Joseph Pinkham to Shoup and Dubois, July 11, 1892; Weldon B. Heyburn to Dubois, July 11, 1892; Willey to Shoup, July 11, 1892; George H. Roberts to Dubois and Shoup, July 12 and 13, 1892; Shoup to President Harrison, July 12, 1892, all in Telegrams and Correspondence, Idaho Congressional Delegation, Pertaining to Coeur d'Alenes, Idaho Historical Society (microfilm copy).

34. J. F. Curtis to Shoup, July 14, 1892, Idaho Congressional Delegation Correspondence; Willey to Charles W. O'Neill, July 15, 1892, Willey Papers; Smith, *Mining War*, pp. 85–89; Daniel McEachern to James H. Hawley, n.d., Hawley Papers.

35. McEachern to Hawley, n.d., Hawley Papers.

36. Smith, *Mining War*, pp. 98–104.

37. Melvyn Dubofsky, "James H. Hawley and the Origins of the Haywood Case, 1892–1899," *Pacific Northwest Quarterly*, LVIII (January 1967), 23–27.

38. *Miners' Magazine*, II (June 1901), 20–24.

39. *Ibid.; Butte Bystander*, May 20, 1893, p. 2.

40. *Butte Bystander*, May 20, 1893, p. 2.

41. Selig Perlman and Philip Taft, *History of Labor in the United States, 1896–1932* (New York, 1935), p. 173.

42. *Miners' Magazine*, II (June 1901), 20–24.

Chapter 3: The Class War on the Industrial Frontier, 1894–1905

1. Vernon H. Jensen, *Heritage of Conflict; Labor Relations in the Non-Ferrous Metals Industry up to 1930* (Ithaca, N.Y., 1930), Ch. 3–10; Melvyn Dubofsky, "The Leadville Strike of 1896–1897: An Appraisal," *Mid-America*, XLVIII (April 1966), 99–118; and "James H. Hawley and the Origins of the Haywood Case, 1892–1899," *Pacific Northwest Quarterly*, LVIII (January 1967), 23–32.

2. See the above citations and also Melvyn Dubofsky, "The Origins of Western Working Class Radicalism, 1890–1905," *Labor History*, VII (Spring 1966), 131–154.

3. *Ibid.*

4. *Miners' Magazine*, II (July 1901), 16; (October 1901), 13–15; (November 1901), 2–3; (December 1901), 21; III (January 1902), 45–46; IV (January 1903), 39–41.

5. *Ibid.*, III (January 1902), 22–23; (May 1902), 15–18; IV (February 1903), 1–3; Western Federation of Miners, *Proceedings of the 1902 Convention* (Denver, 1902), p. 17.

6. Testimony of Moyer and Haywood before the Advisory Board Appointed by Governor James H. Peabody to Investigate and Report upon Labor Difficulties in the State of Colorado, pp. 80–81, 84, 109, 118, in the James H. Hawley Papers, Idaho State Historical Society.

7. *Ibid.*, pp. 158–195.

8. *Ibid.*, pp. 567–594.

9. *Ibid.*, pp. 97, 123–157; W. R. Ennis to Editor, *Miners' Magazine*, IV (April 1903), 43–44.

10.   Advisory Board Hearings, pp. 123–157; *Miners' Magazine*, IV (April 1903), 1–3.
11.   Advisory Board Hearings, pp. 97–100, 109, 123–157.
12.   *Ibid.*, pp. 123–157.
13.   *Ibid.*, pp. 561–562.
14.   For the traditional version of events, see especially Jensen, *Heritage of Conflict*, pp. 96–117. The exception is 58th Cong., 3rd sess., Senate Document No. 122, *A Report on Labor Disturbances in the State of Colorado from 1880 to 1904, Inclusive* (Washington, 1905), pp. 43–50.
15.   Advisory Board Hearings, pp. 45–46, 279.
16.   *Ibid.*, pp. 114–115.
17.   Peabody to H. W. Fullerton, March 6, 1903, and to Brigadier General John Chase, March 7 and 8, 1903, Governor James A. Peabody Papers, Office of the Governor, 1903–1905, Executive Letter Books, Colorado State Archives, Denver.
18.   Peabody to C. M. McNeill, March 7, 1903, and to Fullerton, C. M. McNeill, and Frank C. Peck, March 9, 1903; handwritten note of union proposition received from Mr. Frewen and verified by Mr. Haywood, March 7, 1903, all in Peabody Papers.
19.   H. W. Fullerton, Frank G. Peck, and Charles Moyer to Peabody, March 14, 1903, Peabody Papers; Advisory Board Hearings, pp. 573–574.
20.   *Bill Haywood's Book: The Autobiography of Big Bill Haywood* (New York, 1958 ed.), pp. 117–118; C. M. McNeill and Spencer Penrose to Peabody, March 15, 1903, Peabody Papers.
21.   Peabody to W. R. Van Orden, March 19, 1903, Peabody Letter Books.
22.   *Miners' Magazine*, IV (April 1903), 33–37.
23.   Peabody to United States Reduction and Refining Company; to Moyer; and to Haywood, March 19, 1903, Peabody Letter Books.
24.   *Ibid.*
25.   Advisory Board Hearings, pp. 87–94.
26.   *Ibid.*, pp. 119–120.
27.   *Ibid.*, pp. 204½, 303–304, 336–347, 349, 364.
28.   *Ibid.*, pp. 379–380, 454–455, 456–460.
29.   Concerning the dispute the Peabody Papers contain long reports, too numerous to cite individually, which detail McNeill's delaying tactics.
30.   *Haywood's Book*, p. 128; Emma F. Langdon, *The Cripple Creek Strike* (Denver, 1904–1905), pp. 30–31.
31.   *Labor Disturbances in Colorado*, pp. 46–50.
32.   Peabody to I. F. Parsons, September 14, 1903; to Walter C. Frost, September 18, 1903; to James Turnbull, October 19, 1903, Peabody Letter Books.
33.   Peabody to J. C. Osgood, July 16, 1903; to A. J. Woodruff, March 14, 1903, Peabody Letter Books.
34.   January 25, 1904, Peabody Letter Books.
35.   Peabody to William Howells, August 14, 1903, Peabody Letter Books.
36.   Peabody to Walter C. Frost, September 18, 1903; to Thomas D. Parker, October 3, 1903, Peabody Letter Books.
37.   J. Edward Addicks to Peabody, October 26, 1904, Peabody Papers.
38.   Peabody to Thomas Walsh, *et al.*, August 3, 1903, Peabody Letter Books.
39.   B. M. Rastall, *The Labor History of the Cripple Creek District* (Madison, Wisc., 1908), p. 163.
40.   *Miners' Magazine*, V (September 3, 1903), 4; cf. *Labor Disturbances in Colorado*, pp. 43–44, 146.
41.   Cripple Creek District Citizens' Alliance and Mine Owners' Association to Peabody, September 2, 1903; Mayor F. D. French to Peabody, September 2 and 3, 1903; John Chase, N. C. Miller, and E. McClelland to Peabody, Septem-

ber 4, 1903, all in Peabody Papers; Peabody to Sherman Bell, September 3, 1903, Peabody Letter Books; *Miners' Magazine,* V (September 10, 1903), 5–6.

42. Quoted in Jensen, *Heritage of Conflict,* pp. 130–131.

43. *The Army and Navy Journal,* quoted in *Miners' Magazine,* V (November 5, 1903), 5.

44. Peabody to Benjamin B. Lawrence, September 18, 1903; to John B. Vroom, September 18, 1903; to Meyer Freedman, September 8, 1903, Peabody Letter Books.

45. W. E. Wheeler to Peabody, November 2, 1903, and Congressman H. W. Hogg to Peabody, November 4, 1903, Peabody Papers; Peabody to President Roosevelt, November 16, 1903, Peabody Letter Books; Secretary of War Elihu Root to Peabody, November 17, 1903, and Root to Peabody, November 19, 1903, Peabody Papers.

46. Peabody to Hill, November 23, December 1, 4, 7, 1903, Peabody Letter Books.

47. *Miners' Magazine,* V (November 12, 1903), 6.

48. *Ibid.* (November 26, 1903), p. 7; Bell to Peabody, November 22, 1903, and Commissioner of Mines E. L. White to Peabody, November 30, 1903, Peabody Papers.

49. *Miners' Magazine,* V (December 10, 1903), 9–11.

50. Peabody to Major Zeph T. Hill, December 21, 1903, Peabody Letter Books.

51. Peabody to Hill, December 12, 1903, Peabody Letter Books.

52. Sherman Bell to Bulkeley Wells, March 23, 1904, Peabody Letter Books; *American Labor Union Journal,* March 10, 1904, p. 1.

53. *Miners' Magazine,* V (May 26, 1904), 5.

54. Bell to Peabody, June 6, 1904, Peabody Papers.

55. Ward to Peabody, June 6, 1904, Peabody Papers.

56. Ward to Peabody, June 7, 1904, and Warren A. Haggot, Proclamation of Martial Law, Peabody Papers; Testimony on the Victor Riot in William D. Borah Papers, Idaho State Historical Society.

57. *New York Times* to Peabody, June 13, 1904, Peabody Papers; *Labor Disturbances in Colorado,* p. 272; Jensen, *Heritage of Conflict,* pp. 147–152.

58. Peabody to John A. Inslie, July 2, 1904, Peabody Letter Books.

59. John G. Brooks, *American Syndicalism: The I.W.W.* (New York, 1913), pp. 75–76.

60. Selig Perlman and Philip Taft, *History of Labor in the United States, 1896–1932* (New York, 1935), pp. 169, 178, 189.

61. Quotations come from *ibid.;* Foster R. Dulles, *Labor in America* (New York, 1949), p. 209; Louis L. Lorwin, *The American Federation of Labor* (Washington, 1933), pp. 84–85; Charles A. Madison, *American Labor Leaders* (New York, 1950), p. 264; Selig Perlman, *A History of Trade Unionism in the United States* (New York, 1922), p. 213; Fred Thompson, *The I.W.W.: Its First Fifty Years* (Chicago, 1955), p. 9.

Chapter 4: From "Pure and Simple Unionism" to Revolutionary Radicalism

1. Vernon Jensen, *Heritage of Conflict* (Ithaca, N.Y., 1950), Ch. 6; Minute Books, Silver City, Idaho, Miners' Union, Local 62, WFM, Bancroft Library, University of California, Berkeley.

2. *Butte Bystander,* June 2, October 1, 3, 8, 1894; May 21, November 26, December 3, 1895; the *Populist Courier, Montana Silverite, Populist Tribune,* and *Pueblo Courier* were all labor-Populist propaganda sheets. Cf. *Report of the Industrial Commission on the Relations and Conditions of Capital and Labor*

Employed in Mining, XII (Washington, 1901), 415, 437, 531–532, 537.

3. See the James H. Hawley Papers, Idaho State Historical Society, Boise, for Populism's power in Idaho. On election statistics see W. Dean Burnham, *Presidential Ballots, 1836–1892* (Baltimore, 1955), pp. 306–317, 366–367, 600–601; E. E. Robinson, *The Presidential Vote, 1896–1932* (Palo Alto, 1934), pp. 150–154, 174–177, 256–260.

4. C. Vann Woodward, "The Populist Heritage and the Intellectual," *American Scholar*, XXIX (Winter 1959–60), 55–72, and *Origins of the New South* (Baton Rouge, 1951), Ch. 9; Norman Pollack, *The Populist Response to Industrial America* (Cambridge, Mass., 1962), *passim; Montana Silverite*, November 29, 1895, p. 1; *Butte Bystander*, February 24, 1894, p. 1; May 14, 1895, p. 2.

5. *Butte Bystander*, May 15, 1897, p. 1.

6. *Ibid.*, p. 4; *Miners' Magazine*, I (January 1900), 16–18; (October 22, 1903), 5; Jensen, *Heritage of Conflict*, pp. 70–71.

7. American Federation of Labor, *Proceedings of the 1896 Convention* (Bloomington, Ind., 1896), p. 59. Cf. Philip Taft, *The A.F. of L. in the Time of Gompers* (New York, 1957), pp. 150–152, for an uncritical defense of the AFL's position in the controversy.

8. Biographical data for the following sketch came from Ray Ginger, *The Bending Cross* (New Brunswick, N.J., 1949) and *Age of Excess* (New York, 1965), pp. 166–168, 299–300; David Karsner, *Debs* (New York, 1919).

9. Karsner, *Debs*, p. 168.

10. *Ibid.*, pp. 10–11.

11. Boyce to Gompers, March 16, 1897; Gompers to Boyce, March 26, 1897; Boyce to Gompers, April 7, 1897; Gompers Statement, May 1, 1897, all printed in U.S. Senate, 56th Cong., 1st sess., *Senate Document No. 42*, "Labor Troubles in Idaho," pp. 8–13.

12. All quotes from *Butte Bystander*, July 15, 1897, pp. 1, 4.

13. *Ibid.*, October 16, 1897, p. 1; November 20, 1897, p. 2; November 27, 1897, p. 1; *Miners' Magazine*, I (January 1900), 24–26.

14. Walter MacArthur to Gompers, May 28, 1898, cited in Taft, *AFL in Time of Gompers*, p. 153; *Bill Haywood's Book: The Autobiography of Big Bill Haywood* (New York, 1929), p. 72.

15. Biographical information drawn from M. A. Hutton, *The Coeur d'Alenes* (Denver, 1900), pp. 53–54; WFM, *Proceedings of the 1903 Convention*, p. 17.

16. Hutton, *Coeur d'Alenes*, pp. 53–54; *Haywood's Book*, p. 62.

17. Press Committee, Local 89, to Editor, *Miners' Magazine*, II (December 27, 1901); III (February 1902), 42–43; M. F. Coll to Editor, *ibid.*, III (April 1902), 25–26.

18. *Ibid.*, II (February 1901), 31–33; *Butte Reveille*, September 11, 1900, p. 5; September 18, 1900, p. 6; April 9, 1901, p. 4; May 14, 1901, p. 1; *Butte People*, November 9, 1901, p. 1.

19. *Miners' Magazine*, I (March 1900), 39–40; (June 1900), 41.

20. *Capital and Labor in Mining*, XII, 213–214, 246, 255, 362–363.

21. T. A. Martin to Editor, *Miners' Magazine*, I (March 1900), 22; Speech of T. S. Hogan quoted in *ibid.* (July 1900), 24; *ibid.* (June 1900), 16–17.

22. *Ibid.*, I (November 1900), 6–8; (August 1900), 3; (October 1900), 3; II (July 1901), 18–20; *Butte Reveille*, June 11, 1901, p. 2.

23. *Miners' Magazine*, III (July 1902), 23–33; WFM, *Proceedings of the 1902 Convention* (Denver, 1902), pp. 8–10.

24. WFM, *Proceedings of the 1902 Convention, passim; Miners' Magazine*, III (November 1902), 41–42; IV (January 1903), 16; *Labor World*, June 9, 1902, p. 1.

25. Quoted in *Miners' Magazine*, III (January 1902), 16.

26. John B. Lennon to Frank Morrison, August 8, 1898, AFL Papers, Office of the President, State Historical Society of Wisconsin, Madison; *Butte People*, November 16, 1901, p. 1; November 30, 1901, p. 1; December 21, 1901,

p. 7; WLU Secretary Clarence Smith's reports in *Miners' Magazine,* II (February 1901), 31–33, and (October 1901), 21–23; *ibid.* (December 1901), 4–8; III (January 1902), 10–11; (March 1902), 38–42; (April 1902), 2–5.

27. *Butte People,* December 21, 1901, p. 7; *Miners' Magazine,* II (December 1901), 4–8; III (January 1902), 10–11.

28. *Miners' Magazine,* III (March 1902), 38–42; (June 1902), 4, 14–16; *Butte People,* February 12, 1902, p. 5; March 7, 1902, p. 1; *Labor World,* May 19, 1902, p. 5; June 2, 1902, pp. 1–2; June 9, 1902, pp. 1, 5; *American Labor Union Journal,* November 20, 1902, pp. 1–4.

29. *Labor World,* July 11, 1902, p. 3; *ALU Journal,* October 23, 1902, p. 2; November 1, 1903, p. 4; *Miners' Magazine,* II (November 1902), 23–24.

30. H. L. Hughes to Clarence Smith, March 22, 1903, in *ALU Journal,* April 16, 1903, p. 1; *Labor World,* July 3, 1903, p. 1.

31. *ALU Journal,* September 3, 1903, p. 5; November 19, 1903, p. 1.

32. *Ibid.,* H. Hanson to Editor, December 6, 1902; December 11, 1902, p. 8; *Miners' Magazine,* VI (May 11, 1905), 6.

33. *ALU Journal,* January 7, 1904, p. 2; April 14, 1904, p. 4.

34. *Ibid.,* December 1904, p. 3.

35. *Miners' Magazine,* IV (July 1903), 22; see *ibid.* (May 25, 1903), 27–28, for similar general executive board recommendations.

36. G. A. Hoehn, "The American Labor Movement," *International Socialist Review,* III (January 1903), 410–411; *Labor World,* August 8, 1902, p. 3; *Miners' Magazine,* III (December 1902), 33–42; Ira Kipnis, *The American Socialist Movement, 1897–1912* (New York, 1952), pp. 144–145; Nathan Fine, *Farmer and Labor Parties in the United States, 1828–1928* (New York, 1928), pp. 277–278.

37. Eugene V. Debs, "The Western Labor Movement," *International Socialist Review,* III (November 1902), 257–265.

38. *Miners' Magazine,* V (March 24, 1904), 6.

39. *Haywood's Book,* p. 174; Fred Thompson, *The I.W.W.: Its First Fifty Years* (Chicago, 1955), p. 6; Ginger, *Bending Cross,* pp. 236–237.

40. Official version of the January 1905 conference and manifesto by Clarence Smith in IWW, *Proceedings of the First Convention of the Industrial Workers of the World* (New York, 1905), pp. 83–84.

41. *Ibid.,* pp. 90–99.

42. Hayes to W. L. Hall, December 30, 1904, *ibid.,* pp. 99–100.

43. *Ibid.,* pp. 84–85.

44. *Ibid.,* p. 88.

45. *Ibid.,* p. 86.

46. *Ibid.,* pp. 86–89.

47. Max Hayes, *International Socialist Review,* V (February 1905), 500–501; Gompers to Max Morris, February 2, 1905, Gompers Letterbooks, V. 96, AFL-CIO Headquarters, Washington, D.C.; *American Federationist,* XII (March 1905), 139–141; (April 1905), 214–217; (June 1905), 354–361.

48. Algie M. Simons, *International Socialist Review,* V (February 1905), 496–499; Bohn, "Concerning the Chicago Manifesto," *ibid.* (March 1905), 585–589.

49. Moyer and Haywood, "Open Letter to All WFM Members," April 10, 1905, *Miners' Magazine,* VI (April 13, 1905), 3. The *Miners' Magazine* for April–May 1905 abounds with rank-and-file endorsements of the coming industrial union convention.

50. Quoted in *ibid.,* VI (June 22, 1905), 5–6.

51. *Proceedings of the First IWW Convention,* pp. 1–2.

52. Haywood's estimate in *ibid.,* p. 204; Paul F. Brissenden, *The I.W.W.* (New York, 1957 ed.), pp. 74–75; Jensen, *Heritage of Conflict,* p. 170.

53. Ben H. Williams, "American Labor in the Jungle: Saga of the One Big Union" (unpublished memoirs, Wayne State University Labor Archives);

cf. Brissenden, *IWW*, pp. 76–82; Philip S. Foner, *History of the Labor Movement in the United States*, Volume 4: *The Industrial Workers of the World, 1905–1917* (New York, 1965), p. 31.

54. *Proceedings of the First IWW Convention*, pp. 142–153, 165.

55. *Ibid.*, pp. 152–153; *Miners' Magazine*, VI (February 23, 1905), 3; *Voice of Labor*, III (June 1905), 12.

56. *Proceedings of the First IWW Convention*, pp. 220–221, 247.

57. ALU Secretary Clarence Smith in *ibid.*, pp. 229–230.

58. *Ibid.*, pp. 317, 386.

59. *Ibid.*, pp. 546–547. John Riordan of the ALU was elected to the provisional executive council and Charles Moyer, WFM, was elected permanent representative on the IWW's executive board.

60. *Ibid.*, pp. 153–157.

61. Luke Grant to Gompers, July 8, 1905, quoted in Foner, *IWW*, pp. 39, 560n; Algie Simons, "I.W.W.," *International Socialist Review*, VI (August 1905), 65–77.

62. Quoted in Pollack, *Populist Response*, p. 84.

Chapter 5: The IWW Under Attack, 1905–1907

1. The following biographical sketch of Hagerty is based upon Robert E. Doherty, "Thomas J. Hagerty, the Church, and Socialism," *Labor History*, III (Winter 1962), 39–56, and my own survey of Hagerty's contributions in the *ALU Journal* and the *Voice of Labor*, the latter of which he edited.

2. Gompers to W. D. Mahon, July 15, 1905, Gompers Letterbooks, V. 102, AFL-CIO Headquarters, Washington, D.C.

3. Gompers to AFL Executive Council, July 17, 1905, Gompers Letterbooks, V. 102; Luke Grant to Gompers, July 26, 1905, AFL Papers, Office of the President, Series 11, Box 2, State Historical Society of Wisconsin, Madison.

4. Gompers to Pete Curran, August 3, 1905, Gompers Letterbooks, V. 102.

5. *Butte Reveille*, September 15, 1905, p. 2; for fuller details on AFL attitudes and actions, see Philip S. Foner, *History of the Labor Movement in the United States*, Volume 4: *The Industrial Workers of the World, 1905–1917* (New York, 1965), pp. 62–68.

6. American Federation of Labor, *Proceedings of the 1905 Convention*, pp. 252–256; for an able defense of the WFM, see *Miners' Magazine*, VII (November 23, 1905), 12.

7. Foner, *IWW*, pp. 65–68; Melvyn Dubofsky, *When Workers Organize: New York City in the Progressive Era* (Amherst, Mass., 1968), pp. 46–47.

8. Simons to Paul F. Brissenden, March 26, 1912, quoted in Paul F. Brissenden, *The I.W.W.: A Study of American Syndicalism* (New York, 1957 ed.), p. 66; William Trautmann to James Kirwan, May 22, 1906, cited in WFM, *Proceedings of the 1906 Convention* (Denver, 1906), pp. 287–289; *American Federationist*, XII (August 1905), 514–516.

9. Gompers to Executive Council, July 17, 1905, Gompers Letterbooks, V. 102.

10. Eugene V. Debs, "The Coming Labor Union," *Miners' Magazine*, VII (October 26, 1905), 13; Algie Simons, "IWW," *International Socialist Review*, VI (August 1905), 76–77, and "Plain Words to Socialists," *Industrial Worker*, I (March 1906), 5; cf. Ray Ginger, *The Bending Cross* (New Brunswick, N.J., 1949), pp. 240–241.

11. My version of this bizarre episode in American history is based largely upon an unpublished paper by Michael R. Johnson, "The American Judiciary and Radical Unionism" (1962); and on Pinkerton Reports Relative to the Western Federation of Miners, 1906–1907 (microfilm copy); transcript of the *State of*

Idaho v. William D. Haywood, et al., June 4–July 30, 1907, 8 vols.; the James H. Hawley and the William Borah Papers, all in Idaho State Historical Society, Boise. For different versions of the assassination and the murder trial, see the anti-Haywood, anti-WFM-IWW books by David H. Grover, *Debaters and Dynamiters* (Corvallis, Ore., 1964), and Stewart H. Holbrook, *The Rocky Mountain Revolution* (New York, 1956).

12. See my own "James H. Hawley and the Origins of the Haywood Case, 1892–1899," *Pacific Northwest Quarterly*, LVIII (January 1967), 23–32.

13. On McParland, the Mollies, and the Pinkerton Agency, see Wayne Broehl, Jr., *The Molly Maguires* (Cambridge, Mass., 1964).

14. Gooding to McParland, January 8, 1906, Pinkerton Reports.

15. McParland to Gooding, January 8 and 22, 1906, Pinkerton Reports.

16. McParland to Gooding, January 25, 1906, Pinkerton Reports, explains in full how the detective led Orchard to his extraordinary confession; cf. Harry Orchard, "The Confession and Autobiography of Harry Orchard," *McClure's Magazine*, XXIX (July 1907), 294–306; (August 1907), 367–379; (September 1907), 507–523; (October 1907), 658–672; XXX (November 1907), 113–129.

17. McParland to Gooding, January 25, 1906, Pinkerton Reports.

18. The following account is based upon McParland to Gooding, February 8, 1906, and later correspondence in Pinkerton Reports.

19. *Pettibone v. Nichols* and *Moyer v. Nichols* in *203 United States Reports* (New York, 1907), pp. 192–222.

20. McParland to Gooding, August 26 and December 15, 1906, Pinkerton Reports.

21. McParland to Gooding, March 3, 1907, Pinkerton Reports.

22. Eugene V. Debs, *Writings and Speeches* (New York, 1948), p. 256; *American Federationist*, XIII (April 1906), 233–235; AFL, *Proceedings of the 1906 Convention*, pp. 37–38, 178.

23. *The Works of Theodore Roosevelt* (New York, 1926), XX, 478–482, 485; *Harper's Weekly*, LI (May 18, 1907), 721.

24. *Outlook*, LXXXVI (July 15, 1907), 304.

25. Hawley to McParland, April 15, 1907, Hawley Papers.

26. McParland to Gooding, May 10, 13, and 15, 1907, Pinkerton Reports.

27. Trial Transcript, I, 337ff; George Kibbe Turner on Orchard in *McClure's Magazine*, XXIX (July 1907), 295.

28. Hawley to W. H. Cureton, July 12, 1907, and to Jacob Fillius, July 22, 1907, Hawley Papers.

29. Hawley to Frank ———, July 28, 1907, Hawley Papers; *Outlook*, LXXXVI (August 8, 1907), 715.

30. Hawley to Jacob Fillius, December 7, 1907, and to Bulkeley Wells, December 2 and 6, 1907, Hawley Papers.

31. Hawley to J. Fillius, November 30, 1907, and January 15, 1908; to Borah, November 30, 1907, and January 6, 1908; to B. Wells, December 2, 1907, all in Hawley Papers.

32. Sherman and Trautmann Reports in *Proceedings of the 1906 IWW Convention*, pp. 44–45, 60; W. E. Trautmann to 14th Annual WFM Convention, *Proceedings of 1907 Convention* (Denver, 1907), pp. 130–131.

33. St. John to P. F. Brissenden, October 5, 1911, quoted in Brissenden, *IWW*, p. 130; *Proceedings of the 1906 IWW Convention*, pp. 7–9, 48–59.

34. Max Hayes in *International Socialist Review*, VI (January 1906), 435; *Proceedings of the 1906 IWW Convention*, pp. 323–327.

35. *Proceedings of the 1906 IWW Convention*, pp. 42–72.

36. Gompers to E. N. Nockels, March 28, 1902, Gompers Letterbooks, V. 94.

37. Gompers to Sherman, March 25, 1905, Gompers Letterbooks, V. 94.

38. WFM, *Proceedings of the 1907 Convention*, pp. 612–620.

39. *Proceedings of the 1906 IWW Convention*, pp. 5, 7.

40. *Ibid.*, pp. 48–73; *Solidarity*, June 15, 1912, p. 1.

41. *International Socialist Review*, VI (January 1906), 435.

42. J. Bellow to Editor, *Industrial Worker*, I (July 1906), 7; *Miners' Magazine*, VIII (September 6, 1906), 12–13.

43. *Miners' Magazine*, VIII (August 30, 1906), 6–7; (September 20, 1906), 3, 6.

44. B. H. Williams, "IWW and Politics," *Solidarity*, March 25, 1911, p. 2.

45. *Proceedings of the 1906 IWW Convention*, pp. 5, 7.

46. *Ibid.*, pp. 8–9.

47. *Ibid.*, pp. 80–94.

48. *Ibid.*

49. *Miners' Magazine*, VIII (October 4, 1906), 6–7.

50. *Proceedings of the 1906 IWW Convention*, p. 225.

51. *Ibid.*, pp. 250–254.

52. *Ibid.*, pp. 254–256, 269–271.

53. *Ibid.*, p. 484; C. H. Mahoney to James Kirwan, October 2, 1906, *Miners' Magazine*, VIII (October 11, 1906), 7.

54. *Proceedings of the 1906 IWW Convention*, p. 610.

55. C. O. Sherman to All IWW Members, October 4, 1906, in *Miners' Magazine*, VIII (October 11, 1906), 7; C. O. Sherman, C. E. Mahoney, *et al.*, to Secretaries and Officers of IWW Locals, *ibid.* (October 18, 1906), pp. 12–13.

56. WFM, *Proceedings of 1907 Convention*, pp. 530–531.

57. *International Socialist Review*, VII (November 1906), 311–312.

58. *Industrial Worker* (Joliet), II (January 1907), 10; *IWW Bulletin*, Nos. 1–8.

59. Trautmann, St. John, *et al.*, to IWW Members, in *Miners' Magazine*, VIII (October 18, 1906), 11–12.

60. C. E. Mahoney, Report to WFM Members, October 8, 1906, *ibid.*, pp. 7–10; John O'Neill in *ibid.*, pp. 5–6.

61. Al Ryan and St. John to James Kirwan, n.d., *ibid.* (November 1, 1906), pp. 8–10.

62. Moyer to Kirwan, October 2, 1906, in WFM, *Proceedings of 1907 Convention*, pp. 579–580; Moyer to Mahoney and Kirwan, October 30, 1906, *ibid.*, pp. 580–581.

63. Haywood to Kirwan, October 16, 1906, *ibid.*, pp. 582–583; Haywood to St. John, March 17, 1907, *ibid.*, p. 584; Haywood to Heslewood, April 2, 1907, *ibid.*, p. 621.

64. Haywood to St. John, March 24, 1907, *ibid.*, pp. 584–586.

65. Notice to WFM Locals, *Miners' Magazine*, VIII (November 8, 1906), 3; G.E.B. Report in *ibid.* (December 27, 1906), pp. 3, 9.

66. *IWW Bulletin No. 5*, January 10, 1907, pp. 1, 4; *Industrial Union Bulletin*, March 9, 1907, p. 2.

67. March 24, 1907, in WFM, *Proceedings of 1907 Convention*, p. 586.

68. *Ibid.*, pp. 424, 485–489, 632, 664–665, 680.

69. *Ibid.*, pp. 700–701, 788, 800–801, 870–872.

70. *Industrial Union Bulletin*, July 13, 1907, p. 2.

71. *Chicago Daily Socialist*, March 9, 1908, quoted in *ibid.*, April 18, 1908, p. 2; *Miners' Magazine*, IX (October 31, 1907), 4.

Chapter 6: The IWW in Action, 1906–1908

1. Vincent St. John, *The I.W.W.: Its History, Structure, and Methods* (Chicago, 1919 ed.), p. 18; Russell R. Elliott, "Labor Troubles in the Mining Camp at Goldfield, Nevada, 1906–1908," *Pacific Historical Review*, XIX (November 1950), 369–372; cf. John Dos Passos, *The 42nd Parallel* (New York, 1930), pp. 100–109.

2. Elliott, "Labor Troubles," pp. 370–371; St. John in the *Industrial Union Bulletin*, April 7, 1907, p. 1.

3. On this point see St. John's account in *Industrial Union Bulletin*, April 7, 1907, p. 1, and Elliott, "Labor Troubles," p. 370; cf. Philip S. Foner, *History of the Labor Movement in the United States*, Volume 4: *The Industrial Workers of the World, 1905–1917* (New York, 1965), pp. 93–94.

4. J. H. Walsh's report in *Industrial Union Bulletin*, March 30, 1907, p. 1; cf. Foner, *IWW*, pp. 94–96, for the AFL's role.

5. Elliott, "Labor Troubles," pp. 373–376; *Industrial Union Bulletin*, March 30, 1907, p. 1; April 6, 1907, p. 1.

6. Elliott, "Labor Troubles," pp. 373–375.

7. 60th Cong., 1st sess., *House Document No. 607*, "Papers Relative to Labor Troubles at Goldfield" (Washington, 1908), p. 25.

8. *Ibid.*, p. 25; *Industrial Union Bulletin*, December 14, 1907, pp. 1–2.

9. "Labor Troubles at Goldfield," p. 23.

10. *Ibid.*, pp. 8–9, 23.

11. *Ibid.*, pp. 21–23.

12. *Ibid.*, pp. 15–16, 22–23.

13. George Wingfield to Laura White, quoted in Elliott, "Labor Troubles," p. 384.

14. *Industrial Union Bulletin*, November 9, 1907, p. 1.

15. Stewart Reid to Gompers, August 18 and 22, 1907, quoted in Foner, *IWW*, p. 86.

16. *Schenectady Union*, December 10–11, 1906, quoted in *ibid.*, p. 88.

17. *Industrial Union Bulletin*, March 23, 1907, p. 1; February 1, 1908, p. 3; January 25, 1908, pp. 2–4; April 11, 1908, pp. 1–2.

18. *Ibid.*, May 9, 1908, p. 1; May 16, 1908, p. 3.

19. *Ibid.*, March 16, 1907, p. 1; J. H. Walsh to G.E.B., *ibid.*, March 9, 1907, p. 3; *ibid.*, April 11, 1908, p. 3.

20. *Duluth Herald*, November 17, 1907, quoted in *ibid.*, November 23, 1907, p. 1; *ibid.*, December 14, 1907, p. 3.

21. Cloice Howd, "Industrial Relations in the West Coast Lumber Industry," Bureau of Labor Statistics, *Bulletin No. 349* (Washington, December 1923), pp. 21–23.

22. *Final Report and Testimony of the United States Commission on Industrial Relations* (Washington, 1915), V, 4236–4237.

23. Pope and Talbot to Cyrus Walker, August 10, 1899; Will Ames to Ray O. Hadley, July 1, 1920; Will Ames to Fred Drew, 1904, all in Puget Mill Company Papers, University of Washington Library, Seattle; Carson to Morgan, April 13, 1905, Dolbeer and Carson Company Papers, Bancroft Library, University of California, Berkeley.

24. Fred Drew to Cyrus Walker, August 6, 1906, Puget Mill Company Papers; cf. Howd, "Industrial Relations," pp. 45, 64–65.

25. Howd. "Industrial Relations," pp. 64–65; Robert F. Tyler, "Rebels of the Woods and Fields: The I.W.W. in the Pacific Northwest," unpublished doctoral dissertation, University of Oregon (1953), pp. 47–49; *Industrial Union Bulletin*, March 16, 1907, p. 1.

26. A. B. Ayer to E. C. Griggs, March 6, 1907, Puget Mill Company Papers.

27. Will Ames to R. H. Alexander, March 16, 1907, and to Cyrus Walker, March 7, 1907, Puget Mill Company Papers.

28. Will Ames to R. H. Alexander, March 15 and 18, 1907; E. C. Griggs to Ames, March 18, 1907; Ames to Cyrus Walker, March 22 and 27, 1907; Ames to Fred Talbot, April 2, 1907, all in Puget Mill Company Papers; cf. *Industrial Union Bulletin*, April 20, 1907, p. 1.

29. F. W. Heslewood, "The Great Portland Strike," *Industrial Union Bulletin*, April 27, 1907, p. 2.

30. Will Ames to Cyrus Walker, April 9, 1907, Puget Mill Company Papers;

the Dolbeer and Carson Company Papers detail IWW activities in the California redwood forests.

31. Trautmann's Report in *Industrial Union Bulletin*, October 24, 1908, p. 3; St. John's Report in *ibid.*, November 7, 1908, p. 1.

32. Trautmann's Report, *ibid.*, October 24, 1908, p. 3.

33. *Ibid.*, October 12, 1908, p. 1; February 1, 1908, p. 4.

34. *Ibid.*, October 24, 1908, p. 3.

35. *Ibid.*, February 1, 1908, p. 3; October 19, 1907, p. 1.

36. *Ibid.*, November 7, 1908, p. 1.

37. The biographical information is drawn from William J. Ghent, "Daniel DeLeon," *Dictionary of American Biography*, III, 222–224, and conversations with Professor Bernard K. Johnpoll, State University of New York, Albany.

38. See Don K. McKee, "Daniel DeLeon: A Reappraisal," *Labor History*, I (Fall 1960), 264–297.

39. B. H. Williams, *American Labor in the Jungle: The Saga of One Big Union* (microfilm copy, Wayne State University Labor Archives), p. 25.

40. Statements of Albert Ryan, Percy Rawlings, and Frank Little in WFM, *Proceedings of 1907 Convention* (Denver, 1907), pp. 398, 412–413, 744.

41. *Industrial Union Bulletin*, June 29, 1907, p. 4; October 2, 1907, p. 2.

42. *Ibid.*, February 1, 1908, p. 4; Williams, *One Big Union*, pp. 34–35.

43. *Industrial Union Bulletin*, March 14, 1908, pp. 1, 4.

44. J. Ebert to Editor, April 10, 1908, *ibid.*, April 18, 1908, pp. 1–2; B. H. Williams to Editor, April 16, 1908, *ibid.*, April 25, 1908, pp. 1, 3.

45. Heslewood to Trautmann, n.d., *ibid.*, May 23, 1908, p. 3; K. Rathje to Editor, April 25, 1908, *ibid.*, May 2, 1908, p. 3.

46. J. H. Walsh's reports in *ibid.*, September 19, 1908, p. 1; October 4, 1908, p. 2; October 24, 1908, pp. 1–3.

47. Williams, *One Big Union*, p. 35.

48. *Industrial Union Bulletin*, October 10, 1908, p. 2.

49. *Ibid.*, p. 3, October 24, 1908, p. 3.

50. *Ibid.*, October 10, 1908, pp. 1–2, 4.

51. *Ibid.*, November 7, 1908, pp. 3–4.

52. *Ibid.*, February 20, 1909, p. 2.

53. *Ibid.*, February 27, 1909, p. 2.

54. *Ibid.*, December 12, 1908, p. 3.

55. *Ibid.*, pp. 2–4; October 10, 1908, p. 1.

56. V. St. John to I. S. Bradley, April 21, 1909, State Historical Society of Wisconsin, microfilm copy of the *Industrial Union Bulletin;* Williams, *One Big Union*, p. 37; Ray Ginger, *The Bending Cross* (New Brunswick, N.J., 1949), p. 256.

57. Fred Thompson, *The I.W.W.: Its First Fifty Years* (Chicago, 1955), p. 40; James P. Cannon, *The I.W.W.: The Great Anticipation* (New York, 1956), p. 31.

58. Elizabeth Gurley Flynn, *I Speak My Own Piece* (New York, 1955), pp. 81–84; Cannon, *IWW*, pp. 20–21.

59. *Miners' Magazine*, II (September 1901), 3.

60. Cannon, *IWW*, pp. 20–21; Flynn, *I Speak My Own Piece*, pp. 81–84.

61. V. St. John to Frank Walsh, August 29, 1915; September 28, 1915; October 5, 1915; February 7, 1916; May 23, 1916, Frank Walsh Papers, New York Public Library, Manuscript Division.

62. B. H. Williams to Joyce Kornbluh, October 24, 1963, quoted in Kornbluh, *Rebel Voices: An I.W.W. Anthology* (Ann Arbor, 1964), p. 51.

63. *Solidarity*, May 8, 1915, p. 2; interview with Mrs. Rose Williams, cited in Warren R. Van Tine, "Ben H. Williams: Wobby Editor," unpublished master's thesis, Northern Illinois University (1967), p. 7.

64. Van Tine, "Williams," pp. 33–37.

65. Williams, *One Big Union*, p. 112.

Chapter 7: Ideology and Utopia: The Syndicalism of the IWW

1. Lewis S. Gannett, "The I.W.W.," *Nation*, CXI (October 20, 1920), 448.

2. Joe Hill to Editor, *Industrial Worker*, May 25, 1911, p. 3; *Final Report and Testimony of the United States Commission on Industrial Relations* (Washington, D.C., 1915), V, 4234–4235 (hereafter cited as CIR).

3. B. H. Williams in *Solidarity*, September 14, 1912, p. 2; William E. Bohn, "The I.W.W.," *Survey*, XXVIII (May 4, 1912), 221.

4. Rexford G. Tugwell, "The Casual of the Woods," *Survey*, XLIV (July 3, 1920), 472; Carleton Parker, "The I.W.W.," *Atlantic Monthly*, CXX (November 1917), 651–662.

5. Oscar Lewis, *La Vida* (New York, 1966), p. xlv.

6. *Ibid.*, p. xliii.

7. E. J. Hobsbawm, *Primitive Rebels and Social Bandits* (New York, 1963), p. 108.

8. Lewis, *La Vida*, pp. xiv, xlv–xlvi.

9. CIR, V, 4947; W. D. Haywood, "To Colored Working Men and Women," *Solidarity*, March 10, 1917, p. 2; *Industrial Worker*, April 29, 1909, p. 4; June 17, 1909, p. 2.

10. R. G. Tugwell to Editor, *Survey*, XLIV (August 16, 1920), 641–642; Parker, "I.W.W.," p. 656.

11. Lewis, *La Vida*, pp. xlviii–xlix.

12. Tugwell to Editor, *Survey*, XLIV (August 16, 1920), 641–642.

13. *Solidarity*, July 1, 1911, p. 2.

14. Quoted in Arno Dosch, "What the IWW Is," *World's Work*, XXVI (August 1913), 417.

15. Eric Goldman, *Rendezvous with Destiny* (New York, 1952), pp. 90–97.

16. Ben H. Williams, "Trends Toward Industrial Freedom," *American Journal of Sociology*, XX (March 1915), 627; Williams also in *Solidarity*, April 15, 1911, p. 2, and September 14, 1912, p. 2; John Sandgren, "Industrial Communism," *ibid.*, July 31, 1915, p. 12.

17. E. F. Doree to Fellow Workers, *Industrial Worker*, November 7, 1912, p. 4; Sandgren, "Industrial Communism," p. 12.

18. *Solidarity*, March 22, 1913, p. 2.

19. Hobsbawm, *Primitive Rebels*, p. 57.

20. *Ibid.*, p. 60.

21. *Solidarity*, February 19, 1910, p. 2; CIR, II, 1446, 1449; XI, 10,598.

22. *Industrial Worker*, July 1, 1909, p. 3.

23. *Ibid.*, June 3, 1909, p. 2; Ben Williams to Editor, August 20, 1907, *Industrial Union Bulletin*, September 7, 1907, p. 2.

24. J. J. Ettor, "A Retrospect on Ten Years of the IWW," *Solidarity*, August 14, 1915, p. 2; James Larkin in *International Socialist Review*, XVI (December 1915), 330–331; CIR, V, 4234–4235, 4239.

25. CIR, XI, 10,574, 10,579.

26. *Ibid.*, V, 4239; *Solidarity*, March 14, 1914, p. 2; cf. Hobsbawm, *Primitive Rebels*, pp. 58–59.

27. Jack London, *The Iron Heel* (New York, 1924), pp. 96–99.

28. CIR, V, 4940, 4946–4947; *The Lumber Industry and Its Workers* (Chicago, n.d), p. 59.

29. *Solidarity*, April 2, 1910, p. 2; CIR, XI, 10,574.

30. CIR, V, 4942; *Solidarity*, July 9, 1910, p. 3.

31. V. St. John, "Political Parties Not Endorsed by Us," *Industrial Worker*,

August 12, 1909, p. 3; Vincent St. John, *The I.W.W.: Its History, Structure, and Methods* (Chicago, 1919 ed.), pp. 40–45; CIR, II, 1449; XI, 10,575; *Lumber Industry and Its Workers*, p. 59.

32. *Industrial Worker*, June 6, 1912, p. 2.

33. *Lumber Industry and Its Workers*, p. 73; CIR, XI, 10,575.

34. J. Ebert, "Suppressing the IWW in New York," *Solidarity*, February 14, 1914, p. 20.

35. R. Brazier to Editor, *Industrial Worker*, February 2, 1911, p. 3; *Solidarity*, May 30, 1914, p. 2.

36. *International Socialist Review*, XII (February 1912), 467; XIII (September 1912), 246–247; CIR, XI, 10,580.

37. CIR, V, 4237.

38. *Ibid.*, II, 1451, 1555; V, 4947–4848; Frank Bohn and W. D. Haywood, *Industrial Socialism* (Chicago, 1911), p. 57.

39. CIR, XI, 10,581.

40. Quoted in Dosch, "IWW," p. 417.

41. CIR, II, 1452, 1456; XI, 10,592.

42. *Industrial Worker*, I (June 1906), 8; *Industrial Union Bulletin*, June 29, 1907, p. 2; April 4, 1908, p. 2; *Industrial Worker*, May 8, 1913, p. 2; August 12, 1909, p. 2; *Solidarity*, June 8, 1912, p. 2.

43. *Solidarity*, December 24, 1910, p. 2.

44. *Industrial Worker*, October 8, 1910, p. 2; Arturo Giovannitti, "Syndicalism: The Creed of Force," *The Independent*, LXXVI (October 30, 1913), 210; CIR, XI, 10,578.

45. *Industrial Union Bulletin*, April 6, 1907, p. 2.

46. *Industrial Worker*, May 28, 1910, p. 1; February 23, 1911, p. 2; July 1912–January 1913.

47. *International Socialist Review*, XIII (February 1912), 469; *Solidarity*, February 25, 1911, p. 4.

48. J. Thompson quote from CIR, V, 4240–4241; Haywood in *ibid.*, XI, 10,578–10,579; *Solidarity*, February 25, 1911, p. 4; *Industrial Worker*, March 13, 1913, p. 2.

49. CIR, III, 2482.

50. *Ibid.*, V, 4240–4241; B. H. Williams, *American Labor in the Jungle: The Saga of the One Big Union* (microfilm copy, Wayne State University Labor Archives), p. 45.

51. *Industrial Worker*, May 23, 1912, p. 2; *Industrial Union Bulletin*, September 7, 1907, p. 2.

52. *Industrial Worker*, I (May 1906), 1; W. E. Trautmann, *Industrial Unionism* (Chicago, 1908), pp. 16–18; *Industrial Worker*, May 6, 1909, p. 2; *Solidarity*, June 4, 1910, p. 2; CIR, II, 1450–1451; III, 2598.

53. *Industrial Worker*, May 6, 1909, p. 2; *Solidarity*, June 4, 1910, p. 2.

54. Haywood and Ettor, "What the IWW Intends to Do to the USA," reprinted from the *New York World* in *Solidarity*, June 27, 1914, p. 3.

55. Haywood quoted in Dosch, "IWW," p. 417; Williams, *One Big Union*, p. 45.

56. *Solidarity*, August 24, 1912, p. 2.

57. CIR, II, 1449, 1455, 1459; XI, 10,574, 10,588; *Industrial Worker*, October 3, 1912, p. 2; October 13, 1910, p. 3; *Lumber Industry and Its Workers*, p. 73.

58. CIR, XI, 10,584; *Solidarity*, November 1, 1913, p. 2.

59. *Solidarity*, December 28, 1912, p. 3.

60. For the working-class definition of socialism, see WFM, *Proceedings of 1905 Convention* (Denver, 1905), p. 304; CIR XI, 10,583; W. D. Haywood, "Socialism: The Hope of the Working Class," *International Socialist Review*, XII (February 1912), 461–471.

61. See Philip S. Foner, *History of the Labor Movement in the United*

States, Vol. 4: *Industrial Workers of the World, 1905–1917* (New York, 1965), Ch. 17.

62. Will Herberg, "American Marxist Political Theory," in Donald D. Egbert and Stow Persons, eds., *Socialism and American Life* (Princeton, 1952), I, 491–492.

63. *Industrial Worker*, November 2, 1910, p. 2; October 3, 1912, p. 2; January 9, 1913, p. 2; CIR, XI, 10,587.

64. John Sandgren, "The Syndicalist Movement in Norway," *Solidarity*, February 14, 1914, p. 3; Robert R. La Monte, "Industrial Unionism and Syndicalism," *New Review*, I (May 1913), 527.

65. John Spargo, *Syndicalism, Industrial Unionism and Socialism* (New York, 1913), pp. 13–15.

66. *Industrial Worker*, May 8, 1913, p. 3.

Chapter 8: *The Fight for Free Speech, 1909–1912*

1. IWW, *Twenty Five Years of Industrial Unionism* (Chicago, 1930), p. 20.

2. *Ibid.*

3. *Industrial Worker*, June 3, 1909, p. 2; August 5, 1909, p. 3.

4. *Industrial Union Bulletin*, February 27, 1909, p. 1; J. H. Walsh in *ibid.*, February 21, 1909, p. 1.

5. *Industrial Worker*, April 29, 1909, p. 5.

6. Daniel O'Regan to Dr. Charles McCarthy, November 10, 1914, United States Commission on Industrial Relations Papers, Department of Labor, Record Group 174, National Archives (hereafter cited as CIR Papers); Charles Grant, "Law and Order in Spokane," *Industrial Worker*, March 18, 1909, p. 3.

7. Grant, "Law and Order," p. 3.

8. *Industrial Worker*, August 12, 1909, p. 1.

9. *Ibid.*, October 27, 1909, p. 1; November 3, 1909, pp. 1–2.

10. *Ibid.*, November 10, 1909, p. 1.

11. These descriptions of Spokane justice come from Elizabeth Gurley Flynn, "The Fight for Free Speech at Spokane," *International Socialist Review*, X (December 1909), 483–489; Flynn, "The Shame of Spokane," *ibid.* (January 1910), pp. 610–619; S. Sorenson to V. St. John, n.d., CIR Papers.

12. This account is drawn from Sorenson to St. John, CIR Papers; Robert Ross to CIR, September 19, 1914, CIR Papers; Spokane Free Speech Committee to United Brotherhood of Carpenters and Joiners of America, January 9, 1910, Department of Justice Files, Record Group 60, National Archives (hereafter cited as D/J 60); Flynn, "Shame of Spokane," pp. 610–619; Fred Heslewood, "Barbarous Spokane," *International Socialist Review*, X (February 1910), 705–713; *Industrial Worker*, November 1909–March 1910.

13. Sorenson to St. John, CIR Papers; Flynn, "Free Speech Fight," p. 488.

14. The following sketch is based on Elizabeth Gurley Flynn, *I Speak My Own Piece* (New York, 1955); B. H. Kizer, "Elizabeth Gurley Flynn," *Pacific Northwest Quarterly*, LVII (July 1966), 110–112; "E. G. Flynn: Labor Leader," *Outlook*, CXI (December 15, 1915), 905.

15. Quotations are from Kizer, "Flynn," p. 111; *Outlook*, p. 905; E. G. Flynn to Woodrow Wilson, January 10, 1918, File 188032–146, D/J 60.

16. Kizer, "Flynn," pp. 111–112.

17. Quoted in *ibid.*, p. 112.

18. Flynn, *I Speak My Own Piece*, p. 53.

19. *Industrial Worker*, March 5, 1910, p. 1; February 26, 1910, p. 2.

20. *Ibid.*, March 5, 1910, p. 1; March 12, 1910, p. 1; William Z. Foster, *Pages from a Worker's Life* (New York, 1939), pp. 143–145; Foster, *From Bryan to Stalin* (New York, 1937), pp. 41–42.

21. E. G. Flynn, "Latest News from Spokane," *International Socialist Review*,

X (March 1910), 828–834; *Industrial Worker*, March 12, 1910, p. 1; March 19, 1910, p. 1.

22. *Solidarity*, March 19, 1910, p. 2.

23. W. F. Little to *Industrial Worker*, May 21, 1910, p. 4; F. H. Little to Editor, May 27, 1910, *ibid.*, June 4, 1910, p. 1; F. Little to Editor, May 29, 1910, *ibid.*, June 11, 1910, p. 2; Daniel O'Regan to Charles McCarthy, November 10, 1914, CIR Papers.

24. *Industrial Worker*, September 3, 1910, p. 1; October 1, 1910, p. 1; October 8, 1910, pp. 1, 4; October 5, 1910, p. 4; November 9, 1910, p. 3; November 17, 1910, pp. 1, 3; November 30, 1910, p. 4; December 6, 1910, p. 4; V. St. John to Mayor of Fresno, December 9, 1910, in *ibid.*, December 15, 1910, p. 1; cf. O'Regan to McCarthy, November 10, 1914, CIR Papers.

25. Quoted in *Industrial Worker*, December 22, 1910, p. 1.

26. James P. Cannon, *Notebook of an Agitator* (New York, 1958), pp. 32–36.

27. The following account comes largely from Minderman's diary of the Fresno fight and O'Regan's verification of it in O'Regan to McCarthy, November 10, 1914, in CIR Papers.

28. O'Regan to McCarthy, CIR Papers.

29. Albert Tucker to Vincent St. John, September 21, 1914, CIR Papers; cf. Thomas Whitehead to Editor, *Solidarity*, March 4, 1911, p. 1; and E. M. Clyde to Editor, *ibid.*, April 8, 1911, p. 4; *Industrial Worker*, February 23, 1911, p. 1; March 2, 1911, p. 1.

30. *Industrial Worker*, March 9, 1911, p. 1; *International Socialist Review*, XI (April 1911), 634–636.

31. Hyman Weintraub, "The IWW in California," unpublished master's thesis, University of California, Los Angeles (1947), pp. 23–32.

32. Joe Hill to E. W. Vanderleith, n.d., Frank Walsh Papers, Box 7, New York Public Library, Manuscript Division.

33. Walter V. Woelke, "I.W.W.," *Outlook*, CI (July 6, 1912), 512.

34. Mary A. Hill, "The Free Speech Fight at San Diego," *Survey*, XXVIII (May 4, 1912), 192–194.

35. *Industrial Worker*, February 22, 1912, p. 4; February 29, 1912, p. 4; March 7, 1912, p. 4.

36. Hill, "Free Speech Fight," pp. 193–194; Woelke, "I.W.W.," p. 531, among other non-IWW sources.

37. A. Tucker to Vincent St. John, September 21, 1914, CIR Papers.

38. Chris Hansen to Vincent St. John, n.d., CIR Papers.

39. Woelke, "I.W.W.," p. 531.

40. Harris Weinstock, *Report to the Governor of California on the Disturbance in the City and County of San Diego in 1912* (Sacramento, 1912).

41. Emma Goldman, *Living My Life* (New York, 1934), pp. 495–501; Richard Drinnon, *Rebel in Paradise: A Biography of Emma Goldman* (Chicago, 1961), pp. 135–136.

42. John L. Sehon to George Wickersham, May 2, 1912, File 150139–7; F. C. Spaulding to Wickersham, May 3, 1912, File 150139–8; code message, John McCormick to Wickersham, May 4, 1912, File 150139–6, and May 6, 1912, File 150139–13, all in D/J 60.

43. Senator John D. Works to Wickersham, May 4, 1912, and Wickersham's reply of May 6, 1912, File 150139–10; Congressman J. C. Needham to Wickersham, May 4, 1912, and Wickersham's reply, May 6, 1912, File 150139–12; Mayor James W. Wedham to Wickersham, May 5, 1912, and Wickersham's reply, May 6, 1912, File 150139–11; Wickersham to McCormick, May 6, 1912, File 150139–13; Wickersham to Senator Works, May 9, 1912, File 150139–14, all in D/J 60.

44. McCormick to Wickersham, June 28, 1912; William R. Haar to Wickersham, July 5, 1912, and Wickersham's reply, July 6, 1912, File 150139–20; Wickersham to Senator Works, August 27, 1912, File 150139–26, all in D/J 60.

45. F. W. Estabrook to Charles D. Hilles, September 5, 1912 (with en-

closure: Charles H. DeLacour to Estabrook, September 5, 1912), File 150139–28, D/J 60.

46. Taft to Wickersham, September 7, 1912, File 150139–29, D/J 60.

47. Wickersham to Taft, September 16, 1912, and to C. D. Hilles, September 16, 1912, File 150139–31; Charles DeLacour to Wickersham, November 22, 1912, with marginal note by W.R.H. (William R. Haar?), File 150139–35, all in D/J 60.

48. *Solidarity*, August 24, 1912, p. 3.

49. Quoted in *Industrial Worker*, October 17, 1912, p. 4.

50. *Ibid.*, August 18, 1912, p. 2; Tucker to St. John, September 21, 1914, and Hansen to St. John, n.d., CIR Papers.

51. *Industrial Worker*, January 15, 1910; A. Tucker to Vincent St. John, September 21, 1914, CIR Papers.

Chapter 9: *Steel, Southern Lumber, and Internal Decay, 1909–1912*

1. David Brody, *Steelworkers in America: The Nonunion Era* (Cambridge, Mass., 1960), Ch. 4–6.

2. *National Labor Tribune*, July 29, 1909, quoted in John N. Ingham, "A Strike in the Progressive Era," *Pennsylvania History*, XC (July 1966), 358; M. T. C. Wing, "The Flag at McKees Rocks," *Survey*, XXIII (October 2, 1909), 45.

3. The following account of the McKees Rocks strike is drawn largely from John Ingham's fine article, "A Strike in the Progressive Era," pp. 353–377; a series of reports and articles in *Survey*, including Paul U. Kellogg, "The McKees Rocks Strike," XXII (August 7, 1909), 656–665; Rufus D. Smith, "Some Phases of the McKees Rocks Strike," XXII (October 2, 1909), 38–45; Wing, "The Flag," pp. 45–46; and various articles in the *International Socialist Review*, IX (1909). Unless otherwise noted, my narrative of the strike comes from the above sources.

4. Kellogg, "McKees Rocks," p. 662.

5. *Pittsburgh Leader*, July 15, 1909, quoted in Louis Duchez, "McKees Rocks," *International Socialist Review*, X (September 1909), 197.

6. Quoted in Ingham, "Strike in the Progressive Era," p. 362.

7. Louis Duchez, "Victory at McKees Rocks," *International Socialist Review*, X (October 1909), 290–295, describes the European radical background of several immigrant strike leaders.

8. P. 4.

9. Ingham, "Strike in the Progressive Era," pp. 365–366.

10. Smith, "Some Phases," p. 38.

11. *Ibid.*, p. 39; Kellogg, "McKees Rocks," pp. 664–665.

12. *Survey*, XXII (August 28, 1909), 719.

13. V. St. John to James Wilson, September 8, 1909, in *Industrial Worker*, September 9, 1909, p. 1.

14. *Survey*, XXII (September 11, 1909), 795; Duchez, "Victory at McKees Rocks," p. 290.

15. On this interpretation, see Ingham, "Strike in the Progressive Era," pp. 372–373.

16. See *ibid.*

17. Frank Morris to Editor, September 11, 1909, *Industrial Worker*, September 16, 1909, p. 1; *ibid.*, September 23, 1909, pp. 1–2; *International Socialist Review*, X (October 1909), 360; Louis Duchez, "Passive Strike," *ibid.* (November 1909), pp. 410–411; Duchez, "Victory," *ibid.* (October 1909), pp. 299–300.

18. *Industrial Worker,* October 20, 1909, pp. 1, 4. For *Solidarity's* founding, see Ben H. Williams, *American Labor in the Jungle: The Saga of One Big Union* (microfilm copy, Wayne State University Labor Archives), pp. 38–40.

19. On these matters see Williams, *One Big Union,* pp. 38–40, and Philip S. Foner, *History of the Labor Movement in the United States,* Volume 4: *The Industrial Workers of the World, 1905–1917* (New York, 1965), pp. 299–303.

20. *Industrial Worker,* September 12, 1912, p. 1.

21. The quotations are from Ruth A. Allen, *East Texas Lumber Workers,* (Austin, Tex., 1961), pp. 155–156.

22. *Ibid.,* pp. 168–170.

23. On Emerson, see William D. Haywood, "Timber Wolves and Timber Workers," *International Socialist Review,* XIII (August 1912), 108, and Covington Hall, "I Am Here for Labor," *ibid.* (September 1912), pp. 223–226.

24. Material on the Brotherhood of Timber Workers and the Southern strikes, unless otherwise noted, comes from Allen, *East Texas Lumber Workers;* Charles McCord, "The Brotherhood of Timber Workers," unpublished master's thesis, University of Texas (1959); Covington Hall, "Labor Struggles in the Deep South" (unpublished MS, microfilm copy, Wayne State University Labor Archives); James R. Green, "The Brotherhood of Timber Workers, 1910–1914: A Study in Southwestern Radicalism" (unpublished paper in the author's possession); Covington Hall's reports in the *International Socialist Review, Industrial Worker,* and *Solidarity;* Haywood's reports in the same journals; and H. G. Creel's series in the *National Rip-Saw.*

25. McCord, "B.T.W.," reproduces the original preamble and union constitution, pp. 19–20, 26–28.

26. Biographical information from Allen, *East Texas Lumber Workers,* pp. 180–181.

27. H. G. Creel, "Pinemade Peonage: Or, On the Trail of the Timber Trust," *National Rip-Saw* (February 1912), p. 26.

28. C. Hall, *International Socialist Review,* XIII (July 1912), 51–52.

29. *New Orleans Times-Democrat,* n.d., quoted in *Industrial Worker,* August 10, 1911, p. 1.

30. *Ibid.,* April 20, 1911, p. 1; May 11, 1911, pp. 2–3.

31. *Ibid.,* September 7, 1911, pp. 1, 4; cf. Foner, *IWW,* pp. 239–240, for allegations of a Kirby-Gompers agreement.

32. M. L. Alexander to Little River Lumber Company, October 5, 1911, quoted in H. G. Creel, "Timber Trust Outlaws," *Rip-Saw,* IX (June 1912), 12.

33. *Solidarity,* December 23, 1911, p. 4; *Industrial Worker,* September 26, 1911, pp. 1, 3; Phineas Eastman to Editor, *ibid.,* December 26, 1912, p. 7.

34. Report of organizer George Speed in *Industrial Worker,* August 22, 1912, p. 1; cf. McCord, "B.T.W.," pp. 25–26, for farmers' hostility to the region's lumber companies.

35. *Bill Haywood's Book: The Autobiography of Big Bill Haywood* (New York, 1929), pp. 241–242; Haywood, "Timber Wolves and Timber Workers," pp. 108ff; and *Solidarity,* July 20, 1912, pp. 1, 4.

36. H. G. Creel, "The Timber Trust Answers the *Rip-Saw* with Bullets," *Rip-Saw,* IX (July 1912), 10, 12–14.

37. *Industrial Worker,* August 1, 1912, p. 1; *Solidarity,* August 17, 1912, pp. 1, 4; for whole incident, see McCord, "B.T.W.," pp. 58–64.

38. E. F. Doree to Editor, August 15, 1912, *Solidarity,* August 24, 1912, p. 1; George Speed's report in *Industrial Worker,* August 22, 1912, p. 1.

39. Ed Lehman to Jay Smith and C. Hall, August 11, 1912, in *Industrial Worker,* August 29, 1912, p. 1; C. Hall's report in *ibid.,* September 12, 1912, p. 1; A. L. Emerson to Walker C. Smith, November 4, 1912, in *ibid.,* November 14, 1912, p. 1.

40. Ed Lehman's report in *ibid.,* December 26, 1912, pp. 1, 8; cf. P. Eastman

in *International Socialist Review*, XIII (June 1913), 890–891; C. Hall in *ibid.* (May 1913), pp. 805–806.

41. Reports by C. Hall and Jay Smith in the *Industrial Worker*, January 23, 1913, p. 1; February 20, 1913, p. 1; February 27, 1913, p. 1; March 20, 1913, p. 1.

42. *Ibid.*, June 12, 1913, p. 3; *Solidarity*, May 3, 1913, p. 1.

43. McCord, "B.T.W.," pp. 22–23; Allen, *East Texas Lumber Workers*, pp. 182–183.

44. *Solidarity*, December 10, 1910, p. 3; May 4, 1910, p. 1; December 25, 1911, p. 3.

45. St. John to Brissenden, October 13, 1911, in Paul F. Brissenden, *The I.W.W.* (New York, 1957 ed.), p. 269.

46. XI (July 1911), 42.

47. *Industrial Worker*, August 17, 1911, p. 4.

48. B. H. Williams, "Sixth IWW Convention," *International Socialist Review*, XII (November 1911), 300.

49. William Z. Foster, *From Bryan to Stalin* (New York, 1937), pp. 48–49.

50. Williams, "Sixth Convention," p. 302; Foster, *Bryan to Stalin*, pp. 55–57.

51. *Industrial Worker*, September 28, 1911, p. 4; *Solidarity*, October 7, 1911, p. 2; Williams, "Sixth Convention," pp. 300–302.

52. W. Z. Foster, "As to My Candidacy," *Industrial Worker*, November 2, 1911, p. 3.

53. "Boring or Building," *ibid.*, November 16, 1911, p. 3.

54. Foster, *Bryan to Stalin*, pp. 55–57.

55. *Industrial Worker*, December 28, 1911, p. 4.

56. Foster, *Bryan to Stalin*, pp. 58ff.

Chapter 10: *Satan's Dark Mills: Lawrence, 1912*

1. The following account of the Lawrence strike is drawn largely from 62nd Cong., 2nd sess., *Senate Document No. 870*, "Report on the Strike of the Textile Workers in Lawrence, Massachusetts, in 1912" (Washington, 1912); Massachusetts Bureau of Labor Statistics, *Thirteenth Annual Report on Strikes and Lockouts for the Year 1912* (Boston, 1913), Donald B. Cole, *Immigrant City: Lawrence, Massachusetts, 1845–1921* (Chapel Hill, 1963), pp. 177–194; contemporary newspaper and magazine accounts; also IWW journals, pamphlets, and leaflets.

2. Massachusetts Bureau of Labor Statistics, *Report for 1912*, p. 22; cf. Richard Abrams, *Conservatism in a Progressive Era: Masachusetts Politics, 1900–1912* (Cambridge, Mass., 1964), pp. 226–227, 274–276.

3. Cole, *Immigrant City*, Ch. 3–4.

4. Massachusetts Bureau of Labor Statistics, *Report for 1912*, pp. 31–33; "Strike of Textile Workers in Lawrence," Ch. 2 and 6.

5. 62nd Cong., 2nd sess., *House Document No. 671*, "The Strike at Lawrence, Massachusetts" (Washington, 1912), pp. 139–176.

6. *Ibid.*, pp. 388–394.

7. Harry E. Fosdick, "After the Strike—In Lawrence," *Outlook*, CI (January 15, 1912), 345.

8. Earle Clark, "Wages in Cotton Mills at Home and Abroad," *Survey*, XXVII (March 23, 1912), 1957–1958; W. Jett Lauck, "The Significance of the Situation in Lawrence," *ibid.* (February 17, 1912), pp. 1772–1774.

9. "Strike of Textile Workers in Lawrence," Ch. 3.

10. "Strike at Lawrence," pp. 227–229; Walter Weyl, "The Strikers at Lawrence," *Outlook*, C (February 10, 1912), 309–310.

11. Cole, *Immigrant City*, p. 76; "Strike of Textile Workers in Lawrence," pp. 191–204.

12. "Strike at Lawrence," pp. 86–87.
13. *Industrial Worker*, April 2, 1910, p. 1; Louis Picavet to Editor, January 25, 1911, *Solidarity*, February 4, 1911, p. 1.
14. L. Picavet to Editor, March 10, 1911, *Solidarity*, March 18, 1911, p. 1; *ibid.*, May 13, 1911, p. 4; May 20, 1911, pp. 1, 4; July 1, 1911, p. 3.
15. *Ibid.*, October 21, 1911, p. 1; November 25, 1911, p. 1; *Industrial Worker*, October 26, 1911, p. 1; November 23, 1911, p. 2.
16. Massachusetts Bureau of Labor Statistics, *Report for 1912*, pp. 22–23.
17. Cole, *Immigrant City*, pp. 173, 193–194.
18. Lewis E. Palmer, "A Strike for Four Loaves of Bread," *Survey*, XXVII (February 3, 1912), 1697; Fosdick, "After the Strike," p. 342.
19. "Strike at Lawrence," pp. 74–92, 124–129; *Survey*, XXVI (January 27, 1912), 1634; (February 24, 1912), 1793.
20. J. Ebert, "Joe Ettor," *Industrial Worker*, May 23, 1912, pp. 1, 4.
21. J. Ebert, "Arturo Giovannitti," *ibid.*, May 30, 1912, pp. 1, 4; Mary B. Summer, "Arturo Giovannitti," *Survey*, XXIX (November 2, 1912), 163–166.
22. Biographical sketch drawn from *Bill Haywood's Book: The Autobiography of Big Bill Haywood* (New York, 1929); Haywood's testimony before the United States Commission on Industrial Relations in *Final Report and Testimony* (Washington, D.C., 1915), XI, 10,569–10,573; transcript of *State of Idaho v. Haywood*, June 4–July 30, 1907 (microfilm copy, 8 vols.), Idaho State Historical Society, Boise; *Evidence and Cross-Examination in the Case of U.S.A. v. W. D. Haywood, et al.* (n.p., n.d.); and Haywood's writings in the *Miners' Magazine*, *International Socialist Review*, *Solidarity*, and *Industrial Worker*.
23. Typewritten notes in Frank Walsh Papers, Box 144, New York Public Library, Manuscript Division; also in *Solidarity*, July 31, 1915, p. 6.
24. André Tridon, "Haywood," *New Review*, I (May 1913), 502–506; *Nation*, CXXVI (May 30, 1928), 601; *Literary Digest*, XLVI (May 10, 1913), 1044.
25. *Solidarity*, June 15, 1912, pp. 1, 4.
26. Mary Marcy, "The Battle for Bread in Lawrence," *International Socialist Review*, XII (March 1912), 538.
27. "Strike of Textile Workers in Lawrence," pp. 39–41.
28. Wilbur E. Rowell, "The Lawrence Strike," *Survey*, XXVII (March 23, 1912), 1959; John N. Cole, "The Issue at Lawrence," *Outlook*, C (February 24, 1912), 405–406; Fosdick, "After the Strike," p. 344; "Strike of Textile Workers in Lawrence," pp. 208–210; "Strike at Lawrence," pp. 380–381.
29. Rowell, "Lawrence Strike," p. 1960.
30. Cole, *Immigrant City*, pp. 184–186; Palmer, "Strike for Four Loaves," p. 1692.
31. "Strike of Textile Workers in Lawrence," pp. 42–45, describes the tedious efforts of the state to end the strike.
32. Walter Weyl, "It Is Time to Know," *Survey*, XXVIII (April 6, 1912), 65.
33. *Outlook*, CII (October 19, 1912), 344; Owen R. Lovejoy, "Right of Free Speech in Lawrence," *Survey*, XXVII (March 9, 1912), 1904–1905; *ibid.*, XXVIII (April 6, 1912), 76–77; Weyl, "Time to Know," pp. 65–66; Fosdick, "After the Strike," p. 345.
34. Cole, "Immigrant City," pp. 184–186; "Strike of Textile Workers in Lawrence," p. 39.
35. Cole, *Immigrant City*, pp. 186–189.
36. *Ibid.*
37. Louis Adamic, *Dynamite* (Gloucester, Mass., 1963 ed.), p. 16; Weyl, "Strikers at Lawrence," pp. 311–312; Marcy, "Battle for Bread," p. 538; Constance D. Leupp, "The Lawrence Strike Hearings," *Survey*, XXVII (March 23, 1912), 1954; Massachusetts Bureau of Labor Statistics, *Report for 1912*, p. 27; Cole, *Immigrant City*, p. 189.
38. "Strike of Textile Workers in Lawrence," pp. 64–68.

39. *Survey*, XXVII (February 24, 1912), 1791–1792.

40. "Strike of Textile Workers in Lawrence," p. 51.

41. "Strike at Lawrence," pp. 23–24, 176–226.

42. *Ibid.*, pp. 11–23; "The Lawrence Strike: A Review," *Outlook*, C (March 9, 1912), 531–532, 535–536; Cole, *Immigrant City*, p. 5.

43. "Strike of Textile Workers in Lawrence," pp. 53–59.

44. Leslie H. Marcy and Frederick S. Boyd, "One Big Union Wins," *International Socialist Review*, XII (April 1912), 638; Haywood to Editor, March 18, 1912, *Industrial Worker*, March 21, 1912, p. 4.

45. "Strike of Textile Workers in Lawrence," p. 15; Abrams, *Conservatism in a Progressive Era*, pp. 273–274.

46. On this point see B. H. Williams, "American Labor in the Jungle: The Saga of One Big Union" (unpublished MSS., Wayne State University Labor Archives, microfilm), p. 48.

47. *Industrial Worker*, September 19, 1912, p. 4; October 3, 1912, pp. 1, 4.

48. James P. Heaton, "The Legal Aftermath of the Lawrence Strike," *Survey*, XXVIII (July 6, 1912), 503–510; Heaton, "The Salem Trial," *ibid.* (December 7, 1912), 301–304; Justus Ebert, *The Trial of a New Society* (Cleveland, 1913).

49. *Industrial Worker*, August 1, 1912, p. 1.

50. On these points see, among other sources, Herbert Harris, *American Labor* (New Haven, 1938), p. 337; Paul F. Brissenden, *The I.W.W.* (New York, 1957 ed.), pp. 292–294; Philip S. Foner, *History of the Labor Movement in the United States*, Volume 4: *The Industrial Workers of the World, 1905–1917* (New York, 1965), pp. 348–349; and even B. H. Williams, "One Big Union," pp. 48–50.

51. See the sample of strike literature and leaflets in "Strike of Textile Workers in Lawrence," pp. 496–505.

52. Selig Perlman to Basil M. Manly, December 4, 1913, United States Commission on Industrial Relations Papers, Department of Labor, Record Group 174, National Archives.

53. *Solidarity*, March 29, 1913, p. 1; June 6, 1914, p. 1.

54. William E. Walling, "Industrial or Revolutionary Unionism," *New Review*, I (January 1913), 45; Lincoln Steffens in the Portland, Oregon, *Journal*, March 18, 1912, quoted in *Industrial Worker*, March 14, 1912, p. 3; March 28, 1912, p. 3; Weyl, "Strike at Lawrence," p. 312; *Survey*, XXVIII (April 6, 1912), 1–2.

55. P. Brissenden, *I.W.W.*, p. 283; *Industrial Worker*, March 28, 1912, p. 1.

56. *Industrial Worker*, April 25, 1912, p. 2; *Solidarity*, August 10, 1912, p. 2.

57. Copy of letter from E. F. Doree to John Pancner, n.d., in W. S. Seavey to E. G. Ames, July 22, 1912; Morris Levine to J. Pancner, n.d., Puget Mill Company Papers, University of Washington Library, Seattle.

58. *Industrial Worker*, September 26, 1912, p. 2; *Proceedings of the 1912 IWW Convention*, pp. 13, 19–20; Joe Ettor to Delegates, September 14, 1912, *ibid.*, p. 27.

59. James P. Cannon, "The Seventh IWW Convention," *International Socialist Review*, XIII (November 1912), 424.

Chapter 11: *Satan's Dark Mills: Paterson and After*

1. Elizabeth Gurley Flynn, "Figures and Facts," *The Pageant of the Paterson Strike* (New York, 1913), pp. 15, 19–21; Flynn, "Contract Slavery in Paterson Silk Mills," *ibid.*, pp. 29–31; *Final Report and Testimony of the United States Commission on Industrial Relations* (Washington, 1915), III, 2572–2573 (hereafter cited as CIR); Gregory Mason, "Industrial War in Paterson," *Outlook*, CIV

(June 17, 1913), 286; *Survey*, XXX (April 10, 1913), 81–82; W. L. Kinkead to Editor, *ibid.* (May 31, 1913), p. 315.

2. John Fitch, "The I.W.W.: An Outlaw Organization," *Survey*, XXX (June 7, 1913), 356; Leo Mannheimer, "Darkest New Jersey," *Independent*, LXXIV (May 29, 1913), 1192.

3. Mason, "Industrial War," pp. 286–287; *Survey*, XXX (April 19, 1913), 81–82; CIR, III, 2432–2433, 2572–2573.

4. CIR, III, 2428–2429, 2453–2455, 2596.

5. *Ibid.*, 2432–2433; W. L. Kinkead to Editor, *Survey*, XXX (May 31, 1913), 315–316.

6. Philip Newman, "The First I.W.W. Invasion of New Jersey," *Proceedings of the New Jersey Historical Society*, LVIII (October 1940), 268–283; *Solidarity*, April 6, 1912, pp. 1, 4.

7. CIR, III, 2572.

8. *Ibid.*, 2416–2417, 2432–2433, 2453–2455; *Solidarity*, March 15, 1913, p. 1.

9. CIR, III, 2573; "8 Hour Work Day for All," strike leaflet, Tamiment Institute Library, New York; *Solidarity*, January 18, 1913, p. 4; Elizabeth Gurley Flynn, "The Truth About the Paterson Strike," p. 4, typed copy of speech, Tamiment Institute Library.

10. CIR, III, 2573; *Solidarity*, March 15, 1913, p. 1; March 1, 1913, p. 4; Flynn, "Truth About Paterson," p. 4; Scott Exhibit No. 1. "Diary of Paterson Silk Strike," in CIR, III, 2629.

11. CIR, III, 2416–2417, 2422, 2430–2431, 2612–2613.

12. Flynn, "Truth About Paterson," p. 4; John Reed, "War in Paterson," *The Masses*, IV (June 1913), 16.

13. Fitch, "The I.W.W.: An Outlaw Organization," p. 362.

14. CIR, III, 2452–2453, 2456–2458; *Solidarity*, March 15, 1913, p. 1; W. D. Haywood, "The Rip in the Silk Industry," *International Socialist Review*, XIII (May 1913), 783–788.

15. Flynn, "Truth About Paterson," pp. 4–5; CIR, III, 2456–2458; Haywood, "Rip in Silk Industry," pp. 783–788.

16. Flynn, "Truth About Paterson," pp. 6–7.

17. CIR, III, 2448–2449, 2456–2458, 2572–2573, 2592–2593; Ewald Koettgen, "No Grievances at All!," *Paterson Pageant*, pp. 9–11; strike leaflets, Tamiment Institute Library.

18. Flynn, "Truth About Paterson," pp. 13–14.

19. *Ibid.*, pp. 8–9; CIR, III, 2458–2459; W. D. Haywood, "On the Paterson Picket Line," *International Socialist Review*, XIII (June 1913), 847–851; Frederick S. Boyd, "The General Strike in the Silk Industry," *Paterson Pageant*, p. 5.

20. Mannheimer, "Darkest New Jersey," pp. 1190–1191; Fitch, "I.W.W.: An Outlaw Organization," p. 358; *Survey*, XXX (April 19, 1913), 82.

21. CIR, III, 2490–2491; Mason, "Industrial War in Paterson," pp. 284–285; Mannheimer, "Darkest New Jersey," p. 1192.

22. Fitch, "I.W.W.: An Outlaw Organization," pp. 356–357; Mannheimer, "Darkest New Jersey," p. 1192.

23. CIR, III, 2554–2555, 2583; Kinkead to Editor, *Survey*, XXX (May 31, 1913), 315–316; *ibid.* (April 19, 1913), pp. 82–83; Fitch, "I.W.W.: An Outlaw Organization," pp. 356–358; *Independent*, LVIII (May 22, 1913), 1124.

24. CIR, III, 2576–2577; Fitch, "I.W.W.: An Outlaw Organization," p. 357.

25. CIR, III, 2419, 2593; Boyd, "General Strike," pp. 6–8; Haywood, "On the Picket Line," pp. 847–851.

26. W. D. Haywood, "Smoothing out the Wrinkles in Silk," *Paterson Pageant*, pp. 24–25.

27. Fitch, "I.W.W.: An Outlaw Organization," p. 357; John Reed, "War in Paterson," p. 14.

28. A. Scott, "Strike Diary," February 26–March 14, 1913, CIR, III, 2530–2543, 2562–2569, 2629–2630.

29. *Ibid.*, 2531-2533, and "Scott Diary" (March 30, 1913), 2630; Phillips Russell, "The Arrest of Haywood and Lessig," *International Socialist Review*, XIII (May 1913), 789–792.

30. "Scott Diary" (March 20–July 26, 1913), CIR, III, 2630–2631; cf. Amos Pinchot to Patrick Quinlan, May 2, 1913, in *Solidarity*, June 21, 1913, p. 4; CIR, III, 2530–2531, 2539, 2542–2543.

31. Reed, "War in Paterson," pp. 14, 16.

32. Granville Hicks, *John Reed* (New York, 1936), pp. 100–103; Richard O'Connor and Dale L. Walker, *The Last Revolutionary: A Biography of John Reed* (New York, 1967), pp. 74–75; Mabel Dodge Luhan, *Shakers and Movers* (New York, 1936), pp. 188–189; *Bill Haywood's Book: The Autobiography of Big Bill Haywood* (New York, 1929), p. 262.

33. *Paterson Pageant;* Phillips Russell, "The World's Greatest Labor Play: The Paterson Strike Pageant," *International Socialist Review*, XIV (July 1913), 7–11; *Survey*, XXX (June 28, 1913), 428.

34. Flynn, "Truth About Paterson," pp. 18–20.

35. *Ibid.*, p. 18.

36. *Ibid.*, p. 22; CIR, III, 2603.

37. Alexander Scott, "What the Reds Are Doing in Paterson," *International Socialist Review*, XIII (June 1913), 852–856.

38. Reed, "War in Paterson," p. 17; Jacob Panken's Socialist critique of the strike in the *New York Call*, July 26, 1913, pp. 1, 6; Flynn, "Truth About Paterson," pp. 23, 26–28; Kinkead to Editor, *Survey*, XXX (May 31, 1913), p. 315.

39. Flynn, "Truth About Paterson," pp. 24–25; *Solidarity*, August 16, 1913, p. 1; *International Socialist Review*, XIV (September 1913), 177–178.

40. Flynn, "Truth About Paterson," pp. 26–28; Panken, in *New York Call*, July 26, 1913, p. 1.

41. *Solidarity*, August 16, 1913, p. 1.

42. Flynn, "Truth About Paterson," pp. 1–2, 3, 5, 15–16, 29.

43. *Ibid.*, pp. 2, 30.

44. CIR, III, 2598–2599.

45. Leslie H. Marcy, "800 Per Cent and the Akron Strike," *International Socialist Review*, XIII (April 1913), 711–724; *Solidarity*, June 15, 1912, p. 1; August 17, 1912, p. 1; February 8, 1913, pp. 1, 4; February 22, 1913, p. 1.

46. *Solidarity*, March 15, 1913, p. 1; March 22, 1913, p. 4; Marcy, "800 Per Cent," pp. 711–724; Vincent St. John to Editor, *Survey*, XXX (August 9, 1913), 613–614.

47. See also *Industrial Worker*, April 10, 1913, p. 1.

48. *Solidarity*, April 26, 1913, p. 2.

49. *Ibid.*, June 21, 1913, p. 1; June 28, 1913, p. 1; August 12, 1913, p. 4; *Industrial Worker*, June 26, 1913, p. 1.

50. *Solidarity*, April 26, 1913, p. 2.

51. *Industrial Worker*, April 10, 1913, p. 1; Grover H. Perry's report is in *International Socialist Review*, XIII (May 1913), 812.

52. For the referendum vote, see *Industrial Worker*, March 6, 1913, p. 3; on the Smith affair, *ibid.*, July 17, 1913, p. 2; August 14, 1913, pp. 2–4.

53. *Solidarity*, August 23, 1913, p. 2.

54. *Ibid.*, September 27, 1913, p. 2; October 4, 1913, p. 1; cf. Ralph Chaplin, *Wobbly* (Chicago, 1948), pp. 137–138.

55. *Mother Earth*, VIII (October 1913), 241–242; Robert F. Hoxie, *Trade Unionism in America* (New York, 1921), pp. 139–141, 143–145, 155–156.

56. Tom Mann, "A Plea for Solidarity," *International Socialist Review*, XIV (January 1914), 392–394; *Solidarity*, October 4, 1913, p. 2.

57. Joseph Ettor in the *New Review*, II (May 1914), 283; W. D. Haywood, "An Appeal for Industrial Solidarity," *International Socialist Review*, XIV (March 1914), 544–546.

58. *Solidarity*, October 18, 1913, p. 2; November 22, 1913, p. 2.
59. Vincent St. John to Mark Litchman, May 9, 1914, Mark Litchman Papers, University of Washington Library, Seattle; Paul F. Brissenden, *The I.W.W.* (New York, 1957 ed.), p. 328.

Chapter 12: Back to the West, 1913–1916

1. Carleton Parker, *The Casual Laborer and Other Essays* (New York, 1920), pp. 106–107, and *passim;* P. A. Speek, "Preliminary Investigation of Floating or Casual Migratory Workers," United States Commission on Industral Relations Papers (hereinafter cited as CIR), Department of Labor, Record Group 174, National Archives.
2. Stuart Jamieson, *Labor Unionism in American Agriculture* (Washington, 1945), *passim.*
3. *Solidarity*, February 2, 1913, p. 2; *Industrial Worker*, June 10, 1909, p. 3; July 8, 1909, p. 2; June 25, 1910, p. 1.
4. Paul F. Brissenden, "A Report on the I.W.W. in California" (August 1914), CIR Papers, State Historical Society of Wisconsin, Madison; *Final Report and Testimony of the United States Commission on Industrial Relations* (Washington, 1915), V, 4941, 4945–4946, 5004.
5. This account of the Wheatland riot is derived largely from the report Carleton Parker prepared for the California Commission on Immigration and Housing, copy in CIR Papers, State Historical Society of Wisconsin; for an abridged and more restrained version of the original report, see Parker, *Casual Laborer*, pp. 171–199.
6. Quoted in Philip S. Foner, *History of the Labor Movement in the United States*, Volume 4: *The Industrial Workers of the World, 1905–1917* (New York, 1965), p. 264.
7. CIR, V, 5000–5001, 5011–5018, 5101–5111.
8. *Ibid.*, p. 5000.
9. *Solidarity*, June 20, 1914, p. 2; August 1, 1914, p. 1; September 12, 1914, p. 1; March 14, 1914, p. 4; May 30, 1914, p. 1; Anonymous to Governor Hiram Johnson, September 14, 1915, Department of Justice, Record Group 60, File 150139 after 45, National Archives (hereafter cited as D/J 60).
10. On expenses for detectives and watchmen during 1914 and 1915 harvests, see E. C. Horst to George W. Bell, File 150139 before 37, D/J 60; see the Parker Report and a dissent from it, downgrading IWW influence in California, by a West Coast AFL leader, Paul Scharrenberg, in CIR.
11. Brissenden, "Report on the IWW in California."
12. Simon J. Lubin to Thomas W. Gregory (with enclosures), November 26, 1915, File 150139–46, D/J 60.
13. Daniel O'Regan, "The Situation in Butte, Montana," pp. 1–2, CIR Papers, State Historical Society of Wisconsin; John A. Fitch, "Union Paradise at Close Range," *Survey*, XXXII (August 29, 1914), 538; Vernon Jensen, *Heritage of Conflict* (Ithaca, 1950), Ch. 18.
14. CIR, IV, 3714, 3839, 3874–3879.
15. *Ibid.*, 3724–3726, 3733.
16. Jensen, *Heritage*, p. 314; Fred Isler to Editor, November 10, 1910, *Industrial Worker*, December 3, 1910, pp. 1, 4.
17. On Campbell, see *Industrial Worker*, September 14, 1911, pp. 1, 4; for other points, see CIR, IV, 3747, 3761–3767, 3778–3779, 3860; O'Regan, "Situation in Butte," pp. 2–3; Jensen, *Heritage*, pp. 318–331.
18. O'Regan, "Situation in Butte," pp. 3–5; CIR, IV, 3772–3774.
19. O'Regan, "Situation in Butte," pp. 5–7.
20. *Ibid.*, pp. 7–8.

21. Telegrams, Moyer to Gompers, June 19, 1914; Gompers to Moyer, June 19, 1914; Gompers to M. M. Donoghue, June 19, 1914; O. M. Partelow to Gompers, June 21, 1914; Gompers to Donoghue, June 22, 1914; Moyer to Gompers, June 23, 1914; Gompers to Executive Officers of National and International Unions, June 23, 1914; Gompers to Moyer, June 23, 1914, all in Gompers Letterbooks, AFL-CIO Headquarters, Washington, D.C.

22. W. D. Haywood, "Revolt at Butte," *International Socialist Review*, XV (August 1914), 89; for a complete account, see O'Regan, "Situation in Butte," pp. 8–12; Frank Bohn, "Butte Number One," *The Masses*, V (August 1914), 9–11; cf. Jensen, *Heritage*, pp. 336–337.

23. O'Regan, "Situation in Butte," pp. 12–14.

24. *Ibid.*, pp. 15–16; D. O'Regan to Charles McCarthy, October 10, 1914, CIR Papers, State Historical Society of Wisconsin; CIR, IV, 3733, 3776–3777, 3780–3786; Jensen, *Heritage*, pp. 338–339; Bohn, "Butte Number One," pp. 9–11; Fitch, "Union Paradise," pp. 538–539; *Address of L. O. Evans before the Chamber of Commerce at Missoula, Montana, August 29, 1917* (n.p., 1917), p. 8; W. D. Haywood, "The Battle at Butte," *International Socialist Review*, XV (October 1914), 223–226.

25. O'Regan, "Situation at Butte," pp. 16–21.

26. Gompers to Moyer, August 30, 1914; Gompers to Moyer, September 5, 1914; Gompers to Moyer, September 17, 1914, all in Gompers Letterbooks; O'Regan, "Situation in Butte," pp. 21–23.

27. On military rule, see O'Regan to McCarthy, October 10, 1914, CIR Papers, State Historical Society of Wisconsin; Haywood, "Battle at Butte," pp. 223–226; letter from a Butte Miner, *International Socialist Review*, XV (October 1914), 227–228; on IWW influence, see Jensen, *Heritage*, pp. 346–347; and O'Regan to McCarthy, October 10, 1914.

28. September 26, 1914, p. 1; cf. W. D. Haywood, "Butte Bitter," *International Socialist Review*, XV (February 1915), 473–475.

29. The fullest scholarly treatment of the ensuing Joe Hill case is Philip S. Foner, *The Case of Joe Hill* (New York, 1965); for fictional versions, see Barrie Stavis, *The Man Who Would Not Die* (New York, 1954), especially its nonfictional introduction, pp. 3–114; and Wallace Stegner, *The Preacher and the Slave* (Boston, 1950).

30. A. L. Hall, *et al.* to Editor, April 7, 1914, *Solidarity*, April 18, 1914, p. 2.

31. Foner, *Case of Joe Hill*, pp. 9–11, 16–18; Joe Hill in *Industrial Worker*, May 25, 1911, p. 1.

32. Foner, *Case of Joe Hill*, pp. 23–24; Ed Rowan on the Hill Case in *Solidarity*, June 27, 1914, p. 4.

33. Foner, *Case of Joe Hill*, Ch. 4; W. D. Haywood, "Shall Joe Hill Be Murdered?," *Solidarity*, July 25, 1914, p. 1.

34. Mrs. A. C. Pollok, Theodora Pollok, and Charlotte Anita Whitney to Frank Walsh, August 11, 1915, Frank Walsh Papers, Box 7, New York Public Library, Manuscript Division.

35. Hill to Flynn, July 24, 1915; Hill to E. W. Vanderleith, September 4, 1914, and second undated letter, copies in Walsh Papers; "Joe Hill," *International Socialist Review*, XVI (December 1915), 329–330; *Little Red Song Book*, p. 5.

36. Jim Larkin in *International Socialist Review*, XVI (December 1915), 330–331; cf. Foner, *Case of Joe Hill*, Ch. 5.

37. Vernon H. Jensen, "The Legend of Joe Hill," *Industrial and Labor Relations Review*, IV (April 1951), 356–366; Wallace Stegner, "Joe Hill, The Wobblies' Troubador," *New Republic*, CXVIII (January 5, 1948), 20–24, 38; for Hill's defense by his IWW friends and a rebuttal to Stegner's charge, see Fred Thompson to *New Republic*, CXVIII (February 9, 1948), p. 38, and *ibid.*, CXIX (November 15, 1948), 38; cf. Stegner to *New Republic*, CXVIII (February 9, 1948), 38–39.

38. E. F. Doree, "Gathering the Grain," *International Socialist Review*, XV (June 1915), 740–743; Philip Taft, "The I.W.W. in the Grain Belt," *Labor History*, I (Winter 1960), 53–67.

39. Frank S. Hamilton, "A Screed and a Suggestion," *Solidarity*, November 21, 1914, pp. 2–3.

40. *Solidarity*, July 14, 1914, p. 1; August 8, 1914, p. 4, among numerous such reports.

41. *Ibid.*, August 22, 1914, p. 2; October 3, 1914, pp. 1, 4; J. Gabriel Soltis, "After the Harvest," *ibid.*, October 10, 1914, p. 2; *ibid.*, November 28, 1914, p. 2.

42. W. D. Haywood, "To Migratory Workers," *ibid.*, November 18, 1914, p. 3; *ibid.*, February 6, 1915, p. 1; February 13, 1915, pp. 1, 4; February 20, 1915, p. 2; March 13, 1915, p. 1; April 10, 1915, p. 4.

43. E. Workman, "*History of the '400' A.W.O.* (New York, 1939); *Solidarity*, April 24, 1915, pp. 1, 3.

44. *Solidarity*, June 5, 1915, p. 1.

45. *Ibid.*, June 17, 1915, p. 1; W. T. Nef, "Lessons to be Gleaned from the Kansas Harvest," *ibid.*, July 31, 1915, p. 11; *ibid.*, August 7, 1915, p. 1; August 14, 1915, p. 1; September 18, 1915, p. 1; October 2, 1915, p. 1; Doree, "Gathering the Grain," p. 743.

46. Ben H. Williams, "American Labor in the Jungle: The Saga of One Big Union" (microfilm copy, Wayne State University Labor Archives), p. 54.

47. W. T. Nef, "Let Us Build Up the A.W.O.," *Solidarity*, October 30, 1915, p. 1; *ibid.*, p. 4; December 25, 1915, p. 2; January 8, 1916, p. 1; January 22, 1916, p. 1; February 5, 1916, p. 4; Richard Reese, "The A.W.O.: An Example of a Successful Union," *ibid.*, March 18, 1916, pp. 1, 4; J. A. MacDonald in *International Socialist Review*, XVI (December 1915), 347–349.

48. *Solidarity*, June 3, 1916, p. 1; June 10, 1916, p. 3; July 22, 1916, p. 1; August 5, 1916, p. 1; September 9, 1916, p. 1; September 30, 1916; W. T. Nef in *Internaitonal Socialist Review*, XVII (September 1916), 141–143; Nef, "The Militant Harvest Workers," *ibid.* (October 1916), 229–230.

49. On the splits and factions in the AWO, see Workman, *History of the A.W.O.*, *passim*; *Solidarity*, November 11, 1916; W. T. Nef, "New I.W.W. Plans in Philadelphia," *ibid.*, January 13, 1917, p. 1; P. C. Wetter, "Philadelphia Waterfront and the I.W.W.," *ibid.*, April 15, 1916, p. 1.

Chapter 13: Miners, Lumberjacks, and a Reorganized IWW, 1916

1. C. Whit Pfeffer, "From Bohunks to Finns," *Survey*, XXXVI (April 1, 1916), 8–14; Marion B. Cothren, "When Strike-Breakers Strike," *ibid.* (August 26, 1916), pp. 535–536.

2. See the above articles.

3. Pfeffer, "Bohunks to Finns," p. 10.

4. Proceedings of Meeting: Committee of the Officials of the Range Municipalities with Committee of the Striking Miners from Different Mines, at Virginia, Minnesota, July 7, 1916 (hereafter cited as Meeting of Range Municipalities and Strikers), p. 3, File 33/247; Department of Labor, Record Group 280, National Archives (hereafter cited as D/L 280).

5. Leroy Hodges, "Immigrant Life in the Ore Region of Northern Minnesota," *Survey*, XXVIII (September 7, 1912), 703–709; *Industrial Worker*, August 21, 1913, p. 1; August 24, 1913, p. 1.

6. *Solidarity*, February 12, 1916, p. 1; February 19, 1916, p. 4; May 13, 1916, p. 1.

7. Statement on Strike's Origin by Joseph Greeni, August 10, 1916, File 33/247,

Exhibit B, D/L 280; report by United States Commissioners of Conciliation, W. R. Fairley and Hywel Davies, on the Mesabi Iron Miners' Strike, June 3 to September 17, 1916, File 33/247A, D/L 280 (hereafter cited as Fairley-Davies Report).

8. Fairley-Davies Report.

9. Meeting of Range Municipalities and Strikers, pp. 5, 15.

10. *Ibid.*, p. 13; Fairley-Davies Report.

11. Fairley-Davies Report; *Solidarity*, June 17, 1916, p. 1.

12. E. J. Maney to Fairley and Davies, December 22, 1916, File 33/247A, D/L 280.

13. Fairley-Davies Report; *Solidarity*, July 8, 1916, p. 1.

14. *Solidarity*, July 1, 1916, p. 1.

15. *Duluth News Tribune*, August 19, 1916, in File 33/247, D/L 280; Fairley-Davies Report; "Dollars and Steel against Humanity: Iron Ore Miners' Strike" (IWW pamphlet), File 33/247A, D/L 280; typewritten copy of a report by George P. West for Committee on Industrial Relations, for release in newspapers of August 3, 1916, File 33/247, D/L 280 (hereafter cited as West Report); George P. West, "The Mesabi Range Strike," *New Republic*, VIII (September 2, 1916), 109; *Solidarity*, July 15, 1916, p. 1.

16. Fairley-Davies Report; West Report; Don D. Lescohier and Martin Cole, Report on the 1916 Mesabi Range Iron Miners' Strike, copy in File 33/247, D/L 280.

17. W. D. Haywood to Frank Walsh, August 17, 1916, Frank Walsh Papers, Box 12, New York Public Library, Manuscript Division; *Solidarity*, July 8, 1916, p. 1; July 15, 1916, p. 1; August 9, 1916, p. 1.

18. Meeting of Range Municipalities and Strikers, pp. 8–9; Michael Boylan to Governor J. A. Burnquist, July 8, 1916, and Boylan to O. B. Warren, July 8, 1916, File 33/247, D/L 280.

19. Meeting of Range Municipalities and Strikers, pp. 21, 28; M. Boylan to Company Officials, July 8, 1916, File 33/247, D/L 280.

20. West Report; *Solidarity*, July 22, 1916, p. 2; July 29, 1916, p. 1.

21. Fluvio Pellinelli to William B. Wilson, July 19, 1916; Dante Barton to Louis F. Post, July 21, 1916; W. B. Wilson to Hywel Davies, D. Barton, F. Pellinelli, V. L. Powers, W. E. Webster, and M. Boylan, ali on Juiy 21, 1916, File 33/247, D/L 280.

22. Davies and Fairley, Preliminary Report of July 29, 1916, File 33/247B; Don D. Lescohier to H. Davies, August 11, 1916, File 33/247, D/L 280.

23. Fairley-Davies Report.

24. F. Pellinelli and T. Shragal to Fairley and Davies, September 9, 1916, and memo by Fairley and Davies, October 28, 1916, File 33/247A, D/L 280.

25. Fairley to Davies, September 19, 1916, File 33/247, D/L 280; *Industrial Worker*, September 23, 1916, p. 1; *Solidarity*, September 23, 1916, p. 1; September 30, 1916, p. 1.
Davies to Wilson, January 8, 1917, File 33/247B, D/L 280; Fairley-Davies

26. H. Davies to W. B. Wilson, October 17, 1916, File 33/247; Fairley and Report.

27. *Solidarity*, September 30, 1916, p. 1.

28. F. P. Walsh to Haywood, August 29, 1916; E. G. Flynn to Walsh, September 20, 1916; J. J. Ettor to Walsh, September 21, 1916; Flynn to Walsh, October 16 and 18, 1916; Ettor to Walsh, November 20, 1916; Walsh to Ettor, December 4, 1916; Ettor to Walsh, December 8, 1916; Walsh to Ettor, December 27, 1916, all in Walsh Papers, Box 13. Privately, Walsh admitted his sympathy for the IWW and also for the defendants.

29. *International Socialist Review*, XVII (January 1917), 429; *Solidarity*, December 23, 1916, p. 1.

30. Elizabeth Gurley Flynn, *I Speak My Own Piece* (New York, 1955), pp. 199–203; *Haywood's Book*, pp. 291–292; Foner, *IWW*, pp. 516–517.

31. I.W.W., *Official Proceedings of the 1916 Convention*, pp. 66ff, 114.

32. For Foote's analysis, see *Industrial Worker*, 1909 issues, and especially September 2, p. 1.

33. Mark Reed to E. G. Ames, December 1, 1911, and Ames to Neil Cooney, November 27, 1911, Puget Mill Company Papers, University of Washington Library, Seattle.

34. Ames to Neil Cooney, November 27, 1911, Puget Mill Company Papers; Cloice Howd, "Industrial Relations in the West Coast Lumber Industry," United States Department of Labor: Bureau of Labor Statistics, *Bulletin No. 349* (Washington, 1923), p. 28.

35. E. G. Griggs to E. G. Ames, April 12, 1912; Fred Talbot to Ames, April 5, 1912; John B. Jones to Ames, April 26, 1912; Talbot to Ames, April 26, 1912; Ames to Talbot, April 27, 1912; Talbot to Ames, May 7, 1912; Ames to W. S. Seavey, May 8, 1912; Will Talbot to Ames, May 22, 1916, all in Puget Mill Company Papers; C. Howd, "Industrial Relations," pp. 65–66; *The Lumber Industry and Its Workers* (Chicago, n.d.), p. 78.

36. Seavey to E. G. Ames, July 29, 1912, Puget Mill Company Papers.

37. E. G. Ames to Fred Talbot, April 18, 1913; Talbot to Ames, June 6, 1913; Ames to R. H. Alexander, June 16 and July 17, 1913, all in Puget Mill Company Papers.

38. Employers' Association of Washington to Puget Mill Company, June 16, 1913; Ames to Talbot, June 20, 1913; Ames to W. B. Mark, December 20, 1913; Ames to Tabot, January 19, 1914, all in Puget Mill Company Papers.

39. Howd, "Industrial Relations," p. 69; *Industrial Worker*, July 1, 1916, p. 1; July 8, 1916, p. 1.

40. G. N. Skinner, President, Employers' Association of Washington, Statement of January 15, 1916, in Merrill Ring Company Papers, University of Washington Library; A. A. Baxter to E. G. Ames, June 28 and July 7, 1916; Ames to Mark Reed, July 18, 1916; Ames to Fred Talbot, July 18, 1916; Ames to Jackson, July 25, 1916, all in Puget Mill Company Papers.

41. Ames to Talbot, July 31 and August 14, 1916; Talbot to Ames, July 18, 1916; Ames to Talbot, November 16, 1916; Talbot to Ames, November 25, 1916, all in Puget Mill Company Papers.

42. Ames to Talbot, September 23 and October 6, 1916, Puget Mill Company Papers; Anonymous, n.d.; R. D. Merrill to Colorado Fuel and Iron Company, July 18, 1916; Merrill to C. D. Cummings, March 4, 1916, all in Merrill Ring Company Papers.

43. Ames to Talbot, February 25, March 6, 1914, and March 4, 1915, Puget Mill Company Papers.

44. Norman H. Clark, "Everett, 1916 and After," *Pacific Northwest Quarterly*, LVII (April 1966), 57–64, is the best study of the origins and the implications of the Everett affair.

45. *Industrial Worker*, August 5, 1916, p. 4.

46. Clark, "Everett, 1916," p. 58; *Industrial Worker*, August 26, 1916, p. 1; September 12, 1916, p. 1; September 19, 1916, p. 1; September 30, 1916, p. 1.

47. *Industrial Worker*, November 4, 1916, p. 1; *Solidarity*, October 14, 1916, p. 2; November 4, 1916, p. 1.

48. This account of the Everett Massacre is based upon Clark, "Everett, 1916"; David C. Botting, Jr., "Bloody Sunday," *Pacific Northwest Quarterly*, XLIX (October 1958), 162–172; Robert L. Tyler, "The Everett Free Speech Fight," *Pacific Historical Review*, XXIII (February 1954), 19–30; Anna Louise Strong, "Everett's Bloody Sunday," *Survey*, XXXVII (January 27, 1917), 475–476; for the IWW's official version, see Walker C. Smith, *The Everett Massacre* (Chicago, 1918); *Solidarity*, November 11, 1916, pp. 1, 4; *Industrial Worker*, November 11, 1916, pp. 1–4; November 18, 1916, p. 1.

49. E. G. Ames to Fred Talbot, November 10, 1916, Puget Mill Company Papers.

50. R. H. Mills, *et al.* to Woodrow Wilson, November 5, 1916, File 150139–60; Haywood to Wilson, November 7, 1916, File 150139–49; Attorney Thomas W. Gregory to Haywood, and also to Herbert Mahler, November 15, 1916, File 150139–50; Clay Allen to Gregory, November 17, 1916, File 150139–51, all in Department of Justice, Record Group 60, National Archives.

51. E. G. Ames to Fred Talbot, November 21, 1916, Puget Mill Company Papers.

52. A. Johannsen to Frank P. Walsh, March 10, 1917, Walsh Papers, Box 14.

53. IWW, "Report of the G.E.B.," *Official Proceedings of the 1916 Convention*, p. 146.

54. *Solidarity*, December 2, 1916, p. 1.

55. IWW, "Report of W. D. Haywood," *Official Proceedings of the 1916 Convention*, pp. 33–37; "Report of the G.E.B.," *ibid.*, pp. 73–74.

56. *Ibid.*, pp. 30, 61, 74–80, 105–111.

57. *Solidarity*, January 20, 1917, p. 2.

Chapter 14: The Class War at Home and Abroad, 1914–1917

1. Ralph Chaplin, *Wobbly* (Chicago, 1948), pp. 199–200.

2. *Industrial Worker*, March 28, 1912, pp. 2–4; May 11, 1914, p. 4; *Solidarity*, May 20, 1911, p. 1.

3. *Solidarity*, April 25, 1914, pp. 1–2; May 23, 1914, p. 1.

4. *Ibid.*, August 8, 1914, p. 2; August 15, 1914, p. 2.

5. *Ibid.*, November 13, 1915, p. 2; cf. Vincent St. John, in *International Socialist Review*, XV (August 1914), 117–118.

6. *Solidarity*, October 31, 1914, p. 1.

7. *Ibid.*, September 12, 1914, p. 2.

8. IWW, *Official Proceedings of the 1916 Convention*, p. 138.

9. Douglas Brovett to Editor, February 7, 1917, *Solidarity*, February 17, 1917, p. 4; *ibid.*, p. 2.

10. James M. Slovick to Haywood, n.d., Department of Justice, Record Group 204; Pardon Attorney File 39–240, Folder 4327, National Archives (hereafter cited as D/J 204).

11. Haywood to Slovick, February 9, 1917, D/J 204.

12. *Solidarity*, March 24, 1917, p. 1.

13. *Ibid.*, April 7, 1917, p. 2; Frank Little to Arizona Copper Miners, *ibid.*, April 21, 1917, p. 4; Forrest Edwards to Don Sheridan, April 2, 1917, P.A. File 39–240, Folder 4134, D/J 204; J. A. MacDonald to S. R. Darnelly, April 12, 1917, and MacDonald to Joseph P. Reagan, April 20, 1917, P.A. File 39–240, Folder 4323, D/J 204.

14. George to Walsh, April 19, 1917, Walsh Papers, Box 15, New York Public Library, Manuscript Division.

15. Haywood to Walsh, May 3, 1917, Walsh Papers.

16. *Industrial Worker*, April 14, 1917, p. 1.

17. Richard Brazier to Haywood, May 26, 1917, and Brazier to President Wilson, n.d., both in Pardon Attorney, Report on the I.W.W. Prisoners Convicted in the Haywood (Chicago) Case; Part II, Independent Defendants (December 20, 1922), p. 11; Pardon Attorney, Report on the July general executive board meeting, p. 13, all in Department of Justice, Record Group 60, National Archives (hereafter cited as D/J 60); *Solidarity*, July 28, 1917, p. 8; Chaplin, Wobbly, pp. 206–209.

18. James Rowan to George Hardy, May 23, 1917; Rowan to J. J. Ratti, May 28, 1917; Haywood to Rowan, May 29, 1917, all in P.A. File 39–240, D/J 204.

19. Herbert Mahler to Haywood, June 22, 1917, P.A. File 35–439, D/J 204;

Frank Walsh to Reverend Daniel C. McCorkle, December 26, 1917, Walsh Papers, Box 18.

20. J. A. MacDonald to Burt Kelley, May 25, 1917, and James Rowan to George Hardy, May 23, 1917, File 39–240, Folder 4323, D/J 204.

21. Harry Lloyd to Herbert Mahler (?), April 6, 1917, File 39-240, Folder 4323; Mahler to Lloyd, April 10, 1917, File 35–439, D/J 204.

22. *Solidarity,* June 9, 1917, p. 1; July 21, 1917, p. 7.

23. Thorstein Veblen, memorandum: "Farm Labor and the I.W.W.," n.d., and Maurice G. Bresnan to Veblen, April 8, 1918, Exhibit A, Department of Labor, Record Group 174, National Archives (hereafter cited as D/L 174).

24. *Industrial Worker,* January–March 1917; C. E. Payne, "The Spring Drive of the Lumber Jacks," *International Socialist Review,* XVIII (June 1917), 729–730; Cloice Howd, "Industrial Relations in the West Coast Lumber Industry," United States Department of Labor, Bureau of Labor Statistics, *Bulletin No. 349* (Washington, D.C., 1923), iii; Vernon Jensen, *Lumber and Labor* (New York, 1945), p. 129; Charlotte Todes, *Lumber and Labor* (New York, 1931), pp. 164–165.

25. Payne, "Spring Drive," pp. 729–730; Don Sheridan to W. D. Haywood, April 23, 1917, File 39-240, D/J 204.

26. Francis A. Garrecht to Attorney General Gregory, June 19, 1917, File 186701–49–1, D/J 60; Special Report on Labor Difficulties in the State of Washington, Washington State Council of Defense (1917), and Henry White to William B. Wilson, June 19, 1917, File 33/517, Department of Labor, Record Group 280 (hereafter cited as D/L 280).

27. R. W. Condon to Fred Talbot, May 4, 1917; Talbot to Condon, May 4, 1917; E. G. Ames to Talbot, May 18, 1917; Ames to Talbot, May 28, 1917; Ames to E. G. Griggs, June 20, 1917, all in Puget Mill Company Papers, University of Washington Library, Seattle.

28. *Solidarity,* June 30, 1917, p. 1; Clay Allen to Attorney General Gregory, July 6, 1917, File 186701–49–6; McClean to Gregory, July 11, 1917, File 186701–13–3, D/J 60.

29. *Solidarity,* July 21, 1917, p. 1; Jensen, *Lumber and Labor,* pp. 125–126. My evaluation of employer attitudes is drawn from extensive correspondence in the Puget Mill Company and Merrill Ring Company Papers, University of Washington Library.

30. *Solidarity,* July 21, 1917, p. 4.

31. R. A. Merrill to Alex Polson, July 7, 1917, Merrill Ring Company Papers.

32. Merrill to Polson, July 21, 1917, and Polson to Merrill, July 23, 1917, Merrill Ring Company Papers; cf. Jensen, *Lumber and Labor,* pp. 125–126, and Harold L. Hyman, *Soldiers and Spruce* (Los Angeles, 1963), pp. 50–51.

33. A. F. Pillsbury to General George W. Goethals, July 29, 1917; J. P. Keating to Howard Jayne, July 20, 1917; Willapa Lumber Company to Jayne, July 20, 1917; Henry White to William D. Wilson, July 21, 1917, all in File 33/574, D/L 280; C. Parker to Walter Lippmann, August 15, 1917, File 33/574A, D/L 280; Clay Allen to Gregory, July 14, 1917, File 186701–49–10, D/J 60; Neil Cooney to E. G. Ames, July 21, 1917, Puget Mill Company Papers; Alex Polson to R. D. Merrill, August 9, 1917, Merrill Ring Company Papers.

34. A. Polson to R. D. Merrill, July 23, 1917, Merrill Ring Company Papers; E. G. Ames to Mrs. R. C. Fuller, July 24, 1917, Puget Mill Company Papers; Watson Eastman to F. A. Douty, July 20, 1917, and Gordon C. Corbaley to J. E. Barnes, July 22, 1917, File 33/574; D/L 280.

35. E. G. Ames to Mrs. R. C. Fuller, July 24, 1917; Ames to F. S. Ames, September. 24, 1917, Ames to Daniel Kelleher, September 25, 1917, all in Puget Mill Company Papers; Dillon to Ashmun Brown, July 23, 1917, File 33/574, D/L 280.

36. E. G. Ames to J. H. Weston, August 31, 1917, Puget Mill Company Papers; on efforts to recruit Southern workers, a whole file of correspondence between A. Polson and the Merrill Ring Company, in the company's papers,

reveals the frustrations involved; for the shift in the IWW's strike tactics, see *The Lumber Industry and Its Workers* (Chicago, n.d), pp. 78–81.

37. Council of National Defense Report in File 33/517, D/L 280.

38. Abraham Glasser MS., "Montana Copper," pp. 4–5, D/J 60; Vernon Jensen, *Heritage of Conflict* (Ithaca, 1960), pp. 430–432; *Solidarity*, June 16, 1917, pp. 1, 4.

39. Jensen, *Heritage*, pp. 432–434; *Solidarity*, June 16, 1917, pp. 1, 4.

40. *Helena Independent*, June 13 and 27, 1917, as quoted in A. Glasser MS.

41. Joseph McNulty to William B. Wilson, June 20, 1917; Tom Campbell, Joe Shannon, *et al.*, to Wilson, June 23, 1917, File 33/493, D/L 280.

42. Fitts to Wilson, June 20, 1917; Wilson to W. H. Rogers, June 20, 1917; Rogers to Wilson, June 20, 1917, all in File 33/493, D/L 280.

43. W. H. Rogers to W. B. Wilson, June 26, 1917; Wilson to Gompers, June 27, 1917; Ed Tegtemeyer, *et al.*, to Wilson, June 27, 1917; W. B. Wilson, James B. Lord, S. Gompers, *et al.*, to T. W. Kline, *et al.*, June 27, 1917; B. Baruch to Wilson, June 30, 1917, all in File 33/493, D/L 280; Gompers to Frank J. McNulty, June 30, 1917, Gompers Letterbooks, V. 235, AFL-CIO Headquarters, Washington, D.C.

44. W. H. Rogers to W. B. Wilson, July 9, 12, 14, 16, and 25, 1917; Mary O'Neill to Jeannette Rankin, July 26, 27, and 28, 1917, all in File 33/493, D/L 280.

45. Wade R. Parks to T. W. Gregory, August 29, 1917, File 186701-27-17, D/J 60.

46. *Report of the President's Mediation Commission to the President of the United States* (Washington, 1918), pp. 4–7. For a fuller report and one more favorable to the miners' version of events, see the same commission's "Summary of the Situation in the Arizona Copper Districts," as well as its "Warren Copper District," Department of Labor, Record Group 1.

47. Jensen, *Heritage*, pp. 372–380; IWW, *Official Proceedings of the 1916 Convention*, p. 61.

48. Jensen, *Heritage*, pp. 380–383; *Solidarity*, March 3, 1917, p. 1; President's Mediation Commission, "Warren Copper District."

49. See, for example, Metal Mine Workers' Industrial Union, "To All Metal Mine Workers," leaflet in File 186813, D/J 60.

50. *Solidarity*, May 26, 1917, p. 3; Jensen, *Heritage*, pp. 390–391.

51. J. W. Bennie to W. B. Wilson, May 24, 1917; Preliminary Report of Conciliator Joseph Myers, May 29, 1917; Myers to W. B. Wilson, May 29 and 30, and June 4, 1917, all in File 33/438, D/L 280.

52. Walter Douglas to Franklin K. Lane, June 8, 1917, File 13/82, CIR.

53. *Solidarity*, June 30, 1917, p. 1.

54. Frank McIntyre to W. B. Wilson, July 2, 1917; Governor Thomas E. Campbell to Wilson, July 2, 1917; A. T. Thompson to Franklin K. Lane, July 2, 1917; Norman Carmichael to Wilson, July 6, 1917, all in File 33/438; John McBride and G. W. P. Hunt to Wilson, August 17, 1917, File 33/438A, all in D/L 280; *Solidarity*, July 14, 1917, p. 1.

55. Copy of speech, in File 186813-16, D/J 60.

56. Walter Douglas to Franklin K. Lane, June 8, 1917, File 13/82, D/L 174; A. T. Thompson to Lane, June 29, 1917, and Bernard Baruch to W. B. Wilson, July 3, 1917, File 33/438; John D. Ryan to B. Baruch, July 3, 1917, File 33/438A, all in D/L 280.

57. John McBride to W. B. Wilson, July 11, 1917, File 33/438; McBride and G. W. P. Hunt to Wilson, August 17, 1917, and Globe Loyalty League to Wilson, August 6, 1917, File 33/438A, all in D/L 280.

58. File 33/438A, D/L 280.

59. U.S. Department of Labor, *Sixth Annual Report of the Secretary of Labor* (Washington, 1918), p. 4.

60. Quoted in *Solidarity*, July 28, 1917, p. 3.

Chapter 15: Employers Strike Back

1. 65th Cong., 1st sess., *Congressional Record,* LV, 6104; *Literary Digest,* LV (August 18, 1917), 12.

2. *Literary Digest,* LV (July 28, 1917), 20–21; (August 18, 1917), pp. 12–13; (August 31, 1918), pp. 14–15. For California, see Hyman Weintraub, "The I.W.W. in California," unpublished master's thesis, University of California at Los Angeles (1947), pp. 92–93, 137–138, 151–152.

3. *Outlook,* CXVI (July 25, 1917), 468; (August 15, 1917), p. 572; *Independent,* XCI (July 21, 1917), 87; (July 28, 1917), p. 118; *Nation,* CV (August 23, 1917), 191.

4. M. A. Matthews to Editor, *Survey,* XXXIX (October 20, 1917), 75; *Address of L. O. Evans before the Chamber of Commerce at Missoula, Montana, August 29, 1917* (n.p., 1917), pp. 2, 28–29.

5. 65th Cong., 1st sess., *Congressional Record,* LV, 5499, 6104, 6262–6265.

6. Alex Polson to Charles R. Sligh, August 16, 1917, File 33/574; E. G. Griggs to R. W. Donovan, July 20, 1917, File 33/574C; Griggs to Lynde Palmer, July 28 and August 2, 1917, File 33/574A, all in Department of Labor, Record Group 280, National Archives (hereafter cited as D/L 280); M. A. Kizer to Congressman Burton L. French, June 26, 1917, File 186701–13–1; Western Red Cedar Association to Congressman Addison T. Smith, July 3, 1917, File 186701–49–2; memo, Charles Warren to T. W. Gregory, July 26, 1917, File 186701–38–5, all in Department of Justice, Record Group 60, National Archives (hereafter cited as D/J 60); E. G. Ames to Talbot, June 5, 1917, Puget Mill Company Papers, University of Washington Library, Seattle; A. Polson to Edward N. Hurley, September 20, 1917, Merrill Ring Company Papers, University of Washington Library, Seattle.

7. Norman Carmichael to William B. Wilson, June 28, 1917, File 33/438A; Dwight B. Heard to Walter S. Gifford, June 29, 1917; A. T. Thompson to Franklin K. Lane, June 29 and July 3, 1917; Congressman Carl Hayden to to W. B. Wilson, July 18, 1917, File 33/574, D/L 280.

8. F. Garrecht to Attorney General, June 19, 1917, File 186701–49–1; McClean to Attorney General, July 3, 1917, File 186701–13–2, D/J 60.

9. Clay Allen to Attorney General, July 6 and 30, 1917, Files 186701–49–5 & 20; Garrecht to Attorney General, July 14, 1917, File 186701–49–10, all in D/J 60.

10. T. W. Gregory to Clarence Reames, July 9, 1917, and Reames to Gregory, July 10, 1917, File 186701–38–2–4; Reames to Gregory, July 17, 1917, File 186701–38–11, all in D/J 60.

11. C. Allen to T. W. Gregory, July 14, 1917, and Gregory to Allen, July 18, 1917, File 186701–49–7; Allen to Gregory, July 20, 1917, File 186701–49–9; Allen to Gregory, July 30, 1917, File 186701–49–20, all in D/J 60; William Fitts to W. B. Wilson, July 18, 1917, File 33/574, D/L 280.

12. C. Parker to Newton D. Baker, July 30, 1917, File 33/574, D/L 280.

13. Charles P. Taylor to Frank Morrison, July 25, 1917, File 33/574; on AFL-sanctioned scabbing, see Charles Moyer to Tom White and C. J. Jacobson, July 2, 1917, in Arizonia Attorney General Wiley Jones, "Report on Bisbee Deportations," File 33/438B; copy of notice issued by Miami Local Union, No. 70, IUMMSW, July 4, 1917, File 20/473, all in D/L 280.

14. Eldridge F. Dowell, *A History of Criminal Syndicalism Legislation in the United States* (Baltimore, 1939), a complete study of the various state laws in the area. Alex Polson to R. D. Merrill, July 30, 1917, Merrill Ring Company Papers.

15. For Minnesota and California, see below, pp. 394–395; Washington State

Council of National Defense, "Special Report on Labor Difficulties in the State of Washington," File 33/517, D/L 280.

16. George Bell to Adjutant General, April 21, 1917, Department of War Files, A.G.O. 2581689, as cited in Abraham Glasser MS., D/J 60; Governor Ernest Lister to Newton D. Baker, June 3, 1917, War Department File 3706, as cited in *ibid.*; Governor Thomas Campbell to W. B. Wilson, June 29, 1917, File 33/438, D/L 280.

17. Walsh to Haywood, May 1, 1917, Walsh Papers, Box 15, New York Public Library, Manuscript Division; *Solidarity*, April 17, 1917, pp. 1, 3, 4.

18. *Solidarity*, June 9, 1917, pp. 1, 3; June 16, 1917, p. 1; June 23, 1917, p. 1; June 30, 1917, pp. 3–4; Seattle Strike Committee to Woodrow Wilson, July 21, 1917, File 33/517, D/L 280.

19. See affidavits appended to Thorstein Veblen's 1918 report, "Farm Labor and the I.W.W.," Department of Labor, Record Group 174, National Archives.

20. Minutes of conference between Governor Thomas B. Campbell and Citizens' Committee, Bisbee, Arizona, July 23, 1917, File 186813, D/J 60.

21. President's Mediation Commission, hearings in Phoenix, October 6, 1917, File 33/517, and McCabe to A. B. Bielaski, July 3, 1917, File 33/438, D/L 280; T. A. Flynn to T. W. Gregory, August 1, 1917, File 186813–34, D/J 60; *Outlook*, CXVI (July 18, 1917), 434.

22. Frank E. Jordan to Woodrow Wilson, July 31, 1917, File 186813–35; T. A. Flynn to T. W. Gregory, August 1, 1917, File 186813–34; Carl Hayden to Gregory, August 29, 1917, File 186813–45 3/8; William C. Fitts to Hayden, August 31, 1917, File 186813–45 3/8, all in D/J 60; Charles Moyer to James Lord; W. B. Wilson to Governor Campbell, August 10, 1917; and Campbell to Wilson, August 14, 1917, all in File 33/438A, D/L 280.

23. This account of the Bisbee deportation is based upon hearings held by President Wilson's Mediation Commission, Department of Labor, Record Group 1 (hereafter cited as D/L 1); and on War Department and Bureau of Investigation reports cited in the Abraham Glasser MS.; minutes of conference, Governor Thomas E. Campbell, File 186813; statements in connection with the deportation made to Arizona Attorney General Wiley Jones, July 12, 1917, File 33/438B; and the report of conciliator George W. P. Hunt to W. B. Wilson, September 1, 1917, File 33/438B, all in D/J 60.

24. Report of President Wilson's Mediation Commission on the Bisbee, Arizona, Deportations, November 5, 1917, D/L 1; G. W. P. Hunt to W. B. Wilson, September 1, 1917, File 33/438B, D/L 280; report of John M. Ruckman, August 30, 1917, War Department File, A.G.O. 370.7, File 186813, D/J 60.

25. *Solidarity*, July 21, 1917, p. 8; G. W. P. Hunt and John McBride to W. B. Wilson, July 12, 1917, File 33/438, D/L 280; Rosa McKay to Woodrow Wilson, July 12, 1917, File 186813–9; R. McKay to T. W. Gregory, July 17, 1917, File 186813–11; F. M. H. to Department of Justice, July 12, 1917, File 186813–7, all in D/J 60. Thomas A. French to Gompers, July 15, 1917, and Frank Morrison to W. B. Wilson, July 17, 1917, File 33/438B, D/L 280.

26. W. C. Fitts to J. C. Skemp, July 28, 1917, File 186813–23; T. W. Gregory to Governor Campbell, July 25, 1917, File 186813–19; Burkhart to Gregory, July 25, 1917, Files 186813–22 and –24 1/2, all in D/J 60; for military attitudes, see the Glasser MS.

27. *Solidarity*, August 4, 1917, p. 1; Arizona State Federation of Labor to Gompers, August 21, 1917, D/L 40; Gompers to T. W. Gregory, January 19, 1918, File 186813–55, D/J 60.

28. For Haywood's telegram, see *Solidarity*, August 4, 1917, p. 8; A. S. Embree, *et al.*, to Haywood, July 31, 1917, in War Department report of that date in File 186813, D/J 60; Embree, *et al.*, to Woodrow Wilson, August 3, 1917, File 33/438B, D/L 280.

29. A. S. Embree, *et al.*, to Woodrow Wilson, September 12, 1917, File 186813–46, D/J 60.

30. A. S. Embree to Woodrow Wilson, September 21, 1917, File 186813–46, and S. J. Graham to Embree, September 29, 1917, File 186813–47 1/4, D/J 60.

31. See Ch. 16 below.

32. Report of the President's Mediation Commission on Bisbee, D/L 1; Felix Frankfurter to Dwight B. Heard, October 25, 1917; Governor Campbell to W. B. Wilson, October 26, 1917; W. B. Wilson to Harry Wheeler, October 29, 1917, all in File 33/438B, D/L 280. Wheeler to Woodrow Wilson, October 30, 1917, File 186813-48, D/J 60; W. B. Wilson to Wheeler, November 5, 1917, File 20/473A; Wheeler to W. B. Wilson, November 6, 1917, File 20/473A; Wheeler to F. Frankfurter, November 11, 1917, File 33/438B 1, all in D/L 280.

33. W. C. Fitts, memo to T. W. Gregory, November 23, 1917, and Woodrow Wilson to T. W. Gregory, November 22, 1917, File 186813–50; W. B. Wilson to Gregory, December 4, 1917, File 186813–52; G. C. Todd, memo to T. W. Gregory, December 14, 1917; John Lord O'Brian, memo to Gregory, December 27, 1917; Solicitor General George W. Davis, memo to Gregory, December 18, 1917; and Fitts to Herron, January 14, 1917, Files 186813–53a, b, c, d, all in D/J 60.

34. T. A. Flynn to T. W. Gregory, May 12, 1918, File 186813–69; Flynn to Gregory, May 23, 1918, File 186813–79; G. W. P. Hunt to W. C. Fitts, July 18, 1919, File 186813–91; Fitts to Gregory, August 20, 1918, File 186813–96; Fitts to Claude Porter, December 4, 1918, File 186813–113; Porter, memo to the Solicitor General, December 12, 1918, File 186813–117; John R. Haynes to A. Mitchell Palmer, December 20, 1920, File 186813–138; R. P. Stewart to Walter Nelles, December 31, 1920, File 186813–139, all in D/J 60.

35. Edward Bassett and Joseph McNulty to J. Rankin, July 13, 1917; T. Walsh to W. B. Wilson, July 17, 1917; Mary O'Neill to Rankin, July 30, 1917, all in File 33/493, D/L 280.

36. *Solidarity*, August 4, 1917, p. 1.

37. *Ibid.*, August 11, 1917, pp. 1–3; Senator H. L. Myers to T. W. Gregory, August 3, 1917, File 186701–27–1, D/J 60. W. H. Rogers to W. B. Wilson, August 7, 1917, File 33/493, D/L 280; *Literary Digest*, LV (August 18, 1917), 12–13.

38. *Helena Independent*, August 2, 1917, and Liggett to Adjutant General, August 3 and 4, 1917, War Department Files A.G.O. 370.6, both as cited in A. Glasser MS.; *Solidarity*, August 18, 1917, p. 3.

39. Governor Emmet D. Boyle to Woodrow Wilson, July 3, 1917; Governor Tom Campbell to Wilson, July 15, 1917; J. W. Tumulty to T. W. Gregory, July 17, 1917; Gregory to Tumulty, July 24, 1917, all in File 186813–13, D/J 60; W. E. Gifford to W. B. Wilson, July 19, 1917, File 20/77, D/L 280; W. E. Gifford to William C. Redfield, July 19, 1917, Department of Commerce File 75024/179.

40. Statement of George L. Bell to Council of National Defense, File 20/77, D/L 280.

41. W. B. Wilson to Judge J. Harry Covington, August 7, 1917, File 20/77, D/L 280; George L. Bell to Woodrow Wilson, August 17, 1917, File 186701–1–9, and John M. Sully to Senator Albert Fall, August 28, 1917, File 186701–27–15, D/J 60; Senator H. F. Ashurst to Woodrow Wilson, August 30, 1917, File 33/517, D/L 280.

42. John Lind to T. W. Gregory, July 26, 1917, and Gregory to Lind, July 27, 1917, File 186701–24–1; Lind to Gregory, July 26, 1917, File 186701–24–2; Lind to Gregory, July 28, 1917, File 186701–24–3; Governor J. A. Burnquist to Gregory, July 28, 1917, File 186701–24–4, all in D/J 60.

43. George W. Anderson to T. W. Gregory, August 20, 1917, File 186701–22–1, and Burton K. Wheeler to Gregory, August 21, 1917, File 186701–27–15, D/J 60.

44. W. C. Fitts to A. Fall, August 30, 1917, File 186701–27–16, D/J 60; W. B. Wilson to Judge Covington, August 7, 1917, File 20/77, D/L 280.

Chapter 16: Decision in Washington, 1917–1918

1. *Solidarity*, July 21, 1917, p. 2.

2. F. K. Lane to Newton Baker, June 16, 1917, and Confidential Note, Baker to Lane, n.d.; W. B. Wilson to Baker, June 22, 1917; Woodrow Wilson to W. B. Wilson, June 25, 1917, all in Department of Labor, Record Group 174, File 13/82, National Archives (hereafter cited as D/L 174).

3. Walter Douglas to Newton Baker, July 3, 1917; Bernard Baruch to Baker, July 3, 1917, both in War Department File A.G.O. 370.6, cited in Abraham Glasser MS., "Arizona," p. 23, Department of Justice, Record Group 60, National Archives (hereafter cited as D/J 60).

4. For the argument that federal policy was developed largely in response to Western business pressures, especially from lumbermen, see William Preston, *Aliens and Dissenters* (Cambridge, Mass., 1963), pp. 95, 122–123, and Michael L. Johnson, "The I.W.W. and Wilsonian Democracy," *Science and Society*, XXVIII (Summer 1964), 257–274; *Bill Haywood's Book: The Autobiography of Big Bill Haywood* (New York, 1929), p. 299, includes the conspiracy charge.

5. The Glasser MS. fully documents the origins of military repression in Washington State, Montana, and Arizona.

6. Ralph A. Hayes to Hugh L. Kerwin, September 4, 1917, File 33/438A, D/L 280. On military repression, see entire Files 33/438 *et seq.*, D/L 280, and 20/473, D/L 174, as well as the Glasser MS.

7. Francis Garrecht to T. W. Gregory, July 23, 1917, and Gregory to Garrecht and also to Clay Allen, July 24, 1917, File 186701–49–13, D/J 60.

8. White and Snyder to W. B. Wilson, August 21, 1917, File 33/517, D/L 280; *Solidarity*, September 1, 1917, p. 1.

9. Wheeler to Gregory, File 186701–27–20, D/J 60.

10. See Preston, *Aliens and Dissenters*, Ch. 4–5.

11. Gregory to Charles Warren, July 11, 1917; Assistant Attorney General, memo to A. B. Bielaski, July 12, 1917; Charles Warren, memo to Gregory, July 16, 1917; Gregory to U.S. Attorneys and Special Agents, July 17, 1917, all in File 186701–1–1, D/J 60.

12. Fitts to Clarence Reames, July 28, 1917, File 186701–38–18, D/J 60.

13. Ralph Chaplin, *Wobbly* (Chicago, 1948), pp. 219–220; *Solidarity*, August 11, 1917, p. 8; October 20, 1917, p. 2.

14. Gregory to Woodrow Wilson, August 21, 1917, File 186701–1–9; W. C. Fitts to Frank C. Dailey, August 24, 1917, File 186701–14–26; Gregory to U.S. Attorneys, August 30, 1917, File 186701–14–28; Fitts to Senator Miles Poindexter, August 30, 1917, File 186701–49–33, all in D/J 60.

15. *Solidarity*, September 22, 1917, pp. 2–4.

16. Francis F. Kane to Gregory, September 7, 1917, File 186701–39–4, D/J 60.

17. File 188032 (the Haywood Case file), D/J 60, contains the full text of the indictment, the intra-departmental discussions ·preceding its formulation, and the rationale behind it. Cf. Preston, *Aliens and Dissenters*, pp. 118–122; Chaplin, *Wobbly*, p. 228; and Philip Taft, "The Federal Trials of the IWW," *Labor History*, III (Winter 1962), 60–62.

18. James Keenan to Department of Justice, December 9, 1917, File 188032–97, D/J 60; cf. Hinton Clabaugh to W. C. Fitts, September 29, 1917, File 188032–2, D/J 60.

19. Chaplin, *Wobbly*, p. 228.

20. Woodrow Wilson to Gregory, January 10, 1918, and statement of Colonel M. E. Savile regarding seditious activities in the Northwest, December 29, 1917,

File 186701–61–1; Gregory to Fitts, January 14, 1918, File 186701–61–2; Fitts to Gregory, January 18, 1918, File 186701–61–3; M. A. Matthews to Gregory, January 29, 1918, and Gregory to Matthews, January 29, 1918, File 186701–49–42; Gregory to William B. Mershon, April 3, 1917, File 186813–58 1/4; John Lord O'Brian to C. Reames, June 24, 1918, File 186701–49–98; Louis F. Post to Gregory, March 1, 1918, and Post to H. Powderton, March 1, 1918, File 186701–49–65; Gregory to Reames, March 11, 1918, File 186701–49–76; Fitts to Reames, April 25, 1918, File 186701–49–83; Gregory to Reames, February 27, 1918, File 186701–49–63, all in D/J 60; cf. Preston, *Aliens and Dissenters*, pp. 165–169, 184.

21. Fitts to Senator Henry Ashurst, September 25, 1917, File 186813–47 1/2; to Congressman Carl Hayden, January 31, 1918, File 186701–40; to Ralph M. Easley, February 11, 1918, File 186701–46; to Francis F. Kane, February 15, 1918, File 186701–39–9; to John Preston, March 12, 1918, File 186701–5–40; to Congressman J. W. Fordney, April 8, 1918, File 186813–58 1/2; to W. E. Humphrey, June 13, 1918, File 188032–242; to Ralph M. Easley, July 5, 1918, File 188032–256, all in D/J 60.

22. XXXVIII (August 11, 1917), 429.

23. Gompers to Woodrow Wilson, August 10, 1917, Gompers Letterbooks, V. 237, AFL-CIO Headquarters, Washington, D.C.

24. J. G. Brown to Frank Morrison, July 25, 1917; Baker to Wilson, August 1, 1917; Wilson to Baker, August 3, 1917; cf. Preliminary Report of Commissioner of Conciliation Henry White, August 4, 1917, all in File 33/574, D/L 280.

25. Henry Suzzallo, Carleton Parker, *et al.*, to Council of National Defense, August 7, 1917, File 33/574, D/L 280; on Parker's role, see Harold Hyman, *Soldiers and Spruce* (Los Angeles, 1963), pp. 53–57, a superb and meticulously researched study of federal intervention during the lumber strike.

26. Baker and Wilson to Suzzallo, Parker, *et al.*, August 10, 1917, and Edgar C. Snyder to W. B. Wilson, August 17, 1917, File 33/574, D/L 280.

27. Woodrow Wilson to Newton Baker, September 19, 1917; Baker to W. B. Wilson, September 20, 1917; W. B. Wilson to Woodrow Wilson, September 22, 1917, all in File 20/473, D/L 174.

28. Gompers to C. O. Young, October 16, 1917, Gompers Letterbooks, V. 239; cf. Hyman, *Soldiers and Spruce*, Ch. 1–3.

29. Hyman, *Soldiers and Spruce*, Ch. 2–4; F. Frankfurter to Stanley King, October 25, 1917 (Records of the Mediation Commission), D/L 174; original draft of troop proposal for AFL conference with Gompers, Disque, *et al.*, November 5, 1917, and Assistant Secretary of Labor, memo to Newton Baker, November 6, 1917, File 33/574A, D/L 280.

30. Hyman, *Soldiers and Spruce*, Ch. 4–5.

31. E. G. Ames to Disque, October 30, 1917, Puget Mill Company Papers, University of Washington Library, Seattle; H. Suzzallo and C. Parker to Newton Baker, January 27, 1918, File 33/574A, and Baker to General Squier, January 2, 1918, File 33/574B, D/L 280.

32. H. Suzzallo to W. B. Wilson, February 28, 1918, and Woodrow Wilson to W. B. Wilson, March 2, 1918, File 33/574C, D/L 280; E. G. Ames to R. C. Fulton, April 3 and 9, 1918, Puget Mill Company Papers.

33. E. G. Ames to W. H. Talbot, September 19, 1918, Puget Mill Company Papers; R. D. Merrill to M. T. Jerome, December 10, 1917, Merrill Ring Company Papers, University of Washington Library, Seattle; Hyman, *Soldiers and Spruce*, Ch. 6–7.

34. Hyman, *Soldiers and Spruce*, Ch. 13–14; Henry White to Hugh L. Kerwin, August 12, 1918, File 33/574C, D/L 280; E. G. Ames to W. H. Talbot, August 23, 1918, Puget Mill Company Papers; address by Brigadier General Brice P. Disque to the Loyal Legion of Loggers and Lumbermen, Portland, Oregon, December 6, 1918, and Spokane, Washington, December 9, 1918, copy in Merrill Ring Company Papers; cf. Robert L. Tyler, "The United States Gov-

ernment as Union Organizer: The Loyal Legion of Loggers and Lumbermen," *Mississippi Valley Historical Review,* XLVII (December 1960), 434–451.

35. See Files 33/438 *et seq.,* D/L 280, especially "Mr. Joseph S. Myers' Visit to Clifton: Statement by Manager," sent by Norman Carmichael to W. B. Wilson, August 2, 1917.

36. Gompers to Baker, August 22, 1917, V. 237, and Gompers to Charles Moyer, August 31, 1917, V. 238, Gompers Letterbooks; Gompers to W. B. Wilson, August 27, 1917, File 20/473, D/L 174; cf. Meyer H. Fishbein, "The President's Mediation Commission and the Arizona Copper Strike, 1917," *Southwestern Social Science Quarterly,* XXX (December 1949), 176ff.

37. Governors Emmet D. Boyle (Nevada), Moses Alexander (Idaho), and James Withycombe (Oregon) to Woodrow Wilson, all on August 28, 1917, and Newton Baker to W. B. Wilson, September 1, 1917, all in File 20/473, D/L 174.

38. W. B. Wilson to Woodrow Wilson, August 31, 1917; W. B. Wilson, memo to Woodrow Wilson, August 31, 1917; Woodrow Wilson to Newton Baker, September 19, 1917; Woodrow Wilson, memo to W. B. Wilson, September 19, 1917, all in File 20/473, D/L 174.

39. F. Frankfurter, memo to the Commission, October 5, 1917, File 20/473, D/L 174.

40. President's Mediation Commission, Hearings in Phoenix, Arizona, October 6, 1917, pp. 8–9, File 33/517, D/L 280.

41. Frankfurter to Lewisohn, October 13, 1917; Lewisohn to Frankfurter, October 15, 1917; Frankfurter to Stanley King, October 16, 1917; Frankfurter to Lewisohn, October 17, 1917, all in File 20/473, D/L 174. On his threatened seizure of the mines and Frankfurter's ultimate failure to discover constitutional sanctions for such actions, see Frankfurter to Robert Szold, October 15, 1917; Frankfurter to Samuel J. Rosensohn, October 16, 1917; and Szold to Frankfurter, October 16, 1917, all in File 20/473, D/L 174. Cf. Harlan B. Phillips, *Felix Frankfurter Reminisces* (New York, 1960), pp. 117–121.

42. Frankfurter to F. A. Keppel, October 20, 1917, D/L 1; also correspondence in File 20/473, D/L 174, and File 33/438A [2], D/L 280.

43. Labor Department files cited in note 42.

44. Joseph Myers to Frankfurter, November 28, 1917, File 33/438A [4], D/L 280, and other letters in this file, and A [5] and A [6] for November 1917–January 1918.

45. Davies to W. B. Wilson, "The I.W.W. Menace," March 29, 1918; to Joseph Myers, April 7, 1918; and to H. L. Kerwin, April 8, 1917, all in File 33/517A, D/L 280.

46. W. H. Rogers to W. B. Wilson, September 13, 1917; H. L. Kerwin to W. B. Wilson, November 3, 1917; W. H. Rogers to W. B. Wilson, November 10, 1917; Eugene Meyer, Jr., to Frankfurter, December 10 and 11, 1917; Gompers to W. B. Wilson, December 13, 1917; E. Meyer to Frankfurter, December 20, 1917, all in File 33/493, D/L 280, Box 30, Butte.

47. Frankfurter to Davies, June 18 and 19, 1918, File 20/473, D/L 174; Davies to Frankfurter, July 1, 1918, File 33/1730, D/L 280.

48. Davies to Frankfurter, July 15, 19, and 20, 1918, and Frankfurter to Davies, July 20, 1918, File 33/1730, D/L 280.

49. Robert Bruere, "Copper Camp Patriotism: An Interpretation," *Nation,* CVI (February 1918), 236.

Chapter 17: Courtroom Charades, 1918–1919

1. John Reed as quoted in Ralph Chaplin, *Wobbly* (Chicago, 1948), pp. 244–246.

2. L. H., "The I.W.W. on Trial," *Outlook*, CXIX (July 17, 1918), 448–450.

3. Elizabeth Gurley Flynn, *I Speak My Own Piece* (New York, 1957), pp. 225–226.

4. See the list prepared by Thorstein Veblen, Exhibit D in his report on "Farm Labor and the I.W.W.," Department of Labor, Record Group 174, National Archives (hereafter cited as D/L 174).

5. Elizabeth Gurley Flynn to Woodrow Wilson, January 10, 1918, File 188032–146, Department of Justice, Record Group 60 (hereafter cited as D/J 60); *Solidarity*, August 25, 1917, p. 5.

6. Philip A. Taft, "The Federal Trials of the IWW," *Labor History*, III (Winter 1962), 62, n. 19; Patrick Renshaw, *The Wobblies* (New York, 1967), pp. 222–223.

7. Flynn, *I Speak My Own Piece*, pp. 225–226.

8. George Vanderveer to George Creel, December 21, 1917, and to Woodrow Wilson, February 11, 1918, File 188032–106 1/2; Francis G. Caffey to W. C. Fitts, March 4, 1918, File 188032–190; on Baldwin, see special report on his character and activities by Bureau of Investigation in File 188032–190 (special IWW file), pp. 28–30, all in D/J 60. Cf. William Preston, Jr., *Aliens and Dissenters* (Cambridge, Mass., 1963), pp. 128–139, nn. 31–32, 36–37.

9. John E. Samuelson to John Lind, October 1, 1917, File 188032–28; John Lind to W. C. Fitts, File 188032–20; T. W. Gregory to C. F. Clyne, October 29, 1917, File 188032–51; Gregory to Clyne, *et al.*, December 14, 1917, File 188032–88; Clyne, *et al.*, to Gregory, December 14, 1917, File 188032–91; W. C. Fitts to George W. Whiteside, February 6, 1918, File 188032–147; Whiteside to Fitts, February 7, 1918, File 188032–151; C. R. Porter to C. F. Clyne, March 15, 1919, File 188032–396, all in D/J 60.

10. *Solidarity*, September 29, 1917, p. 8; October 6, 1917, p. 1.

11. Haywood to Walsh, November 2, 1917, Walsh Papers, Box 18, New York Public Library, Manuscript Division; Roger Baldwin to William B. Wilson, February 26, 1918; Baldwin to Newton Baker, February 27, 1918; memo, National Civil Liberties Bureau, February, 1918, all in File 33/517, Department of Labor, Record Group 280 (hereafter cited as D/L 280); A. S. Lanier to Joseph P. Tumulty, January 17, 1919, File 188032–373, D/J 60.

12. A. S. Embree to Editor, September 19, 1917, *Solidarity*, September 29, 1917, p. 8; James Rowan to John Graves, January 10, 1918, in "The U.S.A. vs. William Hood, *et al.*: "A Conspiracy to Violate the Constitution of the U.S., the Espionage Act . . . In the District Court of the U.S.A. in and for the Northern Division of the Northern District of California, First Division," File 186701–57, Section 2, D/J 60.

13. Vanderveer to Walsh, December 31, 1917, Walsh Papers, Box 18; Vanderveer to Creel, December 21, 1917, and to Wilson, February 11, 1918, File 188032–106 1/2, D/J 60.

14. Vanderveer to Wilson, February 11, 1918, File 188032–106 1/2, D/J 60.

15. *Industrial Worker*, December 29, 1917, pp. 1, 4; J. A. Law to Frank Walsh, December 28, 1917, and L. S. Chumley to Walsh, December 29, 1917, Walsh Papers, Box 18.

16. C. F. Clyne to T. W. Gregory, November 9, 1917, File 188032–65; W. C. Fitts to Solicitor, Post Office Department, January 22, 1918, File 188032–129; W. H. Lamar to Fitts, February 9, 1918, File 188032–156; Lamar to Fitts, March 9, 1918, File 188032–196; Clyne to Fitts, March 18, 1918, File 188032–194; Fitts to Lamar, July 25, 1918, File 188032–262; Frank Nebeker to T. W. Gregory, December 6, 1917, File 188032–85; Nebeker to Gregory, January 14, February 19 and 21, 1918, Files 188032–128–163–168, all in D/J 60.

17. E. D. Reed to Woodrow Wilson, May 8, 1918, File 186701–1–56, and W. D. Haywood, *et al.*, to Wilson, May 2, 1918, File 186701–1–60, D/J 60.

18. Easley to W. C. Fitts, February 16, 1918, File 188032–167 1/2, and Ely to John W. Davis, May 14, 1918, File 188032–228, D/J 60.

19. Copy of public statement by W. C. Fitts, *et al.*, File 188032–3; W. C. Fitts to T. W. Gregory, March 11, 1918, File 188032–186 1/2; W. C. Fitts to Nebeker and Porter, February 25, 1918, File 188032–170; Nebeker to Fitts, February 25 and 26, 1918, Files 188032–171–173, all in D/J 60.

20. Abundant evidence was located in the Abraham Glasser MS., D/J 60, especially in the chapters dealing with the Pacific Northwest and in the appended documents. Also see Exhibit C in Veblen's Report on Farm Labor, D/L 174.

21. Josephus Daniels to T. W. Gregory, March 1, 1918, File 188032–176, D/J 60; E. P. Marsh to Hugh L. Kerwin, August 9, 1918, File 33/517A, D/L 280.

22. Vanderveer to Frank Walsh, March 19, 1918, Walsh Papers, Box 19.

23. The background of Clyne's dismissal as chief prosecutor is fully documented in File 188032, D/J 60, on the Haywood Case. Cf. Taft, "Federal Trials," p. 63; Richard Brazier, "The Mass I.W.W. Trial of 1918; A Retrospect," *Labor History*, VII (Spring 1966), 191; *Transcript of Record*, in the United States Circuit Court of Appeals for the Seventh Circuit, October Term, 1918, No. 2721, *W. D. Haywood, et al., vs. U.S.A.*, 5 vols.; Michael R. Johnson, "The Federal Judiciary and Radical Unionism: A Study of the U.S. v. W. D. Haywood, *et al.*," unpublished master's thesis, Northern Illinois University (1963).

24. All this testimony and counter-testimony can be followed tediously in the trial transcript.

25. Carl Sandburg interview with Haywood in the *Chicago Daily News*, as reprinted in *International Socialist Review*, XVIII (November–December 1917), 277–278.

26. St. John to Walsh, August 28, 1918, Walsh Papers, Box 22.

27. L. H., "I.W.W. on Trial," *Outlook*, CXIX (July 17, 1918), 448–450; "IWW as an Agent of Pan-Germanism," *World's Work*, XXXVI (October 1918), 581–582.

28. On the sentences, see Taft, "Federal Trials," pp. 74–75; Ray S. Fanning to A. Mitchell Palmer, March 31, 1919, File 188032–406, D/J 60.

29. *Bill Haywood's Book: The Autobiography of Big Bill Haywood* (New York, 1929), pp. 324–325.

30. The protests are in File 186701, D/J 60.

31. Harrison George, *The IWW Trial* (n.p., n.d.), p. 206.

32. John Preston to T. W. Gregory, October 10, 1917, and Gregory to Preston, October 11, 1917, File 186701–57–1, D/J 60.

33. Governor William D. Stephens to T. W. Gregory, December 29, 1917, File 186701–57–1; Gregory to Stephens, December 29, 1917, File 186701–57–5; Senator Hiram Johnson to Department of Justice, December 29, 1917, File 186701–57–2; John Preston to Gregory, January 24, 1918, File 186701–5–33; original report on Sacramento IWW Case by Special Agent E. F. Morse, sent to Pardon Attorney by W. J. Burns, Director, Federal Bureau of Investigation, March 29, 1923; and memo to Attorney General on the Sacramento Case, July 18, 1923, File 186701–5–33, all in D/J 60. Cf. Preston, *Aliens and Dissenters*, pp. 132–136.

34. V. L. Fox and Frederick Esmond to T. W. Gregory, February 5, 1918, File 186701–5–36; Burnham to Gregory, January 2, 1918, File 186701–57–6; George Vanderveer to Woodrow Wilson, January 3, 1918, File 186701–57–9; J. B. Holohan to Gregory, January 5, 1918, File 186701–57–12, all in D/J 60; Theodora Pollok to Frank P. Walsh, November 20, 1918, Walsh Papers.

35. John Preston to T. W. Gregory, January 26, 1918, File 186701–59–4, D/J 60.

36. Henry B. Twombly to Walter Lippmann, January 30, 1918, and Lippmann to Hugh L. Kerwin, January 31, 1918, File 16/671, D/L 174; T. W. Gregory to Woodrow Wilson, October 18, 1918, "Case of Miss Pollok," File 186701–59–27 1/2, D/J 60; Pollok to Walsh, November 20, 1918, Walsh Papers.

37. Kearful to J. W. Preston, August 30, 1918, File 186701–57–67; T. W. Gregory to Preston, September 13 and 18, 1918; File 186701–59–13 1/2–14;

Preston to Gregory, September 20, 1918, File 186701–59–15; Woodrow Wilson to Gregory, October 1 and 4, 1918, Files 186701–59–23 1/2–24; Gregory to Preston, October 7, 1918, File 186701–59–27 1/2; Preston to Gregory, October 8, 1918, File 186701–59–27 2/3; Gregory to Woodrow Wilson, October 18, 1918, File 186701–59–27 1/2, all in D/J 60.

38. W. C. Fitts to John Preston, February 1, 1918, File 186701–5–33; Preston to T. W. Gregory, February 9, 1918, File 186701–57–25; Fitts to Preston, June 5, 1918, File 186701–57–57; memo to John Lord O'Brian, October 10, 1918, File 186701–59–29; report of Special Agent E. F. Morse, File 186701–5–33; "The U.S.A. vs. William Hood, *et al.*," File 186701–57, all in D/J 60. Cf. "Ol' Rags an' Bottles," *Nation*, CVIII (January 25, 1919), 114–116.

39. See the E. F. Morse report, File 186701–5–33, and "U.S.A. vs. Hood, *et al*," File 186701–57, D/J 60.

40. *The Silent Defense: A Story of the Remarkable Trial of the Industrial Workers of the World Held at Sacramento, California* (Chicago, 1918–1919); Harvey Duff, *The Silent Defenders: Courts and Capitalism in California* (Chicago, n.d.); T. Pollok to Frank Walsh, November 20, 1918, Walsh Papers.

41. Murdock to Claude Porter, January 17, 1919, File 186701–57–113; Louise Connolly to Porter, December 12, 1918, File 186701–59–35; Dr. Millicent Cosgrove to Ada Connolly, May 9, 1919, File 186701–59–44; A. A. Adams to T. W. Gregory, June 20, 1919, File 186701–59–51, all in D/J 60.

42. "The I.W.W. Case in Kansas," n.d., File 186701–17–9; Fred Robertson to Claude Porter, December 3, 1918, File 186701–17–3; Robertson to A. Mitchell Palmer, April 2, 1919, File 186701–17–6, all in D/J 60. Cf. Winthrop D. Lane, "Uncle Sam: Jailer," *Survey*, XLII (September 6, 1919), 806–812, 834; Taft, "Federal Trials," pp. 79–80.

43. Thomas W. Allen to T. W. Gregory, November 14, 1917, File 186701–28–1; Allen to Gregory, January 8, 1918, and Gregory to Allen, January 12, 1918, File 186701–28–3; Allen to Gregory, August 9, 1918; Alfred Bettman to Gregory, August 19, 1918; and John Lord O'Brian to Allen, Auust 19, 1918, all in File 186701–28–8; Allen to Gregory, August 19, 1918, File 186701–28–9; Allen to Gregory, September 7, 1918, File 186701–28–12; Howard Saxton to Gregory, October 4, 1918, File 186701–28–17, all in D/J 60.

44. Allen to A. Mitchell Palmer, April 10, 1919, File 186701–28–23, D/J 60.

45. Fred Robertson to A. Mitchell Palmer, April 2, 1919, File 186701–17–6, D/J 60.

Chapter 18: Disorder and Decline, 1918–1924

1. *Solidarity*, May 28, 1921, p. 2.

2. E. G. Ames to W. H. Talbot, February 1 and August 15, 1919; R. B. Allen to R. W. Condon, August 18, 1919; and Ames to E. S. Grammar, May 19, 1920, all in Puget Mill Company Papers, University of Washington Library, Seattle; R. T. Merrill to J. W. Blodgett, February 5 and 20, 1919; Alex Polson to T. Jerome, August 21, 1919, all in Merrill Ring Company Papers, University of Washington Library, Seattle. Cf. Cloice Howd, "Industrial Relations in the West Coast Lumber Industry," United States Department of Labor, Bureau of Labor Statistics, *Bulletin No. 349* (Washington, D.C., 1929), p. 101.

3. A. S. Embree and George Vanderveer to W. B. Wilson, September 23, 1918, and T. J. Chope to Hugh L. Kerwin, December 6, 1918, File 33/1730; John D. Ryan to H. L. Kerwin, February 17, 1919, and T. S. Chope to Kerwin, February 17, 1919, File 33/438A [10], all in Department of Labor, Record Group 280, Box 30, Butte, National Archives (hereafter cited as D/L 280).

4. John S. Gambs, *The Decline of the I.W.W.* (New York, 1932), pp. 180–

182. See especially *Industrial Pioneer,* July 1924, pp. 4–6, and July 1926, p. 10. Also see J. J. Harder, "Honk, Honk, Hobo," *Survey,* LX (August 1, 1928), 453–455.

5. IWW, *Proceedings of the 1921 Convention* (Chicago, 1921), p. 7. The same convention also suspended the New York Bakery Workers' Industrial Union, Local 146, for the same reason (*ibid.,* p. 13). Cf. Patrick Renshaw, *The Wobblies* (New York, 1967), p. 183; Gambs, *Decline of the IWW,* pp. 135–137.

6. Hywel Davies to H. L. Kerwin, February 17, 1919, and to James Lord, January 7, 1919, File 33/438A [10]; Governor Thomas E. Campbell to Major General D. R. C. Cabell, January 8, 1919; H. S. Babbitt to George W. Coleman, July 19, 1919; and military intelligence reports and memos, File 33/517A, all in D/L 280; Army reports in Files 186701–83, –88, and –107, D/J 60; W. F. Heliker to T. Jerome, February 25, 1919, Merrill Ring Company Papers; E. G. Ames to George S. Long, October 18, 1919, Puget Mill Company Papers.

7. See financial statement in IWW, *Proceedings of the 1920 Convention* (Chicago, 1920), pp. 15a-b.

8. Abraham Glasser MS., "Butte"; "The I.W.W. General Strike in the Northwest," War Department File 10110–753, January 24, 1919; strike leaflet in File 186701–49–119, all in D/J 60.

9. "The IWW General Strike in the Northwest" as cited above; Confidential Report of E. W. Byrn, Jr., to A. B. Bielaski, Bureau of Investigation, File 291596, cited in Glasser MS., "Butte"; B. K. Wheeler to T. W. Gregory, September 18, 1918, File 195397, D/J 60.

10. The quotation is from the Glasser MS., "Butte"; Report on the Labor Situation in Butte, October 16, 1918, by Thomas Barker, Bureau of Investigation, and E. W. Byrn's report for September 1918, File 291596, both cited in Glasser MS., "Butte." See also Newton Baker to T. W. Gregory, October 14, 1918, and Gregory to Baker, October 23, 1918, File 195397–7, D/J 60.

11. Glasser MS., "Butte"; E. W. Byrn, Confidential Report, October 1, 1918, cited in *ibid.*; B. K. Wheeler to Dan M. Kelly, September 28, 1918, cited in *ibid.*; G–2 Files 10110–753, –890, and –903, cited in *ibid.*; B. K. Wheeler to T. W. Gregory, October 4, 1918, File 195397–5, D/J 60.

12. Major A. S. Peske to Director, Military Intelligence, May 5, 1920, G–2 File 10110–1841, cited in Glasser MS., "Butte"; John C. Crowley to Director, Military Intelligence, September 15, 1918, G–2 File 10634–196, and November 20, 1919, G–2 File 10634–606, cited in *ibid.*

13. Robert K. Murray, *Red Scare: A Study in National Hysteria, 1919–1920* (Minneapolis, 1955), *passim;* Stanley Coben, *A. Mitchell Palmer: Politician* (New York, 1963), Ch. 11–12, *passim.*

14. Conversations with Fred Thompson, Fall–Spring 1966–1967; Ed Delaney to J. S. Gambs, July 3, 1921, cited in Gambs, *Decline of the IWW,* p. 134.

15. IWW, *Proceedings of the 1919 Convention* (Chicago, 1919), *passim.*

16. See Murray, *Red Scare,* and Coben, *Palmer.*

17. John Dos Passos, *1919* (New York, 1932), pp. 456–461; Ralph Chaplin, *The Centralia Conspiracy* (Seattle, 1920); Walker C. Smith, *Centralia: Was It Murder?* (n.p., 1925); Robert L. Tyler, "Violence at Centralia, 1919," *Pacific Northwest Quarterly,* XLV (October 1954), 116–124; John M. McClelland, Jr., "Terror on Tower Avenue," *ibid.,* LVII (April 1966), 65–72.

18. T. Jerome to F. B. Hubbard, November 12, 1919, and Hubbard to Jerome, November 20, 1919, Merrill Ring Company Papers; Governor William D. Stephens to A. M. Palmer, November 18, 1919, File 186701–5–43, and J. E. Hoover to Stewart, August 21, 1920, File 195397–37, D/J 60. On Hoover, see William Preston, Jr., *Aliens and Dissenters* (Cambridge, Mass., 1963), pp. 226–227.

19. Mark M. Litchman to Baritz, May 31, 1919, and February 3, 1920; Litchman to Reb, October 2, 1920; Litchman to Slater, March 8, 1921; Litchman to Eugene Balmont, May 27, 1921, all in Mark Litchman Papers, University of Washington Library, Seattle.

20. Ralph Chaplin, *Wobbly* (Chicago, 1948), pp. 256–257.

21. *Proceedings of the 1921 Convention,* p. 10; W. D. Haywood to Roy Dempsey, August 25, 1919, File 186701-57–131, D/J 60. For the entire story of the legal campaign, see Philip Taft, "The Federal Trials of the IWW," *Labor History,* III (Winter 1962), 80–91.

22. Memorandum for the Attorney General from Assistant Attorney General Robert P. Stewart, January 11, 1921, D/J 60.

23. Recommendation of Pardon Attorney Robert H. Turner, January 8, 1921, D/J 60; on Harding and the Appeals Court decision, see Taft, "Federal Trials," pp. 75–76, 82–85.

24. *Proceedings of the 1921 Convention,* pp. 10–13.

25. Mary E. Gallagher, Oral History Interview Transcript, pp. 40–41, Bancroft Library, University of California, Berkeley; Mark Litchman to Reb, June 5, 1921, Litchman Papers.

26. Chaplin, *Wobbly,* pp. 285–286; conversations with Fred Thompson, Fall–Spring 1966–1967; interview with Richard Brazier, May 10, 1965. Cf. Renshaw, *Wobblies,* pp. 241–242; and Taft, "Federal Trials," p. 76.

27. Interview with Brazier, May 10, 1965.

28. *Proceedings of the 1921 Convention,* pp. 11–13, 40; Otto Christensen to Harry Daugherty, July 8, 1921; Daugherty to Christensen, July 8, 1921; and Charles F. Clyne to Daugherty, July 8, 1921, all in Files 188032-620 and –622, D/J 60.

29. Conversations with Alexander Trachtenberg in 1965 and 1966; copy of letter from Haywood to David Karsner, February 11, 1928, given to me by Richard Brazier; R. Walton Morse to Homer Cummings, September 5, 1934, File 188032, D/J 60; cf. *Bill Haywood's Book: The Autobiography of Big Bill Haywood* (New York, 1929), pp. 363–365; Chaplin, *Wobbly,* p. 334.

30. Chaplin, *Wobbly,* p. 323; Chaplin to Dad, February 28, 1922, File 188032-670, D/J 60.

31. C. W. Anderson to Pardon Attorney Finch, March 23, 1923, cited in Preston, *Aliens and Dissenters,* p. 266.

32. The 1922, 1923, and 1924 conventions illustrate the internal bickering at its worst. Also see Walter T. Nef to E. G. Flynn, November 25, 1922, E. G. Flynn Papers (Workers' Defense Union), State Historical Society of Wisconsin.

33. Chaplin, *Wobbly,* pp. 285–288, 298; Report of George Hardy appended to IWW, *Proceedings of the 1922 Convention* (Chicago, 1922); Gambs, *Decline of the IWW,* pp. 89–91; Renshaw, *Wobblies,* p. 262.

34. Chaplin, *Wobbly,* pp. 287–288, 298; *Proceedings of the 1920 Convention,* p. 15, and *Proceedings of the 1921 Convention,* pp. 13–14, 21.

35. George Williams, *Report on the First Congress of the Red Trades Union International* (Chicago, 1921).

36. *The IWW Reply to the Red Trade Union International* (Chicago, 1922), pp. 17–20.

37. J. F. Campbell to Mary Gallagher, July 26, 1930, Gallagher Papers, Bancroft Library, University of California, Berkeley.

38. Chaplin, *Wobbly,* pp. 295–296; IWW, *Proceedings of the 1921 Convention,* pp. 13–14; Robert L. Tyler, "The I.W.W. and the Brain Workers," *American Quarterly,* XV (Spring 1963), 41–51.

39. IWW, *Proceedings of the 1924 Convention* (Chicago, 1924), pp. 1, 30ff.

40. Gambs, *Decline of the IWW,* pp. 60, 110–115; Renshaw, *Wobblies,* pp. 260–263; Hyman Weintraub, "The I.W.W. in California," unpublished master's thesis, University of California, Los Angeles (1947), pp. 250–251; Robert F. Tyler, "Rebels of the Woods and Fields: A Study of the I.W.W. in the Pacific Northwest," unpublished doctoral dissertation, University of Oregon (1953), pp. 189–191; *Proceedings of the 1924 Convention,* p. 3.

41. *Proceedings of the 1924 Convention,* pp. 13–14, 143.

42. M. Gallagher, Oral History Interview Transcript, pp. 37–38.

43. Weintraub, "The IWW in California," pp. 250–251; Tyler, "Rebels of the Woods," p. 192.
44. Dan Wakefield, "The Haunted Hall: The I.W.W. at Fifty," *Dissent*, IV (Fall 1956), 414–419.

Chapter 19: Remembrance of Things Past: The IWW Legacy

1. Mimeographed minutes of the December 1967 meeting provided by Fred Thompson.
2. Conversations with Thompson, Carl Keller, and Walter Westman, 1966–1967. Words from "The Preacher and the Slave," in *The Little Red Song Book* (1964 ed.), p. 9.
3. For a journalistic impression of the old men managing the Chicago office in 1966, see *Chicago Sun-Times*, December 12, 1966, p. 38.
4. See Fred Thompson's review of Philip Foner's history of the IWW in the *Industrial Worker*, February 1966, p. 4. Membership estimates from John S. Gambs, *The Decline of the IWW* (New York, 1932), pp. 165–166.
5. Abundant evidence along this line was found in the archives of the Puget Mill Company and the Merrill Ring Company, University of Washington Library, Seattle; the reports of Labor Department officials from Montana and Arizona as well as military intelligence reports for 1919–1922 profusely cited in the Abraham Glasser MS., Department of Justice, Record Group 60, National Archives.
6. Dan Wakefield, "The Haunted Hall: The I.W.W. at Fifty," *Dissent*, IV (Fall 1956), 414. For dual membership patterns in the pre-war period, see W. D. Haywood to Henry Wilson, May 29, 1917, and Wilson to Haywood, June 9, 1917, Department of Labor, Record Group 280, File 33/517, National Archives.
7. Gambs, *Decline of the IWW*, p. 166; Wakefield, "Haunted Hall," p. 415. The IWW convention proceedings for 1931, 1932, 1934, and 1936 offer no basis for estimating membership. The 1938 proceedings include a financial report that estimates a membership of slightly more than twenty thousand. Yet if that report is to be believed, the IWW received and expended funds far under $1 per member for the entire year 1937–1938. Moreover, at the 1939 convention, which met for only two days, only three unions and five delegates attended. That convention explained the organization's collapse in terms of a March 1939 general executive board decision to suspend from membership a local of Cleveland Stove Makers, the only IWW affiliate then conducting collective bargaining, for signing a time-agreement. Walter Westman and Carl Keller both asserted that this decision split the IWW irrevocably. Thereafter, at the three subsequent conventions—1946, 1950, and 1955—delegates represented neither industrial unions nor local unions; instead, they represented largely propaganda and lodge associations.
8. The IWW also led strikes by construction workers on two major public water projects in the state. See Hyman Weintraub, "The IWW in California," unpublished master's thesis, University of California, Los Angeles (1947), pp. 215–216.
9. *Ibid.*, pp. 220–227; Gambs, *Decline of the IWW*, pp. 138–143.
10. Weintraub, "IWW in California," pp. 227–233.
11. Gambs, *Decline of the IWW*, pp. 44–45.
12. Weintraub, "IWW in California," pp. 235–246; Mary Gallagher, Oral History Project Transcript, pp. 66–67, Bancroft Library, University of California, Berkeley. Photos of the June 1924 vigilante raid are also included in the Gallagher Papers.
13. For an excellent and detailed analysis of the conflict, see Donald J.

McClurg, "The Colorado Coal Strike of 1927—Tactical Leadership of the IWW," *Labor History,* IV (Winter 1966), 68–92. Cf. Charles J. Bayard, "The 1927–1928 Colorado Coal Strike," *Pacific Historical Review,* XXXII (August 1963), 235–250; and Gambs, *Decline of the IWW,* p. 145.

14. The Mary Gallagher Papers include numerous photographs of the car caravans. McClurg, "Colorado Coal Strike," pp. 79, 90–91.

15. McClurg, "Colorado Coal Strike," pp. 88–89.

16. *Ibid.,* p. 90.

17. Lee Tulin to Mary Gallagher, June 21, 1928, Tom Mooney Papers, Box 8, Bancroft Library, University of California, Berkeley.

18. Tom Connors to Mary Gallagher, October 14 and 18, 1928, Mooney Papers.

19. On Harlan County, see Gambs, *Decline of the IWW,* p. 155, and Irving Bernstein, *The Lean Years: A History of the American Worker, 1920–1933* (New York, 1960), pp. 377–381. For the hop pickers' 1933 strike, see correspondence in the Mark Litchman Papers, University of Washington Library, Seattle.

20. Ralph Chaplin, *Wobbly* (Chicago, 1948), p. 361.

21. John Pancner Papers, Wayne State University Labor Archives, Detroit.

22. *Time,* XLVII (April 1, 1946), p. 25; IWW, Minutes of the 1946 Convention.

23. See Ch. 12, n. 37.

24. Philip Taft, "The I.W.W. in the Grain Belt," *Labor History,* I (Winter 1960), p. 67; Michael L. Johnson, "The I.W.W. and Wilsonian Democracy," *Science and Society,* XXVIII (Summer 1964), 274; William Preston, Jr., *Aliens and Dissenters* (Cambridge, Mass., 1963), pp. 150–151.

25. Oscar Lewis, *La Vida* (New York, 1966), p. 1. Cf. Seymour Martin Lipset, *Political Man: The Social Bases of Politics* (New York, 1960), pp. 115–122.

26. For employer resistance to the IWW, see Selig Perlman and Philip Taft, *A History of Trade Unionism in the United States, 1896–1932* (New York, 1935), pp. 280–281. Cf. Walter Galenson, *The C.I.O. Challenge to the A.F.L.* (Cambridge, Mass., 1960); and David Brody, "The Emergence of Mass Production Unionism," in John Braeman, *et al., Change and Continuity in Twentieth Century America* (Columbus, Ohio, 1966), pp. 221–262.

27. Ray Ginger, *The Bending Cross* (New Brunswick, N.J., 1949), p. 257; Bert Cochran, "Debs," in Harvey Goldberg, ed., *American Radicals* (New York, 1957), p. 173; Robert F. Tyler, "Rebels of the Woods and Fields: A Study of the I.W.W. in the Pacific Northwest," unpublished doctoral dissertation, University of Oregon (1953), pp. 2, 21, 204–206; Gambs, *Decline of the IWW,* p. 206; Paul F. Brissenden, *The I.W.W.* (New York, 1919 ed.), pp. xx–xxi, among numerous other works.

A NOTE ON SOURCES

The Industrial Workers of the World has been ill-treated by history and government. Government, of course, practically eradicated the IWW as a labor organization; worse, Justice Department authorities confiscated *all* the organization's official records and correspondence during the 1917 raids, then held these materials in Chicago until 1923 when, by federal court order, they were incinerated. Even the correspondence used as official exhibits by the prosecution during the federal trials of IWW members disappeared without a trace. Thus scholars face the unenviable, though not impossible, task of reconstructing the history of the IWW without access to the organization's basic records during the period of its most vital activity: 1908–1918.

Little wonder, then, that until recently there have been no thorough studies of the IWW and that few historians have dared approach the topic. The best of the early studies of the organization remain Paul F. Brissenden's "The Launching of the Industrial Workers of the World" (*University of California Publications in Economics,* IV, No. 1, pp. 1–82, Berkeley, 1913) and *The I.W.W.: A Study of American Syndicalism* (originally published by Columbia University Press, New York, 1919, but going through three later revisions, the latest in 1957, without substantial change); John S. Gambs, "The Decline of the I.W.W." (*Studies in History, Economics and Public Law,* No. 361 [New York, Columbia University Press, 1932]); John G. Brooks, *American Syndicalism: The I.W.W.* (New York, Macmillan, 1913). Two official histories should also be mentioned: Vincent St. John, *The I.W.W.: Its History, Structure, and Methods* (Chicago, 1919 ed.), and Fred Thompson, *The I.W.W.: Its First Fifty Years* (Chicago, 1955).

Brissenden's work, superlative at the time of publication and still wearing well, is concerned largely with the internal, institutional development of the IWW. It is based mostly on the official publications and convention proceedings of the IWW; it treats in only cursory fashion the interaction between Wobblies and American society, and it necessarily neglects the most crucial period of organization history: the war years, 1917–1919. Nevertheless, it remains invaluable for its portrait of internal IWW intrigue and conflict and for its analysis of the organization's ideology and structure. John Brooks's book, though it has many striking insights, is largely personal in content and approach, a firsthand observer's immediate impressions of the forces that produced syndicalism and the IWW in America. John Gambs's scholarly account deals mostly with the post-1920 years, relies heavily upon published sources, is biased against the Wobblies, and understates the impact of government repression in weakening the IWW. The first of the two official IWW histories was written by St. John, the organization's most important official during its halcyon years, 1908–1915; the second by Thompson, a man who stayed with the IWW during the lean years after 1919. Both suffer from the sins and virtues of official histories; they offer intimate descriptions and insights, but they lack objectivity. They are also too brief to probe very deeply beneath the surface of the Wobblies' history.

Three other early treatments of the pre-war IWW should be noted. Louis Levine, in "The Development of Syndicalism in America," *Political Science Quarterly*, XXVIII (September 1913), 451–479, offers a mature, sophisticated, and scholarly account which places American syndicalism in an international as well as a domestic context. André Tridon in *The New Unionism* (New York, B. W. Huebsch, 1913) offers a sympathetic sketch of the IWW and also considers syndicalism as an international phenomenon. Carleton H. Parker's seminal study, *The Casual Laborer and Other Essays* (New York, Harcourt, Brace, & Howe, 1920), uses the techniques of social psychology to analyze the migratory laborers attracted to the IWW. Although Parker's approach reveals many little-known facets of the migratory's existence and personality, it mixes antipathy with sympathy in unequal doses. Parker was eager to improve living conditions among oppressed migrants and to reform the environmental factors in American life that produced such men, but he viewed the IWW as a destructive, anti-social agency and most of its members, if not its leaders, as mental defectives. He shared the typical middle-class progressive reformer's abhorrence of radicalism from below.

The autobiographies of two prominent Wobblies, William D. Haywood and Ralph Chaplin, cannot be neglected. *Bill Haywood's Book: The Autobiography of William D. Haywood* (New York, International Publishers, 1929 and 1958 ed.) was written while the author was in exile in Moscow, a desperately ill and defeated man. Completed with the assistance of Communist party ghostwriters, the autobiography rings true in many places, yet it is replete with errors a healthy and observant Haywood would never have tolerated. Chaplin's *Wobbly: The Rough and Tumble Story of a Radical* (Chicago, University of Chicago Press, 1949) is the reminiscences of a former Wobbly editor and poet (never a strike leader or organizer) who later found salvation in Christianity and anti-communism, a not uncommon Cold War phenomenon. Although his remembrances of the early Wobblies, especially Haywood, appear fair and revealing, at many points Chaplin's newly discovered religion colors his attitudes. Three more autobiographies by individuals who broke with the IWW and later found their utopia in the Communist party offer perceptive critical comments on the IWW: Elizabeth Gurley Flynn, *I Speak My Own Piece: Autobiography of the "Rebel Girl"* (New York, Masses and Mainstream, 1955); William Z. Foster, *Pages from a Worker's Life* (New York, International Publishers, 1939)—also his *From Bryan to Stalin* (New York, International Publishers, 1937); and James P. Cannon, *Notebook of an Agitator* (New York, Pioneer Publishers, 1958). One unpublished memoir must also be mentioned: Ben H. Williams, "American Labor in the Jungle: The Saga of One Big Union" (microfilm copy, Wayne State University Library, Labor Archives). Written by a prominent Wobbly and longtime editor of *Solidarity*, it contains astute comments about the personality of the committed Wobbly and about the dynamics of IWW factionalism, particularly for the years 1905–1908.

Most other historical treatments of the IWW written before 1950, which usually are brief portions in general histories of the American labor movement, are based upon the works described above and add little or nothing to the Wobbly story. Some are sympathetic, others hostile, and none is quite sure about the IWW contribution to American radicalism or about its impact upon society. Most follow the pattern set by the deans of American labor history, Selig Perlman and Philip Taft (*History of Labor in the United States, 1896–1932* [New York, Macmillan, 1935]), in viewing the IWW primarily as the unique response of libertarian Westerners to the singular American frontier environment. Few scholars have returned to the theme of internationalism pursued originally by Brissenden and Levine.

In the past two decades, however, there has been a resurgence of scholarly interest in the IWW. The most noteworthy products of this renewed interest are Philip S. Foner's *History of the Labor Movement in the United States,* Volume 4: *The Industrial Workers of the World, 1905–1917* (New York, International Publishers, 1965); Patrick Renshaw, *The Wobblies: The Story of Syndicalism in the United States* (New York, Doubleday, 1967); Robert L. Tyler, *Rebels of the Woods: The I.W.W. in the Pacific Northwest* (Eugene, University of Oregon Press, 1967); and Joyce L. Kornbluh, ed., *Rebel Voices: An I.W.W. Anthology* (Ann Arbor, University of Michigan Press, 1964).

Gratifying as these new studies are to anyone interested in the IWW, they are all to some extent deficient. Tyler's is restricted geographically, and it fails to transcend Brissenden's and Parker's earlier observations. Renshaw inflates minor aspects of IWW history out of proportion, neglects essential events, and (his impressive scholarly apparatus of footnotes notwithstanding) makes numerous factual errors and gross distortions of events. Of all the recent works on the IWW, Foner's is the most serious and the most professional. Yet he, too, fails at important junctures. His reader is left not knowing the circumstances that produced the IWW or brought it down so rapidly from the heights it had conquered during World War I. Foner explains most IWW failures according to his own version of Marxism-Leninism. This is an egregious mistake, for of all radical labor organizations the IWW is the hardest to cast in a rigid Marxist mold.

In addition to these writers, several graduate students have chosen aspects of the IWW's history as thesis subjects. The results of their research have been most uneven. Tyler undertook the most ambitious of these studies, "Rebels. of the Woods and Fields: A Study of the I.W.W. in the Pacific Northwest" (unpublished doctoral dissertation, University of Oregon, 1953). Like his later book, the dissertation relied mostly on newspapers and published sources and tended to patronize the IWW as a group of folk-singing troubadours: the *minnesingers* of the labor movement. In two articles also derived from his dissertation and published prior to his book—"I.W.W. in the Pacific N.W.; Rebels of the Woods," *Oregon Historical Society Quarterly,* LV (March 1954), 3–44, and "The Rise and Fall of an American Radicalism: The I.W.W.," *Historian,* XIX (November 1956), 48–65—Tyler describes the IWW as primarily a Western organization responsive to frontier conditions. Yet in a 1960 essay, "The I.W.W. and the West," *American Quarterly,* XII (Summer 1960), 175–187, he implicitly contravenes his earlier writings by reverting to the Brissenden-Levine thesis concerning the international matrix out of which the IWW emerged. Another unpublished University of Oregon dissertation, Claude W. Nichols, Jr., "Brotherhood in the Woods: A Twenty Year Attempt at 'Industrial Cooperation'"

(1959), also based mostly on newspapers and published sources, criticizes sharply, without substance or careful analysis, the IWW's wartime activities in the lumber industry. Donald M. Barnes, "The Ideology of the Industrial Workers of the World, 1905–1921" (unpublished doctoral dissertation, Washington State University, 1962), is just what the title implies. Based on sources available to previous scholars such as Brooks and Brissenden, it adds little to their analysis of the IWW and is less understanding of a strange and non-systematic ideology. A similar dissertation that concentrates upon the ideology of the IWW is Joseph R. Conlin, "The Wobblies: A Study of the Industrial Workers of the World Before World War I" (University of Wisconsin, Madison, 1966). Although Conlin is more sympathetic to the Wobblies than Barnes, he is equally tendentious in his analysis of IWW doctrines. The best of the unpublished theses is Hyman Weintraub's "The I.W.W. in California, 1905–1931" (master's thesis, University of California at Los Angeles, 1947), a sympathetic study of the IWW in a Western state that was not one of its strongholds.

Although the IWW's organizational records through 1918 were destroyed by federal authorities, and those for the years 1919–1923 were lost as a result of a fire at IWW headquarters, more than enough unpublished and published sources are available from which to re-create the organization's history. Before discussing the sources that illuminate specific aspects of IWW history, I should mention those which shed light on the organization's entire history and which are the most valuable.

No history of the IWW can be written without perusing carefully the organization's official publications: the *Industrial Worker, Industrial Union Bulletin, Solidarity,* and *One Big Union Monthly,* as well as numerous special regional and foreign-language periodicals. Wobblies, whether learned or not, liked to write, and the IWW journals, which opened their columns freely to all shades of opinion within the organization, included correspondence from rank-and-filers on any and every matter of interest to the membership. The periodicals reported in detail on all events of significance to the IWW, and recorded best the organization's internal, institutional history. They must, however, be supplemented by the IWW's *Official Convention Proceedings,* particularly for the crucial 1905, 1906, and 1916 conventions.

Of no less importance are the holdings in the National Archives in the collections of the Labor and Justice Departments. Labor Department Record Groups 174 (fragments of the President's Mediation Commission files) and 280 (Federal Mediation and Conciliation reports) together contain the most complete and objective accounts of IWW organizing activities and industrial disputes among iron miners, copper miners, lumber workers, and harvest hands from 1916 to 1918. These papers include the unpublished reports and transcripts of hearings conducted by the President's Mediation Commission; field reports and general correspondence filed by investigators and conciliators representing the Federal Mediation Service; and proposals that originated at various levels within the department to cope with the IWW wartime menace.

Justice Department Record Groups 60 (general records) and 240 (Pardon Attorney's Office) are unsurpassed for their accounts of the federal government's response to the IWW threat. R.G. 60 includes some revealing correspondence on the pre-war IWW free-speech fights and the full record of the wartime prosecutions of the Wobblies, except for what J. Edgar Hoover has restricted (see below). R.G. 240, though of less value, includes, among the pardon petitions of IWW prisoners, revealing portions of correspondence concerning attitudes toward and responses to American involvement in World War I.

Of great value for gleaning insights into the IWW's ideology and its activities before World War I are the published and unpublished reports of the United States Commission on Industrial Relations (Washington, D.C., Government Printing Office, 1915, 15 volumes). The published reports contain lengthy testimony by W. D. Haywood, Vincent St. John, James Thompson, George Speed, Joe Ettor, and other IWW leaders, as well as detailed analyses of the Paterson silk strike and the Wheatland, California, riot. The unpublished reports, seldom seen or used, are located either in the National Archives (Department of Labor, Record Groups 1 and 174) or the State Historical Society of Wisconsin, Madison. They cover topics as diverse as the free-speech fights, inter-union conflict in Butte, and the Lawrence textile strike.

The official papers of the American Federation of Labor at AFL-CIO headquarters in Washington (Gompers Letterbooks) and at the State Historical Society of Wisconsin (files of the Office of President) were of surprisingly slight help. Much correspondence was apparently destroyed, whatever the reason, and little dealing with the IWW remains, although the two rival labor organizations clashed often and bitterly.

Origins, 1890–1905

The sources concerning the IWW's Western origins are so extensive and varied that I will mention only those which proved to be most important for this book. Government documents and state archives contain the best materials on industrial disputes in the mining West and the emergence of the Western Federation of Miners. Idaho developments are treated in the papers of Governor Norman Willey, James H. Hawley, William Borah, and Telegrams and Correspondence of the Idaho Congressional Delegation Relative to the 1892 Coeur d'Alene Dispute, all in the collections of the Idaho State Historical Society, Boise. The same ground is covered in a series of congressional reports: 56th Cong., 1st sess., *House Report No. 1999,* "Coeur d'Alene Labor Troubles"; *Senate Document No. 24,* "Coeur d'Alene Mining Troubles"; and *Senate Document No. 42,* "Labor Troubles in Idaho."

The Colorado labor wars, which were so basic to the history of the WFM and to the creation of the IWW, assume new import when viewed through the perspective provided by the papers and letterbooks of Governors Davis H. Waite (1893–1895), Albert A. McIntyre (1895–1897), Alva Adams (1897–1899), and James H. Peabody (1903–1905), all in the Colorado State Archives (Record Groups 1 and A-69). These collections, except for the Waite papers, reveal the full extent of the working alliance in Colorado between mining industry employers and state officials, especially in the case of Governor Peabody, who was determined to destroy the WFM. A federal government report (58th Cong., 3rd sess., *Senate Document No. 122*, "A Report on Labor Disturbances in the State of Colorado from 1880 to 1904") presents a detailed and fair overview of the Colorado industrial conflicts.

Three books also explain how labor conflict in the Mountain West resulted in working-class radicalism and led to the formation of the IWW. Vernon H. Jensen, *Heritage of Conflict: Labor Relations in the Nonferrous Metals Industry up to 1930* (Ithaca, Cornell University Press, 1950), is an outstanding history of the WFM, though the author sympathizes with the more moderate faction in the Federation and has little liking for Haywood, St. John, and other Wobblies. Robert W. Smith's *The Coeur d'Alene Mining War of 1892: A Case Study of an Industrial Dispute* (Corvallis, Oregon State University Press, 1961) is a dull but nevertheless detailed and equitable version of the Idaho conflict that led directly to the establishment of the WFM. B. M. Rastall, "The Labor History of the Cripple Creek District," *Bulletin of the University of Wisconsin*, No. 198: *Economic and Political Science Series*, III, No. 1 (Madison, 1908), provides excellent insights into the industrial war that gripped Colorado's mining districts from 1903 to 1905. Rastall does not veil his antipathy to radical labor, which he defines loosely and broadly.

The WFM's flirtation with Populism and its increasing radicalism can be traced in the organization's *Official Convention Proceedings* and in newspapers such as the *Butte Bystander* (1892–1897), *Butte Reveille* (1900–1905), *Pueblo Courier*, and, after 1900, in the union's own fine publication, *Miners' Magazine*.

The evolution from Western Labor Union to American Labor Union to Industrial Workers of the World is covered in the above papers as well as in the *Labor World* (Butte, 1902–1903), the *American Labor Union Journal* (*Butte*, 1902–1904), the *Voice of Labor* (Chicago, 1904–1905), and the *International Socialist Review* (Chicago, 1900–1918). Of course, the definitive source on the first IWW convention is the official stenographic record of the sessions, which runs more than six hundred printed pages (New York, Labor News Company, 1905). Strangely, the papers of Daniel DeLeon and Algie Simons (two of the original founders of the IWW, whose papers are in the State Historical Society of Wisconsin) contain no references to the organization.

Formative Years, 1905–1908

Two books treat the most important event in the early years of the IWW: the Haywood trial. Stewart H. Holbrook, in a colorful journalistic version of the trial's background, *The Rocky Mountain Revolution* (New York, Henry Holt, 1956), accepts without reservation Harry Orchard's confession, which implicated the WFM in a conspiracy of murder and mayhem and which held the union responsible for almost every heinous outrage committed during the Western industrial conflicts from 1899 to 1904. David H. Grover's more recent and scholarly version of the same event follows the Holbrook tradition. In his *Debaters and Dynamiters: The Story of the Haywood Trial* (Corvallis, Oregon State University Press, 1964), Grover also accepts Orchard's veracity, does not doubt the guilt of either Haywood or the WFM, and, still worse, makes errors of fact which prejudice the case against Haywood.

The whole strange and scarcely believable affair is laid out in all its gruesome reality and confusion in the James McParland Pinkerton Reports to Idaho Governor Frank Gooding, the trial transcripts, the notes of prosecutors James H. Hawley and William Borah, and the personal papers of Hawley and Borah (all in the Idaho State Historical Society). About the only solid conclusions to be inferred from the thousands of pages of evidence and correspondence concerning the case are Orchard's guilt in the assassination of Frank Steunenberg and the recurrent theme of violence in Western labor conflicts.

Internal conflicts within the IWW can be readily discerned in the pages of the *Miners' Magazine* and the *Industrial Worker* (1906–1907) for the Sherman faction, the *Industrial Union Bulletin* (1907–1909) for the St. John faction, the *International Socialist Review,* and the 1906–1908 convention proceedings of the IWW and the WFM. Jensen's *Heritage of Conflict* presents the WFM leadership's case against the IWW and the basis for its secession.

Free Speech and Free Men, 1909–1917

The famous free-speech fights are adequately described in lengthy articles in the IWW press and in the *International Socialist Review.* The United States Commission on Industrial Relations' unpublished field reports on the fights, however, offer much interesting and little-known information about the participants and their motives. Justice Department File 150139 (R.G. 60) describes the singular role played by President William Howard Taft and the Republican National Committee in the San Diego fight. Materials in this file illustrate how government officials well before World War I sought grounds upon which to eliminate the IWW.

Industrial conflict at McKees Rocks, Pennsylvania, and in the Louisiana timber fields can be followed in the IWW press and also in the *International Socialist Review, Survey* (Charity Organization Society journal), and the commercial press. Covington Hall, an IWW member from New Orleans, describes organization efforts among timber workers and longshoremen in a long unpublished manuscript (Tulane University Library; microfilm copy, Wayne State University Labor Archives).

Nationwide publicity insured that the sources concerning the Lawrence and Paterson strikes would be extensive. The Commission on Industrial Relations investigated both conflicts; its Paterson findings were published in the *Final Reports;* the Lawrence investigation conducted by Selig Perlman turned up interesting observations and is available in the National Archives, Department of Labor, R.G. 174. The usual journalistic and magazine sources covered the strikes widely, and the IWW itself ground out hundreds of pages of propaganda. Of particular interest is a speech by Elizabeth Gurley Flynn ("The Truth About Paterson," typescript copy, Tamiment Institute Library, New York City) which analyzed the Paterson strike's result from the IWW perspective. For the

Lawrence conflict, see also: 62nd Cong., 2nd sess., *Senate Document No. 870*, "Report on the Strike of the Textile Workers in Lawrence, Massachusetts, in 1912," and *House Document No. 671*, "The Strike at Lawrence, Massachusetts."

The IWW's decision to return to the West and the founding of the Agricultural Workers' Organization are covered in *Solidarity*, the *Industrial Worker*, and the convention proceedings for 1914–1915. The type of migratory worker to whom the IWW appealed is perceptively surveyed in Nels Anderson (though he is more interested in the individualistic, less organization-inclined migratories), *The Hobo: The Sociology of the Homeless* (Chicago, University of Chicago Press, 1923). Anderson, himself a hobo, or migratory worker, at one stage in his life, sympathetically delineates the factors causing labor transiency in the America of 1890–1920, the life-style of the transients, and the barriers to their organization in unions. A more recent, more impressionistic, and less valuable study (especially the error-filled section on the IWW) is Kenneth Allsop's *Hard Travelin': The Hobo and His History* (London, Hodder & Stoughton, 1967). The Wheatland riot was investigated by the state of California and the United States Commission on Industrial Relations, and the reports prepared for both by Carleton Parker describe the "riot" objectively. The violence in Butte and the ensuing struggle between the IWW and the WFM were investigated by a Commission on Industrial Relations agent (whose report is in the State Historical Society of Wisconsin collections), who held Wobblies responsible for the violence; the Butte affair's seriousness is reflected in the volume of correspondence about it in the Gompers Letterbooks. Jensen, in *Heritage of Conflict*, once again fully presents the WFM version.

Industrial conflict on the Mesabi Iron Range is completely and competently described and analyzed in the field reports prepared by conciliators from the Federal Mediation and Conciliation Service (Department of Labor, R.G. 280, File 33/247). The roles of Elizabeth Gurley Flynn, Joe Ettor, and Carlo Tresca can be followed in the IWW press and in the papers of Frank Walsh (Manuscript Division, New York Public Library), prominent attorney, friend of radicals, and former chairman of the Commission on Industrial Relations, with whom Flynn and Ettor corresponded regularly during the strike.

IWW interest and activities in the Pacific Northwest lumber industry are treated in a number of published studies. Cloice R. Howd, "Industrial Relations in the West Coast Lumber Industry," Bureau of Labor Statistics, *Bulletin No. 349* (Washington, D.C., Government Printing Office, 1923), provides the best overview. Vernon Jensen's *Lumber and Labor* (New York, Farrar & Rinehart, 1945) gives an excellent but sketchy account, and Charlotte Todes' *Lumber and Labor* (New York, International Publishers, 1931) is a similar study but from an avowedly Marxist, anti-IWW perspective. The inside story of labor relations in the area is strikingly revealed in the papers of the Puget Mill Company and the Merrill Ring Company (University of Washington Library, Seattle), two of the larger West Coast lumber firms. The gory details of the Everett Massacre are treated in these sources as well as in the IWW and commercial presses.

Trials and Tribulations, 1917–1924

Two books, neither of which is concerned primarily with the IWW, provide an excellent introduction to the Wobblies' wartime difficultes. Harold Hyman's *Soldiers and Spruce: Origins of the Loyal Legion of Loggers and Lumbermen* (Los Angeles, University of California Press, 1963), a thoroughly researched study of the 1917–1918 events in the Northwest lumber industry, focuses upon government efforts to insure uninterrupted spruce production and the use of federal troops to curb the IWW. It shows clearly how progressive reformers like Carleton Parker could not tolerate the Wobblies and were quite willing to use repression to drive the IWW from the woods. William Preston's *Aliens and Dissenters: Federal Suppression of Radicals, 1903–1933* (Cambridge, Harvard University Press, 1963) is the definitive study of federal attempts to curb radicals, and as such it naturally devotes considerable attention to the wartime campaign against the IWW. One could scarcely improve upon Preston's analysis of the government's strategy to repress the IWW; but he relies largely upon the usual published materials to relate the history of the IWW and its activities during the war years. Preston discovered, as I did, that all Bureau of Investigation and Military Intelligence reports are classified indefinitely and closed to scholars. Also, after Preston completed his research, J. Edgar Hoover restricted and removed from the open archives additional Justice Department files and papers so that I was unable to see these "sensitive" items. I was able, however, to obtain from the archives a microfilm copy of the Abraham Glasser manuscript, which is an authoritative study (prepared during the New Deal) of the use of military force to cope with domestic disturbances. Glasser studied World War I labor conflicts in the Pacific Northwest, Arizona, and Montana, and he quotes verbatim from significant portions of Bureau of Investigation and Military Intelligence reports. I compared some of his direct quotations from non-classified sources to the originals and found them entirely accurate, leading me to conclude that Glasser's use of classified items was equally scrupulous. His manuscript thus provides a unique source from which to observe military efforts to crush the IWW.

An older, still valuable account of wartime attempts to curb dissent in general and the IWW in particular is Eldridge F. Dowell, "A History of Criminal Syndicalism Legislation in the United States," *The Johns Hopkins University Studies in Historical and Political Science Series*, LVII, No. 1 (Baltimore, 1939).

The Federal Mediation and Conciliation Service records offer insights into another aspect of the IWW story: the organization's objectives and tactics in the 1917–1918 lumber and copper strikes. These files in Department of Labor R.G. 280, 33/438A–A [10], and 33/574A–C, illustrate how the Labor Department and its conciliators preferred reform but tolerated repression when reforms failed to remove the IWW from the scene. R.G. 174, the records of the President's Mediation Commission, is particularly revealing on the Arizona situation and the immense power and influence wielded by the young Felix Frankfurter, the commission's secretary.

Three huge Justice Department files contain the bulk of materials relevant to the campaign to eliminate the IWW. File 186701 includes reports to and from district attorneys in every state in the Union referring to radicals, and it also contains the background information on the Wichita, Omaha, and Sacramento IWW cases. File 186813 includes the complete reports on the infamous Bisbee, Arizona, deportations and demonstrates clearly the double standard employed by Justice Department officials in dealing with Wobblies. File 188032 is devoted entirely to the major prosecution effort against the IWW: the case of the *United States v. W. D. Haywood, et al.*

For the IWW's own version of its attitudes and activities during the war years, one should consult *Solidarity*, the *Industrial Worker*, various publications of the organization's general defense committee, and sympathetic pamphlets published by the National Civil Liberties Bureau. Some idea of Wobbly responses to the war can be gleaned from correspondence in Justice Department R.G. 204, Pardon Attorney File 39–240. This file, as well as several smaller ones in the same record group, contains the only remaining copies of actual IWW correspondence, and these are *copies*, not originals.

The sources cited above, as well as Gambs's *The Decline of the IWW*, cover the years 1919–1924. For that period one should also consult the IWW convention proceedings, *One Big Union Monthly, Industrial Pioneer,* and *Industrial Solidarity.*

The IWW's dismal decline after 1924 can be followed in Gambs, *Industrial Solidarity, Industrial Pioneer,* the *Industrial Worker,* other organization publications, and convention proceedings for the years during whch the IWW was fortunate enough to hold conventions.

Illuminating views of postwar industrial disputes can be found in the papers of Mark Litchman (University of Washington Library), former Wobbly, Seattle attorney, and adviser in 1933 to striking IWW hop workers; and Mary Gallagher (Bancroft Library, University of California at Berkeley), IWW sympathizer and observer of the 1924 San Pedro conflict and the Colorado coal miners' strike of 1927–1928.

A NOTE ON
LITERATURE PUBLISHED
SINCE 1970

In the nearly twenty years that have passed since the first edition of this book was originally published in 1969, no other scholarly general history of the IWW has appeared in print. Yet the scholar or student who begins research today on the Wobblies is in a far more advantageous and enviable position than I was when I initially started on the project, for two primary reasons. First, we now have available Dione Miles's marvelous bibliographical tour de force on the IWW: *Something in Common—An IWW Bibliography* (Detroit: Wayne State University Press, 1986). In her bibliography of printed literature on the IWW, Miles includes more than 200 books and over 3,000 articles and essays, many in foreign languages and most with useful annotations. The book also lists nearly everything published by and about the IWW from its founding in 1905 through 1985. Second, scholars today can use two sets of archival records unavailable to me during the 1960s. The Archives of Labor and Urban History at the Walter Reuther Library, Wayne State University, are the official depository for all of the IWW's own records, which cover the organization's post-1919 history in detail. Moreover, the declassified records of the Bureau of Intelligence and the separate military intelligence agencies, which contain many detailed reports on the Wobblies from the era of World War I through the 1930s, are available for use at the National Archives and also through selected microfilm series published by University Publications of America.

Much new scholarship has also been published about the IWW since 1969, and it adds to or revises parts of *We Shall Be All* in four ways. David Montgomery and other historians have related the history of the IWW more directly to the most salient features of American labor history. In his collection of essays entitled *Workers' Control in America* (New York: Cambridge University Press, 1979), Montgomery relates the syndicalism of the IWW both to the strain of job control stressed by highly skilled workers and to the needs of less-skilled, newer immigrant workers neglected by mainstream craft unions. He also analyzes why the Wobblies failed to widen their appeal among the skilled or to build durable unions for the unskilled. Bruno Ramirez, in *Why Workers Fight: The Politics of Industrial Relations in the Progressive Era, 1898–1916* (Westport, Conn.: Greenwood Press, 1978), also places the IWW at the center of the struggle by American workers to obtain greater control of the shop floor in the years before World War I. Three other books deal with the subject less successfully. Joseph R. Conlin's *Bread and Roses Too: Studies of the Wobblies* (Westport, Conn.: Greenwood Press,

1970) asserts that the IWW was nonrevolutionary, nonviolent, and very much in the American tradition of industrial unionism which flowed from the Knights of Labor through the IWW directly to the CIO. Donald E. Winters, Jr., in *The Soul of the Wobblies: The I.W.W., Religion, and American Culture in the Progressive Era, 1905–1917* (Westport, Conn.: Greenwood Press, 1985), tries to prove that the ideology and practices of the IWW drew directly on Christian traditions and sought to make a reality out of the Social Gospel. Unfortunately, Winters defines religion so elastically that his definition explains everything and nothing. Finally, Aileen S. Kraditor, in *The Radical Persuasion: Aspects of the Intellectual History and Historiography of Three American Radical Organizations* (Baton Rouge: Louisiana State University Press, 1981), seeks to prove that the IWW as well as the Socialist Labor and Socialist parties were at odds with mainstream American values and traditions. Her analysis is quite imaginative, even partly believable, yet ultimately unconvincing.

Two exceptional essays point out aspects of the IWW neglected in *We Shall Be All.* In a long review of that book and also Conlin's *Bread and Roses Too,* William Preston, Jr., criticizes the authors for failing to provide fuller data about the leaders and members of the IWW and hence doing an injustice to the Wobblies' sound and sensible radical critique of American society and economics ("Shall This Be All? U.S. Historians versus William D. Haywood, et. al.," *Labor History,* 12 [Summer 1971], 435–53). A Japanese historian, Tatsuro Nomura, has successfully answered some of the questions raised by Preston and, in the process, confirmed my own more impressionistic portrait of the leaders of the IWW: "Who Were the Wobblies? The Defendants of the Chicago IWW Trial of 1918: Collective Biographies," *Journal of Aichi Prefectural University,* Twentieth Anniversary Number [1985 (Nagoya, Japan)], 135–50). In another context Mike Davis has related the history of the IWW to the struggle over scientific management waged between workers and employers in the early twentieth century: "The Stop Watch and the Wooden Shoe: Scientific Management and the IWW," *Radical America,* 9 (January–February 1975), 69–95.

Two books, one a revised IWW-sponsored history of the organization and the other a popular history intended for a younger audience, provide by far the most complete picture of the IWW's history after 1919. Fred Thompson and Patrick Murfin, in *The I.W.W., Its First Seventy Years, 1905–1975* (Chicago: I.W.W., 1977), brings Thompson's history of the first fifty years up to date. Len DeCaux, in *The Living Spirit of the Wobblies* (New York: International Publishers, 1978), does the same thing in much more spritely prose. One might also wish to consult DeCaux's autobiography, in which he has much of interest to say about the IWW and its links to other strains of American labor radicalism: *Labor Radical: From the Wobblies to the CIO, a Personal History* (Boston: Beacon Press, 1970).

Three exceptionally fine biographies offer information and insight into the lives and careers of a trio of radicals indelibly associated with the IWW: William D. "Big Bill" Haywood, Eugene V. Debs, and Daniel DeLeon. Peter Carlson's *Roughneck: The Life and Times of Big Bill Haywood* (New York: Norton, 1983) tells the story of its subject in rollicking and dramatic fashion. If it adds little of substance to historical analysis and interpretation, Carlson's biography proves a marvelously good read. Equally easy to read and far more impressive for its scholarly and interpretative qualities is Nick Salvatore's *Eugene V. Debs: Citizen and Socialist* (Urbana: University of Illinois Press, 1982). Salvatore makes Debs's initial marriage to the IWW and his subsequent early divorce understandable. In *Daniel DeLeon: The Odyssey of an American Marxist* (Cambridge: Harvard University Press, 1979), L. Glen Seretan provides a sympathetic portrait of the stormy petrol of American radicalism, a man whose idiosyncratic beliefs and practices fundamentally shaped the early years of the IWW.

The greatest contribution to the history of the IWW during the past two decades has come in the form of books and articles detailing the story at the local and state levels. That literature has grown so enormously that I will cite only its best and most representative products. Three books fill in thoroughly the gaps in the prehistory of the IWW, that is, the origins of working-class radicalism among western mine workers. Richard Lingenfelter, in *The Hardrock Miners* (Berkeley: University of California Press, 1974), provides the fullest narrative history of western miners and their efforts to build unions from the 1850s to the founding of the Western Federation of Miners in 1893. Mark Wyman, in *Hard Rock Epic: Western Miners and the Industrial Revolution, 1860–1910* (Berkeley: University of California Press, 1979), offers fresh glimpses and insights into the nonviolent, nonradical aspects in the history of western miners as well as explaining fully the factors and influences that turned many of his subjects into radicals or violent men. George G. Suggs, Jr., in *Colorado's War on Militant Unionism: James H. Peabody and the Western Federation of Miners* (Detroit: Wayne State University Press, 1972), analyzes how events in the state of Colorado in the years 1903–5 precipitated the founding of the IWW. Three other books not only add to the story from different perspectives but also draw on the history of workers in Canada. A. Ross McCormack's *Reformers, Rebels, and Revolutionaries: The Western Canadian Radical Movement, 1899–1919* (Toronto: University of Toronto Press, 1977) tells the story of syndicalism north of the border and relates it to events in the United States. In *Fools and Wise Men: The Rise and Fall of One Big Union* (Toronto: McGraw-Ryerson, 1978), David J. Bercuson examines how syndicalism culminated in the One Big Union (OBU) movement in Canada and why it failed. Approaching the same subject from a different angle, Carlos Schwantes, in *Radical Heritage: Labor, Socialism, and Reform in Washington State and British Columbia* (Seattle: University of Washington Press, 1979), explains through comparative analysis why labor radicalism had a more durable impact among workers in western Canada.

Other books and articles elaborate the history of western workers and labor radicalism. In a series of articles and essays James C. Foster has provided new data on western miners, their working conditions, union traditions, and links to the IWW. Among Foster's most important contributions are three articles on the WFM and the the IWW in Alaska, published in *Alaska Journal*, 4–6 (1974–76), 130–41, 66–77, and 2–11 respectively; "The Ten Day Tramp," *Labor History*, 23 (Fall 1982), 608–23; and "The Western Wobblies," in James C. Foster, ed., *American Labor in the Southwest* (Tucson: University of Arizona Press, 1982). The events that led to the infamous Bisbee, Arizona, deportations of July 1917 can best be comprehended by reading James Byrkit's *Forging the Copper Collar: Arizona's Labor-Management War* (Tucson: University of Arizona Press, 1982).

Arnon Gutfeld tells a similar story about workers and radical labor in wartime Montana in *Montana's Agony: Years of War and Hysteria, 1917–1921* (Gainesville: University Presses of Florida, 1979). Finally, Cletus E. Daniel, in *Bitter Harvest: A History of California Farm Workers, 1870–1941* (Ithaca: Cornell University Press, 1981), covers the history of the Wobblies in that state's "factories in the field" in substantial and sympathetic detail.

A variety of publications fill in the local history of the IWW in other parts of the United States. To sample that literature, perhaps the best place to begin is with Joseph R. Conlin, ed., *At the Point of Production: The Local History of the IWW* (Westport, Conn.: Greenwood Press, 1981). Not all the essays in the collection are equally good, but I would single out for careful attention the following: James E. Fickle, "Race, Class, and Radicalism: The Wobblies in the Southern Lumber Industry"; Patrick Lynch, "Pittsburgh, the IWW and the Stogie Workers"; James D. Osborne, "Paterson, Immigrant Strikers, and the War of 1913"; Robert E. Snyder, "Women, Wobblies, and Workers' Rights: The 1912 Textile Strike in Little Falls, New York"; David G. Wagaman, "*Rausch Mit:* The IWW in Nebraska during World War I"; and Roy Wortman, "The IWW and the Akron Rubber Strike of 1913." Among the articles on the local history of the IWW, none surpasses in quality or level of interpretation James R. Green's "Brotherhood of Timber Workers, 1910–1913: A Radical Response to Industrial Capitalism in the Southern U.S.A.," *Past and Present*, (August 1973), 161–200. Of nearly equal quality are two articles by Steve Golin which focus on the strike of 1913 in the Paterson, New Jersey, silk industry and offer new interpretations of both the strike's significance and the meaning of the Paterson Pageant: "Defeat Becomes Disaster: The Paterson Strike of 1913 and the Decline of the IWW," *Labor History*, 24 (Spring 1983), 223–48; and "The Paterson Pageant: Success or Failure," *Socialist Review*, 69 (May–June 1983), 45–78. Anne Huber Tripp provides a detailed analysis in *The I.W.W. and the Paterson Silk Strike of 1913* (Urbana: University of Illinois Press, 1987).

Several other articles round out the best of the local histories. Among them are: Merl Reed, "Lumberjacks and Longshoremen: The IWW in Louisiana," *Labor History*, 13 (Winter 1972), 41–59; Robert E. Ficken, "The Wobbly Horrors: Pacific Northwest Lumbermen and the Industrial Workers of the World," *Labor History*, 24 (Summer 1983), 325–41; and Michael H. Ebner, "The Passaic Strike of 1912 and the Two I.W.W.s," *Labor History*, 11 (Fall 1970), 452–66. Two articles by Al Gedicks trace the connections between labor radicalism and ethnic culture among Finnish nonferrous metal miners in the upper Midwest: "The Social Origins of Radicalism among Finnish Immigrants in Midwestern Mining Communities," *Review of Radical Political Economics*, 8 (Fall 1976), 1–31; and "Ethnicity, Class Solidarity, and Labor Radicalism among Finnish Immigrants in Michigan Copper Country," *Politics and Society*, 7 (1977), 127–56. Finally, a scholarly history by Roy T. Wortman traces the history of the IWW in one state (Ohio, where the organization had its greatest successes from the 1930s through the 1950s), from its founding to its decline and disappearance: *From Syndicalism to Trade Unionism: The IWW in Ohio* (New York: Garland Publishing, 1985).

INDEX

545

5 5 9

United States Commission on Industrial Relations, 155, 160, 164, 210–211, 238, 257, 270, 328
United States Reduction Co., 40
United States Steel, 6, 198–199
United States Supreme Court, 33, 100, 390, 422, 459
United Textile Workers of America: and Lawrence strike, 233, 234, 235, 245; and Paterson strike, 268, 276
"Unknown Committee," 204–205

Valentino, Modestino, 278, 280
Vanderveer, George, 408, 427, 430–431, 434–436
Veblen, Thorstein, 360, 447
Victor, Colo., 21, 47
Vigilantes: in Akron, 286; in Bisbee, 385–386, 387–389; in Butte, 391–392; in Everett, 339–341; in Jerome, 384–385; and San Diego free-speech fight, 191–193; in San Pedro, 475; during World War I, 383–384
Vindicator Mine, 52
Violence, 19; in Akron, 286; during BTW Strike, 216–217, 218; in Butte, 303–305; in Coeur d'Alenes, 1892, 31, 32; and 1928 Colorado coal strike, 476; in Cripple Creek (1903–1905), 52–53; in Everett, 338–341; and industrial conflict, 36–37; and IWW, 146, 160–164; and Lawrence strike, 228, 246–249; and McKees Rocks strike, 204, 205–206; on Mesabi Range, 325–327; in Paterson, 276–278; in San Pedro, 475; and Wheatland incident, 296
Virginia City Miners' Union, 24
The Voice of Labor, 76, 92

Wages: in Lawrence, 227–228, 230–232; in McKees Rocks steel, 199, 200–201; on Mesabi Range, 321, 322–324; in mining and smelting, 40; in Paterson, 265, 267; in U.S., 7–8; in Wheatland, 294; during World War I, 370
Wagner Act (National Labor Relations Act), 478
Waite, Davis, 37

Wakefield, Dan, 467, 473
Wald, Lillian, 7
Waldheim Cemetery, 312, 461
Walker, John H., 415, 416–417
Wall Street Journal, 377
Walling, William E., 259
Walsh, Frank P., 238, 310, 328, 331, 335, 429, 431, 436
Walsh, J. H., 176–177; versus DeLeonism, 137–138; and Japanese-Americans, 127
Walsh, Thomas, 391
War Department, 382, 398–400, 401–403, 413, 417
Wardner, Idaho, 28
War Industries Board, 415, 420
Warren, Charles, 404
Warren, Ariz., 23, 369, 386, 417
Washington State Council of Defense, 365, 382, 411
Weinstock, Harris, 160, 192
Welfare capitalism, 445, 482
Wells, Bulkeley, 53
West Coast Lumbermen's Association, 335–336, 447
West Coast Seamen's Union, 474
Western Federation of Miners (WFM), 24, 25, 28, 38–39, 92, 106, 108, 109, 121–124, 148; and AFL, 65, 70–71, 94–95; and ALU, 71, 74–75; in Butte, 301–307; in Colorado, 39–40; creation of, 34–35; strike in Colorado City, 40–46; 1898 convention, 65; 1900 convention, 68–69; 1902 convention, 69, 70–71; 1903 convention, 73; 1904 convention, 54, 76; 1905 convention, 80; 1907 convention, 118; strike in Cripple Creek, 47–55; goals, 35, 57–58; and Haywood Case, 97–105; ideology, 56, 57–58, 60, 65, 67–68, 68–69; and industrial conflict, 35, 36–38; and 1906 IWW convention, 110–112; and origins of IWW, 76, 78, 81–82, 86; and IWW 1906 split, 115–118, 119; and Mesabi Range strike, 324; and politics, 59; secession from IWW, 119; and socialism, 59–60, 69; and WLU, 66, 70–71
Western governors, and federal repression of IWW, 393–394

A Note on the Author

Melvyn Dubofsky studied at Brooklyn College and the University of Rochester, where he earned a doctoral degree. He is a professor of history at the State University of New York at Binghamton and the author of *When Workers Organize: New York City in the Progressive Era.* He is also co-author of *John L. Lewis: A Biography* and co-editor of *Labor Leaders in America,* recently published by the University of Illinois Press.